CAREER OPPORTUNITIES IN THE NONPROFIT SECTOR

Jennifer Bobrow Burns

Foreword by
Timothy P. Shriver, Ph.D.
Chairman and CEO,
Special Olympics, Inc.

Ferguson
An imprint of Infobase Publishing

Career Opportunities in the Nonprofit Sector

Copyright © 2006 by Jennifer Bobrow Burns

Ferguson
An imprint of Infobase Publishing
132 West 31st Street
New York NY 10001

Library of Congress Cataloging-in-Publication Data
Burns, Jennifer Bobrow.
   Career opportunities in the nonprofit sector/Jennifer Bobrow Burns; foreword by Timothy P. Shriver.
     p. cm.
   Includes bibliographical references and index.
   ISBN 0-8160-6003-7 (hc : alk. paper)
   1. Nonprofit organizations—Vocational guidance—United States. 2. Nonprofit organizations—Employees—Job descriptions—United States.
   I. Title.
   HD2769.2.U6B87 2006
   331.702′0973—dc22   2005009495

Ferguson books are available at special discounts when purchased in bulk quantities for businesses, associations, institutions, or sales promotions. Please call our Special Sales Department in New York at (212) 967-8800 or (800) 322-8755.

You can find Ferguson on the World Wide Web at http://www.fergpubco.com

Cover design by Nora Wertz

Printed in the United States of America

VB Hermitage 10   9   8   7   6   5   4   3   2   1

This book is printed on acid-free paper.

CONTENTS

FOREWORD

The nonprofit sector offers a wealth of options often untapped by job seekers. By picking up this book, you have taken the first step to learn more about such a career. *Career Opportunities in the Nonprofit Sector* is a great book, and I highly recommend it to everyone. It is full of information that is accurate, comprehensive, and applicable within any nonprofit setting.

But this book is important for reasons beyond the skills and techniques it presents to the reader; it is important because it invites people into the nonprofit sector. No sector—not the corporate, private, or government sector—could be more crucial to understand right now than the nonprofit sector. Nonprofits need to be more efficient, more effective, and more agile than ever. To meet the challenges they face, they need the best talent, too.

Now more than ever, the world faces environmental challenges: overwhelming poverty, widespread disease, unrelenting intolerance, and growing hunger, to name a few. Never before have problems seemed so intractable, but at the same time, never before have the means to attack major problems seemed so attainable. In this day of globalization and enormously fast exchanges of ideas and ingenuity, the nonprofit sector must emerge as a key player.

One of the major elements of this shift is that nonprofits must become more entrepreneurial. We need to embrace business disciplines without losing any of our passion for helping others. Just like successful leaders in the corporate world, we must use performance measurement, strategic allocation of resources, competitive analysis, and partnership development to run nonprofit organizations successfully. We must become accountable in demanding results, dedicated to focusing on needs, and passionate in the pursuit of visionary goals. We must attain all of these goals with the urgency and creativity of entrepreneurs, developing new solutions and operational patterns wherever the need exists.

For all these reasons and more, I encourage you to study this book carefully. Future nonprofit workers must be people of skill, humor, and efficiency—not just great leaders, but also great managers. The nonprofit sector is a place for people with diverse skill sets. Writers, mathematicians, artists, and engineers can all find a place here where they can use their talents while also helping others.

Furthermore, nonprofit professionals must be dedicated. As the CEO and chairman of Special Olympics, I work every day with committed individuals who strive to make an impact on society and to change attitudes around the world. Their passion for what they do is unparalleled in the corporate sector. Their work, as well as the work of their nonprofit colleagues, touches the lives of millions worldwide.

The time is now for students to explore nonprofit careers and the wealth of opportunities they offer. By working as a volunteer or an intern, you can explore different career possibilities to achieve a realistic understanding of the work involved. You will gain valuable experience that will help you forge a path upon graduation. And there is nothing like the satisfaction you will feel from using your time to make a difference.

Career Opportunities in the Nonprofit Sector contains the tools and information needed to help talented and visionary people become tomorrow's successful leaders and managers of the nonprofit sector. For that alone, this book's contribution to the world will be invaluable.

— Timothy P. Shriver, Ph.D.
Chairman and CEO, Special Olympics, Inc.

INTRODUCTION: INDUSTRY OUTLOOK

Choosing a career is one of the most challenging decisions you'll have to make during your life. In addition to finding an occupation that fits with your skills and interests, you want to also make sure that your job fits with your lifestyle needs and values. For many people, it is of crucial importance that they find work that is both personally meaningful and is socially responsible. They seek ways to make a living while making a contribution to society. This is where the nonprofit sector comes in.

There is an old saying that states, "If you do what you love, it will never feel like work." Nowhere is this truer than in the nonprofit sector. In the nonprofit sector, your values and passion lead the way. Career paths are chosen based both on job tasks as well as on enthusiasm for a cause. You might enter the nonprofit world by deciding that you want to be a social worker, lawyer, or controller at any type of organization. On the other hand, you may decide you feel so strongly about working for immigrant's rights, the environment, or cancer prevention, that you find yourself in a position such as fund-raiser or activist that you never even knew existed.

Currently, approximately 13 million Americans are employed in the nonprofit sector. Ranging from advocacy and community groups to museums and foundations, nonprofits are often at the forefront of major issues and represent diverse interests, activities, and passions. Nonprofits are driven by a mission; to carry out this mission, they frequently promote causes and provide public services. Working for these organizations enables people to reconcile their work with their social conscience.

According to Independent Sector, a coalition of leading nonprofits, foundations, and corporations strengthening not-for-profit initiative, philanthropy, and citizen action, there are more than 1.5 million nonprofits in the United States with combined revenues of more than $670 billion. However, the nonprofit sector is often misunderstood by job seekers. Some assume *nonprofit* means that volunteers perform all work and there are no positions that pay an actual salary. Others believe nonprofit opportunities involve only stuffing envelopes and raising money. The fact is, job seekers with diverse interests can apply their strengths in the nonprofit sector and earn a good living doing so. Representing more than 10 different industries and hundreds of job functions, opportunities abound for those skilled in research, writing, mathematics, and more.

The economic impact of nonprofit organizations in our society is huge. In addition to the millions they employ, nonprofits have the potential to help communities and individuals become productive financial contributors. They conduct research to wipe out disease, and they are clearinghouses of education and progressive thought. They provide job training and shelter to the underrepresented. They advocate for those who do not have the means to fight for themselves and their rights. The potential of these changes is boundless.

Nonprofit professionals are tremendously dedicated and committed. Their passion for their organizational missions drives their work and enables nonprofit organizations to advance society. They use their creativity to deal with the less glamorous realities of working at a nonprofit—long hours, limited resources, and sometimes low pay.

What Is a Nonprofit?

Legally, a nonprofit is defined as any organization that has been granted tax exemption status by the Internal Revenue Service (IRS) under Section 501(c)(3) of the Federal Tax Code. According to the United States Census Bureau, a nonprofit (or not-for-profit) organization is an organization that is not operated for the purpose of making a profit for its owners or shareholders. It may or may not also be a tax-exempt organization. While some nonprofits do engage in commercial profit-generating activities, the profit is used to support the organization rather than financially benefit the individuals at the organization.

This legal definition only begins to scratch the surface of understanding nonprofits. Nonprofits toe the line between the public sector (government) and the private sector (business). For this reason, they are sometimes referred to as the "third" or "independent sector." While they all exist to serve the public good without the incentive of profit, they vary tremendously in terms of activities, programs, missions, goals, issues, and functions.

What Industries Make Up the Nonprofit Sector?

It is difficult to pin down a definitive list on the industries comprising the nonprofit sector. According to the Foundation Center, the National Taxonomy of Exempt Entities (NTEE) uses 10 basic subject groups to classify nonprofit organizations. These include:

– Arts, culture, and humanities
– Education
– Environment and animals
– Health
– Human services
– International/Foreign affairs
– Religious organizations
– Public/society benefit
– Mutual membership benefit organizations
– Nonclassifiable organizations

Many organizations do not just fit into one classification, but actually can be grouped under several. This book serves to present a broad representation of the nonprofit sector by both combining and expanding upon some of these categories. Areas are included such as social services, advocacy and community development, and professional, business, and trade associations.

What Makes Nonprofits Unique?

Nonprofits are driven by a mission that is the underlying checkpoint for all the work they do. For example, if the mission of a particular organization is to fight hunger in developing nations, every activity from programming to budgeting is viewed in the context of how it is furthering that mission. This creates a challenge in that nonprofit organizations must also reach financial goals in order to stay alive. Each nonprofit must find a way to reconcile the tension between these two bottom lines—mission versus financial. For this reason, fund-raising is a part of life at all nonprofits. The exception are foundations and philanthropic organizations that are on "the other side." They are in the position of distributing existing funds to other nonprofit organizations.

Furthermore, a board of directors governs nonprofit organizations. The board comprises some combination of community leaders, community members, donors, employees, and other professionals. The board is responsible for both helping the organization to be successful, as well as making sure its mission is carried out. They have unique legal and ethical responsibilities that are theirs alone and cannot be transferred. While the roles of board members vary depending on the organization, the board is trusted with hiring and firing the executive director and making major financial and programming decisions.

Another major feature of nonprofit organization is the role of volunteers. From large hospitals and museums, to international relief programs, to three-person grassroots organizing campaigns, nonprofits depend on volunteers to manage their work load. These committed individuals donate their time and energy because they care about the mission. Nonprofits work to find ways to recruit and retain volunteers and keep them motivated.

How Is Working for a Nonprofit Different from Working at a Corporation?

At nonprofit organizations, the general career trajectory is typically more flexible than in the private sector. With more to do and fewer resources, people are less confined by their job description or defined by a hierarchy. Everyone from the administrative assistant to the executive director has a hand in the work. There is usually a less-structured advancement process, with promotion common at any time for individuals with the right combination of education and experience.

Also, work environments tend to be more relaxed and informal. At many organizations, professionals dress casually. Insiders who have prior business experience also cite friendliness and camaraderie in the atmosphere that they feel was lacking at their corporate jobs. There is an overall feeling of "we're all in this together" where opinions are invited and voices heard.

Furthermore, there is often more opportunity to take on increased responsibility at nonprofit organizations, particularly at the entry level. Students right out of college often run programs, make decisions, and even manage interns and volunteers. If they are creative and can take initiative, new professionals can carve out niches for themselves and design their own careers, based on their interests and talents. Due to the diversity of positions and roles, employees at nonprofit organizations often have mixed skill levels, providing the opportunity for retraining and growth. It is easier to be a generalist and enjoy more autonomy.

While there is no denying that salaries are lower than their comparable corporate positions and resources can be scarce, there are other benefits that can be more important in securing a comfortable and satisfying lifestyle. Those employed in the nonprofit sector work hard, long hours, but often feel motivated to do so based on their commitment. They may profit from programs such as tuition reimbursement and generous vacation time to prevent them from burning out.

Nonprofit professionals can use their skills to create more lucrative paths if they desire. Larger organizations offer more competitive pay, as do those on the East and West Coasts. Individuals with advanced degrees often earn more as well, depending upon their areas of expertise. Furthermore, nonprofit gurus often use their experience to work as consultants to other nonprofits and businesses, helping them to write grants, run programs, plan events, create policy, and more. They may do this as full-time work, or concurrently with other nonprofit employment.

How Do Nonprofit Jobs Differ from One Another?

Since it is so diverse, it is virtually impossible to make generalizations about career opportunities in the nonprofit sector.

Several factors determine differences in position titles, job responsibilities, and salary. The first of these factors is size. Nonprofits range from one-room homeless shelters and grassroots community agencies to world-renowned hospitals and prestigious universities. Some have tremendous endowments, while others struggle to find funding to maintain their programs. Titles have very different meanings as one program assistant may work directly for an executive director in an office of three employees, whereas another program assistant is part of a staff of more than 1,000 employees. Salaries vary greatly as well, depending upon the organization's budget.

Furthermore, geographical location greatly influences opportunities and types of jobs. Nonprofits can be found in every region of the country, serving every area of the world. The larger nonprofit organizations tend to be on the East and West Coasts, with concentrations of headquarters in New York and Washington, D.C.; San Francisco, Chicago, Minneapolis, Los Angeles, Seattle, and Boston are also the home to many organizations. However, there are locally based community groups in small towns nationwide.

Some locations are specific to certain types of organizations. For example, environmental groups may be plentiful in the Pacific Northwest, and suburban Virginia houses many professional and trade associations. As does size, geography influences salary, with higher earnings on both coasts and lower paychecks in the South and Midwest. However, bear in mind that with higher salaries come higher costs of living.

Finally, nonprofits differ by industry. A program director for a social services agency has a very different job than a program director for a museum or foundation. Each industry employs people ranging from those without a high school education to Ph.Ds. Salaries vary across industries, as do job descriptions.

What Is the Outlook for Nonprofit Jobs?

According to Action Without Borders—Idealist.org, the nonprofit sector is a growth industry. New nonprofits spring up on a regular basis in need of talented staff to manage their budgets, run their programs, recruit volunteers, and raise funds. Furthermore, the Bureau of Labor Statistics states that much of the sector including membership organizations (business and professional organizations, social and civic organizations, labor organizations, and religious orga-

nizations) will see a 10 percent increase by 2010. As changes in the economy cause layoffs in the private sector, nonprofits will provide additional opportunities and alternatives for those skilled in multiple fields.

How Do I Get Started in the Nonprofit Sector?

There is no one path to follow to break into the nonprofit sector. People enter at all levels, with high school diplomas, bachelor's degrees, and advanced credentials. Educational training specific to your industry of interest becomes critical down the road. Many nonprofit professionals hold master's and professional degrees in fields such as nonprofit management, law, public policy and administration, and social work, to name just a few.

For a sector based on serving the public good and helping others, volunteering is an invaluable nonprofit learning experience. The best advice insiders have is to tap into your interests and go with them. Whether you want to tutor children in math, travel abroad to build playgrounds, conduct policy research, or provide museum tours, there are many opportunities to enable you to do so. Not only will you feel good about your work, but you will also gain information about yourself and your likes and dislikes, which will be crucial in making career decisions.

Internships are also plentiful in the nonprofit sector and an excellent way to explore your interests further. Internships are structured learning programs that may be similar to volunteer opportunities at some organizations. They may be paid or unpaid, and some schools may grant academic credit for your experience. Internships offer unique insight into careers because they are geared at providing professional exposure to students.

Because nonprofit people are passionate about their work, they often are excited to share this passion with others. Take the time to speak to professionals working in your area of interest. Mentors will help you find your niche and answer your questions.

In Conclusion

If you are looking for a way to combine your passion with a career where you can use your best skills, read on. If you are flexible, curious, committed, and compassionate, you won't be disappointed. There is something for everyone in the nonprofit sector.

ACKNOWLEDGMENTS

I would like to extend my appreciation to all those who participated in some way in the creation of this book. Without their assistance, this book would not have been possible.

First, I would like to thank Dr. Timothy P. Shriver, for both his exemplary career in the nonprofit sector and his belief in the importance of this project. His foreword adds a great deal of inspiration to its contents. A big thank-you also goes to Stephanie Garibaldi, in Dr. Shriver's office, who offered her help and guidance. Furthermore, I am grateful to my editor, James Chambers, for his flexibility, patience, and valuable input.

Next, I would like to express my gratitude to the many people who took the time to speak to me (or e-mail) about their jobs. The insight they shared contributed invaluably to my research and helped to make the career profiles more interesting and realistic. In addition to those who prefer to remain anonymous, they include:

John Albert; Alejandro Amezcua, Associate Director of Communication and Outreach, National Council of Nonprofits; Signe Anderson, Program Coordinator, Visions in Action; Mike Armstrong, Pacific Region Logistics Manager, Outward Bound West; Amy Barer, Director of Special Events, Jewish Theological Seminary; Rachel Benevento, former Corporate Relations Manager, American Cancer Society; Jayne Bigelsen, Director of Communications and Public Affairs, Association of the Bar of the City of New York; Douglas Bohn, Assistant Vice President for Academic Affairs and University Registrar, Sacred Heart University; Matthew Bolton, International Aid Worker and Development Consultant; Susan Booth, Artistic Director, Alliance Theatre; Miriam Buhl, former Executive Director, New York Women's Foundation; Milan Bull, Director of Science and Conservation, Connecticut Audubon Society; Katherine Burgueno, Business Manager, Yale Repertory Theatre; Virginia Clairmont, Director of Member Services, American College Personnel Association; Julia Parsons Clarke, Associate Attorney, Perkins Coie; Kristen Conte, Vice President of Finance and Administration, Eugene and Agnes E. Meyer Foundation; Sandy Dalious, Director of Membership Services and Human Resources, National Association of Colleges and Employers; Christina Darnowski; Debra Felix, Program Officer, Howard Hughes Medical Institute; Brooke Fitzgerald, College Coach; Megan Frison, Human Resources Director, Outward Bound; Elisabeth Gehl, Grassroots Organizer, BPWUSA; Patti Hanson, Membership Manager, Brooklyn Botanic Garden; Shelley Hassman-Kadish, Reporter, WSHU; Meital Hershkovitz; Maia Hurley, Policy Analyst, Alliance for Children and Families; Dan Kessler and Russ Finkelstein, Action Without Borders, Idealist.org; Bonnie Koenig, Consultant, Going International; Carol Kratzman, Naturalist, Connecticut Audubon Society; Leeann Lavin, Director of Public Affairs, Brooklyn Botanic Garden; Marie Leahy, Marketing Manager, Brooklyn Botanic Garden; Wanda Little-Coffey, Manager, Component Relations and Finance and Business Operations Sections, American Society of Association Executives; Camille Luckenbaugh, Research Director, National Association for Colleges and Employers; Susan Mascareillo, Director of Volunteers, Greater Baltimore Ronald McDonald House; Heather Maxson, Museum Educator, Museum of Modern Art; Dr. Reed Morton, Director, Healthcare Executive Career Resource Center, ACHE; Jane Penn, Nonprofit Consultant; Rachel Peris, Public Color; Ellen Quinn, Fund Manager, Community Development Fund; Laura Reed, Political Scientist and Research Fellow, Kennedy School of Government, Harvard University; Angela Raven-Roberts, UNICEF; Dr. Sherry Rosen, Prospect Researcher, Jewish Theological Seminary; Anthony Sarmiento, Journal Editor, the *CPA Journal;* Julie Savino, Dean of Financial Aid, Sacred Heart University; Jacqueline Skinner, Director of Educational Programs, American College Personnel Association; Dee Slater, Administrative Director, Dekko Foundation; Susan Spagnuolo, Director of Training and Technical Assistance, Mid-Atlantic Network for Youth and Family Services; Robert Taylor, Associate Director of Student Affairs, Columbia University; Jeanne Marie Tokunaga, Publications Manager, California Dental Association; Angie Wang, Program Director, New York Women's Foundation.

Additionally, I would like to thank the individuals who provided me with crucial information, whether it was statistics, contact names, books, or Web sites, which added to my research.

Donia Allen; Dixie Arthur, ASAE; Leslie Bedford, Director, Leadership in Museum Education Program Bank Street College of Education; Tara Benson; Carolyn Cail, Information Coordinator NCRTM; Janice Dluzynski, Director, Information/CEO Central ASAE; Susan Echoare McDavid; Bonnie Figgett, SHU Librarian; Allison Foster, Association of Schools of Public Health; Stephanie Frydman; Clifton Guterman, Artistic Assistant, Alliance Theatre; Berta James, North Texas Make a Wish Foundation; Nina Jenson, Bank Street College of Education; Gail Johnson, Evergreen State

College; Scott Joy, Human Resources Director, Outward Bound West; Erin Leonard, North Carolina Outward Bound; Nancy Raphael, Chief/Human Resources, UNICEF; Jeff Schulman, McKinsey & Co.; Susan Shiroma, Foundation Center; Cara Smith; Joel Treisman; Ludmilla Trigos; Anne Williams, UNICEF.

Last, but not least, I want to thank my family for their love and support. My parents, Ellen and Robert, who have always encouraged my writing; my sister, Heather, the best writing coach and sibling anyone could have; and most of all, my husband, Bryan, and daughter, Sophie: my love goes to you for sharing my time with this project and helping me all the way.

HOW TO USE THIS BOOK

By considering a career in the nonprofit sector, you are exploring ways to do what you love and use your strengths in a socially responsible setting. You will be not only advancing your own career, but also making a contribution to the greater good of society in some way.

As you can see from the Table of Contents, the nonprofit sector is very diverse in terms of both the industries it encompasses and possible job titles. This book is broken down into 10 categories—nine for specific industries represented by the nonprofit sector, and one that includes many positions frequently found in each of these 10 industries. However, even among the positions listed by industry, there is much overlap. For example, the job title "Grassroots Organizer" is put under the category "Advocacy and Community Development," but it could also belong under "Environment and Conservation," "Health and Science," and "Business, Professional, and Trade Associations," among others. For these reasons, make sure to peruse the entire Table of Contents to read about any job titles that catch your eye.

Because it is so varied, no one book could possibly contain all the potential job titles to be found in the nonprofit sector. There are many more positions to be found than the 78 listed by this book. Use this sampling as a starting point for further research into any and all titles and industries of interest.

This overlap of positions and diversity of roles is part of the beauty of the nonprofit sector, and one of its most distinguishing features. There is the opportunity for new professionals to take on much responsibility early on and wear many hats, so to speak. Without the hierarchy found in many corporations, nonprofits offer tremendous learning experiences for their employees, who, due to understaffing and budget constraints, are often not limited by their job titles.

Contrary to what the name *nonprofit* implies, those who work for these organizations actually can make a profitable living. It is important to remember that *nonprofit* refers to their tax status, not the ability of their employees to make money. Even with inadequate funding, nonprofits find ways to pay their staffs, as well as nurture their minds and hearts in intangible ways. From Web developers to marketing managers, most positions found in the private sector also exist in nonprofits. So get ready to discover what the nonprofit sector has in store for you.

The Career Profiles

Each of the 78 career profiles in this book describes a different job found in the nonprofit sector. It contains useful infor-

mation that can serve as a starting point for further research into each specific profession and general field. The following sections are included in each career profile.

Career Profile Snapshots and Career Ladders

Each career profile begins with a snapshot of information that will be found in more detail by reading further. At a quick glance, you can get a general sense of basic duties, salary ranges, employment and advancement prospects, and education, training, and skill requirements. The best geographical location to find employment is also included here. In most fields, the locations listed are by no means the only options, but just the areas with the highest concentration of jobs.

Opposite the career profile snapshot is a career ladder, containing three job titles. The profiled job will always be in the middle of the three in order to provide an idea of the typical career path.

Position Description

The position descriptions offer an overview of the basic duties and responsibilities of each career that is profiled. The goal of the position descriptions is for you to come away with an understanding of what someone in this occupation actually does on a regular basis. Information is included such as daily tasks, type of projects, and how each job fits in with other professions in the field. They may contain insight into typical hours, work environments, and the types of activities involved. Furthermore, the position descriptions share any background information about the industry that is needed to understand the career profile.

Salaries

More than in the private sector, nonprofit salaries vary tremendously at different organizations. For example, a Director of Development at one organization can earn $40,000, whereas another organization might pay its Director of Development more than $100,000.

There are several factors that contribute to this salary disparity. The first is size of the organization, including both the sizes of the budget and the staff. Smaller organizations might have budgets under $100,000, while large ones can have budgets over $10 million. As it would logically follow, nonprofits with smaller budgets pay considerably less than those with higher budgets. Additionally, those with smaller budgets employ less staff. Organizations may range in size from a few staff members to several thousand.

Another key factor that affects salary is geographic location. Major cities such as New York, Washington, D.C., and San Francisco offer higher salaries, as well as an inflated cost of living. The East and West Coasts usually pay more than the Midwest and the South to compensate for other expenses.

Furthermore, since the nonprofit sector encompasses so many industries, this affects salary as well. A Special Events Director working for a social services organization may earn less than a counterpart working for a hospital or university. Education and experience also play a major role in determining salary.

The salary information in this section is compiled from several sources, including the Bureau of Labor Statistics, professional associations, salary surveys, employees in the field, and others. Since salary information becomes outdated very quickly, make sure information is accurate by checking recent sources. As you read over the figures, you can also use salary calculators from sites such as http://www.salary.com to compare salaries based on region.

Employment Prospects

Employment prospects are variable and often are directly affected by the economy. As with the salary data, the projections in this section come from the Bureau of Labor Statistics, professional associations, and employees in the field. Be sure to check updated information about the careers that interest you as prospects are constantly changing. They also vary based on the size, budget, location of the position, as well as by type of organization.

Advancement Prospects

This section covers the advancement prospects for the career being profiled. It may include next steps within the same type of organization, as well as possible moves to other types of organizations that can result in higher salaries or more responsibility. It also discusses any training or other requirements that might be needed for advancement. Although many professionals move between the public and the private sector, most of the advancement prospects covered here focus on nonprofit options.

Education and Training

Some nonprofit positions require specific educational backgrounds and degrees, while others have more flexible requirements. This section includes the required credentials, as well as the credentials that may not be essential, but are widely preferred for employment. It discusses helpful undergraduate majors, course work, and graduate degrees. It also covers any training needed such as certificates or internships.

Special Requirements

Some of the profiled careers have special requirements such as licensure or certification. They might require certain degrees from accredited programs or the passing of specific exams for entry. This section handles these important facts and provides resources such as the Web sites and phone numbers for organizations that offer additional information.

Experience, Skills, and Personality Traits

Each career that is profiled requires certain skills, experience, and personality traits in order to be entered. This section discusses necessary skills, such as computer programs, foreign languages, public speaking, or other learned expertise. It also highlights personality traits and innate abilities, such as flexibility, curiosity, or patience, which will enable one to be successful in this field. The positions that are being profiled range from entry level to those that require 10 years or more of experience. This section lets you know about experience required as well.

Unions and Associations

Professional associations are an excellent way to gain valuable information about a career field as well as participate in its growth. This section lists associations that may be useful to those in each job.

Tips for Entry

Here you can find helpful tips to learn more about each career. The tips may include insider advice from professionals, useful Web sites, and books. It also may include suggestions relating to course work or internships, and lets you know how to get involved. The information is geared to offering additional information that can help you learn more about each position and the field. Repeatedly, you will see tips that advise gaining experience through volunteer work and internships with nonprofit organizations.

Additional Resources

Beyond the career profiles, there are several appendixes that have practical information to be used in your exploration. Here you can find contact information and other concrete resources to help you learn more about each field. The appendixes in this book are as follows:

Graduate Schools

People employed in the nonprofit sector hold a vast range of graduate degrees. Because they could not all be included here, eight fields were selected that are frequently helpful and can be applied to many different types of positions. They are arranged by state and provide addresses, telephone numbers, and Web sites.

As you read the various profiles, you can learn what types of degrees are required for each position. Do not be concerned if the degrees mentioned are not in one of the eight fields detailed in this section; links about the relevant degrees can be found in each individual profile.

Professional Associations

In this section, the associations that are mentioned in the career profiles are listed alphabetically by industry. They can be found nationwide and many have worldwide members. Each association is listed, along with its mailing address, telephone number, and Web site.

List of Nonprofit Organizations

This section includes a list of the 100 largest nonprofit organizations, as designated by the *NonProfit Times* in 2004. This list can serve as a useful reference for exploring opportunites. Each organization is listed with its mailing address, telephone number, and Web site.

Web Sites

The Internet is one of the best ways to learn about different careers. Web sites that are in this section may provide job listings, industry information, or other helpful tips about the nonprofit sector. As URLs get updated frequently, check each site to make sure the information is still current. If you find a site is no longer valid, try typing the name into a search engine such as Google or Yahoo to find an updated link.

Bibliography

In order to learn more about the many careers represented in this book, a bibliography for further reading is provided. The bibliography is listed by the same industries that are included in the Table of Contents for easy organization. Most books should be easy to find through local libraries, bookstores, and sites such as http://www.amazon.com.

GENERAL NONPROFIT POSITIONS

MANAGEMENT

EXECUTIVE DIRECTOR

CAREER PROFILE

Duties: Provides leadership to a nonprofit organization including managing staff, reporting to the board of directors, and overseeing all financial, administrative, and programmatic functions

Alternate Title(s): President, Chief Executive Officer (CEO)

Salary Range: $40,000 to $150,000 and up

Employment Prospects: Good

Advancement Prospects: Good

Best Geographical Location(s): All, especially major cities

Prerequisites:

    Education or Training—Bachelor's degree; master's or professional degree often preferred

    Experience—Five to 10 years; significantly more at large organizations

    Special Skills and Personality Traits—Excellent organizational, communication, and management skills; ability to work well with people; capable of creating and implementing strategic vision

CAREER LADDER

```
┌─────────────────────────────────────┐
│         Executive Director           │
│  (larger organization); Consultant   │
└─────────────────────────────────────┘

┌─────────────────────────────────────┐
│         Executive Director           │
└─────────────────────────────────────┘

┌─────────────────────────────────────┐
│  Departmental Director; Vice President │
└─────────────────────────────────────┘
```

Position Description

The Executive Director shapes, promotes, and implements the mission of a nonprofit organization. Whether the organization's ultimate objective is to protect the environment, fight domestic violence, or stamp out disease, it is the Executive Director who is charged with making sure the programmatic and administrative support is in place to accomplish these goals. Brought on as a leader and visionary by the board of directors, there is an expectation that the Executive Director will produce results that may include strengthening an organization, rescuing it from financial difficulty, increasing revenue or membership, developing new programs, or changing its image. This job, the highest position at a nonprofit organization, brings with it much responsibility, but also great rewards for those who are up for the challenge.

Executive Directors have the primary responsibility for the operations of an organization. They must assure a long-range strategy for the organization to achieve its mission, as well as handle the everyday details in order to get there. In addition to developing programs and organizational and financial plans with the board of directors and staff, they carry out plans and policies authorized by the board.

Another key role of the Executive Director is to work closely with the board of directors of the organization. The board, a group of individuals participating on a voluntary basis who are legally and financially responsible for the actions of the organization, is responsible for hiring (and if need be, firing) the Executive Director. In turn, the Executive Director is often responsible for recruiting board members. Therefore, it is crucial that they get along well and have good lines of communication. The Executive Director reports to the board on financial, administrative, and programmatic functions. Often, members of the board oversee some of these functions. The Executive Director manages and informs the board so that they can carry out these responsibilities.

Day-to-day responsibilities of the Executive Director may vary based on the size of the organization. For example, most will have some responsibility for fund-raising and development, but the role and involvement with donors and actual fund-raising activity differs. Also, some Executive Directors are involved with providing direct services, while others do not. At a larger organization, they may delegate responsibility for staffing to a human resources director, while at a smaller organization they may be more involved and will oversee all the human resources functions such as compensation, benefits, hiring, and firing.

Overall, their duties can be broken down into the following areas:

- Administration, which includes resource allocation; securing office needs such as supplies or space; various human resources functions; establishing an organizational structure and appropriate staffing; overseeing grants management
- Leadership and community relations, which includes working to meet the needs of the community; promoting the organization internally and to the community; educating the public about the organization's current goals and accomplishments; serving as a representative and spokesperson of the organization; establishing relationships with the media, corporations, and other local/national organizations; additional public relations and marketing duties
- Financial, which includes preparing and submitting the budget for board approval; ensuring availability and access of funds to do organization's work; working with accountants and financial/investments managers; maintaining financial information
- Fund-raising, which can include developing fund-raising goals and strategies; grant writing; prospect research; cultivating relationships with donors and organizations
- Program development, delivery, and evaluation, which includes developing initiatives for new programs; assessing the current programs and their effectiveness; reporting on organizational activities
- Board of directors, which includes providing advice, counsel, and information to the board with regard to creating programs, policies, and strategy; informing the board of organizational and financial activity; educating members about carrying out their roles; working to develop annual plan and strategy

Successful Executive Directors believe strongly in their organizations' missions and are passionate about their cause. Because the hours are extremely long, the position can run the risk of becoming all consuming. The work is intense and can be physically and emotionally draining for those who are not expecting the level of commitment required.

Furthermore, Executive Directors must enjoy motivating and managing people. They may act at times as parent or coach to their staff, particularly at small organizations. They are called upon to handle crises, resolve disputes, and to teach, encourage, and develop their employees. Working for an Executive Director who enjoys serving as a mentor and

role model can be an invaluable professional experience for staff members.

Additional tasks may include:

- Promoting volunteer participation in all areas of the organization's work
- Maintaining a working knowledge of significant developments and trends in the field
- Recruiting staff and developing job descriptions
- Attending regular meetings with board, community and corporate leaders, media, and staff

Salaries

According to an article on www.philanthropicservice.com, a 2002 survey by the *NonProfit Times* reported the average salary for an Executive Director of a nonprofit organization as $90,903. Furthermore, the same survey shares the breakdown for Executive Directors by sector within nonprofits as:

Association—$120,044
Foundation—$107,145
Religion—$104,085
Cultural—$95,828
Education—$95,514
Health—$93,983
Social/Welfare—$83,901
Civic—$65,246

Salary varies greatly not only by type of organization, but by size and location. Small, grassroots organizations with budgets under $500,000 often have under 10 total staff members; this is a significant difference from large, international organizations that employ thousands of people. Thus, the salary for the Executive Director depends on the budget of the organization as well.

Employment Prospects

Overall, employment prospects are good for Executive Directors. Virtually all nonprofit organizations, large or small, have an Executive Director or comparable professional. Since the nonprofit sector is growing so rapidly, positions are available at a wide variety of organizations for those that have the appropriate educational background and work experience. Additionally, many Executive Directors are brought in to institute change within an organization or solve problems. Once the desired result occurs, which may take five to 10 years, Executive Directors may leave to pursue other opportunities, thus creating relatively high turnover and new jobs.

Advancement Prospects

After accomplishing their goals at one organization, Executive Directors may go on to lead different organizations with larger budgets, more staff, or varied responsibilities. Prospects for advancement are good because having worked successfully as an Executive Director at an organization prepares someone to take on a multitude of leadership roles within the public or private sector. Some Executive Directors go on to serve as consultants to nonprofit organizations.

Education and Training

In addition to a bachelor's degree, most Executive Directors have advanced degrees. These include master's degrees in business administration (MBA) or public administration (MPA) with a nonprofit focus, nonprofit management, or additional subject areas based upon the field. For example, the Executive Director of an arts organization may hold a degree in arts administration or fine arts, while the Executive Director of a social service agency may have a master's degree in social work or public health. Furthermore, professionals with law degrees may be uniquely qualified for Executive Director positions based upon their analytical training.

A 2000 study conducted by Seton Hall University found that more than 242 college and universities offer courses in nonprofit management, including undergraduate programs, graduate programs, and noncredit courses. In addition to degree programs, nonprofit management certificate programs are available, such as the Duke University Certificate Program in Nonprofit Management. While these programs are by no means required for entry, they may provide valuable skills and knowledge to professionals without considerable management or nonprofit experience.

Experience, Skills, and Personality Traits

Before becoming an Executive Director, considerable work experience is necessary. Typically, Executive Directors have at least five to 10 years of prior nonprofit experience (depending on the size of the organization) in areas such as development, communications, administration, public affairs, or volunteer management. Those Executive Directors who have actually done the work of the staff they manage are often the most respected and productive.

Executive Directors need strong management skills and proven leadership ability. They need to be able to command respect, yet work alongside their staff as team players. They must be open to criticism, both the giving and taking, and be generous with praise. They need to enjoy working with people and be able to motivate, inspire, and guide. Also important are creativity, excellent communication skills, financial knowledge, and analytical/strategic thinking.

Unions and Associations

There are many professional organizations for Executive Directors of nonprofits including the American Society of Association Executives, the National Council of Nonprofit Associations, the Alliance for Nonprofit Management, and the Association of Fund-raising Professionals.

Tips for Entry

1. Be aware of leadership style of favorite bosses and professors. Learn how to manage well and take note of dos and don'ts from them when it is your turn.
2. Research organizations of interest to you and set up informational interviews with their Executive Directors. Ask them how they began their nonprofit career.
3. Explore graduate and certificate programs in nonprofit management. The Appendix on p. 258 of this book will help you get started.
4. Get to know people who serve on the board of directors of various organizations. Most nonprofits include this information on their Web site.

CHIEF FINANCIAL OFFICER

CAREER PROFILE

Duties: Overseeing, directing, and managing all finances and financial operations for a nonprofit organization

Alternate Title(s): Director of Finance, Director of Finance and Administration

Salary Range: $50,000 to $200,000 and up

Employment Prospects: Good

Advancement Prospects: Good

Best Geographical Location(s): All; best opportunities in major cities

Prerequisites:

Education or Training—Bachelor's degree; advanced degree in business, finance, accounting, or economics highly preferred

Experience—Ten years of increasingly responsible financial positions; nonprofit experience

Special Skills and Personality Traits—Excellent financial skills and knowledge; business understanding; analytical and problem-solving skills; strong communication skills; strategic thinking ability

CAREER LADDER

```
┌─────────────────────────────────┐
│  Chief Financial Officer (larger │
│  organization); Executive Director │
└─────────────────────────────────┘

┌─────────────────────────────────┐
│    Chief Financial Officer       │
└─────────────────────────────────┘

┌─────────────────────────────────┐
│    Vice President of Finance     │
└─────────────────────────────────┘
```

Position Description

In the nonprofit sector, everyone wants to talk about the mission. For many, the mission is why they get up and go to work every day; the cause is where the passion is. Talking about money may be less idealistic; however, without the financials being in order, nonprofits would cease to exist.

The Chief Financial Officer, or CFO, is essentially the executive director of finances. As the top financial officers, CFOs shoulder the fiduciary responsibility of their organization, making sure that their money will enable them to meet their missions. While it may be up to the executive director to have the vision, the CFO makes sure the vision is feasible and does not lead the organization into bankruptcy.

One of the major challenges faced by the Chief Financial Officer is the conflict of interest between the organization's mission and finances. While their corporate counterparts can make business decisions solely based on their bottom line, nonprofits are not profit-driven. Even if they are not financially sound, nonprofits cannot and will not cut pro-

grams and services that are part of their mission. CFOs, who usually have extensive business and financial education and training, learn on the job to see things differently under the nonprofit lens.

This challenge means that Chief Financial Officers often must make decisions that will cause their finances to take a hit, but will further the mission of their organization. For example, would a CFO of a major hospital opt not to authorize a life-saving surgery on a child without health insurance? Certainly, it would cost the hospital money, but the human cost is more important. While these decisions might not make financial sense, they enable the CFO to sleep at night, knowing his or her ethical responsibility has been carried out.

Furthermore, it can be formidable for nonprofit CFOs to spend money when there are not immediate results. Allocating a huge chunk of the annual budget for a new computer system may not meet yearly programming goals, but it will help meet those goals in the future. Chief Financial Officers must look at the big picture, and they need to be able to justify spending, reassuring the board that all decisions are made in keeping with the organization's mission.

A common term in financial management is *return on investment,* or ROI. Chief Financial Officers must help the board understand this concept in a different way. Good CFOs look to the private sector for tips. They may model some practices on the private sector, but adapt them to meet the needs of nonprofits. Sometimes, a decision is made that might not be a good financial investment, but is ultimately an investment in the organization's mission. This is how nonprofit CFOs try to balance these two conflicting forces of their job.

Additionally, Chief Financial Officers participate in fund-raising. They work with the board, executive director, and fund-raising staff to develop strategies and goals for raising money. CFOs educate and advise the fund-raising staff about the organization's financial status and needs to help them do their jobs. Often it takes spending money to make money, and they may recommend splurging on events and other programs that can lead to large donations.

Chief Financial Officers are both visionaries and strategists. In addition to managing the organization's investment portfolio, they also develop a long-term plan to make the money grow. They share information with the public about what they are doing with the money, adding the human quality that brings the mission to life.

Additional duties may include:

- Overseeing accounting, payroll, and controlling functions
- Preparing and managing budgets
- Meeting with the board of directors and presenting on financial concerns
- Meeting with high-level donors and developing fund-raising goals
- Developing financial tracking systems
- Supervising financial, accounting, and fund-raising staff
- Managing real estate investments and insurance policies
- Working as liaisons with investment committees

Some Chief Financial Officers also have responsibility for administration along with finance. In these cases, they may handle human resources issues such as hiring, salaries, and benefits; technology initiatives; and office operations.

The job of a Chief Financial Officer is high-powered and intense. It involves long hours, and at times, high stress. In many ways, the future of the organization is on the line with most decisions they make. Nonprofit CFOs thrive on this challenge and the balancing act they must perform between money and mission.

Salaries

Compensation for Chief Financial Officers can vary greatly depending on the size and type of organization. A top-level position in an organization of 20 has different implications from the same position in an organization of 1,000.

A November 2002 article in *CFO* magazine titled, "Facing the Bear: The 2002 Compensation Survey" written by Tim Reason, showed the average nonprofit CFO compensation (including salary and bonuses) was approximately $175,000. However, additional sources reflect considerably lower salaries.

According to the *NonProfit Times 2003 Salary Survey,* the mean projected 2003 salary for a Chief Financial Officer was $60,675. Another survey, *Compensation in Nonprofit Organization, 16th Edition,* a 2003 survey report of 131 benchmark jobs from Abbott, Langer & Associates, Inc., lists the median income of Chief Financial Officers as $74,893. Yet another survey summarized at www.workforce.com, citing a 2003 study about pay in the not-for-profit sector shows median cash compensation for Chief Financial Officers as $110,000. These studies show the tremendous variation in compensation for this position.

Employment Prospects

Employment prospects are good for Chief Financial Officers. Nonprofits are paying more attention to the financial aspects of their operations, and talented professionals are needed with expertise in this area. Opportunities are best in large cities and growing industries.

However, not every nonprofit financial professional is well suited for a CFO job. In addition to the business and accounting skills, prospective Chief Financial Officers also must have the experience and desire to be in nonprofit management.

Advancement Prospects

Advancement prospects are also good because Chief Financial Officers develop a skill set that affords them many options. While CFO is often the ultimate goal of one's career, one can move to different organizations to achieve new results. Some CFOs may decide to take on nonprofit management as executive directors or work as consultants helping other organizations develop business and financial plans.

Education and Training

To become a Chief Financial Officer, one needs a minimum of a bachelor's degree. Any field of study is possible, but course work in finance, accounting, business, and technology is essential.

Most CFOs have graduate degrees, commonly a master's of business administration (MBA). Others may be certified public accountants (CPAs). Degrees in nonprofit management or public administration can also be useful.

Most Chief Financial Officers say that the best training they received was on the job. Schooling is necessary to understand the financial principles, but putting them into practice in the nonprofit sector can really be learned only by doing it, say CFOs.

Experience, Skills, and Personality Traits

Ethics are a key component of the Chief Financial Officer's job. He or she must be able to stand by the financials if they are under scrutiny, confident that choices were made in the best interest of the organization.

In addition to integrity, Chief Financial Officers must have excellent relationship-building skills. The CFO and executive director of an organization must get along well as it is the job of the CFO to translate the executive director's vision into a reality. They also work closely with the board of directors; it is essential to have their respect and trust.

Chief Financial Officers also need specific technical skills to do their jobs. They need expertise in accounting and accounting principles, budgeting and budget management, grant management, and understanding the financial reporting required of 501(c)(3) nonprofits. Furthermore, they need a broad business background that enables them to understand all components of business operations. Prior nonprofit experience provides the necessary context through which to understand the business. Ten years of experience or more are typically needed for a CFO job, although at smaller organizations, less may be possible.

Unions and Associations

Chief Financial Officers may belong to associations including the Association for Financial Professionals, the American Society of Association Executives, and the Alliance for Nonprofit Management.

Tips for Entry

1. Explore the site www.cfo.com to learn more about the responsibilities and issues specific to a Chief Financial Officer.
2. Take courses in business, finance, and accounting to become familiar with terms and principles. Also, read publications such as the *Wall Street Journal* and the *NonProfit Times* to get acquainted with investing, as well as the nonprofit sector.
3. Try an internship where you can work in a financial capacity for a nonprofit. Take a look at http://www.idealist.org for ideas and visit your campus career center.
4. Gain leadership experience through campus organizations. Try running for office in positions such as president or treasurer.

DIRECTOR OF SPECIAL EVENTS

CAREER PROFILE

Duties: Planning, overseeing, and managing events for a nonprofit organization

Alternate Title(s): Event Planner, Event Manager, Special Events Director, Director of Meeting Planning

Salary Range: $40,000 to $80,000 and up

Employment Prospects: Good

Advancement Prospects: Good

Best Geographical Location(s): All

Prerequisites:

Education or Training—No specific requirements, but a minimum of bachelor's degree preferred for most positions

Experience—Two to five years of nonprofit or event planning experience

Special Skills and Personality Traits—Excellent networking skills; written and verbal communication ability; meticulous organization and attention to detail

CAREER LADDER

```
┌─────────────────────────────────────┐
│   Director of Special Events         │
│   (larger organization), Vice President, │
│         or Consultant                │
└─────────────────────────────────────┘

┌─────────────────────────────────────┐
│     Director of Special Events       │
└─────────────────────────────────────┘

┌─────────────────────────────────────┐
│      Special Event Coordinator       │
└─────────────────────────────────────┘
```

Position Description

Nonprofit organizations host a variety of special events each year to raise money for their cause and/or to thank donors or community members for their participation. These events, often called "benefits," range from black-tie galas, silent auctions, and formal dinners, to concerts, golf tournaments, and carnivals. There is a multitude of details that go into making each event run smoothly and seamlessly. The Director of Special Events is the person responsible for managing the planning, execution, and follow-up for these events.

The Director of Special Events plans the annual calendar of events for the organization. Depending on the size of the organization, it may have several large evening events and some smaller daytime events each year. Directors of Special Events may plan three events per year; they may plan 20. These can range in size from 30 attendees to more than 1,000.

Planning includes preparing the guest list, ordering the invitations, working with designers, and managing the mailing process. In order to plan the guest list, many Directors of Special Events use a database to track donors and select criteria for invitations based on donation level. The invitations often include information about the organization, donor listings by levels of gifts, and a bio of the honoree, if appropriate. He or she also works with a committee for each event, composed of a chairperson or co-chairperson, as well as volunteers.

The Director of Special Events also oversees all event logistics. This includes finding an appropriate venue, negotiating contracts, and hiring vendors such as florists, caterers, musicians, lighting companies, entertainers, and more as necessary. For some events, they may decide to have giveaways like promotional items or gift bags for all attendees. The Director of Special Events usually attends all events to ensure that everything is in place at the time of the event and manages crisis control if anything goes wrong.

Some events are planned in order to honor a specific individual. The individual selected to honor is usually someone who has a notable history of good work and has given generously to the organization. Furthermore, it is often someone who is well connected with generous friends, usually those in the corporate world that are looking for a philanthropic cause. If there is an honoree, the Director of Special Events will work as a liaison with this person.

As central to many nonprofit positions, fund-raising is also a part of the job. Another role of the Director of Special Events is the solicitation and tracking of funds. He or she must be involved with tracking the responses and maintaining records of who has already given money. Then they must follow up with those that have not already given. The Director of Special Events manages the budgets for all events and works collaboratively to set ticket prices with the director of development for their organization.

Additional duties may include:

- Writing auction catalog copy and other materials
- Writing remarks for honoree or other speakers
- Selecting and tasting menus for events
- Listening to bands and orchestras
- Maintaining financial records for each event
- Recruiting volunteers to assist with fund-raising
- Overseeing support staff
- Visiting and choosing locations for events
- Meeting with other hospitality industry professionals such as restaurant and hotel managers
- Acting as a liaison with corporations
- Maintaining donor database
- Hiring and training on-site personnel
- Managing deadlines

Depending on the size of an organization, the Director of Special Events may manage a staff of five to 10 people, may work with one assistant, or may work completely as a one-person shop. This determines whether the job is involved with the day-to-day logistics of each event, or if it involves delegating and managing the process. Furthermore, some nonprofit organizations do not have Directors of Special Events. The director of development, communications director, or even the executive director may take on the role. Other organizations choose to outsource the work to special event consultants or consulting firms that deal specifically with nonprofit organizations.

Directors of Special Events who work for business, trade, and professional associations are also involved with planning meetings and conferences for members. These annual conventions and expositions are frequently the main income-producing events for the organization, so a lot of care goes into making them run successfully. This includes working closely with hotels, airlines, and tourism professionals, as well as collaborating with the education, finance, and executive departments within their association. The Director of Special Events also coordinates meetings, develops brochures, plans programs, and secures advertisements to market the conference and ensure strong member participation.

Since events may take place during the day, in the evening, or on the weekends, Directors of Special Events often work long hours. Some local travel may be required to visit possible venues for events, or more extensive travel for attending national or international conferences.

Salaries
According to a 2003 *ASAE Association Executive Compensation and Benefits Study* published every two years by the American Society of Association Executives, the average salary for a director of meetings/conventions was $67,997. Depending upon the size of the organization, the geographical location, and their years of experience, Directors of Special Events may earn between $40,000 and $80,000 and up.

Employment Prospects
Employment prospects for Directors of Special Events are good. Although many nonprofit organizations may need to cut these positions in tough economic times and delegate the work to the development director or another administrative staff person, all nonprofit organizations plan events, so there is opportunity for those who are flexible. Directors of Special Events can also specialize in different functions such as meetings, conferences, and fund-raisers.

Advancement Prospects
Some Directors of Special Events seek advancement through moving to larger organizations or building on their event planning and fund-raising experience to seek high-level positions such as vice president or executive director. Others prefer to go out on their own and work for themselves or consulting firms as special events consultants. Furthermore, Directors of Special Events may move over to the development side if they have worked extensively with donors and gift solicitation.

Education and Training
Directors of Special Events have a variety of educational backgrounds. While it is not required to have a bachelor's degree for entry-level positions, most Directors of Special Events do have them and some also hold advanced degrees. Courses in business, finance, communications, and public relations may be helpful.

Some universities and continuing education programs offer certificates in event planning, such as New York University's School of Continuing and Professional Studies' Certificate in Meeting, Conference, and Event Management. These programs teach useful skills, but are not required for entry into the field.

Experience, Skills, and Personality Traits
To get hired as a Director of Special Events for a nonprofit organization, one either needs to have experience and knowledge of event planning, or experience and knowledge of development and the nonprofit world. For entry-level

positions, internship experience and good organizational skills are valuable. A Director of Special Events will usually have at least three years of experience in the corporate or nonprofit world; one who manages a department will often have five to 10 years of experience.

It is important for a Director of Special Events to be a good networker who understands the value of building relationships. Communication skills, both written and verbal, are crucial in interacting with vendors and donors alike and preparing materials.

Events can be unpredictable, so the Director of Special Events must be able to stay calm under pressure and be resourceful. If disaster strikes, he or she cannot panic, but instead find solutions to ensure the event can still take place. They should be very organized with an excellent attention to detail. When working with high-level donors, minutia-like spelling errors on a place card may make the difference in gift amounts to the organization.

Financial skills are very useful in managing a budget. Creativity is also necessary for a successful Director of Special Events to make events fun, different, and memorable.

Unions and Associations

Directors of Special Events may belong to organizations such as the International Special Events Society, the Inter-national Association for Exhibition Management, the American Society of Associations Executives, and Meetings Professionals International.

Tips for Entry

1. Plan an event for family or friends and pay attention to all the details that go into the event from beginning to end. See if you would enjoy this type of work on a larger scale for an organization.
2. Make a list of all the steps needed to run a successful fund-raising event. Have you ever attended a benefit? Which events have you personally attended that you have enjoyed the most? How would you have planned it differently?
3. Visit Web sites such as http://www.asaenet.org and http://www.idealist.org to see job descriptions for Directors of Special Events.
4. Learn about courses in meeting, conference, and event management. Take a look at the program offered by New York University at http://www.scps.nyu.edu/departments/certificate.jsp?certId=168.
5. Another good way to gain event-planning experience is through campus clubs or groups with which you are involved. Offer to work on their annual car wash, fashion show, pledge drive, or other fund-raising events.

HUMAN RESOURCES DIRECTOR

CAREER PROFILE

Duties: Manages employee relations functions for a non-profit organization including staffing, recruiting, benefits and compensation, and policies and procedures

Alternate Title(s): Human Resources Manager, Director of Staffing, Recruitment Manager, Employment Manager, Personnel Director, Training and Development Director

Salary Range: $45,000 to $125,000

Employment Prospects: Good

Advancement Prospects: Good

Best Geographical Location(s): All

Prerequisites:

Education or Training—At larger organizations, minimum of a bachelor's degree; master's degree in human resource administration or business preferred

Experience—Two to 10 years, depending on the size of the organization

Special Skills and Personality Traits—Excellent interpersonal skills; enthusiasm; good organization and attention to detail; flexibility; professionalism

CAREER LADDER

```
┌─────────────────────────────────────┐
│   Vice President or Deputy Director   │
└─────────────────────────────────────┘

┌─────────────────────────────────────┐
│      Human Resources Director         │
└─────────────────────────────────────┘

┌─────────────────────────────────────┐
│ Human Resources Assistant, Associate, │
│            or Coordinator             │
└─────────────────────────────────────┘
```

Position Description

Human Resource Directors are the advocates for the employees of their organizations. As representatives of their organizations, they project consummate professionalism and a positive image. They are the first line of contact for all personnel issues, and are often the first people a candidate for employment will meet. They handle "people" concerns, ranging from hiring, firing, and interviewing to mediating problems, administering benefits, and coordinating training.

Human Resources Directors may be generalists or specialists. In some organizations, the Human Resources Director may oversee all of the following aspects as a generalist, or focus in on one area such as recruiting, as a specialist. The basic functions that fall under human resources may include the following:

- Compensation and benefits, including salaries, major medical and dental insurance, vacation time, and pension plans (such as 401K)
- Hiring, including recruiting, interviewing, and generating job offers
- Employee relations, including mediation, employee assistance programs, and counseling
- Training and development, including employee education and programming
- Policy and procedures

As the administrators of benefits and pension programs, Human Resources Directors work with insurance companies to process claims and invoices for provider payment. They also handle monthly transfers and remittances for 401K and pension plans. Furthermore, they maintain benefits records and compare benefit plans and salary information with similar organizations. In a case where their organization provides reimbursement to employees for education or child care, they work to ensure that employees receive these credits as well. Additionally, they track other benefit usage such as vacation time and sick leave. The

Human Resources Director needs to understand all the available benefits thoroughly and may meet with new employees to review the benefits package and help them to make selections. For compensation, Human Resources Directors maintain salary records for all employees and determine appropriate salary ranges. They work with the different departments within the nonprofit to ensure fair compensation for new hires.

In terms of recruiting and hiring, Human Resources Directors are responsible for much of the process. Along with the various hiring departments, they develop job descriptions and then create a recruiting strategy. While most nonprofit organizations do not have large recruiting budgets like corporations, some may visit college campuses to participate in their interviewing programs for graduating students; attend career fairs; advertise in newspapers, professional newsletters, and online job search engines; and post jobs on internal and external Web sites. They screen candidates through résumé and cover letter review, and often conduct initial interviews. During these screening interviews, they look to see if candidates meet the basic job requirements and are a good fit for the organization before advancing them to meet with other staff members. While the final hiring decisions are usually made by the individual departments or managers, Human Resource Directors may play a role as well. Once the decision has been made to offer the candidate a position, they often generate the offer letter, manage communication with the candidate, register for any necessary testing (such as mandated drug testing), and negotiate salary.

Employee relations involve staff management issues including training and development, solving problems, and mediating between employees and supervisors. Human Resources Directors can develop training goals for their organizations and organize programs for employees to receive all sorts of educational seminars ranging from cultural sensitivity training to Microsoft Excel workshops. Also, employees sometimes view Human Resources Directors as a safe harbor within the organization to voice their work-related concerns or personal difficulties. They must be tactful and objective in listening to complaints or problems and choosing an appropriate course of action. Some organizations offer confidential counseling through employee assistance programs or community referrals for employees. Human Resources Directors may also develop and conduct annual performance evaluations of employees, along with direct supervisors.

Many policies contribute to helping a nonprofit organization run smoothly and many fall under the human resources department. Human Resources Directors develop policy for issues ranging from fair hiring practices, to posting vacant positions, to producing training manuals for the organization. By documenting policy and making sure all employees are aware of rules and procedures, this can prevent misun-

derstandings and even lawsuits in the unfortunate event that an employee is terminated.

Additional duties may include:

- Ensuring personnel policy compliance with state and federal employment laws
- Managing volunteers for the organization
- Handling union grievances and arbitration
- Developing personnel manuals
- Conducting new employee orientation
- Benchmarking with other organizations
- Preparing and monitoring budgets
- Piloting new programs
- Working with the board of directors and other committees
- Attending board meetings
- Using software and databases to track information
- Maintaining employee records
- Conducting job evaluations
- Developing policies for filling vacant positions

It is important for Human Resources Directors to be proud of their organizations and committed to their missions. As one Human Resources Director put it, they must be "cheerleaders" for their organization to be successful. If the person responsible for recruiting new employees is not enthusiastic and positive, how can the organization expect to hire and retain a quality staff?

Some travel may be required for Human Resources Directors involved with nationwide recruiting, as well as to attend national meetings. Hours usually keep to a 40- to 45-hour workweek, with longer hours expected during busy times of the years, such as benefit deadlines and hiring seasons.

Salaries

According to information on http://www.careerjournal.com, from a study titled *Compensation in Nonprofit Organizations, 16th Edition,* 2003, by Abbott, Langer & Associates, Inc., the average salary for a Human Resources Director was $51,677. If the Human Resources Director is an executive-level position, is combined with additional responsibilities such as membership or volunteer management, or is at a large organization, the range is from about $60,000 to $125,000. As is usually the case in the nonprofit sector, smaller organizations offer lower salaries.

Employment Prospects

Overall, employment prospects are good, especially in larger organizations. However, in times of budget constraints, the human resources department is often one of the first cut, since there is less hiring to be done. Also, some nonprofit organizations, particularly small ones, do not have designated Human Resources Directors. The administrative work is delegated to an office manager or assistant and the hiring to the individual departments.

Advancement Prospects

Human Resources Directors often advance by moving from smaller organizations to larger ones. They might also take on new areas of responsibility such as volunteer management or educational programming, or develop specialty areas for consulting. As nonprofit organizations evolve, Human Resources Directors have more opportunity to wear different hats and take on new responsibilities as people retire and retrain.

Education and Training

To become a Human Resources Director, an undergraduate background in business, psychology, human resources, English, or communications is helpful. Many high-level professionals also hold master's degrees in fields such as human resources management, business, or organizational psychology. In the past, it was possible to become a Human Resources Director at a small organization without a bachelor's degree, working up from an administrative position. However this is rarely possible in today's market, as the nonprofit sector grows more competitive.

Experience, Skills, and Personality Traits

While entry-level positions in human resources are available right out of college, positions as a Human Resources Director can require up to 10 years of experience. Smaller organizations are more apt to try someone with only two or three years of experience, while large organizations look for professionals who have proved themselves with a long list of accomplishments.

Human Resources Directors must display professionalism and good judgment. They need to be articulate, well organized, and have the ability to juggle multiple projects. They also must be flexible to adapt to the changing needs of their organization. Strong interpersonal skills and enthusiasm are an absolute must.

Unions and Associations

Human Resources Directors may belong to the American Society of Association Executives, the Society for Human Resources Management, and the American Society for Training and Development.

Tips for Entry

1. Take a look at job listings particularly for nonprofits on sites such as http://www.idealist.org.
2. Volunteer in your career services office on campus. Opportunities may be available as a peer counselor to review résumés and help fellow students prepare for interviews.
3. Join a professional organization for networking.
4. Research graduate programs in human resources management through the Society for Human Resources Management at http://www.shrm.org/foundation/directory.
5. Speak to a Human Resources Director at a nonprofit organization to learn about various specialties.
6. Have you ever been involved in an organization's hiring process? Consider an internship or volunteer position that exposes you to human resources. You may be able to sit in on interviews or recruit volunteers.

DIRECTOR OF VOLUNTEERS

CAREER PROFILE

Duties: Creates, develops, and runs volunteer programs for a nonprofit organization; recruits, trains, and manages volunteers

Alternate Title(s): Manager of Volunteer Services, Coordinator of Volunteers, Volunteer Resources Manager

Salary Range: $25,000 to $85,000

Employment Prospects: Fair

Advancement Prospects: Good

Best Geographical Location(s): Major cities

Prerequisites:

Education or Training—Bachelor's degree or higher required for most positions

Experience—Volunteer, internship, or prior nonprofit experience needed

Special Skills and Personality Traits—Responsible; patient; good communicator; strong manager

CAREER LADDER

```
┌─────────────────────────────────┐
│   Executive Director, Director   │
│     of Development, or Director  │
│  of Volunteers (larger organization) │
└─────────────────────────────────┘

┌─────────────────────────────────┐
│      Director of Volunteers      │
└─────────────────────────────────┘

┌─────────────────────────────────┐
│   Volunteer Coordinator, Intern, │
│           or Volunteer           │
└─────────────────────────────────┘
```

Position Description

Most nonprofit organizations could not function without their dedicated staff of volunteers. Volunteers perform a tremendous variety of tasks in different settings ranging from comforting ill patients at hospitals, to providing tours at museums, to making phone calls to support legislation for grassroots environmental groups. The Director of Volunteers must assess the needs of the organization and then find a way to staff those needs with able and willing volunteers.

A challenge for Directors of Volunteers is not only to create job descriptions, but also to find creative and innovative ways to recruit volunteers for these unpaid positions. Since money is not at stake, they need to find other motivators to appeal to people's sense of goodness, community, or social conscience. Marketing is a key factor in getting the organization known and the volunteer program appealing. The Director of Volunteers often markets programs to local businesses, schools, religious organizations, and service groups that are likely to be receptive. Word of mouth is also a big factor in recruiting volunteers, through the connections of board members, staff, and most important, other volunteers who have been in the program and could share their positive experiences.

Once a pool of volunteers is established, the Director of Volunteers deals with appropriate placement within the organization. He or she usually conducts interviews with the volunteers to get to know them better and find a role that best suits both the personality, skills, interests, and availability of the volunteer as well as the needs of the organization. Helping to find the right fit can be a time-consuming process, but it is beneficial in the end because it is much easier to retain satisfied and successful volunteers than those who are not working in conjunction with their potential and talents.

Background checks for volunteers will vary depending on the organization and the population they serve, but all volunteers generally go through an application process that includes checking of character references. The Director of Volunteers must be a good judge of people and as one director put it, "go with their gut" in terms of holding off on placing any individuals about whom they doubt their professionalism and ability to serve as an appropriate volunteer.

Another important part of the job of a Director of Volunteers is training. There are many ways that the Director of Volunteers can train his or her volunteer staff, including creating policy and procedure manuals, informational brochures, position descriptions, newsletter articles, and bringing in speakers for training on a variety of issues. Some Directors of Volunteers hold regular volunteer supervision meetings at which issues and concerns are raised.

Volunteers who share their free time to help others appreciate recognition for their efforts, and the Director of Volunteers works to create mechanisms to recognize this service. Programs such as annual award dinners, certificates of honor, Volunteer of the Month programs, and newsletter articles are some of the ways that volunteers can be commended for their accomplishments. However, not all volunteers appreciate such public recognition and many Directors of Volunteers agree that one-on-one acknowledgment goes a long way. One Director of Volunteers commented on the amount of time she spends writing personal thank-you notes, and how important she feels this is to the field.

The Association for Volunteer Administration (AVA), the top international professional organization for Directors of Volunteers, identifies several core competencies as critical for the successful management of volunteer resources. The core competencies are as follows:

• Professional Principles—ethical practice, pluralism, professional development, advocacy
• Leadership—types of leadership, decision making
• Organizational Management—models and management, tools such as communication and team building, financial and program accountability
• Planning—strategic and operational planning, risk management
• Human Resources Management—volunteer program management, supervision, staff/volunteer relationship, information collection and reporting

If you ask a Director of Volunteers why he or she has chosen this field, you are not likely to hear that the answer relates in any way to benefits, perks, or compensation. They often work long hours for little pay. Directors of Volunteers do not do their work for the money, but rather, for the gratifying feeling of not only helping others, but also helping others to help others, which only multiplies the satisfaction.

Salaries

According to a 2003 *Nonprofit Times* survey on the Association for Volunteer Administration's (AVA) Web site, the average salary for a Director of Volunteers was $35,267. However, this same survey shows some variation for geographic location, ranging from a low of $26,191 in the central U.S. region to a high of $35,230 for the mid-Atlantic states. Even a wider disparity occurs based on the size and budget of the organization. The fol-

lowing chart depicts salary difference based on organizational budget size:

$50 million +	= $51,953
$25 to $49.9 million	= $29,000
$10 to $24.9 million	= $34,986
$1 to 9.9 million	= $35,411
$500k to $999.9k	= $30,599

Another survey found on the AVA Web site, the *Towers Perrin 2000 Survey of Management Positions in Nonprofit Organizations,* demonstrates the distinction in salary between Directors of Volunteers who serve as volunteer managers and Directors of Volunteers who hold senior-level positions within the organization. The data for volunteer managers shows $32,900 as minimum annual salary; $41,300 as midpoint annual salary; and $50,200 as maximum annual salary. This contrasts with the data for senior-level positions: $65,300, minimum annual salary; $86,300, midpoint annual salary; and $108,500, maximum annual salary.

Employment Prospects

Currently, employment prospects are fair for several reasons. As organizations downsize due to economic hardship, the Director of Volunteers is often one of the first positions to be cut. The job is often delegated to someone else in the organization such as the executive director or other senior manager. Additionally, some boards of directors do not recognize the value in having a specific professional designated to do this job. However, studies have shown that organizations with professional Directors of Volunteers have better volunteer retainment, better community relations, and therefore, ultimately raise more money for the organization.

Advancement Prospects

For some Directors of Volunteers, their current position is the highest level that they seek. Others may go on to manage or establish larger volunteer programs at bigger organizations. Still others take their skills and apply them to other senior-level positions in the nonprofit sector such as executive director or director of development.

Education and Training

There is no standard education required for a Director of Volunteers. People come to this profession from a variety of backgrounds and can bring their unique skills to their job. Most job listings require a bachelor's degree. Course work or experience in teaching, social work, writing, and public relations can be helpful, as well as, of course, having been a volunteer.

Recently, a movement has begun to "professionalize the profession" by establishing various certificate credentialing programs. While these programs are voluntary, they can help individuals gain valuable skills, as well as professional credibility to enter and advance within the field. Certificate programs include the Certificate in Volunteer Management from Washington State University and Certificate of Excellence in Nonprofit Leadership and Management from the University of Wisconsin–Madison. Additionally, the Certified in Volunteer Administration (CVA) credential is offered by the Association for Volunteer Administration (AVA) for practitioners in volunteer resources management.

Experience, Skills, and Personality Traits

Above all, a Director of Volunteers should be a people person. Excellent communication, interpersonal, and listening skills are important, as is the ability to build teams that can bond with each other as well as the agency. Often, this position can be a one-person department and requires the capacity to handle a lot of responsibility. In order to understand the commitment and concerns of volunteers, they should have served as volunteers themselves.

Successful Directors of Volunteers are positive, compassionate, nurturing, and patient. They have good teaching and leadership skills and can train, manage, and motivate people with ease. In addition, strong sales, marketing, and recruiting skills are beneficial in order to help build a volunteer program.

Unions and Associations

The international professional membership association for Directors of Volunteers is the Association for Volunteer Administration, an organization with more than 2,100 members representing 16 countries. Other Directors of Volunteers may belong to other nonprofit associations such as the American Society of Association Executives or the Society for Nonprofit Organizations.

Tips for Entry

1. Volunteer! Try out different volunteer roles to help out at organizations of interest.
2. Visit Web sites such as http://www.volunteertoday.com and http://www.managingvolunteers.com that are geared toward professionals who manage volunteer programs.
3. Find a mentor in the field who can help you with job leads and making the transition into a professional position.
4. Join professional associations, both locally and nationally. Check out the Web site of the Association for Volunteer Administration at http://www.avaintl.org.
5. Learn as much as you can through conducting online research, reading articles, and reviewing policy and procedure manuals.

RESEARCH DIRECTOR

CAREER PROFILE

Duties: Manages the research efforts for a nonprofit organization, including conducting, coordinating, and disseminating research; devising strategies; implementing plans; and synthesizing information

Alternate Title(s): Statistician, Director of Institutional Research, Research Manager, Director of Research and Evaluation

Salary Range: $45,000 to $75,000 and up

Employment Prospects: Fair

Advancement Prospects: Fair

Best Geographical Location(s): All, with the majority of positions in or near major cities

Prerequisites:

Education or Training—Minimum of a bachelor's degree; many organizations require master's or doctoral degrees

Experience—One to 10 years of research experience, depending on the organization

Special Skills and Personality Traits—Excellent attention to detail; superior research, writing, and analytical skills; strong communication skills; good grasp of quantitative concepts and statistics

CAREER LADDER

```
┌─────────────────────────────────┐
│   Vice President of Research      │
└─────────────────────────────────┘

┌─────────────────────────────────┐
│        Research Director          │
└─────────────────────────────────┘

┌─────────────────────────────────┐
│  Research Assistant or Associate  │
└─────────────────────────────────┘
```

Position Description

Nonprofit organizations conduct research for various reasons. For some, it is to support their agenda on legislative issues. For others, it is to provide relevant data to their membership. Yet others use research to further scientific studies and expand public knowledge about important issues. For all, however, it is to advance the mission of their organization in some way.

Particularly for organizations seeking funding for specific projects, research studies prove the validity of their position. For example, if a youth development nonprofit wants to secure funding for an after-school program, research studies can help make this happen in the following way. First, the organization asserts that after-school programs can help keep teenagers out of trouble and enhance their academic performance. Then, by producing reports

that contain data supporting this claim, investors may be more likely to finance this program. Research can often provide the proof that nonprofit programs actually work.

Research Directors are responsible for leading the research efforts of their organization. Whether it is to push a policy through in Washington or to inform members of a profession about recent salary trends, they conduct studies aimed at getting the necessary information for their organization, whatever that might be. In addition to supervising other researchers and overseeing projects, most Research Directors also work in the trenches, conducting research themselves.

The process of research can be intense, involving many steps until completion. Research Directors begin by strategizing not only what types of research studies make sense for their organization at the current time, but also what type of studies best meet their long-term goals. This is called determining the research methodology. Some research projects may require quantitative studies, which depend on numbers and statistics, while others may call for qualitative studies, which involve using words and speaking to people for more anecdotal evidence. Most organizations have research projects that require both these methods, either used together in one study or separately in different studies.

To get the necessary data, Research Directors may design questionnaires and interview people. They may determine subjects and devise ways to secure their participation. Also, they may conduct scientific analyses or study groups over longer periods of time. Furthermore, they spend time contacting respondents through letters, e-mail, and telephone calls to obtain information.

Once data returns from a survey, Research Directors lead the process of collating and analyzing the data. They may supervise a staff who keys it in to the databases and runs reports. Then they must make sense of the findings and determine how it meets their goals. They coordinate with editorial and design staff to produce research reports that can be sent to members, potential funders, policy makers, and other interested parties. At times, they may be called upon to formally present their findings.

It is essential for Research Directors to keep up on any and all trends and issues pertinent to their organization. They scan the media and hunt for anecdotal information. Some are also responsible for public policy and keep up on all legislative developments relevant to their area of public interest. Also, some Research Directors may be responsible for benchmarking studies. Benchmarking is the process of measuring organizations against their competitors to determine who is the best, who sets the standard, and what that standard is.

Additional duties may include:

- Initiating relationships with academic institutions as research partners
- Outsourcing research responsibilities to other professionals
- Creating instruments for research and evaluation
- Overseeing departmental budgets
- Supervising a research team
- Developing and delivering presentations
- Managing Web information sites
- Acting as a spokesperson for the media
- Writing reports and fact sheets
- Attending national meetings
- Analyzing and comparing other research studies
- Producing statistical reports
- Conducting literature reviews
- Developing new research ideas and initiatives

Research Directors play an important role in nonprofits since they have the ability to further their mission by validating their work. They spend time working independently, but also as part of a team that collaborates to produce results.

Salaries

Salaries for Research Directors vary depending on the size and type of their organization, as well as by their level of education and experience. Research Directors with a bachelor's degree working for small associations may earn in the $45,000 range, while those holding a doctoral degree and employed by large organizations may earn upwards of $75,000.

According to a summary at www.workforce.com citing a 2003 study about pay in the not-for-profit sector, the median cash compensation for a research position (not top-level) was $53,200. However, the same summary cited the median compensation for a statistician as $100,000 and the top position in scientific research as $117,900.

Employment Prospects

Employment prospects are fair for Research Directors. While not all nonprofit organizations have the capacity for this position, for many others, particularly those in public policy, advocacy, science, and associations, it is crucial. Opportunities are available for those professionals with the appropriate combination of research experience and education.

Advancement Prospects

To advance as a Research Director, one needs an advanced degree. A Ph.D. is required for complex research studies and provides the necessary background to develop research initiatives and lead a team. Research Directors may work for one to 10 years as assistants and associates before moving into their role. Then they may transition from there by moving to larger organizations with more responsibility or taking on more organizational leadership as a vice president or comparable position.

Education and Training

Education and training requirements vary for Research Directors depending on the size and type of their organization, but require a bachelor's degree at the very least. Many organizations prefer or require at least a master's degree, and those who conduct more complex research studies seek professionals with a doctoral degree. Subjects of study vary depending on the organization, but coursework in psychology, public policy, and even investigative journalism may be helpful. An understanding of statistics is necessary.

While they usually do not receive formal training on the job (with the exception of specific database and computer programs), the expectation is that Research Directors come in with a solid background in research. Whether it comes from working as a research assistant for a professor as an undergraduate, conducting research studies independently as a graduate student, or working as part of a team of researchers as an assistant, it is crucial to have this experience and knowledge base.

Experience, Skills, and Personality Traits

Research Directors must be highly computer literate. They need to be experienced with spreadsheets such as Microsoft Excel and Access, as well as statistical programs such as SPSS and additional quantitative analysis software.

Also, they need to be able to manage their time well, multitask, and meet deadlines. They should be superb researchers with inquisitive minds and excellent analytical skills. It is also important for Research Directors to pay careful attention to detail and to have the patience to see studies through.

Unions and Associations

Research Directors may belong to professional organizations, including the American Society of Association Executives, the Alliance for Nonprofit Management, the Independent Sector, the Association for Research on Nonprofit Organizations and Voluntary Action, and the Association of Professional Researchers for Advancement.

Tips for Entry

1. While a student, work as a research assistant for a professor. Learn about the various types of research methodologies and become skilled in their practices.
2. Explore nonprofit organizations that correspond with your area of study and research interests.
3. Take courses in statistics and become familiar with the related software. Brush up on your computer skills by learning more about spreadsheets and databases.
4. Speak to entry-level researchers at nonprofit organizations, such as research assistants. Find out about how they found their positions and what path they followed.
5. Read the job descriptions for Research Directors on nonprofit sites such as http://www.opportunitynocs.org/index.jsp.

DIRECTOR OF MEMBERSHIP

CAREER PROFILE

Duties: Manages the membership process for a nonprofit organization; devises strategies for recruiting and retaining members

Alternate Title(s): Membership Director, Membership Manager, Director of Membership Services, Recruiting Director

Salary Range: $30,000 to $75,000 and up

Employment Prospects: Good

Advancement Prospects: Good

Best Geographical Location(s): Major cities

Prerequisites:

Education or Training—No formal requirements, but bachelor's degree is standard; courses in English and marketing helpful

Experience—Prior work or volunteer experience in nonprofits

Special Skills and Personality Traits—Excellent writing and interpersonal skills; organization; creativity

CAREER LADDER

```
┌─────────────────────────────────────┐
│  Director of Membership (larger      │
│  organization) or Vice President     │
└─────────────────────────────────────┘

┌─────────────────────────────────────┐
│       Director of Membership         │
└─────────────────────────────────────┘

┌─────────────────────────────────────┐
│    Membership Coordinator            │
│  or Sales/Customer Service Associate  │
└─────────────────────────────────────┘
```

Position Description

If you have ever joined a club or organization, chances are good that someone in the membership department made you aware of the program, as well as processed your application. Directors of Membership run the process of recruiting and retaining members of different types of nonprofit organizations, including zoos and conservation; arts and culture; religious organizations; and business, professional, trade, and charitable associations.

At a cultural or conservation institution, the job of a Director of Membership is twofold since it involves the cultivation of both current members and new members. The Director of Membership makes sure that current members are satisfied and that they take advantage of the benefits of membership. The idea is that support goes both ways: you support us and we will support you. Benefits may include receiving publications such as newsletters in the mail, attending special members-only events or programs, and obtaining other individual tours and services. By providing members with strong customer service and recognition for

their support, the Director of Membership encourages the possibility of members taking their patronage to the next level—becoming a donor. They work with the directors of major gifts and development to target individuals likely to upgrade their membership status. The bottom line is that members who are happy with the organization are more likely to show their appreciation by ensuring its continuation through financial support.

In addition to meeting the needs of current members and working to upgrade membership, Directors of Membership also work to recruit new members; approaches include on-site sales, direct mail, and other media marketing campaigns. The goal of the organization is to focus efforts toward those individuals most apt to become members. Thus, on-site sales is one way to target people who are already interested in the organization. For example, Directors of Membership may assume that people who are visiting their museum have an interest in supporting it. Direct mail is most effective when there is a list exchange with similar institutions. In this case, when members of a community zoo demonstrate that they support conservation they may be good candidates to approach for membership in a local botanic garden.

Marketing and sales are also a key part of the job of Directors of Membership. They need to be able to make membership look desirable and to produce materials that back up this claim. They must know who to target and what approach to take in order to market membership successfully. In addition, they may work with the marketing and communications departments to create brochures, advertisements, and Web site content to promote membership. The ability to sell the institution and its programs is crucial.

Directors of Membership who work at museums or cultural institutions may run individual membership, as well as corporate membership. Membership is often separated into various levels such as friend, supporter, and patron, distinguished by the membership price and benefits. They also may organize additional programs for companies, such as sponsorship of an exhibition, a chance for high visibility for the company looking for philanthropy. These can be motivating opportunities to attract new members and raise more money for the organization. Together with the director of special events and director of development, they plan members-only events to encourage giving and meet their fundraising goals.

Working as liaison with other departments within the organization is necessary to achieve the ultimate goal for nonprofits to carry out their missions: raising money. The Director of Membership works in conjunction with visitor services, volunteer services, education, fund-raising and development, special events, and others in order to identify new members and cultivate existing ones.

At business, professional, and trade associations, Directors of Membership play a slightly different role since their members are individuals who belong to their organization because of their professional affiliation. They also strive to recruit and retain members, but keep within this pool, rather than the general public. They focus on customer service, collecting dues, and promoting member satisfaction. They may deal with issues such as continuing education, certification, and chapter relations. Annual conventions are an opportunity for them to work hand in hand with other departments within their association to improve their membership numbers. At many associations, when people let their memberships lapse, a campaign is waged as to how to get them back. As one Director of Membership stated, her job is "to make membership sexy" and to strategize ways to make it appealing. Directors of Membership at business, professional, and trade associations also spend much time meeting the needs of current members, making themselves accessible through telephone conversations and e-mails.

Additional duties for all Directors of Membership may include:

- Maintaining a database of member information
- Evaluating programs and recommending improvements
- Writing newsletters and other promotional material
- Developing new programs
- Identifying cultivation strategies
- Designing member benefits
- Performing administrative tasks
- Ensuring that membership goals are met and that desired numbers are achieved
- Preparing membership renewal forms
- Meeting with current and prospective members to discuss programs and involvement
- Working with other similar nonprofit institutions to share information to increase membership
- Providing follow-up to members
- Observing trends in member feedback and satisfaction
- Processing invoices
- Working as a liaison with the board of trustees
- Managing a customer call center
- Answering members phone calls and e-mails
- Meeting financial target goals for their organization

The job of a Director of Membership will vary depending on the size and location of the organization. Cultural icons such as the Metropolitan Museum of Art in New York City, or the Kennedy Center for the Performing Arts in Washington, D.C., have huge membership bases and large departments to support membership, whereas small theater companies and local museums often have only one person to handle membership, as well as other responsibilities. The same goes for large versus small professional associations. Some Directors of Membership are at the executive level of their organization and manage large staffs, while other positions are considered more mid-range within the organization.

Salaries

According to the 2003 *ASAE Association Executive Compensation and Benefits Study* from the American Society of Association Executives, the average total compensation for a Director of Membership was $72,953. However, this figure is for executive-level Directors of Membership at large organizations. Salary will vary depending on the size and location of the organization, as well as the level of the position. Mid-range salaries are typically in the $40,000 to $60,000 range.

Employment Prospects

Employment prospects are generally good. Membership is vital to many nonprofit organizations, so they take it seriously. Those institutions with dedicated professionals for membership services are more successful at recruiting and retaining members, cultivating relationships, and encouraging giving. Opportunities exist at a number of different types of organizations as well.

Advancement Prospects

Advancement prospects are also good. Directors of Membership develop a skill set that includes writing, fund-raising, and marketing, which can be applied to many areas of the nonprofit sector. Advancement can be achieved by moving from a small institution to a larger one, or by transitioning into positions in development, major gifts, marketing, communications, or executive administration.

Education and Training

While there is no formal educational path to take, most positions require at least a bachelor's degree. In some settings, it is common for Directors of Membership to have a master's degree in business or nonprofit management, which may provide a competitive edge for job hunting and advancement. Professionals who become Directors of Membership often have either work experience in the nonprofit sector or in sales and marketing. Courses in nonprofit management, sales and marketing, English, writing, public relations, and communications are often useful.

Experience, Skills, and Personality Traits

Directors of Membership must be customer-service focused. They need to enjoy working with people and helping to meet their needs, answer their questions, and address their complaints. Also, strong writing skills are helpful in order to work on grant proposals, correspond with members, and create membership materials. Good organization,

database management skills, creativity, and the ability to sell are also key.

It is also important for Directors of Membership to fully understand the goals of their organization in order to sell it to prospective members. They need to be aware of when to initiate programming, how to generate revenue, and how to work well with others as part of a team.

Unions and Associations

Directors of Membership can belong to a number of nonprofit professional associations, including the Association of Fund-raising Professionals and the American Society of Association Executives, as well as local, specific organizations such as Women in Development in New York City, Boston, and Chicago.

Tips for Entry

1. Volunteer within the membership services department of a nonprofit organization.
2. Get involved with an organization on campus. How does this organization recruit new members and work with existing ones? Talk to the people responsible for these roles to learn about the skills required.
3. Pick up membership brochures from a local museum or cultural institution. Evaluate them for effectiveness as both a prospective member as well as a Director of Membership who may have produced them.
4. Try a temporary job at a nonprofit to learn the ropes. Don't be afraid to start at the bottom: this could be a great introduction to the field and a good way to get your foot in the door.

BOARD MEMBER

CAREER PROFILE

Duties: As part of a board of directors, provides governance and support to a nonprofit organization

Alternate Title(s): None

Salary Range: $0 to a small stipend

Employment Prospects: Excellent

Advancement Prospects: Fair

Best Geographical Location(s): All

Prerequisites:

Education or Training—Varies from no formal education to advanced professional degrees

Experience—Corporate or community experience, or life experience relevant to the organization

Special Skills and Personality Traits—Good leadership and decision-making skills; ethical, honest, and open-minded; analytical and strong problem-solving abilities; team player

CAREER LADDER

```
┌─────────────────────────────────────┐
│   Board Chairperson or President     │
└─────────────────────────────────────┘

┌─────────────────────────────────────┐
│           Board Member               │
└─────────────────────────────────────┘

┌─────────────────────────────────────┐
│      Volunteer or unrelated          │
│      professional position           │
└─────────────────────────────────────┘
```

Position Description

As you read over nonprofit job descriptions, you can see that many state duties such as "working with the board of directors." The board of directors (sometimes also called board of trustees) is the governing body of a nonprofit organization. In addition to making sure the mission of the organization is carried out, they are responsible for major financial and programming decisions. Executive directors must get board approval for the budget, new positions, new programs, new fund-raising campaigns, and any other significant undertaking.

Board Members are, for the vast majority, volunteers. Most are employed elsewhere in full-time professional positions, or have other sources of income. While they do not get paid for serving on the board, they will tell you the other advantages are exceptional. Many Board Members come from the corporate world, resulting in a mutually beneficial relationship. For the nonprofit organization, they enjoy corporate ties that can result in significant giving. For the Board Member, the opportunity to serve the greater good and help a nonprofit to succeed is extremely rewarding.

The composition of nonprofit boards varies depending on the organization. Boards usually comprise some combination of high-level donors, community leaders and other prominent professionals, community members, and senior staff of the organization. It logically follows that local organizations have more Board Members from their communities, while national and international organizations may have Board Members from all over the country and even the world.

Serving as a Board Member may bring with it some financial expectations. To serve on some boards, Board Members may be required to donate a certain amount each year, but this is not always the case. However, giving is always encouraged and often expected, depending on the Board Member's financial position. They may be asked to fund specific projects on an as-needed basis. Those Board Members who are not in the position for major giving can provide support in other ways, such as bringing in other donors or recruiting volunteers. The situation is understood and explained when the Board Member begins his or her service, so there won't be complications or misunderstandings later on.

Additionally, many Board Members find their experience serving on a nonprofit board to be excellent for personal networking. Nonprofit boards generally have a large number of wealthy individuals with prominent careers. In some society circles, being part of a certain nonprofit board is prestigious. Board Members not only have the opportunity to work together for a common cause, but also can make connections that could advance their own careers. All the while, they are still legally and ethically bound to do their duty to serve the nonprofit.

Because of their frequent wealth and prominence, Board Members assist nonprofits in several ways. First, they bring their own networks that are excellent sources for fund-raising. For each event, Board Members provide the organization with their guest list of attendees to invite, all of whom are expected to attend and pay top dollar for their seats. Furthermore, Board Members can offer additional help based on their own personal backgrounds. For example, a Board Member who professionally is a public relations executive may be able to get free publicity for events and programs. Also, Board Members are often paramount in recruiting volunteers. Since the majority of Board Members are employed elsewhere, they can tap into their colleagues and friends to support an organization they believe in.

Some Board Members may not be wealthy, yet they may be from the community that the nonprofit serves, which is just as important, if not more. They are part of the leadership that makes decisions that affects their own lives, not just the lives of disadvantaged people the Board Members have never met. Also, they have a constituency base and access to inside resources. This gives them, as well as their fellow Board Members, an invaluable perspective to be taken into account with all decisions. These community Board Members are in the unique position of making recommendations based on knowledge of how the results will affect them and their neighborhoods.

Board Members may meet monthly, quarterly, or less frequently depending on the organization. They form committees to head different projects or aspects of management that are appropriate to the size and structure of their organization. Board Members lead various committees and take on roles based on their interests and specialty areas, as well as the needs of the organization. For example, one Board Member may serve as a treasurer and another might lead a marketing or personnel committee.

Furthermore, they are called upon to provide approval for major decisions, such as the budget or new programming. From a financial standpoint, Board Members review the feasibility of these initiatives, always taking the organization's mission into account. They also listen closely to the executive director and other senior staff members who may explain why these programs make sense. It helps Board Members when they hear presentations not only from the executive director, but other staff members as well.

Following are the "Ten Basic Responsibilities of Nonprofit Boards," as published by BoardSource on their Web site http://www.boardsource.org:

1. Determine the organization's mission and purpose. It is the board's responsibility to create and review a statement of mission and purpose that articulates the organization's goals, means, and primary constituents served.
2. Select the chief executive. Boards must reach a consensus on the chief executive's responsibilities and undertake a careful search to find the most qualified individual for the position.
3. Provide proper financial oversight. The board must assist in developing the annual budget and ensuring that proper financial controls are in place.
4. Ensure adequate resources. One of the board's foremost responsibilities is to provide adequate resources for the organization to fulfill its mission.
5. Ensure legal and ethical integrity and maintain accountability. The board is ultimately responsible for ensuring adherence to legal standards and ethical norms.
6. Ensure effective organizational planning. Boards must actively participate in an overall planning process and assist in implementing and monitoring the plan's goals.
7. Recruit and orient new board members and assess board performance. All boards have a responsibility to articulate prerequisites for candidates, orient new members, and periodically and comprehensively evaluate its own performance.
8. Enhance the organization's public standing. The board should clearly articulate the organization's mission, accomplishments, and goals to the public and garner support from the community.
9. Determine, monitor, and strengthen the organization's programs and services. The board's responsibility is to determine which programs are consistent with the organization's mission and to monitor their effectiveness.
10. Support the chief executive and assess his or her performance. The board should ensure that the chief executive has the moral and professional support he or she needs to further the goals of the organization.

Source: Reprinted with permission from www.boardsource. org. BoardSource, formerly the National Center for Nonprofit Boards, is the premier resource for practical information, tools, and training for board members and executive directors of nonprofit organizations worldwide. For more information about BoardSource, visit www.boardsource.org or call 800-883-6262. BoardSource (c) 2003. Text may not be reproduced without written permission from BoardSource.

Because Board Members are volunteers, they get great satisfaction from their work. They choose only to serve on the board of organizations they truly support. Serving on a nonprofit board may require only a few hours per year, or many hours each week, depending on the expectations of the organization and involvement level of the individual Board Member.

Salaries

The overwhelming majority of Board Members do not receive financial compensation for their service. According to a 2003 article in *Philanthropy News Digest* (http://fdncenter.org/pnd/), some nonprofits report paying Board Members a range between $5,000 and $70,000 per year. However, this is not common. Board Members are rarely, if ever, motivated by money to serve on nonprofit boards.

Employment Prospects

Prospects are excellent for those who want to volunteer as Board Members. However, Board Members go through a more extensive recruitment process than other volunteers.

First, they need to be nominated. Current Board Members often strategize about whom they want to serve on their boards. They often are looking to meet a specific need with each member, such as someone working for a large financial company, arts organization, or member of a certain community. Likely Board Members are those who are expected to be accessible and involved.

After nomination, the current president and other members interview the potential Board Member. They must agree to appoint each Board Member. The responsibilities for Board Members are outlined, and they usually attend orientation and training to get fully up to speed with the inner workings of the organization.

Advancement Prospects

Board Members seeking additional leadership can become board presidents or chairpersons. Furthermore, the networking that comes from board membership can also lead to advancement in their own professional careers.

Education and Training

Board Members may have a whole range of educational backgrounds. Most Board Members have college degrees and often hold graduate or professional degrees. Doctors, lawyers, teachers, social workers, investment bankers, stay-at-home mothers, and artists alike may serve together at various organizations. However, there may be Board Members at some organizations who have never completed high school, yet they add specific knowledge or life experience to the board on which they serve. Bringing something of special value to the board, whether it is money, connections, or expertise, is the most esteemed credential a Board Member can offer.

Some organizations look to recruit Board Members who are alumni of various programs. Colleges and universities look to their graduates, and different social service or other educational programs may look for those who have successfully completed their programs.

Board Members receive training on the job to learn the ins and outs of their organization. They may receive training manuals, attend orientation sessions, and spend time with the executive director and other Board Members.

Experience, Skills, and Personality Traits

While there is no specific experience that Board Members must have to serve on a nonprofit board of directors, it is expected that they have relevant work and/or life experience that will enable them to contribute to the organization. They must be committed to the mission of the organization and willing to dedicate their time and/or money as needed.

Board Members should expect to contribute leadership as well. They are often asked on an interview by a nominating committee "What do you bring to us?" and they are expected to lead committees and projects throughout their tenure.

Organizations differ in the way they handle length of service. Some nonprofits impose term limits of one to two years on Board Members and may require a hiatus between reappointments. Others choose to stagger terms of service where different Board Members are elected every few years for varying terms. They do this to keep a balance of veteran leadership and fresh ideas.

In terms of personal qualities, Board Members should take their jobs seriously. They need to feel vested in decision making and knowledgeable about the issues at hand. However, at the same time, they need a sense of humor and enthusiasm in order to keep the atmosphere productive and congenial.

Furthermore, Board Members need to be honest and ethical. They must be able to objectively analyze the situation at their organization and make decisions that not only benefit the organization financially, but also further its mission. It is valuable for them to be fair and impartial, and not forceful with opinions or contrary. Their ideas should be respected without their having to force the issue.

Unions and Associations

There are a number of organizations that offer support to nonprofit Board Members. These include Board Source (http://www.boardsource.org/), Management Assistance Program for Nonprofits (http://mapnp.nonprofitoffice.com/ http://www.mapnonprofit.org/), and boardnetUSA (http://www.boardnetusa.org).

Tips for Entry

1. Take a look at the Free Complete Toolkit for Boards, offered by the Management Assistance Program for Nonprofits at http://www.mapnp.org/library/boards/boards.htm.
2. Board Cafe is a newsletter for nonprofit boards. See their helpful resources at: http://www4.compasspoint.org/p.asp?WebPage_ID=652.

3. Do you have any friends or family members who are part of a nonprofit board of directors? Ask them how they got involved as a Board Member and what they like about their experience.

4. Consider opportunities to join a board of directors either through your community, the schools you have attended, or any service programs in which you participated.

5. The site http://www.nonprofits.org/npofaq has excellent resources in their Frequently Asked Questions section about serving on a board of directors.

FUND-RAISING
AND DEVELOPMENT

DIRECTOR OF DEVELOPMENT

CAREER PROFILE

Duties: Develops and manages specific plans for fund-raising activities of an organization

Alternate Title(s): Director of Fund-raising, Development Manager

Salary Range: $40,000 to $100,000 and up

Employment Prospects: Excellent

Advancement Prospects: Good

Best Geographical Location(s): Major cities

Prerequisites:

Education or Training—Bachelor's degree; master's degree may be preferred for some positions

Experience—Five to 10 years

Special Skills and Personality Traits—Creativity, confidence, strong leadership and management skills, excellent interpersonal ability

CAREER LADDER

```
┌─────────────────────────────────────┐
│ Executive Director or Vice President │
└─────────────────────────────────────┘

┌─────────────────────────────────────┐
│      Director of Development         │
└─────────────────────────────────────┘

┌─────────────────────────────────────┐
│  Development Assistant, Associate,   │
│           or Coordinator             │
└─────────────────────────────────────┘
```

Position Description

Did you ever participate in a high school car wash or dance-a-thon? If so, then you have been a fund-raiser. In order to carry out their good work and run successfully, nonprofit organizations of all kinds need to raise money. Whether it is the college that needs a new library or the museum that needs a space to house a special exhibition, they are dependent on fund-raising in order to meet their goals. The job of the Director of Development is crucial to the heart of nonprofit organizations because this individual leads the fund-raising efforts and is responsible for their achievement or failure. They are the strategizers and the networkers, often acting as their executive director's right-hand person.

Directors of Development work to develop annual fund-raising strategies that will fit the needs of their organizations. This approach may involve direct mail; phone appeals; foundation, government, and corporate grant proposals; special events; or other activities that will strengthen their donor base. In order to create the right approach, Directors of Development review prior mailings and other plans to analyze the results. While some donors will be contacted by mail, large donors are often contacted personally,

and it is up to the Director of Development to arrange these meetings and speak for the cause.

Many Directors of Development are in charge of major gift solicitation. A major gift is a high-level donation. The amount of what is considered a major gift varies from organization to organization and depends on their size and budget. While a large hospital might consider anything over $2 million a major gift, a small grassroots environmental group might label a donation of $200,000 a major gift.

The act of identifying potential donors is called prospect research. The type of organization dictates the type of donors and donations that are sought. For example, Directors of Development at colleges and universities often appeal to wealthy alumni for donations, while those employed by social service agencies may appeal to large corporations looking for a philanthropic cause. While some organizations have designated individuals for prospect research, Directors of Development often conduct extensive research to find appropriate donors that may include learning about their educational, family, and financial histories.

The Director of Development works as a liaison with the executive director and other organizational staff, the board of trustees, and external supporters of the organization. He or she usually works quite closely with the executive director, whose job also involves much development and fund-raising. As part of a team, they strategize and meet with potential donors. The Director of Development also manages a staff and delegates responsibility to them.

Not only is the Director of Development responsible for developing relationships with those expected to give monetarily, but he or she is also expected to interact with those who might provide the organization with favorable publicity and other advantages. Because a large part of the job depends on cultivating relationships, a successful Director of Development must be a people person who is persuasive and willing to work long hours to plan fund-raising events and campaigns. Furthermore, once the relationship has been initiated, follow-up is key to its longevity.

Additional duties may include:

- Maintaining a computer database and other records of past, present, and potential future donors
- Supervising an annual membership campaign with prospects lists ranging from hundreds to hundreds of thousands
- Assisting in developing the annual budget
- Working on an annual fund-raising plan
- Establishing an annual giving program
- Soliciting major gifts for development of an endowment
- Reporting on grants received
- Seeking corporate sponsorship for specific programs
- Creating and managing special events
- Overseeing the board of trustees and major gift solicitation
- Planning and attending fund-raising events
- Writing, editing, or overseeing grant proposals
- Researching potential funding sources
- Meeting with prospective and current donors
- Managing a development staff

The five major areas of development opportunity for a nonprofit organization are major giving, planned giving, corporate giving, member/donor mailings, and foundation giving. Some Directors of Development specialize in one or several of these areas, while others are generalists who oversee all areas as they are carried out by different development team members.

Directors of Development may find employment at a large range of nonprofits including educational, religious, arts, social welfare, health, membership, and environmental organizations. Many specialize and find a niche for themselves in one of these areas as well, getting to know the most likely donors and sources for raising money related to each industry. Travel, evening/weekend hours, and attending fund-raisers, parties, and other social events are often required to meet with donors, board members, and executives.

Salaries

Salaries of Directors of Development can vary greatly depending on the size and type of organization. According the the *Nonprofit Times* 2004 Annual Salary Survey, the average salary for a Director of Development was projected as $55,569, a $1,436 decrease from 2003, reflecting budget cuts and economic conditions. However, geography and budget play a large role as well. The same survey states an average salary low of $45,828 for Directors of Development working for organizations with budgets between $500,000 and $999,999 and an average salary high of $102,462 for those employed by organizations with budgets over $50 million. Additionally, by location the range is also significant, but not quite so drastic. Directors of Development in the southern United States earn the least of all regions, averaging $43,457, while those in the mid-Atlantic states earn the most at $68,636.

It is apparent that a Director of Development who manages a sizeable staff at a large, well-established organization can make upward of $95,000, while someone employed by a small shop with a total staff of 10 and no management responsibility may earn $40,000. Also, the salary of the Director of Development may be proportional to his or her performance at certain organizations.

Employment Prospects

Since all nonprofit organizations large and small need to raise money, there is excellent opportunity for Directors of Development. Employment prospects are also strong because they are needed within virtually all types of nonprofits. Typically, working for several years as a development assistant, associate, or fund-raiser, professionals can then move to larger or different types of organizations to find positions as Directors of Development.

Advancement Prospects

The opportunity is also good for Directors of Development to advance. Directors of Development who can demonstrate their accomplishments at one organization will be very attractive to another organization that hopes to match the financial rewards. Since in most organizations, this is a relatively high-level position, the next step for many is work as an executive director. Others leave to go to larger organizations for more money and responsibility, while others capitalize on their experience to become independent consultants or public relations executives. As consultants, their expertise in running successful fund-raising campaigns is in high demand.

Education and Training

While there is no particular type of education required to be a Director of Development, virtually all professionals have bachelor's degrees and many have master's degrees as well. Much of the job is learned through hands-on work experience. It generally takes from five to 10 years to reach a Director of Development position, with most candidates having proved themselves by holding increasingly responsible fund-raising positions.

Undergraduate degrees may be in any liberal arts discipline, but courses in business, communications, finance, and public relations may prove especially useful. Some Directors of Development have a master's degree in related fields depending on their specialty such as public administration, nonprofit management, arts administration, or higher education administration. Some colleges, universities, and professional organizations offer courses in fund-raising, which may also be helpful. Examples include the Columbia University School of Continuing Education in New York City, which offers a master of science in fund-raising management for nonprofit administration (http://www.ce.columbia.edu/smp/courses/year/fund-raising.cfm), the University of Pennsylvania's College of General Studies certificate in fund-raising (http://www.sas.upenn.edu/CGS/certificate/cfr/), and Goucher College in Baltimore, which offers a professional certificate in fund-raising management (http://www.goucher.edu/professionalprograms/index.cfm?page_id=673).

Experience, Skills, and Personality Traits

The job of a Director of Development is about building relationships. Above all, a Director of Development must be a good people person. He or she must have the confidence and comfort level to get along with all kinds of people, particularly wealthy people, and ask them for money. Networking is a key skill, and the Director of Development must understand the finer points of networking and have the ability to develop a strong personal network of contacts.

It is also important for a Director of Development to have a broad knowledge base. Although some professionals specialize, it is still necessary to be a generalist and understand the whole development process ranging from planning special events to soliciting corporate sponsorship in order to be informed and do the job well. Knowledge of specific fund-raising and development software such as Raiser's Edge is expected by many organizations. Also valuable are creativity, high energy, good writing skills, and the ability to work with numbers.

Unions and Associations

Professional associations that Directors of Development can join include the American Association of Fund-Raising Counsel, the Association of Fund-raisers and Direct Sellers, and the Association of Fund-raising Professionals. Furthermore, Directors of Development often belong to additional organizations that reflect their specialty area.

Tips for Entry

1. Visit the Web site http://www.afpnet.org/ to learn more about careers in fund-raising and development.
2. As a college student, participate in a campus fund-raising activity such as a telethon. Many colleges look for volunteers to call alumni for donations. Contact your development office to find out how you can help.
3. Explore graduate programs in nonprofit management and local fund-raising courses.
4. Conduct an informational interview with a Director of Development at an organization you admire.
5. Gain experience planning an event for an organization to which you belong.

DEVELOPMENT ASSISTANT

CAREER PROFILE

Duties: Provides fund-raising support for a nonprofit organization by assisting the fund-raising and development staff with administrative and programming responsibilities

Alternate Title(s): Fund-raising Assistant, Development Coordinator

Salary Range: $25,000 to $50,000

Employment Prospects: Good

Advancement Prospects: Excellent

Best Geographical Location(s): All

Prerequisites:

Education or Training—Bachelor's degree preferred
Experience—Position is usually entry-level, with some volunteer or internship experience in fund-raising helpful
Special Skills and Personality Traits—Excellent written and verbal communication skills, attention to detail; good organizational skills; relationship-building ability

CAREER LADDER

```
┌─────────────────────────────────┐
│     Development Officer,         │
│   Director of Development,       │
│ or other development professional│
└─────────────────────────────────┘

┌─────────────────────────────────┐
│     Development Assistant        │
└─────────────────────────────────┘

┌─────────────────────────────────┐
│      Intern, Volunteer,          │
│  or Administrative Assistant     │
└─────────────────────────────────┘
```

Position Description

In many ways, Development Assistants are like the structural foundation of many nonprofit organizations. By providing support, they ensure that the entire fund-raising operation is able to run smoothly. While they may not have the glamour of meeting with high-level donors and sealing deals as do directors of development, they handle the day-to-day tasks that enable fund-raising.

Development Assistants provide support for the development operations of a nonprofit organization. Fund-raising is usually broken down within an organization to include major giving, planned giving, corporate giving, member/donor mailings, and foundation giving. Development Assistants may work for a specific director in one of these areas or the department as a whole. Administrative responsibilities include answering telephone calls and e-mails, filing and organizing papers, maintaining development databases, and clerical tasks such as data entry and mailing coordination. They may also handle financial administration such as processing deposits, matching gifts, and handling credit card charges.

Development Assistants also serve as implementers for the development department, participating in meetings, brainstorming ideas, and then carrying out the tasks that will make the programs happen. They might conduct donor research, find the right venue for an event, work with vendors, draft letters or invitations, create a more efficient database, and more. Depending on their particular skills and abilities as well as the needs of their department, they contribute to the overall goal of helping their organization gain the funds to carry out their mission. To do this, they become experts about their particular organization and what it strives to accomplish.

Depending on the work setting and the individual goals of each Development Assistant, they may have a little or a lot of responsibility. For those Development Assistants who see their job as primarily administrative, they go to work and get their tasks done. However, for those Development Assistants who want to build a career in nonprofit fund-raising, the position is an opportunity to learn and grow. They may accompany their directors to donor meetings, sit in on strategy sessions, draft proposals, independently plan events, and more. Furthermore, they may take on responsibility for particular fund-raising programs or goals, such as annual benefits, pledge drives, or direct mail campaigns.

Their duties may include:

- Tracking contributions in a database
- Following up with donors and answering questions
- Scheduling appointments
- Planning meetings or travel arrangements
- Coordinating volunteers
- Generating computerized reports
- Soliciting donations through cold calling
- Initiating cultivation efforts
- Maintaining mailing lists
- Performing background research on donors or prospective donors

It is important for Development Assistants to have a strong customer service focus. In addition to dealing with supervisors who are under pressure to reach donation goals, they also must cater to donors who need personal attention. At some organizations, they need to check their egos at the door and be willing to complete any task asked of them, no matter how menial. However, most Development Assistants see this as "paying their dues," and enjoy being part of the excitement of successful fund-raising campaigns. They may build their experience in particular areas of the nonprofit sector, specializing in the arts, health care, education, religious organizations, or social services.

Furthermore, Development Assistant positions are often ideal ways for recent college graduates to break into the development field and nonprofit organizations in general. While in the past, many organizations saw their fund-raising options as limited to foundation grants and corporate philanthropy, many now recognize the value of individual gifts, and people are needed to manage this process. Development Assistants can be especially valuable to smaller organizations with limited budgets, since they are cheaper to hire than more experienced candidates. These Development Assistants may initiate annual campaigns, write grant requests, or focus on sending individual letters to prospective donors.

Salaries

According to a survey by the Association of Fundraising Professionals, fund-raisers such as development coordinators (which can be comparable in many organizations to Development Assistants) made a median $46,000 in 2003. Salaries vary depending on the size, budget, and location of the organization, as well as the level of position. Some Development Assistants might be next in line for director positions, while others may have to go through the ranks of assistant director, associate director, and so on. A typical range is between $25,000 and $50,000.

Employment Prospects

Employment prospects for Development Assistants overall is quite good. Nonprofit organizations cannot sustain themselves without fund-raising, and employees who assist with this process will always be needed. Prospects for employment are good in times of economic prosperity because then donors generally have more money to give. However, even in poor economic times, nonprofits cannot do without their development staff. As they try to accomplish their goals with even tighter budgets, nonprofits need to try harder to raise money. In either of these situations, directors of development usually cannot accomplish these tasks alone, and Development Assistants are needed and valued.

Advancement Prospects

Advancement prospects are excellent for Development Assistants who have used their job as a learning experience. Since they already have inside knowledge of the fund-raising process and demonstrated success as part of a fund-raising team, they are often ideal candidates to advance to other development positions. After a period ranging from a few months to a few years, they may become development officers. After several more years of experience, they might become development directors, prospect researchers, major gifts officers, or managers of specific programs.

Education and Training

While it is not required by all organizations, most Development Assistants have college degrees. Liberal arts disciplines are common fields of study. Courses in business, communications, English, finance, or public relations are helpful as well. At large organizations, some may even hold a master's degree in nonprofit administration or have completed course work or certificate programs in fund-raising.

After five years of experience, a development professional may seek the Certified Fund Raising Executive (CFRE) credential. This credential, offered by the Association of Fundraising Professionals, demonstrates "an individual's mastery of the standards set for core knowledge and skills required of fund-raising executives after five years of experience," according to their Web site (http://www.afp-net.org). It is not required, but may be helpful for advancement later on.

Experience, Skills, and Personality Traits

Most Development Assistant positions are entry-level and usually last between one to five years before people either advance or move on. Prior interest and experience in fund-raising while in college is helpful, such as planning events to raise money for campus organizations or working in the alumni office.

Development Assistants juggle many responsibilities at once, therefore requiring superior organizational skills.

Prior knowledge of specific fund-raising software is helpful, but can often be learned on the job. They also need attention to detail, good computer skills, and excellent communication and writing ability. Furthermore, an outgoing personality and skill at building relationships will be needed for success in upper-level development positions.

Unions and Associations

Development Assistants may belong to the Association of Fundraising Professionals, the American Association of Fund-Raising Counsel, the Association of Fundraisers and Direct Sellers, and additional organizations based on their specialty area.

Tips for Entry

1. Learn more about fund-raising through courses. Many associations and schools offer classes such as the Association of Fundraising Professionals (http://www. afpnet.org/education_and_career_development/first_ course_in_fund-raising), New York University's School of Continuing and Professional Studies (http://www. scps.nyu.edu/departments/certificate.jsp?certId= 100), and the University of Washington at Tacoma (http://www.tacoma.washington.edu/pdc/schedule/ fundraising_cert.html).

2. Get involved with student organizations on campus. Participate in fund-raising events such as car washes and concerts to find out how the process works.

3. Contact your alumni office on campus to learn about cultivating relationships with alumni for fund-raising and participation in campus events. Students often play strong roles in the process of getting alumni involved.

4. Consider an internship with a nonprofit organization. Working in development, special events, or grant writing would all be helpful ways to gain a background understanding of the field.

5. Learn more about the certified fund raising executive (CFRE) credential at http://www.cfre.org/index.php.

CORPORATE RELATIONS MANAGER

CAREER PROFILE	CAREER LADDER

Duties: Establishes, maintains, and develops relationships with companies and corporations to seek their support in helping a nonprofit organization achieve its mission

Alternate Title(s): Director of Corporate Relations, Company Relationship Manager, Employer Relations Manager

Salary Range: $35,000 to $70,000

Employment Prospects: Good

Advancement Prospects: Good

Best Geographical Location(s): Major cities

Prerequisites:

Education or Training—Minimum of a bachelor's degree required for most positions

Experience—Fund-raising or communications experience helpful

Special Skills and Personality Traits—Team-building; excellent written and verbal communication; ability to prioritize, multitask, and meet deadlines; good networking skills

```
┌─────────────────────────────────┐
│  Senior Director or Vice President │
│      of Corporate Relations        │
└─────────────────────────────────┘

┌─────────────────────────────────┐
│    Corporate Relations Manager     │
└─────────────────────────────────┘

┌─────────────────────────────────┐
│   Corporate Relations Coordinator  │
└─────────────────────────────────┘
```

Position Description

In order to carry out their goals, nonprofit organizations depend on aid from the corporate world. Through donations of both time and money, companies can show their support for various philanthropic causes. The Corporate Relations Manager serves as a liaison between the organization and different corporations to foster mutually beneficial relationships for both parties.

Corporations assist nonprofits with carrying out their missions in two major ways. First, and most obviously, they can donate money through a number of different avenues. For a charitable organization this can consist of sponsoring events or participating in a payroll deduction program, while for a cultural organization it can comprise sponsoring exhibits, buying ticket blocks, or group membership. For a university or hospital, it can include a building naming opportunity for a high-level donation. The second way companies can contribute to nonprofits is by providing volunteers. Corporate Relations Managers will often recruit corporate volunteer teams for large fund-raising events such

as walk-a-thons. They work with an on-site contact to coordinate and manage these volunteers. Through both of these types of assistance, companies help nonprofits promote their cause and educate the public.

Corporate Relations Managers strive to forge connections. In order to identify the companies most likely to participate in fund-raising and educational programs, first they must conduct research using the Internet, online databases such as Hoovers, and personal contacts. Rather than wasting time contacting all local prospects, Corporate Relations Managers are strategic, asking questions such as—which companies are the best match for our organization based on their employee base, philanthropic interests, and mission statement? Common alliances also come through board members, friends, and family members. Everyone knows someone, and working through these networks is more apt to produce positive results. Through these contacts, the senior-level decision-makers are identified and relationships are cultivated. While it is beneficial to reach the highest level professional possible, it depends on where the logical relationships lie. Corporate Relations Managers may start by contacting those in corporate responsibility/philanthropy or human resources departments. Contact methods include writing letters, making cold calls, and crafting numerous e-mails.

In addition, Corporate Relations Managers must come up with a strategy for targeting companies. They take many factors into consideration, including the size of the company, their current programs and activities, and what makes sense for them. Then they target the approach accordingly—there isn't a "one size fits all" approach in terms of both method of contact and type of proposal. Some companies that are already extended with volunteer projects may be more willing to buy tables at a fund-raising gala, while others may be looking to participate in direct service programs. Also, e-mail may be the best initial contact in some cases, while word of mouth might reveal that a certain executive prefers telephone calls to her assistant. This needs to be handled with finesse in order to nurture the alliance.

As much time as possible is spent in face-to-face meetings with the companies. Corporate Relations Managers have numerical goals to fulfill related to meetings set up and money raised. At these meetings, they make their pitch to the companies as to what they are asking for, be it time or dollars. They customize the presentations to meet each company's specific needs and values. Corporate Relations Managers work with internal teams to collaborate on a well-rounded approach. They need to be knowledgeable about their own organization and its programs in order to solicit support.

Their duties may include:

- Writing proposals, letters, and e-mails to companies
- Making telephone calls
- Attending meetings
- Initiating new programs
- Developing solicitation strategies
- Maintaining databases of company contacts and participation records
- Researching companies and individuals on the Internet
- Coordinating volunteer programs
- Educating companies about the mission of the organization to garner support
- Developing an annual sales plan and negotiating contracts (at cultural institutions)
- Designing sales and marketing brochures
- Overseeing outreach efforts
- Staying aware of current events and trends
- Following up with contacts and maintaining ongoing relationships
- Working to create a brand for the organization as a recognizable philanthropy
- Coordinating corporate recognition and gift materials such as signs, fund-raising templates, and site visits

Corporate Relations Managers are good networkers. Once developed, they are able to maintain relationships and help companies to understand the benefits they are getting in return for supporting their cause. An e-mail here or phone call there keeping donors and participants up to date with recent organization events and programs can go a long way. Corporate Relations Managers may work at cultural institutions, charitable organizations, colleges and universities, and hospitals, among others. They typically work a 40- to 50-hour week, with some overtime for evening and weekend events.

Salaries

As with many nonprofit positions, salaries vary depending on organizational size and geographical location. Salaries can range from $35,000 to $70,000 and up. Corporate Relations Managers who supervise assistants and other staff earn at the higher end of the spectrum, while those in entry to mid-level positions earn less.

Employment Prospects

Employment prospects are good in that nonprofit organizations continue to work to further develop their relationships with the corporate sector. Since they depend on companies for a portion of their funding, the job of the Corporate Relations Manager becomes increasingly important. Opportunities are particularly plentiful with colleges and universities looking to strengthen their corporate ties.

Advancement Prospects

Corporate Relations Managers can advance to senior level director or vice president positions. Also, they can capitalize on their relationship-building and writing skills and move to other nonprofit roles such as general development work, major gifts, prospect research, communications, or special events.

Education and Training

Corporate Relations Managers often come to their positions from various backgrounds in both the corporate and nonprofit sectors. A bachelor's degree is required; useful fields include English, communications, public relations, or finance. Often they have prior work experience in writing, public relations, fund-raising and development, or sales. They need to understand the nonprofit sector and the relationship it has with corporations.

Experience, Skills, and Personality Traits

Corporate Relations Managers need excellent writing and interpersonal skills. It is important that they are outgoing and articulate, able to represent their organization while they meet with company contacts at all levels. They should be good organizers who are able to prioritize, multitask, and meet deadlines. Also, they need the ability to make decisions, as well as work independently and as a team player.

Unions and Associations
Corporate Relations Managers may belong to nonprofit and development-related organizations such as the American Association of Fund-Raising Counsel, the Association of Fund-raising Professionals, and the National Council of Nonprofit Associations.

Tips for Entry
1. Research corporate philanthropy departments to learn about corporate giving. Consider the various philosophies as to how companies support the nonprofit sector.
2. Improve writing skills through courses in English, journalism, and communications.
3. Visit your campus career center or contact your alma mater. Find out more about corporate relations and how employers support their programs.
4. Get an internship in the nonprofit sector. Learn about the different roles in the development department.

MAJOR GIFTS OFFICER

CAREER PROFILE

Duties: Solicits substantial donations from wealthy individuals to raise money for a nonprofit organization

Alternate Title(s): Director of Major Gifts, Planned Giving Officer, Director of Capital Campaigns

Salary Range: $45,000 to $80,000 and up

Employment Prospects: Good

Advancement Prospects: Good

Best Geographical Location(s): All

Prerequisites:

Education or Training—Bachelor's degree

Experience—Several years of development experience, particularly with some in individual gifts

Special Skills and Personality Traits—Excellent written and verbal communication skills; superior interpersonal ability; tact and diplomacy; persuasive skills; confidence

CAREER LADDER

```
┌─────────────────────────────────┐
│   Senior Major Gifts Officer    │
│   or Director of Major Gifts    │
└─────────────────────────────────┘

┌─────────────────────────────────┐
│      Major Gifts Officer        │
└─────────────────────────────────┘

┌─────────────────────────────────┐
│ Development Assistant, Associate,│
│          or Officer             │
└─────────────────────────────────┘
```

Position Description

While every little bit that an individual gives helps a nonprofit organization, it is the major contributions from individual donors that really get things done. Whenever you see a hospital or university building named for an individual, this is a visible result of major giving. Many other major gifts take place that have more subtle recognition, but the results are no less important. Wealthy individuals are in a position to make changes to the organizations they support: funding programs, projects, and overall operations.

With other members of the fund-raising team dedicated to working with corporations and foundations to raise money, Major Gifts Officers work specifically with high-level donors, cultivating relationships and developing strategies geared toward encouraging giving. Their jobs are an eclectic combination of marketing and public relations, writing, persuading, and handholding. They may be responsible for everything from drafting material about their organization and writing solicitation proposals, to planning events and meeting with donors at unusual times or places.

To begin their work, Major Gifts Officers first must identify prospects for giving. In conjunction with prospect researchers, they investigate high net-worth individuals who have demonstrated interest in their organization. By finding out details about their financial and personal backgrounds, they learn where they have given before and what position they may be in for giving now, and how much. This creates a list of prospects for major giving.

Cultivating relationships is a key part of fund-raising in general, but is particularly important for Major Gifts Officers. How individuals choose to express their philanthropy is a very personal decision and can be influenced by minute factors. Major Gifts Officers need to be intuitive and skilled at working with people in order to match appropriate donors with different goals of their organization. For example, a donor who prides herself on being well read and having an extensive book collection will likely be more interested in funding a library or literacy program rather than a sports complex. Sometimes, giving opportunities are created specifically to meet a donor's giving requests. It is up to the Major Gifts Officer to get to know the donors and make giving a positive experience for both the donor and the organization. It is the cultivation that makes the solicitation (actually proposing the request for giving) happen.

The definition of what constitutes a major gift varies among organizations. Depending on the size and budget of the nonprofit, a major gift may be considered upward of $10,000 or upward of $1 million. The distinction is decided by each organization independently.

Acknowledgment of major gifts is also a key part of the role of Major Gifts Officers. While some donors prefer to remain anonymous, many like to see different types of recognition for their generosity. Some of the most major acknowledgments are the naming opportunities, where entire buildings, libraries, rooms, programs, scholarships, fellowships, and so on are dedicated in someone's honor, bearing their name. Other recognition possibilities include discreet signage outside of buildings, honorary events such as formal dinners on behalf of the major gift donors, and advertisements in local publications publicly thanking specific donors for their contributions. Personal notes and e-mails from not only the Major Gifts Officer, but also from other executives within the organization, can go a long way to make the donors feel appreciated.

Their duties may include:

- Attending fund-raisers and cultural events
- Training and managing volunteers to help with gift solicitation
- Developing gift acceptance policies and procedures
- Expanding and managing donor bases
- Raising current donors to higher levels
- Developing a major gift strategy and plan
- Maintaining contact with past and present donors
- Analyzing fund-raising activities to determine areas for improvement
- Helping to set and meet income goals for major gift prospects
- Keeping informed about laws and tax changes that may affect major gift giving
- Writing and editing proposals and reports

It is valuable for Major Gifts Officers to have understanding of complicated tax issues, such as trusts and annuities. They also need to understand the mission of their organization completely and feel committed to its purpose. In order to persuade others to give, their passion for their cause should be obvious. Travel and/or long hours may be required to meet with donors and attend events.

Salaries

Salaries vary greatly depending on the size and budget of the organization, as well as what constitutes a major gift. Clearly, organizations that anticipate major gifts worth hundreds of thousands of dollars are going to have more money to pay their staff. According to an annual salary survey by the *Nonprofit Times,* the mean projected 2003 salary for Major Gifts Officers was $56,850, though the same survey reports a higher projected figure for the previous year, 2002, at $62,951.

Employment Prospects

As wealth is projected to move from one generation to the next, there will be increased opportunity for major giving. Many smaller nonprofits that have previously depended on corporate and foundation giving have shifted their efforts to add major gifts staff. Expanded openings may also come from regional organizations. These organizations are moving toward cultivating relationships with donors in their geographical location who may be motivated to give based on regional loyalty.

Advancement Prospects

Major Gifts Officers may advance to lead departments of major gift giving, or development operations overall as directors of development. They may also move on to larger organizations where the major gifts are higher and they are responsible for generating more money, thus resulting in higher salaries. Furthermore, they may transition into other fund-raising specialties such as planned gifts, which includes donations involving complicated tax or financial arrangements, and running full fund-raising campaigns.

Education and Training

Virtually all Major Gifts Officers have bachelor's degrees in a wide variety of subjects. A liberal arts education that has provided strong research, writing, and communication skills is valuable, as are courses in business and finance.

Understanding of fund-raising practice is essential. While Major Gifts Officers receive training on the job, they should come in with a base of knowledge about how fund-raising is accomplished, as well as an understanding about their particular industry. For example, a Major Gifts Officer for a large city opera company should have education or experience related to music in addition to fund-raising skills.

Experience, Skills, and Personality Traits

Most Major Gifts Officers have several years of fund-raising experience before coming to their positions. Depending on the size of the organization and the level of the position, experience can range from one to 10 years.

In addition to superb written and verbal communication skills, Major Gifts Officers should be scrupulously ethical. They must respect confidentiality in working with donors and sensitive personal information such as finances. They should also have a keen sense about people and the ability to understand motivations for giving, as well as the ability to negotiate, charm, and persuade as expert networkers and relationship builders. A good memory for personal details can go a long way.

Because much donor information is computerized, Major Gifts Officers need to have knowledge of donor databases and various computer programs, including Microsoft Office. Excellent organizational skills enable them to keep track of donor information and donation records. Experience with business, finance, and event planning is also helpful.

Unions and Associations

Like other fund-raising professionals, Major Gifts Officers may belong to the Association of Fundraising Professionals, the American Association of Fund-Raising Counsel, the Association of Fundraisers and Direct Sellers, and additional organizations based on their specialty area.

Tips for Entry

1. Learn more about fund-raising by visiting the Web site of the Association of Fundraising Professionals (http://www.afpnet.org). You can find out about education and courses in fund-raising, as well as recent developments in the field.

2. Virtually all college campuses have at least one staff member responsible for major gift solicitation. Search your university Web site to determine who this individual is, and then arrange an informational interview with him or her.

3. Pay attention to the way donors are recognized on your campus, in hospitals, and in cultural institutions. See if you can recognize plaques and other acknowledgments. This will give you insight into major gift donation.

4. Hone your communication skills through coursework. Advance your writing and research skills through English courses and take a class in public speaking to become comfortable speaking in front of groups.

5. Develop strong networking skills by joining campus organizations and by attending events where you will meet new people.

PROSPECT RESEARCHER

CAREER PROFILE

Duties: Conducts research on prospective donors for a non-profit organization; compiles personal and financial information

Alternate Title(s): Prospect Research Analyst, Prospect Research Associate, Research Manager

Salary Range: $30,000 to $60,000 and up

Employment Prospects: Fair

Advancement Prospects: Good

Best Geographical Location(s): Major cities

Prerequisites:

Education or Training—Bachelor's degree; graduate degree is preferred

Experience—One to three years nonprofit or research experience

Special Skills and Personality Traits—Excellent research skills; careful attention to detail; creativity; good networker

CAREER LADDER

```
┌─────────────────────────────────┐
│      Director of Research        │
│   or Director of Development     │
└─────────────────────────────────┘

┌─────────────────────────────────┐
│       Prospect Researcher        │
└─────────────────────────────────┘

┌─────────────────────────────────┐
│   Research Assistant/Associate   │
│ or Development Assistant/Associate│
└─────────────────────────────────┘
```

Position Description

To put it bluntly, Prospect Researchers get paid to snoop into wealthy people's business. Part of the fund-raising and development team at nonprofit organizations, they are skilled researchers who investigate potential donors, discovering information such as educational background, family status, business details, and sources of wealth. They research information using the Internet, databases, and personal contacts and prepare complete donor profiles for the frontline fund-raisers to use as background when approaching high-level donors.

Through print resources and high-tech databases such as LexisNexus and Hoover's, as well as Internet search engines such as Google and Yahoo, they investigate details about people that may reveal who is in a position to give to their organization this year. They can find out details such as when people have sold stock or what their recent real estate transactions have been. Prospect Researchers will choose their prospects with care, and they are skilled at recognizing what makes a good prospect for their particular organization as well as understanding and evaluating wealth indicators.

In educational institutions, they may focus on alumni or parents; in cultural institutions, they may focus on donors or collectors. In any case, they consider who has the proclivity to give to an organization such as theirs. Another important fact to find out about their prospects is where else they give. Based on their prospects' existing affiliations, Prospect Researchers hope to learn who is most likely to be interested in giving to their organization.

Prospect Researchers are masters of networking. While the Internet and database research can yield critical tidbits and necessary financial details, uncovering relationships can yield even greater results. Making phone calls to see who knows who, finding high-level friends of board of director members, and learning through word of mouth who may have a specific and personal reason to want to give to their organization this year goes a long way. Prospect Researchers can spend hours, even days or weeks, chasing one particular lead if the payoff looks promising. The preliminary research they conduct can help prepare the development team before they approach major donors.

Not just research skills but research savvy is required. Prospect Researchers uncover much information, and they need to be able to determine the relevant and strategic points buried within. They both take the lead on identifying and qualifying new prospects, as well as following up on research requests. They are constantly aware of their environment and have good recall for names and faces. Also, they are able to identify multiple research sources, including books, newspapers, journals, magazines, internal files and records, and even through passing conversations with colleagues in order to expand their organization's list of potential donors.

It is also important for Prospect Researchers to thoroughly understand fund-raising, as well as how it relates to the mission and goals of their organization. Good institutional knowledge is necessary; in order to identify appropriate prospects, they must be well versed in their organization's mission, goals, history, and programs, as well as familiar with their fund-raising needs. They must have experience with the fund-raising cultivation process as defined by the Association of Professional Researchers for Advancement: identification, qualification, cultivation, solicitation, and stewardship.

Their duties may include:

- Using the Internet and computer databases to review recent articles and press materials
- Developing and maintaining donor databases
- Recommending cultivation strategies to development team and/or major gifts officer
- Managing prospect tracking system
- Preparing background materials for fund-raisers to use on visits with high-level prospects
- Keeping up on current news and industry trends
- Conducting financial analysis on prospects' wealth capacity
- Reviewing reports for information updates and prospect identification leads
- Analyzing information to rate prospects
- Synthesizing information to create clear profiles
- Understanding legal and government documents such as IRS From 990 and wills and trusts
- Writing grant proposals

Prospect Researchers must have great respect for and awareness of privacy issues. They need to distinguish between public and private information, understand donors' rights, and take an ethical approach to the entire process. They work in settings that include higher education, charities, health care, arts and cultural institutions, religious institutions, and environmental organizations.

Salaries
According to a 2001 study by the Association of Professional Researchers for Advancement, most advancement research professionals including Prospect Researchers earned between $30,000 and $44,999; 4.9 percent made less than $24,999 and 1.6 percent made more than $85,000. This varies depending on the size, location, and type of organization.

A more recent study made in 2003 by Abbott, Langer and Associates, Inc. about pay rates in nonprofit organizations listed the median income of donor research managers, which would include Prospect Researchers, as $38,250.

Employment Prospects
Employment prospects are fair, since departments tend to cut research budgets before other areas. Prospect Research positions may be absorbed by other professionals in the development team. Opportunities are better for those who have experience in both fund-raising and research. The greatest area for employment opportunity tends to be in higher education.

Advancement Prospects
Because Prospect Researchers have a skill set that is very marketable in the nonprofit world, advancement prospects are good. They may advance to lead a research department, manage a development and fund-raising department, or work as private consultants.

Education and Training
Prospect Researchers often come to their positions from other fields, including library science, journalism, public relations, or marketing. They hold bachelor's degrees in a variety of fields, often in the liberal arts and humanities. Many also have a master's degree, which is a preferred credential for many positions. Some Prospect Researchers who focus heavily on research, policy studies, and evaluation may have doctorates. Within departments, it is often beneficial to have Prospect Researchers with a variety of educational backgrounds, since they all bring different strengths to the table.

Experience, Skills, and Personality Traits
Prospect Researchers need to enjoy research and have a good eye for detail. They need to be interested in people and the intricacies of their lives. Successful Prospect Researchers have excellent memories and can remember things they read several years ago about a potential donor that may have relevance today. They also need the patience to follow up on leads that may not produce results immediately.

Writing skills help to produce reports that are easy for others to follow, while knowledge of finance and accounting enables Prospect Researchers to understand and analyze the data they examine. They also should be tactful, discreet, and ethical, with a respect for confidentiality and appropriate boundaries. Prior research experience, typically ranging from one to three years and encompassing both the academic and professional, is necessary to find a job as a Prospect Researcher.

Unions and Associations

The main professional association for Prospect Researchers is the Association of Professional Researchers for Advancement (APRA). They also may belong to the Association of Fundraising Professionals, the New England Development Research Association, and others related to their specialty area.

Tips for Entry

1. Practice conducting Internet searches using search engines such as Google. Choose a person or topic and then try to find as much detail as possible.
2. Visit the APRA Web site at http://www.aprahome.org/ to learn more about the field.
3. Take courses with large research components to enhance skills.
4. Learn how to read and analyze financial documents such as tax returns and trusts and estates.

COMMUNICATIONS

DIRECTOR OF COMMUNICATIONS

CAREER PROFILE

Duties: Directs all communications activities for a non-profit organization, including public relations, print, audio, broadcast, and electronic media

Alternate Title(s): Communications Director, Director of Public Relations, Communications Manager, Director of Media Relations, Director of Publishing

Salary Range: $40,000 to $75,000 and up

Employment Prospects: Good

Advancement Prospects: Good

Best Geographical Location(s): All

Prerequisites:

Education or Training—Bachelor's degree; master's degree preferred for some positions

Experience—Five years or more of work experience; will vary by size and type of organization

Special Skills and Personality Traits—Superior written and editorial skills; excellent verbal communication skills; strong management, planning, and organizational skills

CAREER LADDER

```
┌─────────────────────────────────────┐
│   Director of Communications         │
│ (large organization) or Vice President│
└─────────────────────────────────────┘

┌─────────────────────────────────────┐
│   Director of Communications         │
└─────────────────────────────────────┘

┌─────────────────────────────────────┐
│   Communications Coordinator,        │
│      Writer, or Journalist           │
└─────────────────────────────────────┘
```

Position Description

Image is everything, or so the saying goes. Whether or not you agree with that statement, it is certain that the image of a nonprofit organization helps define its work and goals for the general public. Generally, what people see through commercials, billboards, magazine and newspaper advertisements, and brochures is the way they develop their understanding about the message of an organization and what it is aiming to achieve. It is the job of the Director of Communications to manage this image through educational and promotional media material, including print, audio, broadcast, and the Internet.

Nonprofit organizations educate people about their mission through the way they market their programs. In order to create a recognizable "brand" for the organization, the Director of Communications is responsible for both the internal publications produced by the organization, as well as organization's external image and media portrayal. This can include coordinating and producing presentations in a variety of mediums such as print, Internet, audio, and broadcast media. Because people usually base their opinions on what they see or hear, Directors of Communications may work on the organization's representation through Web sites, videos, brochures, and advertisements.

The responsibilities of the Director of Communications vary depending on the size and structure of the organization. At a small association, the Director of Communications may write and edit all printed materials including newsletters, press releases, advertising copy, speeches, and brochures. At a larger organization, the Director of Communications oversees final copy and manages a large staff, in which each member has specific areas of responsibility. A Director of Communications may supervise a department made up of several specialty areas including public relations, creative services, interactive media, and public information. The Director of Communications may work in one of these areas specifically, or in all of them.

The Director of Communications may work to create marketing campaigns designed to educate the public about the services of the organization, as well as to encourage or solicit donations. These campaigns may be viewed through videos, brochures, and Web sites. When the projects are very large, the Director of Communications can serve as a liaison to outsource assignments to public relations firms and other consultants.

Sometimes Directors of Communications need to provide damage control. If something negative has come up about the organization in the media, they might recommend how to handle the crisis situation and educate and advise staff about handling interviews and public appearances. In all circumstances, their goal is to make sure the organization is portrayed in the most positive light.

Setting communications policy is also important for nonprofit organizations. Directors of Communications may conduct surveys to analyze current policy and make recommendations for changes and improvements. They also work to develop media relations policies.

Their duties may include:

- Serving as the organization's spokesperson
- Producing videos and multimedia presentations and overseeing the production process
- Writing news releases and other publicity materials
- Arranging for television or radio guest spots
- Working with celebrities to promote the mission of the organization
- Conducting studies and research on policies to share with general public, as well as internal staff
- Working with outside vendors to coordinate large events and services
- Preparing representatives for interviews
- Initiating, developing, and maintaining media contacts
- Researching materials and writing speeches for organizational leaders
- Coordinating press conferences and special events
- Enhancing visibility for the organization
- Putting together press kits
- Drafting and designing educational and/or advocacy materials

It is useful for the Director of Communications to have good relationships with the media and to have a strong network of contacts. The job involves a high energy level and an ability to interact with people around the clock as a frontline representative of his or her organization.

Many professionals who become Directors of Communications for nonprofit organizations have prior experience as writers, journalists, or public relations executives in either the nonprofit or corporate world.

Salaries

Salaries for Directors of Communications vary greatly depending on location and size of organization. According to a 2003 *Association Executive Compensation and Benefits Study* by the American Society of Association Executives (ASAE), the average salary for a director of publishing, which can be comparable with a Director of Communications, was $73,138. However, this figure would be for a professional at a large organization with considerable professional experience. Most Directors of Communications earn between $40,000 and $75,000.

Employment Prospects

Employment opportunities are good for Directors of Communications, as all organizations have a need to create media material and manage their public relations. As multimedia outlets increase, so does demand for professionals to work on these resources, as well as to manage departments. Directors of Communications can find also find opportunities by focusing on one of their specialty areas such as writing, media, or public relations.

Advancement Prospects

Advancement prospects for Directors of Communications are good, but they may depend on how geographically flexible one is willing to be. Some professionals move from a smaller to a larger organization, while others take on further leadership positions within the organization, such as executive director or vice president. Another opportunity for Directors of Communications to advance in the nonprofit sector can be found through work as a private consultant.

Education and Training

Directors of Communications can have varied backgrounds. While it is common for some to have strong backgrounds in writing, English, and journalism, others have business, public relations, and management training. In addition to a bachelor's degree, some Directors of Communications may have a master's degree in journalism or business (MBA).

Experience, Skills, and Personality Traits

Before becoming a Director of Communications, an individual may work for several years as a writer, editor, journalist, or public relations specialist. He or she may also start out in an organization as a communications coordinator or assistant. Some leadership experience or experience managing a staff is also necessary, especially for a Director of Communications who will be responsible for supervising a large staff.

As their title implies, Directors of Communications must be excellent communicators. They must be articulate and comfortable with presenting to different types of people. It is also important for them to be both media savvy and aware of human nature. Having a keen understanding of the connection between image and perception helps them to be successful at their jobs. Also, they must be skilled writers and able to translate industry jargon into language that is catchy and easy for people to understand.

Unions and Associations

Directors of Communications may belong to professional associations, including the American Society of Association Executives, the Public Relations Society of America, and the National Council of Nonprofit Associations, among others related to the specialty of their organization.

Tips for Entry

1. Apply for an internship at a public relations firm to learn more about communications areas such as media relations, writing press releases, and creating a publicity campaign.
2. Hone your writing skills and gain experience through courses, the school newspaper, yearbook, and other campus publications.
3. Take a public speaking course to brush up on verbal communication skills.
4. Talk to Directors of Communications at various nonprofit organizations to learn more about their jobs.

MARKETING MANAGER

CAREER PROFILE

Duties: Promotes the programs, events, and services of a nonprofit organization; increases brand awareness

Alternate Title(s): Communications Manager, Advertising Manager

Salary Range: $40,000 to $70,000 and up

Employment Prospects: Good

Advancement Prospects: Good

Best Geographical Location(s): All, with emphasis in major cities

Prerequisites:

Education or Training—Bachelor's degree; master's degree helpful for advancement

Experience—One to five years of marketing experience

Special Skills and Personality Traits—Creativity; flexibility; good analytical skills; understanding of advertising and promotions; excellent communication skills

CAREER LADDER

```
┌─────────────────────────────┐
│     Director of Marketing    │
│      or Communications       │
└─────────────────────────────┘

┌─────────────────────────────┐
│      Marketing Manager       │
└─────────────────────────────┘

┌─────────────────────────────┐
│      Marketing Assistant     │
└─────────────────────────────┘
```

Position Description

Nonprofit organizations need buy-in from the public in order to achieve their goals. Membership organizations, whether professional associations or cultural institutions, need people to see their value and join. Charities need people to see the benefits of their programs and give money to fund them. Marketing Managers are responsible for promoting these programs, events, and services in order raise money and awareness for their organization. They may be responsible for creating new earned income–generating opportunities as well in order to meet their objectives.

Whereas in the corporate world, the Marketing Manager markets the company's products, in the nonprofit realm, the organization's programs are the "product" to be marketed. Instead of creating and branding a product, Marketing Managers develop a brand and recognizable image for their organization. They work to define materials and messages that bring brand recognition to their institution. Marketing Managers are often members of the communications team, working closely with specialists in public relations, advertising, and media relations. Together, they determine the prime targets to convey their message, including newspaper, magazines, radio, television, and the Internet.

Furthermore, Marketing Managers must know their organization well, understanding its mission, history, goals, and all programs and services. For example, for a Marketing Manager at a botanic garden to promote the benefits of membership, first he or she must know what these benefits are and why they were established. The Marketing Manager may even have a role in developing these benefits as part of the marketing campaign. If an organization develops new programs or is hosting a major event, it is up to the Marketing Manager to get the word out. Part of the job is to decide the best way to promote these programs and develop a plan to do so.

Marketing Managers also play a major role in the development of marketing collateral. Marketing collateral refers to the collection of media used to identify and present information about an organization. It may include brochures, Web pages, logos, posters and signs, flyers, direct mail pieces, fact sheets, catalogues, and reports. This development needs to be very strategic since visual images contribute strongly to perception and recognition.

Nonprofit marketing also differs from corporate marketing in another way. As companies develop their marketing strategies, they often use a combination of positive and negative campaign tactics. In promoting the positive attributes of their product, they often cite the negative qualities in the products of competitors to drive consumers toward buying their product. This tactic is nonexistent in nonprofits—can you imagine a museum encouraging you to join by telling you what is wrong with other museums? Instead, Marketing Managers focus only on the positive, concentrating on their advantages without resorting to any insults to others. For many, this is a challenging and enjoyable aspect of their work.

Marketing Managers determine what is unique about their organization and use it to their advantage. They conduct research about what similar organizations are doing to help develop the angle they want to pursue. Additionally, they decide to whom they should be marketing—the general public, corporations, or specific groups. They also work to identify new markets, finding untapped groups for new membership bases, fund-raising opportunities, corporate sponsorship, program participation, partnership, and more. Partnership opportunities are key here, offering companies a chance for philanthropy that will benefit both parties.

Their duties may include:

- Monitoring trends
- Planning and promoting special events
- Developing opportunities for sponsorship and media access
- Launching marketing initiatives
- Securing advertisement placements
- Developing event giveaways such as promotional items
- Working with external vendors
- Creating marketing material on the organization's Web site
- Developing marketing strategies to launch new programs
- Expanding membership bases
- Campaigning for subscription services
- Writing, editing, and proofreading sales copy
- Conducting and analyzing market research including studies, reports, trends, and new developments among similar organizations
- Deciding on pricing strategies for saleable materials

The results of their work are tangible, and Marketing Managers can determine their success based on giving rates, membership rises, event attendance, and other factors. At some organizations, pressure may be on for Marketing Managers to achieve certain financial or numerical goals; new professionals may be hired and brought in for exactly that purpose. Knowing their jobs may be on the line if they fail to deliver can be stressful for some Marketing Managers, but others thrive on the challenge and realize it pushes them to work harder and be more creative.

Salaries
According to the Bureau of Labor Statistics, median annual earnings in 2002 were $78,250 for Marketing Managers.

However, this figure almost exclusively represents the corporate world. A 2003 survey report of 131 benchmark jobs from Abbott, Langer & Associates, Inc., *Compensation in Nonprofit Organizations, 16th Edition,* lists median incomes for Marketing Managers in the nonprofit sector as $50,783. Additionally, according to a summary at www.workforce.com citing a 2003 study about pay in the not-for-profit sector, the median cash compensation for a nonprofit marketing position was $54,100, with the top marketing position as $87,800.

Insiders say that typical salaries for nonprofit Marketing Managers are in the $50,000 to $60,000 range. They vary depending on the size and location of the organization, as well as the level of the position.

Employment Prospects
Employment prospects are good for Marketing Managers. As nonprofits look to find new and innovative ways to promote themselves, more marketing staff will be hired. Branding is increasingly important for organizations to make themselves recognizable. Opportunities will be best for those who have advanced education and experience in marketing, as well as a background at nonprofit organizations. Marketing Managers may come to nonprofits from the corporate sector, but knowledge of the way nonprofits work is required.

Advancement Prospects
Marketing Managers may advance by moving from smaller organizations to larger ones, or by continuing their education or training. At this level, it may be difficult to move up in the hierarchy of one institution, so turnover is relatively high as professionals seek opportunities at new organizations. Marketing Managers may also advance to lead staff teams as directors of marketing or communication.

Education and Training
Marketing Managers hold bachelor's degrees in a variety of subjects. Majors or course work in marketing, advertising, public relations, English, communications, statistics, business, and finance are helpful. Some positions require a specific type of training; for example, a job that involves developing collateral marketing materials such as brochures may also require graphic design experience.

Many Marketing Managers begin their careers in marketing at the entry level as assistants with only a bachelor's degree. However, as they advance, an advanced degree becomes more important, particularly at larger organizations. Useful degrees include a master's of business administration (MBA) with a specialization in marketing or nonprofit management. Additional training may also be available through the American Marketing Association (http://www.ama.org).

Experience, Skills, and Personality Traits

Marketing Managers should be excellent communicators who work well with people and are able to be collaborative. They should have a combination of creative and analytical abilities in order to generate new ideas as well as understand statistics and financial data. Another asset is the ability to take a variety of opinions and combine them to develop a cohesive message. They must be flexible and be able to juggle many tasks simultaneously.

Generally, Marketing Managers have three to five years experience in marketing, although at smaller organizations, less may be required. Experience can be gained at other organizations, or through internships while a student.

Unions and Associations

Professional associations for Marketing Managers include the American Marketing Association, Sales and Marketing Executives International, and the Arts & Business Council (for those working for cultural institutions).

Tips for Entry

1. To learn more about careers in marketing, including definitions of terms, articles, and resources, contact http://www.knowthis.com/careers/careersmkt.htm.
2. The Arts and Business Council is a great source of networking opportunity for those interested in marketing for cultural institutions. Explore their Web site at http://www.artsandbusiness.org.
3. Visit the Web site http://www.idealist.org to search job descriptions for Marketing Managers in the nonprofit sector. This will give you an idea of how these jobs differ from corporate marketing positions.
4. Become aware of collateral marketing tools such as letterhead, posters, brochures, and newsletters. Think about the strategy behind the logo—does it seem successful to you? Try to speak with someone who was involved in designing the logo and planning the campaign.
5. Since marketing is about presentation, make sure your résumé is in top shape. Stop by your campus career center for a critique.

DIRECTOR OF PUBLIC AFFAIRS

CAREER PROFILE

Duties: Oversees the relationships with the public for a nonprofit organization, institution, or association; may include media relations, community relations, and public information

Alternate Title(s): Director of Public Relations, Director of Media Relations, Director of Community Relations, Director of Public Information

Salary Range: $35,000 to $75,000 and up

Employment Prospects: Good

Advancement Prospects: Good

Best Geographical Location(s): All, especially major cities

Prerequisites:

Education or Training—Bachelor's degree

Experience—Three to seven years of experience in communications, marketing, journalism, or public relations

Special Skills and Personality Traits—Excellent written and verbal communication skills; media savvy; ability to develop relationships and stay calm under pressure; articulate and professional

CAREER LADDER

```
┌──────────────────────────────────────┐
│   Director of Public Affairs (larger  │
│   organization) or Vice President     │
└──────────────────────────────────────┘

┌──────────────────────────────────────┐
│       Director of Public Affairs      │
└──────────────────────────────────────┘

┌──────────────────────────────────────┐
│         Account Coordinator           │
│      or Public Affairs Specialist     │
└──────────────────────────────────────┘
```

Position Description

Directors of Public Affairs are responsible for representing their organization in its relationships with the public. The public consists of many groups. It can encompass community members, the government, private corporations and businesses, the press/media, other nonprofit organizations, visitors, members, and donors. The process of imparting information to the public is very powerful. Public image can greatly affect nonprofit organizations and make a great difference in meeting financial and programming goals.

Because the definition of *public* has so many components, the field of public affairs is not simple to define. Public affairs is a multidisciplinary field that may combine aspects of communications, community relations, corporate relations, and public policy. Depending on the employment setting, the job of a Director of Public Affairs may touch on all or some of these things.

Directors of Public Affairs work to safeguard the image of their organization. Working closely with other profes-

sionals responsible for communications and marketing, they determine the "brand" they want to promote. With nonprofit organizations, that brand is often driven by the mission. Directors of Public Affairs try to figure out the best way to make sure their institution's mission reaches and is understood by the largest number of people.

In terms of communications, Directors of Public Affairs may supervise all aspects of publications for their organization. They ensure that each conveys the mission and message desired. Furthermore, they also can take a role in educational programs in order to both guarantee community participation as well as corporate sponsorship. They work to facilitate communication on an internal and external level.

Furthermore, Directors of Public Affairs are often liaisons with the media. They are frequently the point people for their organization and the interface with the press. They alert the media about recent events and programs in order to promote their mission to the public. For example, if the Chinese government donated a panda bear to a Cleveland zoo, the Director of Public Affairs would notify the press if a Chinese dignitary came to visit. They stay on top of all opportunities to get recognition for their organization.

It is common for Directors of Public Affairs to meet with reporters and answer their questions. Throughout, they are conscious about what they are saying and how it will affect the image of their organization. Additionally, they may work on marketing aspects such as creating specific promotions as ways to increase awareness about their organization.

Another responsibility of many Directors of Public Affairs is to be the face of their organization. They may greet visiting dignitaries, appear on radio or television spots, or attend press conferences and answer questions. For this reason, it is crucial for Directors of Public Affairs to know the mission and history of their organization inside and out. The more passionate they are about it, the better they can share that with the public. They also need to be extremely articulate and well spoken, at ease talking in front of large groups of people.

Their duties may include:

- Representing their institution at events
- Marketing products and/or services to the public, government, or corporations
- Writing publicity brochures, press releases, or Web copy
- Developing other written materials for media distribution
- Planning and coordinating public forums
- Meeting with community groups and other public groups
- Conducting outreach to various public groups
- Devising a long-range public affairs strategy
- Using e-mail and telephone conversations to communicate their messages
- Managing the public affairs budget

Directors of Public Affairs may work for many types of nonprofits, including cultural or conservation institutions such as museums or zoos, professional or trade associations, charities, research institutes, universities, and advocacy groups. Depending on the industry of employment, the job may vary. For example, at a professional association, the Director of Public Affairs may focus more on public policy work and government relations, while at a botanic garden, he or she may spend more time working on communications.

Also, Directors of Public Affairs may develop specialty areas. One may deal specifically with community groups, while another cultivates corporate relationships. The challenge for many Directors of Public Affairs is that their field is all-encompassing and may not offer the option of creating a narrow focus. However, many thrive on this challenge and find that it helps them never becoming bored.

Directors of Public Affairs may work in departments that vary in size from a one-person shop to groups of 10 or more. They usually have supervisory responsibilities for both administrative and professional staff. Because they often attend evening and weekend events, they may work long or nontraditional hours to meet the needs of their job.

Salaries
Based on a Workforce Management survey from November 2003 on http://www.workforce.com that studied pay in the not-for-profit sector for 92 jobs, the median total cash compensation for a public relations manager, comparable to a Director of Public Affairs at many organizations, was $70,000. The median cash compensation for a public relations position, nonmanagement, was $51,200, according to the same survey.

Another survey report of compensation in nonprofit organizations by Abbott, Langer & Associates in October 2003 showed the median income of directors of public relations at $50,327 and directors of information at $47,330. Overall, Directors of Public Affairs typically earn in the $50,000 range, but can have salaries of considerably less or more based on the nature of their position and type of organization.

Employment Prospects
Employment prospects are good for Directors of Public Affairs. All nonprofit organizations need to maintain good relationships with the public, and it is important to have someone to manage this process. The majority of opportunities are found at larger organizations that have more involvement with the media, the community at large, and other groups.

Advancement Prospects
Advancement prospects are also good based on the strong skill set that Directors of Public Affairs develop. While they are already at a high-level position, they can advance by moving to a larger organization or by becoming a vice president. Also, they may choose to carve out a specialty area in terms of whom they work with (donors, corporations, community) or what they do (public relations, writing, marketing).

Education and Training
Directors of Public Affairs hold bachelor's degrees in a variety of fields that emphasize communications. Common majors are English, journalism, public relations, or marketing. Some hold graduate degrees in these fields as well. They have excellent command of written and verbal language. Directors of Public Affairs that also do policy work may hold degrees in public policy.

Some professionals come to the field through previous work as journalists, reporters, public relations specialists, writers, or corporate communications specialists. They may receive ongoing training through seminars held by organizations such as the American Management Association and the American Public Relations Society. It is also important for Directors of Public Affairs to be knowledgeable about the industry in which they are involved.

Experience, Skills, and Personality Traits

Depending on the level of their position, Directors of Public Affairs may have between three and 10 years of experience. In addition to their superior communication skills, they also need to be able to deal with people. They must be proficient and polished, able to project the image and mission of their organization with both conviction and professionalism.

Directors of Public Affairs thrive under pressure and are able to troubleshoot in difficult situations. They seek out press opportunities and are savvy enough to know how to put a positive spin on a bad situation. It is also important that they are strategic thinkers who can help drive the consensus by understanding what makes a good news story. Their enthusiasm for their mission is apparent in what they do.

Unions and Associations

Directors of Public Affairs may belong to professional associations such as the Public Affairs Council, the American Management Association, the American Public Relations Society, the American Society of Association Executives, and the American Marketing Association, depending on their industry and specialty.

Tips for Entry

1. Gain communications experience through an internship. Try out roles in advertising, public relations, or marketing for a nonprofit organization to understand different roles and responsibilities.
2. Improve your writing skills by taking courses in English or journalism. Try your hand at writing for the campus newspaper or newsletters of various students groups.
3. Do a search for "Director of Public Affairs" using an Internet search engine such as Google to learn more about various available positions and job descriptions.
4. Explore nonprofit organizations of interest. Try to speak to three separate Directors of Public Affairs in different industries to find out the differences in their jobs. Consider choosing one cultural institution, one university, and one professional association.

PUBLICATIONS MANAGER

CAREER PROFILE

Duties: Handles all publications for a nonprofit organization, including newsletters, journals, membership directories, brochures, convention guides, and annual reports

Alternate Title(s): Publisher, Associate Publisher, Publications Director, Director of Publishing

Salary Range: $40,000 to $75,000 and up

Employment Prospects: Fair

Advancement Prospects: Fair

Best Geographical Location(s): All, with most opportunities in major cities

Prerequisites:

Education or Training—Bachelor's degree, preferably in English or journalism

Experience—One to seven years in publishing, depending on the organization

Special Skills and Personality Traits—Excellent writing, editing, and grammatical skills; knowledge of graphic design and good artistic sense; strong organization and management ability

CAREER LADDER

```
┌─────────────────────────────┐
│   Vice President or Director │
│      of Communications      │
└─────────────────────────────┘

┌─────────────────────────────┐
│     Publications Manager     │
└─────────────────────────────┘

┌─────────────────────────────┐
│        Writer/Editor         │
└─────────────────────────────┘
```

Position Description

Most nonprofit organizations produce a multitude of publications each year. Newsletters go out to members, donors, or other involved parties to inform them about recent happenings. Annual reports let board members as well as the general public understand the financial and administrative results accomplished by year's end. Brochures announce programs and key mission highlights.

While some types of publications are common to all nonprofits, others are dictated by industry. Professional associations often have scholarly journals. Arts organizations often have event calendars and exhibit flyers. Colleges and universities have alumni magazines. Membership organizations often have membership directories. Charities and other philanthropic organizations often have publications that honor their donors. In addition to these examples, there are many more that are tailored to each organization's specific needs.

Publications Managers oversee the process of all of these publications. They have a part in the writing, editing, design, printing, production, and mailing. In terms of writing and editing, they both write and edit material themselves, as well as delegate tasks to staff writers and editors. At smaller organizations, they often do the more hands-on work. They may select writers for various jobs and manage the editorial process. Furthermore, Publications Managers play a large role in determining the content for the various publications. They pay close attention to detail since the final results often reflect upon them.

Public relations savvy is useful for Publications Managers because they create the angle they want their publications to have. This is particularly important for the pieces that will be used as publicity materials such as brochures and member correspondence. They ask, "What are we trying to accomplish here?" and tailor the content accordingly. They strategize with writers, editors, designers, and additional marketing and communications staff to meet their goals. Some Publications Managers focus on specific types of writing. For example, one Publications Manager may be responsible for all publications dealing with fund-raising, while another may handle all member correspondence.

Additionally, Publications Managers need to be experienced in the publishing process from conception to print. They need to understand layout and graphic design, and have an eye for artwork and aesthetics. As managers, they often have administrative responsibilities as well. They develop yearly publications budgets and work with independent contractors to find services that are top quality but stay within the realm of the budget. They lead meetings and supervise staff.

Their duties may include:

- Obtaining bids for publications projects
- Maintaining publication and production schedules
- Conducting press checks
- Working with artists, designers, editors, and writers
- Negotiating contracts for services
- Collaborating with other departments
- Managing page layout process
- Overseeing printing process
- Selecting topics, authors, articles, and ideas for content

At some organizations, Publications Managers may also be responsible for online publications such as all or some of the Web page content. While technical staff often handles the programming, it is helpful for them to know about Web design and creating a Web page. They need a sense of design and work to create a format that flows clearly for their audience. They may make updates to the Web site as needed.

Publications Managers typically work a 40- to 50-hour workweek, with longer hours as major publications deadlines approach. They usually spend their time in an office, looking at pages or computer screens for extended periods of time.

Salaries

A 2003 survey report of 131 benchmark jobs from Abbott, Langer & Associates, Inc., *Compensation in Nonprofit Organizations, 16th Edition,* lists median incomes of publishers as $67,810. Furthermore, according to the 2003 *ASAE Association Executive Compensation and Benefits Study* from the American Society of Association Executives, the average total compensation for a director of publishing was $73,138. As with all positions in the nonprofit sector, salary varies based on size and type of organization, as well as the level of the position of the Publications Manager.

Employment Prospects

Employment prospects are fair for Publications Managers. The main reason for this is that not all nonprofit organizations have a full-time Publications Manager on staff. It is more typical for many nonprofits to have a communications manager or director who also handles publications among other communications functions.

Since Publications Manager is a specialized job, they can often be found only at larger organizations. Those looking for employment should focus on building a network of contacts. The greatest opportunities will be found in larger cities.

Advancement Prospects

Publications Managers may advance by moving to even larger organizations where they have more responsibility. For example, they may move from an organization where they handle only newsletters and brochures to an association that publishes several professional journals and a membership directory as well. Additionally, they may advance to take on a role of more leadership within their current organization, such as vice president or director of communications.

Education and Training

Publications Managers frequently hold bachelor's degrees in English, communications, or journalism. As part of a solid liberal arts background, courses that hone writing and editing skills are helpful. Also, coursework in business, public relations, and marketing are useful as well. Some Publications Managers hold a graduate degree, as well as a degree in a field relevant to their organization.

While much of the training comes while working full time, prior publications experience is a must for anyone considering this career. Insiders recommend internships for college students at magazines, newspapers, literary journals, or book publishers that provide extensive exposure to the field. While corporate experience can also offer the necessary skill set, Publications Managers at nonprofits also need to understand how the public sector differs from the private. They must be committed to the mission of their organization and see the publications as a reflection of these ideals.

Experience, Skills, and Personality Traits

It is essential for Publications Managers to have a way with words. They are excellent writers and editors themselves, with a sharp eye for grammar. They know not only what makes good writing from an editorial perspective, but also what makes dynamic publications from a visual and artistic perspective. Furthermore, they are meticulous and pay close attention to detail, with the ability to work well under pressure and meet deadlines.

In order to become a Publications Manager, one to seven years of work experience is required. The length of time varies depending on the size and structure of the organization. At large organizations where the Publications Manager supervises a sizeable staff, business and management experience is crucial.

Unions and Associations

Publications Managers may belong to the American Society of Association Executives, the International Association of Business Communicators, the Newsletters and Electronic Publishers Association, and the Small Publishers, Artists, and Writer's Network. They may belong to others based on the specialty of their organization as well.

Tips for Entry

1. Try out different publishing venues such as your campus newspaper and/or literary magazine to learn more about the publishing process.
2. Explore Web development by learning how Web sites are created, updated, and maintained. Find out how writing for the Web differs from other formats and what makes a successful webpage.
3. Hone your writing and editing skills through courses that challenge you to conduct research, write papers, and review your own writing, as well as the writing of your peers.
4. Gain exposure through internships. It can be valuable to intern at a commercial book or magazine publisher, as well as at a nonprofit organization to learn more about the field overall.
5. Take a look at http://www.idealist.org to view publishing and communications jobs in the nonprofit sector.

OTHER

CONSULTANT

CAREER PROFILE

Duties: Assists a nonprofit organization with determining long-term goals and provides guidance as to the most effective way to achieve these goals

Alternate Title(s): Independent Contractor, Adviser, Nonprofit Specialist

Salary Range: $55 to $250 per hour

Employment Prospects: Excellent

Advancement Prospects: Good

Best Geographical Location(s): Major cities

Prerequisites:

Education or Training—Bachelor's degree; some consultants have graduate degrees

Experience—Five to 10 years of nonprofit work experience

Special Skills and Personality Traits—Excellent organization and analytical skills; strong verbal and written communication skills; flexibility; tolerance for ambiguity

Licensure/Certification—Some states require consultants involved with fund-raising to register with the state Attorney General

CAREER LADDER

```
┌─────────────────────────────────┐
│   President of Consulting Firm    │
│     or Executive Director         │
│   of Nonprofit Organization       │
└─────────────────────────────────┘

┌─────────────────────────────────┐
│           Consultant              │
└─────────────────────────────────┘

┌─────────────────────────────────┐
│    Nonprofit Professional         │
│  (such as Director of Development │
│    or Special Events Manager)     │
└─────────────────────────────────┘
```

Position Description

The Merriam-Webster online dictionary defines a "Consultant" as someone "who gives professional advice or services." Consultants are experts who capitalize on their experience in order to assist organizations with achieving their goals. They are hired by a wide variety of nonprofit organizations in order to help with strategic planning and developing long-term objectives. Rather than focusing on day-to-day operations, Consultants look ahead and help organizations with their vision and plans for the future.

All Consultants have experience and expertise in some aspect of the nonprofit sector. Many have worked in areas such as fund-raising, development, event planning, and grant writing and may have industry specialties such as the arts, health care, social service, or education.

Before beginning a project with an organization, first a Consultant must learn about the organization in order to best help formulate its goals. Part of their background research includes reading all printed materials such as annual reports, newsletters, brochures, and Web sites to gain a better understanding of its mission and recent accomplishments.

Then Consultants usually spend much time conducting interviews with staff members. They often meet with all level of staff from the administrative assistant to the executive director and ask questions about their views of the organization, including likes and dislikes and areas for improvement. People often feel free to speak frankly with a Consultant because he or she is not a supervisor who has any bearing on their promotion or job status. After conducting research and interviewing staff members, Consultants will assess the situation and make recommendations for goal setting and change.

Some Consultants come in to train or present programs to nonprofit organizational staff or board members. They may provide training about organizational planning, fundraising campaigns, marketing, event planning, and grant seeking.

Consultants are attractive to organizations for many reasons. As outsiders who are removed from organizational bureaucracy, Consultants are able to offer a fresh perspective without office politics getting in the way. Furthermore, because they are paid by the hour or project and do not receive benefits, it is often cost-effective for organizations to hire them. Some consultants are brought in to complete specific projects such as writing a specific grant proposal or planning a large event. This frees up the rest of the organizational staff to continue with their regular work while the project is able to meet its deadline. Additionally, an organization will often choose to use a Consultant when there is no one internally with expertise in the current area of need and/or the organization has already tried to meet the need unsuccessfully.

Their duties may include:

- Conducting prospect research
- Working on an annual fund-raising appeal
- Providing board of directors development such as educating board members about their role
- Working on strategic plans
- Writing reports that assess findings
- Attending meetings with staff and board members
- Devising an instructional manual for staff and/or board members
- Planning special events
- Writing grant proposals
- Helping to prepare and create appropriate budgets
- Mentoring staff and providing opportunities for staff development

Consultants may be self-employed or they may work for nonprofit consulting firms. Those who are self-employed enjoy the flexibility of working on their own schedule, rather than a typical nine-to-five workday. While they spend some time at the organization, their work is completed in their own space, usually a home office, shared office space, or even a library or anywhere one can bring a laptop computer. However, during large projects, Consultants may work extremely long hours to complete the work within the required deadline. Projects may range in length from several days to several months or longer. Some Consultants take one project at a time, while others manage to juggle several smaller assignments at once.

Salaries

Most Consultants are paid by the hour, and depending on their level of experience and expertise, they can charge anywhere from $50 to $250 per hour. Usually, if Consultants are at a level where they can charge more than $250 per hour, they earn a set fee for the entire project. Some projects usually pay a set fee as well. For example, a Consultant may earn $3,000 for writing a grant proposal, and more for writing a strategic plan.

Employment Prospects

As many nonprofit organizations downsize with fluctuations in the economy, there is currently excellent employment opportunity for Consultants. Although their hourly rates may be high, it often ends up being cheaper for organizations to outsource their work by hiring Consultants rather than full-time employees. Because Consultants do not receive benefits and do not need a physical space within the organization to work, it is financially beneficial for many organizations to choose Consultants for their projects. In this way, organizations can essentially get a senior-level professional for an entry-level price, and both organizations and Consultants benefit.

Advancement Prospects

Consultants can advance by joining larger consulting firms, taking on more clients if they work independently, or starting their own consulting firms. They may advance by becoming highly specialized in one particular area of the nonprofit sector. Also, some Consultants may seek leadership roles such as executive director at nonprofit organizations after building up specialty experience.

Education and Training

Although there is not one particular educational path to follow to become a Consultant, virtually all Consultants have a bachelor's degree and many have a master's degree as well. Courses in subjects such as English, writing, communication, fund-raising, public relations, and finance may be helpful. Also useful can be additional training in nonprofit management and grant writing.

Experience, Skills, and Personality Traits

Since Consultant means "expert," one cannot become a Consultant until he or she has several years of related experience. Most successful Consultants have worked for five to 10 years in the nonprofit sector including roles in fund-raising and development, grant writing, special events planning, and prospect research.

Unlike general staff members who often must take instruction, a Consultant must be comfortable in a position of authority where he or she is giving advice. They also must be able to handle great amounts of responsibility. It is crucial for Consultants to work well with people. Many different types of people must view them as credible, and they must be good communicators, as well as effective listeners.

Since they are often self-employed, Consultants also must be very self-motivated. Prior work experience is key in order to develop a network of contacts that will help Consultants find work. It is the job of a self-employed Consultant to get clients, and his or her networking skills must be honed. They must also be able to financially and emotionally handle the fluctuations of work. Certain cycles may be very busy, while others may be slow.

Special Requirements

For Consultants who work independently and are involved specifically with fund-raising, some states require them to register with the Attorney General. These Consultants may need to get a government bond if they will be soliciting funds.

Unions and Associations

Consultants can belong to a variety of professional associations depending on their specialty area. These may include the Association of Fundraising Professionals, the Associa-

tion of Professional Researchers for Advancement, the American Association of Grants Professionals, the American Marketing Association, and the International Special Events Society.

Tips for Entry

1. Talk with consultants to learn about their career path. Find out about their educational and professional backgrounds, as well as their current day-to-day work.
2. Research the pros and cons of working as an independent consultant or a consultant at an established consulting firm.
3. Consider how you would market yourself for a service you could provide. Develop a campaign, including publicity and business plans.
4. Speak to friends, family members, and other professionals working for nonprofits. Find out if their organizations have ever hired consultants and for what types of projects.

GRANT WRITER

CAREER PROFILE

Duties: Writing proposals to help an organization secure funding for specific projects and general support from foundations, corporations, and individuals

Alternate Title(s): None

Salary Range: $30,000 to $70,000 and up

Employment Prospects: Good

Advancement Prospects: Good

Best Geographical Location(s): All

Prerequisites:

Education or Training—Bachelor's degree; an advanced degree and courses on grant writing helpful

Experience—Writing or nonprofit experience required

Special Skills and Personality Traits—Excellent writing skills; creativity; understanding of nonprofit sector; marketing and public relations abilities

CAREER LADDER

```
┌─────────────────────────────────────────┐
│   Director-level Position or Consultant   │
└─────────────────────────────────────────┘

┌─────────────────────────────────────────┐
│              Grant Writer                 │
└─────────────────────────────────────────┘

┌─────────────────────────────────────────┐
│  Journalist, Administrative Assistant,    │
│              or Intern                     │
└─────────────────────────────────────────┘
```

Position Description

Nonprofit organizations depend on grants in order to fund many of their programs. They may seek grants for specific projects, general operating support, or to fund start-up ventures, to name a few. Grant Writers put together these proposals targeted at different foundations, corporations, and individuals that have been identified as good prospects for giving. They synthesize research conducted by the development department, as well as perform research themselves to understand the past history and interests of these potential donors. This helps them to determine which have funding priorities that are similar to those of their own organization. They also use this research to create a personalized approach for each proposal.

Grant proposals often begin with a tailored cover letter. In this letter, Grant Writers include quotes and details about their organization that they believe will appeal to the potential donor. This is why the more they know about the foundations, corporations, and individuals they solicit, the better the chance for success. If they feel a specific layout for the proposal might be effective, they might even work with graphic designers to target this cover letter and make it aesthetically pleasing. They also describe the kind of funding they seek, whether it is for a specific project or more general support.

After the initial cover letter, which enables them to make a case for a specific program and target it to a specific source, most organizations use standard proposals that share their information. These proposals can be about 10 pages long and often include the following information:

- Executive summary
- Background of the organization, including history and mission
- Needs and problems addressed by the organization
- Program goals of the organization
- Organization accomplishments
- Program descriptions
- Methods of evaluation, including quantitative and qualitative research studies

In addition to the cover letter and general proposal, most organizations also send a press kit, an audit report, and their 501(c)(3) form confirming that they are a valid nonprofit. Some states require certain application forms for proposals and adhere to strict guidelines. Grant Writers are attuned to all this information and put together a package they feel will be most effective.

Grant Writers also work to determine where to send proposals. They track past sources of funding and maintain databases. Since some organizations will not accept unsolicited proposals, they work with board members and executive staff to gain networking contacts. They might be responsible for cold calling potential donors, making inquiries by telephone or writing to see if they could submit formal proposals, and always following up and tracking deadline dates. Sometimes they will also arrange site visits, where they bring donors into the office or to see specific programs to get them involved.

In addition to writing grant proposals, Grant Writers also do grant reporting. Many funding groups require annual and even midyear reports about where their money has gone. Grant Writers write up a report that includes details such as how the money was spent, photos of projects, and a narrative description. They also may add information about how to provide renewed support. Even when this report is not mandatory, Grant Writers may provide them to other donors anyway, as a method of soliciting ongoing support.

Additional duties may include:

* Working with the executive director, board of directors, and fund-raising/development staff
* Identifying new funding sources and grant opportunities
* Writing and editing additional material for newsletters, cultivation, and reports
* Maintaining tracking calendars and deadlines
* Building relationships with donors
* Working on direct mail campaigns and annual reports
* Developing budgets to accompany funding requests

The job of a Grant Writer varies depending on the size and set up of the organization. Some nonprofits have large grant writing staffs in which the writers solely focus on grant writing, while other Grant Writers juggle many responsibilities including fund-raising and development in addition to grant writing. Regardless of their responsibilities, many Grant Writers tell of the sense of satisfaction they feel when a grant comes through. Although they are not on the front lines of fund-raising, they can see the influence they have when programs get funding.

Salaries

According to an October 2003 survey report of compensation in nonprofit organizations by Abbott, Langer & Associates, Inc., the median salary for Grant Writers was $38,812. However, this figure varies depending on the size and location of the organization. A 2003 annual salary survey of New York City nonprofits by Professionals for Nonprofits stated the average salary for Grant Writers in New York City to be between $50,000 and $70,000.

Employment Prospects

Due to the growing need for funding among nonprofits, employment prospects are good for Grant Writers to write those proposals. Grant Writers can work for all different types of nonprofits and can be part of the development staff or work within other departments. With a good knowledge of fund-raising and the nonprofit sector overall, there are a variety of positions available. Also, some organizations hire Grant Writers on a part-time basis, which enables Grant Writers to do freelance or consulting work if they choose.

Advancement Prospects

Advancement prospects are also good. With their writing, editing, research, and fund-raising skills, Grant Writers can move into director-level positions in communications, development, or administration, as well as develop more flexible freelance consulting careers as stated above.

Education and Training

While there is no specific education required for becoming a Grant Writer, virtually all Grant Writers have a bachelor's degree, and many have an advanced degree as well. Since writing ability is so important, majors in English or other humanities subjects can be helpful. Grant writing has also become a popular career path for Ph.D's who choose not to enter academia, since many of them have personal experience with writing grants through their course of education and research.

A variety of school and agencies offer grant writing courses, a good way to gain expertise in grant writing by investing only a small amount of time and money. Programs include the Foundation Center in New York City, which offers courses throughout the country (http://fdncenter.org/learn/), and The Grant Institute (http://www.thegrantinstitute.com/), which travels to university campuses for presentations nationwide. There are also many online courses at sites such as http://www.grantwriting.com and http://www.classesusa.com.

Experience, Skills, and Personality Traits

Writing, editing, and research skills are crucial for success as a Grant Writer. A background in the nonprofit sector is also valuable, through internships and volunteer work. An understanding of the fund-raising process and any personal experience with writing grants helps. Some people come to the field from journalism, public relations, and other positions that require extensive writing.

Grant Writers need not only to be able to write, but also to be able to tailor their writing to meet the needs of their organization and/or potential donors. Persistence and resilience enable them to keep at it and not to take rejection personally. For those also doing development work, good interpersonal skills will help with networking and solicitation of donors.

Unions and Associations

Grant Writers may belong to national organizations such as the Association of Fund-raising Professionals, and other local groups or associations related to the mission of their organization.

Tips for Entry

1. Conduct research into grant writing. There are a multitude of Web sites that offer information and advice about writing grant proposals, including http://cpmcnet. columbia.edu/research/writing.htm, http://www.cpb.org/grants/grantwriting.html, http://www.seanet.com/~sylvie/grants.htm, http://www.hamptonu.edu/bsrc/CMSE/grtmn.html, and http://www.fundsnetservices.com/grantwri.htm.

2. Gain experience in the nonprofit sector through internships and volunteer work.

3. Consider taking a grant-writing course. The sites listed throughout this profile will give you ideas about how to get involved.

4. Talk to current Grant Writers to learn more about the job. Gain their perspectives about the best ways to prepare for a career.

WEBMASTER

CAREER PROFILE

Duties: Develops, manages, and maintains the Web site(s) and overall Internet presence for an organization

Alternate Title(s): Web Site Administrator, Web Developer, Web Producer

Salary Range: $40,000 to $60,000 and up

Employment Prospects: Fair

Advancement Prospects: Fair

Best Geographical Location(s): All, especially larger organization in major cities

Prerequisites:

Education or Training—Bachelor's degree in computer science preferred, but not required; knowledge of computer programming

Experience—Related experience creating and managing Web sites through full-time work or internships

Special Skills and Personality Traits—Excellent computer programming skills; understanding of Internet and online communication technologies; strong organizational skills; ability to meet deadlines and work well under pressure; knowledge of graphic design

CAREER LADDER

```
┌─────────────────────────────────────┐
│  Webmaster (larger organization) or  │
│  Director of Information Technology   │
└─────────────────────────────────────┘

┌─────────────────────────────────────┐
│             Webmaster                 │
└─────────────────────────────────────┘

┌─────────────────────────────────────┐
│   Web page Designer or Programmer     │
└─────────────────────────────────────┘
```

Position Description

The Internet is one of the most important tools that nonprofit organizations can use to further their missions. Through their Web sites, they can promote their programs, create awareness for their issues, register members, tell people how to volunteer or donate money, provide public education and information, and sell revenue-generating products, among others. To accomplish their goals, even the smallest nonprofits recognize the need for their own Web site. Since most nonprofit professionals do not have the skills and expertise needed to achieve this on their own, that is where a Webmaster comes in.

Webmasters at nonprofit organizations create and implement Internet visions. Starting from scratch, they strategize as to what will make a successful Web site based on the goals of their organization. They gather information from all the departments and key players to determine what will be included and a layout that will work. Their aim is to command the attention of visitors and to make them want to linger on the site long enough to learn about the organization. For some nonprofits, visibility can make a huge difference in their funding and continued existence, so the task is of the utmost importance. A user-friendly site can mean a considerable difference in donations, volunteers, and overall support.

Web sites of nonprofit organizations differ from those of corporations, and Webmasters in this sector must be aware of the distinctions. First, sites of different organizations often cover the same specific topics. For example, they often contain detailed information about staff, including major leaders and the board of directors. Another important feature of each site is to make sure visitors to the site know how they can support the organization. Whether this involves direct donations, support through events, membership, programs, or performances, or volunteering time, the giving options are often outlined. Public policy and advocacy is another important area to click on where the public can get educated and involved.

The job of a Webmaster is often defined differently at varying organizations. It may include programming, graphic design and determining the "look" of the site, content development, and production. Most Webmasters continuously maintain and update their sites after development, troubleshooting problems. They create the links that visitors use to navigate the site. Also, they record the "hits" so they know the parts of the site people most often visit and whether or not they complete any online registrations.

Additionally, Webmasters may work on both the back end and the front end of a Web site. The back end involves the database and hardware infrastructure that supports the site, requiring the Webmaster to be skilled at programming. The front end relates to the aspects that users can see, such as design and navigation tools, requiring the Webmaster to be up to speed on graphics and content development. Webmasters must decide on the hardware needed to build the site and the software needed to make it work properly.

Webmasters must continuously communicate with staff members at their organization to make sure that the information on the Web site is up to date and reflects the most current vision. Information gets outdated in the blink of an eye, so they must be on top of all new developments. They work with all departments such as communications, which may handle writing the copy, editing, and public relations; and development, which can outline their fund-raising achievements and goals. Usually, they serve as internal liaisons and do little work with external vendors.

Their duties may include:

- Setting up and managing internal and external listservs
- Fixing software bugs
- Brainstorming ideas
- Adding new features such as discussion boards and registration capabilities
- Researching Web sites of similar organizations
- Writing code
- Responding to visitor feedback
- Supporting users nationwide and worldwide
- Posting content pages
- Editing and reviewing content
- Testing the links on the site to make sure they work properly
- Dealing with security issues

For many Webmasters, their job is a way to get paid while spending time on one of their favorite hobbies: surfing the Net. Most are passionate about the Internet and are very involved in their work. Since the World Wide Web does not function on a nine-to-five schedule, neither do most Webmasters. Their jobs may involve long, nontraditional hours to enable sites to go live and to fix any problems.

Salaries

Salaries of Webmasters vary based on the size and budget of the organization, as well as the job responsibilities. According to a summary at www.workforce.com citing a 2003 study about pay in the not-for-profit sector, the median cash compensation for a nonprofit Webmaster was $55,000. The summary also reported a low of $26,000 and a high of $165,000. These figures demonstrate the huge range for these types of positions.

Employment Prospects

Unfortunately, not all nonprofit organizations have the budget for their own full-time Webmaster. It is often cheaper to outsource the work to a consultant. However, there are Webmasters who make a good living working as consultants primarily to nonprofit organizations.

Large organizations often do hire on-site Webmasters, and more nonprofits are recognizing this need as budgeting allows. Opportunities are better than they were after the crash of many Internet companies in the late 1990s. In fact, many Internet professionals sought out the nonprofit sector as another arena for opportunity while the corporate sector floundered, and they continue to do so. As the Internet capabilities increase and are used more frequently by nonprofits to meet their goals and increase their visibility, so do positions for Webmasters.

Advancement Prospects

Webmasters may advance by moving to larger organizations with more complex Web sites. They may seek out positions that enable them to build more online features such as registrations and discussion boards, and even cutting-edge technologies such as streaming videos or live chats. Webmasters at larger organizations can earn higher salaries. Webmasters may also decide to become self-employed, working as consultants for nonprofit organizations to build their Web sites.

Education and Training

While formal education is less important for Webmasters than having the required skill sets, most position listings ask for bachelor's degrees, particularly in computer science. They want to be sure that Webmasters have the appropriate training to carry out their jobs, and a degree can often add this credibility.

This is a field where training comes from actually doing the work, not just learning about it. Most Webmasters gain experience through internships and part-time jobs while they are students. As they design Web sites for campus organizations or companies, they receive the valuable training needed to perform this job on a regular basis. Furthermore, constant training is needed to keep skills up to date with new technologies.

Experience, Skills, and Personality Traits

Clearly, computer skills are the main qualification for positions as a Webmaster. Depending upon the position, different programming languages may be needed. Some common requirements may include HTML, XML, CGL, SQL, Java, Java Script, ASP, Cold Fusion, and C++. Web development and design tools such as Acrobat, Dream Weaver, Flash Animation, and Photoshop can also be required. Webmasters should be experienced and familiar with Internet technologies, having already had the experience of personally building and maintaining several Web sites in order to get hired.

In addition to technical skills, Webmasters need to be excellent organizers. They need to have creative vision combined with the ability to manage projects, meet deadlines, and work well under pressure. Those Webmasters who write and develop content should have strong writing skills as well.

Unions and Associations

Webmasters may belong to a variety of professional associations including the World Organization of Webmasters and the Internet Society, as well as regional groups. New associations are frequently forming since the field is still so new.

Tips for Entry

1. Volunteer to create and maintain the Web site for a student organization on campus. This will provide firsthand experience on the work of a Webmaster.
2. Visit the Web sites of several nonprofit organizations that interest you. Notice what features they all have in common, as well as their design and layout.
3. Take courses that will help you enhance your computer skills. In addition to those offered by local universities, there are hundreds of online tutorials. Conduct a search engine query for the programs you want to learn to explore the options.
4. Apply for a formal internship in Web development. This will provide you with skills, as well as mentors who may be able to help you find a job.
5. Learn more about the job of a Webmaster and other careers in Web site development by visiting links such as http://www.wetfeet.com/asp/careerprofiles_overview.asp?careerpk=45 and http://www.course.com/careers/dayinthelife/webdev_jobdesc.cfm

CONTROLLER

CAREER PROFILE

Duties: Preparing financial analyses of operations for a nonprofit organization; overseeing accounting, auditing, and budgeting practices

Alternate Title(s): Accountant, Bookkeeper, Comptroller

Salary Range: $50,000 to $138,000

Employment Prospects: Good

Advancement Prospects: Good

Best Geographical Location(s): All

Prerequisites:

Education or Training—Bachelor's degree in accounting or finance

Experience—Several years of bookkeeping or accounting experience

Special Skills and Personality Traits—Attention to detail; well-organized; knowledge of accounting and nonprofit guidelines

Licensure/Certification—Some Controllers may be Certified Public Accountants (CPAs)

CAREER LADDER

```
┌─────────────────────────────────┐
│   Controller (larger organization) │
│       or Director of Finance      │
└─────────────────────────────────┘

┌─────────────────────────────────┐
│           Controller            │
└─────────────────────────────────┘

┌─────────────────────────────────┐
│       Assistant Controller       │
└─────────────────────────────────┘
```

Position Description

Controllers help nonprofit organizations manage their financial affairs, looking at both the big picture and day-to-day operations. They direct financial plans and policies, as well as accounting practices, taking into consideration the mission of the organization at all times. It is their job to prepare reports that reflect the organization's financial position, summarizing the present and forecasting the future. These reports include balance sheets, income statements, and analyses of future earnings or expenses. Controllers also help organizations manage their relationships with lending institutions and the financial community, as well as maintaining all fiscal records.

Acting as liaisons between the organization and regulatory authorities, Controllers are responsible for preparing required information for tax purposes and independent audits. In the nonprofit sector, their job takes on a different component than their corporate counterparts. Since all nonprofit organizations are required by law to undergo independent audits, the Controller ensures that accounting guidelines are followed appropriately. They pay close attention to "GAAP," which stands for "Generally Accepted Accounting Principles." These are a set of accounting standards established by the Financial Accounting Standards Board and used to standardize financial accounting of public companies. Most nonprofits receive 501(c)(3) status, which makes them exempt from paying federal income taxes. Since it is crucial for the IRS to approve this designation of nonprofits, the Controller needs to make sure that all documents are in compliance.

Coding is another facet of the job of a Controller in a nonprofit organization. He or she codes all deposits according to IRS and GAAP standards, based on their specific expenses. For example, donations must be coded to show if they have been designated for fund-raising, programming, or administrative use. Every dollar must be accounted for, requiring the Controller to pay close attention to detail.

Controllers also plan and establish the annual budget for their organization at the beginning of each fiscal year. They analyze their organization's finances to determine where the money will come from and where it will go for the coming year. They pay attention to quarterly reports to make sure that plans are on track. It is important that they make sure that the organization is able to achieve its goals. As one Controller put it, "in the nonprofit sector, we recognize how every number relates to human lives."

Furthermore, Controllers oversee payroll and purchasing, as well as accounts payable functions. In many organizations, particularly small ones, they also handle salary and benefits administration. In addition to their financial skills, Controllers must be discreet and tactful. They are privy to confidential information such as how much each employee earns. It is important for them to remain professional at all times and not breach confidentiality in these matters.

Their duties may include:

- Writing and cutting checks
- Keeping track of donations
- Receiving deposits
- Balancing books
- Detailing entries for donations
- Analyzing statistical and accounting information
- Working with accounting firms
- Maintaining books, accounts, and records, as well as implementing new systems for organization and reporting
- Creating financial policy and procedure
- Managing financial/accounting assistants
- Providing effective financial controls for the organization
- Evaluating and recommending insurance coverage
- Establishing economic objectives for the organization
- Developing cash handling procedures for special events
- Performing bank reconciliations
- Coordinating annual audit
- Maintaining general ledger
- Responding to inquiries from grantors
- Writing expense reports
- Preparing 1099 forms annually for independent contractors

Controllers generally work a 40- to 45-hour workweek. Those who move from the corporate sector to the nonprofit sector find it important to understand the structure of nonprofit organizations and the tax guidelines they must follow. Also, they find it rewarding to be able to manage finances that will be used to contribute to good causes and improving society.

Salaries

According to the Occupational Outlook Handbook online, a 2002 survey by Robert Half International, a staffing services firm specializing in accounting and finance professionals, showed corporate controllers earning between $54,000 and $138,750. Additionally, the same site also quotes the Association for Financial Professionals' 14th annual compensation survey, showing average total compensation for

Controllers in 2002 to be $134,300. However, Controllers in the nonprofit sector typically earn at the lower end of the spectrum. Bonuses and other financial perks may augment their salaries.

Employment Prospects

Employment prospects are good for Controllers in the nonprofit sector. Complying with government regulations is essential for organizations, and the Controller has an important job in making that happen. Opportunities are the most plentiful for those with a master's degree and work experience. Most positions require an accounting degree and three to five years of experience.

Advancement Prospects

Controllers may advance by moving to larger nonprofit organizations, or through additional training or education. Many choose to go back to school for master's degrees in accounting, finance, or business, while others take courses to develop additional skills. Controllers with the right skill set and experience may advance to become directors of finance and administration.

Education and Training

Most Controllers at nonprofit organizations have a minimum of a bachelor's degree, usually in accounting or finance. It is becoming more common for them to hold graduate degrees in accounting or business administration (M.B.A.). In the past, Controllers may have been hired without college degrees if they had bookkeeping experience, but today this is less likely due to increased competition for positions. In smaller organizations, however, Controllers may still be hired by trade rather than education, with a bookkeeping background rather than an undergraduate degree.

Special Requirements

Controllers who specialize in accounting may earn the Certified Public Accountant (CPA) or Certified Management Accountant (CMA) designations. Check out the Web site of the American Institute for Certified Public Accountants at http://www.aicpa.org/index.htm for more information. Furthermore, the Institute of Management Accountants (http://www.imanet.org/) offers a Certified in Financial Management designation to members with a bachelor's degree and at least two years of work experience who pass the institute's four-part examination and fulfill continuing education requirements.

Experience, Skills, and Personality Traits

Controllers must be well organized and meticulous, able to focus on minute details and follow rules carefully. They should have excellent computer skills, as well as strong communication skills to share information with others in their organization and work with external agencies. They need to be good at multitasking and have a firm ability to work with numbers. Basic accounting and financial skills are essential, as is knowledge of the nonprofit sector.

Unions and Associations

Controllers may belong to professional associations, including the Association for Financial Professionals, the Financial Management Association International, the National Association of State Auditors, Comptrollers, and Treasurers, and the Institute of Management Accountants. They may also belong to additional associations based on the specialty of their organization.

Tips for Entry

1. Learn more about the U.S. "GAAP" by looking at the Web site http://cpaclass.com/gaap/gaap-us-01a.htm.
2. Speak to a Controller at a nonprofit organization to learn more about his or her job. Find out how the job differs from that of a Controller in the corporate sector.
3. Take courses in accounting or finance to see if they interest you. Learn more about accounting and becoming a certified public accountant (CPA) by visiting the Web site http://www.aicpa.org/index.htm.
4. Do you know what a 990 is? Nonprofits have very specific forms that they are required by the IRS to file each year. Learn more about these special tax regulations by visiting http://www.nonprofits.org/npofaq/18/85.html.

ADMINISTRATIVE ASSISTANT

CAREER PROFILE

Duties: Provides administrative support to various departments within a nonprofit organization, performing such tasks as customer service, coordinating mailings, handling telephone calls, and others

Alternate Title(s): Executive Assistant, Secretary, Coordinator, Receptionist

Salary Range: $20,000 to $50,000

Employment Prospects: Good

Advancement Prospects: Good

Best Geographical Location(s): All

Prerequisites:

Education or Training—Bachelor's degree preferred for some positions but not required

Experience—Prior exposure to an office setting

Special Skills and Personality Traits—Excellent organization skills; strong customer service focus; ability to multitask; flexibility and calmness

CAREER LADDER

```
┌─────────────────────────────────┐
│      Program Coordinator         │
│   or other entry-level position  │
│       based on department        │
└─────────────────────────────────┘

┌─────────────────────────────────┐
│     Administrative Assistant     │
└─────────────────────────────────┘

┌─────────────────────────────────┐
│  Temporary Worker, Volunteer,    │
│      Intern, or Student          │
└─────────────────────────────────┘
```

Position Description

Few nonprofit organizations would be able to function at the level they do without the aid of Administrative Assistants. Although the position may be low on the hierarchical ladder, it is utmost in importance to keep operations running smoothly.

Administrative Assistants may be asked to take on varying roles depending on the organization and department for which they work. Each department within a nonprofit may have an Administrative Assistant, such as development or volunteer services. Furthermore, the executive director may have his or her own Administrative Assistant. However, in smaller organizations, several departments will share one assistant who supports their various responsibilities. In very small organizations, there may be one Administrative Assistant to support the entire staff. Responsibilities for Administrative Assistants may be specialized or diverse, depending on the situation.

Commonly, Administrative Assistants handle basic office support tasks such as answering the telephone, greeting visitors, and performing data entry. They may order supplies, furniture, and deal with problems that arise with equipment, such as hiring a worker to come and fix the copy machine if necessary. Part of their role is to make sure that the staff has everything they need to perform their jobs well, whether that means a comfortable office temperature or light bulbs in all their lamps. As troubleshooters, Administrative Assistants get things done.

Often, Administrative Assistants perform other tasks related to their strengths and are often hired based on how their backgrounds fit with the needs of the organization. For example, some Administrative Assistants work on human resource projects, maintaining personnel files and setting up interviews and orientations for new employees. Others work on budgeting, bookkeeping, or accounting, making use of their training in the financial realm. Yet others who are skilled at writing may draft letters, e-mails, and other correspondence. Administrative Assistants who are particularly strong at working with people may set up appointments and talk to donors, making sure their needs are being met.

Additionally, Administrative Assistants can be the eyes and ears of their organization. They know what is going on, who is responsible for what, and the protocol to handle different situations. Whether it is a simple task like getting coffee or a creative project like designing flyers, they pitch in where needed and know who to ask for support.

Because of the diversity and potential of their tasks, Administrative Assistants can be poised to become professionals in the nonprofit sector with the appropriate education and experience. This is more common in the nonprofit sector, where less of a hierarchy exists than in the corporate world. While some Administrative Assistants are satisfied with the secretarial nature of their jobs and prefer to carry out their assigned tasks only, others take initiative and use this opportunity to gain experience and learn more about the nonprofit field. It can be an entry-level way for a recent graduate to get a foot in the door of an organization of interest.

Also, for some Administrative Assistants, their positions may be a means to an end. College or graduate students may seek positions as Administrative Assistants in order to help finance their education. Others may find opportunities that offer part-time or flexible hours in order to meet other personal needs.

Their duties may include:

- Maintaining files or records
- Organizing daily schedules
- Updating databases of donors or members
- Answering initial correspondence
- Attending meetings
- Taking notes or minutes at meetings
- Providing reports to supervisors
- Supervising volunteers or other support personnel
- Interacting with vendors
- Conducting background research
- Scheduling meetings and appointments
- Making travel arrangements
- Tracking grant proposals
- Assisting with donor correspondence and solicitations
- Helping with day-to-day operations
- Supporting the board of directors

Administrative Assistants frequently serve as their supervisors' right hand. Their managers depend on them to make sure that all runs smoothly. At some organizations, their tasks may run into the personal. It is not unheard of for bosses to ask their Administrative Assistants to pick up their dry cleaning, baby-sit for their children, or water their plants while they are on vacation. However, those kinds of relationships are unusual, and it is understood right away that this may be part of the job. Although some Administrative Assistants are resentful of such tasks, others welcome them with the perks that may come along as well, such as house-sitting or invitations to glamorous events.

Administrative Assistants need to be computer literate and comfortable in an office environment. They should be familiar with fax machines, photocopy machines, voice mail systems, and other office equipment. It is important for them to be excellent organizers with the ability to gather data. Usually, they work a 40-hour workweek, but may work additional hours on special projects. They may receive overtime pay in some organizations. Administrative Assistants who work directly for the executive director may have longer hours, but also higher salaries.

Salaries

Salaries for Administrative Assistants vary greatly depending on the location, size, and budget of the organization. They also vary depending on education and experience, as well as on departmental responsibilities. Administrative Assistants may earn as little as $20,000 or as much as $50,000 or more.

According to a summary at http://www.workforce.com citing a 2003 study about pay in the not-for-profit sector, the median cash compensation for an executive assistant is $50,300. Executive assistants reporting directly to executive directors are at the highest end of the salary range. The same survey cites median earning for a program assistant as $32,800.

Employment Prospects

Employment prospects for Administrative Assistants are good. In organizations large and small, assistants are always needed to support the professional staff. While opportunities are expected to grow slowly in the corporate world, nonprofit organizations will not experience the same slowdown since they rely on Administrative Assistants to perform many roles. Opportunities are the greatest in organizations heavily involved with fund-raising.

Advancement Prospects

Good Administrative Assistants are hard to find, and managers may fight tooth and nail to keep the ones who have performed well for them. However, they usually are fiercely loyal and staunch supporters when their assistants want to move on to bigger and better roles.

For Administrative Assistants with a bachelor's degree, the next step would be to move into an entry-level professional role within their department of interest, whether it is development, communications, administration, or others. The experience they receive from their work as an Administrative Assistant, along with the recommendation by a supervisor, is usually sufficient to get that promotion. Administrative Assistants without a bachelor's degree may advance by going on for additional education, taking computer courses, or moving from a small organization to a larger one. They may seek to work as an executive assistant for more money and responsibility.

Education and Training

Education and training for Administrative Assistants varies. A bachelor's degree is not required, but many Administrative

Assistants do hold bachelor's degrees in a variety of liberal arts fields. The degree can make them more competitive for positions at large or prestigious organizations that see their Administrative Assistants more like entry-level professionals.

It is important for Administrative Assistants to have worked in an office before. In addition to knowing how to operate office equipment, they should be especially skilled with computers and have an excellent command of the Microsoft Office programs such as Word, Excel, and PowerPoint.

Experience, Skills, and Personality Traits

Administrative Assistants deal with difficult personalities on a daily basis. For this reason, it is necessary for them to be calm and unflappable, able to handle stressful situations with ease. It is also important for them to be customer-service focused and thick-skinned, with the ability to handle criticism. Good Administrative Assistants are detail-oriented to a fault and are superior organizers.

Furthermore, Administrative Assistants should have excellent communication skills. Depending on the organization, they may be communicating with donors, sponsors, members, and visitors on a daily basis. Strong writing skills are helpful for correspondence.

Unions and Associations

Administrative Assistants may belong to professional associations depending on their type of organization. In addition to general nonprofit associations, they also may belong to the International Association of Administrative Professionals or the National Association of Executive Secretaries and Administrative Assistants.

Tips for Entry

1. Find an Administrative Assistant position in the industry that interests you in order to gain experience in that area. For example, if you are interested in museum work, an administrative positions at a museum can help you learn the ropes and make valuable contacts.
2. Try work-study or other part-time position in an office on campus. Learn how to operate office equipment and try out your customer service skills.
3. Take a course to become proficient in Microsoft Office. Their Web site at http://www.microsoft.com/learning/default.asp will help you figure out where to start.
4. Speak to Administrative Assistants in the nonprofit sector to find out what they like best and least about their jobs.

BUSINESS, PROFESSIONAL, AND TRADE ASSOCIATIONS

DIRECTOR OF GOVERNMENT RELATIONS

CAREER PROFILE

Duties: Advocates on the local, state, or federal level on behalf of issues important to members of an association and the profession as a whole

Alternate Title(s): Director of Public Policy, Director of Public Affairs, Government Relations Manager

Salary Range: $60,000 to $120,000 and up

Employment Prospects: Good

Advancement Prospects: Good

Best Geographical Location(s): Washington, D.C., and other major cities

Prerequisites:

Education or Training—Minimum of a bachelor's degree; graduate degree in law, public policy, political science, or other discipline required for most positions

Experience—Depending on the size of the association, three to 10 years in politics, law, or advocacy

Special Skills and Personality Traits—Excellent written and verbal communication skills; relationship-building and networking; understanding of the legal process

CAREER LADDER

```
┌─────────────────────────────────────────┐
│  Vice President of Government Relations   │
│           or Public Policy                │
└─────────────────────────────────────────┘

┌─────────────────────────────────────────┐
│   Director of Government Relations        │
└─────────────────────────────────────────┘

┌─────────────────────────────────────────┐
│   Assistant Director of Government        │
│     Relations or Policy Analyst           │
└─────────────────────────────────────────┘
```

Position Description

In each profession, there are hot-button issues that affect its members. Teachers may be concerned with state regulations determining tenure and required student testing, while physicians may worry about health care reform and laws favoring insurance companies. Legislation is constantly being considered at the local, state, and federal level that affects members of various professional associations. The Director of Government Relations serves as a liaison between his or her association and the government, guiding and influencing the association's legislative programs.

Directors of Government Relations meet with local, state, or federal senators and legislators in order to lobby and advocate on behalf of their organization. Since some professional membership associations are quite large with thousands of members, committees are formed that represent various special interests within the profession. For example, the American Bar Association has committees with members in corporate law, environmental law, employ-

ment law, and so on. Since the committees are a manageable way to reach out to the members, the Director of Government Relations works closely with these groups, bringing the issues of most importance to the forefront. The committees work together to determine their public policy position on different laws—for or against—and they share it with the Director of Government Relations so he or she can bring their voice to the lawmakers.

Communication is a two-way street for Directors of Government Relations. On the one hand, they work with their members and committees, not only hearing their areas of concern, but also advising them on what issues they should be thinking about. Since they spend much of their time researching issues of importance, they hold meetings at which they educate their members about recent developments that affect the profession. They help to translate the legal jargon from the legislators into language members can understand, and so they help them to be clear on exactly how certain legislation will relate to them and their profession. It is their job to help members understand how different bills will impact them and what they can do about it.

On the other hand, Directors of Government Relations work with the politicians, whether in their state capitals or Washington, D.C. The better their lines of communication are with the legislators, the better position they are in to get the concerns of their association heard and addressed. They report about the position of the association and in this case, make sure to translate any industry jargon that would not be clear. When the legislature is in session, they spend much time on the phone, writing letters, and setting up face-to-face meetings. Initial meetings might involve a formal presentation with regard to the association's legislative position, but follow-up meetings are usually more informal.

Relationships are everything here, and a good Director of Government Relations is an effective networker who knows how to build ongoing alliances and make contacts. Politicians rely on professional associations to be credible sources of information on important issues. Whereas private lobbyists often have their own financial interests at heart, Directors of Government Relations see themselves as advocates rather than lobbyists, working to implement change for their associations without a personal financial benefit. As the voice for their members, they are passionate about their issues and use this passion and insider knowledge to influence government activities. They use grassroots advocacy with their members to organize rallies, coalitions, and campaigns to lobby the government.

It is essential for Directors of Government Relations to have a keen understanding of the issues that are important to the professional association they represent. They are aware of any news, trends, and recent developments through research and speaking to people. Also, they need to be government experts who understand the legislative process and how public policies are written and regulations are determined. They are constantly monitoring government activities so they can discover public policy issues that will affect their members.

Additional duties may include:

- Hiring and supervising staff
- Creating a budget
- Writing letters, presentations, and proposals
- Writing briefs and policy statements
- Meeting with politicians
- Speaking on the telephone with legislators and members
- Developing Web site content for their associations related to public policy and advocacy issues
- Performing outreach to members and committees to get them involved in issues
- Providing government relations and congressional updates to members
- Mobilizing members to vote or take political action
- Drafting public relations pieces

- Serving as a spokesperson for his or her association on legislative issues
- Handling union and labor issues

Directors of Government Relations often travel to Washington, D.C., or their state capitals in order to meet with legislators. Their hours will often encompass evenings so they can accommodate their members who work during traditional hours. A typical workweek is between 45 and 50 hours, but may vary as bills are up for consideration.

Furthermore, Directors of Government Relations are genuinely interested in people, getting to know them on an ongoing basis. Maintaining good government relations benefits the association greatly. By understanding who does what, as well as who supports what, in the government, they know exactly whom to call when important legislation is up for review. These friendships will make their job more efficient, effective, and enjoyable.

Salaries

Salaries vary depending on the education and experience held by the Director of Government Relations, as well as on the size, budget, and location of the association. According to the 2003 *ASAE Association Executive Compensation and Benefits Study,* which the American Society of Association Executives publishes every two years, the average total compensation for a Director of Government Relations is $98,377. Another survey, *Compensation in Nonprofit Organizations, 16th Edition,* a 2003 survey report of 131 benchmark jobs from Abbott, Langer & Associates, Inc., shows the average salary for a Director of Government Relations as $77,176.

Employment Prospects

Because public policy will always be important to professional associations, employment prospects are good. There will always be legislation affecting members, and a professional will be needed to serve as a liaison between the association and the government. The greatest opportunities will be found at large organizations with substantial member bases. These are often located in major cities or in Washington, D.C.

Advancement Prospects

Advancement prospects are also good. Directors of Government Relations hold relatively high positions within most associations, so they can use their experience to advance to the vice president level. They may also move from smaller organizations to larger ones, to positions of more leadership, responsibility, and visibility.

Education and Training

Directors of Government Relations need a minimum of a bachelor's degree, but to be an effective Director of Government Relations, one should have an advanced degree. Because of the legal understanding needed to interpret legislation, Directors of Government Relations often hold law degrees. While this is common, it is not the only credential accepted by the field. Master's degrees in public policy or political science are also helpful, as they, too, provide an understanding of the political and legal process.

Furthermore, Directors of Government Relations are often specialists within the specific industry they represent. For example, it would be likely that the Director of Government Relations for the National Association of Social Workers would have a master's degree in social work (MSW) in addition to any public policy or legal training. While this is not required, this inside experience within the profession is often helpful in connecting with issues and members.

Experience, Skills, and Personality Traits

In addition to a thorough understanding of law and public policy through education, work experience is very valuable. Directors of Government Relations may have three to 10 years of work experience before coming into this position, depending on the size of the association. Prior work experience with lobbying, grassroots organizing, and working on political campaigns is important.

Furthermore, Directors of Government Relations have superior writing and public speaking skills. They are articulate and confident, able to express themselves well in all the writing and presenting they must do. They have the ability to use language to persuade and collaborate, not alienate. Also, they should be committed, determined, and flexible.

Unions and Associations

Professional associations for Directors of Government Relations include the American Society of Association Executives, as well as specific groups by state.

Tips for Entry

1. Gain experience working on a political campaign to learn more about the political process. Pay attention to everyone's role from the volunteers stuffing envelopes right up to the candidate in order to gain insight into the whole picture.
2. Check out the Web site of a professional association that interests you. Look at the section for advocacy, public policy, or government relations to understand more about the issues affecting the profession and the work that went into creating this site. You can find lists of associations on sites such as http://www.ipl.org/div/aon/ and http://directory.google.com/Top/Society/Organizations/Professional.
3. Some states have associations that bring together a variety of government relations/public policy professionals. Take a look at the Government Affairs Council in Illinois: http://www.ilchamber.org/ga/gacouncill.asp.
4. Explore graduate programs in public policy and political science, in addition to law school programs.

DIRECTOR OF EDUCATION

CAREER PROFILE

Duties: Creates and implements educational programming and professional development opportunities for members of an organization

Alternate Title(s): Director of Continuing Education, Director of Member Programming, Director of Certification

Salary Range: $45,000 to $75,000 and up

Employment Prospects: Good

Advancement Prospects: Good

Best Geographical Location(s): Major cities; association headquarters

Prerequisites:

Education or Training—Bachelor's degree required; advanced degree preferred

Experience—Previous work experience related to field of association

Special Skills and Personality Traits—Creativity; strong writing and interpersonal ability; marketing and strategic thinking; meeting planning and organizational skills

CAREER LADDER

```
┌────────────────────────────────────┐
│   Vice President, Deputy Director    │
│ of Programming, or Executive Director│
└────────────────────────────────────┘

┌────────────────────────────────────┐
│        Director of Education         │
└────────────────────────────────────┘

┌────────────────────────────────────┐
│   Assistant Director of Education    │
└────────────────────────────────────┘
```

Position Description

Virtually all professions have at least one national professional association that sets standards, provides programming, and generally supports people in the field. Depending on the nature of the profession, the organization may offer licensure or certification, participate in lobbying and reform, and/or publish journals, job listings, and other career resources for members. Although the needs of the members of the American Medical Association differ from those of the American Marketing Association, they both need Directors of Education to serve their membership base and help achieve their goals. Directors of Education are responsible for professional development. They ensure retention and satisfaction through providing programs geared to meet the constantly changing needs of members in various professions today.

Directors of Education must keep their eyes on current trends and industry information. Often having a background in the profession of the association they represent, they understand their membership. They are avid readers, researchers, and planners who keep close to the pulse of their association and are aware of education and training needs within their industry. In order to offer quality educational programs that will keep members involved and interested, they must stay on the cutting edge of new developments themselves.

Professional associations provide various kinds of programming, but commonly, most run an annual conference, as well as smaller specialty events. The Director of Education is involved in all aspects of this convention from conceptualizing ideas and securing speakers to coordinating on-site logistics and collaborating with colleagues. In addition, they work with state and regional offices to plan local workshops. Overall, these events are geared at developing the professionals in the field and can include angles such as continuing education, skills training, e-learning, scholarly lectures, team-building exercises, and leadership seminars.

In some industries, certification or licensure is required, and this can be part of the responsibility of the Director of

Education. He or she must make certain that by attending specific programs, members are eligible for continuing education credits, or other requirements dictated by the profession. Also, some professional associations grant licensure and the Director of Education can be part of that process, including organization of state and national exams.

Since it is important for professional associations to be visible to their own members, as well as to other organizations, Directors of Education need to market their programs. In order to project an image of high standards and excellence in their field, they work closely with directors of marketing in order to put a positive spin on all ideas, both short- and long-term. They also need to find the best target markets to reach the maximum number of people. They want members to know about offerings so they can attend conferences, get involved in leadership, subscribe to publications, and last but not least, pay their dues.

Their duties may include:

- Writing proposals for new professional development programs
- Restructuring and expanding existing programs
- Grant writing
- Negotiating speakers' fees
- Selecting program locations and facilities
- Designing Web site content and distance learning seminars
- Promoting programs and other events
- Developing materials for members, prospective members, the general public, and the government
- Selecting topics for conferences and meetings
- Creating brochures and other educational materials
- Coordinating online and in-person educational programs
- Overseeing research studies
- Collaborating with other organizations
- Writing letters and reports
- Assisting chapters with educational needs
- Being aware and knowledgeable about government regulations affecting their industry

Some travel is required for Directors of Education as they attend conferences and other programs they have organized. These events are crucial to the functioning of all associations since they are a major part of fund-raising and revenue generating. The Director of Education plays a key role in these events as they are the idea people, as well as the logistics people, and need to be decisive, flexible, and detail-oriented.

Salaries

According to the 2003 *ASAE Association Executive Compensation and Benefits Study* from the American Society of Association Executives, the average total compensation for a Director of Education is $74,355. Keep in mind that this average is for executive-level Directors of Education at large membership associations, and Directors of Education at smaller organizations may make considerably less, ranging from $45,000 to $65,000 on average.

Employment Prospects

Since education is an important department of professional associations, employment prospects are good. Even in times of budget cutbacks, it will always be necessary to have someone handling certification issues in fields with such requirements. Opportunities are particularly strong for those with experience not only working for associations, but also with professional experience in the industry that the association represents.

Advancement Prospects

Advancement prospects are also good. Directors of Education may advance through moving from smaller organizations to larger ones, consulting on educational issues, or obtaining continuing education themselves that may make them eligible for higher salaries.

Education and Training

When working for a business, trade, or professional association, it is extremely important to have credibility with its members. In particular, Directors of Education who work for associations that represent highly trained and educated professionals often hold the same degree is its members in order to be seen as a peer. For example, at the American Bar Association, it is likely that the Director of Education would hold a law degree and has spent some time as a practicing attorney. By the same token, the Director of Education for the American Institute of Constructors should have experience in the construction industry in order to better understand his or her members' needs. Although this is not required, it can be quite helpful, depending on the association.

Directors of Education hold bachelor's degrees in a variety of fields, as well as a wide range of advanced degrees. Additional background in education, meeting planning, communications, writing, human resources, business, and public relations is a plus.

Experience, Skills, and Personality Traits

Directors of Education usually get into the field with formal education and training in their own industry, or through considerable work experience in associations or education, marketing, or public relations. To do their jobs well, they must be creative and innovative so they can plan new programs and stay fresh. They must also be successful at planning meetings and special events, logistics and organizing, and writing.

Also important are excellent communication skills. Directors of Education not only interact with members, but also association chapters, higher education institutions, governing boards, and others. Since e-learning is a growing part of the role of Directors of Education, good computer skills are also necessary.

Unions and Associations

Even those professionals working for associations have associations of their own. Directors of Education may belong to the American Society of Association Executives, among others.

Tips for Entry

1. Join a professional association, which will help give you an understanding of educational offerings.
2. Speak to members in various professions to find out about the associations to which they belong and the educational programs in which they participate.
3. Gain event planning experience by organizing a program on your campus.
4. Take an education course or work as a teaching assistant to learn about educational theory and curriculum development.

DIRECTOR OF COMPONENT RELATIONS

CAREER PROFILE

Duties: Providing support and leadership to the subgroups of an association, including chapters, councils, sections, special interest groups, and societies

Alternate Title(s): Director of Chapter Relations, Director of Constituent Relations, Chapter Relations Professional

Salary Range: $40,000 to $65,000 and up

Employment Prospects: Fair

Advancement Prospects: Good

Best Geographical Location(s): Major industrial centers, including Washington, D.C.; New York City; Chicago; and state capitals.

Prerequisites:

Education or Training—Bachelor's degree; some associations require graduate degrees

Experience—Prior association experience; five years or more for the director level

Special Skills and Personality Traits—Excellent verbal and written communication skills; ability to develop relationships; knowledge of some marketing and public relations practices; problem-solving and analytical skills

CAREER LADDER

```
┌─────────────────────────────────────┐
│  Director of Component Relations     │
│  (larger organization), Vice President, │
│  or Executive Director               │
└─────────────────────────────────────┘

┌─────────────────────────────────────┐
│  Director of Component Relations     │
└─────────────────────────────────────┘

┌─────────────────────────────────────┐
│  Component Relations Professional    │
│  such as Assistant, Associate,       │
│  or Manager                          │
└─────────────────────────────────────┘
```

Position Description

Business, professional, and trade associations are large entities that often serve a diverse group of members. In any one profession, there are people employed in different areas that have various issues, needs, and expectations. Subgroups may exist related to job description, work setting, or geographic location, among others.

For example, the National Education Association has members working in K–12 schools and colleges and universities. They range from anthropology professors on rural campuses to kindergarten teachers in inner cities. At an organization like the American Bar Association, there are members employed in both the public and private sectors. Although they are all attorneys, they face huge discrepancies in salary, work environment, and job descriptions. Furthermore, associations also have subgroups by state, region, and even country. Licensure requirements and employment outlook are just some of the issues that vary depending on location.

Because of the diversity of members within associations, a department is needed to manage these constituencies and make sure no one gets lost in the shuffle. The Director of Component Relations hears these different voices and addresses their individual concerns, as well as brings them together in collaboration for their profession as a whole.

As one association executive put it, Directors of Component Relations are like "mini-CEOs or management consultants." They need knowledge across all disciplines of association management, including marketing, finance, event planning, and volunteer management. Volunteer management is the closest link, since Directors of Component Relations actually spend much of their time as volunteer managers, assisting various chapter leaders who are most often volunteers, rather than paid staff. They must be able to look at the big picture to help each chapter build and grow.

Chapters and their leadership play a crucial role in associations. Directors of Component Relations cannot possibly know everything about each special interest group and committee of their association, particularly at large organizations with more than 100 subgroups. Therefore, they depend on the chapters for expert guidance. Each chapter is made up of people who are working in a particular sector of their profession and are uniquely qualified to understand current issues and concerns. It is the members who sustain each association, and their efforts enable their profession to grow.

At most associations, the chapters comprise volunteers who govern themselves. Directors of Component Relations consult with these chapters to provide management support. They advise chapter leaders on staffing, volunteers, finances, and other leadership issues. They help them to recruit and retain members as well as provide guidance on legalities. Also, they serve as liaisons between the various chapters, the association's national administration, and the board of directors. It is their job to ensure that each chapter's activities support the association's overall mission and goals.

Directors of Component Relations think about how the various constituents can work together to influence the future of their association. They collaborate on various policy concerns, lobbying the government on new legislation. Chapters often conduct grassroots efforts, getting local members mobilized and involved.

While the association is located at a national headquarters, the chapters are spread out throughout the country and sometimes even worldwide. Directors of Component Relations are able to bring their local efforts together to garner national attention.

According to the American Society of Association Executives, the duties for an advanced chapter relations professional may include:

- Developing and implementing an overall strategic plan for the local chapter activities in support of the association's goals and direction.
- Creating a communications plan linking the national organization with the local chapters/sections to create an awareness of the association's programs, products, and services.
- Developing new tools and services to support chapter/section operations.
- Supporting leadership activities for staff development of chapter officers.
- Taking responsibility for the oversight of chapter/section development, including creation of new chapters/sections, reorganization activities, and mergers and closures.
- Promoting programs for membership recruitment and retention at the chapter level.
- Managing dues-related activities.
- Acting as a liaison to several committees, councils, and/or task forces.
- Preparing an annual budget and periodic monitoring to ensure fiscal responsibility.

At the entry level, component relations professionals spend time learning the ropes. They are more involved with day-to-day chapter operations and reporting. Additionally, they often produce and provide materials for chapter support, such as manuals and guides, newsletters, and statistical reports. While Directors of Component Relations interact heavily with the board of directors, those new to the profession have minimal contact with them.

To be successful, Directors of Component Relations must know a little bit about a lot of things. Insiders say their job is constantly changing and requiring them to learn new skills. One day they may be helping a special interest group to create a marketing plan; the next day they might consult with a regional committee about a new member recruitment strategy. Directors of Component Relations are rarely bored and thrive on brainstorming, strategizing, and building relationships.

Salaries
Since Directors of Component Relations are usually found within larger associations only, their salaries reflect that distinction. Earnings are typically in the $40,000 to $65,000 range, with geography and size of the association playing a strong role. Experience is also a factor in determining salary.

Employment Prospects
Employment prospects for Directors of Component Relations are fair. While there are jobs to be found for those with association experience, only large associations with a number of chapters and special interest groups employ component relations professionals. Turnover for positions tend to be relatively low, with most current Directors of Component Relations reporting that they have been at their jobs five years or more. Starting out in other areas of association management such as volunteer management could be a good way to get into the field.

Advancement Prospects
Because Directors of Component Relations develop such a broad skill set from doing their jobs, their opportunities for advancement are good. As generalists, they can move into other areas of association management since they have had a hand in other roles. They can move to larger associations as Directors of Component Relations or as directors of volunteer management or directors of communications. Furthermore, they often look to become executive directors or independent consultants.

Education and Training
A bachelor's degree is expected for component relations professionals, and can only be supplemented by extensive

association experience. Directors of Component Relations have degrees in many subjects. A background in business or communications is especially helpful.

Furthermore, in some associations it is necessary (or preferred) for the Director of Component Relations to hold the degree and/or certification of the profession or trade of the association. For example, the Director of Component Relations for the American Nurses Association might be a registered nurse.

Experience, Skills, and Personality Traits

Component relations professionals must be excellent communicators, both verbally and in writing. Public speaking is a must, as is the desire to build and nurture relationships. They need to be extroverted, gregarious, and flexible as they are constantly meeting new people and adapting to new responsibilities.

Since chapters look to the Director of Component Relations for advice and support, he or she must have the confidence and expertise to guide them. Directors of Component Relations are skilled at program development, program planning, organizational management, and project management. They need to be strong leaders and managers who are results-oriented and able to multitask. Professionals who become Directors of Component Relations often have significant association experience ranging from five to 10 years.

Unions and Associations

The main association for Directors of Component Relations is the American Society of Association Executives. They might belong to additional organizations depending on the profession they represent, as well as other nonprofit professional groups such as the Society for Nonprofit Organizations and the Alliance for Nonprofit Management.

Tips for Entry

1. Learn more about careers in association management through the American Society of Association Executives (ASAE). Visit their Web site at http://www.asaenet.org and browse at their career headquarters.

2. Research the Certified Association Executive Program offered through ASAE at http://www.asaenet.org/asae/cda/index/1,1584,ETI1571_MEN3_NID3956,00.html. This program offers a voluntary credential that may be helpful for advancement.

3. Sharpen your presentation skills through courses on public speaking. In addition to academic classes, for more advanced training consider programs such as Toastmasters International at http://www.toastmasters.org/.

4. Intern at a professional association to explore different positions in association management.

5. Are you the member of a campus organization that has other chapters? If so, contact the national office to see how you can work on collaborative projects with other chapters.

LIBRARIAN

CAREER PROFILE

Duties: Provides research and reference assistance to members of a professional association; coordinates resource library

Alternate Title(s): Professional Resource Manager, Resource Center Director, Director of Resources, Information Professional

Salary Range: $35,000 to $65,000

Employment Prospects: Good

Advancement Prospects: Good

Best Geographical Location(s): Major cities

Prerequisites:

Education or Training—Bachelor's degree and master's degree in library science (MLS) required

Experience—Entry-level following graduate school; several years of experience helpful

Special Skills and Personality Traits—Excellent organization and research skills; patience; strong computer skills; good interpersonal relations; ability to read, write, and synthesize detailed information

Licensure/Certification—May require accreditation by the American Library Association

CAREER LADDER

```
┌─────────────────────────────────┐
│         Head Librarian          │
│   or Director of Library Services │
└─────────────────────────────────┘

┌─────────────────────────────────┐
│            Librarian            │
└─────────────────────────────────┘

┌─────────────────────────────────┐
│  Assistant Librarian or Library Intern │
└─────────────────────────────────┘
```

Position Description

Professional associations house a myriad of information that is useful to their members, as well as the general public. When a member of a profession needs to conduct research, he or she often turns to their association for access to archives that include journals in the field, research studies, and more.

Furthermore, when a writer is conducting research about a particular career field, he or she will turn to professional associations as the most credible source to find statistics, job descriptions, and accurate depictions of responsibilities. Librarians manage these resources for many associations in a role that is continuously changing and evolving.

While Librarians can work in many settings in the nonprofit sector, including traditional libraries, museums, hospitals, and foundations, those working for associations enjoy becoming experts about their particular field. They are knowledgeable about every resource related to the profession their organization represents, including books, magazines, newspapers, and Web sites. In addition to outside resources, they are the keepers of internal information. Professional associations may have publications such as journals, newsletters, and academic papers. Without Librarians, this material cannot be managed in a useful way. Librarians catalog and organize these publications, making the wealth of information they hold available to members in need.

At a professional association, membership is the key factor in survival and growth. The executive staff is constantly thinking of ways to promote member satisfaction and encourage new membership. One of the ways they achieve these goals is through programs that establish value to their members. Librarians play a critical role here because in many professions, research services are something that members need and want. Access to journals, articles, books,

Web sites, and archives is the first piece of it; a professional dedicated to helping them find what they seek makes the service, and thus, the association, even more valuable.

The role of Librarians is changing as organizations move into the technological age. Librarians today need to be extremely computer savvy, learning complex databases and Internet searches during their professional schooling. The days of microfiche and paper storage are giving way to CD-ROMs and databases. They are often called upon to computerize archives, organizing material for their associations.

While cataloging was the way of the past, Librarians now form taxonomies, classifying and organizing material into related groups or categories. In this way, they help the association increase revenue since once these publications are organized they can be sold externally and promoted internally.

Their duties may include:

- Maintaining a database of internal publications
- Communicating with members through phone and e-mail
- Preparing indexes of current periodicals
- Organizing bibliographies
- Compiling reports on areas of interest to members
- Training users to develop database-searching skills
- Making presentations to members or the public
- Acquiring new resources
- Writing grants for new programs
- Answering questions and recommending resources to members and staff

Librarians at professional organizations have responsibilities that combine user services, technical services, and administrative services. The members are the users, and first and foremost, Librarians provide a service to them, making sure they are finding the information they need. Furthermore, the technical services, such as providing remote access to databases and all other technology-based projects, are a big part of their jobs. Finally, Librarians spend some time handling administrative tasks and may supervise staff members, manage resource budgets, and even take on some fund-raising or public relations duties.

While public Librarians often must work weekends and evenings, Librarians at professional associations enjoy 40- to 50-hour weeks, mainly during typical business hours. Insiders say that although the salaries are better in the corporate sector, Librarians at associations enjoy less stress and more autonomy. They add a professional component to their organizations, and since the work they do is not done by any other department, they make themselves indispensable.

Salaries

According to the Bureau of Labor Statistics (BLS), median annual earnings of Librarians in 2002 were $43,090. Librarians working for other information services, which include nonprofit organizations and professional associations, have a slightly lower median at $37,770. Experience and education also play a role in salary figures.

A survey of Librarians working at nonprofits in the Washington, D.C., Metro area, shows a median annual salary for Librarians at $58,329, with staff librarians earning $50,598 and information specialists at $40,850.

Source: "2003 Salary Survey of Nonprofit Organizations," Cordom Associates, Washington, D.C., (202) 296–3337. (Careerjournal.com)

Employment Prospects

According to the BLS, jobs for Librarians outside traditional settings, including nonprofit organizations, will grow the fastest among Librarian jobs over the decade. As many traditional Librarians retire, the need will arise for professionals who represent the future with new skills and training.

As associations look to move forward and update their paper resources, more jobs will open up for Librarians. They will be valued because of their research and computer skills, and associations will seek them out to manage information and meet their members' needs.

Advancement Prospects

Librarians at professional associations can advance by moving from smaller associations to larger ones. They may also choose to manage departments and research services for associations. Additionally, Librarians can advance by moving to other areas of the nonprofit sector such as museums or hospitals, public libraries, or colleges and universities. This transition is especially easy if it relates to the industry of the professional association. For example, a Librarian for the American Medical Association may go on to work at a hospital. Librarians also may choose to enter the corporate sector or government system.

Education and Training

In addition to a bachelor's degree, a master's degree in library science (MLS) is required for one to be considered a professional Librarian. Some resource managers at professional associations might not have this credential, but they will not be able to advance or likely find employment elsewhere, as the credential is becoming even more valuable.

Course work in an MLS program usually takes between one to two years and is typically 36 credits. Undergraduate background can be in any field, but usually includes liberal arts, research, and writing. Also, some Librarians at professional associations have training in the field of the association in addition to their MLS degree. For instance, a Librarian at the Public Relations Society of America may have prior public relations experience before completing his or her library degree.

Some MLS programs train Librarians to work is specific settings such as museums, public or academic libraries, or law firms. Other specializations may be available such as music, information technology, reference, or school media specialization.

Special Requirements

Employers may require Librarians to have completed an MLS program accredited by the American Library Association (ALA). There are approximately 56 accredited schools. See the ALA's Web site for more information at http://www.ala.org.

Experience, Skills, and Personality Traits

Librarians should be well read and well organized. They need excellent research skills and the ability to arrange and compile information in a clear manner. Furthermore, they should be good at analyzing information and knowledgeable about publishing trends and recent events within the field of their association. Also, good communication skills are valuable for the customer-service component of their jobs.

Additionally, Librarians must have superb computer skills. They should be familiar with LexisNexis and other databases, as well as skilled at Internet searches.

Unions and Associations

Librarians may belong to the American Library Association, the Special Libraries Association (specific to professionals in nontraditional settings such as nonprofit organizations), and also may gain information from the Association for Library and Information Science Education.

Tips for Entry

1. Spend time speaking with the Librarian at your local public library. Ask him or her about graduate training and possible employment settings.
2. Visit the Web site of a professional association that interests you. See if you can discover any links for resources. Many of the services are for members only, so speak to people you know who belong to various associations. Find out what kinds of information services are available to them.
3. Learn how to use databases such as LexisNexis. They can be found in most college and university libraries.
4. Research graduate programs in library science by visiting the Association for Library and Information Science Education's Web site at http://www.alise.org.

JOURNAL EDITOR

CAREER PROFILE

Duties: Reviews and edits submissions to a professional journal for a professional association

Alternate Title(s): Editor, Associate Editor

Salary Range: $25,000 to $50,000 and up

Employment Prospects: Fair

Advancement Prospects: Fair

Best Geographical Location(s): New York City, Washington, D.C., and other major cities

Prerequisites:

Education or Training—Bachelor's degree in English, communications, or journalism

Experience—Several years of publishing and editorial experience

Special Skills and Personality Traits—Excellent writing and editing skills; careful attention to detail; strong grammatical skills and grasp of the English language; technical knowledge based on field of association

CAREER LADDER

```
┌─────────────────────────────┐
│   Senior Journal Editor      │
│   or Editor in Chief         │
└─────────────────────────────┘

┌─────────────────────────────┐
│   Journal Editor             │
└─────────────────────────────┘

┌─────────────────────────────┐
│   Editorial Assistant        │
│   or Assistant Journal Editor│
└─────────────────────────────┘
```

Position Description

Professional journals are the academic cornerstone of many professional associations. Here, issues are examined, positions debated, and new discoveries are unveiled to the community. Some associations have one journal, while others have many to reflect all the specialties within their field. In order for each journal to provide the wealth of information that it does, a Journal Editor is at the helm of the process.

Journal Editors oversee the content of each publication for which they are responsible. They plan each issue with regard to submissions, schedules, and deadlines. Their goal is to produce the highest quality published journal they can by ensuring that the submissions are of the best caliber. At most journals, Journal Editors work together with an editorial board comprising professionals in the journal's field in order to review submissions. The review process can be extremely time-consuming as some journals get thousands of unsolicited manuscripts each month. Reviewers and the Journal Editors examine the contents and writing style of each article, as well as the credentials of the writers. Furthermore, they assess the topics of the upcoming issues and

determine which articles fit best with the needs of their members.

Once articles have been selected for publication, Journal Editors make sure that each piece and every issue is consistent with the journal's mission and voice. They pay attention to the presentation and make sure that the journal will be aesthetically pleasing to readers. Furthermore, they coordinate the publication process with other staff members responsible for production, advertising, and marketing to make certain each issue goes to the printer on time. The size of the journal staff determines how much time the Journal Editor spends working on other aspects of the publication process. At smaller journals, it is typical for each staff member to play a larger role in overall administration. Larger associations tend to have more staff members who can be more specialized in their tasks.

The editorial process requires excellent grammatical skills and sharp command of the English language. Many Journal Editors are responsible for line editing, which involves checking every line in each piece. Every word in each article is scanned carefully and read over several times to catch errors of spelling, syntax, grammar, or usage. While some may think this sounds tedious, Journal Editors thrive on sculpting articles until they shine. They are skilled at reworking sentences to read better and more clearly. With a tangible end result that will be read by thousands, Journal Editors find the process satisfying and worthwhile.

In addition to their editorial skills, Journal Editors also must have knowledge of the field their association represents. Other editors in the nonprofit sector often have a wide breadth of knowledge and training in English or journalism only. However, because professional journals are so specific, Journal Editors are usually experienced members of their professional or academic community. This background is essential to effectively assess and review the content of the publication for accuracy and understanding.

Additional duties may include:

- Supervising editorial assistants and other administrative workers
- Consulting with internal staff members in marketing, circulation, design, and so on
- Communicating with authors
- Establishing editorial policy
- Determining themes for issues
- Reviewing final proofs
- Verifying facts and clarifying information
- Writing editorial content
- Assigning pieces to freelance writers
- Organizing material and planning page layout
- Conducting research

Journal Editors need to have excellent verbal communication skills in addition to their written talents. In their work with authors, they must be tactful but authoritative in terms of explaining any changes they must make in their writing. They must be persuasive in their opinions to make authors, as well as other staff members within their association, understand their choices and why they make sense.

Insiders say they enjoy the nonprofit publishing world as opposed to the commercial one. Commercial publishing has a reputation for being highly competitive and cutthroat, with many years of paying dues doing grunt work for little pay. Nonprofit organizations generally offer a more cooperative workplace, with everyone committed to the mission of the association. Teamwork is prevalent, as is the opportunity to take on more responsibility at a quicker pace.

Salaries

According to the Bureau of Labor Statistics, median annual earnings for salaried editors, including Journal Editors, were $41,170 in 2002. Another survey, *Compensation in Nonprofit Organizations, 16th Edition,* a 2003 survey report of 131 benchmark jobs from Abbott, Langer & Associates, Inc., lists median incomes of editors (books and periodicals) as $50,000. Additional information comes from a summary at

http://www.workforce.com citing a 2003 study about pay in the not-for-profit sector. According to this study, the median cash compensation for a nonprofit editor was $44,200 and a managing editor (journals and books) was $67,000.

Insiders in the field say that entry-level salaries are typically in the $25,000 to $30,000 range, and move up to $45,000 to $50,000 with three to five years of experience.

Employment Prospects

Jobs for Journal Editors tend to be easier to obtain than editorial jobs for commercial publishers or magazines. Although their reputation is not as glamorous, it is an excellent way for a recent graduate to get experience in the field and take on much responsibility early on, since associations have smaller staffs.

Also, the commercial publishing industry is centered in several cities, primarily New York, Boston, and San Francisco. Since professional associations are found in a variety of regions of the United States, Journal Editors have more geographic flexibility and locations for employment.

Growth is expected to occur particularly in new or growing occupations that are forming and expanding professional associations. Professions that are trying to standardize and become more academic may add or expand journals that will need Journal Editors.

Advancement Prospects

At the entry level, Journal Editors can start out as editorial assistants, where they learn the ropes by working for specific editors. These positions are excellent opportunities to build skills and make valuable contacts with editors and writers. After several years with good performance evaluations, they often can move up to a full editorial role.

For advancement at a professional journal, Journal Editors must have not only editorial experience, but also some professional training in the field their association represents. For example, the editor in chief of the American Accounting Association is a certified public accountant in addition to an editor. Furthermore, for journals that are especially academic, a doctorate may be required. Journal Editors can also move up by going from small associations to larger ones or by leaving associations to work for other publications in the nonprofit sector, such as university presses and internal newsletters.

Education and Training

Many Journal Editors have undergraduate degrees in English, communications, or journalism. This background in reading, research, and editing their own writing, as well as the writing of their peers, is excellent preparation for an editorial career. Many also have experience working on campus newspapers, magazines, or literary journals while in school.

Most successful Journal Editors at large associations have additional academic training. Associations with scholarly journals often require the Journal Editors to have doctoral degrees, or at minimum, the professional degree of the association.

Experience, Skills, and Personality Traits

Journal Editors should be well read and knowledgeable about their field. A keen sense of what is interesting and engaging to readers helps their publications to be successful and well respected. For line editing, they need to pay close attention to detail and have the patience to read over material numerous times until they get it right.

As the publishing industry grows and changes with technology, Journal Editors should be extremely computer literate. They may have responsibility for writing and editing Web site content, and some Web publishing experience is valuable.

Unions and Associations

Journal Editors often belong to the professional and/or academic associations popular in their field. In addition, they may belong to organizations specifically for editors, including the American Society of Magazine Editors, the Society of Professional Journalists, the Society of American Business Editors and Writers, the Society for Technical Communication, the Council of Science Editors, and the Council of Editors of Learned Journals.

Tips for Entry

1. Take courses in English, writing, or journalism in which you can read and edit the writing of your peers. This will help you to not only improve your writing skills, but also to recognize the writing strengths of others.
2. Editors commonly use specific proofreading marks as they review writing. These marks are symbols and shorthand for the corrections that need to be made. Learn about these marks by checking out the list at http://www.m-w.com/mw/table/proofrea.htm.
3. Consider a publishing course as a way to get a foot in the door to the editorial field. Although these courses might be more geared toward commercial book and magazine publishers, they may prove to be a good investment if you do not have any experience with writing and editing. Several schools offer these courses, including Columbia University in New York City (http://www.jrn.columbia.edu/admissions/programs/publishing/); Stanford University in Palo Alto, Calif. (http://publishingcourses.stanford.edu/); and the University of Denver, in Denver, Colo. (http://www.du.edu/pi/).
4. Work as a Journal Editor is also a good career transition for a professional who is a member of an association and wants to get more involved with editing journals. If you already hold the credentials for a particular field, this is an important first step. You can use this experience and your personal familiarity with the journals to investigate full-time opportunities.

FOUNDATIONS, GRANT-MAKING ORGANIZATIONS, AND PHILANTHROPY

PROGRAM OFFICER

CAREER PROFILE

Duties: Reviewing and recommending grant proposals for funding by their foundation; carrying out additional programming responsibilities such as research, program development, and evaluation

Alternate Title(s): Program Associate

Salary Range: $45,000 to $120,000 and up

Employment Prospects: Fair

Advancement Prospects: Fair

Best Geographical Location(s): Foundation cluster regions such as New York metropolitan area, Washington, D.C., San Francisco Bay Area, Los Angeles area

Prerequisites:
Education or Training—Bachelor's degree required; many foundations strongly prefer master's or doctoral degrees
Experience—Varies from three to 10 years
Special Skills and Personality Traits—Creativity; analytical thinking and intellectual curiosity; knowledge of specific subject area; good judgment and communication skills

CAREER LADDER

```
┌─────────────────────────────────────┐
│  Senior Program Officer, Program     │
│  Director, or Vice President         │
│  for Programs                        │
└─────────────────────────────────────┘

┌─────────────────────────────────────┐
│  Program Officer                     │
└─────────────────────────────────────┘

┌─────────────────────────────────────┐
│  Program Assistant                   │
└─────────────────────────────────────┘
```

Position Description

To understand the job of a Program Officer, it is important first to understand more about foundations—what they are and how they are categorized. The Web site of the Minnesota Council on Foundations (http://www.mcf.org) offers this definition of foundations: "A foundation is a nonprofit organization that supports charitable activities in order to serve the common good. Foundations are often created with endowments—money given by individuals, families or corporations. They generally make grants or operate programs with the income earned from investing the endowments." They also clarify the difference between types of foundations. According to their site, there are three basic types of grant-making foundations, with a fourth type that runs programs but does not make grants:

• **Independent Foundations (also known as Family Foundations)** Independent foundations are the most common type of private foundation. They are generally

founded by an individual, a family or a group of individuals. They may be operated by the donor or members of the donor's family—a type often referred to as a family foundation—or by an independent board.

• **Corporate Foundations** Corporate foundations are created and funded by companies as separate legal entities, operated by a board of directors that is usually made up of company officials. Corporations may establish private foundations with endowments, make periodic contributions from profits, or combine both methods to provide a foundation's resources. Some companies operate in-house corporate giving programs, which unlike corporate foundations are under the full control of the company and are not required by law to follow the same IRS regulations. Many corporations maintain both a foundation and a corporate giving program.

• **Community/Public Foundations** Community and other public foundations are publicly supported foundations operated by, and for the benefit of, a specific community or geographic region. They receive their funds from a variety of individual donors, and provide a vehicle for donors to establish endowed funds without incurring the costs of starting a foundation. Community/public foundations are administered by a governing body or distribution committee representative of community interests.

- **Operating Foundation** There is also a type of foundation that does not generally make grants, called an operating foundation. The majority of an operating foundation's funds are expended to operate its own charitable programs.

Source: Minnesota Council on Foundations
http://www.mcf.org/mcf/whatis/founda.htm

Within foundations in general, there is a wide variation in terms of their issue area, programs, missions, and goals. Each of them was started for reasons such as to help increase awareness of a specific health, economic, or social problem; fund research to eradicate disease; promote education or the environment; and so on. Nonprofit organizations of all sizes seek out foundations to fund specific programs and offer general support. On the flip side, foundations accept grant proposals from organizations whose funding needs match their funding interests. The job of a Program Officer involves reviewing these proposals to find the best fit for his or her foundation. He or she writes reports and provides recommendations to senior staff as to which organizations and individuals should receive grants.

Reviewing grant proposals is an enormous task. First, Program Officers may be involved in the process of soliciting proposals or determining proposal criteria such as time lines or Web site content that advises grantees about the process. Then, once the proposals are submitted, Program Officers must evaluate them on several points. They look to ensure that the proposal fits the scope of their foundation, consider who will benefit from the proposed program, and evaluate costs.

Program Officers need to understand the overall feasibility of each of the proposals and may gain this knowledge base through research, site visits, questioning, and analysis. Site visits to the grantee organizations can be very informative and a good way to get to know the organization better to determine their goals. Once they have studied the proposals, they make recommendations and rank them in terms of their funding priority. They often write summaries and present their findings to a grants committee that may include members of the board of directors, the executive director, and other senior staff members. Their analysis is one of the primary methods used to make funding decisions.

Program Officers also handle administrative functions, and attention to detail is crucial. They often inform organizations as to whether their grant request has been approved or denied—imagine the chaos that would ensue if they sent an incorrect letter. They advise grantees with regard to poli-cies and procedures, and help them to evaluate their own program success.

Their duties may include:

- Analyzing and understanding public policy
- Motivating peers in shared program efforts
- Researching, designing, and implementing new grant-making programs
- Conducting educational presentations
- Maintaining a monitoring and tracking database
- Managing specific groups of grants
- Monitoring annual reports from grantees
- Evaluating programs for effectiveness
- Soliciting professionals and volunteers to be part of grant-making process
- Processing grant requests
- Sending out checks

In large foundations with several interest areas, Program Officers may specialize in specific areas. For example, within the same foundation, there may be a Program Officer who works on arts programs, and another who works on community development. These Program Officers are experts in their area, usually having functional work experience in that field. These foundations may have 20 Program Officers or more, while others have one or two. In many foundations, Program Officers report directly to a program director, but others may not have program directors in their hierarchy. Program Officers may report to senior program officers, vice presidents for programs, or even the executive director in a very small foundation.

Salaries

Because foundations vary in size, scope, and structure, so do the salaries of Program Officers. A 2003 Compensation Summary for New Health Foundations as part of a joint survey of the Council on Foundations, along with Grantmakers in Health, showed different median salaries for Program Officers based on the foundation's budget. At foundations with assets between $5 million and $99.9 million, Program Officers earned a median salary of $51,000; with assets between $100 million and $249.9 million, $57,995; and with assets greater than $250 million, $86,000.

Employment Prospects

Positions as a Program Officer are very competitive, and they tend to be few and far between. Also, turnover is relatively low, and people stay in their positions for a while. The best opportunities are for those who have functional work experience and/or specific educational training in the interest area of the foundation. Positions become known through word of mouth, so networking is important. Some Program Officers begin through internships at foundations, administrative assistant or temporary positions, or program assistant positions.

Advancement Prospects

Advancement prospects are also fair because many Program Officers stay in their positions over time if they are satisfied with their work. Also, while many foundations have several Program Officers, they will have fewer senior-level positions. Some may advance to become senior program officers, program directors, vice presidents for programs, or executive directors. Others may find a niche as consultants, advising organizations on writing successful grant proposals.

Education and Training

Education and training requirements vary according to the foundation. Small foundations may hire Program Officers with bachelor's degrees, but at larger foundations in bigger cities, many Program Officers have master's and doctoral degrees. For example, at a foundation that provides grant money for scientific research, it is common for most of the Program Officers to have Ph.D.'s in the sciences. In fact, foundation work has become a popular alternative for Ph.D.'s who choose not to enter the academic job market. Program Officers may also have master's degrees in a wide variety of fields, including public policy and international affairs, depending upon their focus.

In terms of training, most of it comes on the job. Familiarity with grants and grant making is useful.

Experience, Skills, and Personality Traits

In addition to education, several years of experience in the nonprofit sector may be very helpful as well, particularly in the interest area of the foundation. If one is interested in grant making to help the homeless, having worked directly with that population is a big asset and helps with program evaluation and grant assessment.

Additionally, Program Officers should be passionate and informed about the issues of their foundation in order to be successful. They should be meticulous and well organized, paying careful attention to detail. They need good judgment and analytical ability to evaluate proposals and strong communication skills to work with grantees, as well as to relay their opinions internally.

Since monitoring, tracking, and processing grants are done via computer, good computer skills are crucial. Knowledge of Microsoft Office, such as Word, Excel, and PowerPoint is a good base to learn the customized spreadsheet and Internet-based software that is often designed specifically for each foundation to meet their needs.

Unions and Associations

Program Officers may belong to professional associations including the Grant Managers Network, the Council on Foundations, Grantmakers for Effective Organizations, and Grantmakers for Education.

Tips for Entry

1. Gain foundation experience through internships or temporary work.
2. Get involved in professional associations to learn more about the field. Take a look at the Web site of the Grant Managers Network at http://www.gmnetwork.org.
3. Learn more about grant making through courses and certificate programs. Take a look at the Certificate in Grantmaking and Foundations offered by New York University at http://www.scps.nyu.edu/departments/certificate.jsp?certId=101.
4. Hone your writing and communication skills by preparing a cover letter for an internship with a foundation. Highlight related coursework, volunteer experience, and other important skills.

PROGRAM DIRECTOR

CAREER PROFILE

Duties: Oversees grant-making work for a foundation; manages staff; makes decisions regarding grant proposals and programming; initiates new programming

Alternate Title(s): None

Salary Range: $50,000 to $120,000 and up

Employment Prospects: Fair

Advancement Prospects: Fair

Best Geographical Location(s): Foundation cluster regions such as New York metropolitan area, Washington, D.C., San Francisco Bay Area, Los Angeles area

Prerequisites:

Education or Training—Bachelor's degree required; graduate degree preferred or required for many positions

Experience—Three to 10 years, depending on the organization

Special Skills and Personality Traits—Excellent writing, research, and communication skills; intellectual curiosity; understanding of the nonprofit sector and grantmaking process

CAREER LADDER

```
┌─────────────────────────────────┐
│   Vice President of Programs     │
└─────────────────────────────────┘

┌─────────────────────────────────┐
│        Program Director          │
└─────────────────────────────────┘

┌─────────────────────────────────┐
│ Program Assistant or Program Officer │
└─────────────────────────────────┘
```

Position Description

Some foundations receive hundreds of grant proposals every year from a variety of nonprofit organizations seeking funding for projects, programs, and general support. Proposals must be analyzed and decisions must be made about who will receive funding and why. The Program Director of a foundation ensures that the grant-making process is carried out. He or she supervises program officers, assistants, and other program staff; initiates and develops new programming; and works on long-range strategic planning with senior staff.

Because foundations vary so greatly, they have different criteria for the proposals they will consider and the projects they seek to fund. Grants may be awarded for general operating support, for specific projects or programs, to fund new ventures and start-ups, to provide technical assistance, to add to endowments, and for facilities and equipment. Not only are there several types of foundations such as family, community, international, and corporate foundations, but

they also have very different goals and agendas based on their issues. For example, a community-based women's foundation may look to finance programs that support female victims of domestic violence, and a cancer prevention and research foundation may offer funding for educational programming designed to promote healthy behaviors and eliminate risk factors such as smoking. Most foundations include detailed descriptions of their funding criteria on their Web sites, as well as downloadable grant applications. Often, they separate their grant criteria into several categories that may include grants for education, research, travel, domestic and international programming, and economic development. They also describe in detail their time line for the grant application process.

Along with the program officers they supervise, Program Directors sift through these proposals to see which ones most closely meet their criteria for funding. They oversee research and further investigation of the proposals as well as site visits to potential grantees. In addition, some foundations also work with volunteer teams that participate in the review process. The Program Directors train these volunteers to go out into the field and visit the prospective organization, teaching them how to evaluate their proposals and report back on their findings. After the grants are reviewed, a funding summary is submitted that goes to a grants or review committee, usually made up of board members and senior staff, but sometimes will include Program Directors as well. The board has final say, and their approval is needed to move forward. Program Directors use their persuasive skills to encourage funding for the programs they support. While the programming staff shares in this responsibility, it is the Program Director who is ultimately responsible and constantly must make sure all is running smoothly.

Program Directors also offer ongoing and technical support to the grantee organizations. After the programs have been funded, they evaluate progress and check up on how the organization is managing as well as how their money has been put to use. They receive regular quantitative and qualitative reports from the grantee organization to determine effectiveness. Program Directors maintain productive relationships with the grantees, often helping them to develop and grow. They serve as a resource, providing one-on-one support through personal meetings and phone calls to offer advice and insight about their programs. Furthermore, they might conduct surveys assessing grantee needs and providing optional training or consultants if necessary as an opportunity for professional development. Sharing information and assistance with nonfinancial resources, they keep the lines of communication open and encourage feedback for more successful programming overall.

In addition to grant-making responsibilities and technical support, many foundations run their own programming as well, such as educational or leadership development programs. They use programming to carry out their missions and goals. The Program Director develops, initiates, and designs this programming, determining areas of need and collaborating with their team for implementation and staffing.

Additional duties may include:

- Presenting to board members on foundation initiatives and grant recommendations
- Writing Web site content and other literature related to grant making requirements and time lines
- Staying informed about the issues relevant to their foundation
- Preparing reports
- Conducting program evaluation
- Sharing information with policy makers, professionals, and community members
- Pursuing opportunities to further their foundation's agenda and goals
- Hiring consultants and program staff

- Working closely with the vice president of programs, executive director, and board members
- Soliciting grant requests from specific organizations

The responsibilities of a Program Director will vary depending upon the size of the foundation. The largest foundations may have more than 20 Program Directors, not to mention program officers and assistants, while small foundations may have only one working alone. This affects whether the Program Director will be expected to wear many hats and take on a variety of tasks, or will specialize in targeted areas.

Salaries

Salaries for Program Directors vary not only by size and location of the foundation, but also by their years of education and experience. Since the field draws in people with diverse backgrounds, the salary for a professional with a bachelor's degree and three years of experience versus a Ph.D. with 10 years of work will not be the same. A general range can be anywhere from $50,000 to $100,000 and up. Foundations also may be willing to pay specific individuals more based on their salary history and expectations, as well as the experience they bring along.

A 2003 Compensation Summary for New Health Foundations as part of a joint survey of the Council on Foundations, along with Grantmakers in Health, showed different median salaries for Program Directors based on the foundation's budget. At foundations with assets between $5 million and $99.9 million, Program Directors earned a median salary of $75,037; with assets between $100 million and $249.9 million, $79,330; and with assets greater than $250 million, $97,169.

Employment Prospects

Program Director jobs are quite competitive, with many more interested candidates than available positions. Prior nonprofit experience is often essential, as is networking within the field. Many foundations do not post their available positions on the Web, as they do not want to be inundated with thousands of résumés. Instead, people often find out about positions through word of mouth. It is not uncommon for specific professionals to be recruited from one foundation to another.

Advancement Prospects

Advancement prospects are also fair, due to the competitiveness and small number of positions. Program Directors may move from a smaller organization to a larger one, or advance to a vice president of programs role.

Education and Training

Program Directors often hold not only bachelor's degrees, but advanced degrees as well. The majority of Program

Directors at large foundations hold a master's degree or Ph.D. Depending upon the focus of the foundation, it may look to hire people with a master's degree or a doctorate in the arts, humanities, sciences, public affairs, public policy, international affairs, human services, or public health.

Most of the training for foundation work comes on the job. It may be difficult to understand exactly what is required until one does the job oneself. This is why it is extremely helpful for Program Directors to have prior work experience in the nonprofit sector.

Experience, Skills, and Personality Traits

Before getting into foundation work, insiders say it is beneficial to have actual field experience within the nonprofit sector first. For example, people who are interested in working for a foundation that supports literacy programs will be more effective if they have spent several years working on the ground level at a literacy program. This provides a more thorough, personal understanding of the issues the foundation is funding, and an invaluable expertise that cannot be taught. Anywhere from three to 10 years of experience may be required, depending on the foundation.

Because of the level of a Program Director and supervisory responsibilities, leadership and management skills are essential. Intellectual curiosity and the desire to gain, organize, and analyze information is key. Since organizations depend on foundations for funding, Program Directors should be articulate in describing their requirements to grantees. They should be clear communicators, but also diplomatic and take care not to raise grantees expectations.

In addition, Program Directors have the opportunity to be creative, designing programs that reach new heights and take a different approach.

Unions and Associations

Program Directors may belong to a variety of organizations. There are many different grant-making organizations by subject area as well as organizations that support foundations. These include Grantmakers in Health, the Regional Association of Grantmakers, the Council on Foundations, the Foundation Center, the Women's Funding Network, the National Center for Family Philanthropy, the Association of Small Foundations, and Emerging Practitioners in Philanthropy.

Tips for Entry

1. Take a look at these grant-making resources provided by the Kellogg Foundation, one of the nation's largest family foundations: http://www.wkkf.org/Grants/Grantseeking_Resources.aspx

2. Conduct informational interviews with Program Directors at foundations. Find out what their jobs are like on a daily basis and how you can gain experience.

3. Decide which area of the nonprofit sector appeals to you and gain field experience. Research which foundations fund these types of programs as a next step for future employment.

4. Consider a position as a program assistant or administrative assistant to learn more about working at a foundation.

INVESTMENT PROFESSIONAL

CAREER PROFILE

Duties: Manages the financial resources and endowment for private foundations; makes investment decisions; may manage several specific sources of money for a foundation, including active, semiactive, and inactive funds

Alternate Title(s): Chief Investment Officer, Director of Finance and Administration, Director of Investments, Director of Finance, Fund Manager, Financial Analyst, Vice President for Finance and Administration

Salary Range: $40,000 to $150,000 and up, depending upon the position and level

Employment Prospects: Fair

Advancement Prospects: Fair

Best Geographical Location(s): Foundation cluster regions such as the New York metropolitan area, Washington, D.C., San Francisco Bay Area, Los Angeles area

Prerequisites:

Education or Training—Bachelor's degree required; graduate degree often preferred; background in basic accounting or finance

Experience—Entry-level to 15+ years of experience, depending on the position

Special Skills and Personality Traits—Knowledge of finance and nonprofits; diplomacy and tact; attention to detail; leadership and management skills; excellent organizational skills

CAREER LADDER

```
┌─────────────────────────────────┐
│  Vice President for Finance and  │
│    Administration or Chief       │
│      Investment Officer          │
└─────────────────────────────────┘

┌─────────────────────────────────┐
│ Investment Professional (including│
│  titles such as Director of Finance,│
│     Endowment Management          │
│        or Investments)            │
└─────────────────────────────────┘

┌─────────────────────────────────┐
│ Funds Manager or Financial Analyst│
└─────────────────────────────────┘
```

Position Description

For better or worse, money drives everything else in foundation work. Most private foundations have a permanent endowment, meaning that the foundation was started with an initial sum of money and the founder's goal is for that money to essentially last forever, replenishing itself through prudent investments. If the endowment on which the foundation is built is not well managed, then there will be fewer grants to make. Eventually, the money will run out over time and the foundation will have to close down. On the other hand, however, if the money is well cared for, this assures the foundation of longevity and more grant making in the long run. It is up to the various Investment Professionals within a foundation to protect this money, strategizing on investments that will enable the foundation to carry out its charitable purpose for years to come. Investment Professionals include vice presidents of finance and administration, chief investment officers, directors of investments, and fund managers.

Vice presidents of finance and administration or chief investment officers are the primary relationship-holders with the financial managers hired by their foundation. The vice president of finance and administration must understand investment strategy, make recommendations, and carry out decisions made by the board about their investing goals. They look at factors such as asset allocation, growth, value, index, risk tolerance, and determine what the foundation needs to accomplish with this money. Also, they monitor and watch these investments, constantly thinking and learning about current investments and new possibilities.

Furthermore, vice presidents of finance and administration manage the cash flow after grants have been awarded. They monitor the active portfolio for the grants, as well as develop and operate overall budgets. They work as liaisons to the investment committee to implement decisions and bring the necessary information to the board to help facilitate decision making. While chief investment officers may handle only financial responsibilities, vice presidents of finance and administration might also spend approximately half their time managing general office operations; human resources functions such as hiring, discipline, compensation issues, and benefits; and technology planning.

Foundations are in a unique position among nonprofits because instead of needing to raise money, they need to give money away. They have several sources of money that need to be monitored. The funds manager is responsible for overseeing various funds and sharing information about their status with board members, foundation executives, and any other shareholders. Funds managers are financial whizzes who try to ensure that the assets of a foundation are earning as much as they can. They analyze risk and offer recommendations to board members and executive staff as to how to best manage the funds of the foundation.

Inactive funds are those that have ceased operations. While funds managers do not have much day-to-day involvement with these funds, they do need to keep track of them. They post monthly interest statements, quarterly reports to board of trustees and shareholders, and conduct annual wrap-ups with auditors. With semiactive funds, there is more frequent reporting on activity, and they supervise the paying out of loans and grants. In addition to quarterly reports, they follow up and make sure all involved parties are aware of how much the fund is earning, as well as where earnings may be used.

Active funds take up most of the time of funds managers. Active funds are those that currently have shareholders and are being purchased and sold. The board of trustees is watching these funds, so funds managers are careful with reporting detail. They post interest, send out quarterly reports, and ensure that they get payment when it is due. Since some foundations provide funding that supports an entire nonprofit organization, funds managers are particularly diligent about getting those reports done and working with the executive director to ensure necessary transactions.

The responsibilities of a funds manager are both administrative and strategic. Administrative duties include keeping books and files, financial reporting, preparing for board meetings, and using financial software. While administration requires attention to detail, strategizing involves more

forward thinking and looking at the big picture. Funds managers ask questions like "How can we work with other organizations to maximize our dollars?" and "How can we use our money better to achieve our foundation's goals?" They consider both the long- and short-term goals of their organization and explore sources for extra funding.

Large foundations may have additional Investment Professionals. Directors of investments or finance may oversee the financial books and records of the foundation, while financial analysts may conduct forecasting and financial analysis. They may also have staff members who analyze the financial feasibility of each grant proposal the foundation is considering. Some large foundations employ in-house money managers, but for the most part, at least some of the work is contracted out.

Duties for various Investment Professionals may include:

- Evaluating grantees financial capacities
- Analyzing specific funds and investments; making recommendations
- Reporting to the board of directors
- Setting financial policies and procedures
- Working with external investment professionals
- Implementing investment strategies

Most Investment Professionals work very closely with the board of directors. The board constantly wants to know how the endowment and specific funds are doing, and the Investment Professionals must be responsive and open to their questions. They need to understand what the board wants from the funds and what their goals are. It is important for them to be knowledgeable and diplomatic in order to manage not only the funds themselves, but also these sometimes complicated relationships.

Working as an Investment Professional for a foundation is a way that someone who is business-oriented can utilize his or her skills to contribute to the nonprofit sector. Insiders say the work is extremely satisfying, as they are growing investments to benefit others rather than "helping rich people to grow richer," as is often the case in the corporate world. Also, the work is so important to the existence of a foundation since foundations can survive failed programs, but not failed investment decisions that dwindle down their endowments. It can also be quite lucrative for those with the right combination of education and experience.

Salaries

Salaries of Investment Professionals are as diverse as their titles, variable based on level, education, and experience. While funds managers at small foundations may earn $40,000 to $60,000 per year, salaries for chief investment officers or vice presidents for finance and administration are quite high. A recent study by the Council on Foundations showed the median salary for vice presidents for finance and administration as $123,900. Other Investment Professionals fall somewhere in between.

Employment Prospects

Although there are many types of Investment Professionals within foundations, employment prospects are still fair because not all foundations employ them, particularly those at lower levels. Since their work is very specialized, not many positions are available. Since external financial professionals are used so frequently, many foundations do not have in-house funds managers, financial analysts, or directors of finance. The best opportunities can be found in large foundations and through networking in the field.

Advancement Prospects

Advancement prospects are also fair due to the scarcity of positions. Investment Professionals at the lower end of the hierarchy may advance through additional education and training; at the higher end, through moving to larger foundations that offer greater responsibility. They also may move from private to operating foundations and become more involved with grant making and programming.

Education and Training

Education and training requirements also vary depending upon the position. Although it is possible for a funds manager at a small foundation not to have a bachelor's degree, it is very unlikely in current conditions due to the high level of competition for positions. Most director-level Investment Professionals not only hold a bachelor's degree, but an advanced degree as well, especially the master of business administration (M.B.A.) degree.

Experience, Skills, and Personality Traits

While a funds manager or financial analyst may be hired directly out of college or graduate school, chief investment officers often have 15 to 20 years of professional experience. Many Investment Professionals have prior work experience in finance in the private sector for investment banks and consulting firms. However, combination experience in both the public and private sector is best, because nonprofit understanding and sensitivity is a must.

Basic computer and accounting skills are necessary to get into the field, including understanding spreadsheets such as Excel. Attention to detail, analytical skills, and a background in economics are also important. Good interpersonal skills come into play while dealing with board members, external money managers, and staff alike.

Unions and Associations

Within the foundation world, there is no one group that focuses on the business practices of foundations; most groups focus on the programming and grant-making functions. However, there are still a number of associations to which Investment Professionals can belong. These include the Foundation Financial Officers Group, the Council on Foundations Technology Affinity Group, Grantmakers for Effective Organizations, and the American Society of Association Executives, a good forum for exchanging best practices. Also, anyone who handles human resources also would likely belong to the Society for Human Resources Management.

Tips for Entry

1. Take a course in business, economics, or accounting to better understand financial analysis and money management.
2. Try your hand at investing money earned from part-time or summer jobs. This can be an excellent way to learn firsthand about making sound investment decisions. Before you do so, follow some particular stocks on the New York Stock Exchange to watch their progress (http://www.nyse.com/).
3. Visit the site http://www.mba.com to learn more about the master of business administration degree.
4. Speak to an Investment Professional at a foundation to learn more about job responsibilities and career paths.

GRANTS ADMINISTRATOR

CAREER PROFILE

Duties: Oversees the centralized processing of grants through a foundation from intake to follow-up

Alternate Title(s): Grants Manager, Administrative Director, Program Administrator, Foundation Administrator

Salary Range: $45,000 to $85,000 and up

Employment Prospects: Fair

Advancement Prospects: Fair

Best Geographical Location(s): Foundation cluster regions such as New York metropolitan area, Washington, D.C., San Francisco Bay Area, Los Angeles area

Prerequisites:

Education or Training—Bachelor's degree preferred; required for most positions

Experience—Some nonprofit experience and technical background

Special Skills and Personality Traits—Multitasking skills; customer service; attention to detail; administrative and organizational skills

CAREER LADDER

```
┌─────────────────────────────────────┐
│  Director of Grants Administration   │
└─────────────────────────────────────┘

┌─────────────────────────────────────┐
│        Grants Administrator          │
└─────────────────────────────────────┘

┌─────────────────────────────────────┐
│     Administrative Assistant,        │
│ Grants Assistant, or Program Assistant│
└─────────────────────────────────────┘
```

Position Description

Since awarding grants to organizations to support their projects, programs, and operations is a big part of the mission for most foundations, the process of managing these grants is crucial. Grants Administrators are the professionals responsible for overseeing grants management. They ensure data integrity, legal compliance, and grant-making policy and procedure. At the heart of the foundation, they serve as the clearinghouse for all grant-related functions, and they feed material to all other foundation departments.

There are four centralized functions applied to each grant that comes through a foundation: intake, review, award, and follow-up. The Grants Administrator is involved in each of these processes. When a grant is submitted to the foundation, the proposal must first be entered into the computer system. A file is created and the grant is coded. The Foundation Center offers the following classification system for how grants are coded:

- field of activity (subject or program area)
- type of recipient organization (museum, school, and so on)
- population groups served (blacks, children, etc.)
- type of support awarded (general, capital, etc.)
- geographic focus (domestic/foreign/international)

Copyright © 1995–2004 The Foundation Center

After coding the grants and creating the files, Grant Administrators evaluate what may be missing and will request materials from the grant seekers as necessary. Then staff members in programming, finance, communications, and technology are assigned to the proposals. In some small foundations, the Grant Administrator has program responsibilities as well, and may be involved in the proposal review process.

During the review process at large foundations, however, Grants Administrators are more involved in the due diligence, rather than the decision making about which proposals will be recommended to the grants committee or board members. They work to ensure that the grant goes through the proper channels to avoid problems. They consider issues such as whether or not the grant meets the criteria supplied by the foundation and if the staff has the necessary data.

After the review process, Grants Administrators apply tasks such as approving or denying the grant in the data system. This is an important part of quality control and making sure that the grant is listed and coded properly affects the foundation. Project descriptions must be accurate and reflect clearly what the grant is funding since this information will appear on the foundation Web site, in annual reports, and in industry publications and press releases to represent the foundation.

Also, because reporting grants to the IRS is required by foundations, it is essential for the Grants Administrator to make sure that the grant is legal and follows the correct IRS regulations and exemption status. Each year the IRS requires that every private foundation file a form called a 990-PF. This form includes, among other information about finances, trustees, and officers, a complete grants list. While the detail about each grant may vary from foundation to foundation, it is important for all information to be correct and for the path of each grant to be tracked and documented by the Grants Administrator.

Once a grant is approved, Grants Administrators run award agreements, which are documents signed by both the foundation and grantees. Grants Administrators may also schedule requirements and payments in the data system and process them. The monitoring and follow-up process includes Grants Administrators receiving interim and year-end reports from grantees. They analyze and determine if the grantee has met the objectives of the grant, and then finally, they close it out in the system.

Additional duties may include:

* Ensuring compliance with IRS regulations
* Preparing materials for board and committee meetings
* Creating and updating policy and procedures manual
* Maintaining systems and grant management software
* Analyzing grant reports and program trends
* Serving as liaison for all foundation staff
* Analyzing budget and expenditure reports
* Assuring data integrity
* Researching programs and foundation management issues
* Creating budgets and financial reports

Furthermore, Grants Administrators handle training and systems administration. They provide for staff training on all data systems, design templates, and run special reports. Also, they provide data and information to both internal board and staff members, as well as external stakeholders. They make sure procedures are in place to for each policy ranging from payments to reports to lobbying.

Within the last 10 years, Grants Administrators have become "professionalized." While they used to be seen by some as glorified administrative assistants, they now are viewed as integral to the functioning of a foundation, and their role is acknowledged as essential.

Salaries

According to a 2003 salary survey by the Grants Managers Network, the Grants Administrators surveyed reported a median income between $50,000 and $60,000 annually. Twenty-five percent also reported receiving an annual cash bonus. Additionally, a 2003 Compensation Summary for New Health Foundations as part of a joint survey of the Council on Foundations, along with Grantmakers in Health, showed different median salaries for Grants Administrators based on the foundation's budget. At foundations with assets between $5 million and $99.9 million, Program Directors earned a median salary of $44,404; with assets between $100 million and $249.9 million, $43,300; and with assets greater than $250 million, $52,185. The reason for the discrepancy of higher salaries at foundations in the first category compared to the second may be due to the high level of responsibility of Grants Administrators at small foundations where they may be required to wear many hats.

Salary also varies depending on the structure of the foundation, number of grants administration staff, and management responsibilities of the Grants Administrator. Insiders say that a typical range is from $45,000 to $85,000, with Grants Administrators at large foundations sometimes earning $100,000 and up.

Employment Prospects

As with most foundation positions, employment prospects are fair due to the small number of available jobs and limited number of foundations. While there are clusters of foundations in many U.S. regions including Minnesota, Indiana, and Atlanta, and small family foundations in small towns everywhere, the majority of foundations are in New York City, Washington, D.C., and Northern and Southern California. The best job opportunities are in these locations. People tend to stay in their positions fairly long term, so there is not much turnover. Also, some small foundations do not have a centralized grants administration staff and may delegate the responsibility to a program officer. Networking through professional organizations is a key way to get in the door.

Advancement Prospects

Grants Administrators may advance to become directors of grants administration or more senior administrative directors. Sometimes, Grants Administrators who have programming responsibilities may move onto the programming side as program officers or directors. They also may advance from more administrative positions if they complete additional education or training.

Education and Training

Education and training requirements are dependent on several factors, including the level of the Grants Administrator position. At some small foundations where the position is more administrative, candidates may be hired with some bookkeeping experience but no college degree, or more commonly, a recent bachelor's degree. At large foundations where the Grants Administrator will be supervising others, a master's degree may be required.

Experience, Skills, and Personality Traits

Grants Administrators need to be mulitaskers. They must be able to handle multiple projects at once and balance specific tasks and functions. A strong customer-service orientation is required to work with both internal and external professionals.

It is also necessary to understand how foundations work, grant making and the grant-making cycle, and IRS regulations. Information technology skills and knowledge of grant-making software and databases such as Microsoft Access are needed as well.

With the heavy administrative capacity of their jobs, Grants Administrators must be detail-oriented and able to apply procedure, policy, and practice. The position is a great opportunity for someone with a strong administrative background to use his or her skills to work in the nonprofit sector and make a contribution.

Unions and Associations

The main professional association for Grants Administrators is the Grants Managers Network, an association for foundations professionals responsible for grants management. The group is working to develop curriculum and career path information for Grants Administrators and further professionalize the occupation. They have members nationwide and hold meetings in locations including Ohio, the Midwest, and the Pacific Northwest. Grants Administrators also may belong to the Council on Foundations and other associations based on their foundation interest area.

Tips for Entry

1. Visit the Grants Managers Network Web site at http://www.gmnetwork.org. Read job descriptions for Grants Administrators and learn about the board of directors, professionals in the field from all over the country.
2. Learn more about grant coding by visiting the Foundation Center Web site at http://fdncenter.org/research/grants_class/index.html.
3. Go to http://www.irs.gov to learn more about foundation grants regulations.
4. Take a computer course to gain skills in databases such as Microsoft Access.

HEALTH AND SCIENCE

HEALTH POLICY ANALYST

Duties: Researches and analyzes health policy issues; lobbies and advocates for and against specific legislation on public health issues; develops policy and policy recommendations

Alternate Title(s): Public Health Policy Analyst, Health Care Policy Analyst, Program Analyst, Legislative Analyst or Adviser

Salary Range: $30,000 to $60,000 and up

Employment Prospects: Good

Advancement Prospects: Good

Best Geographical Location(s): All, with particular concentration in Washington, D.C.

Prerequisites:

Education or Training—Minimum of a bachelor's degree; typically a master's degree in public health, public policy, or related field

Experience—One to five years

Special Skills and Personality Traits—Excellent analytical and problem-solving abilities; strong research and writing skills; knowledge of public health issues, policy, and the legislative process

CAREER LADDER

```
Policy Director
```

```
Health Policy Analyst
```

```
Policy Assistant
```

Position Description

The field of public health seeks to protect people's health and safety throughout the world. Different public health practitioners contribute to this mission in many ways, through direct care, through education, and through academic research. Health Policy Analysts study public health issues, offering analyses and making recommendations from an expert's point of view. These recommendations can influence worldwide health policy.

Health Policy Analysts review public health issues piece by piece in order to interpret all data. They are concerned with the big picture and how public health challenges such as access to health care and environmental protection affect people's lives. They look to find solutions and methods for dealing with complex problems ranging from vaccination and smoking to clean water and family planning in order to make communities healthier and safer. Additionally, they share information with policy makers as well as the public

to determine which policies will make our society a better place.

A typical day for a Health Policy Analyst will likely include a combination of research, communication, and analysis. Research involves investigating the issues, analyzing the data, and synthesizing the policy information. It can include data collection, quantitative and qualitative methods, literature reviews, and extensive interviews. Using writing as a tool to impart their message, Health Policy Analysts write reports, policy briefs, action alerts, articles and fact sheets that summarize this information.

Health Policy Analysts may be responsible for creating a policy or advocacy plan related to a certain issue, reviewing proposals, and drafting policy updates to be distributed to the government or the public. They may meet with the media to discuss their positions and determine an advocacy strategy that will reach as many people as possible.

Some Health Policy Analysts work closely with legislation. They serve as advisers to help lawmakers on Capitol Hill understand the different policies up for votes so they can make informed decisions. As advocates for various issues, they work to convince politicians to vote in the best interest of public health and their constituents. Part of their job is also to remain objective in their research, portraying divergent views on controversial issues in order to make sure all information is presented.

Public education and advocacy go hand in hand. Many Health Policy Analysts coordinate education efforts, creating public health curricula and working with health educators to deliver these programs. They may also offer advice and training materials. Furthermore, they develop advocacy plans and strategies. It is important to create community partnerships so those people affected by public health issues can participate in influencing their own future. Health Policy Analysts may help them get mobilized and take action at the grassroots level.

Their duties may include:

- Writing briefs
- Developing policy recommendations
- Analyzing research findings
- Advising constituents as to how they are meeting their objectives
- Writing and tracking program and grant proposals
- Developing grassroots campaigns
- Building coalitions
- Serving as consultants to state and local organizations
- Engaging in strategic planning
- Creating new programs
- Conducting outcomes assessments

While a number of Health Policy Analysts work on Capitol Hill or for various government agencies, they also have many employment options in the nonprofit sector. They may work for public and private foundations, think tanks, advocacy groups, domestic and international health organizations, universities and schools of public health, and professional associations.

Health Policy Analysts care about public health. They feel passionate about their issues and motivated to work toward change. They may specialize in analyzing policy related to specific issues such as the environment, disease, or safety. Furthermore, they may specialize to work with particular populations and their health policy concerns such as women, children, senior citizens, or different minority groups. Often Health Policy Analysts use their skill to focus on the effect legislation has on health services for special populations. They work to determine how best to help these populations prepare for the implementation of new laws and policy.

Salaries

Salaries for Health Policy Analysts fluctuate based on the type of employment setting and level of the position. According to insiders, most entry-level positions are in the $30,000 to $45,000 range. However, Health Policy Analysts can earn more at the director level. They may also command higher salaries if they have advanced degrees in public health, public policy, or law.

Employment Prospects

Employment prospects for Health Policy Analysts are good. The importance and awareness of public health issues is increasing, and people are becoming more concerned about how public health concerns affect their lives.

As communities take more control of their health and the government tries to address various problems, Health Policy Analysts are needed to make sense of these issues and legislation. The field is expected to continue to grow over the next decade.

Advancement Prospects

Health Policy Analysts have a number of opportunities for advancement. With their skill set, prospects are good as they can move from one type of work setting to another. They may move from local grassroots associations to state and national health organizations. Another option is to advance to direct policy and policy issues as a manager and supervisor. Some Health Policy Analysts go on to work as consultants, advising government, nonprofit, and private sector clients on public health issues.

Education and Training

Health policy is an interdisciplinary field. Different positions may draw from public policy and administration, public health, politics, law, communications, advocacy, political science, nonprofit management, economics, and education. Health Policy Analysts may hold bachelor's degrees in any of these fields and others.

Most professionals hold graduate degrees; during this course of study they get more specialized training. The most common graduate degrees in the field are in public health or public policy/administration. Here, Health Policy Analysts learn how to analyze policy, understand the legislative process, and evaluate programs. Those Health Policy Analysts who plan to work in the international health arena also have experience abroad and have an international focus to their studies.

Some schools offer specific degrees in health policy research such as Florida State University in Tallahassee (http://www.coss.fsu.edu/academics/health.shtml). Complete listings of graduate programs in public health and public policy/administration can be found in Appendix I of this book.

Experience, Skills, and Personality Traits

In order to be successful at their work, Health Policy Analysts should be excellent communicators, both verbally and in writing. Their command of language comes into play as they write reports and lead meetings. For those who work with legislators, relationship-building and public speaking skills are essential.

Furthermore, Health Policy Analysts need analytical minds. They must be skilled researchers and problem solvers, able to break down complex issues and present multiple possibilities. It is important for them to understand the U.S. government and policy analysis strategies. Management skills are also useful.

Health Policy Analysts have special skills and experience based on their specialty area. For example, those who work in women's health often have backgrounds in women's studies as well as experience working for women's advocacy groups. Those Health Policy Analysts who work in international health are expected to have foreign language skills and knowledge of international relations.

Depending on the position, Health Policy Analysts may come to their positions directly after graduate school or with several years of experience. Internships and prior research experience are helpful.

Unions and Associations

There are a number of professional associations for Health Policy Analysts. They include the American Public Health Association, the Association of Schools of Public Health (ASPH), the Public Health Foundation, the National Environmental Health Association, the Public Health Law Association, the Public Health Leadership Society, and the Association for Public Policy Analysis and Management.

Tips for Entry

1. There are a number of Web sites that maintain job listings for Health Policy Analysts. The following site, http://www.uic.edu/sph/resources/careers/policyg2test. htm, part of the ASPH employment council, maintains an extensive list.
2. Become well informed about public health issues. A good link to connect you to various topics comes from the library of the University of California, Berkeley at: http://www.lib.berkeley.edu/PUBL/internet.html.
3. How well do you understand public policy? Learn more by visiting Web sites such as http://www.aei.org/, http://www.rand.org/, and http://www.publicagenda. org/.
4. Hone your research and analytical skills through courses in the social, natural, and biological sciences.
5. Find the area of health policy that inspires you. Volunteer your time or apply for an internship to develop experience in this area.

HEALTH EDUCATOR

CAREER PROFILE

Duties: Promote, maintain, and improve health among individuals and communities by providing information, education, and support related to adopting healthy behaviors

Alternate Title(s): Public Health Educator

Salary Range: $25,000 to $50,000 and up

Employment Prospects: Good

Advancement Prospects: Good

Best Geographical Location(s): Major urban areas

Prerequisites:

Education or Training—Bachelor's degree required; master's degree preferred and/or required for many positions

Experience—One to two years of experience in public health or health education through full-time work, internships, or volunteer work

Special Skills and Personality Traits—Excellent interpersonal skills; strong verbal and written communication skills, analytical and research abilities

Licensure/Certification—Health Educators may seek voluntary national certification through the National Commission for Health Education Credentialing, Inc.; state requirements may vary

CAREER LADDER

```
Director of Health Education
or Senior Health Educator
```

```
Health Educator
```

```
Education Assistant
```

Position Description

Health can be a very personal issue, and people are not always as informed as they could be about how their lifestyle may affect their own health and the health of their families. The main goals of Health Educators are to help people and communities adopt healthy lifestyles, make effective use of health services, and practice self-care. They achieve their goals through education that is geared at promoting healthy behaviors and preventing disease and disability. Through education, they can positively influence people at risk to make behavioral changes and improve their attitudes, skills, and knowledge. They strive to empower people to take control of their health, understand their options, and make informed decisions.

Health Educators are responsible for planning, implementing, monitoring, and evaluating programs designed to

encourage healthy environments and policies. In addition to evaluating current services, they may make recommendations for changes and improvements. Often, they serve as a resource to other health professionals, as well as to individuals and communities.

In order to accurately assess community health needs, Health Educators must collect and analyze data. This data is also useful for researching, designing, and presenting preventative health care programs. Health Educators are sometimes responsible for administering financial resources for public health programs as well. Furthermore, Health Educators strategize about the best ways to promote public awareness for their specific health issues. They may interact with the media or write educational materials, brochures, newsletters, and reports as a way to get their message across. Community outreach is another leading way for Health Educators to reach individuals at risk.

As is common in the nonprofit sector, Health Educators may also be involved with fund-raising and gaining support for their programs. They may write grants and meet with community members, corporations, and foundations to obtain funding for special projects.

There are many public health issues addressed by Health Educators, including HIV/AIDS, smoking, pregnancy, substance abuse, sexually transmitted diseases, nutrition, high blood pressure, and diabetes. Most Health Educators have specializations such as public, clinical, community, industrial, or school health. Additionally, they often focus on the issue represented by their organization of employment. For example, a Health Educator working for Planned Parenthood might lecture to teenagers about sexually transmitted diseases and protection. Furthermore, they may lecture or present on these topics to schools and community groups.

Their duties may include:

- Planning and implementing effective health education programs
- Teaching or lecturing to groups about health issues
- Providing educational opportunities for other health personnel
- Collaborating with community leaders and health professionals in order to assess health care needs and plan programs and services accordingly
- Conducting community surveys to evaluate health needs, develop health goals, and determine availability of quality services
- Preparing and distributing educational and informational materials
- Collecting data for researching, designing, and presenting preventative health care programs
- Evaluating available health services and helping people to develop desirable health goals
- Organizing community coalitions to address community health issues
- Dealing with social, behavioral, legal, and economic issues
- Administering fiscal resources for health education programs
- Advocating for health education and services
- Mobilizing communities for action
- Developing visual, print, or audio materials and media campaigns for health education
- Training peer counselors, advocates, or educators

Health Educators generally work a 40-hour workweek, including some weekends and evenings for meetings and programs. Local travel within their communities to schools or agencies may be required. They can work in settings such as hospitals, colleges and universities, government agencies, health-related nonprofit organizations, and social service organizations.

Within communities, Health Educators draw on members to mobilize resources, solve problems, and identify needs to improve health status. In schools and universities, Health Educators may teach health as a subject, develop curriculum and workshops, advocate as part of a health team, and promote healthy choices. In health care settings, they may educate patients, create activities and incentives for at-risk groups, and train staff members.

Salaries

According to a salary survey at http://www.healthcarejobstore. com, the average salary for Health Educators in the United States in 2004 was approximately $36,600. Salary ranges vary both by geographical location and workplace setting. Health Educators with master's degrees and those working for large nonprofit organizations or universities can earn considerably more.

Employment Prospects

As insurance companies and government agencies become increasingly conscious of the cost effectiveness of preventative health measures, the need for Health Educators will rise. The Bureau of Labor Statistics states that the profession is expected to grow faster than average through 2012, due to the growing importance of preventative health care and health improvement and awareness issues. Opportunities for Health Educators will be found in large urban areas, as well as in smaller communities where the need for services is strong.

Advancement Prospects

For a Health Educator to advance, additional education and experience is often required. Health Educators who hold master's degrees and have worked in the field for several years may advance to senior or director-level positions that involve supervisory responsibility. Also, Health Educators may find opportunities for advancement by developing a specialization in working with a particular population or health care issue.

Education and Training

To become a Health Educator, the minimum requirement is a bachelor's degree. However, most Health Educators hold master's degrees in health education, health science, public health, public administration, or related field. Also helpful are courses in behavioral sciences, biological sciences, management, economics, and communications. Health Educators take courses and receive ongoing training through conferences and workshops to hone their skills.

Special Requirements

At the national level, voluntary certification as a certified health education specialist (CHES) is available from the

National Commission for Health Education Credentialing, Inc (NCHEC). Various credential competencies are offered, including service coordination, resource communication, and program planning. Health Educators can seek this credentialing regardless of their work environment. CHES are recertified every five years based on documentation of participation in 75 hours of approved continuing education activities. For more information, visit http://www.nchec.org.

Experience, Skills, and Personality Traits

Health Educators must have excellent analytical and communication skills in order to evaluate data and present it to the public. They must be comfortable with speaking to large groups of people and being persuasive when necessary. It is also important for Health Educators to be knowledgeable about health care issues and current events. They often have volunteer, internship, or a few years of work experience demonstrating their interest in health issues, working with people, and teaching.

In addition to these skills, Health Educators must have flexible and adaptable personalities. They need the ability to work with different types of people and to impart information without passing judgment. Depending on their geographical region and population with which they work, foreign language skills can be very beneficial for Health Educators and even required by some employers. Furthermore, some positions require Health Educators to have a valid driver's license in order to travel locally.

Unions and Associations

Professional organizations for Health Educators include the American Alliance for Health, Physical Education, Recreation & Dance; the National Commission for Health Education Credentialing, Inc.; the Society for Public Health Education; and the American Public Health Association.

Tips for Entry

1. As a student, get involved with campus groups that promote healthy behaviors. They can often be found through the student health services or counseling centers on campus. Volunteers often speak at campus events about pertinent issues such as substance abuse, alcohol abuse, communicable diseases, and more.
2. Research graduate programs in health education and public health. Check out school Web sites to see where recent graduates are employed.
3. Explore a health issue of personal interest. Search the Internet and read articles to learn more about the issue and what services are currently being offered for education and prevention.
4. Contact professional associations for more information about training, graduate programs, and employment options.
5. Learn more about job opportunities and descriptions at http://www.healtheducationjobs.com.

HOSPITAL ADMINISTRATOR

CAREER PROFILE

Duties: Manages hospitals to ensure efficiency of functioning and quality of medical care for patients; plans, directs, and organizes the delivery of health-care services

Alternate Title(s): Hospital Director, Health-care Administrator

Salary Range: $50,000 to $140,000 and up

Employment Prospects: Good

Advancement Prospects: Fair

Best Geographical Location(s): All, particularly regions with growing populations

Prerequisites:

Education or Training—Advanced degree in related field required for most positions

Experience—Graduate school residency or post-graduate fellowship for entry-level position; five to 15 years for senior-level position

Special Skills and Personality Traits—Strong leadership abilities; good analytical and financial skills; tact, diplomacy, and decision-making ability

CAREER LADDER

```
┌─────────────────────────────────────┐
│  Chief Executive Officer or Hospital │
│      Administrator (large facility)  │
└─────────────────────────────────────┘

┌─────────────────────────────────────┐
│       Hospital Administrator         │
└─────────────────────────────────────┘

┌─────────────────────────────────────┐
│   Department Director or Assistant   │
│              Director                │
└─────────────────────────────────────┘
```

Position Description

On television, hospitals are often portrayed as exciting, glamorous, and hectic workplaces where life and death decisions are constantly at stake. Doctors, nurses, and patients are featured prominently in the center of the action. However, behind the scenes, there are professionals hard at work in order to make certain that all is running smoothly and that clinicians, administrators, and patients alike can all function in the best possible facility.

As their title implies, Hospital Administrators are the chief managers of health care facilities, including hospitals, clinics, hospices, and drug treatment centers. They make sure that resources are available and well organized in order to provide optimum treatment for patients. Furthermore, in order to maintain safe and up-to-date facilities, they use quality mechanisms to evaluate the hospital and level of care it provides.

Hospital Administrators have a vision for their organization and a plan to put it into action. While coordinating the operations of various branches of the hospital, they are constantly looking toward the future to improve programs and facilities. They are challenged by the vast structure of hospitals and must take a multidisciplinary approach to lead a team including doctors, nurses, other clinical staff, and administrators. They consider the big picture and how the interrelated areas within health care can work together, ranging from research and insurance to inpatient care and outpatient follow-up.

As the leaders of these organizations, Hospital Administrators have supervisory responsibilities that may include managing and hiring administrative and support staff. Their job includes leading human resources and acquiring staff in areas of need. Currently, nurses are in short supply nationwide, so this is one challenge that Hospital Administrators may work to overcome through creative recruiting strategies. They also need to ensure that all staff, clinical and administrative, are practicing within their specific areas of competency. Because hospitals include both clinical and administrative staff, a successful Hospital Administrator will have not only a strong business background, but also a clear clinical understanding.

Hospital Administrators work as liaisons between medical, administrative, and governing groups. They carry out policy set by a governing board of trustees, and they frequently work with governing boards, government officials, and the general public to meet the needs of the hospital and the community. Work with boards may include educating them about their realm of responsibility and involving them in decision making. Furthermore, Hospital Administrators often serve as ambassadors to their communities. They need to meet community expectations and make sure they contribute, often serving on health-related community organizations.

Many of the responsibilities of a Hospital Administrator are financial. They must have the ability to manage hospital finances, both in terms of day-to-day revenue, as well as long-term strategic plans. They plan budgets and determine rates for health services. Furthermore, they may be responsible for allocating funds for research and educational programs.

Hospital Administrators have faced many challenges in recent years. They must work within regulations and with limited resources to make decisions that directly affect peoples lives. One challenge comes with the changes in the structure and financing of health care. The focus has shifted to preventative care and dealing with insurance regulations and payment for services. Another comes with the changes in society since September 11th. Hospitals are now often first-response units for bioterrorism threats, and the Hospital Administrator must be sure the facility is prepared. Finally, it is a challenge to deal with competing authority structures that comprise a hospital, such as doctors, nurses, and administrators. However, those Hospital Administrators who can navigate this leadership seamlessly and efficiently are among the most personally gratified and professionally successful managers in any field.

Their duties may include:

- Planning, organizing, and controlling the delivery of health-care services
- Staying abreast of medical advances, insurance changes, technology innovations, and government regulations
- Creating and maintaining policies
- Participating in fund-raising, marketing, and public relations for the hospital
- Evaluating employees
- Attending staff meeting
- Organizing department activities
- Implementing business strategies
- Securing new technologies
- Working on policy directives and creating public policy
- Developing treatment policies and procedures

Hospital Administrators often work long hours, including early mornings, late nights, and weekends, since hospitals are open around the clock. Some travel may be required to attend meetings or make site visits. Also, some Hospital Administrators work as generalists, while others specialize and manage particular types of facilities such as children's hospitals.

Salaries

Salaries for Hospital Administrators vary greatly depending on the size of the facility they manage. According to the 2003 Hospital Compensation Report, published by the American Hospital Association and HAY Consultants, the average salary for chief executives of smaller facilities (total revenue under $25 million) is $143,000 per year, compared with $345,000 for chief executives at the largest facilities (total revenue over $200 million). However, these salaries reflect those Hospital Administrators who are the chief executives of their organizations and have considerable work experience.

According to the Bureau of Labor Statistics, median annual earnings of all medical and health services managers, including Hospital Administrators, were $61,370 in 2002. This takes into account those working in middle management and various aspects of health care administration.

Furthermore, entry-level salaries for those completing a postgraduate fellowship are approximately $39,055, according to a 2002 Postgraduate Fellowship Compensation Survey on the Web site of the American College of Healthcare Executives.

Employment Prospects

Overall, employment opportunities for Hospital Administrators are expected to grow faster than average over the next 10 years, as hospitals continue to consolidate. However, this merging also means that many hospitals will close, offering fewer jobs at the highest management level since there will be fewer facilities. Hospital Administrators will need to be flexible and seek opportunity within their broader health-care networks. The settings with the most jobs will include home health-care services and outpatient care centers.

Advancement Prospects

Advancement prospects for Hospital Administrators are fair, as there is much competition for top positions. Depending on their level of experience and education, they may find opportunities for advancement by moving from smaller facilities to larger ones where they can take on more responsibility at a higher level. Also, they may move on to work as independent consultants or chief executive officers in other health care settings.

Education and Training

It is crucial for a Hospital Administrator to have a background in management. With competition so great, it is virtually required for Hospital Administrators to have related master's degrees in order to not only obtain jobs, but also to have the understanding and education to perform the job well, including master's degrees in health-care administration, public administration, business, public health, or health sciences, with specialties in health care management. Some Hospital Administrators may be licensed medical doctors or nurses with additional education and experience in management.

Typically, graduate programs are two to three years and include a required, supervised internship where students can gain hands-on experience in a health-care setting. Through course work and internships, students learn about hospital organization and management, marketing, accounting and budgeting, human resources, economics, and strategic planning. Some graduate programs such as Xavier University in Cincinnati, Ohio, and George Washington University, in Washington, D.C., require a one-year "residency," where students must work in a hospital supervised by a preceptor, and rotate through different hospital departments and completing projects. Furthermore, other students opt to complete a postgraduate fellowship, a supervised, one- to two-year program after the completion of the master's degree that provides valuable experience and exposure to hospital departments and boards.

In order to reach the position of Hospital Administrator, professionals must pay their dues, working in entry-level positions after graduate school, then moving up to manage a department within five years. After gaining experience at the director level, one may move to an assistant vice president role before eventually finding a chief role as a Hospital Administrator.

Experience, Skills, and Personality Traits

Running a hospital or other health-care facility requires both business and people skills. In order to succeed as a Hospital Administrator, one must have strong business and management skills combined with tact and diplomacy. It is necessary to have knowledge of finance and economics for running a hospital smoothly, but just as important is a strong sense of ethics and the ability to communicate well. Hospital Administrators should also be good decision makers who employ forward thinking and strategic vision. Excellent leadership and analytic skills are valuable as well.

Unions and Associations

Professional organizations for Hospital Administrators may include the American Hospital Association, the American College of Health Care Administrators, the American College of Health Care Executives, and the Association of University Programs in Health Administration.

Tips for Entry

1. Read about current issues facing the health-care industry today to learn more about the challenges facing Hospital Administrators.
2. Visit the Web site http://www.healthmanagementcareers. com to explore career information and job descriptions.
3. Shadow current Hospital Administrators to see the job on a daily basis. Spend time talking with them to learn about their career paths, educational background, and professional training.
4. Research graduate programs that have specialties in health-care management. The Association of University Programs in Health Administration (http://www. aupha.org) is a good place to start.

EPIDEMIOLOGIST

CAREER PROFILE

Duties: Studying and tracking the genetic, health, and social determinants that cause disease; establishing interventions to control and prevent health problems

Alternate Title(s): Medical Scientist

Salary Range: $35,000 to $85,000

Employment Prospects: Good

Advancement Prospects: Good

Best Geographical Location(s): Cities with major research centers

Prerequisites:

Education or Training—Minimum requirement is master's degree in science or public health; some positions may require a Ph.D. in epidemiology or M.D. degree

Experience—Prior work or internship experience necessary

Special Skills and Personality Traits—Excellent analytical skills; strong research, math, and basic science ability; logical; curious; patient; flexible; good writing and communication skills

CAREER LADDER

```
┌─────────────────────────────────┐
│     Director of Epidemiology     │
└─────────────────────────────────┘

┌─────────────────────────────────┐
│          Epidemiologist          │
└─────────────────────────────────┘

┌─────────────────────────────────┐
│  Epidemiology Intern or Trainee  │
└─────────────────────────────────┘
```

Position Description

Epidemiologists can be seen as health detectives. They search for patterns and investigate *why*—why specific ethnic groups are prone to certain types of diseases, why women living within a 30-mile radius of each other suddenly develop breast cancer, and why eating dark green vegetables can help people to live longer.

Through researching human health and disease worldwide, Epidemiologists study different populations and communities to understand determinants for disease and to help identify and prevent health problems. They consider risk factors such as environment, occupation, and nutrition and how they relate to the cause of disease. Furthermore, they are often called in to examine infectious disease outbreaks to determine causes and control outcomes. With the threat of bioterrorism a real problem in the world today, the job of an Epidemiologist carries great importance in influencing and maintaining public health and safety.

Epidemiologists investigate disease clusters and determine links in cause. They look not only to study what causes these diseases, but also to understand how to prevent these diseases and treatment options. This work can be carried out in a number of different ways and various types of Epidemiologists work together to achieve this ultimate goal.

Field Epidemiologists conduct studies through gathering information on specific populations. They may conduct surveys, personal interviews, or even observe people in order to understand the factors that may contribute to disease and health problems. Research Epidemiologists may work in labs or teach at universities where they analyze research data and reports. They often focus on preventing chronic disease through identifying risk factors. Some Epidemiologists work for the government, where they contribute to devising and executing health policy. They explore health issues and conduct studies related to both prevention and outcomes. Their work also helps influence the decisions of government officials and policy makers to take measures to defend against disease.

Also, as a public health discipline, Epidemiologists work with communities. They look at current conditions and conduct needs assessments to identify key health issues and evaluate the effectiveness of present interventions. Furthermore, they might plan and implement surveillance programs to monitor health status and trends. After establishing their findings, they will work with the community to promote education and prevention options to eliminate risk factors.

An Epidemiologist's job may consist of the following chain of responsibilities: investigating a disease outbreak or cluster, generating and testing a hypothesis, entering data and using computerized data analysis tools, performing statistical analysis of data, and developing reports.

Additional duties may include:

- Designing and implementing health outcomes surveys
- Identifying technologies and strategies to provide better care to prevent and treat disease
- Recruiting people to participate in studies
- Attending meetings
- Obtaining funding for studies by writing grant proposals
- Evaluating reports and making recommendations
- Writing articles for scientific journals
- Serving as an epidemiological consultant within an organization
- Preparing clinical notes and reports
- Presenting findings to groups
- Supervising staff, students, or trainees
- Developing informational materials
- Proposing intervention methods

Epidemiologists in the nonprofit sector may work at universities, research institutes, foundations, or other health organizations. Field Epidemiologists may travel frequently throughout the world to conduct studies and investigate outbreaks, whereas other types of Epidemiologists travel less often, usually just to attend professional conferences.

Also, Epidemiologists can have specializations. They can focus by group such as women, children, or low-income populations, by issue such as environmental or occupational health, or by disease such as exclusively studying cancer or communicable diseases.

Overall, epidemiology is a field that couples science with public service. It is attractive to investigative types with scientific orientations who also want to contribute to society and help others.

Salaries

According to the Bureau of Labor Statistics (BLS), median annual earnings of epidemiologists were $53,840 in 2002. The middle 50 percent earned between $44,900 and $66,510. The lowest 10 percent earned less than $35,910, and the highest 10 percent earned more than $85,930.

Employment Prospects

In 2002, 3,900 Epidemiologists were employed in the United States. The Bureau of Labor Statistics indicates that the job outlook remains good. The current focus on research and disease prevention helps employment prospects. Also, Epidemiologists are frequently less affected by recessions than are other medical scientists because they work on long-term research projects.

Advancement Prospects

Positions are competitive, but still growing as awareness about disease and bioterrorism increases in importance. Epidemiologists may seek further training in order to advance to leadership positions running a lab or research staff. Degrees beyond the master's level are essential for considerable advancement.

Education and Training

Depending on their work setting and responsibilities, Epidemiologists may hold a master of public health (M.P.H.) degree, master of science in epidemiology (M.S.) degree, a doctor of philosophy (Ph.D.) degree, and/or a medical doctor (M.D.) degree. A minimum of a master's degree is required for all positions. Some jobs may require a Ph.D. for conducting research, or an M.D. for administering drugs in clinical trials. A medical degree and training in infectious diseases is particularly important for work in hospitals and health-care settings.

Those with an M.P.H generally seek employment in the more practice-oriented arena, such as a local or state public health department. Students earning an M.S. usually pursue careers in research with responsibilities including study design, data analysis, grant and report writing, publication preparation, and study coordination. Career opportunities for Ph.D.'s and M.D.'s include university faculty, principal investigator at research institutes (both federal and nonprofit), and researcher at large health maintenance organizations.

Helpful courses at the undergraduate level include math, statistics, basic science, and computer science.

There is another program that trains Epidemiologists who have already completed their graduate work. The national Centers for Disease Control and Prevention (part of the U.S. Department of Health and Human Services) in Atlanta, Ga., runs a program called the Epidemic Intelligence Service (EIS). This is a two-year, postgraduate program of service and on-the-job training for health professionals interested in practicing epidemiology. For more information, see http://www.cdc.gov/eis/.

Experience, Skills, and Personality Traits

One can enter the field of epidemiology through completing a master's degree in epidemiology. The field attracts not only recent college graduates and people with several years of work experience in health care, but also seasoned medical professionals such as doctors and nurses.

Epidemiologists must be adept at conducting research and analyzing data. They need sharp critical thinking skills and good intuition to look at information and determine patterns. Also, strong communication skills are important. They must interface with people through clinical studies and research teams where it is necessary to be able to work well with others. Furthermore, they should be good decision makers and have planning and organizational skills.

Unions and Associations

Epidemiologists can belong to a variety of professional associations including the American College of Epidemiology, the American Epidemiology Society, the American Public Health Association (Epidemiology Section), and the Society for Epidemiological Research.

Tips for Entry

1. Explore the Web site for the Centers for Disease Control and Prevention at http://www.cdc.gov.
2. Talk to Epidemiologists who work in different settings such as universities, hospitals, and government to learn about the differences in skills and responsibilities.
3. Become familiar with job descriptions at www.sciencejobs.com.
4. Explore graduate schools of public health and epidemiology requirements and course work.
5. Improve research skills through taking scientific and analytical courses.

LABORATORY TECHNICIAN

CAREER PROFILE

Duties: Performs tests and experiments in medical laboratories to further research into disease diagnosis, treatment, and prevention

Alternate Title(s): Medical Technician, Clinical Laboratory Technician, Medical Laboratory Technician, Research Laboratory Technician

Salary Range: $20,000 to $42,000

Employment Prospects: Excellent

Advancement Prospects: Good

Best Geographical Location(s): All

Prerequisites:

Education or Training—Associate's degree; some jobs may require bachelor's degree; high school or advanced course work in the basic sciences also required

Experience—Entry-level with prior scientific background or training/clinical education in a medical laboratory technician (MLT) program

Special Skills and Personality Traits—Curious; good problem-solving skills; accurate and detail-oriented; good manual dexterity required for some positions

Licensure/Certification—Some states require Laboratory Technicians to be licensed or registered; one such accrediting agency is the National Accrediting Agency for Clinical Laboratory Sciences (NAACLS)

CAREER LADDER

```
┌─────────────────────────────────┐
│       Medical Technologist,       │
│       Laboratory Director,        │
│   or Senior Laboratory Technician │
└─────────────────────────────────┘

┌─────────────────────────────────┐
│       Laboratory Technician       │
└─────────────────────────────────┘

┌─────────────────────────────────┐
│             Student               │
└─────────────────────────────────┘
```

Position Description

Laboratory Technicians play a crucial role in understanding and fighting disease. They assist scientists with the research and experiments that advance medicine, clarify problems, and benefit society. Their job focuses on the practical aspects of experiments and may include setting up equipment, preparing slides, and running tests. Performing tests of blood, tissue, and other bodily substances, they follow instructions and pay close attention to detail, making sure the experiments are running smoothly.

Laboratory Technicians are needed for all areas of lab work including blood banking, chemistry, hematology, immunology, microbiology, pathology, and biochemistry. They work alongside other medical laboratory personnel such as medical technologists and scientists who supervise their work. Each lab is centered on a particular research goal, and everyone works together to support this mission. For example, one lab may focus on isolating a hormone that affects weight patterns in mice, or another may study the chemical reactions of different cancer drugs. Therefore, the experiments will vary depending upon the focus and goals of the research studies.

In addition to providing practical assistance with experiment tasks, Laboratory Technicians also use their own scientific knowledge to observe and draw conclusions. They may compare results with past studies to analyze any differences. Furthermore, they perform troubleshooting if something goes wrong, figuring out why and what can be done differently.

Their duties may include:

- Preparing specimens
- Making observations
- Operating and maintaining equipment such as microscopes, centrifuges, and spectrophotometers
- Ensuring laboratory is stocked with reagents and supplies
- Preparing solutions for experiments
- Maintaining records of techniques and procedures
- Assisting with research papers
- Reviews and records results of experiments
- Evaluating test results
- Operating automated analyzers

Some Laboratory Technicians perform specialized work and have specific training in these areas such as histotechnicians, who cut and stain tissue specimens for pathologist to examine under microscopes, and phlebotomists, who collect blood samples. Laboratory Technicians with four-year college degrees may be more directly involved with research, assisting scientists with publishing research papers by conducting literature searches and gathering data for studies.

Many people choose to become Laboratory Technicians because they enjoy science and the structured process of working in a lab, conducting experiments, and seeing results. Some may desire to stay in the field, continue their education, and become medical technologists who perform more complex tests and analysis. Other college graduates may work for several years as Laboratory Technicians in order to gain more clinical and research experience before applying to medical school.

Laboratory Technicians in the nonprofit sector may work in hospitals, colleges and universities, clinics, public health facilities, and other laboratories. They usually work a 40-hour workweek, but their hours may vary depending upon the size of the facility; in large hospitals where labs run around the clock, they may work shifts that include both day and night. Furthermore, they must take care to protect themselves from infectious specimens by wearing gloves, masks, and goggles.

Salaries

A 2002 Wage and Vacancy Survey of Medical Laboratories conducted by the American Society for Clinical Pathology's Board of Registry in conjunction with MOR-PACE International (Detroit, Mich.) details salary information for Laboratory Technicians. According to this biennial survey, the average salary for Medical Laboratory Technicians is $31,928, with a range between $27,040 and $35,776. For those Laboratory Technicians in a supervisory role, the average salary is $39,520, with a range between $33,280 and $41,600. Salaries vary depending on the size and geographic location of the hospital or research facility. The same survey also shows an 8.8 percent increase in Laboratory Technician salaries between the years 2000 and 2002.

In addition, the Bureau of Labor Statistics reported the median annual earnings of medical and clinical Laboratory Technicians as $29,040 in 2002. The middle 50 percent earned between $23,310 and $35,840.

Employment Prospects

Employment prospects are excellent, according to the Bureau of Labor Statistics, because the number of job openings is expected to continue to exceed the number of job seekers. Also, as technology continues to advance, more diagnostic tests will be developed, creating greater opportunities. For those who have the appropriate training, there will be a variety of options for employment.

Advancement Prospects

Advancement prospects are also good. For Laboratory Technicians looking to advance, the path to becoming a laboratory or medical technologist is very clear through obtaining additional education and experience. One can become a medical technologist by receiving a bachelor's degree and getting three years of experience or attending a NAACLS accredited medical technologist program. Once becoming a medical technologist, he or she would then be able to perform a full range of complex lab tests with little or no supervision. Others may choose to leave the field and go back to school in other medical and science-related fields.

Education and Training

In order to become a Laboratory Technician, an associate's degree is necessary for many positions, and some more research-oriented positions may require a bachelor's degree. A strong background in high school or advanced sciences, including biology, chemistry, math, and computer science, is needed.

There are also a variety of programs available through community colleges and hospitals that offer clinical education as a medical laboratory technician (MLT). These programs are accredited by the National Accrediting Agency for Clinical Laboratory Sciences (http://www. naacls.org/). According to the American Society for Clinical Pathology, approximately 200 community colleges and hospitals offer these programs.

Special Requirements

The Bureau of Labor Statistics reports that some states require laboratory personnel to be licensed or registered. State departments of health or boards of occupational licensing offer information on licensure. Voluntary certification through NAACLS is also widely required by many health industry employers and necessary for advancement. To learn more about certification, visit http://www.naacls.org.

Experience, Skills, and Personality Traits

Laboratory Technicians should enjoy scientific exploration. They need to like challenge, responsibility, and solving problems. It is also important for them to pay close attention to detail and to be able to follow instructions and supervision. Manual dexterity and normal color vision can also be essential for analyzing specimens. Computer skills are valuable for operating increasingly more complex equipment.

Students may work in labs part-time in order to gain experience before working full-time. Experience also can be gained through course work and clinical education programs. After completing an accredited MLT program, students are eligible for jobs immediately.

Unions and Associations

Professional associations include the American Society for Clinical Pathology, the National Accrediting Agency for Clinical Laboratory Sciences, and American Medical Technologists, a nonprofit certification and professional member association.

Tips for Entry

1. Check out the Board of Registry for the American Society for Clinical Pathology, which provides information about careers and certification for clinical laboratory personnel, http://www.ascp.org/bor/about.
2. Also, take a look at the information on certification and careers provided by American Medical Technologists at http://www.amt1.com/site/epage/15319_315.htm.
3. Explore course work in the sciences and medical technology such as biology, chemistry, and courses with lab requirements.
4. Research programs that offer the CLT/MLT: clinical laboratory technician/medical laboratory technician certification at http://www.naacls.org/search/programs.asp.

NUTRITIONIST

CAREER PROFILE

Duties: Promotes nutrition as essential to a healthy lifestyle by planning meals for organizations and advising individuals and groups about healthy eating

Alternate Title(s): Dietician; Nutrition Specialist; Community Nutritionist

Salary Range: $30,000 to $60,000 and up

Employment Prospects: Fair to Good

Advancement Prospects: Fair to Good

Best Geographical Location(s): All

Prerequisites:

Education or Training—Bachelor's degree required; many positions also require a master's degree

Experience—Minimum of one to two years of internship or work experience

Special Skills and Personality Traits—Knowledge of nutritional science and dietetics; excellent interpersonal skills; strong verbal communication ability; patience, sensitivity, and tolerance

Licensure/Certification—Many states and employers require a registered dietician (RD) degree for employment; some states also regulate who can use the title "Nutritionist"

CAREER LADDER

Director of Nutrition

Nutritionist

Student or Intern

Position Description

As experts on the effects different foods have on the human body, Nutritionists promote dietary health. They help individuals and groups to understand how the food choices they make can affect their long-term wellness. They also plan and prepare menus in public settings including hospitals, schools, and community agencies to ensure the quality of the food meets the highest nutrition standards.

There are a number of employment options for Nutritionists in the nonprofit sector. Nutritionists in hospitals and health care are commonly called clinical nutritionists or dieticians. In hospitals, nursing homes, and other nonprofit health facilities, they are on staff to plan menus, as well as arrange specific diets for patients based on their health concerns. Based on their knowledge of vitamins, digestion, and the human body, they advise patients. They can teach them how to modify their diet due to certain illnesses that may require them to avoid the intake of sugars, salts, or alcohol.

In addition to hospitals and health organizations, Nutritionists are needed by community agencies that feed homeless and disadvantaged populations. Here, they are often called community nutritionists. Nutritionists plan the menus at soup kitchens and shelters to ensure that the most nutritious meals possible are being planned with the limited resources available. Also, they pay attention to how meals are prepared to prevent disease or illness through unsanitary practices.

Furthermore, Nutritionists may work for relief and development organizations where they focus on domestic and international nutrition issues. They may design programs, conduct research, and perform behavioral counseling to help individuals and groups adopt healthier lifestyles. Nutritionists also promote other issues that go hand in hand with better eating, including exercise and physical activity. The idea is not just to foster the right diet, but to encourage people to make the best possible choices for their overall health.

Nutrition is an important public health issue, since attitudes about nutrition can shape the health and well being of various communities. A big part of the role of Nutritionists is also as educators. By working with specific groups in communities such as adolescents or pregnant mothers, they can impart the importance of eating balanced meals and healthy lifestyles. They discuss the way the body digests different foods and the results they have on the body. Some Nutritionists are professors at colleges and universities, instructing those new to the profession and shaping educational curriculum. Nutritionists also partner with community groups to promote health awareness.

Another way Nutritionists influence public health is through policy. Federal, state, and local policies regarding nutrition affect people in many ways. For example, the content of school lunches and introducing children to healthier foods at young ages can fight obesity and disease. Nutritionists often lobby for changes in meals at schools, agencies, and organizations to make the meals healthier. They also decide what should and should not be included. Furthermore, they may plan campaigns to promote and publicize these new policies.

Additional duties may include:

- Lecturing different groups about nutrition and health awareness
- Providing one-on-one counseling to individuals
- Determining eligibility for federal programs
- Partnering with other health professionals including nurses, physicians, psychologists, and physical therapists
- Teaching classes in healthy food preparation
- Conducting research on nutrition
- Working with chefs and other food preparers
- Developing brochures and other educational materials promoting nutrition
- Working with volunteers
- Coordinating a food pantry
- Conducting community outreach
- Designing programs and software for nutritional analysis

Nutritionists may specialize to work with different populations including children, the elderly, or specific ethnic groups. They also may create a niche by working with those suffering from certain diseases such as diabetes or facing genetic predispositions such as obesity. In working with these groups, Nutritionists can focus in and target specific strategies geared toward their needs.

The hours for Nutritionists may include some evening and weekend shifts in health-care settings, but are generally within a 40-hour workweek range. Insiders say that they enjoy their jobs and like the results-oriented component. It is gratifying to see patients and clients see the immediate and long-term benefits that come from altering their diets.

Salaries

Salaries for Nutritionists vary depending on their work setting as well as their education level. According to *Compensation in Nonprofit Organizations, 16th Edition,* a 2003 survey report of 131 benchmark jobs from Abbott, Langer & Associates, Inc., the median income for a Nutritionist working in the nonprofit sector is $35,546.

Additionally, the Bureau of Labor Statistics (BLS) cites that median annual earnings of dietitians and Nutritionists were $41,170 in 2002. The BLS also quotes a 2002 survey from the American Dietetic Association that shows the median annual income for registered dietitians in a variety of practice areas. That survey cites the following figures for nonprofit settings: $55,000 in food and nutrition management; $54,800 in education and research; $44,000 in clinical nutrition/ambulatory care; $43,300 in clinical nutrition/long-term care; $43,200 in community nutrition; and $40,800 in clinical nutrition/acute care. Nutritionists working in business, consulting, or private practice can earn upward of $60,000 and more.

Employment Prospects

Employment prospects for Nutritionists are expected overall to be good. While the BLS states that opportunities will grow at an average rate through 2012, growth is expected in public and community nutrition. Awareness is increasing for public health issues, and concerns such as obesity in the United States are garnering much attention. With the implementation of prevention programs and healthy eating campaigns, especially for children, opportunities for Nutritionists will be available.

Advancement Prospects

For advancement, Nutritionists can take on leadership positions directing programs or departments. They may also become affiliated with colleges or universities, working as full professors who conduct research or adjuncts who teach in addition to working in other settings. Nutritionists may also choose to maintain private practices where they advise individuals or act as consultants to nonprofit organizations or businesses.

Education and Training

Nutritionists must hold either undergraduate or graduate degrees in nutrition or dietetics. These courses cover the physiology of the human body, including digestion, food balance, and vitamin needs. They may focus on food science, biology, physiology, chemistry, biochemistry, and institution management, as well as courses that develop an understanding of human behavior such as psychology and counseling.

Both undergraduate and graduate programs include required clinical internships in addition to academics.

As of 2003, there were about 230 bachelor's and master's degree programs approved by the ADA's Commission on Accreditation for Dietetics Education (CADE). To meet necessary clinical experience for licensure as registered dieticians (RDs), Nutritionists must either complete a CADE-accredited program or complete 900 supervised hours in a CADE-accredited internship program. See this link for more information: http://www.eatright.org/Public/Careers/94_20037.cfm.

Most practicing Nutritionists are registered dieticians, holding RD licensure. In addition to RD licensure, professionals at the associate's degree level may become licensed as DTRs, or dietetic technicians, registered.

However, while in most states licensure does not regulate who can call themselves a Nutritionist, there is professional certification for Nutritionists through the International and American Associations of Clinical Nutritionists. The requirements also include a combination of education, practical experience, and a licensing exam. Information provided by the Clinical Nutrition Certification Board offers more specifics at: http://www.cncb.org/default.htm.

For work in community agencies, some Nutritionists hold a master's degree in public health and have an undergraduate degree in nutrition. Courses or specialization in community nutrition is important.

Special Requirements

According to the BLS, 46 states and jurisdictions have laws governing the profession of dietetics. Of these states, 30 require licensure, 15 require certification, and one requires registration. The American Dietetic Association (ADA) awards the registered dietitian credential to those who pass a certification exam after completing their academic coursework and supervised experience. Since requirements vary by state, see the ADA's Web site at: http://www.eatright.org/Public/Careers/94.cfm.

Also, the Clinical Nutrition Certification Board (http://www.cncb.org/default.htm) of the International and American Associations of Clinical Nutritionists offers licensure as a clinical Nutritionist. While this licensure is not required to work in most states, it can be a helpful credential for employment.

Experience, Skills, and Personality Traits

Nutritionists need excellent communication skills in order to work with a variety of clients. They must be persuasive and command authority, while being approachable and sympathetic to concerns and issues. Also, many positions involve public speaking and presentations.

Furthermore, Nutritionists need to be experts about food and the human body. They need to understand different combinations and their chemical breakdowns, as well as the effects of diet on overall health. In order to work with diverse populations, they must be culturally sensitive and skilled at counseling.

Unions and Associations

The nation's largest professional association for food and nutrition practitioners is the American Dietetic Association. Nutritionists may also belong to the International and American Associations of Clinical Nutritionists.

Tips for Entry

1. How much do you know about healthy eating? Take a look at the Food Guide Pyramid, developed by the United States Department of Agriculture (USDA) to learn more about what makes a serving and what types of daily food combinations are recommended: http://www.pueblo.gsa.gov/cic_text/food/food-pyramid/main.htm.
2. Continue to learn about dietary guidelines and nutrition facts through the American Dietetic Association's food and nutrition information at http://www.eatright.org/Public/NutritionInformation/92.cfm.
3. Take courses in nutrition and food science to get a feel for the subject. Speak with the professors of these courses about career options.
4. Set up an informational meeting with a Nutritionist working at a hospital or community agency. Learn about his or her career path and get advice about how to begin.
5. Try an internship or volunteer position to gain experience with diverse populations. Explore local soup kitchens, homeless shelters, senior citizen centers, and community agencies.

SOCIAL SERVICE AND RELIGIOUS ORGANIZATIONS

SOCIAL WORKER

CAREER PROFILE

Duties: Helps people identify and overcome social and health problems in order to best function in their environment; works with communities and organizations to improve social and health services

Alternate Title(s): Therapist, Case Manager

Salary Range: $25,000 to $60,000 and up

Employment Prospects: Excellent

Advancement Prospects: Good

Best Geographical Location(s): All

Prerequisites:

Education or Training—Bachelor's degree in social work (BSW) required; many positions also require the master's degree in social work (MSW)

Experience—Positions range from entry level to requiring several years of work experience

Special Skills and Personality Traits—Sensitivity and maturity; excellent interpersonal and listening skills; ability to be objective

Licensure/Certification—All states and the District of Columbia require practicing social workers to be licensed, registered, or certified for professional practice; however, these standards vary by state

CAREER LADDER

```
┌─────────────────────────────────┐
│      Social Work Manager         │
│    or Director of Social Work    │
└─────────────────────────────────┘

┌─────────────────────────────────┐
│          Social Worker           │
└─────────────────────────────────┘

┌─────────────────────────────────┐
│      Social Work Assistant       │
│      or Graduate Student         │
└─────────────────────────────────┘
```

Position Description

If you care about people and want to improve their quality of life, consider a career as a Social Worker. It is impossible to pigeonhole the job of a Social Worker. Social Workers in the nonprofit sector conduct short-term therapy at colleges and universities and run programs on stress management. They counsel middle school students faced with peer pressure and gangs. For people who are homeless, they are advocates who help find shelter and work programs. They facilitate adoption procedures to join infertile couples with the babies they so desire. They help non-English speakers navigate the United States court system. In hospitals, they help people understand and cope with difficult diagnoses and get the services they need. They create and analyze policy, call for reform, and fight for the rights of underrepre-

sented individuals and groups. While one Social Worker is not trained to do all of these things, it is a career with much opportunity for additional skill building and transitioning to new challenges.

Social Workers strive to improve quality of life, relieve suffering, and enable people to function in the best way they can within their environment. They accomplish their goals through providing direct services to their clients or working for change to improve overall social conditions. They are set apart from other helping professionals in that in addition to helping clients cope with their feelings about a situation, they also provide assistance to deal with it. They counsel their clients within a broader social framework. For example, a Social Worker may assist a homeless client with the physical and emotional stress of homelessness by providing therapy, but also may work to find a spot in a shelter, an after school program for the client's children, and a job training program.

Some social workers create and administer plans for their clients in order to help them obtain services. For their case load of clients, they conduct meetings, develop a case plan design to obtain needed resources, and maintain case notes and goal plans for each client. Furthermore, as advocates for their clients, Social Workers identify appropriate providers and facilities for services, understand eligibility requirements for programs such as Medicare and Welfare, and act as liaisons between their clients and various service personnel.

In addition to direct service, many Social Workers also work for social change, calling for policy reform within larger social issues such as health care, crime, and the legal system. They act as a voice for those in need who cannot advocate for themselves. Through conducting research and analyzing policy, they make specific recommendations for legislation or other improvements.

Social work is made up of a diverse group of professionals acting as teachers, therapists, and advocates in many types of employment settings and specialties. They enjoy a tremendous amount of variety in work tasks, as well as work environments. Social Workers can have a wide variety of expertise areas such as child welfare, child protection, mental health, substance abuse, criminal justice, policy and administration, and new program development. Furthermore, some Social Workers specialize in working with specific populations, including children, teenagers, adults, senior citizens, the homeless, substance abusers, or cancer patients.

Their duties may include:

- Providing counseling to individuals, groups, or families to assist them with social, emotional, or economic needs
- Running support groups for clients and/or their families
- Offering training for clients to improve personal or emotional functioning and assist them with issues of everyday living
- Assisting clients with navigating social systems such as hospitals, adoption and foster care, courts, and others
- Assessing, diagnosing, and treating forms of mental illness
- Referring clients to appropriate professionals for additional care or services
- Working within a community to best allocate resources for social services
- Developing programs, resources, and policies to address social issues and community needs; working to implement change
- Planning for services to facilitate clients' assimilation back into their communities
- Initiating legal action, when necessary, to protect the welfare of clients
- Conducting research to improve, plan, and develop social programs and health services

- Coordinating and working with organizations to combat social problems through community awareness and response programs

Social Workers in the nonprofit sector can find employment in hospitals, clinics, nursing homes, mental health and social service agencies, community service organizations, K–12 schools, colleges and universities, correctional facilities, and rehabilitation facilities. Additionally, many maintain private practices as therapists or consultants. They may work a typical 9 to 5 workweek or more flexible hours that include evenings and weekends, depending on their work setting. Because of the emotional nature of their jobs, Social Workers tend to burn out from working hours that are too long. Overall, however, they are passionate about what they do, and the feeling they are making a difference in people's lives compensates for low pay and long hours.

Salaries

Salaries for Social Workers vary by employment setting and amount of experience. According to the 2002 Practice Research Network Survey by the National Association of Social Workers, the median annual income for Social Workers in 2001 was $44,400. However, Social Workers in the nonprofit sector tend to earn less than Social Workers working for corporations or in private practice. The same survey found the median annual salary for Social Workers employed specifically in the nonprofit sectarian sector to be $41,300. One of the most lucrative nonprofit options for Social Workers is through employment by public K–12 schools and colleges and universities. Social Workers employed in the nonprofit sector may supplement their income by also maintaining private practices.

Employment Prospects

According to the Bureau of Labor Statistics, employment for Social Workers is expected to grow faster than average through 2012. There are several reasons for this projected increase, including rapid growth of the geriatric population, as well as continued demand for social services to help people deal with increased mental and physical illness, crime, delinquency, and other crises.

Employment opportunities for Social Workers will grow in cities and rural areas alike. As cities continue to deal with social problems and help their communities deal with issues such as violent crime, HIV, and substance abuse, the demand for social services and Social Workers will rise. Furthermore, in rural areas, growth will occur because there is less competition for positions as they become open when experienced Social Workers retire. Employment for Social Workers in settings such as hospitals and health-care facilities, social service agencies, and substance abuse treatment centers is expected to experience particular growth.

Advancement Prospects

Because there are so many settings in which Social Workers can find employment, advancement prospects are good. Positions tend to have high turnover, and professionals may choose to move around frequently to avoid burnout. Advancement opportunities may include running agencies and/or managing other Social Workers, as well as other professional and paraprofessional staff, but will vary depending on the specialty, work setting, and geographic location. Social Workers also may move to the corporate sector or develop private practices. A master's degree and related work experience are necessary for leadership and management positions.

Education and Training

In order to become a Social Worker, the minimum requirement is a Bachelor of Social Work (BSW), from a four-year college or university accredited by the Council on Social Work Education. However, many employers require the 60-credit Master of Social Work (MSW) degree, and it is required for ultimate advancement. Furthermore, the master's degree is required by many states for professional practice and licensure.

To be accepted into a master's degree program, the undergraduate degree in social work is not required, but a demonstrated interest in helping others is. Courses in psychology, sociology, English, communications, and economics may be useful, in addition to volunteer work and internship experience. It is also possible to get an advanced graduate degree, including the Doctorate in Social Work (DSW) or Ph.D., for those who plan to teach or conduct research at the college level.

Social Work training includes practical field experience as well as classroom study. Students can expect required fieldwork and internships at both the undergraduate and graduate levels. These required experiences are excellent opportunities for students to decide which area of social work is the best fit, as well as providing good leads for potential employment.

Special Requirements

All states and the District of Columbia have licensing, certification, or registration requirements regarding social work practice and the use of professional titles. Standards for licensure vary by state, but professional ethics, cultural sensitivity, and communication skills are emphasized. Additionally, the National Association of Social Workers (NASW) offers voluntary credentials.

Experience, Skills, and Personality Traits

Helping people to deal with crises is difficult work. Social Workers must be compassionate and sensitive listeners, yet be able to remain objective and detached when necessary. They must have superior communication skills, empathy, and the ability to be nonjudgmental and work with many types of people. Also important is the ability to remain calm in stressful situations. Knowledge of their communities and the social networks and services available is crucial.

Experience working with people in need is crucial. Prior to attending graduate school, aspiring Social Workers may volunteer at their campus crisis hotline, work at soup kitchens, or tutor low-income students. They must respect diversity and demonstrate an understanding of people's differences. This experience will also help prepare them for the task ahead. The work of a Social Worker can be frustrating, with caseloads that are too high, and not enough time and/or money. They see abuse, neglect, and societies and systems that are unfair and biased. Yet, Social Workers continue on and try not to get discouraged because the work they do has a direct, immediate impact on those they serve.

Unions and Associations

The largest membership association for Social Workers worldwide is the National Association for Social Workers (NASW). Certain settings for Social Workers may require specific union membership as well. The American Association of State Social Work Boards has information about state licensure requirements (www.aswb.org), and for information about accredited schools of social work, contact the Council on Social Work Education (www.cswe.org).

Tips for Entry

1. Conduct informational meetings with Social Workers in various specialties and work settings to learn about the different career paths within Social Work.
2. Gain experience helping others from diverse backgrounds through volunteer work and community involvement.
3. Visit the National Association of Social Workers Web site at http://www.naswdc.org/ for helpful career information.
4. Spend time conducting research about graduate programs in social work. Talk to current students and arrange with the admissions office to sit in on a class.
5. Improve communication and interpersonal skills by taking speech courses and joining extracurricular clubs.

REHABILITATION COUNSELOR

CAREER PROFILE

Duties: Provides counseling and services to help people cope with the personal, social, and vocational effects of disabilities

Alternate Title(s): Vocational Counselor, Job Placement Specialist, Independent Living Specialist

Salary Range: $16,000 to $40,000

Employment Prospects: Excellent

Advancement Prospects: Good

Best Geographical Location(s): All

Prerequisites:

Education or Training—A master's degree in rehabilitation counseling is the standard for most positions

Experience—Completion of the required graduate school supervised fieldwork in rehabilitation counseling

Special Skills and Personality Traits—High energy; patience; compassion and respect for different types of people; creativity

Licensure/Certification—National certification to obtain the credential of Certified Rehabilitation Counselor (CRC) offered by the Commission on Rehabilitation Counselor Certification (CRCC); while this certification is voluntary, many employers require it

CAREER LADDER

Director of Rehabilitation Counseling

Rehabilitation Counselor

Rehabilitation Counseling Intern or Assistant

Position Description

According to the American Medical Association, an estimated 43 million Americans have physical, mental, or psychological disabilities that restrict their activities and prevent them from obtaining or maintaining jobs. Whether someone is born with a genetic mental disability or acquires a physical disability late in life due to an accident, a Rehabilitation Counselor can help that individual function in the best way possible. Rehabilitation Counselors help people with all kinds of disabilities to achieve independence. Working with clients one-on-one and in conjunction with their families and a variety of health professionals, they coordinate a treatment plan designed to develop skills, increase employability, and enhance quality of life. Their main goal is to help people with disabilities to become self-sufficient.

Rehabilitation Counselors take a multidisciplinary approach to counseling and work with clients on psychological, social, vocational, and economic issues. They spend much time getting to know the individual and learning about their interests, motivations, and aptitudes. They focus on the whole person and take family, work, and socioeconomic factors into account rather than just looking at the disability. They assess an individual's strengths and weaknesses, as well as evaluate medical and psychological reports in order to gain the most comprehensive understanding of service, program, and resource needs. These rehabilitation services may include employment, school-to-work transition service, disability management, employee assistance, personal adjustment counseling, environmental modification through technology, and independent living.

Because their job is so multidisciplinary, Rehabilitation Counselors work as part of a team with health-care and other professionals such as doctors, nurses, occupational and physical therapists, social workers, teachers, and attorneys to create an individual rehabilitation plan. They can be seen as the link and liaison between the entire team and the professional responsible for the organization and coordination of services. This way, they try to avoid gaps in service and letting anyone "fall through the cracks" in the system. Furthermore, they often provide community outreach to dispel myths and educate the public about disabilities and to eliminate environmental barriers that people with disabilities may face.

In terms of vocational counseling, Rehabilitation Counselors help people with disabilities to adapt to the world of work. Since it is difficult to achieve economic independence without employment, this is a key aspect close to the mission of most Rehabilitation Counselors. They provide vocational assessment, career planning, and job training so individuals can obtain employment skills and appropriate job placements. They may organize classes that teach a specific trade, assist with application or interview preparation, conduct job development, and arrange for on-site job coaching. Additionally, they work with employers to educate them about hiring people with disabilities and figure out how everyone's needs can be met through the hiring process.

Their duties may include:

• Determining clients' needs and eligibility for rehabilitation services
• Arranging for special services within a school or workplace such as hearing devices or wheelchair-accessible ramps
• Administering vocational inventories and other psychological and aptitude tests
• Staying informed and educated about physical, psychological, developmental, emotional, and learning disabilities
• Maintaining records and reports
• Developing community referral sources for services
• Monitoring cases to ensure that treatment plan is being followed
• Delivering presentations to community or other professionals about disability issues

Rehabilitation Counselors typically work a 40-hour workweek that may include some evening or weekend shifts. Nonprofit work environments can include community rehabilitation programs, social services agencies, residential/ group homes, schools, and hospitals. They may specialize to work with specific populations including children, geriatrics, or individuals with particular types of disabilities.

Salaries
Each year, the American Medical Association publishes a Health Professions Career and Education Directory. According to the 2004–2005 directory, the National Council on Rehabilitation Education states the average starting salary for rehabilitation counselors in the public sector as more than $23,000 and can range between $16,000 and $32,000. Including Rehabilitation Counselors working in the private sector, the average overall salary for all Rehabilitation Counselors is estimated at more than $30,000.

Employment Prospects
The Bureau of Labor Statistics states that 122,000 people in the United States were employed as Rehabilitation Counselors in 2002. However, this number does not come close to meeting the high demand. As the population continues to age, medical advances save lives that formerly would have been lost, and legislation strives to promote equal rights for people with disabilities; more and more Rehabilitation Counselors are needed to serve this growing population. The Web site www.rehabjobs.org further emphasizes that the demand for Rehabilitation Counselors is expected to increase over the next few years. The effect of vocational rehabilitation has been gaining momentum since Congress passed the Rehabilitation Act of 1973 and after subsequent groundbreaking legislation, including the 1990 Americans with Disabilities Act. Many of the professionals who have contributed to this field since the 1970s are preparing for retirement.

Advancement Prospects
Advancement prospects are good as well. Because employment prospects are growing at such a rapid rate, opportunities are available for Rehabilitation Counselors with experience to take a more senior role where they may supervise other Rehabilitation Counselors and manage a staff.

Education and Training
The standard educational requirement is a master's degree in Rehabilitation Counseling. The program is usually one and a half to two years in length and includes 600 supervised clinical fieldwork hours in addition to academic coursework. The fieldwork, or practicum, as it is often called, can take place within a range of rehabilitation-related settings. The coursework consists of classes related to individual and group counseling, psychosocial and medical aspects of disability, human growth and development, vocational and career counseling, principles of rehabilitation, case management and planning, and issues and ethics. The Council on Rehabilitation Education (CORE) accredits graduate programs in Rehabilitation Counselor Education (RCE).

There are no formal undergraduate requirements to be admitted to the master's program. However, most applicants have bachelor's degrees or significant course work in psychology, sociology, human service, or rehabilitation services. A background in interpersonal communications and commitment to service is also helpful.

Special Requirements

National certification as a certified rehabilitation counselor (CRC) is available for graduates of accredited master's degree programs through the Commission on Rehabilitation Counselor Certification (CRCC). Although this certification technically is voluntary, it is standard for employment in the rehabilitation field. In addition to the master's degree, candidates must complete an approved internship and take a certification exam to receive the credential. Additionally, some Rehabilitation Counselors may seek additional state or national counselor licensure through the National Board of Certified Counselors.

Experience, Skills, and Personality Traits

Rehabilitation Counselors should be flexible, compassionate, and creative. They need excellent interpersonal skills and sensitivity in order to work with diverse populations including clients, their families, other professionals, and the community. Furthermore, they must have patience and the ability to work at the pace and aptitude level of each individual. Also important are good judgment and analytical skills.

Unions and Associations

Many Rehabilitation Counselors belong to the National Rehabilitation Counseling Association, which began in 1958 and is a division of the National Rehabilitation Association. They may also belong to the American Rehabilitation Counseling Association (ARCA), the International Association of Rehabilitation Professionals, and the National Council on Rehabilitation Education.

Those who focus on vocational counseling may also belong to the National Employment Counseling Association, or other divisions of the American Counseling Association. In addition to national organizations, there are many local and state professional associations for Rehabilitation Counselors as well.

Tips for Entry

1. Learn more about certification issues by visiting the Web site of the Commission on Rehabilitation Counselor Certification (CRCC) http://www.crccertification.com/.
2. Conduct research on the field by looking at sites such as http://www.ed.gov/about/offices/list/osers/rsa/about.html, www.rehabjobs.org, and http://www.nchrtm.okstate.edu/.
3. Meet with Rehabilitation Counselors to see the job in action. Ask them what they like best and least about their jobs.
4. Be aware of and sensitive to disability issues. Take notice of such things as wheelchair-accessible ramps, closed-captioning for the hearing impaired, and other environmental modifications.
5. Speak with people with disabilities to discover what some of their biggest challenges are. Think about how you could help.

HUMAN SERVICE WORKER

CAREER PROFILE

Duties: Assists a variety of human service professionals to care for people in need; provides direct and indirect services to improve people's functioning

Alternate Title(s): Human Service Aide, Case Management Aide, Social Work Assistant, Community Support Worker, Mental Health Aide, Community Outreach Worker, Life Skill Counselor, Gerontology Aide

Salary Range: $17,000 to $32,000

Employment Prospects: Excellent

Advancement Prospects: Good

Best Geographical Location(s): All

Prerequisites:

Education or Training—High school diploma or GED; associate's degree or additional education helpful

Experience—One to two years working directly with people, or equivalent education

Special Skills and Personality Traits—Patience; flexibility; good communication skills; interest in helping people; nonjudgmental; ability to stay calm in a crisis situation

Licensure/Certification—Some positions may require a valid driver's license

CAREER LADDER

```
┌─────────────────────────────┐
│  Human Service Professional │
│        or Supervisor        │
└─────────────────────────────┘

┌─────────────────────────────┐
│     Human Service Worker    │
└─────────────────────────────┘

┌─────────────────────────────┐
│      Student or Trainee     │
└─────────────────────────────┘
```

Position Description

Human Service Workers provide a needed service to some of the country's most underserved populations. They counsel, support, and teach the elderly, the homeless, the impoverished, the physically and mentally disabled or ill, and the abused, to name just a few. By assisting professionals such as social workers, doctors, nurses, psychologists, physical therapists, and counselors, they help clients to achieve their maximum level of functioning and to meet their own needs in order to lead more productive lives.

Human Service Workers have evolved as a profession over the past 50 years. According to the National Organization for Human Service Education, the 1950s and 1960s saw changes in helping those in need, leading to the deinstitutionalization of people formerly serving in state mental hospitals. The reintegration of people back into their communities required new training for professionals in the helping services. This legislation, coupled with the human rights movement around the same time, brought on a new class of workers dedicated to helping clients to advocate for themselves and providing services to meet their needs.

There are many ways that Human Service Workers provide support and help to their clients. Firstly, they assess their needs, whether they require food, shelter, medication, or employment. Then they work to meet these needs through services such as Medicare and welfare, all the while advocating for their clients and teaching them how to become more self-sufficient. Also, Human Service Workers help their clients navigate through any bureaucracy and red tape that may delay services. Their tasks are diverse and may include arranging transportation for clients leaving the hospital, making home visits to those who are unable to get dressed or bathe alone, or taking members of a group home on a trip and leading their activities.

Because they can work in such a wide variety of settings, the jobs of Human Service Workers vary as well in terms of responsibility level. Human Service Workers with little education or experience primarily carry out orders from supervisory professionals, while those with more education and experience enjoy more autonomy. They may work in environments including hospitals, social service agencies, substance abuse clinics, correctional facilities, group homes, shelters, and community centers, serving a variety of populations.

Because other social service professionals are burdened with higher levels of responsibility, it is often the Human Service Worker who develops a close relationship with clients and their families. Many are close companions to their clients as they accompany them on a daily basis. Families lean on them in times of crisis because they have been there to understand the situation. Therefore, the job requires patience, compassion, and sensitivity.

Additional duties may include:

- Monitoring clients' progress and keeping notes and records
- Reporting on progress to supervisors
- Making referrals to other social service programs
- Helping with crisis intervention
- Providing hygiene care
- Teaching clients to master daily living tasks
- Keeping track of medication
- Assisting clients with finding employment and coordinating job skill trainings

Human Service Workers generally work a 40-hour week, although many positions are part-time. Local travel may be required to visit clients in their homes. Since group homes and other programs often operate on a 24-hour basis, evening and weekend shifts may be required. The shifts are draining, the pay is low, and the work is demanding; Human Service Workers have high turnover and can experience burnout rather quickly. However, those in the field find their work very rewarding and may move between different work settings and populations to avoid becoming overburdened.

Salaries

According to the Bureau of Labor Statistics (BLS), median annual earnings of social and human service assistants were $23,370 in 2002. The middle 50 percent earned between $18,670 and $29,520. The top 10 percent earned more than $37,550, while the lowest 10 percent earned less than $15,420. These figures will vary depending upon education, experience, and work setting.

Employment Prospects

Employment prospects for Human Service Workers are excellent, with the occupation being among those targeted for the most rapid growth until 2012 by the BLS. As the demand for social services increases, so does the need for Human Service Workers, particularly because they are some of the cheapest available labor in the social services industry.

The BLS expects demand for social services to expand with the growing elderly population, as well as services to grow for pregnant teenagers, the homeless, the mentally disabled and developmentally challenged, and substance abusers. Furthermore, job training is becoming increasingly important as more people are laid off and work-based programs are more prevalent. Human Service Workers can help clients enroll in these programs for retraining and skill building.

Advancement Prospects

The best way for Human Service Workers to advance is through additional education. Advancement prospects are quite good for those interested in building a career in the social services. Coursework and certificate programs that provide additional training can advance Human Service Workers to positions of more autonomy and responsibility. Additional schooling that leads to an associate's or bachelor's degree can make a big difference in terms of job title, duties, and salary.

Education and Training

While Human Service Workers are required to have a high school diploma or GED, any additional education can be very helpful in finding employment. Courses in the social and behavioral sciences, psychology, gerontology, human services, English, and human development are valuable assets.

Many community colleges offer associate's degrees in human services, as well as specializations or certificates to work with specific populations. According to the National Organization for Human Services, each of the 50 states offers at least one training program for human services education and many have more. Check out their Web site for more information at http://www.nohse.org/. Bachelor's degree programs are available for those seeking more extensive training as well.

In addition to education, Human Service Workers receive continuous on-the-job training in counseling and crisis intervention through in-service events, lectures, and seminars.

Special Requirements

Some positions may require a valid driver's license and/or a criminal background check. Driving may be required to make home visits to clients.

Experience, Skills, and Personality Traits

According to the Web site of the National Organization for Human Services (http://www.nohse.org), there are six competencies that describe the major generic knowledge, skills, and attitudes that appear to be required in all human service work. Training varies depending on the work setting, client population, and level of organization work.

1. Understanding the nature of human systems: individual, group, organization, community and society, and their major interactions.
2. Understanding the conditions that promote or limit optimal functioning and classes of deviations from desired functioning in the major human systems.
3. Skill in identifying and selecting interventions which promote growth and goal attainment. Interventions may include assistance, referral, advocacy, or direct counseling.
4. Skill in planning, implementing and evaluating interventions.
5. Consistent behavior in selecting interventions that are congruent with the values of one's self, clients, the employing organization and the Human Service profession.
6. Process skills that are required to plan and implement services.

Additionally, Human Service Workers should enjoy working with people and helping them to the best of their ability. They need to be calm and understanding, helping people patiently and without judgment. Good communication skills are essential for gaining the respect of their clients, their families, and the other professionals working as part of their team.

Unions and Associations

To gain more information about becoming a Human Service Worker, contact the National Organization for Human Services and the Council for Standards in Human Services Education.

Tips for Entry

1. Volunteer to work with people in need. Choose an agency or work environment that interests you and call them to find out about volunteer opportunities. This will provide an understanding of the demands of working with different populations.
2. Take a look at these links provided by the National Organization for Human Service Education to learn more about careers in human services: http://www.nohse.org/links.html.
3. Explore this site, which provides a list of schools that are members of the Council for Standards in Human Service Education: http://www.cshse.org/members.html.
4. Search the Web for information about certificate programs in gerontology and substance abuse. Many schools nationwide offer this type of training. See this link from Indiana University East to get an idea of some of the requirements: http://www.iueedu/bulletin/B_G/degreeprograms/bss/gerontology.htm.
5. Take courses in social and behavioral science. Develop listening, counseling, and mediating skills that will make you competitive in the workplace.

PSYCHOLOGIST

CAREER PROFILE

Duties: Studies and researches the connection between the mind and behavior of humans and animals

Alternate Title(s): None

Salary Range: $35,000 to $80,000 and up

Employment Prospects: Good

Advancement Prospects: Good

Best Geographical Location(s): All

Prerequisites:

Education or Training—Doctoral degree in psychology required with the exception of school psychology, where a master's degree is sufficient to work in most school systems

Experience—Graduate school internship/externship required

Special Skills and Personality Traits—Analytical mind; good judgment; patience and respect for others; excellent communication and listening skills

Licensure/Certification—The American Psychological Association (APA) accredits doctoral programs in clinical, counseling, or school psychology; school psychologists may also receive certification from the National Council for Accreditation of Teacher Education, with the assistance of the National Association of School Psychologists

CAREER LADDER

```
┌─────────────────────────────────────┐
│        Head Psychologist             │
│ or Director of Counseling or Research│
└─────────────────────────────────────┘

┌─────────────────────────────────────┐
│           Psychologist               │
└─────────────────────────────────────┘

┌─────────────────────────────────────┐
│           Intern/Extern              │
└─────────────────────────────────────┘
```

Position Description

Contrary to popular images, few Psychologists sit behind a big desk, taking notes while their patients lie on a couch. Furthermore, most do not wear white coats and work in labs, watching rats run through a maze. From learning disabilities and phobias to depression and anxiety, there are multitudes of problems people face that interfere with their lives. In many cases, these disorders can be cured, controlled, or at least better understood. Through research and practice, Psychologists (both directly and indirectly) help individuals with just that. They bring to light the connection between mind and behavior that drives all living creatures. As they learn more about the human mind and behavior, they can do more to help people alleviate or cope with pre-existing conditions that impair their functioning. While some Psychologists provide the counseling and treatment for these problems, others conduct the research and experiments to lead to these discoveries. Still others use their talents to consult with organizations, helping to foster communication in the workplace, in courts, in schools, and other settings.

Psychologists use a combination of intuition and science to do their jobs. They adhere to the scientific method of observation, experimentation, and analysis, but they use their creativity for interpretation and application. They pose questions and strive to answer *"why"*—why do many little girls pay with dolls and why do some people fear spiders. The theories they develop are tested through both research and practice to see which will stand up over time.

The field of psychology is so diverse that Psychologists can have a variety of specialties and take on different roles. For example, they may teach future Psychologists, test intelligence or personality, help communities, conduct research, or work as health-care providers. Often they play several roles simultaneously or throughout their careers. The various specialties within psychology are all linked by their shared interest in the connection between the mind and behavior. Different branches of psychology include:

- Clinical: Diagnosing and treating mental, emotional, and behavioral disorders
- Counseling: Helping people cope with and understand their problems across the life span
- Cognitive: Studying perception, thinking, and memory
- Developmental: Focusing on child, adolescent, or adult development
- Experimental: Performing research and controlled experiments to advance scientific knowledge
- Educational: Understanding how people learn most effectively
- Forensic: Monitoring jury/client behavior and working with the court system and legal issues
- Industrial: Focusing on workplace and human resources issues
- School: Working in public and private schools with students, parents, and staff to conduct testing, assessment, and counseling

Not all Psychologists work directly with people. Some solely conduct research and perform experiments, never providing counseling, while others meet with patients or clients one-on-one. Psychologists can be divided into researchers and practitioners, although some may do both. Researchers study behavior, whereas practitioners apply this knowledge to help people. Either way, Psychologists provide a major influence on the way people understand themselves and the world around them.

In a mental health or hospital setting, Psychologists may supervise counselors, social workers, paraprofessionals, and other counseling staff. They work in multidisciplinary teams alongside psychiatrists in order to diagnose and determine proper treatment. They may help people with issues ranging from substance abuse and domestic violence to schizophrenia and bipolar disorder. Furthermore, they may serve as consultants in times of crisis, helping victims of disasters such as earthquakes and plane crashes cope with their losses and deal with post-traumatic stress syndrome.

Their duties may include:

- Providing counseling to individuals, couples, families, and groups
- Analyzing and interpreting data
- Researching effective treatments
- Performing crisis intervention

- Administering personality, intelligence, and other types of psychological tests
- Conducting assessments and making recommendations for treatment
- Working with psychiatrists to get patients on needed medication
- Directing a variety of social service or community programs
- Developing psychological test and measures
- Leading research studies and recruiting research subjects
- Reading professional journals and papers

Many Psychologists consider their jobs to be both an art and science, requiring creativity as well as logic. They enjoy a tremendous amount of flexibility and freedom in both work tasks and hours. Often, they create flexible schedules that may include some nights and weekends, but have shorter weeks or flexible days. Some Psychologists teach, conduct research, work for nonprofit agencies, and maintain private practices, all at the same time, just several hours a week in each. It helps them to have variety, while also enabling them to keep up with the constant education and contact with colleagues needed to stay fresh and informed.

Also, many Psychologists specialize by population or issue. They may work with children, teen mothers, or senior citizens, or focus on alcoholics, obsessive-compulsives, or cancer survivors. They work in diverse settings, including clinics, hospitals, colleges and universities, schools, government agencies, nonprofit organizations, social services agencies, correctional facilities, corporations, and laboratories.

Salaries

According to the Bureau of Labor Statistics, median annual earnings of wage and salary clinical, counseling, and school Psychologists in 2002 were $51,170. The middle 50 percent earned between $38,560 and $66,970. Those employed by nonprofit agencies tend to earn at the low end of the spectrum, with Psychologists working for individual and family services averaging $37,490. Psychologists who maintain private practices in addition to work in other settings can earn considerably more if they have a strong client base.

Employment Prospects

Current employment prospects for Psychologists are good. Opportunities are expected to grow as early intervention and prevention becomes increasingly important. In particular, jobs are expected to grow over the next 10 years in health and substance abuse clinics, as well as social service agencies. Also, it is clear that respect for diversity and cross-cultural understanding are invaluable to solving world problems both large and small. Psychologists are among the professionals who train and educate people to respect one another and acknowledge differences.

Advancement Prospects

Because of the many options Psychologists have with their education and training, advancement prospects are good as well. Some Psychologists may advance to leadership positions where they run a lab, program, or department, supervising the work of a large staff. Others may find opportunities for advancement through additional specialty training, consulting, private practice, lecturing, and writing books and articles.

Education and Training

In addition to a bachelor's degree, Psychologists must have a doctoral degree as well, except for school psychologists who can work in schools with a master's degree. Many future Psychologists major in psychology at the undergraduate level, but courses in math, science, English, sociology, history, and anthropology are also helpful. While an undergraduate degree in psychology is not required for graduate school admission, a certain number of credits in psychology are necessary. The Graduate Record Exam (GRE) is also required. For more information about graduate school requirements, consult the American Psychological Association's (APA) student section at http://www.apa.org/students/student3.html.

Graduate school admission to doctoral programs in psychology is highly competitive. In addition to excellent grades and exam scores, students are expected to have research and related work experience. Doctoral programs in psychology include the Ph.D. (Doctor of Philosophy), the Psy.D. (Doctor of Psychology), and the Ed.D. (Doctor of Education). Typically, they take between four and seven years to complete and include the writing of a dissertation or other original research paper that proposes and tests a hypothesis, a one-year required internship or externship that provides practical experience, and final comprehensive exams.

Many graduate schools of education offer master's degree programs in school psychology. These programs are usually 60 credits and can be completed in two to three years, including required field work experience. They lead to certification as a School Psychologist and prepare professionals for work in private and public school settings. For more information about these programs, see the National Association of School Psychologists at http://www.nasponline.org.

Special Requirements

The American Psychological Association accredits doctoral training programs in clinical, counseling, and school psychology. Psychologists must attend accredited programs in order to practice professional psychology in the United States. In addition, each of the 50 states and the District of Columbia requires licensure for Psychologists providing patient care. See the Association of State and Provincial Psychology Boards at http://www.asppb.org for more information.

The National Council for Accreditation of Teacher Education, with the assistance of the National Association of School Psychologists, also is involved in the accreditation of advanced degree programs in school psychology. For details, see the National Association of School Psychologists at http://www.nasponline.org.

Experience, Skills, and Personality Traits

Because graduate programs in psychology are so competitive, most students gain work experience while in college, working as research assistants for professors or volunteers at crisis hotlines. Also, most applicants to graduate school work for one to four years after finishing their undergraduate studies, honing their research and/or therapeutic skills.

Psychologists should possess a combination of intellectual curiosity and compassion. They need analytical minds and exceptional judgment, but the ability to remain nonjudgmental. Psychologists who work with people should have excellent listening and communication skills; those who conduct research should be thorough, patient, and detail-oriented. All should have superb intuition and a desire to better understand the mind.

Unions and Associations

The largest professional association for Psychologists is the American Psychological Association, with more than 150,000 members worldwide. The APA has more than 50 divisions for psychological specialties including military psychology, humanistic psychology, and psychoanalysis. School Psychologists may also belong to the National Association of School Psychologists.

Tips for Entry

1. Learn more about graduate study in psychology. The APA publishes a book, *Graduate Study in Psychology, 2002 Edition,* which provides information about accreditation and program requirements.
2. There are many career paths in psychology depending upon your area of interest. Consult "Psychology as a Career" on the APA Web site at http://www.apa.org/students/student1.html. It provides detailed descriptions of different specialties and their job responsibilities.
3. Find out about the GRE exam by going to their Web site at http://www.gre.org.
4. Take courses in both normal and abnormal psychology to see what areas interest you. See about working as a teaching assistant or research assistant to a psychology professor.

CLERGY

CAREER PROFILE

Duties: Provides religious and spiritual guidance to a congregation; counsels congregation members; presides over religious ceremonies throughout the life cycle relating to birth, marriage, and death

Alternate Title(s): Minister, Pastor, Priest, Rabbi (among many others)

Salary Range: $15,000 to $100,000 and up

Employment Prospects: Good

Advancement Prospects: Good

Best Geographical Location(s): All

Prerequisites:

Education or Training—Varies by religion, ranging from no formal requirements to graduate degrees in theology

Experience—Varies, but includes extensive involvement with and understanding of one's religion

Special Skills and Personality Traits—Religious conviction; compassion and tolerance; dynamic communication, listening, and public speaking skills

Licensure/Certification—Ordination by a seminary or approved leader

CAREER LADDER

```
┌─────────────────────────────┐
│    Senior Clergy Member      │
└─────────────────────────────┘

┌─────────────────────────────┐
│          Clergy              │
└─────────────────────────────┘

┌─────────────────────────────┐
│ Assistant or Junior Clergy Member │
└─────────────────────────────┘
```

Position Description

Whether you are a believer or an agnostic, it is undeniable that religion plays a substantial role in the lives of people all over the world. Throughout history, people have fought, died, and been persecuted for their beliefs, their faith remaining steadfast in times of adversity. For many, religion is the driving force of their thinking, their values, and their homes. It is their code of ethics, affecting their actions and understanding of right and wrong. In fact, according to a survey reported on http://www.religioustolerance.org, 44 percent of Americans report that they attend religious services on a weekly basis.

Members of the Clergy are leaders who guide, teach, and interpret their religious doctrines for their followers. Many lead congregations on a daily or weekly basis, giving sermons meant to inspire. They make their sacred texts—whether the Bible, the Torah, or the Koran, among others—accessible to

their congregations, providing interpretation and understanding. They lead members in prayer and supervise the religious education that affects the future and continuation of their religion.

Clergy do not necessarily go about the career development process like other professionals. Many feel they are "called" to their work through divine intervention, rather than through career exploration and choice. It is not a nine-to-five job, but rather a vocation that permeates all aspects of their lives. Rather than working on a time clock, they are often available for their congregations at all hours, whenever they might need them.

As they nurture and support their congregations, Clergy preside over the religious rites that have taken place for generations. Beginning at birth, Clergy officiate at the ceremonies that bring new members into the world including baptisms, christenings, and circumcisions. From confirmations to Bar Mitzvahs, Clergy members also perform rites that initiate their members into adulthood. They join them in marriage based on the traditions of their faith, and they bury the dead with the same traditions, reciting speeches and prayers at funerals. They are a source of comfort to families in times of joy and pain alike.

Clergy members are powerful figures in their communities. Their speaking abilities command a room and make people pay attention and motivate them to believe. Their congregations look to them for answers to often impossibly difficult questions, so they must have the confidence and the faith to offer advice and guidance.

In addition to providing spiritual counsel, in many denominations, Clergy also have administrative responsibilities as the leader of a congregation. In these circumstances, they need to be effective managers as well as compassionate listeners. Some may be involved with fund-raising, including bringing in new members or meeting with donors who may offer support such as new buildings. Furthermore, they may meet with other community members in business, nonprofit, and other religious denominations to discuss issues of importance to their communities. They may work to develop a curriculum of tolerance and inclusion that educates other faiths about their religion.

Since the youth is the future of each religion, Clergy are often involved with teaching and youth services, providing some instruction and delegating lessons to teachers. Some Clergy provide specific religious services for children and adolescents in order to facilitate their understanding at an early stage.

Their duties may include:

- Visiting the sick or bereaved
- Serving as an authority to answer questions of religious integrity
- Providing counseling to members with personal problems
- Serving as a spokesperson for their congregation or faith
- Attending events and meetings
- Writing articles, columns, or newsletters
- Keeping up on new developments in their own and other religions
- Performing outreach and volunteer work
- Serving as missionary or supervising missionary work
- Traveling on behalf of their congregation
- Getting members involved in activities
- Providing referrals for social services, counseling, and health
- Attending conferences for continuing education

Not only are variations in jobs great for clergy members in different religions, but also within each religion, there are different denominations with unique specifications. Clergy members must believe passionately in their faith, for they are choosing not only a career, but also a lifestyle that brings with it some restrictions. For example, women may not be able to become clergy members in all religions. The Roman Catholic priesthood is not open to women, nor can women become rabbis in Orthodox Judaism and certain Protestant denominations. Furthermore, Catholics priests cannot marry.

Clergy who work with congregations must be prepared to often have very long hours. According to the Bureau of Labor Statistics, in 2002, almost one-fifth of full-time clergy worked 60 or more hours a week, more than three times that of all workers in professional occupations. Clergy are often "on-call" for their congregants, visiting their homes and offering advice day and night. It can be stressful to shoulder the weight of this responsibility; for this reason, Clergy must be comfortable with themselves and the commitment they have made to this profession.

Salaries

Salaries for Clergy vary greatly according to religion, denomination, work settings, and more. On the low end, religious priests take a vow of poverty and only receive a stipend that covers their room and board. On the high end, some ministers and rabbis working for large, wealthy congregations can earn salaries of $80,000 and above, with additional income from performing weddings and other religious ceremonies.

Additional salary information about Clergy comes from Gale Research's *American Salary and Wages Survey,* seventh edition by Helen S. Fisher, editor. These statistics state a salary range for Clergy based on geographical location, ranging from $54,040 in Washington, D.C., to $31,150 in Indiana.

Employment Prospects

Employment prospects are good overall for Clergy. As with many other nonprofit fields, they vary depending on the geographic location as well as the religion and denomination, and. However, even in the lower-need, more saturated areas, all signs show that jobs will continue to grow. Because religion is a crucial part of the lives of so many people, religious leaders will always be needed, regardless of the economy.

Advancement Prospects

Most Clergy begin at small congregations and may work to advance within that congregation or to take more senior positions at other congregations that are larger or in different locations. Once Clergy find a position in a community in which they want to settle, they tend to stay for a long time and experience great job satisfaction. In addition to congregations, they may work at colleges and universities, teaching in seminaries, or at religious and community social service agencies.

Education and Training

Each religion has its own set of educational and training requirements. The majority of Clergy hold bachelor's degrees and advanced degrees or training from a theological seminary. For example, some Protestant ministers are required to complete a three-year Master of Divinity degree from a seminary; rabbis may be required to study for five years in a Jewish theological seminary; and training for the Catholic priesthood usually involves eight or more years of study beyond high school at a seminary.

Regardless of religion, education and training for Clergy shares certain similarities. All require careful reading, understanding, and interpretation of sacred texts; basis of religious laws; history of religion; and instruction in counseling, teaching, and leading a congregation. Many also provide course work in education, psychology, and public speaking, as well as an in-depth understanding of theology and the beliefs of other major religions.

Also similarly for all religions, individuals who want to join the Clergy are never turned away if they cannot afford the cost of training. Scholarships are generally available for all that want to study and choose this path.

Special Requirements

For Clergy to begin their work after training, they must be ordained by a seminary or authorized religious leader. Each religion has different requirements for ordination, and they can be obtained from seminaries or religious leaders.

Experience, Skills, and Personality Traits

Because of their in-depth work with people, Clergy should be compassionate, patient, and nonjudgmental. They need to exercise a number of dichotomies: be excellent listeners as well as communicators; give people guidance without forcing the issue; command respect but be approachable. Clergy also should be comfortable with the rich and the poor, the sick and the well. A day may range from visiting people with terminal cancer to having dinner with wealthy board members. Although no one is perfect, Clergy should have a strong sense of ethics and morality—in a sense, be able to "practice what they preach." They must maintain strict confidentiality, as they hear about various sins and transgressions.

Furthermore, they should be knowledgeable not only about their own religion, but other religions as well and help to develop cross-cultural understanding and tolerance. They need the strength and sensitivity to use their positions as leaders to influence their members in a positive way, to become not only better Christians, Jews, Muslims, and so on, but better people.

Unions and Associations

There are many associations and training institutes for Clergy depending upon faith and denomination. These include the Jewish Theological Seminary of America, Hebrew Union College-Jewish Institute of Religion, the National Federation for Catholic Youth Ministry, the African American Ministers Association, the Center for Applied Research in the Apostolate (CARA), the National Conference of Diocesan Vocation Directors, Catholic Online, and the American Association of Rabbis.

Tips for Entry

1. There are virtually hundreds of religions with different titles and expectations for their religious leaders. Consult the Web site for the Hartford Institute for Religion Research at http://www.hirr.hartsem.edu/org/faith_denominations_homepages.html for links to many denominations.
2. Speak to the Clergy member that leads your current religious congregation. Find out how he or she prepared for such a career and what advice he or she may have for you.
3. Take college courses in religion and theology to become more knowledgeable about your own religion, as well as others from an academic rather than religious standpoint.
4. Volunteer your time working with people in need. Perform selfless acts such as working in a soup kitchen or staffing a crisis hotline to understand how to listen and provide support for those who depend on you.

PROGRAM DIRECTOR

CAREER PROFILE

Duties: Manages all aspects of a program for a social service agency; specific programs may include domestic violence or homeless services, among others

Alternate Title(s): Program Manager, Program Coordinator, Director of Programs and Services

Salary Range: $35,000 to $65,000

Employment Prospects: Fair to Good

Advancement Prospects: Fair to Good

Best Geographical Location(s): All

Prerequisites:

Education or Training—Bachelor's degree required for most positions; many positions require advanced degrees in social work, counseling, public administration, or related fields

Experience—Three to five years in social service work

Special Skills and Personality Traits—Excellent communication skills; strong managerial, leadership, and organizational skills; cultural sensitivity and ability to work with diverse populations

Licensure/Certification—Licensure in social work or counseling may be required for some positions only

CAREER LADDER

```
┌─────────────────────────────────────┐
│      Director of Social Services,    │
│ Agency Director, or Executive Director│
└─────────────────────────────────────┘

┌─────────────────────────────────────┐
│          Program Director            │
└─────────────────────────────────────┘

┌─────────────────────────────────────┐
│    Program Assistant or Assistant    │
│         Director, Counselor,         │
│          or Social Worker            │
└─────────────────────────────────────┘
```

Position Description

Social service agencies run many programs that are essential in communities. From substance abuse and homelessness to domestic violence and child protection, they provide counseling, shelter, food, and support to people in need. To ensure that each of these programs run smoothly and provide the necessary services, they need to be managed by Program Directors.

Program Directors oversee specific program areas within social services. While some of their responsibilities differ depending on the program, many basic components are the same. In all positions, they evaluate and monitor existing programs for effectiveness, as well as generate ideas for new programming or more efficient ways to do things. Program Directors think strategically about both the mission of their agency, as well as the practical aspects of offering their services such as funding and budgeting. They manage the financial aspects such as allocating funds, soliciting donations, and balancing a budget.

Furthermore, Program Directors are supervisors. They often lead staffs made up of professional social workers and counselors as well as paraprofessional aides. Frequently, they are involved with recruiting and managing volunteers as well. Since much of the work in social service agencies includes direct service with clients, Program Directors may run case meetings where individual clients' cases are discussed and analyzed in a confidential setting. Together with their staff, they develop a team treatment approach.

Some Program Directors are also direct service providers who counsel clients, while others supervise the counseling process and serve more as administrators. This situation causes mixed feeling for those in the field. Many Program Directors who have worked for a number of years as counselors or social workers feel burned out and welcome the opportunity to take on a purely administrative role. However, others find that the direct service is the part they love about the field, and they find roles that enable them to combine this with management.

Additionally, Program Directors may serve as advocates for their client populations. For example, a Program Director of a domestic violence support program may work with national domestic violence groups to set standards and policy. They may represent the field to lobby in Washington, D.C., or in state legislatures for reform.

At times, Program Directors may serve as legal advocates for their clients. They may testify on their behalf, as well as accompany them to court and explain the legal system to them, working together with attorneys. Furthermore, Program Directors also may educate legal service providers on cultural or other issues specific to their population. They are knowledgeable about all referral sources and can get their clients the assistance they need, be it legal, medical, psychological, or referrals to other social service agencies.

While managing crisis intervention on a daily basis on-site, Program Directors also look toward the big picture as to how their work can influence prevention. Social service agencies exist because people have needs that cannot be met by their current conditions. Whether it is working to educate people about substance abuse, child abuse, or providing work training for those whom are homeless, Program Directors seek to fight the causes of these problems. In an ideal world, the work they do would make their jobs obsolete by stamping out these issues and removing the need for support services.

Their duties may include:

- Writing grant proposals to support programs
- Conducting training sessions for staff members and volunteers
- Partnering with local and national advocacy groups
- Designing publicity materials
- Writing brochures, newsletters, or Web site content
- Planning events to raise money for awareness and issues
- Organizing and staffing a crisis hotline
- Presenting educational programs to the community
- Conducting client assessment and/or intake
- Serving as a liaison in the community to businesses and other agencies
- Managing a number of program sites at once
- Hiring new staff members and conducting performance appraisals
- Helping clients integrate back into the mainstream of society

Program Directors often work very closely with the executive directors and board of directors of their organization. Their jobs often require long hours, including evenings and weekends, and can be emotionally draining. Yet most Program Directors feel tremendously committed to their work. They believe in their cause and the satisfaction they feel from helping people overcome adversity makes it worthwhile.

Salaries

Depending on the size and type of program they manage, salaries for Program Directors will vary. In mid-size agencies, salaries are typically in the $40,000 range for Program Directors with at least two years of experience and graduate degrees. However, at large agencies, salaries may be in the $60,000 range and up for Program Directors with five years or more of experience. Programs that are looking to expand and have secure funding may offer higher salaries to lure in experienced candidates.

According to *Compensation in Nonprofit Organizations, 16th Edition,* a 2003 survey report of 131 benchmark jobs from Abbott, Langer & Associates, Inc., the median income for a Director of Program Services was $50,259.

Employment Prospects

Employment prospects are dependent on budgeting and may range from fair to good for Program Directors. As more awareness develops for social issues such as homelessness and violence, agencies are created and expanded to meet these needs. However, funding is often dependent on the political administration in a given city. Opportunities are best for those Program Directors with graduate degrees and several years of experience. These professionals bring a proven track record of success and are attractive to executive directors and nonprofit boards when they look to hire.

Advancement Prospects

Advancement prospects are also fair to good for Program Directors. Those with advanced degrees and experience can go on to become executive directors of agencies or comparable positions. Having learned the ropes from both a direct service and managerial standpoint, they are often well prepared for these positions. Program Directors may also serve as consultants, activists, or in other roles to assist agencies run effective programs.

Education and Training

Program Directors come to their positions from a variety of backgrounds. A bachelor's degree in a human service related field is usually a minimum requirement. Most Program Directors have graduate degrees in human service fields including social work, counseling, or psychology.

Also, some Program Directors, particularly those who are more involved with administration, advocacy, and policy, rather than direct service, have advanced degrees in public administration, nonprofit management, or law. To run a large agency successfully, degrees or course work in these areas is important.

All Program Directors experience some kind of training through their work in social service agencies. They become familiar with the different social welfare systems in various cities and the appropriate chain of command and referrals.

Additionally, they may be trained in crisis intervention, mediation, and other types of counseling strategies.

Special Requirements
For some positions, Program Directors may need to be licensed as social workers or counselors. For information about social work licensure, contact the Association of Social Work Boards at http://www.aswb.org/lic_req.shtml. For counselor licensure, contact the National Board of Certified Counselors at http://www.nbcc.org.

Experience, Skills, and Personality Traits
Program Directors must be culturally sensitive in order to work with a diverse group of clients. In some settings, specific cultural knowledge or language ability is required when working with many non-English speakers.

Even if the job of Program Director does not require direct service, most positions call for Program Directors to have previous direct service experience. Many have worked for several years as counselors, social workers, or at the minimum, volunteers who have counseled people in need. This experience is necessary in order to credibly supervise a staff of service providers. In cases where the Program Director has a different background, such as public administration, law, or nonprofit management, he or she often employs a licensed counselor, social worker, or psychologist to supervise those counseling services.

Additionally, Program Directors must be well organized, with very strong leadership skills. They need to multitask and manage many different projects at once. As strong leaders, they need to motivate staff as well as be team players. They need to retain their compassion, yet be thick-skinned and resilient.

Unions and Associations
Program Directors may belong to a variety of professional associations depending on their specialty area. These include National Association of Social Workers, the American Counseling Association, and the American Public Human Services Association.

Tips for Entry
1. Which social service issue stirs the passion in you? Volunteer your time to help homeless people, battered women, abused children, violence victims, and other populations in need.
2. Develop leadership experience through campus involvement. Take on a position that requires you to supervise others and delegate responsibility, as well as work as part of a team.
3. Work on perfecting your résumé. Make sure each description reflects the skills you have developed, especially those related to helping people, communication, and advocacy.
4. Check your local phone book to learn about social service agencies in your area. Visit an organization of interest and see if you can arrange an appointment to speak with a Program Director.
5. Explore graduate programs in social services. Check Appendix I in this book for social work and counseling programs.

ADVOCACY
AND COMMUNITY
DEVELOPMENT

PUBLIC INTEREST LAWYER

CAREER PROFILE

Duties: Provides free legal services to clients who cannot afford representation; represents nonprofit organizations

Alternate Title(s): Legal Services or Legal Aid Lawyer, Pro Bono Lawyer

Salary Range: $40,000 to $80,000 and up

Employment Prospects: Fair

Advancement Prospects: Good

Best Geographical Location(s): Large cities and rural areas

Prerequisites:

Education or Training—Bachelor's degree, followed by a law degree (JD)

Experience—Public interest internship or volunteer experience while in law school; some positions require several years of post–law school work experience as well

Special Skills and Personality Traits—Compassionate and respectful of diversity; critical thinking and analytical mind; excellent written and verbal communication skills

Licensure/Certification—All lawyers in the United States, including Public Interest Lawyers, must pass the bar exam in order to legally practice law.

CAREER LADDER

```
┌─────────────────────────────────────┐
│   Executive Director, Legal Services │
│  Director, or Nonprofit Board Member │
└─────────────────────────────────────┘

┌─────────────────────────────────────┐
│      Public Interest Lawyer          │
└─────────────────────────────────────┘

┌─────────────────────────────────────┐
│     Law student Intern, Extern,      │
│           or Volunteer               │
└─────────────────────────────────────┘
```

Position Description

There are multitudes of people in the United States who have legal concerns but cannot afford the high price of private legal counsel. As the Latin term *pro bono* suggests, derived from the Latin *pro bono publico—for the public good,* Public Interest Lawyers serve these underrepresented populations. They provide a range of legal services for low-income individuals who do not have they money for representation. They also may work for public interest groups on specific advocacy issues such as women's rights, adoption, immigration, or the environment.

There are several different settings in which Public Interest Lawyers may work. First, they may be employed by in legal aid or legal services clinics, which are generally government-funded. They provide direct service and representation in court matters to underrepresented clients. Second,

they can work for nonprofit organizations where they are hired to lobby, advocate, protect constitutional rights or help low-income people. Additionally, they can work directly for the government in such roles as prosecutors and public defenders. Finally, they can work for private law firms for designated full-time pro bono work. Many Public Interest Lawyers develop private practices representing clients in cases that they feel will help to bring about a more equitable and accessible justice system.

As attorneys for low-income people, Public Interest Lawyers meet with their clients to explain and interpret the law. They give advice, help negotiate agreements and draft contracts, intervene with other involved parties on behalf of their clients, and assist clients with the completion of government forms such as Social Security or unemployment. Furthermore, they assist and represent clients in court. The people-oriented law issues they assist with may include domestic relations, landlord/tenant, consumer protection, debtor/creditor law, administrative law, and civil rights law.

As advocates for their clients, Public Interest Lawyers assure people that they will get the help they need. In addition to providing representation, Public Interest Lawyers also act as referral sources, matching up clients with the most appropriate legal service provider depending on their needs. A large part of their time is spent networking, meeting with other service providers to share ideas and strategies, participating in listservs, and recruiting other lawyers to volunteer their expertise. As one Public Interest Lawyer put it, their goal is to consider "how we can best help people who need help." To achieve this goal, their work is very collaborative.

In public interest law centers and social action organizations, Public Interest Lawyers may research, lobby, organize and litigate. Rather than working with individual clients, they are more broad-based advocates who work on policy, reform, and class-action litigation. They are concerned with issues of human rights and social justice such as employment discrimination, fair housing, and education, to name a few.

Their duties may include:

- Conducting legislative advocacy on the federal, state, and local levels
- Writing grant proposals to fund work
- Meeting with potential funders
- Training and mentoring law students and newcomers to the field
- Marketing services to gain visibility with clients, volunteers, and potential funders
- Organizing individuals and community groups
- Increasing community outreach
- Meeting with partners at law firms to recruit pro bono volunteers
- Serving as a spokesperson for their organization, clients, or issues

Many students graduate from law school with student loans totaling $50,000 to $80,000 and above. Those students who choose to enter public interest law will not earn the high salaries of their counterparts who join the private sector, yet they often feel a sense of fulfillment that is rare in this profession. Although large case loads and poor funding may frustrate them, they are committed to their work, their causes, and their clients, and they feel they are making a difference.

Salaries

According to 2000–2004 salary information on the Web site http://www.PayScale.com, the median salary for Public Interest Lawyers in the United States is $53,000. A typical salary range shown on that same site is from $40,000 to $79,085. Jobs in the federal government tend to be at the high end of the spectrum compared with legal services and organization jobs.

As stated earlier, Public Interest Lawyers do not choose this field for the money, but for their commitment to social justice and helping others, like many others in the nonprofit sector. However, as one of the lowest-paying careers in the legal field, there are a number of grants and fellowships, as well as law school, employer, state, and federal loan repayment assistance programs (LRAPs) to help offset student debt and encourage students to enter this profession.

Employment Prospects

Despite the long hours and low pay, positions in public interest law are very competitive. Since funding for such positions is scarce, there are more lawyers looking for public interest work than there are available jobs. It is rare for recent law school graduates to obtain these jobs unless they have significant internship experience; most candidates work for several years or complete fellowships first. The best employment prospects can be found working for the government.

Advancement Prospects

Many Public Interest Lawyers continue doing the same work for many years because they enjoy it. Although competition for positions make for tight advancement opportunities, prospects are still good because of the variety of settings in which Public Interest Lawyers can work and use their skills. They may choose to seek high-level government positions such as attorney general or positions as directors of legal services or executive directors of nonprofit organizations.

Education and Training

To become a Public Interest Lawyer, one must complete an undergraduate degree as well as a law degree from an accredited law school. The Law School Admission Test (LSAT) is a standardized test required for admission. Undergraduate majors can include anything, but often courses in English, history, political science, social work, and economics are useful. Many people take time off between completing their bachelor's degree and attending law school, which can be a valuable time to gain work experience. Particularly for public interest law, prior work experience serving low-income people is helpful. Some applicants to law school interested in becoming a Public Interest Lawyer hold a master's degree in social work or nonprofit management.

Law school is the time for anyone interested in public interest law to begin gaining experience. Many law schools offer courses, clinics, and journals related to public interest law, and involvement in them is crucial to enter the field.

Students should volunteer their time, even interning for free if necessary, and gain experience providing legal services to people in need.

Additionally, because positions are so competitive, there are a number of one-year fellowships available after law school. Programs such as the Equal Justice Works Fellowship and the Skadden Fellowship Program offer recent graduates a one-year paid experience to provide legal services. These experiences are excellent preparation for a career as a Public Interest Lawyer and provide an edge in the hiring process. Bear in mind, however, that these fellowships are as competitive, if not more so, than full-time jobs.

Special Requirements

In order to practice law, Public Interest Lawyers (as well as lawyers of any kind) must be admitted to the bar of the state in which they want to work by passing a written bar examination. To qualify to take the bar exam, candidates must graduate from a law school accredited by the American Bar Association (ABA).

Experience, Skills, and Personality Traits

Experience with public interest work is an absolute must in order to break into the field, either through law school internships, volunteer work, or pre–law school, post-college work demonstrating an understanding and involvement of working with underserved populations.

Public Interest Lawyers must be able to balance their time and juggle conflicting responsibilities with ease. There is always more work to be done than hours in the day, so they need to be energetic, optimistic, compassionate, and dedicated. Furthermore, they should be outgoing, with superior written and verbal communication skills and the ability to take criticism and deal fairly with difficult people. Clients who are upset with the system may take their frustrations out on their attorneys, and Public Interest Lawyers need to be able to understand the issues and remain calm and professional. Also important are critical thinking and analytical skills.

Unions and Associations

Public Interest Lawyers may belong to a variety of professional associations, including the National Legal Aid and Defense Association, the Pro Bono Institute and the pro bono section of the American Bar Association. Furthermore, Equal Justice Works (formerly the National Association for Public Interest Law) is another important organization for law students interested in public interest careers. According to its Web site, http://www.napil.org/about.php, Equal Justice Works is an organization dedicated to "organizing, training and supporting public service-minded law students, and in creating summer and postgraduate public interest jobs."

Tips for Entry

1. Gain experience working with low-income people through volunteering at a homeless shelter or soup kitchen.
2. Learn more about public interest law through the Public Interest Law Network worldwide—http://www.pslawnet.org.
3. Sit in on a law school class and talk to law students for tips about getting into law school and preparing for a career in public interest.
4. Research different advocacy organizations that represent causes of interest.
5. Participate in community outreach projects.
6. Investigate the Law School Admissions Council and LSAT exam by going to the Web site http://www.lsat.org.

GRASSROOTS ORGANIZER

CAREER PROFILE

Duties: Lobbies through constituents to support the legislative priorities of a nonprofit organization; works with members of organization to promote activism and advocacy

Alternate Title(s): Community Organizer; Organizer; Grassroots Activist; Field Organizer

Salary Range: $25,000 to $40,000

Employment Prospects: Good

Advancement Prospects: Good

Best Geographical Location(s): All

Prerequisites:

Education or Training—No formal requirements, but most have a bachelor's degree; master's degree helpful

Experience—Entry level to several years of experience, depending on the organization

Special Skills and Personality Traits—Strong verbal and written communication skills; energy and enthusiasm; good interpersonal skills; team player

CAREER LADDER

```
┌─────────────────────────────────────┐
│   Grassroots Manager, Grassroots     │
│  Director, or Director of Public Policy│
└─────────────────────────────────────┘

┌─────────────────────────────────────┐
│        Grassroots Organizer          │
└─────────────────────────────────────┘

┌─────────────────────────────────────┐
│        Grassroots Assistant          │
│        or Nonprofit Intern           │
└─────────────────────────────────────┘
```

Position Description

Grassroots Organizers help their organizations to achieve their missions and legislative goals. Through education efforts, they motivate and mobilize local constituents to advocate and lobby on behalf of the organization. The American Heritage Dictionary (dictionary.com) defines *grassroots* as "people or society at a local level rather than at the center of major political activity." Thus Grassroots Organizers work with people in their own communities, encouraging them to take action and make a difference in the big picture.

Much of the job of Grassroots Organizers centers on lobbying and program development. They work with Capitol Hill and members of federal and state government, but unlike lobbyists, they do not lobby directly with Washington. Instead, they provide information to their organization's members to do it on their behalf. A Grassroots Organizer works with local volunteers and members to generate support for a particular program. He or she will educate community members about the pertinent issues and encourage them to contact politicians for the cause. By building community alliances, Grassroots Organizers strive to build net-

works of local leaders and create bridges to legislators through outreach.

Grassroots Organizers are policy experts. They work closely with the director of public policy in order to understand the most important issues to their cause. Furthermore, they conduct research in order to stay up to speed on all recent developments. Their days can include scanning Web sites, reading newspapers, and making phone calls to policy makers.

Education plays a major role in the work of Grassroots Organizers. They need to think of creative and effective ways to engage and inform community members. They need a firm understanding of the issues their organization supports and why. They need to be able to answer members' questions and believe in the mission and goals to convince others. Also, they should be visible and often come face-to-face with their constituents at conferences and meetings. They develop presentations as another way to explain the issues and motivate members to get involved. Writing is another way Grassroots Organizers can educate people; they may create brochures, newsletters, and other material designed to provide information.

The Internet is a major source for education, lobbying, and program development. The days of sitting at the typewriter composing letters to senators have changed. Through computers, Grassroots Organizers, constituents, and politicians all have access to e-mail and can make their concerns known quickly and directly. Many Grassroots Organizers also use the Internet to keep in touch with their members, providing weekly legislative alerts and using other strategies to keep them abreast of all current information. Grassroots Organizers must use their creativity and writing skills to keep the language simple but straightforward.

Their duties may include:

• Working with other nonprofit organizations in coalitions for related issues
• Collaborating with local, regional, and national staff and community members
• Developing campaign strategies
• Providing training and support to local members
• Creating goals and implementing education efforts
• Identifying methods for sharing grassroots information
• Meeting with groups to share information and find organizing models
• Recruiting members for activist roles
• Facilitating media outreach
• Coordinating outreach to legislators and organizing policy meetings
• Cultivating financial support and fund-raising opportunities
• Working with member groups on college campuses

Grassroots Organizers have to love advocacy, know how to lobby, and are often self-described "policy-junkies." They need to be passionate themselves in order to get others to take action and to keep finding ways to get them involved. Also, they find rewards not only in helping their organization to accomplish their goals, but also in empowering members and promoting community education. They enable people to be on the front lines, making changes for things they care about, rather than waiting for someone else to do it for them.

Grassroots Organizers may work a typical nine-to-five workweek, or longer, nontraditional hours depending upon their organization and involvement in the community. Some Grassroots Organizers travel to different regional communities, and these jobs may require a valid driver's license.

Salaries
Salaries for Grassroots Organizers vary depending on the size and location of the organization. They generally fall within the $25,000 to $40,000 range.

Employment Prospects
Employment prospects are good. Nonprofit organizations throughout the country need committed individuals to organize grassroots campaigns, so many opportunities exist

nationwide. Candidates who are knowledgeable about a variety of social issues, are familiar with lobbying, and work well with people can find a variety of positions available. Also, some organizations hire part-time Grassroots Organizers, so people may choose to combine these part-time positions with related work.

Advancement Prospects
Advancement prospects for Grassroots Organizers is also good. They may move up within their current organizations or move to larger organizations, taking on roles of increasing leadership and responsibility such as Grassroots Manager. Some may advance to become Directors of Public Policy, which is a high-level, well-compensated position. Others may choose to branch into community development, lobbying, or even political jobs.

Education and Training
There is no particular path required to become a Grassroots Organizer. While bachelor's degrees are not technically required, most position listings require them and insiders say that master's degrees can be helpful as well. Also, certain organizations may require specific degrees; for example, a job with the Sierra Club may require a bachelor's degree in environmental science or political science. A firm knowledge base in the issues and related subjects of the organization for which one wants to work is crucial.

Experience, Skills, and Personality Traits
Enthusiasm and energy, combined with leadership ability, are important traits for Grassroots Organizers. They should enjoy working with different types of people and have a good sense of what motivates and excites them. Strong writing and editing skills are necessary as well in order to produce clear written material such as newsletters and Web content. For some positions, language skills may also be an asset.

Grassroots Organizers should also have a good understanding of the legislative process and how to lobby on a national and/or state level. Experience can often be gained through campus activism, work with community organizations, internships, and other nonprofit positions. Some organizations hire Grassroots Organizers directly from college or graduate school with volunteer experience, while other expect a few years of related experience in the nonprofit sector.

Unions and Associations
Grassroots Organizers may belong to professional organizations such as the National Organizers Alliance, which promotes progressive organizing for social, economic, and environmental justice and supports organizers nationwide, or Women in Governmental Relations. They also may belong to local or issue-based organizations.

Tips for Entry

1. Get involved! Try out campus organizing or join a community development organization for a cause you care about. Learn about what it takes to motivate others.
2. Determine the issues most important to you. What cause would you be willing to work for and why?
3. Learn more about lobbying. A good example of grassroots organizing comes from the Humane Society of the United States, which has a Citizen Lobbyist Center on their Web site at http://www.hsus.org/ace/11589.
4. Become educated about the legislative process. The following links explain legislative process: House of Representatives, http://thomas.loc.gov/home/lawsmade.toc.html; Senate, http://thomas.loc.gov/home/enactment/enactlawtoc.html; tracking of federal bills, http://thomas.loc.gov/.

URBAN PLANNER

CAREER PROFILE

Duties: Develops land use plans to provide for growth and revitalization of urban, suburban, and rural communities; helps local officials make decisions concerning social, economic, and environmental problems

Alternate Title(s): Community, City, or Regional Planner

Salary Range: $36,000 to $60,000 and up

Employment Prospects: Good

Advancement Prospects: Good

Best Geographical Location(s): Major urban areas

Prerequisites:

Education or Training—Bachelor's degree required; master's degree in urban planning or related fields is strongly preferred and may be required for many positions

Experience—One to two years experience through internships or full-time work; training through graduate programs

Special Skills and Personality Traits—Excellent spatial and visual skills; good verbal and written communication skills; strong analytical abilities

Licensure/Certification—Can obtain optional certification through the American Institute of Certified Planners (AICP)

CAREER LADDER

```
┌─────────────────────────────┐
│    Director/Senior Planner   │
└─────────────────────────────┘

┌─────────────────────────────┐
│        Urban Planner         │
└─────────────────────────────┘

┌─────────────────────────────┐
│            Intern            │
└─────────────────────────────┘
```

Position Description

In the most basic terms, Urban Planners build cities, determining everything from the width of streets to the height of buildings. The job of the Urban Planner is to design and promote the best use of a community's land and resources. This includes land used for residential, commercial, recreational, and institutional purposes. Through analyzing data related to the physical, economic, and social aspects of communities, they prepare reports and recommendations and administer government plans and policies on issues affecting land use, zoning, public utilities, community facilities, housing, and transportation.

Urban Planners initially examine and assess a community's present resources and land use including streets, highways, airports, houses, schools, and libraries. They accomplish this through surveying sites, conducting research, meeting with constituents, and keeping up on current issues specific to the population such as employment and economic trends. After reporting on land use, they prepare plans for community development, using computer databases, spreadsheets, and other analytical techniques.

Urban Planners spend much time collaborating with others, including local residents, special interest groups, politicians, land developers, and civic leaders. Their goal is to create and implement a vision for each community that meets the needs of its members. Working with many different types of communities—such as small villages, large cities, suburban towns, even counties, states, and federal agencies—they analyze the problems and resources at hand and help the community to determine its best options for growth and change. Urban Planners in the nonprofit sector want to better the communities they represent by empowering their members to become involved in the proposed changes.

Their duties may include:

- Developing land use plans for aspects including housing, parks and recreation, highways and transportation, and economic development
- Compiling and analyzing data on factors affecting land use through field investigation, surveys, and research
- Running public meetings with community members and officials in order to formulate land use and community plans by uniting social, budgetary, and developmental concerns
- Designing and managing the planning process
- Assessing feasibility and cost-effectiveness of projects and making recommendations on proposals
- Preparing narrative reports such as detailed maps on land use
- Being knowledgeable about topics such economics, legal issues, and environmental regulations affecting land use
- Projecting program costs by using computer databases, spreadsheets, and analytical techniques
- Refurbishing zoning regulations on building usage, in the manner that is best for the region

Urban Planners often work in state or local government and community development organizations. They typically work 40 to 45 hours a week, with extended hours as necessary. Urban Planners employed by large organizations may have specializations, in areas including transportation, housing, economic development, international planning and development, environmental planning, policy making, urban design, or historic preservation.

Salaries

According to the Bureau of Labor Statistics, median annual earnings of Urban Planners were $46,500 in 2000. Salary can vary depending upon the type of work setting. Median annual earnings in local government, the industry employing the largest numbers of Urban Planners, were $45,300.

Employment Prospects

Employment for Urban Planners is expected to experience average growth through 2012. Opportunities will arise as a result of additional government land regulation, historic preservation initiatives, and redevelopment. Growth will also occur as a result of openings created as experienced Urban Planners change careers or retire.

The strongest area of new opportunity for Urban Planners will be within more affluent and rapidly expanding communities. Local governments will need Urban Planners to address concerns in these areas as they experience population growth.

Advancement Prospects

The abundance of advancement prospects varies by employer, geographical location, and specialization. Promotions are often dependent on size of the organization, as well as on community trends. Cities and communities that are growing have more overall advancement prospects. Without a master's degree, advancement for Urban Planners is limited; leadership positions are virtually impossible without graduate work. Some Urban Planners advance to become consultants or begin their own planning organizations.

Education and Training

There are a limited number of accredited bachelor's degree programs in urban planning; graduates from these programs may qualify for many entry-level positions. However, future opportunities will be limited without an advanced degree. Most entry-level jobs in federal, state, and local government agencies require a master's degree in urban or regional planning, urban design, geography, or a similar course of study. Other related fields of study include landscape architecture, civil engineering, transportation, or environmental studies.

Graduate programs in Urban Planning are commonly two years in length. Specializations and popular offerings may include environmental planning, land use and comprehensive planning, economic development, housing, historic preservation, social planning, community development, transportation, and urban design. Internships are often required for graduate students and provide valuable hands-on experience in learning to analyze and solve planning problems.

Because Urban Planners complete much of their data analysis using computers, computer and statistical course work and training is helpful. Also recommended are courses in disciplines such as law, earth sciences, demography, economics, finance, health administration, geographic information systems, and management.

Special Requirements

The American Institute of Certified Planners (AICP), a professional institute within the American Planning Association (APA), grants certification to individuals who have the appropriate combination of education and professional experience and pass an examination. Certification may be helpful for promotion, but is not required.

Experience, Skills, and Personality Traits

It is crucial for Urban Planners to understand physical design and the way cities and communities work. They must have excellent creative, analytic, and problem-solving abilities, as well as a strong understanding of plans and the way they are developed. Knowledge of local and state government, as well as social issues and trends, is useful. Also important is the ability to communicate well. Urban Planners meet with many constituents and often need to serve as a mediator or facilitator between the groups.

Unions and Associations

There are a variety of professional associations that Urban Planners can join for networking and professional development. These include the American Institute of Certified Planners, a division with the American Planning Association, the Urban Land Institute, and the Association of Collegiate Schools of Planning.

Tips for Entry

1. As a college student, volunteer for a local community development organization to get a feel for the work of an Urban Planner. Organizations such as Habitat for Humanity and Americorps have related programs.

2. Internships are an important way to get in the door. Contact related employers about opportunities even if internships are not required.

3. Research graduate programs to learn more about specializations within urban planning.

4. Join professional associations to network with experts in the field. Conduct informational interviews to learn more about job requirements and career paths.

5. The Web site for the American Planning Association has useful career and graduate school information at http://www.planning.org.

LOBBYIST

CAREER PROFILE

Duties: Represents a specific interest group; advocates for issues and persuades politicians to vote on legislation that supports their cause

Alternate Title(s): None

Salary Range: $30,000 to $80,000 and up

Employment Prospects: Good

Advancement Prospects: Good

Best Geographical Location(s): Washington, D.C., state capitals, and other major cities

Prerequisites:

Education or Training—No formal requirements; however, most Lobbyists have at least a bachelor's degree and many hold a graduate degree

Experience—Significant work experience required (at least three to five years), often in politics, government, or public relations

Special Skills and Personality Traits—Excellent communication skills, confidence and persuasive abilities, good understanding of the legislative and political process

CAREER LADDER

```
┌─────────────────────────────────────┐
│  Director of Policy, Independent     │
│  Lobbyist, or Consultant             │
└─────────────────────────────────────┘

┌─────────────────────────────────────┐
│  Lobbyist                            │
└─────────────────────────────────────┘

┌─────────────────────────────────────┐
│  Policy Assistant , Activist,        │
│  or other Public Policy Position,    │
│  among others                        │
└─────────────────────────────────────┘
```

Position Description

Decisions are made in Washington every day that affect the general public. Whether it is a ban on smoking, a decision about health insurance, or an environmental policy change, individuals and groups have strong feelings about these issues and the effect they will have on our society. Lobbyists can be seen as professional persuaders. They represent different public and political special interest issues such as equal rights or gun control. Their job is to determine the best way to convince politicians to vote favorably on legislation supporting the interest they represent. Lobbyists tailor their appeals both to specific individuals, as well as to group voting blocs. The act of creating these appeals that reach out to influence politicians is called lobbying.

Lobbyists can work through direct or indirect lobbying. Direct lobbying includes face-to-face meetings with members of Congress in order to provide information about upcoming bills that are awaiting votes. In contrast, indirect lobbying enlists the help of the community in order to sway political votes. These Lobbyists enlist the help of grassroots organizers and community activists. These activities can include writing articles, letters, and press releases; telephoning community members to rouse involvement; and through media appearances on television and radio.

Many Lobbyists in the nonprofit sector work for public interest organizations including environmental groups, women's organizations, and civil rights associations. Their jobs are often broken down into four functional areas:

- Advocacy
- Campaign strategy
- Media outreach
- Fund-raising

They act as advocates as well as strategists for their cause, identifying and prioritizing the issues of greatest concern. They bring both problems and potential solutions to the attention of lawmakers to get recognition for their issues and bring about change. Also, they often create campaigns or plans as ways to garner support and tackle pressing problems. Methods they use can include grassroots organizing, coalition building, community outreach, and media publicity. Media outreach includes serving as a spokesperson for their campaigns through media events, press releases, and board meetings. Furthermore, they often take part in fundraising activities such as writing grant proposals, and reaching out to foundations and donors for support.

Additional duties may include:

- Working with politicians in order to draft legislation that supports their interest area
- Maintaining strong relationships with supporters, community members, and politicians
- Serving as spokespeople for their issues
- Fund-raising for support, as well as reelection campaigns for politicians who support their cause
- Researching and analyzing legislation
- Attending congressional hearings
- Using graphs, charts, polls, and reports to provide information about issues
- Reporting to politicians about concerns and reactions from the community
- Researching issues and checking legislator's positions on various bills
- Writing newspaper and magazine articles
- Making television and radio appearances in order to garner support, interest, and awareness for their issues
- Attending parties, social events, and political functions
- Developing new policy areas
- Analyzing issue areas and determining new places to focus

To be successful, Lobbyists must be passionate about their causes and believe in the work they do. They must also have a keen understanding of the United States government, politics, and the legislative process. Since different organizations hire Lobbyists to advocate for their points of view, Lobbyists can work for the federal or state government, public interest groups, labor unions, trade and professional associations, or lobbying firms. They often work long hours, ranging from 40 to 80 hours per week. When a bill is up for vote, it is not uncommon for them to work through the night.

Salaries

The salary of a Lobbyist ranges greatly based on experience and whether they work in the private or nonprofit sector. Lobbyists may earn only $30,000 during their first year, but increase to $80,000 and above after 10 years. Some Lobbyists earn set salaries, while others work on commission.

Prior work experience can play a significant role in the salary of a Lobbyist. People coming into the field with considerable professional accomplishments and a large network of political contacts often command higher salaries. How-

ever, most Lobbyists working for nonprofits earn between $30,000 and $50,000.

Employment Prospects

Employment opportunities for Lobbyists in the nonprofit sector are good because there will always be legislation affecting various groups, and advocates and activists will always be needed. Because there are a wide variety of potential employment settings for Lobbyists in nonprofit and government, employment opportunities for Lobbyists are constantly available.

Advancement Prospects

Advancement prospects for Lobbyists are also good, since there are a number of ways that Lobbyists can advance their careers. After working for several years, Lobbyists may become partners in lobbying firms, or even start their own firms. Others may choose to take leadership positions in nonprofit organizations where they can direct government relations or public policy.

Education and Training

No specific formal education is required to become a Lobbyist. Although no set standards are established, there are many aspects of education and background that most Lobbyists have in common.

Most Lobbyists hold a minimum of a bachelor's degree; many hold an advanced degree in law, journalism, social work, economics, public affairs/policy, or political science. Other academic subjects of value for a career as a Lobbyist include public relations, communications, education, and history. Those who lobby for a particular issue, for example environmental Lobbyists, usually have a related degree in that field, such as environmental science.

Experience, Skills, and Personality Traits

Since many Lobbyists come from other fields, relevant knowledge and experience is a key factor in securing a job. Prior experience on Capitol Hill is very helpful, particularly as a congressional or legislative aide. Other Lobbyists have experience in a variety of nonprofit organizations, as well as government or political offices, lobbying firms, law firms, or public relations firms. Additionally, the field may attract former legislators or politicians who use their connections to lobby successfully.

Lobbyists are passionate about their issues and confident about their positions. To succeed as a Lobbyist, one must be outgoing and charismatic. Lobbyists must excel at all types of communication, particularly public speaking. They must enjoy meeting people and have the ability to be persuasive. Also important is a strong knowledge base of United States government and the legislative process, in order to understand the issues and processes involved.

Unions and Associations

There are several professional organizations of interest to Lobbyists. These include the American League of Lobbyists (www.alldc.org), the American Society of Association Executives (www.asaenet.org), the American Association of Political Consultants (http://www.theaapc.org/), and Women in Government Relations (http://www.wgr.org/).

Tips for Entry

1. While a student, consider a government internship. There are many semester and summer programs available in Washington, D.C. Also, explore local government opportunities on the state level.
2. Research political issues of interest to you. Take a stand and determine how you would garner support for that issue.
3. Take a public speaking class to hone your communications skills. Attend networking events to practice meeting and talking to different types of people.
4. Explore state Public Interest Research Groups (PIRGs) by visiting the Web site http://www.pirg.org/. They are an alliance of state-based, citizen-funded organizations that advocate for the public interest.

COMMUNITY DEVELOPER

CAREER PROFILE

Duties: Works to influence the economic, social, and physical transformation and development of a community

Alternate Title(s): Real Estate Developer, Economic Development Associate, Community Development Corporation Associate

Salary Range: $25,000 to $45,000 and up

Employment Prospects: Good

Advancement Prospects: Good

Best Geographical Location(s): All with a focus on inner cities and rural areas

Prerequisites:

Education or Training—At the grassroots level, no formal requirements; at larger organizations, bachelor's degrees are required and master's degrees are preferred in fields such as city planning or public policy

Experience—Combination of education and one to five years of work experience

Special Skills and Personality Traits—Excellent communication skills; background knowledge of community development and grassroots organizing; good financial skills; flexibility and passion; good problem-solving skills

CAREER LADDER

```
┌─────────────────────────────────┐
│       Associate Director         │
│   or Director of a Community     │
│  Development Corporation (CDC)   │
└─────────────────────────────────┘

┌─────────────────────────────────┐
│       Community Developer         │
└─────────────────────────────────┘

┌─────────────────────────────────┐
│  Community Development Assistant  │
└─────────────────────────────────┘
```

Position Description

There are virtually thousands of struggling communities throughout the world. While many professionals work to improve communities and the lives of those who live there, the field of community development is unique because it incorporates community residents into the decision-making process and empowers them to better to their own neighborhoods. According to Paul C. Brophy and Alice Shabecoff in their book *Careers in Community Development,* the definition of community development is "the economic, physical, and social revitalization of a community, led by people who live in the community."

Nonprofit organizations that aim to enhance communities are generally called community development corporations or CDCs. They are frequently locally based, grassroots groups who are led in part by members of the neighborhoods undergoing the change. Their board of directors encompasses both community members and leaders. CDCs take a three-pronged approach to revitalizing communities, focusing on economic, social, and physical enhancement.

Community development organizations cannot possibly do their work alone. They have many partners who enable them, as well as their community members, to see positive change. These partners include businesses (from supermarket chains opening new stores to real estate developers); service providers (offering health care, counseling, and so on); academic institutions (providing funding, research, and volunteers); policy, advocacy, and trade organizations (working on legal and policy issues); and consultants who can provide guidance.

There are several ways in which Community Developers can work to bring about economic change. They work to get private investors involved. By encouraging corporations, businesses, and wealthy individuals to come into low-income areas, they seek to spread the economic benefits to the people living there. To get investors interested, Community Developers appeal to both their softer and practical sides, playing up both the economic benefits as well as the social ones of doing something for the greater good.

Another way to influence change is through workforce development. Community Developers help create jobs for neighborhood residents. They collaborate with local employers to build job descriptions and advertise opportunities. Additionally, they may develop training and certification programs to get community members up to speed on necessary skills. These activities help residents find viable work so they can become an economic force in their neighborhood.

Housing plays a major role in community development, affecting economic, social, and physical factors. Some Community Developers are real estate experts, working together with commercial developers to buy and renovate properties. Others provide financial counseling to community members and find ways to finance low-cost mortgages, turning them from renters to homeowners who are further vested into their neighborhoods. For those who still will not be able to afford that transition, the development of affordable housing options is paramount. The removal of unsafe and unsightly buildings does a lot for physical improvement. Imagine the difference in a community once buildings are taken down that have broken windows, barbed wire, and burned-out walls.

Community Developers also work to affect social change. One way is through youth organizing, by working with community youth and getting them involved in after-school programs, academics, and advocacy. As the future of their communities, youth are targeted to become community organizers so they can learn about their neighborhoods and how to lead. They may serve as mentors and plan projects for improvements.

Working with service providers is another way Community Developers fight for social change. By partnering with various agencies, they can ensure that residents will get their social needs met, such health care and vaccinations, literacy programs, parenting resources, crime control, disability services, mental health counseling, and more.

Furthermore, Community Developers can influence public policy. They may meet with lawmakers to advocate on behalf of community issues. Also, they may mobilize community groups to do their own grassroots organizing and activism.

While Community Developers and CDCs cannot change a community from poor to rich, they can make it safer, cleaner, and more inhabitable, thus transforming the lives of its residents. They use a philosophy of self-help and self-improvement to offer the tools and teach residents the skills they need to be self-sufficient. By mobilizing community residents and serving as advocates, they inspire members to take pride in their communities and become involved.

Additional duties may include:

- Working with community youth to forge new enterprises
- Starting new businesses
- Supporting entrepreneurs interested in contributing to the community
- Raising capital and other types of funding
- Analyzing and assessing community needs
- Running meetings
- Balancing annual budgets
- Initiating new programs
- Securing zoning approval for buildings

There are a number of options and paths one can take in a community development career. Community Developers can work at the local, national, or international level. They can focus on specific places such as inner city Chicago or rural North Dakota. Additionally, they can work to serve specific populations such as Chinese immigrants or victims of domestic violence.

Community Developers may also choose to focus in a specific area of community development as a full-time job. There are specialists who do real estate development, economic development, youth organizing, job development, and more.

Overall, Community Developers are passionate about their work. They are committed to their cause and their jobs, often working long hours into evenings and weekends.

Salaries

Salaries for Community Developers are determined by several factors. One is the size of the CDC or other organization of employment, as well as the geographical location. Another factor is the education and experience level of the Community Developer. The type of position also plays a role. For example, those working in real estate or economic development tend to earn more than those do in job or youth development. Generally, Community Developers may begin their positions in the $25,000 to $45,000 range, but can advance from there.

Employment Prospects

Employment prospects for Community Developers are good as the field continues to evolve and grow. According to Brophy and Shabecoff's book, CDCs grew by 64 percent between 1997 and 2001, and such growth is expected to continue. Other nonprofit groups, such as faith-based and social service organizations, will also grow and expand the jobs they offer in the community development field. Because the field offers diverse opportunities for those with different skill sets, more jobs will be available. People find employment in the field through grassroots volunteering, internships, and educational programs.

Advancement Prospects

Advancement prospects will also be good for Community Developers, due to the flexibility of the field. Whether one's niche is as a community organizer, policy analyst, or housing professional, all Community Developers have multiple responsibilities and gain many skills that will help them move up. Graduate and training programs provide another avenue for advancement, often enabling a professional to become eligible for a higher-level position with a higher salary.

Community Developers may also go from working or even directing a CDC to beginning their own. They may also move from small local organizations to larger national or international ones.

Education and Training

To get into the field of community development, there are several different academic paths to take. At the grassroots level within small CDCs, it may be possible to get started without a bachelor's degree, but it will be needed eventually for advancement. Most Community Developers have a minimum of a bachelor's degree, and many have a master's degree as well.

Educational requirements vary depending upon area of specialty. For example, a Community Developer who wants to focus on housing development may study urban planning, architecture, engineering, real estate, or business/finance. One who is interested in pursuing social issues may study social work or public health. Other helpful fields are public policy, public administration, and economics. Knowledge of low-income financing programs is also useful.

Experience, Skills, and Personality Traits

An excellent way to get started in the community development field is through internships and volunteer work. Not only will this provide valuable experience to get in the door, but it also helps individuals to determine which aspect of community development is most interesting to them.

Most Community Developers are like entrepreneurs, in that they need to determine what initiatives are important and then figure out ways to manage and fund them. They need a good business sense and financial background, combined with a sensitivity and understanding of lower-income populations. It is crucial that they are able to work with a wide variety of people.

Furthermore, they should be excellent communicators, as both writers and speakers. Organizational, project management, and analytical skills are especially important, as is an ability to focus on details as well as see the big picture. Flexible and resilient, Community Developers must have thick skins to accept failure of their CDCs. They must be able to solve problems, come up with creative alternatives, and bounce back from adversity. Also, they must deeply

committed in order to work the long hours needed to get their job done.

Unions and Associations

Community Developers may belong to the National Congress for Community Economic Development (NCEED) which is the main trade association for the field. Also, the Community Development Leadership Association (part of NCEED) is a good resource for new practitioners in the field. Other associations include the National Neighborhood Coalition, the National Community Reinvestment Coalition, the National Association of Community Action Agencies, InterAction (American Council for Voluntary International Action), and the Community Development Society.

Tips for Entry

1. Join the Community Development Leadership Association (CDLA) (http://www.ncced.org/programs/cdla/index.html), an association specifically geared toward new professionals in the field. Funded by the Ford Foundation, it keeps students who have participated in NCEED programs engaged in the community development field. Some of its services include discussion groups, newsletters, and training programs.

2. Volunteer your time in local communities in need. Volunteering or interning can introduce you to community organizing and development as a career, make valuable contacts in the field, and give you the opportunity to help others. Try contacting programs such as Habitat for Humanity (http://www.habitat.org/) and Americorps (http://www.americorps.org), as well as local neighborhood organizations that can be found in the phone book.

3. There are several "intermediaries" in the community development field: organizations with missions to help community development groups. Learn more by going to the Web site of three big ones: the Neighborhood Reinvestment Corporation (http://www.nw.org/network/home.asp), the Local Initiatives Support Corp. (http://www.lisc.org/), and the Enterprise Foundation (http://www.enterprisefoundation.org/).

4. Some colleges and universities offer degrees in community economic development. Take a look at Cornell University's master's degree program in community and rural development (http://www.cals.cornell.edu/dept/cardi) and Los Angeles Trade-Technical College's certificate and associate's degree program (http://www.cdtech.org)

5. Explore training programs in community development through organizations such as the Community Development Training Institute (http://www.ncdaonline.org/cdti) and the Community Revitalization Training Center (http://www.netwalk.com/~crtc).

YOUTH ORGANIZER

CAREER PROFILE

Duties: Mobilizes and motivates young people in a community to take action; works on behalf of specific causes geared at enhancing and developing the lives the community youth

Alternate Title(s): Youth Activist, Youth Developer, Program Coordinator, Youth Worker, Lead Organizer, Youth Development Professional, Youth Leadership Trainer

Salary Range: $18,000 to $40,000

Employment Prospects: Good

Advancement Prospects: Good

Best Geographical Location(s): All, with particular emphasis in inner cities and rural areas

Prerequisites:

Education or Training—Bachelor's degree required for many positions, but not all

Experience—Prior work or volunteer experience with youth

Special Skills and Personality Traits—Patience, flexibility, and understanding; ability to develop rapport with young people; good leadership skills; excellent communication and interpersonal skills

Licensure/Certification—Some positions require a valid driver's license and car

CAREER LADDER

```
┌─────────────────────────────┐
│  Director of Youth Services │
└─────────────────────────────┘

┌─────────────────────────────┐
│      Youth Organizer        │
└─────────────────────────────┘

┌─────────────────────────────┐
│     Volunteer or Intern     │
└─────────────────────────────┘
```

Position Description

Although it sounds trite, the youth really are the future of our communities. As they grow up and make different life choices, they will become the adults who can affect what will happen to their neighborhoods. For this reason, an important component of the community development field is youth development. Youth Organizers work with young people, usually between the ages of 10 and 20, mobilizing and motivating them to take action and effect change within their communities.

According to the National Youth Development Information Center, youth development is "a process which prepares young people to meet the challenges of adolescence and adulthood through a coordinated, progressive series of activities and experiences which help them to become socially, morally, emotionally, physically, and cognitively competent." The goal is to concentrate on the broad development needs of youth, which is positive, rather than focusing on eliminating youth problems, which is negative. Youth Organizers have a background in youth development, enabling them to understand the needs and goals of the population with which they work.

Youth Organizers coordinate campaigns to be led and launched by adolescents in their communities. They ask: "What are the important issues facing young people here?" "How can change occur?" and "How can we get our message across?" Rather than coming up with the answers themselves, they are trained facilitators who can work with the experts—the young people—to develop the ideas on their own.

The campaigns may include topics such as fighting crime, promoting diversity, voter registration, social justice, and preventing violence as well as issues such as safety, immigrant rights, domestic violence, sexual harassment, and school change. Youth Organizers meet with young people at community centers and classrooms to develop plans. They strategize about education and advocacy programs to get their messages across and get other community members involved.

Youth Organizers may focus in fund-raising, programming, research, policy, advocacy, or job and training opportunities, among others. Youth organizing is a collaborative field. In order to promote public awareness of youth issues, Youth Organizers work with other organizations and agencies that provide youth services, including schools, clinics, and religious institutions. Together they may plan programs such as cultural events (shows and concerts) and community service projects ("clean-up-the-park day").

Another aspect of youth organizing is leadership development. Youth Organizers work to identify and nurture young leaders. Their goal is for young people to become productive contributors to their neighborhoods. They build on existing competencies and empower youth to develop their strengths. Young people are encouraged to lead meetings, create teams, research issues, and devise their own campaigns.

Youth Organizers are both mentors and teachers. They help teens learn problem-solving skills and independence. Furthermore, they often demonstrate socially appropriate behavior through their own models. Youth Organizers motivate young people to feel a sense of purpose and plan for their future. By bringing issues such as vocational awareness, health, and creativity to light, they foster personal responsibility and understanding.

Their duties may include:

- Providing leadership training seminars
- Developing training manuals
- Creating action plan and organizing strategies
- Building and maintaining relationships with other youth development agencies
- Writing monthly reports of activities
- Making classroom presentations
- Producing flyers and outreach materials
- Conducting community outreach
- Planning schedules and work hours
- Supervising staff
- Identifying key issues
- Recruiting and retaining youth volunteers
- Developing a youth advisory board
- Building relationships with local businesses, government, and nonprofit groups

Youth Organizers may work for groups at both the national and local level. National organizations may have different strategies for mobilizing youth. They can reach out to specific chapters, sometimes on college campuses. Local organizations do more grassroots organizing, meaning they concentrate their efforts within their own communities. However, this is not to say that both national and local groups do not spend time getting all interested citizens involved.

Youth organizing is not a nine-to-five job. Youth Organizers often must work some evenings and weekends to accommodate the school schedules of teens. One of the most important factors for success as a Youth Organizer is the ability to develop rapport with youth. Someone in this position must be able to treat young people with respect and tolerance, maintaining credibility as both one who understands them but also as an authority figure.

Salaries

Youth Organizers typically earn between $18,000 and $40,000, according to experts in the field. Average starting salaries are usually in the low to mid $20,000 range. Some positions that are national in scope may pay more, especially for Youth Organizers with considerable education and experience.

Employment Prospects

Employment prospects are good for Youth Organizers. As the field of community development grows and more community development corporations (CDCs) spring up nationwide, there is a greater need for Youth Organizers to work within these neighborhoods. While community developers work with the overall population, Youth Organizers get the buy-in for change from the young people who can help contribute to the mission.

Positions for Youth Organizers exist nationwide, but the greatest number of opportunities will be found in rural and inner city areas.

Advancement Prospects

Youth Organizers may advance to a variety of positions in the youth development or community development field. They may take leadership positions directing youth services for a nonprofit organization, or they might decide to specialize in another area of community development such as housing. Furthermore, they can continue on in advocacy, working as organizers or lobbyists for a variety of causes. Others may seek graduate degrees in fields such as social work, counseling, education, urban planning, or law, where they can continue to work with young people.

Education and Training

While it is not always necessary, many positions for Youth Organizers do require bachelor's degrees. Fields of study are diverse and can include education, political science, sociology, psychology, human development, social work, and communications.

Equally important to education is experience working with young people and knowledge of the issues at hand. Internships or volunteer experience working with this age group is crucial in demonstrating that one understands their needs. Some students begin working part-time as Youth Organizers while in college.

Additionally, whether the job involves immigrant rights, literacy, or promoting diversity, Youth Organizers need to be cognizant of the facts and ideas associated with these issues. A background in public policy can be helpful for advocacy work.

Special Requirements
Some positions for Youth Workers require them to have a valid driver's license and a car.

Experience, Skills, and Personality Traits
As the title implies, it is valuable to be organized as a Youth Organizer. They should also be self-motivated and creative, able to work independently as well as part of a team as both a leader and member.

Youth Organizers do not need to be from the community in which they work, but any personal background they have is helpful and adds to their credibility. It is crucial that they project understanding and tolerance without ever being condescending. They need to be comfortable working with young people from a wide variety of backgrounds. Prior volunteer experience demonstrates that they can relate to those who are younger with humor and ease.

Also, Youth Organizers must be ethical and trustworthy. They often handle confidential and sensitive information from their groups. They should be excellent communicators who can teach, enlighten, and build relationships. With creativity, they help young people devise ways to get their ideas across and find their voices. Additionally, they need to be compassionate and dynamic, able to lead, motivate, and mentor young people.

In some communities where different languages are spoken, positions for Youth Workers may require specific language skills.

Unions and Associations
Youth Organizers may belong to professional associations such as the National Assembly of Health and Human Services Organizations, America's Promise: The Alliance for Youth, the Center for Teen Empowerment, and the American Youth Policy Forum. Furthermore, they may gain valuable information from the National Youth Development Information Center.

Tips for Entry
1. Explore this link, http://www.ssw.umich.edu/youthAndCommunity/pubs/Community_Youth_Organizers_Bookshelf.pdf, compiled by the University of Michigan's School of Social Work. It is a comprehensive list of resources to help community Youth Organizers do their jobs.
2. The Web site of the National Youth Development Information Center offers extremely helpful information to those interested in the youth development field. It provides a youth development library, policy and advocacy information, and job listings, among other resources. Consult http://www.nydic.org.
3. There are many organizations that provide leadership training and activism resources for young people. See Youth on Board (http://www.youthonboard.org/) and What Kids Can Do (http://www.whatkidscando.org/) for ideas.
4. If you are committed to working with young people, demonstrate this interest through an internship or volunteer position. Work as a tutor or youth program coordinator for a local nonprofit. Try sites such as http://www.servenet.org/ and http://www.volunteermatch.org/ to get started.
5. Consider mentoring as an excellent way to gain experience helping young people. These mentoring organizations have information as to how you can get involved: Big Brothers Big Sisters, http://www.bbbsa.org; MENTOR/National Mentoring Partnership, http://www.mentoring.org; Boys and Girls Clubs of America, http://www.bgca.org; National Dropout Prevention Centers, http://www.dropoutprevention.org; Points of Light Foundation, http://www.pointsoflight.org; 4-H, http://www.4-h org/fourhweb.

ECONOMIST

CAREER PROFILE

Duties: Researches and analyzes the way society uses resources to turn out goods and services for use

Alternate Title(s): Economic Research Analyst, Economic Affairs Officer

Salary Range: $50,000 to $125,000 and up

Employment Prospects: Fair

Advancement Prospects: Fair

Best Geographical Location(s): All, with emphasis on major research centers

Prerequisites:

Education or Training—Bachelor's degree required for entry-level research positions; master's degree and preferably Ph.D. needed for all other positions

Experience—Several years of academic or work experience

Special Skills and Personality Traits—Excellent analytical, problem-solving, and numerical skills; strong research and writing ability

CAREER LADDER

```
┌─────────────────────────────┐
│      Senior Economist       │
└─────────────────────────────┘

┌─────────────────────────────┐
│          Economist          │
└─────────────────────────────┘

┌─────────────────────────────┐
│      Research Assistant     │
└─────────────────────────────┘
```

Position Description

People always struggle to do their best to meet their needs with the resources they have. In many ways, this basic human struggle is the definition of the social science of economics. Economists study the ways in which society uses its resources to meet its needs.

Economists examine resources across societies such as land, labor, machinery, and raw materials. Then they consider how these resources will be able to produce the goods and services that will satisfy material and human needs. They analyze the costs and the benefits involved with the production process, taking into account the principle of supply versus demand. Because resources are scarce while wants are often unlimited, this makes the study a challenge.

Using scientific models, Economists strive to understand human behavior. Faced with limited resources, why do people make the choices they do and how does it affect society overall? Economists conduct both quantitative (number and statistic-based) and qualitative (word and narrative-based) research, using these methods to study relationships between people and money, policy, and industry. They may examine tax rates, inflation, unemployment, and energy costs.

Through their research, Economists can also affect policy. They conduct independent research, as well as review and analyze existing studies. After conducting their research, Economists generate reports on their findings. The reports often make connections between policy and economic trends and effects. It is crucial for these reports to written clearly so they can be understood by people in other professions and government leaders, since they may be used as persuasive tools. Their findings and recommendations can play a major role in influencing policy.

Economists in the nonprofit sector may work in the domestic or international realm. They serve a role in addressing important public needs. Domestically, they may work for professional associations conducting research into employment trends and their economic causes and effects, and forecasting labor trends. They may work for community development organizations studying the options for growth and investment. Furthermore, they may work for think tanks or research institutes on projects related to agriculture, rural development, urban development, labor issues, policy, or industrial trends.

For advocacy groups, Economists can make recommendations that will help affect policy and funding. For example, an Economist working for the Environmental Defense Fund can study the economic impact of overdeveloping a specific wetland area. This study can ensure that the land will be preserved.

Internationally, Economists work for organizations such as the United Nations or the World Bank, conducting research on the world economic spectrum. They may analyze issues including foreign trade and trade policies, the impact of world economies on one another, exchange rates, and international urban, agricultural, or rural development. Furthermore, Economists are employed by colleges and universities where they often have both teaching and research responsibilities.

Also, some Economists conduct research specifically about the nonprofit sector. They might identify problems (such as the demand for volunteer labor), measure outputs and results, analyze organizational structure and behavior, and forecast trends. Nonprofits have an important economic function as the third sector between private (business) and public (government), and they both affect and are affected by both these areas.

Additional duties may include:

- Formulating development proposals
- Drafting reports, tables, and statistical charts
- Organizing and attending seminars
- Preparing policy briefs
- Assisting in trade negotiations
- Maintaining and analyzing large databases
- Developing empirical (evidence-based) models and studies
- Presenting results to business and nonprofit leaders, as well as to policy makers
- Designing analytical frameworks for data and methods for data collection
- Conducting mathematical modeling
- Monitoring legislation and its effect on various organizations and industries
- Keeping abreast of world financial news

Economists work independently, spending many hours alone with their research. However, they also are frequently part of teams in which they work together to share information and collaborate on reports. Occasional travel may be required for empirical research, depending on the Economist's specialty.

Salaries

Salaries for Economists in the nonprofit sector vary depending on their work setting and level of education and experience. According to the Bureau of Labor Statistics, median annual wage and salary earnings of Economists were $68,550 in 2002. This figure includes those working in both the nonprofit and private sectors.

Additional information comes from a summary at www.workforce.com citing a 2003 study about pay in the not-for-profit sector. According to this study, the median cash compensation for a nonprofit Economist at the top of the field was $96,200.

Employment Prospects

Employment prospects for Economists are fair. There is a growing movement to provide more extensive research into the nonprofit sector, which may add jobs at nonprofit-related research institutes. As the economy gets even more complex with technological advancements, opportunities will also arise in growing fields such as community development, professional associations, and advocacy groups, as well as at international nongovernmental organizations (NGOs).

The Bureau of Labor Statistics expects average growth for Economists through 2012. Jobs will be most plentiful for those Economists with Ph.D.'s.

Advancement Prospects

Economists can advance through extended education and training. For those Economists without a Ph.D., this credential is critical for advancement. A Ph.D. degree in economics or related fields usually takes between five and seven years to complete.

Additionally, Economists may move to different types of nonprofit organizations or take on leadership positions where they can lead research teams or departments.

Education and Training

With a bachelor's degree, those who majored in economics are eligible for jobs as research assistants in the nonprofit sector or for entry-level government positions. Professional Economist positions require advanced degrees, usually a doctorate in economics. In addition to several years of course work, a doctorate also requires an original, extensive research paper or dissertation, which takes several more years to finish.

Economics is broken down into two areas of study: microeconomics (study of supply and demand of individual areas of activity such as a household or organization) and macroeconomics (study of whole systems and total production of goods and services). Related fields can include mathematics, history, philosophy, business, statistics, public policy, urban development, econometrics, and political science.

Economists may also specialize in a number of economic sectors such as health, the environment, education, law, or housing development.

Experience, Skills, and Personality Traits

Economists are required on a daily basis to analyze complex information. They must be able to conduct statistical analyses and often need advanced computer skills as well. Excellent research, writing, and organizational skills are essential for producing in-depth reports; strong communication skills are crucial for presenting findings.

Furthermore, Economists working for international organizations may be required to speak and understand several languages, depending on the position.

Unions and Associations

There are a number of professional associations to which Economists may belong, including the American Agricultural Economics Association, the American Economics Association, the National Association for Business Economics, the Association of Environmental and Resource Economists, the American Real Estate and Urban Economics Association, and the Society of Labor Economists.

Tips for Entry

1. Many Economists are employed by international organizations such as the World Bank or the United Nations. Take a look at their Web sites at http://www.worldbank.org/ and http://www.un.org/.

2. The American Economics Association lists jobs for Economists on their Web site: http://www.aeaweb.org/joe/. Many of the jobs are in the nonprofit sector.

3. Explore different areas of economics by taking a wide variety of courses. In addition to required courses that cover basics such as microeconomics and macroeconomics, consider electives on topics such as industrial organization, globalization, environmental economics, the public economy, political economy, and international trade.

4. Learn more about the principle used by Economists called game theory, a field of study that bridges mathematics, statistics, economics, and psychology. It is used to study strategic choices and economic behavior and the way organizations act when their actions affect the behavior of others. This site can help you begin: http://www.gametheory.net/.

5. Speak to professors of economics about work as a professional Economist in the nonprofit sector.

ARTS AND CULTURE

MUSEUM EDUCATOR

CAREER PROFILE

Duties: Educates the public about museum information, programs, services, and exhibits; creates learning opportunities

Alternate Title(s): Educational Program Manager; Coordinator of School or Family Programs

Salary Range: $20,000 to $40,000

Employment Prospects: Fair

Advancement Prospects: Fair

Best Geographical Location(s): Major cities

Prerequisites:

Education or Training—Bachelor's degree; master's degree is also helpful. Course work related to education or specialty of museum, such as art history or science

Experience—Prior work, volunteer, or internship experience at museums and/or teaching

Special Skills and Personality Traits—Excellent communication skills; creativity, flexibility, and multitasking skills; ability to work well with people

CAREER LADDER

```
Director or Curator of Education
```

```
Museum Educator
```

```
Education Assistant or Administrative
Assistant, Intern, or Volunteer
```

Position Description

Museum Educators develop high-quality educational programs, materials, and activities for all kinds of museums including museums of art, history, science, culture, and children's museums. Museum Educators serve as liaisons between the museum collection and visitors, creating both informal and curriculum-based learning opportunities. They help disseminate information to the public, plan exhibitions, work with families, lead scholarly panels, and work to provide accessibility of programs. Depending upon the type of museum, the work of a Museum Educator will vary, ranging from planning hands-on exhibits at a science museum to arranging tours at an art museum.

Education departments also vary between museums in terms of the population they serve. Large museums cater to a wide audience, and Museum Educators plan programs for children (grouped by age range), adolescents, adults, families, senior citizens, and people with disabilities and special needs. Since each of these groups is different, so are the pro-

grams and education offered by the museum, ranging from film showings to scholarly symposiums.

In terms of work specifically with children, Museum Educators often collaborate with schools and community organizations to expose children to museums and create educational programs geared toward different age groups. For example, they may lead creative art projects for elementary school groups and provide multimedia lectures on museum pieces and tours for middle and high school students. Also, there is a movement to bring museum education into the actual classrooms, so Museum Educators make visits to public schools where they plan and write an educational curriculum for teachers and students. Whether the topic is Impressionist artists or prehistoric dinosaurs, they devise ways to make it engaging for students and provide professional development workshops for teachers to learn the process.

Museum Educators serve as the link between the museum and the public. One of their goals is to make the museum accessible to the public through planning programs, writing brochures and Web site content to increase understanding, and training other museum staff in the educational mission. They may write educational guides for families visiting the museum.

Another major part of the job can include recruiting, hiring, and supervising interns, volunteers, or docents. In managing these groups along with the director of education, they provide ongoing training and may delegate such tasks as tours and projects.

Additional duties might include:

- Performing outreach for community involvement
- Developing resources for schools
- Running after-school or holiday programs for families and children
- Coordinating speakers
- Creating new programs and educational strategies
- Engaging children and adults in museum collections
- Writing curriculum for both museum and school programs
- Expanding museum audience through research, teaching, and outreach activities
- Presenting to large and small groups
- Developing educational content for the museum's Web site

In order to support and promote the mission of the museum, Museum Educators interact with people of all ages and cultural backgrounds. They have pride in their museums' collections and enjoy sharing their knowledge with others. They encourage visitors to think critically, look carefully, explore, and analyze. Because they are educators themselves, they are dedicated to receiving ongoing training and learning themselves. They typically work a 40-hour workweek, but it may include evenings and weekends to match the museum's hours.

Salaries

Salaries for Museum Educators tend to start out low, usually in the low $20,000 range. Larger museums can offer higher salaries, but an entry-level position will rarely offer more than the high $20,000 range. With experience, Museum Educators can earn into the $30,000 range. According to insiders, advanced degrees help Museum Educators to command more money.

Employment Prospects

Because there are a limited number of museums, especially large museums, employment prospects are fair. There is great competition for positions at prestigious institutions, with more applicants than job openings. Graduate programs in museum studies, internships, and volunteer work can help prospective Museum Educators make the necessary connections to find a job. Smaller museums may hire Museum Educators for seasonal work only, during the school year or during the summer.

Advancement Prospects

Advancement prospects are also fair, due to the limited number of positions. Museum Educators may try to move from a smaller museum to a larger one, or to move up within their current institution to a director of education or other senior position. Others may focus on a different area of museum work, such as visitor services, curatorial, or development, while some may go on to further pursue arts education through full-time teaching.

Education and Training

It is beneficial for Museum Educators to have a background in the specialty of the museum (such as art, history, or science) as well as knowledge of educational theory and practice. A bachelor's degree is required, and a master's degree preferred for most positions.

A master's degree in museum studies is becoming an increasingly important credential for employment in the field. There are a number of programs throughout the United States, and most offer specialization in museum education. Through these programs, students complete required internships at museums that help them get in the door for permanent positions.

Experience, Skills, and Personality Traits

Volunteer work or internships in a museum, as well as teaching or training experience, is invaluable for learning about the job and is a prerequisite for most positions. Good writing and interpersonal skills, combined with strong content knowledge related to the museum's offerings are key. Museum Educators should also be creative and flexible, with a customer-service focus.

Foreign language skills are often very helpful as well, especially in large museums that attract many international visitors. Sign language skills can also be an asset.

Unions and Associations

Museum Educators may belong to the American Association of Museums and its related organization, the Standing Professional Committee on Education (EdCom); and local organizations for Museum Educators such as the New York City Museum Educator's Roundtable.

Tips for Entry

1. Find a local museum of interest and volunteer. There are many opportunities that include interfacing with the public, giving tours, and working with children.

2. Learn more about museum careers through the following link: http://www.aam-us.org/resources/reference_library/3careers.cfm.
3. Check out job descriptions for Museum Educators at Web sites such as http://www.museumjobs.com and http://www.aam-us.org/aviso/index.cfm.
4. Research graduate programs in museum studies to learn more about the work. *Graduate Training in Museum Studies: What Students Need to Know* by Marjorie Schwarzer, published by the American Association of Museums, is a good place to start.
5. Gain teaching experience through one-on-one tutoring, after school programs, and other opportunities available through your campus.
6. Visit museums and pay attention to all the educational programming and materials you see.

CURATOR

CAREER PROFILE

Duties: Oversees and preserves objects in a museum's collection; plans and prepares exhibits; participates in obtaining new acquisitions

Alternate Title(s): None

Salary Range: $25,000 to $60,000 and up

Employment Prospects: Fair

Advancement Prospects: Fair

Best Geographical Location(s): Major cities

Prerequisites:

Education or Training—Undergraduate and advanced degree, preferably in art history or other area of specialization

Experience—Extensive art history or other appropriate academic background including museum experience; contribution within one's specialty field

Special Skills and Personality Traits—Strong writing skills; excellent judgment and analytical abilities; creativity and flexibility

CAREER LADDER

```
┌─────────────────────────────────────┐
│   Chief Curator or Museum Director   │
└─────────────────────────────────────┘

┌─────────────────────────────────────┐
│              Curator                 │
└─────────────────────────────────────┘

┌─────────────────────────────────────┐
│          Assistant Curator           │
└─────────────────────────────────────┘
```

Position Description

When you visit a museum and admire the work that went into planning a particular exhibition, you have a Curator to thank for your experience. Curators oversee and preserve the collections in museums, zoos, aquariums, botanical gardens, nature centers, and historic sites. This job has many components and includes maintaining, preserving, cataloging, studying, displaying, and analyzing the components of the collection. Curators also plan and prepare exhibits. They take pride in the aesthetic value of the exhibits and their organization and arrangement. In order to decide how an exhibition should be arranged, Curators should have a strong sense of artistic vision. The work on the exhibitions ranging from writing brochure copy, to selecting music to played in the background, to producing multimedia presentations aimed at explaining the work.

Curators are also responsible for developing the collection through acquisition. They acquire items of cultural, biological, or historical significance through purchases, gifts, field exploration, and intermuseum exchanges. Furthermore, many Curators educate the community about the museum's holdings through coordinating tours, lectures, workshops, and other public outreach programs. They promote the museum's collection and take opportunities to make it more visible. They also conduct research and contribute to scholarly articles.

Curators use computer databases to catalogue and organize their collections. Many also use the Internet to make information available to other curators and the public. Increasingly, Curators are expected to participate in grant writing and fund-raising to support their projects. Collaboration with museum staff in fund-raising and development, education, and visitors' services is frequent. Some Curators maintain the collection, others do research, and others perform administrative tasks. In small institutions, with only one or a few Curators, one Curator may be responsible for multiple tasks, from maintaining collections to directing museum affairs.

Most Curators have a specialization in a field, such as art, botany, paleontology, or history. They also may have a specialty in a particular type of art form such as sculpture or photography, as well as knowledge from a specific historical era.

Additional duties may include:

- Conducting scholarly research and overseeing projects
- Negotiating and authorizing the purchase, sale, exchange, or loan of collections
- Acquiring objects for permanent collections, as well as temporary special exhibitions
- Balancing budgets and hiring new curatorial staff
- Designing and preserving exhibits
- Educating and presenting collections to the public
- Acquiring new materials to contribute to scholarly studies
- Managing professional and paraprofessional staff including students, interns, volunteers, research associates, and assistant curators
- Teaching classes within museums or at local colleges and universities
- Participating in field work
- Working with boards of various institutions to administer plans and policies
- Completing written work such as labeling exhibits and preparing brochures
- Formulating policies and procedures
- Implementing educational programs

Supervising junior staff, interns, and even volunteers is also a part of the job of many Curators. For people with a scholarly orientation, this can be a welcome part of their work and a way to teach and share their knowledge with other. Generally, Curators work more than a 40-hour workweek, due to weekend public programs, evening meetings, and research hours. Travel may be required for Curators involved in fieldwork at large museums.

Salaries

The salary of a Curator can vary considerably by size, location, and type of institution. According to the Bureau of Labor Statistics (BLS), median annual earnings for Curators in 2002 were $33,720 in museums, historical sites, and similar institutions, while a nonprofit compensation survey by Abbott, Langer and Associates, Inc. showed the 2003 median salary for Curators to be $42,328. Additionally, salaries of Curators in large, well-funded museums can often be several times higher than those working for small organizations. The BLS states the average annual salary for museum Curators working for the federal government in 2003 as $70,100.

Employment Prospects

The Bureau of Labor Statistics expects growth for Curators to be average among occupations through 2010. The increased public awareness and interest in visiting museums is balanced by tight funding constraints.

Art and history museums remain the largest employers for Curators. While more opportunities will arise at larger institutions, the competition for these positions will increase as well, requiring substantial experience for top jobs. Art museums at universities are an additional option for Curators to find employment.

Advancement Prospects

Most Curators follow a specific career ladder for advancement ranging from Assistant Curator to Chief Curator or Museum Director. The more specialty experience, training, education, and research credits a Curator has, the better the opportunities are for advancement. Some Curators move up the ranks within the same institution; other Curators seek advancement through moving from a small museum to a larger one.

Education and Training

In order to obtain a position as a Curator, it is crucial to have the appropriate combination of education and experience. Only in a very small museum would a Curator have only a bachelor's degree. Most Curators hold a master's degree or a doctorate in fields including art, art history, history, historic preservation, archaeology, or museum studies. Curators with particular specialty areas (such as the sciences) usually have degrees in those fields. Also helpful for administrative responsibilities are courses in business, public relations, and fund-raising. A background combining a specific academic expertise with a museum studies degree may be especially attractive to some employers.

The job of a Curator requires lifelong on-the-job training and education. Much is learned through the actual work and the research and publication that goes along with it. Many Curators gain experience through volunteering and interning as students. Courses in grant writing may also be an asset.

Experience, Skills, and Personality Traits

Curators must have superior writing, research, and analytical skills in order to evaluate collections and contribute to scholarly works. In addition, they must be flexible and adaptable to handle the many varied responsibilities of their job. Also important are creativity, insight, and clear judgment in order to maintain and enlarge collections with high standards.

Knowledge of more than one academic subject and foreign languages can be helpful for Curators as they work across varied disciplines. Managerial and leadership skills are also crucial for upper-level positions.

Unions and Associations

There are several professional associations that Curators can join for networking and development. These include the

American Association of Museums (http://www.aam-us.org), the Regional Alliance for Preservation (http://www.rap-arcc.org), and the Association of Science and Technology Centers (http://www.astc.org/).

Tips for Entry

1. Explore various academic subject areas of interest and identify museums with that specialty.
2. Visit museums and try to observe and evaluate collections from a Curator's standpoint.
3. Schedule an appointment with a Curator in order to learn more about what he or she does.
4. Research graduate programs in Museum Studies in order to find out about the various topics of studies. *Graduate Training in Museum Studies: What Students Need to Know* by Marjorie Schwarzer, published by the American Association of Museums, is a good place to start.
5. View the job listings on *Aviso,* the monthly newsletter of the American Association of Museums (http://www.aam-us.org/aviso/index.cfm) in order to become more familiar with jobs and their requirements.
6. Spend time on museum Web sites to find out about internship and volunteer opportunities.

DIRECTOR OF VISITOR SERVICES

CAREER PROFILE

Duties: Manages everything related to the experience of visitors to an arts or other cultural institution

Alternate Title(s): Director of Visitor Programs, Director of Visitor Experience, Visitor Services Manager

Salary Range: $35,000 to $75,000

Employment Prospects: Fair

Advancement Prospects: Fair

Best Geographical Location(s): Major cities and towns with cultural resources

Prerequisites:

　Education or Training—No specific requirements, but bachelor's degree standard

　Experience—Ranges from two to 10 years, depending on the size of the institution

　Special Skills and Personality Traits—Excellent customer-service orientation; strong communication skills; understanding of public relations; good management ability

CAREER LADDER

```
┌─────────────────────────────────────┐
│   Director of Public Programming,    │
│ Vice President, or Director of Visitor│
│     Services (larger institution)    │
└─────────────────────────────────────┘

┌─────────────────────────────────────┐
│     Director of Visitor Services     │
└─────────────────────────────────────┘

┌─────────────────────────────────────┐
│      Visitor Services Specialist     │
│   or Assistant/Associate Director    │
└─────────────────────────────────────┘
```

Position Description

Directors of Visitor Services monitor the visitor experience to their institutions. When visitors enter a cultural institution such as a museum, Directors of Visitor Services want their experience to be inviting and welcoming from the moment they walk in the door. While experts may deem a museum great, it is the people who visit every day that guarantee it a spot in cultural history. Furthermore, the contributions from visitors who want to see what they have to offer keep museums going.

Directors of Visitor Services head the department that is responsible for informational materials for visitors. While education departments handle material geared toward educational programs and offerings, not all content produced is educational. There are maps, directories, and other pieces of practical information that are crucial for visitors to receive.

Collaboration is integral to the job of Directors of Visitor Services. They collaborate with many other museum departments, such as membership services, where they strive to use the positive visitor experience to turn visitors into members. They also work together with the education and public programming departments to ensure that visitors will have a choice of programs to attend to enhance their visit. Tours are often joint efforts between visitor services and education. Furthermore, by working with the communications department, Directors of Visitor Services are involved in brochures, newsletters, press releases, and other content that may affect visitors and their perception of the institution.

Some Directors of Visitor Services may also be involved with public programming. Programs are often targeted to specific audiences such as children, families, or international visitors. This involves even further collaboration with the education department, where they will work together to develop programming that supports the mission and develops audience attendance. The job can also include supervising interns or volunteers, as well as program evaluation.

Since museums bring in such a wide array of visitors, Directors of Visitor Services work to accommodate all populations and meet their needs. Some may specialize in providing services for visitors with disabilities, making sure stairways and exhibits are wheelchair accessible, offering sign language interpreters, and featuring brochures written in Braille. Others may work with international guests, coordinating translation services and ensuring the availability of materials in many languages. These services help to enhance the overall visitor experience for everyone.

Additionally, Directors of Visitor Services are strategic. They seek not only to provide services for their current visitor base, but also to expand their audience. They may market their programs through meetings with community groups, advertising, and conducting outreach. It is important for them to be responsive to the needs of various groups and work to create a vision that is inclusive and far-reaching. By evaluating and analyzing current programs, it helps them to determine direction for the future.

Furthermore, Directors of Visitor Services are managers. Their positions are often within management of their institution. They can supervise large staffs, including those who work in admission, coat check, security, and other front line customer-service roles, providing and coordinating work schedules. They also coordinate admission procedures such as ticketing. They can oversee special events as well. Additionally, they manage the budget for their departments.

Think of all the times you have been hungry while visiting a museum, as well as the souvenirs you have purchased. At many museums and cultural institutions, the gift shop and on-site restaurant are an important part of a visitor's experience, as well as an important area for profitability. The Director of Visitor Services, who makes sure their day-to-day operations are going well, frequently oversees these. Directors of Visitor Services may update menus, order new gift items, and create inviting displays in the windows of these venues to lure visitors in.

Additional duties may include:

- Developing research methods to determine visitor expectations
- Using technology to create a more effective visitor experience
- Writing copy related to visitor information on the institution's Web site
- Analyzing inventory of shops and restaurants and preparing quarterly reports
- Screening and hiring new employees
- Answering visitors questions, e-mails, and phone calls
- Creating phone tree messages for visitors
- Overseeing a visitor center
- Planning special events
- Assessing public offerings
- Writing copy for visitor information materials
- Participating in fund-raising goals and initiatives

Directors of Visitor Services have a strong commitment to customer service. They need to have a basis in public relations; as a representative of their institution, they should have both the knowledge and the desire to constantly portray it in a positive light. As the front line professionals to see visitors, they should project their museum's mission. They must know about all programs and services inside and out.

Also, they need to be excellent troubleshooters. Visitors who have complaints are often referred to them. They accept criticism and do not take it personally. The hours for Directors of Visitor Services may include evenings and weekends, to reflect museum schedules.

Salaries

Salaries vary for Directors of Visitor Services. The main factor influencing earnings is the level of the position combined with the size of the organization. Some Directors of Visitor Services may manage more than 30 employees for a large, urban institution that gets millions of visitors each year. Others may serve as coordinators, with little or no supervisory responsibilities and a much smaller visitor base. Therefore, salaries may range from the low $30,000s to the high $70,000s depending on these factors.

Employment Prospects

Employment prospects are fair for Directors of Visitor Services. Opportunities are dependent on the budget of the institution. At smaller museums, jobs may combine visitor services with public programming or education.

However, since museums depend on their visitors to keep running, this position is quite important. Positions are available for those with experience in cultural institutions. The majority of jobs will be found in highly populated and touristed urban areas.

Advancement Prospects

Directors of Visitor Services may pursue different paths for advancement depending on their current position. Those at smaller institutions may look to move to larger ones, while Directors of Visitor Services who manage big departments may seek more leadership as a vice president or senior manager.

In addition to the arts, Directors of Visitor Services may move to other areas of the nonprofit sector. Colleges and universities often have large visitor centers employing directors. Additionally, conservation parks such as zoos, aquariums, nature centers, and botanic gardens all feature visitor services.

Education and Training

Most Directors of Visitor Services hold a bachelor's degree; many at large institutions have advanced degrees as well. At art museums, common majors include art history, history, fine arts, or museum studies, while at science museums, natural and biological sciences are frequent. Degrees in education and arts administration are also helpful.

For Directors of Visitor Services who work with special populations, specific knowledge and training is required. For example, those who work with people with disabilities should be well versed in the Americans with Disabilities Act (ADA) regulations, and those who work with international groups may speak several languages. Also, Directors of Visitor Services who work with children may have a background in teaching.

Experience, Skills, and Personality Traits

It is essential for Directors of Visitor Services to have excellent communication skills. They should be able to develop rapport with many different types of people. Articulate and gregarious, they need to interact with visitors, donors, support staff, and executives with ease.

Directors of Visitor Services also need to be strong managers. It is crucial for them to be well organized and able to manage many different tasks at once. They must provide distinct leadership that motivates those working in the front line areas to be friendly, yet efficient. Knowledge of managerial principles such as budgeting is also helpful.

Depending on the level of their position, Directors of Visitor Services may have between two and 10 years of experience. Prior work in museums or other cultural institutions, including internships and volunteer jobs, is invaluable.

Unions and Associations

Directors of Visitor Services may belong to a number of associations related to the arts and nonprofit sector. Associations specifically for museum professionals include the American Association of Museums and the Association of Science-Technology Centers. Those Directors of Visitor Services employed by conservation organizations might belong to the Wildlife Society or the Nature Conservancy.

Tips for Entry

1. In order to learn more about job descriptions, consult sites such as http://www.museumjobs.com, http://www4.wave.co.nz/~jollyroger/GM2/jobs/jobs.htm, http://www.museum-employment.com/, and http://www.globalmuseum.org/. Professional associations often list positions on their sites as well. Additionally, most museums and cultural institutions list their job openings directly on their Web sites.

2. Check out undergraduate, graduate, and certificate programs in museum studies. Schools nationwide offer these degrees, including New York University in New York (http://www.nyu.edu/fas/program/museum-studies/), Baylor University in Waco, Tex. (http://www.baylor.edu/Museum_Studies/), and the University of Hawaii at Manao in Honolulu (http://www.hawaii.edu/amst/museum_certificate.htm).

3. Visit a museum and spend time at the visitor's center. Speak to the Director of Visitor Services to learn more about his or her job.

4. Schedule an appointment at your campus career center to find out about internship and volunteer opportunities at museums. This is a great way to get in the door, as well as to learn about various career paths.

ARTISTIC DIRECTOR, THEATER

CAREER PROFILE

Duties: Directs artistic programming for a theater such as play selection, design team, and casting; acts as chief executive officer of a theater

Alternate Title(s): Theatrical Director

Salary Range: $0 to $100,000 and up

Employment Prospects: Poor

Advancement Prospects: Fair

Best Geographical Location(s): Major cities; summer resorts; artistic communities

Prerequisites:

Education or Training—No formal requirements, but theater training and graduate study is common

Experience—Five to 10 years in directing

Special Skills and Personality Traits—Creativity; artistic vision; ability to multitask and juggle many responsibilities; excellent writing and interpersonal skills

CAREER LADDER

```
┌─────────────────────────────────────┐
│  Artistic Director (larger institution) │
│       or Executive Director          │
└─────────────────────────────────────┘

┌─────────────────────────────────────┐
│          Artistic Director           │
└─────────────────────────────────────┘

┌─────────────────────────────────────┐
│ Assistant or Associate Artistic Director │
└─────────────────────────────────────┘
```

Position Description

An Artistic Director is the creative equivalent of a chief executive officer. He or she leads a theater as the primary person in charge of programming who creates, protects, and promotes the artistic mission of the institution. They are the visionaries who develop the focus for their organization. Along with the executive director, Artistic Directors make major decisions about the ongoing development of artistic values and activities.

More hard work than meets the eye goes into the theatrical productions that the world enjoys. There is someone behind the scenes managing the whole creative process, from cultivating the talent of the performers and musicians, to overseeing the technical components such as lighting and set production. Artistic Directors are responsible for all content including selecting plays, hiring cast and design teams, and commissioning writers. They decide what will be performed, when, and why. At a large theater with a broad range, play selection is a huge job and involves knowledge of many genres including classics, international works, children's theater, and up-and-coming playwrights.

In addition, a large part of their job includes community relations and outreach. Artistic Directors work to create partnerships with other producing organizations and regional theaters. They seek to build relationships with artists and artistic institutions, as well as those corporations or private individuals who support the arts. By setting up a dialogue with business, political, and financial community leaders, they advocate for their theaters and make a case for their continued existence. They use public relations skills to show the arts as a community revenue draw.

As high-ranking professionals for their theater, although they may not be involved in the day-to-day aspects of fundraising, Artistic Directors are often the main fund-raising closers. They work with their executive directors, board of directors, and development staff, and they may meet with high-level donors, government officials, or committee members and present proposals for continued funding and support. Additionally, they are involved in human resources functions such as hiring, supervising, and evaluating artistic and technical staff, including performers, designers, stage managers, and technical directors. They may also manage assistant or associate artistic directors who work directly with them.

Artistic Directors frequently serve as the spokespeople for their institutions. They are responsible for shaping and preserving the artistic image they want the public to see. They assist with all marketing and communications through public appearances, media presentations, and other speaking engagements, as well as approving advertisements and other publicity materials.

Their duties may include:

- Directing a limited number of productions each season
- Updating board of directors on artistic activity
- Developing an annual program budget
- Creating and evaluating programs
- Implementing short-term plans and developing long-term goals
- Negotiating fees and contracts
- Overseeing production activities for individual plays
- Determining artistic policy
- Writing proposals and papers to secure government and corporate/foundation funding, as well as individual support
- Supervising visiting artists and directors
- Reading scripts and meeting with playwrights
- Keeping up to date with artistic issues and current events

Being an Artistic Director is not just a job; it is a passion. In addition to running an institution, they also strive to maintain their work as artists. It is unlikely for Artistic Directors to work less than 60 hours per week, factoring in rehearsal time and performances, as well as daily operations. They must be available during regular nine-to-five hours, in addition to attending evening and weekend functions and performances.

Salaries

Salaries for Artistic Directors can run the gamut from no salary for someone who serves in this position on a volunteer basis, or $100,000 and up for someone with an extensive artistic background who is leading an extremely large institution. Prior experience of the Artistic Director, funding, seasonal work, and most crucial, the size of the organization, all play a role in affecting salary.

Employment Prospects

Because of the limited number of theaters and low turnover in the field, employment prospects for Artistic Directors are poor. There are approximately 450 members of the national service organization Theatre Communications Group, with one Artistic Director each, demonstrating the slim number of possible options. When positions do open, they go to those professionals with extensive directing, acting, and/or leadership experience.

Advancement Prospects

Advancement prospects are fair. Artistic Directors can advance by moving from smaller institutions to larger ones.

Sometimes, they may seek positions as executive directors of theaters or other leadership positions within artistic and cultural institutions. Additional opportunities may be found at theaters affiliated with universities.

Education and Training

Since there are no formal educational requirements, backgrounds of Artistic Directors vary greatly. It is common to see undergraduate study in the arts and humanities, as well as graduate work. Master of fine arts (MFA) degrees are the most valuable, as students can specialize in theater programs including directing, production, management, acting, and playwriting. These programs also provide students with access to the local artistic community and creative leaders, offering precious networking opportunities. Some colleges and universities offer bachelor of fine arts (BFA) programs as well.

Experience, Skills, and Personality Traits

Artistic Directors frequently have five to 10 years of experience as directors before taking on the artistic leadership of an entire institution. They have often made a name for themselves as an actor, director, or producer (and less commonly, a playwright) before taking on this type of role. With this experience, they bring a national network of artists, colleagues, and funding opportunities to help their new organization grow and flourish.

Creativity and artistic vision are key qualities for Artistic Directors. They must have outstanding written and verbal communication skills, and the ability to command respect as a leader, as well as to be part of a team. Dealing with diverse creative personalities and handling conflict comes into play. Also, public relations, marketing, and fund-raising experience are helpful.

In order to become an Artistic Director, individuals need to be knowledgeable about all genres of dramatic literature. They require an understanding of and appreciation for diverse communities and different sized institutions. Furthermore, they should have a broad understanding of the artistic audience that ranges beyond just theater.

Unions and Associations

Organizations for Artistic Directors include Theatre Communications Group, the National Organization for the American Theatre; the League of Resident Theatres; the Society of Stage Directors and Choreographers; and Actors Equity, among others.

Tips for Entry

1. Seek out a mentor in the field. Joining professional associations related to theater will help you meet Artistic Directors.
2. Gain experience in directing while a student by becoming involved in campus theater. Most colleges

and universities have theaters that are run by students and professional staff alike.

3. Research MFA programs to learn about theater arts graduate programs. Try the *Directory of Theatre Training Programs: 2003–2005; Profiles of College and Conservatory Programs Throughout the United States* by Jill Charles to start.

4. Search for "Artistic Directors" on the Internet for more information about job descriptions.

BUSINESS MANAGER

CAREER PROFILE

Duties: Manages the financial, administrative, and business operations for a cultural or artistic institution; implements policy and procedures

Alternate Title(s): Operations Manager, Financial Manager, Administration Manager, General Manager

Salary Range: $30,000 to $80,000 and up

Employment Prospects: Fair

Advancement Prospects: Fair

Best Geographical Location(s): Major cities or cultural hubs

Prerequisites:

Education or Training—Bachelor's degree strongly preferred in the arts, business, or public administration

Experience—Prior experience in nonprofits and/or administration, ideally both

Special Skills and Personality Traits—Excellent organizational skills; strong business, management, and supervisory skills; knowledge of financial principles such as accounting and budgeting

CAREER LADDER

```
┌─────────────────────────────────┐
│      General Manager             │
│      or Managing Director        │
└─────────────────────────────────┘

┌─────────────────────────────────┐
│      Business Manager            │
└─────────────────────────────────┘

┌─────────────────────────────────┐
│   Assistant Business Manager     │
│   or Business Manager            │
│   (smaller institution)          │
└─────────────────────────────────┘
```

Position Description

In addition to all the creative arts professionals who contribute to museums, theaters, symphonies, and other cultural institutions, there are also businesspeople who make the operations run smoothly. Business Managers are creative as well, but they use their creativity to manage the operations and financial responsibilities for their organizations. From behind the scenes, they ensure that visitors have the maximum experience when the curtain goes up or the doors are opened. They use their business knowledge and judgment to guide the financial and administrative operations of their organizations.

In terms of finances, Business Managers handle the budget for their organization. They prepare it annually, and project both revenue and expenses in order to make sure it will balance. They may also have responsibility for setting and managing the budget. They may write budget reports or narratives, as well as constantly monitor expenditures. Whenever someone in the organization needs to make a purchase, attend a seminar, or participate in any activity that

will cost the organization money, the Business Manager usually must approve it.

Additionally, Business Managers determine salary lines for different positions based on the budget and work together with other departments to write job descriptions. They handle payroll duties such as submission of time sheets and distribution of checks, as well as any payroll disputes.

Business Managers are frequently their main office administrators. They can take on many human resource roles involved with employee relations, particularly in organizations that do not have human resources departments. In organizations that do have human resources department, the Business Managers are often the liaison for their particular office or group. They might provide performance appraisals, participate in hiring and firing, and deal with benefits and grievances. They often supervise paraprofessional staff themselves, sometimes a considerable amount. In addition, they set staffing policy and procedures.

Also, Business Managers check and update inventory, determining not only what supplies are needed, but also how much can be spent on them. They handle all things relating to the office running as it should including heating and cooling systems, electricity, custodial needs, and maintenance. If the air-conditioning malfunctions, staff will call on the Business Manager. Whether they actually perform these tasks or delegate them depends on the size of the organization, but either way, they are ultimately responsible.

For an institution with performances such as a theater company or orchestra, Business Managers handle the performance logistics. They may coordinate auditions, plan schedules, and oversee issues such as lighting and sound. Also, they may order equipment, arrange rehearsals, and participate in setup. Business Managers often attend many performances to make sure all is going well.

In museums, Business Managers often take responsibility for on-site features such as shops and restaurants. They oversee security, which can be quite important in museums with prestigious collections worth millions of dollars. As facilities managers, they supervise the grounds the building is on as well as the actual building itself.

Business Managers work as liaisons with many other staff members in their organization. They work closely with the executive director and board of directors to ensure that the vision and mission for the institution is supported financially. In terms of events, they may work in conjunction with the special events department to provide logistics and staff. Furthermore, they must also use their communication skills to collaborate with others in the arts world such as donors, patrons, and artists.

Their duties may also include:

- Inspecting the facilities
- Negotiating with lessees
- Providing permits and services needed for events
- Writing correspondence related to special events, advertising, and rentals
- Developing rules and regulations
- Providing scheduling for employees
- Making hiring recommendations
- Working as a liaison with the business community to provide support to the arts
- Generating financial reports and submitting budgets and spreadsheets
- Managing special projects
- Reviewing labor needs and making personnel recommendations
- Tracking and monitoring the budget on a quarterly basis

Business Managers are often well-organized people with a keen business sense, who are also passionate about the arts. They want to be around artistic institutions, and their talent lies in enabling them to run more efficiently.

Since the cultural arts do not operate on a nine-to-five schedule, Business Managers often work long or nontraditional hours. At theater companies, they may attend evening and weekend performances, and museums can require evening and weekend work as well.

Salaries

Depending upon the institution, Business Managers may be executive-level staff who report directly to an executive director, or they may be more in middle management. Their level will directly affect their salary. A Business Manager for a small, independent theater company may earn less than $30,000, while Business Managers at a large museum may earn more than $80,000.

Employment Prospects

Employment prospects for Business Managers are fair. There are a limited number of institutions that need Business Managers each year. Also, people tend to stay in their jobs long-term, with little turnover. The best opportunities are for those with experience in the field through work, volunteering, internships, and school programs.

Universities also provide additional employment options for Business Managers in the arts. Most schools have several theater companies and museums on campus. An aspiring Business Manager can gain experience as a student by working or volunteering for one of these organizations. Considering work at a university also opens up the number of choices for job seekers. Other options for Business Managers in the arts might include public radio and television.

Advancement Prospects

Business Managers might advance to general manager or managing director positions within theater companies or museums. In order to get these types of positions, additional training such as a graduate degree can be helpful. Additionally, some Business Managers may move from smaller institutions to larger ones, or try different settings within the arts.

Education and Training

While it is not required, most Business Managers have at least a bachelor's degree. Most job postings ask for candidates with nonprofit arts experience in theaters or museums and an undergraduate degree. The best training comes from hands-on work in the field through volunteering.

In addition to traditional liberal arts courses, helpful subjects include business, public administration, finance, fine or performing arts, or arts management. Some Business Managers may hold a master's degree in fine arts, business, public administration, or arts management.

Experience, Skills, and Personality Traits

Business Managers should be exceptionally organized, efficient, and meticulous. They should be able to set and follow schedules, as well as give and receive directions. It is important for them to be good supervisors as well as communicators. They need to be able to multitask, juggle many tasks at once, and stay calm under pressure.

In terms of business, Business Managers should have a firm understanding of accounting and budgeting principles. They should be computer literate with knowledge of spreadsheets and budgeting software. Furthermore, they should be well versed in finance and business theory and practice.

To complement their business expertise, Business Managers in this setting should also have a great appreciation for and interest in the arts. They should understand how business is conducted in the nonprofit sector and believe strongly in the missions of their organizations.

Unions and Associations

There are a number of professional associations to which Business Managers may belong, including Theatre Communications Group, the National Organization for the American Theatre, the American Association of Museums, the International Society for the Performing Arts Foundation, the Arts and Business Council, Inc., and Americans for the Arts.

Tips for Entry

1. Check out certificate programs in arts management offered by community colleges and other schools throughout the country. One such program is at Seattle Central Community College in Seattle, Wash.: (http://www.seatlecentral.org/sccc/spotlight.php).
2. Visit the local museum on campus. Learn more about its operations and speak to the Business Manager about his or her job.
3. Attend a performance by a campus theater companies. Consider a volunteer or work-study position to gain the behind the scenes perspective.
4. Have you ever balanced a budget? Take an accounting course to learn basic principles.

REPORTER, PUBLIC RADIO

CAREER PROFILE

Duties: Develops and delivers news and feature stories for a public radio station

Alternate Title(s): Correspondent, Broadcaster, Newscaster

Salary Range: $25,000 to $50,000 and up

Employment Prospects: Fair

Advancement Prospects: Fair to good

Best Geographical Location(s): Major cities or college towns

Prerequisites:

Education or Training—Degree or background in journalism or communications is helpful and may be required for some positions

Experience—Experience through work or internships in radio, typically at least three years

Special Skills and Personality Traits—Excellent communication and public speaking skills; investigative mind; good research skills

CAREER LADDER

```
Senior Reporter or News Director
```

```
Reporter
```

```
Production Assistant, Intern,
or expert in other field
```

Position Description

Have you ever turned on your favorite radio station and felt frustrated to hear lengthy commercials instead of music or news? On public radio, that would not be possible. Public radio differs from commercial radio in that no commercial advertising is allowed. Like other nonprofit organizations, it depends on fund-raising from listeners and other supporters to sustain its existence. While different corporations that underwrite public radio programs by giving money may be mentioned on air in the context of "this program is funded in part by…," no products are endorsed or advertisements aired.

Nearly 700 public radio stations operate in the United States today. Public radio meets a need in communities that is not met by commercial radio. It often features classical or niche music and human-interest stories as well as news programs that highlight issues in depth. Although important happenings in the news are covered, it is not the goal of public radio to provide traffic reports, weather updates, or to let you know if there was a local shooting. Instead, public radio seeks to provide original programming and news that gets to the heart of important issues and discusses and analyzes perspectives.

Reporters for public radio stations wear many hats compared to their commercial counterparts. In addition to reporting on assigned stories, they are responsible for coming up with their own stories that will engage and enlighten their audience. They will often rely on their own areas of personal interest to get ideas for stories. For example, a Reporter with an interest or background in health care may choose to focus on health-related stories of interest. Reporters who do not have a built-in specialty will usually develop a niche area for themselves early on.

In order to get story ideas, Reporters must be news junkies themselves. They must scan the local and national media, including newspapers, magazines, and the Internet. Radio stations also receive press releases informing them about different stories, and they subscribe to a news wire service that fills them in on the latest happenings on a daily basis. The Associated Press is one source that comes through the wire, as is Reuters for business news.

Once Reporters have their story ideas, they sit down and write their pieces. They choose the angle they want to take and the ideas they want to highlight to inform and engage their listeners. Feature stories may take several days or even weeks to write, while spot news stories are done on a daily basis. After writing their stories, Reporters edit their own work, and then they are checked over and edited by a news director or other editorial staff member.

Public radio Reporters do not face the same pressure as television reporters when they go on air. They do not need to spend hours in hair and makeup, worry about their wardrobe, or read from a teleprompter. Since their audience can hear but not see them, they are able to read their pieces directly from their script. However, they do need to be excellent public speakers who can handle tight deadlines and work under pressure.

Some public radio Reporters host their own programs that are aired at regular times. These Reporters might interview guests or take phone calls from listeners. Call-in shows require much collaboration with producers, booking agents, and other broadcasting professionals.

Additional duties may include:

- Preparing and presenting reports
- Conducting live and studio interviews
- Researching and writing stories on issues
- Interviewing people for background information
- Reporting on breaking news stories
- Operating a broadcast console, digital sound editor, and other radio/satellite equipment
- Substituting for other reporters to host programs as needed
- Keeping abreast of current news and events
- Generating program ideas
- Assisting with special programming
- Producing segments

Reporters in public radio may work for national nonprofit radio networks such as National Public Radio (NPR), or they may work for local affiliates. The national or local affiliation will affect the types of news and feature stories they cover. Some travel may be required for national correspondents.

Reporters may work nontraditional hours since radio does not end when the typical workday does. However, most news stories and programs are delivered during heavy listening times such as commuting hours.

Salaries

Salaries for public radio Reporters vary depending on their experience, as well as their network. New Reporters may earn less than $30,000, but seasoned journalists with expertise may earn $50,000 and up. Just as in any media field, high-profile experts with national reputations will command more money. Salaries at medium-market public radio stations often range between $38,100 and $48,900.

In general, however, salaries for public radio Reporters are not high. An article on NPR's Web site states that public radio salaries are notoriously low and do not represent the value of public radio to the communities it serves.

Employment Prospects

Opportunities are fair for Reporters in public radio. Although public radio has a growing audience and a lack of competition, there are not a large number of available positions. According to Transformations Consulting Group/Livingston Associates, more than 60 percent of public radio stations are licensed to universities. In this case, hiring is dependent on the overall hiring trends and current budget limitations of the university. There is a steady stream of employment for those who are well connected in the field.

Advancement Prospects

It is easier to advance within public radio than to break in from the outside. However, most Reporters who are happy with their network and its programming stay in their jobs for a while. They may move on from local to national affiliates, or decide to take on more management responsibility as a news director. Others may aspire to host their own programs, giving them more autonomy over content.

Education and Training

No particular educational path is required to become a Reporter on public radio, but most Reporters have bachelor's degrees. Many hold graduate degrees as well. Those without degrees often have considerable experience. Helpful fields include journalism, broadcasting, and communications.

Furthermore, Reporters with specialty areas often have educational backgrounds and work experience in their field. A Reporter who covers stories on politics may have a degree in law, political science, or public administration, while a business Reporter may hold a master's of business administration (M.B.A.).

Training for Reporters mostly occurs through internships. In order to get a job, one must have prior on-air experience and familiarity with radio. College and even high school is the ideal time to volunteer and learn the ropes. It is typical for employers to ask candidates to submit audition tapes when applying for jobs, and internships can help budding professionals gather those necessary tools. It also familiarizes them with the crucial radio equipment and station environment. A minimum of three years of prior experience is typical for entry-level Reporter jobs.

Nonprofit experience in public radio is also important. While there is some movement from commercial to public radio, it is important for those making the move to have an understanding of the differences. Other Reporters may come over from print or television journalism.

Experience, Skills, and Personality Traits

Public radio Reporters must be able to meet deadlines and manage stress. As excellent communicators, they must be articulate speakers who are able to handle the challenge of live broadcasts. They must be able to present professional on-air broadcasts. Furthermore, Reporters should be strong writers as well.

To be a good Reporter, one should also be curious about people. An investigative mind drives research and makes for finding interesting stories that engage listeners. Reporters should also be very well read on current events and attuned to the issues facing their listeners. They should be culturally aware and sensitive, with strong listening skills. Additionally, Reporters should be thick-skinned, as they often try to speak to people who are less than willing to be interviewed in controversial cases.

Unions and Associations

Reporters in public radio may belong to the Public Radio News Directors, Inc., the Public Radio Programmer's Association, Inc., Americans for Radio Diversity, American Women in Radio and Television, the National Association of Broadcasters, the American Federation of Television and Radio Artists, and the Corporation for Public Broadcasting.

Tips for Entry

1. In addition to listening to their programming, you can learn a lot about public radio by going to the Web site of National Public Radio (NPR) at http://www.npr.org/. According to their site, "NPR is an internationally acclaimed producer and distributor of noncommercial news, talk, and entertainment programming. A privately supported, not-for-profit membership organization, NPR serves more than 750 independently operated, noncommercial public radio stations."

2. Consult http://www.current.org, the newspaper for people in public broadcasting in the United States. It comes out bimonthly and has important news about the field, as well as job listings.

3. Internships at radio stations are a must as a student. Check out your campus radio station and find out what kinds of programming they offer.

4. Volunteer at a radio station during a busy time such as election night. Although you won't get on-air experience, it will be an excellent way to make contacts and learn more about how radio stations operate.

5. Find a mentor. Contacts are essential in this field, and a mentor can provide support, encouragement, and an invaluable insider's network. Explore the Web site "Radio College," offering information about mentoring, to get started: http://www.radiocollege.org/.

HISTORIAN

CAREER PROFILE

Duties: Researches and analyzes past events, putting them into a context to understand their effect on society

Alternate Title(s): Conservator, Archivist, Historic Preservation Specialist

Salary Range: $30,000 to $70,000

Employment Prospects: Poor/Fair

Advancement Prospects: Poor/Fair

Best Geographical Location(s): Major cities or cultural centers; university towns

Prerequisites:

Education or Training—Minimum of a bachelor's degree; the majority of positions require a master's or doctoral degree

Experience—Several years of academic, museum, or research work

Special Skills and Personality Traits—Outstanding research skills; excellent writing ability; intellectual curiosity; strong problem-solving and analytical skills; ability to understand and synthesize complex historical information

CAREER LADDER

```
┌─────────────────────────────────────┐
│   Historical Director, Museum Director, │
│   or History Department Chairperson   │
└─────────────────────────────────────┘

┌─────────────────────────────────────┐
│              Historian               │
└─────────────────────────────────────┘

┌─────────────────────────────────────┐
│  History Student or Assistant Historian │
└─────────────────────────────────────┘
```

Position Description

We've all heard variations on the 1905 quote by Spanish-American philosopher George Santayana that "those who cannot remember the past are condemned to repeat it." Regardless of which version you have heard, the importance of studying history is clear. By understanding where we have been, we can determine where we are going. Studying the past enables societies to learn from their mistakes and move forward.

Historians research the past, organizing and synthesizing their findings to share information with the public. They often specialize in working with a particular period (ancient history, Renaissance history), a particular region (Japan, New Zealand), or a particular field (social history, political history). Some Historians are so specialized that they may study all three (ancient Japanese political history). They review all materials, such as books, journals, newspaper, letters, and diaries, that will help them understand the way things were at that time.

According to the American Historical Association as delineated in their online publication *Careers for Students of History,* several key characteristics define the work of a professional historian. These are:

1. Use of the historical method: This is a systematic approach to understanding the past that includes phrasing questions or describing problems in historical terms. Historians ask who, what, how, and why?
2. Use of historical context: Historians discover connections between objects and events. They do not look at an object or event by itself, but instead learn how it was part of a chain of events or a web of connected happenings from a specific time and place.
3. Use of primary and secondary sources: In their research, Historians know how to use both primary and secondary sources. Primary sources are firsthand; either as actual historical documents or first-person

accounts by those who have witnessed events, such as letters, diaries, or oral histories. Secondary sources include articles, reports, and papers that have been written about events or objects. It can be complicated to make sense of these resources, but Historians are trained to know how to study these materials and find relevant information.

4. Ability to organize and communicate their insight to others in a convincing and accessible way: After Historians discover information, they must be able to synthesize it in a way that the public can understand. This is how they express the significance of their findings. Historians may share information with the public through scholarly papers, articles, books, museum exhibitions, essays, documentaries, and more.

Historians spend much of their time conducting research into the past. They are adept at searching for complex information and analyzing both visual materials and material culture. To some extent, Historians must piece together a modern replica of past events in order to fully understand them. Furthermore, their expertise enables them to determine the authenticity of findings and sources.

Historians with archival responsibilities also protect collections of historical source materials. They work with both the collections of their own institution as well as others. They may organize, catalog, display, and process these collections.

Additional duties may include:

- Interviewing people to gather information and oral histories
- Lecturing and writing about their research findings
- Traveling to see artifacts and remnants of the past
- Selecting research topics
- Leading museum seminars
- Designing museum exhibitions
- Maintaining and caring for historical artifacts
- Providing recommendations and advice to government or business about historical objects
- Serving as an advocate to protect historical buildings or collections

There are a number of areas in the nonprofit sector in which Historians may work. Many Historians are employed by universities where they may teach and/or conduct research. Outside of academia, they are often called "Public Historians" because their activities seek to serve the public. In museums, they may plan exhibitions and determine ways to creatively display artifacts. Historians may also work at nonprofit preservation organizations, local community historical societies, and national parks, where they may preserve and protect buildings, landmarks, or environmental resources. In some of these settings, they may also have responsibility for budgeting, advocacy, fund-raising, teaching, and maintaining local resources.

Historians are experts on their particular subjects. They are scholars of their regions, populations, and eras who have a keen understanding about what life was like at that time. No matter what their specialty, they have knowledge about many aspects of culture including religion, customs, politics, art, economy, science, leisure, intellectual pursuits, and more. They work with other professionals with whom their work may overlap such as anthropologists, archaeologists, curators, and others.

Salaries

According to the Bureau of Labor Statistics, the median annual earnings for Historians in 2003 were $42,030. Salaries vary depending on work setting, education and training, and type of position. Historians employed by colleges and universities as full professors may earn considerably more, typically in the $70,000 range. While Historians at small museums or historical societies may earn less than $40,000, those in prestigious positions at large institutions may earn more than $60,000.

Employment Prospects

Employment prospects for Historians are poor to fair. Opportunities often depend on the funding level of institutions to maintain a Historian on staff. Museum jobs are very competitive, and once a Historian is employed by a museum, there is little turnover. The greatest job availability for Historians is in academia, as university professors and researchers. The next area is historic preservation, as there is a growing movement to protect and preserve significant places, buildings, and artifacts.

Advancement Prospects

Advancement prospects for Historians are also poor to fair. Historians tend to stay in their positions long-term, particularly after being granted tenure (at a university). They may advance to direct a museum or department, or all historical activities for an organization. Many Historians seek out additional opportunities by working as consultants and experts on authenticity of objects or other features. They also may write books, articles, or lecture on historical topics for added income.

Education and Training

In rare cases (and at small institutions), Historians may be hired with a bachelor's degree, but the vast majority have an advanced degree, usually a Ph.D. Historians work across multiple disciplines and may be educated and trained in several fields. While most were straight history majors as undergraduates, others studied related fields such as anthropology, sociology, archaeology, art, ancient studies, philosophy, economics, and languages.

At the graduate level, Historians become experts in their particular area. They may write their dissertations on 18th-century Belgian painters or the weapons or cultural impact of the Civil War. They may study historical preservation or get a degree in museum studies or administration. Public history is another common field of study for Historians at museums and other organizations that serve the public.

Historians receive most of their training through their academic study. By conducting extensive research as students, they gather the expertise they will use as professional researchers later on. They also develop the writing and lecturing skills that will prepare them for public work.

Experience, Skills, and Personality Traits

Historians are intellectually curious and are fascinated by the past. They are skilled investigators often driven by questions that will reveal answers and clues about why things are the way they are. They have superb research and writing skills and can make sense of complex information. Furthermore, they are experts in research strategy and knowledgeable about databases such as LexisNexis and other research sources.

Unions and Associations

There are a variety of professional associations to which Historians may belong, depending on their specialty area, including the Organization of American Historians, the American Historical Association, the Society of American Archivists, the American Association for State and Local History, the National Council on Public History, the American Association of Museums, and the National Trust for Historic Preservation.

Tips for Entry

1. Consider the field of public history, which prepares Historians for work outside of academia. The National Council on Public History (http://www. ncph.org) offers useful resources. A list of university programs can be found at http://www.ncph.org/ degree.html. Their directory of professional history consultants at http://www.ncph.org/consult.html is ideal for networking.

2. The American Historical Association has excellent career information for Historians on their Web site (http://www.historians.org).

3. Visit the Web site of the Smithsonian Institution at http://www.si.edu. It contains valuable information for those looking for public Historian careers.

4. Most states and communities have historical societies; join yours for the opportunity to learn about where you live as well as to speak to Historians and volunteers about their jobs.

COLLEGES AND UNIVERSITIES

PROFESSOR

CAREER PROFILE

Duties: Serves on the faculty of a college or university; teaches courses, conducts research, and publishes scholarly works

Alternate Title(s): Faculty Member, Adjunct Instructor or Lecturer

Salary Range: $30,000 to $125,000 and above

Employment Prospects: Fair

Advancement Prospects: Good

Best Geographical Location(s): All

Prerequisites:

Education or Training—Ph.D. required at most colleges and universities; master's or professional degrees may be accepted at smaller or professional schools, or for adjunct positions

Experience—Graduate school and dissertation completion; research in specialty area

Special Skills and Personality Traits—Excellent research and writing skills; intellectual curiosity; analytical mind; good communication skills

CAREER LADDER

```
┌─────────────────────────────────┐
│  Department Chairperson, Dean,   │
│    or University President        │
└─────────────────────────────────┘

┌─────────────────────────────────┐
│           Professor              │
└─────────────────────────────────┘

┌─────────────────────────────────┐
│ Teaching Assistant or Adjunct Instructor │
└─────────────────────────────────┘
```

Position Description

Professors are responsible for training and nurturing the minds of the future leaders and contributors to society. They are teachers who are so passionate about their subject matter that they spent an average of seven years after their undergraduate degree conducting research, writing, and teaching their topic. Although the work of a advanced statistical analysis professor will vary greatly from someone who teaches 18th-century British literature, what they have in common is their commitment to academia and quest for knowledge.

The proportionate value placed on teaching and research for a Professor varies depending on the type of educational institution at which he or she is employed. At large, research-based universities, Professors are often hired based on their research interests and accomplishments. There is a common saying in the academic world, "publish or perish," which refers to the pressure put on faculty by their university to have a certain number of published scholarly works

each year. While they will teach several classes, their teaching ability is secondary to what they offer the university in terms of securing research grants and publishing prestigious papers. On the other hand, at smaller colleges and community colleges, the focus is often on teaching. Professors are selected based on teaching experience, methods, and theory and previous student satisfaction.

Professors may teach exclusively undergraduate students or graduate students, or a combination of both. They have an assigned course load per semester, usually about 12 to 16 teaching hours per week. In addition to actually standing up and teaching these courses, there is an enormous amount of preparation required. Professors develop curriculum, prepare syllabi, select texts to use, create assignments, design exams, and determine all grades. Flexibility and creativity are major components of course design, and each course can be tailored to the Professor's strengths and interests. Some Professors may deliver lectures to auditoriums filled with more than 500 students; others focus on class participation to spark lively debates in rooms of 10.

The academic job search process that leads to professorship is one of the most grueling of all professions. As graduate students, individuals are expected to produce an extensive thesis, called a dissertation, in order to receive their doctorate. The dissertation must be an original scholarly exploration of their topic that uncovers new information, tests a hypothesis, or presents points differently than has been done before. In the sciences, this will consist of laboratory work, while in the humanities, it will involve literature and original document review. In addition to the completion of the dissertation, graduate students also must pass oral comprehensive examinations, where they "defend" their dissertation in front of several faculty members.

After completing the Ph.D., graduate students "go on the market," meaning they make themselves available for the academic job search. At their home institutions, they set up files called dossiers that contain confidential recommendations from their advisers and other faculty members. When they apply for various Professor positions, they submit a cover letter and a curriculum vitae; they also request that their school send the official dossier. The letters of recommendation are a very important part of the application process. If students are invited for campus interviews, they may be required to present a lecture to a class, answer questions from a faculty panel, or discuss their teaching philosophy and/or research interests in depth. In some fields, such as the sciences, students then go on for one to two years of postdoctoral research before applying for faculty positions.

A major goal for many new Professors is the ever-elusive tenure. After a period of approximately seven years under contract, the instructor's accomplishments are reviewed and tenure may be awarded. Those granted tenure enjoy job stability essentially for the rest of their lives; they can teach, conduct research, and explore new ideas without the fear of losing their jobs for being unpopular or controversial. Instructors who are denied tenure must leave the institution immediately.

Two-year colleges, community colleges, and smaller colleges and universities tend to hire Professors who are not full-time employees of the institution. This is cost-effective, as they do not have to pay for overall salary and benefits, but just per class that they teach. These Professors are generally called adjunct instructors. Working as an adjunct instructor can be a good way for recent graduates to gain more teaching experience or otherwise employed professionals to share their skills and teach on the side. However, it is not financially feasible for most people looking to support themselves.

The amount of student-Professor contact varies at different institutions, as well as by Professors' own preferences and personalities. Many Professors take on advising and mentoring students as part of their jobs, and it is something

they enjoy. Others will advise only graduate students who are working on the same type of research as they are. Professors collaborate with other departments and professionals on campus such as deans, career counselors, and academic advisers to ensure that students' goals are met.

Additional duties may include:

- Writing grant proposals to fund research
- Consulting with business, government, or community organizations
- Attending professional conferences
- Participating in faculty meetings
- Supervising graduate student research
- Writing textbooks and other publications
- Teaching online courses
- Collaborating with campus administrators
- Holding office hours for students

Professors enjoy flexible schedules and often those who do not like to work traditional hours are attracted to the field. With teaching schedules usually not taking up more than 16 hours per week, Professors can conduct research, write, grade papers, and meet with students during the evening, on weekends, and as their schedule allows. Many also enjoy reduced course loads or no courses over the summer and during school breaks. Professors need to be self-motivated in order to accomplish many of their objectives on their own time. Travel may be required for research purposes and to attend meetings and conferences.

Salaries

The 2003–04 survey by the American Association of University Professors states that salaries for full-time faculty with doctorates averaged $75,863. By rank, the average was $100,682 for Professors, $68,640 for associate professors, $58,576 for assistant professors, $39,476 for instructors, and $45,763 for lecturers. Faculty in private four-year institutions earn higher average salaries than those teaching at community colleges or state colleges and universities. At the master's level, the average salary for all types of Professors combined was $59,400.

In addition to their base salaries, many Professors also earn additional income from writing, consulting, and speaking engagements. They also may receive special university benefits such as tuition for dependents, housing allowances, and other perks.

Employment Prospects

The 2004–5 Occupational Outlook Handbook online states that "opportunities for Ph.D. recipients seeking jobs as postsecondary teachers are expected to be somewhat better than in previous decades." With college enrollment up, more faculty must be hired. However, while this is encouraging, prospects are still fair for full Professors and positions are very competitive.

The most plentiful opportunities will be positions at two-year or community colleges, and part-time positions. Candidates who are willing to relocate, especially to smaller schools in rural communities looking to build their reputations, may find more available jobs.

Advancement Prospects

Although jobs as a Professor are difficult to attain, when someone breaks in and makes it through the tenure process, they can relax with excellent job security and freedom. The advancement structure usually follows from assistant professor, to associate professor, to full Professor. Some Professors strive to become department chairpeople, deans, or university presidents. Others use their job flexibility to pursue related goals as well.

Education and Training

For the majority of Professor positions, a doctoral degree is required. As undergraduates, students who are thinking about careers as Professors should do very well in their majors. They should take their grades seriously, get involved with research, and most important, get to know their professors so they will be able to get personal letters of recommendation. If they have the opportunity to write an undergraduate honors thesis, they should take it, as graduate schools look favorably on these accomplishments. Some stellar students will get accepted to Ph.D. programs directly after undergraduate work; others work for several years in related areas or obtain a master's degree first. Competition for acceptance is keen, particularly to prestigious programs with strong reputations.

Graduate school is an extensive commitment of time and money. Most Ph.D. students receive all or partial funding while they spend the six to eight years in school studying for their doctorate, accompanied by a small stipend. While the money is enough to get by, it is often not much, and graduate students become experts at living frugally. Unfortunately, funding is not as plentiful for master's programs, and many students incur large debts to finance their education.

Once a student is in graduate school, working as a teaching assistant is one of the best ways to prepare for a career as a Professor. Teaching assistants may assist Professors, but often have the opportunity to independently develop curriculum, teach courses, and determine grades. Many graduate students are required to work as teaching assistants as part of their acceptance package. Some students may also be able to work as teaching assistants during their undergraduate years. Positions as a research assistant are also very useful.

Some smaller schools, community colleges, and professional schools will hire instructors with a master's degree and related experience. For example, to teach at a school of the arts, many faculty members may hold professional experience and a master's in fine arts (MFA) degree in lieu of a doctorate.

Experience, Skills, and Personality Traits

In addition to teaching and research experience obtained through graduate work, Professors should be creative, flexible, and have a thirst for knowledge. They need to be able work independently without supervision; many thrive on it. In order to work with students, they should be good communicators, and they need the base of excellent research and writing skills for their academic credibility. They should appreciate the expression of new ideas and be open-minded and tolerant.

Unions and Associations

Professors may belong to the American Association of University Professors, the Association of American Colleges and Universities, and the American Association of Community Colleges.

Tips for Entry

1. Learn more about the academic job search by reading *The Academic Job Search Handbook* by Mary Morris Heiberger and Julia Miller Vick.
2. Read the online version of *The Chronicle of Higher Education,* the leading publication in the academic world, at http://www.chronicle.com.
3. Speak to your professors about getting involved with research projects. Talk to them about the graduate school process and academic career paths.
4. Take a look at rankings through *US News and World Report* to learn about the top doctoral programs in your field of study at http://www.usnews.com/usnews/edu/grad/rankings/rankindex_brief.php.

ADMISSIONS OFFICER

CAREER PROFILE

Duties: Evaluating, developing, and recommending admissions criteria for student acceptance to college and university programs

Alternate Title(s): Admissions Counselor

Salary Range: $22,000 to $50,000 and up

Employment Prospects: Good

Advancement Prospects: Good

Best Geographical Location(s): All

Prerequisites:

Education or Training—Bachelor's degree required; master's degree is often helpful for competitive positions and advancement

Experience—Entry-level; may require one to two years of part-time, full-time, internship, or volunteer experience in an admissions office, including responsibilities such as a tour guide or student interviewer

Special Skills and Personality Traits—Flexibility; willingness to travel; excellent communication skills and personal judgment

CAREER LADDER

```
┌─────────────────────────────────┐
│   Assistant or Associate Director │
│         of Admissions             │
└─────────────────────────────────┘

┌─────────────────────────────────┐
│        Admissions Officer         │
└─────────────────────────────────┘

┌─────────────────────────────────┐
│   Admissions Assistant or Intern  │
└─────────────────────────────────┘
```

Position Description

Admissions Officers play a major role in deciding whether students are accepted or rejected from the college and university programs to which they apply. They evaluate each application to determine if the student meets the academic and personal criteria required by the school for admission. Admissions Officers often help to develop these admissions requirements as well. In this way, they are responsible for shaping the future student bodies of their schools.

Much of the work of an Admissions Officer flows in a cycle like the academic year. Schools may vary in terms of their admissions deadlines and acceptance dates, but frequently the time line is similar to the following.

During the fall, most Admissions Officers travel for periods of time ranging from the beginning of September to late November or early December. Each Admissions Officer is assigned to a region of the United States or an international region and makes visits to high schools in these regions. At these high schools, Admissions Officers may make presentations to students and their parents, answer questions, and attend college fairs.

After the travel season is over, Admissions Officers spend much of January, February, and March reading applications. They evaluate each student on criteria such as grades, standardized test scores, extra curricular activities, and colleges essays. They may also conduct interviews with students at this time. A selection committee will then meet to make final decisions before the acceptance letters go out.

After acceptance letters are sent out, often in early April, Admissions Officers are involved with planning campus events for the prospective students in the hope that these students will accept their admissions offers. Events may include open houses, campus tours, programs with current students, and presentations by campus faculty and administrators. Admissions Officers may spend the summer analyzing the results of the past year and preparing recruitment strategy for the upcoming year.

Another main responsibility of Admissions Officers is student recruitment. Admissions Officers are the salespersons for their schools; thus it is important for them to believe in the missions of the schools in order to promote them to students.

Their duties may include:

- Evaluating, developing, and recommending admissions criteria and policies
- Evaluating applicant credentials
- Reading and voting on applications
- Interviewing prospective students either on campus or on the road
- Participating in discussions regarding enrollment management
- Working with high school guidance counselors to discuss students and special admissions requirements
- Giving presentations for large and small groups of high school students about college programs and admissions requirements
- Developing and managing on and off campus recruitment events such as tours and class visits
- Advising potential and new students on various curriculum and academic preparation issues
- Serving as liaison to student groups, alumni, and faculty members to develop initiatives to improve the admissions process
- Managing student workers and/or tour guides

Admissions Officers may work with undergraduate or graduate degree programs. Some Admissions Officers may specialize with recruiting and assisting certain groups of the student population such as student athletes, students of color, and transfer students.

Admissions Officers tend to work long hours that include evening and weekend programs in addition to the regular workweek. Travel is also a large component of the job. At small local schools, the travel is concentrated, while national universities often require Admissions Officers to go long distances. Admissions Officers must be comfortable with airplane travel, visiting different regions of the country and/or world, and driving or using public transportation. Reimbursed for all travel expenses, including meals, gasoline, airfare, and hotels, Admissions Officers may travel with colleagues or alone.

Salaries

Salaries for Admissions Officers vary based on their school of employment, as well as their experience and background. Entry-level salaries can range from $22,000 per year to $35,000 and up. According to *Facts & Figures—Median Salaries of College Administrators by Type of Institution, 2002–3,* on the Chronicle of Higher Education online, the median salary for associate directors of admissions is

$46,329; for the chief admissions officer, it is $68,000. With several years of experience, salaries can improve by more than 20 percent. Furthermore, some schools may pay Admissions Officers for overtime, which could make a big difference in overall salary. Admissions Directors, particular at competitive colleges with large endowments, can make considerably more money.

Employment Prospects

There will always be a need for Admissions Officers to guarantee new students at colleges and universities. Currently, employment prospects for Admissions Officers is good. Many colleges and universities are experiencing increased enrollment, which leads to the need for more staff to review applications. Furthermore, as college programs grow more competitive, there is more of a need for professionals to evaluate admissions criteria, meet with students, and manage the process.

Advancement Prospects

Advancement opportunities for Admissions Officers are good. The field often experiences high turnover for several reasons. The work is intensive and time-consuming, thus often leading to burnout. Many professionals work as an Admissions Officer for several years and then use this experience as a springboard for other opportunities in nonprofit, business, or human resources. They may become admissions directors or other university administrators. Others may decide to attend graduate school. This can create a multitude of advancement opportunities for Admissions Officers with experience, especially if they are willing to switch schools.

Education and Training

While it is not required for Admissions Officers to hold a master's degree, many of them do, in fields such as higher education administration, counseling, psychology, education, or management. This can help with advancement to higher levels of responsibility, particularly at more academically competitive schools.

For those Admissions Officers who work with graduate or professional school admissions, many of them hold the same degree as the students they recruit. While schools can rarely staff their entire admissions office with alumni, some do prefer to hire those Admissions Officers who have graduated from their program.

Experience, Skills, and Personality Traits

Because of all the interpersonal activity the job requires, it is necessary for Admissions Officers to have superb communication skills. They must enjoy meeting many different people and be skilled at public speaking with high levels of energy. Admissions Officers need clear judgment and the ability to be objective when evaluating applications. Also important is the ability to be organized.

Additionally, it is helpful for Admissions Officers to have previous experience working in an admissions office. While students, many future Admissions Officers volunteer their time, read applications, or work as tour guides.

Unions and Associations

There are various professional organizations for Admissions Officers to join for networking and professional development. The main organization for professionals is the National Association of College Admissions Counselors in Washington, D.C. (http://www.nacac.com/index.html). This group comprises more than 8,000 professionals helping students make decisions about higher education and they hold a yearly national conference. They also have state and regional offices.

Another organization for Admissions Officers is the College Board (http://www.collegeboard.com/splash), which is the umbrella organization for the Scholastic Achievement Test (SAT), and the American Association of Collegiate Registrars and Admissions Officers.

Tips for Entry

1. According to insiders, the hiring window for jobs as an Admissions Officer is small, ranging from May to July. It is important to conduct research and apply for jobs early before the academic year gets under way.
2. Speak to current professionals working in college admissions offices for advice about the profession.
3. Volunteer in the admissions office of a local college during winter or spring break.
4. Take a course in public speaking to brush up on presentation skills.
5. Visit the Web site for the *Chronicle of Higher Education* (http://www.chronicle.com) to view job listings for Admissions Officers.
6. Find out about working as a tour guide on your campus.

CAREER COUNSELOR

CAREER PROFILE

Duties: Provides career and vocational counseling to individuals and groups; assists job seekers with career development and job search techniques

Alternate Title(s): Vocational Counselor; Placement Counselor; Employment Counselor, Career Adviser

Salary Range: $25,000 to $50,000 and up

Employment Prospects: Good

Advancement Prospects: Good

Best Geographical Location(s): All

Prerequisites:

    Education or Training—Bachelor's degree for most positions; some positions may require a master's degree

    Experience—One to two years' prior counseling experience through internships, volunteer, or full-time work

    Special Skills and Personality Traits—Excellent interpersonal skills; strong listening and empathetic abilities; good communication skills; knowledge of job market

    Licensure/Certification—Licensure as a professional counselor may be required in some states

CAREER LADDER

```
┌─────────────────────────────────┐
│       Assistant, Associate,      │
│  or Director of Career Counseling│
│      or Career Development       │
└─────────────────────────────────┘

┌─────────────────────────────────┐
│        Career Counselor          │
└─────────────────────────────────┘

┌─────────────────────────────────┐
│        Graduate Intern           │
└─────────────────────────────────┘
```

Position Description

Everyone wants an answer to the question "what should I do with my life?" This is complicated, since on average, people have 10 jobs and five careers throughout their lifetimes. Career Counselors help individuals make career decisions. On a college campus, they review and evaluate each student's education, training, work history, interests, skills, and personal traits in order to help them better understand themselves and their goals. Through one-on-one appointments, they assist them with all aspects of the job search process ranging from self-assessment to negotiating offers of employment. They help people to explore their vocational interests, skills, and values and to develop a plan of action.

Career Counselors help students assess themselves in many ways. In addition to appointments where they ask questions about the client's past experiences, they often use interactive exercises and vocational inventories in order to help people determine their interests and career preferences. Common inventories include the Strong Interest Inventory and the Myers Briggs Type Indicator, as well as computer-based programs such as SIGI-Plus. These inventories work best in conjunction with counseling so that the results can be interpreted and put into a context that is helpful for the client.

Once students know their careers of interest, Career Counselors can help them research different career fields and career paths, as well as learn about specific job opportunities. They have access to a variety of resources, including career libraries with guidebooks that describe different jobs, helpful Web sites, and databases of job listings. Furthermore, they teach students techniques such as networking and informational interviewing as a way to explore opportunities. Career Counselors also help students obtain internships, part-time jobs, and volunteer work to learn more about their career preferences.

Career Counselors also work with students to develop job search skills and to locate and apply for jobs and internships. They provide support and coaching with résumé and cover letter writing and interviewing techniques. Often they can role-play a situation, such as a job interview or networking conversation to help students understand how to improve their communication skills. Most college career centers offer programs such as campus recruiting, job databases, career fairs and networking nights to put student in touch with employers who have positions to fill.

In addition to providing counseling and job search resources, Career Counselors also present workshops to groups related to the whole spectrum of career issues, including professional etiquette, job searching, and applying to graduate school. They may present to groups as small as two and as large as 100. Many Career Counselors write and develop the curriculum for these workshops. On some campuses, Career Counselors have the opportunity to teach a required career development course or credit-bearing seminar.

In colleges and universities, Career Counselors may work with undergraduate students, graduate students, and alumni, and are part of a larger career services office that may include directors, employee relations specialists, and support staff. Depending on the size of the school, Career Counselors may be generalists or work with specialty populations divided by major, career interests, class year, or other designations. While they clearly are not expected to know everything about all careers, it is important for Career Counselors to maintain a knowledge base of different industries and employment trends through research, conferences, and speaking with employers.

Career Counselors generally work a 40-hour week, with some evening hours for counseling and programming. Career Counselors employed in higher education usually work all 12 months of the year and can expect longer hours during busy student recruiting periods.

Their duties may include:

- Providing career counseling to individuals and groups
- Critiquing résumés, cover letters, and other job search correspondence
- Administering vocational inventories as part of the counseling process, when appropriate
- Presenting workshops on career-related topics to groups
- Planning career programs for students such as panels or site visits to organizations
- Working with employers to learn about job opportunities
- Scheduling appointments
- Supervising other career counselors, graduate assistants, interns, or work-study students
- Collaborating with faculty, deans, and other advisers for student programming
- Writing brochures, tip sheets, and other career-related material
- Participating in the hiring process for new career counselors
- Running career counseling support groups
- Organizing career fairs

- Attending conferences
- Keeping abreast of employment trends and job market information
- Training new counselors and other staff members
- Developing student outreach programs
- Publicizing and marketing programs and other events

Salaries

The Salary Wizard report on http://www.salary.com shows the 2004 median expected salary for a typical Career Counselor working in higher education as $37,910. Average salaries tend to range from $35,000 to $50,000. Colleges and universities usually offer strong employee benefits, including four weeks of paid vacation, medical and dental insurance, and reimbursement for continuing education. Career Counselors working for nonprofit organizations other than colleges and universities usually have slightly lower salaries and less-comprehensive benefits.

Employment Prospects

According to the Bureau of Labor Statistics, employment of all counselors, including Career Counselors, is expected to grow faster than average for all occupations through 2012. As the economy experiences ups and downs, the demand for Career Counselors grows. Many schools now offer tours of the career center to prospective freshmen, and parents and students alike are interested in placement statistics and services offered. Career Services is becoming an increasingly important department in colleges and universities, with many schools adding additional counselors to their staff in order to assist students with their job searches and to expand the number of organizations who recruit on campus.

Advancement Prospects

Advancement as a Career Counselor depends upon the work environment. Some Career Counselors work in offices where they already at are the highest professional level. Others may seek leadership positions within their setting and move to become assistant or associate directors, and then directors of career counseling or career services. The abundance of advancement prospects varies by geographical location. For example, a Career Counselor employed by a university in a major urban area would likely find many opportunities for advancement within all local schools.

Furthermore, Career Counselors who are trained in counseling have other nonprofit opportunities for advancement if they choose to leave the university setting. Many community organizations and state and local governments are adding Career Counselors to their staffs in order to provide training and other services to laid-off workers, experienced workers seeking a new or second career, full-time homemakers seeking to reenter the workforce, and workers who want to update their skills.

Education and Training

A four-year college degree is typically the minimum requirement for a position as a Career Counselor; often a master's degree in counseling, psychology, higher education administration, or another related field is preferred or required. While some Career Counselors have strong backgrounds in education, counseling, and psychology, other Career Counselors have coursework in business and human resources. Accredited master's degree programs usually include a minimum of two years of full-time study and a supervised internship experience. Career Counselors who work with specific populations such as law students or engineers sometimes, but not always, have degrees or work experience in those fields.

Work experience or internships in the counseling field are helpful for obtaining entry-level jobs. Career Counselors must have strong listening skills, excellent verbal communication skills, and a high degree of empathy. Also important is having knowledge of career development theory, career fields, and the current job market.

Special Requirements

While most colleges and universities do not expect Career Counselors to be certified, there is a certification process available and/or required by some states. In 2001, 46 states and the District of Columbia had some form of counselor credentialing, licensure, or certification. In some states, credentialing is mandatory; in others, it is voluntary. Many counselors elect to be nationally certified by the National Board for Certified Counselors, Inc. (NBCC), which grants the general practice credential "national certified counselor (NCC)." To be certified, a counselor must hold a master's or higher degree with a concentration in counseling from a regionally accredited college or university; have at least two years of supervised field experience in a counseling setting; provide two professional endorsements; and have a passing score on the NBCC's National Counselor Examination for Licensure and Certification (NCE). For more information, see http://www.nbcc.org.

This national certification is optional, and it differs from state certification. However, in some states, those who pass the national exam are exempted from taking a state certification exam. Even if Career Counselors do not need certification for university employment, it may be valuable for those seeking additional opportunities.

Experience, Skills, and Personality Traits

Career Counselor positions are often entry-level within career services offices for candidates graduating from related master's degree programs. One to two years of work experience may be expected but can include internships, graduate assistantships, or work in another industry.

Furthermore, Career Counselors must have the ability to work well with diverse groups of people and display empathy and concern for their problems. In order to gain the respect and confidence of their clients, Career Counselors must display good judgment, patience, and the ability to remain calm. Strong verbal communication and presentation skills are also important. Good writing skills are useful for providing critiques of résumés and other written materials. A working knowledge of the current job market and career-related resources that clients can use is also necessary for success as a Career Counselor.

Unions and Associations

Career Counselors can join a variety of professional associations for networking and professional development. Career Counselors working in higher education can join the National Association of Colleges and Employers (NACE) and the American College Personnel Association (ACPA). Other organizations include the American Counseling Association (ACA) and the National Career Development Association (NCDA). Many professional associations for Career Counselors are also organized by state and by region.

Tips for Entry

1. Gain experience as a student through volunteer work that reflects an interest in helping people. Look at programs including tutoring, crisis hotlines, and other community service.
2. While in college, visit the campus career center and speak to the Career Counselors to find out more about what they do. Using the career center will not only put you in touch with Career Counselors, it will also benefit you by providing access to job resources.
3. Explore internship opportunities by contacting local university career centers and community organizations to find out about positions.
4. Learn more about various career fields through browsing at libraries and bookstores. Reading books about résumés, interviewing, and job searching is very helpful.

ACADEMIC ADVISER

CAREER PROFILE

Duties: Advises students with regard to academic issues such as course selection, schedule planning, and fulfilling requirements

Alternate Title(s): Academic Counselor, Academic Advisor

Salary Range: $25,000 to $45,000 and up

Employment Prospects: Good

Advancement Prospects: Good

Best Geographical Location(s): All

Prerequisites:

Education or Training—Bachelor's degree required; master's degree preferred and may be required for many positions

Experience—One to two years of experience as an adviser through full-time work, peer advising, or internships

Special Skills and Personality Traits—Excellent verbal and written communication skills, strong interpersonal skills, sensitivity and patience, knowledge of academic requirements

CAREER LADDER

```
┌─────────────────────────────────┐
│    Senior Academic Adviser       │
│  or Director of Academic Advising│
└─────────────────────────────────┘

┌─────────────────────────────────┐
│        Academic Adviser          │
└─────────────────────────────────┘

┌─────────────────────────────────┐
│        Graduate Intern           │
└─────────────────────────────────┘
```

Position Description

Students often begin college confused about their academic plans. This is where the job of an Academic Adviser comes in. Academic Advisers help students with all aspects of their academic experience in higher education, including community colleges, four-year colleges and universities, and graduate programs. At the beginning of the process, they meet with their caseload of students and discuss their future goals. They assist them with planning a schedule that will meet their requirements and put them on a path to graduate on time.

Academic Advisers also help students select their majors. They review the requirements for each major and help students find the best fit to achieve their goals. At some campuses, the major selection process is a big deal, and Academic Advisers plan events to help students learn about the various majors and celebrate the declaration. These events may include presentations by professors, as well as alumni working in a variety of career fields. Academic Advisers may also assist students with applying to graduate school and explaining the application process. They work collaboratively with other campus professionals such as faculty members, deans, and career counselors to help students explore and research their options.

If students run into academic difficulties, Academic Advisers help them navigate their choices. Sometimes students who are having problems will seek out their Academic Adviser first because it feels "safer" than going for more traditional counseling, with which some students may attach a stigma. They need to be attuned to the student's concerns and listen to not only what is presented, but also what is not said. Many students face an enormous amount of pressure from their parents, as well as themselves, to choose a certain major or receive high grades. A student may come into college as a pre-med, but find that freshman year she is failing biology, and see her Academic Adviser for advice. Academic Advisers need to acknowledge this pressure and help students make choices that are satisfying to both their families and themselves. They must exercise good judgment; rather than telling a student what he should do, they empower them to make their own, informed decisions.

If a student is failing a course, an Academic Adviser can recommend tutoring or help the student to drop the course before the grade appears on the transcript. Often they will act as the student's advocate if they see the student wants to succeed. They also counsel students on barriers to their academic success, and will refer them to the necessary campus support services when appropriate. Certain situations call for a red flag such as sudden drop in grades, absenteeism, or suspected depression, drug use, or suicidal tendencies. Academic Advisers are well versed in their campus support systems and can refer them to the counseling center to get the services they need.

Also, Academic Advisers also may run workshops for students to help them better understand the academic process and college achievement. These workshops may include topics such major selection, time management, study skills, graduate school admissions, and graduation requirements. Academic Advisers may be responsible for designing, creating, and publicizing these workshops, in addition to the presentation.

Additional duties may include:

- Meeting with students individually and in groups to plan their academic schedules
- Monitoring students' progress by holding regular meetings each semester
- Presenting seminars and workshops related to the academic process
- Advising students' on university policies and procedures
- Assisting students with enrollment of academic courses
- Maintaining student records
- Working with students in collaboration with other campus offices to eliminate barriers to academic success
- Supervising student workers
- Developing and implementing academic skill-building programs
- Running computer reports to track enrollment statistics
- Advising transfer students

In order to meet the needs of student schedules, Academic Advisers often work more than 40 hours per week, including occasional evenings and weekends. At large colleges and universities, there may be a team of Academic Advisers working alongside deans and professors, while at small schools there may be only one. Academic Advisers may work with specialty populations, divided by major, academic class, or academic program. Student caseload varies depending on the type and size of the institution of employment.

Salaries

Salaries for Academic Advisers vary depending on the size, location, and budget of the institution for which they work. According to data on Salary Wizard at http://www. salary. com, the median salary for Academic Advisers is 35,944.

Starting salaries are often between $25,000 and $35,000. Also, they can take advantage of many other benefits offered to employees by colleges and universities, including reimbursement for continuing education, comprehensive health insurance, and four weeks of paid vacation.

Employment Prospects

Employment prospects for Academic Advisers are good. As college enrollment continues to grow on many campuses, so does the need for professionals to advise these students. The majority of opportunities can be found in areas with high concentrations of colleges and universities, and within institutions experiencing growth.

Advancement Prospects

Advancement opportunities become available for Academic Advisers as other professionals leave for new positions or retire. There is relatively high turnover for Academic Advisers, with many people leaving positions within five years. This creates good opportunity for promotion to senior adviser or director-level positions. Academic advising also provides a good springboard for those interested in other positions in higher education administration. Some move over to student affairs, while others stay on the academic side to become deans or academic program directors.

Education and Training

To become an Academic Adviser, the minimum requirement is a bachelor's degree. Many employers prefer and/or require a master's degree. Academic Advisers may hold a master's degree in counseling, higher education administration, social work, psychology, or a variety of academic disciplines. Some professionals may go on to study for their master's degree part-time at the institution where they are employed. Academic Advisers who work with students of particular majors often have a background in that major.

Advising experience as a peer Adviser, tutor, or counselor is good preparation for an entry-level job as an Academic Adviser.

Experience, Skills, and Personality Traits

Because Academic Advisers work with students from diverse backgrounds, it is important for them to be sensitive and empathetic toward their concerns. They must have excellent analytical, organizational, and interpersonal skills. Also important is the ability to listen and communicate well. A background in counseling or work directly advising others is helpful.

Academic Advisers must have a strong understanding of overall academic curriculum, as well as knowledge of specific requirements within their institution of employment. Much of this comes from on the job training, but requires

Academic Advisers to be quick learners. They must become experts on their school and all its academic programs. It is also necessary to be computer literate to maintain student records and run reports.

Unions and Associations

The National Academic Advising Association (NACADA) (http://www.nacada.ksu.edu/) is a professional association specifically for Academic Advisers working in higher education. With more than 6,500 members representing all 50 states, they offer regional divisions, conferences and events, and leadership opportunities. For those Academic Advisers who specialize in working with athletes, there is the National Association of Academic Advisers for Athletics (http://www.nfoura.org/).

Tips for Entry

1. Talk to current Academic Advisers at a variety of college and universities to learn more about their jobs and academic backgrounds.
2. Spend time reviewing course catalogs to better understand academic policies and major and graduation requirements.
3. Enhance your listening skills by working as a volunteer on campus.
4. Practice your communication and public speaking skills by taking a speech course.
5. As a student, volunteer as a peer adviser. Many schools have programs where juniors and seniors mentor freshman and sophomores with the same major area of study.

REGISTRAR

CAREER PROFILE

Duties: Oversees record keeping, registration, and scheduling process for a college or university

Alternate Title(s): University Registrar; Director of Enrollment Services; Director of Records

Salary Range: $50,000 to $80,000 and up

Employment Prospects: Good

Advancement Prospects: Good

Best Geographical Location(s): All

Prerequisites:

Education or Training—Minimum of a bachelor's degree; master's degree or higher often preferred

Experience—Three to five years of university administration

Special Skills and Personality Traits—Attention to detail; mathematical skills; good interpersonal ability

CAREER LADDER

```
┌──────────────────────────────────┐
│ Vice President or Dean of Student │
│  Services or Academic Affairs     │
└──────────────────────────────────┘

┌──────────────────────────────────┐
│            Registrar              │
└──────────────────────────────────┘

┌──────────────────────────────────┐
│ Assistant or Associate Registrar  │
└──────────────────────────────────┘
```

Position Description

Registrars serve as official university record-keepers and certifiers. They manage the student registration process, grade collection, the certification process for the federal government and professional organizations, and verifying grades and degrees. For example, if a student is receiving a bachelor's degree in nursing, the Registrar signs off on the degree, letting the American Nurses Association know that the student has completed the requirements to obtain professional nursing certification.

Registrars are also university leaders, since their function is so crucial to the running of academic and student services. Together with the deans, they help create and implement effective academic policies and procedures regarding student registration and records across their campuses. They often manage a staff made up of professional and administrative members, which will vary in size depending on the size of their school. The staff is divided up by specialty area, with one person designated to handle a single area, such as graduation, transcripts, certification, bookkeeping, and so on.

With the technological advancements that computers have brought to college campuses, many schools have already implemented an electronic registration process that may also include grade reporting and retrieval. Registrars have played an integral role in that process, and on campuses that have not yet made the switch, they are working to make it happen. It is important for them to be up to date on the computer programs, technologies, and academic software used to advance their services through technology.

Course registration is an involved process that entails analyzing, juggling, and even smoothing over some ruffled feathers at times. Registrars prepare class lists and designate classrooms for faculty members. This can involve finessing sometimes when professors get very particular about where and when they want to teach their classes. Registrars are customer-service focused and try to work with both students and faculty to ensure satisfaction.

Registrars collaborate with both the administrative and academic departments within a university. They work with faculty and department heads to plan class schedules, evaluate transfer credits, and determine academic standing; they work with administrative deans and counselors to process leaves of absence and advise students about policy. For this reason, they need to flexible and skilled with numbers as well as interpersonal communication.

Their duties may include:

- Managing a staff
- Monitoring students progress toward filling graduation and degree requirements
- Running reports about topics such as student retention, degree completion, and enrollment
- Analyzing registration data to create policy
- Ensuring compliance with federal laws concerning student records
- Maintaining academic partnerships with other institutions
- Assuring timely creation of student transcripts
- Recording and processing grades
- Managing modifications in curriculum
- Evaluating and implementing new technologies
- Participating in campus committees
- Arranging exam schedules
- Working with the student accounts office to determine fiscal clearance for registration
- Interpreting registration policies for students, faculty, and staff
- Evaluating programs and creating new policies
- Developing strategic initiatives

Depending on the college or university, Registrars may be in the reporting structure of either student services or academic affairs. As with most university professionals, they typically work a 12-month year, with longer working hours during busy times of the academic year and lighter schedules during the summer months.

Registrars also keep up with the constantly changing government laws and regulations that affect their profession. The Federal Educational Rights and Privacy Act (FERPA), also called the Buckley Amendment, protects the rights of students by guaranteeing their access to their academic records while prohibiting unauthorized access by others. The law has been updated and revised many times, so Registrars need to know current status to determine when they can or cannot release data in specific circumstances. Also, another current issue in the field is the debate over what constitutes an official signature. With the advent of technology and electronic completion of many student forms, it becomes questionable whether a student can be held financially accountable for courses he or she has not paid for if there is no actual signature present. By keeping up on the legalities and paying careful attention to detail, Registrars can protect both students and the university in various situations.

Salaries

According to a 2002–3 survey of median salaries of college administrators by type of institution from the *Chronicle of Higher Education* Web site, the median salary for Registrars at all types of institutions was $59,206. Depending on the size and location of the institution, as well as the education and experience of the Registrar, salaries ranged from $51,960 for those with a baccalaureate degree to $80,922 for those with a Ph.D. Like other university administrators, Registrars often enjoy generous vacation time, tuition reimbursement, and a comprehensive benefits package.

Employment Prospects

Overall, employment prospects for Registrars are good. As older people in the field retire, new opportunities arise at colleges and universities across the country. Particularly for those living in cities with many schools, or those who are geographically flexible, there are many positions available.

Advancement Prospects

Registrars may use their skill set to advance to other areas within university administration and prospects are good. Some may go on to become vice presidents or deans, while others may choose to work as Registrars for larger universities that offer better pay, more prestige, or other benefits.

Education and Training

While a bachelor's degree may be listed as the minimum requirement, to get hired as a Registrar today, most candidates hold a master's degree. Since it is a management position, a business or math background is helpful to provide the necessary financial and number skills, either as an undergraduate course of study or through an MBA degree. Also, many Registrars currently entering the field hold a master's degree in higher education administration. During this program, they complete internships in the Registrar's office that provide invaluable job training and employment contacts. At larger and more competitive schools, the Registrar might even have a doctorate and be involved with research studies. Furthermore, many people take advantage of free tuition benefits and study for advanced degrees in the evening at their school while working full-time.

Experience, Skills, and Personality Traits

Registrars need to be meticulous and thrive on paying careful attention to detail. They should be organized and work well with numbers. However, math-orientation on its own will not make a successful Registrar. Because they are often the frontline staff dealing with students, parents, other administrators, and faculty, they must have excellent interpersonal skills. They need management and analytical skills, as well as public relations and customer-service abilities. Computer skills and experience with student information systems is required. Registrars often gain experience through working their way up in the Registrar's office, in other university departments, in other business-focused roles, or as graduate students.

Unions and Associations

The main professional association for Registrars is the American Association of Collegiate Registrars and Admissions Officers (AACRAO), an organization of more than 9,000 professionals representing 2,300 institutions. They also may belong to the American College Personnel Association, as well as regional branches of organizations.

Tips for Entry

1. Take courses in math and business to gain a better understanding of financial and economic principles.

2. Speak to a Registrar to learn more about the job responsibilities.

3. Research graduate programs in Higher Education Administration. The appendix in the back of this book is a good place to begin.

4. Read job descriptions for Registrars on sites such as http://www.chronicle.com and http://www.higheredjobs.com.

5. Take a look at different college and university home pages and visit the sites for the Registrar's Office. This will help clarify the role of the Registrar's office and job functions.

STUDENT ACTIVITIES COORDINATOR

CAREER PROFILE

Duties: Develops activities designed to promote student development; advises student organizations; plans and manages student activities such as workshops and events; develops leadership programs

Alternate Title(s): Student Affairs Coordinator; Student Activities Counselor; Coordinator of Student Life

Salary Range: $30,000 to $50,000

Employment Prospects: Good

Advancement Prospects: Good

Best Geographical Location(s): All

Prerequisites:

    Education or Training—Master's degree in student personnel or higher education administration preferred for most positions

    Experience—One to two years of experience in student affairs for those with only a bachelor's degree; master's degree and internship experience can substitute for professional work experience

    Special Skills and Personality Traits—Excellent interpersonal skills; patience and flexibility; teamwork ability; good multitasking, organization, and event planning

CAREER LADDER

```
┌─────────────────────────────────┐
│   Assistant or Associate Director│
│      of Student Activities       │
└─────────────────────────────────┘

┌─────────────────────────────────┐
│   Student Activities Coordinator │
└─────────────────────────────────┘

┌─────────────────────────────────┐
│     Graduate Assistant or Intern │
└─────────────────────────────────┘
```

Position Description

Student Activities Coordinators are a vital part of the student affairs staff on a college campus. As student advocates, as well as experts in student development theory, they oversee the planning of activities that will help to promote student development. They juggle a multitude of responsibilities, all with the same overriding goal of enhancing the academic, social, and cocurricular experience students receive in college.

One of the major responsibilities of most Student Affairs Coordinators is to advise student organizations. Depending on the size of the campus, hundreds of student organizations may exist. They can include activity-based groups such as the chess club or yearbook; preprofessional groups such as the prelaw society or the biomedical engineering society; issue-based groups such as the Young Democrats or students for peace; and cultural heritage groups such as the black students organization or the Turkish students association. As students take leadership of various campus groups for the first time, they are often unsure about how to navigate the university system, be effective leaders, and balance their involvement with their course load. Student Activities Coordinators provide guidance to these new leaders with regard to financial management, university policy, and group dynamics. They help them with setting up their annual schedule of events and programming. In addition, they often run programs on leadership development to help the students become effective managers.

In this way, Student Affairs Coordinators also serve as counselors, advising student leaders on how to budget their time and get the most out of their leadership role without letting the rest of their educational experience suffer. They work with them on becoming savvy in navigating the university system and help them to understand how the skills they develop through their leadership will translate into real world opportunities. They often work in conjunction with the career services office to develop workshops related to résumé preparation or job opportunities for student leaders. In addition, they also work with academic advisers and deans to help students choose an academic program that will help them to achieve their ultimate goals.

Another portion of the job of Student Activities Coordinators consists of programming. The programming is often done on a developmental model by class year and covers a variety of student life topics such as adjusting to college for freshman and transitioning to the professional world for seniors. They also conduct or arrange for skill training and help with large-scale events such as orientation and graduation. Sometimes the Student Activities Coordinators present these programs themselves, while other times they will collaborate with other campus offices or solicit outside speakers.

Depending on the campus, the work of a Student Activities Coordinator may also include and overlap with residential life, Greek life (fraternities and sororities), housing, academic advising, and others.

Their duties may include:

• Enforcing laws and policies of the university
• Attending committee meetings to represent student activities among the overall student affairs staff
• Monitoring budgets for events
• Negotiating contracts and fees for event services
• Conducting regular meetings with student organizations
• Helping student groups to transition between leaders
• Evaluating leadership of different student organizations
• Preparing advertising and marketing materials for events
• Ensuring safety for events
• Delivering workshops, lectures, and trainings
• Producing annual financial and activity reports
• Evaluating programs for success
• Assisting with operations
• Promoting programs and policies
• Researching and designing workshop topics

Most offices of student activities have at least one Student Activities Coordinator who reports to an assistant or associate director, in addition to a director or dean. Larger schools have several Student Activities Coordinators, which gives them the flexibility to focus in on specific activities or populations. For example, an office might have a Student Activities Coordinator for each class year, or for specialty areas such as cultural heritage clubs, social activity clubs, or media and communication clubs.

Student Activities Coordinators tend to be young and energetic, fresh out of college or graduate school. This can be an asset in the field, as students can relate to them better and develop good communication and rapport. However, they must strive to maintain their sense of authority, while being friendly. They are the professionals who must sign off on events, and they are the ones responsible if things go wrong. They need to ensure no policies are being violated and that students are respecting their input.

Another reason Student Activities Coordinators are often young and full of energy is that the job requires many hours, including evenings and weekends for programming. It is a 12-month job that could require up to 50 hours per week during the busy times of year. It is difficult for people with families or many outside obligations to meet the demands of this nontraditional schedule and balance it with their personal life. People usually do not stay in the position for more than four years, to avoid burnout and to allow for more growth.

Salaries

According to data on the Salary Wizard at http://www.salary.com, the median salary for a student activities officer in higher education is $41,173. This figure varies depending on the size and geographical location of the institution. Many Student Activities Coordinators take advantage of other benefits offered by colleges and universities such as taking classes or enjoying vacation time.

Employment Prospects

Employment prospects for Student Activities Coordinators are good. As enrollment grows, so does the need for professionals to work with students. Opportunities within student life are extensive, and many community colleges, colleges, and universities need to hire professionals to work with students in this capacity. Because of the high turnover in the field (each professional staying in a job for about three to four years), positions become available on a regular basis.

Advancement Prospects

Advancement prospects are also good. Particularly for those with a master's degree, Student Activities Coordinators can advance to become assistant directors, associate directors, or directors of student activities. With the skills they develop, they can also transition to other areas of student affairs such as career services, academic advising, residential life, and others.

Education and Training

A master's degree in student personnel or higher education administration is the preferred credential for the field. While earning the master's degree, students gain experience in student activities through required internships. Smaller schools may be willing to hire candidates with only a bachelor's degree if they have had experience in student activities while completing their undergraduate work. Helpful undergraduate majors include psychology, sociology, human development, and English. Often, they will take courses in student development or pursue a master's degree while employed. It is important for Student Activities Coordinators to have an understanding of student development theory and the college process.

Experience, Skills, and Personality Traits

Many Student Activities Coordinators have had experience as student leaders or members of a student organization while in college or graduate school themselves. This experience, along with internships or work-study positions in student affairs, provides a helpful background for the field.

Student Activities Coordinators should be enthusiastic and enjoy working with people. They need to have respect for multicultural issues and knowledge of higher education administration. Skills in writing and budgeting are helpful, as are the abilities to manage time well and plan events.

Unions and Associations

Student Activities Coordinators may belong to a variety of professional associations, including the American College Personnel Association and the National Association of Student Personnel Administrators.

Tips for Entry

1. While in college, get involved with student organizations. Consider taking a leadership role and learn how students and the administration work together.
2. Look at the big picture. Most people do not stay as Student Activities Coordinators for more than five years, so think about your ultimate goals.
3. Explore graduate programs that prepare student affairs professionals by visiting the Web site: http://www.acpa.nche.edu/c12/directory.htm.
4. Talk to current Student Activities Coordinators to learn more about their jobs. Ask them about the pros and cons and what tips they have for those just starting out.

FINANCIAL AID DIRECTOR

CAREER PROFILE

Duties: Supervises the distribution of federal, state, and institutional dollars to students for their educational experience

Alternate Title(s): Financial Aid Manager, Financial Aid Administrator

Salary Range: $50,000 to $80,000 and up

Employment Prospects: Good

Advancement Prospects: Good

Best Geographical Location(s): All

Prerequisites:

Education or Training—Bachelor's degree; master's degree helpful for some positions

Experience—Work-study or internship position in financial aid office for entry-level position; three years or more for director level

Special Skills and Personality Traits—Excellent financial and interpersonal skills; attention to detail; flexible

CAREER LADDER

```
┌─────────────────────────────────┐
│      Financial Aid Director      │
│       (larger institution)       │
└─────────────────────────────────┘

┌─────────────────────────────────┐
│      Financial Aid Director      │
└─────────────────────────────────┘

┌─────────────────────────────────┐
│      Financial Aid Officer       │
└─────────────────────────────────┘
```

Position Description

With the rising cost of higher education in the United States, many students and their families seek assistance to offset expenses and make the dream of college or graduate school a reality. Money is out there, including resources from the federal government, state governments, and various educational institutions. Financial Aid Directors are responsible for the management and allocation of these funds. They meet with students and families, conduct financial review, determine eligibility, and present award packages. Furthermore, they are experts on the rules, regulations, policies, and procedures related to these loans, grants, and scholarships, and have in-depth knowledge of what is available.

Financial Aid Directors spend time meeting with prospective, recently accepted, current, and transfer students and their families. During these meetings, they review the families' financial profiles, including tax returns, assets, adjusted gross income, and other data in order to determine eligibility for different types of funding. After calculating the federal, state, and institutional award amounts, they oversee the processing of the loan and financial aid application. They explain what types of aid students qualify for

once they have been accepted, and go over some of the financial alternatives for coming up with the rest of the money. In this way, they serve as financial planners to help students and families create a budget that will meet their needs and enable them to pay for their education.

As one Financial Aid Director put it, "Needs analysis is both an art and a science." Because the process of financial aid is neither perfect nor exact, it is imperative to understand the intricacies and details that go into a financial analysis. Financial Aid Directors must remain objective when they meet with families as they explain the decisions they made regarding their children's educational future and why.

The U.S. government plays an important role in educational funding, and the Financial Aid Director must work in compliance with government policies and regulations. First, they need to make sure that students are not being overawarded. Colleges and universities are constantly being audited and need to be cautious about accounting for every dollar. Also, Financial Aid Directors need to follow policy in order to make sure their institutions meet eligibility requirements for federal aid. They participate in a constant monitoring and give-and-take with the government—receiving information and reporting back on status.

At private colleges and universities, there are institutional dollars to be awarded in addition to federal and state loans. Scholarships, both need and merit-based are available through private donors, endowments, tuition money, and other specific school-based programs. This process is called "tuition discounting" and is practiced by schools to attract a high-quality and diverse group of students. Here, Financial Aid Directors are decision makers, playing a part in deciding who gets these awards and justifying why. They also work with other university officials to determine what is valued by their specific institution. For example, some schools offer scholarships for athletes, musicians, community service participants, and so on. Tuition discounting is not without controversy and is constantly being reviewed, researched, and monitored by the profession.

Their duties may include:

- Researching and interpreting federal, state, and private financial aid regulations and sources
- Establishing departmental policies and procedures
- Analyzing trends, budgeting, and forecasting
- Using software such as Banner Software, Banner Web, Guarantor software, and state and federal proprietary programs
- Designing quality control mechanisms for technology programs
- Running reports on status of students and funds
- Transitioning data from different computer systems
- Providing information to external auditors
- Managing annual departmental budget
- Running a work study or student employment office
- Preparing and submitting reports for continued federal and state funding of financial aid programs
- Keeping up to date on new legislation affecting financial aid
- Hiring, supervising, and training employees

Financial Aid Directors manage an office staff that may include associate or assistant directors, counselors, information technology specialists, administrative assistants, work-study students, and graduate assistants or interns. Within the office, staff members may be divided by their specific responsibilities such as managing federal funds, transfer students, academic merit scholarships, graduate students, and so on. Each of these groups has varying needs and requires different types of counseling and support. For example, graduate students are eligible for government aid separate from undergraduates and also are usually in another type of social and financial situation, perhaps having worked for several years and functioning independently from their parents. However, it is up to the Financial Aid Director to be knowledgeable about all the areas in order oversee the department.

Salaries

According to *Facts & Figures—Median Salaries of College Administrators by Type of Institution, 2002–3*, on the *Chronicle of Higher Education* online, the median salary for Directors of Financial Aid at all institutions is $60,356. Additional data on http://www.salary.com, shows a typical Financial Aid Director as earning a median base salary of $63,984, according to their analysis of data reported by corporate human resources departments. Half of the people in this job earn between $53,851 and $76,741.

Employment Prospects

Employment aspects are good for Financial Aid Directors, since all colleges and universities need professionals to manage this process. There are usually more open positions than qualified applicants to fill them. Positions often get filled through word of mouth, alumni contacts, and graduate school assistantships. They are also listed on Web sites with student affairs jobs such as http://www.higheredjobs.com and http://www.chronicle.com.

Advancement Prospects

Financial Aid Directors gain a specific set of skills that they can apply to several different areas within colleges and universities, other nonprofits, or the private sector. While Financial Aid Directors are almost always the head of their own departments, they may seek advancement by moving from a smaller school to a larger one, transitioning into the student lending field, or taking on new roles in higher education such as that of a dean.

Education and Training

Financial Aid Directors should have a bachelor's degree. A financial background including accounting, business, finance, economics, and computer science is useful. Many Financial Aid Directors (particularly at large universities) hold a master's degree in fields such as business, higher education administration, public relations, or educational administration. Because regulations are always changing, Financial Aid Directors are always learning, and they receive ongoing training through government workshops and professional development seminars.

Experience, Skills, and Personality Traits

Successful Financial Aid Directors strike a balance between numbers and people skills. As counselors, they are skilled at dealing with students and their parents, assuaging fears and handling delicate subjects such as personal finance. As financial administrators, however, they can read a tax return, review formulas, and spot errors a mile away. They need to have a strong financial background in order to make sense of the data they analyze.

Also important are excellent technical skills. Many computer databases and customized software programs focus specifically on financial aid data, and while Financial Aid Directors receive training on all of them, any previous computer knowledge or expertise is helpful. They also need knowledge of the state and federal regulations and guidelines that govern financial aid, as well as an understanding of basic accounting, budget, and fiscal reporting techniques.

Unions and Associations

Financial Aid Directors can belong to a variety of professional associations, including the National Association of Student Financial Aid Administrators (NASFAA), the National Association of College and University Business Officers, and the American College Personnel Association (ACPA).

Tips for Entry

1. Review Web sites such as http://www.finaid.org to learn about educational funding.
2. Work in the financial aid office on campus to learn more about what the various professionals there do.
3. Learn more about graduate programs in higher education administration using the Appendix in this book.
4. Take a course in business or accounting to brush up on financial principles.
5. Have you ever applied for financial aid? Consider the process you went through and the professionals who advised you.

DEAN OF STUDENTS

CAREER PROFILE

Duties: Oversees the links between academic and student life on a college or university campus, including student acquisition, retention, housing, orientation, and graduation; administers academic policy

Alternate Title(s): Dean of Student Services, Dean of Student Affairs

Salary Range: $55,000 to $90,000 and up

Employment Prospects: Good

Advancement Prospects: Good

Best Geographical Location(s): All

Prerequisites:

Education or Training—Minimum of a bachelor's degree; advanced degree required for most positions

Experience—Five to 15 years of academic and student services experience

Special Skills and Personality Traits—Excellent interpersonal skills; strong written and verbal communication; knowledge of student development and academic environment; good leadership and management skills

CAREER LADDER

```
┌─────────────────────────────────┐
│   Dean, College or University   │
└─────────────────────────────────┘

┌─────────────────────────────────┐
│        Dean of Students         │
└─────────────────────────────────┘

┌─────────────────────────────────┐
│   Assistant or Associate Dean   │
└─────────────────────────────────┘
```

Position Description

College is a time of great transition for many students. Often, it is the first time they are away from home, and students need to learn how to juggle their academic responsibilities with their newfound social freedom. Living in a dormitory, planning a course schedule, joining clubs and activities, and considering career options are just some of the issues they face. Deans of Students are top-level administrators who help facilitate the academic and social process for students.

Most Deans of Students have responsibilities that fall into both the academic and student development realms. In terms of academics, Deans of Students are involved with curriculum development for their schools. Some assist students with program planning and major selection themselves; others work extensively with their staff to train them to advise students.

When students are having particular academic concerns, they often see the Dean of Students. If they need to change their major, are failing a course, or are having medical or personal problems that are affecting their grades, the Dean of Students can advise them on next steps. They may help identify issues, review records, and take action on behalf of the student. Deans of Students may also work closely with faculty to determine different academic requirements and an advising structure.

Student affairs and development responsibilities encompass much policy and procedure. Deans of Students establish rules and set policy as to the way things must be done and handled. They may advise student clubs and organizations and work with those administrators to develop structure and programming. They are involved with students throughout their time on campus, from managing orientation to supervising graduation. They frequently set the procedure and establish the paperwork students need to complete for processes such as major selection and graduation. Furthermore, they often determine housing assignments and deal with difficulties that come up related to the dormitories.

Discipline also plays a major role in the job of Dean of Students, for both academic and personal issues. They may write a disciplinary code of conduct, conduct disciplinary hearings, and investigate charges brought against students regarding problems such as sexual harassment, plagiarism, or drug use.

Together with faculty, Deans of Students rule on academic issues and determine when to make exceptions to the rules. They decide when a student should be suspended, be put on academic probation, or given a leave of absence. Students often petition the Dean of Students when they want to drop a course after the designated time or get excused from assignments due to personal situations.

As campus leaders, Deans of Students often have responsibility for several major campus components. These may include student affairs, student activities, residence life, career services, disability services, academic advising, multicultural affairs, international student services, Greek life (fraternities and sororities), and health services, among others. Deans of Students supervise associate deans and directors; they usually report to a college dean or vice president.

Additional duties may include:

- Preparing and editing university publications
- Developing a policy and procedure manual
- Managing specific scholarship programs
- Assessing the performance of staff
- Meeting with parents, alumni, and trustees of the college
- Advising university officials on appropriate courses of action in different situations
- Mediating disputes between students and faculty or administrators
- Maintaining student records and files
- Leading staff meetings
- Conducting follow-up surveys
- Participates in the faculty tenure process
- Serving as an adviser to student government
- Evaluating current programs and implementing change where necessary

In some colleges and universities, there is a conflict of interest between the academic and administrative staff. The academics often want to preserve the notion of higher education for the sake of knowledge, while administrators bring in the practical aspect of applying this knowledge outside of academe. Deans of Students play an interesting role straddling these two disciplines. At some schools, they may be part of the faculty, but more frequently, they are solely administrators in the department of student affairs. Either way, one challenge of their work is to play to both sides and smooth out edges between them.

Deans of Students may work at two-year community colleges, four-year public and private colleges, and large international public and private universities. Their hours are lengthy, with many meetings extending into the evenings and even weekends. Some Deans of Students may be required to live near campus and are even offered subsidized housing, while others are not.

Additionally, Deans of Students may have specific responsibilities based on the campus at which they work. Some are required to teach one or more courses, while others are responsible for students with particular majors or students at a particular level such as master's degree students or sophomores.

Salaries

Salaries for Deans of Students vary depending on the size and geographical location of the college, as well as the educational level required for the position. According to data from a survey on the Web site http://www.salary.com, a typical Dean of Students in higher education earns a median base salary of $77,632, according to an analysis of data reported by corporate human resources departments.

Additionally, a 2002–2003 survey of median salaries of college administrators by type of institution from the *Chronicle of Higher Education* Web site, the median salary for Deans of Students at all types of institutions was $72,823.

Employment Prospects

Overall, employment prospects are good for Deans of Students. With enrollment up on many campuses despite rising costs, Deans of Students are needed to provide leadership to student affairs. Opportunities are greatest for those who are geographically flexible, and for those with advanced degrees.

Advancement Prospects

Some Deans of Students may advance to become dean of their entire college or university, or dean of a specific college within their university. For example a Dean of Students serving both an engineering and liberal arts college may go on to become dean of the engineering school. These deans have responsibility for overall academics and administration, rather than student affairs.

However, only Deans of Students with strong academic credentials can make this move. A doctorate is required to become dean of a college, and a doctorate in an academic discipline, rather than an educational field like student affairs, is highly preferred.

At some colleges and universities, Deans of Students are part of the faculty and can receive tenure, the process by which after a certain number of years, a position is reviewed and then virtually guaranteed to that individual until retirement.

Education and Training

Only at very small schools could a Dean of Students be hired with a bachelor's degree. On most campuses, a minimum of a master's degree is necessary, and many require a doctorate. The most common field of study at the graduate level for a Dean of Students is a degree in higher education administration, student personnel administration, or student development. However, many Deans of Students also have degrees in the liberal arts or other educational fields such as counseling or international education.

While it is important for Deans of Students to be knowledgeable about student development theory and issues, they may need specialized degrees for serving certain populations. For example, a Dean of Students at an art school will likely have a degree in art history, arts administration, or fine arts.

Additionally, most Deans of Students work extensively with students during their graduate studies. Most programs require internships and fieldwork that enable new professionals to gain valuable hands-on experience.

Experience, Skills, and Personality Traits

Dean of Students is a management position. Deans of Students often begin as assistant or associate deans, or in another area of student services such as admissions or career planning. It usually takes between five and 15 years of experience to move to a position at this level. Deans of Students must have excellent leadership and supervisory skills as they often must manage large staffs.

Deans of Students may serve as teachers, advisers, mentors, counselors, disciplinarians, and therapists all at once to their students. In order to do their jobs, they must be fair, impartial, and ethical. Yet, they must also be sensitive, with good listening skills, in order to hear students' needs and gain their respect.

Unions and Associations

Deans of Students may belong to professional associations, including the National Association of Student Personnel Administrators, the American Association for Higher Education, the Association of College Administration Professionals, and the American College Personnel Association.

Tips for Entry

1. While a student, get involved with student affairs on your campus. Try a position as a resident adviser (RA) or join an organization related to one of your interests.
2. Explore graduate programs in higher education administration, listed in Appendix I, section B.
3. Gain experience in teaching by working as a teaching assistant or tutor in one of your strong subjects. Ask professors and other teaching assistants how you can get started.
4. Have you ever had contact with your Dean of Students or another dean on campus? Next time you need to make an appointment, schedule some extra time to speak to him or her about the chosen career path.
5. Browse the Web site of the *Chronicle of Higher Education* (http://www.chronicle.com) for job listings and information about the higher education field.

ENVIRONMENT, NATURE, AND CONSERVATION

NATURALIST

CAREER PROFILE

Duties: Educates public visitors to parks about the environment; teaches classes about wildlife, plants, and the geology of a particular region

Alternate Title(s): Teacher Naturalist, Interpretive Naturalist, Environmental Educator

Salary Range: $20,000 to $30,000

Employment Prospects: Fair

Advancement Prospects: Fair

Best Geographical Location(s): All, particularly regions with parks, water, and conservation needs

Prerequisites:

Education or Training—Bachelor's degree in science or conservation field

Experience—Teaching experience and some knowledge of plants, animals, and geology

Special Skills and Personality Traits—Love of nature and the outdoors; excellent communication skills including public speaking and teaching skills; knowledge of the environment, science, and conservation

CAREER LADDER

```
┌─────────────────────────────────┐
│      Senior Naturalist or       │
│ Director of Education or Conservation │
└─────────────────────────────────┘

┌─────────────────────────────────┐
│           Naturalist            │
└─────────────────────────────────┘

┌─────────────────────────────────┐
│         Intern/Volunteer        │
└─────────────────────────────────┘
```

Position Description

Naturalists are passionate about nature and strive to share their passion with others. They love the outdoors and are fascinated by the plant and animal life found in different geographical regions. They work for parks, nature centers, wildlife refuges, museums, and other conservation organizations. As experts on the flora and fauna of their particular park, Naturalists study different species and teach others not only about these living things, but also why it is important to protect them.

Many Naturalists spend the bulk of their time teaching. They often work with groups ranging from preschool to older adults, providing programs catered to different age groups. Programs can include lectures, tours, or walks. For young children, they may offer a program about owls where they can see an owl in its natural habitat, followed by an arts and crafts project. For senior citizens, they may run bird walks or classes on conservation issues. They develop the

plans for these programs and think of ideas that will be interesting to visitors.

For programs with school-age children, Naturalists often collaborate with local school districts. They write curriculum to be used both on their own site, as well as in schools. They update current offerings and adapt them to meet the needs of teachers and different student groups. As they turn the outdoors into a classroom, they engage students and help them to see the wonder of nature.

While all Naturalists focus on the conservation and preservation of ecosystems, the topics for Naturalists to teach will vary depending on their geographical region and organization of employment. For example, a Naturalist working in a beach community will be concerned about wetlands preservation and its related animal and plant species. Those Naturalists employed by organizations such as the Audubon Society have a focus on birds and other wildlife. From the woodlands to the desert, they may run programs about bears, arctic foxes, or cacti, depending on where they live.

In addition to teaching, Naturalists also spend their time interfacing with the public in other ways. As resources of information, they may staff visitor's centers and answer questions there. People may bring in interesting plants they have found growing in their backyards that they would like identified. Also, Naturalists field telephone calls and e-mails on a variety of conservation issues.

Naturalists may also take on some administrative responsibilities within their organizations. They may supervise volunteers, oversee the care for any on-site animals used for education, and participate in public communication such as writing press releases, program flyers, or newsletter copy. Furthermore, they often travel the trails themselves on a regular basis to notice any changes, as well as new and interesting things to share with visitors.

Some Naturalists also conduct research. They may be involved with projects that study different endangered species or ecology. The projects may be involved with helping to further the known information about these life-forms, as well as to set or change public policy. Naturalists may participate in population studies, track bird migration, or sample streams to test water condition. Most research studies are affiliated with universities and based there, so Naturalists collaborate with the university research team.

Other Naturalists may seek positions that enable them to work with special populations, such as young children. At times, they may need to adapt their lessons to serve people with disabilities and other special needs. In parks and preserves with many visitors who speak other languages, foreign language skills are helpful.

Their duties may include:

- Monitoring and preserving plants and animals
- Identifying and studying different wildlife species
- Leading nature walks and tours
- Designing exhibits and display areas for artifacts
- Publishing a newsletter
- Writing Web copy
- Assisting with fund-raising efforts
- Gathering information on local ecology
- Keeping aware of public policy and issues affecting the environment
- Ensuring safety of guests during nature excursions
- Working directly with animals used for visitor programs
- Developing programming schedules
- Using multimedia to create and deliver presentations
- Running summer camp programs for children

Naturalists need to enjoy working outside, even in inclement weather. They usually work a 40-hour workweek, but it may include evenings and weekends for public pro-grams. Even though salaries tend to be low, Naturalists often report high job satisfaction because they are able to earn a living while expressing their passion for nature.

Salaries

Salaries for Naturalists can range from about $20,000 to $30,000. Because of these low numbers, some Naturalists supplement their income with additional teaching or research positions. Naturalists who advance to a senior level within a large organization may earn more.

Employment Prospects

Employment opportunities for Naturalists are fair. There are not a large number of possible employers, and additional positions may be cut due to budget limitations. Those who have interned in the field have a distinct advantage.

While most Naturalists work for parks, nature preserves, and conservation organizations, others may find positions in private and public schools. In private schools, especially schools with an experiential education component, Naturalists can find work more similar to that which they would experience at a park. For work in most public school systems, Naturalists need to be certified science teachers. Positions as a science teacher are more plentiful and can offer considerably better salaries and working hours that those of traditional Naturalists. However, many Naturalists love the autonomy that comes from working outside with nature and would never trade that for a school classroom.

Advancement Prospects

Naturalists may advance to positions with more responsibility within their organization. Possible next steps can include director of education, director of programming, or director of conservation. Others may decide to become more heavily involved with teaching and research and find positions in schools, colleges, and universities.

Education and Training

Naturalists should hold a bachelor's degree in a scientific field. Popular majors include biology, ecology, environmental science, natural resource management, and botany. Others may have a degree in education, which can also be helpful. Prior teaching experience is an asset and may be necessary for employment. The fieldwork that accompanies the academics is good preparation in practical learning. Additionally, Naturalists have usually spent much time at parks and nature preserves throughout their lives, which provides a background that cannot be learned in school.

Experience, Skills, and Personality Traits

Naturalists are committed to environmental issues and the protection of the earth's species and land. They are innate observers who are curious about the world around them, aware of their surroundings, and they pick up on subtle environmental changes. Knowledgeable about plants, animals, and geology, they are also well informed about the natural history of their regions.

Furthermore, they are excellent communicators and strong public speakers who are able to work with people of all ages. They are good teachers, with flexibility and patience to answer questions and deal with the public. Those who conduct research need to be adept in this area as well.

Unions and Associations

Naturalists may belong to the Association for Environmental and Outdoor Education, the North American Association for Environmental Education, and the National Science Teachers Association. They also may belong to conservation associations such as the Nature Conservancy, the Sierra Club, and the Wildlife Society.

Tips for Entry

1. Internships are the best way to get involved in environmental education. One site to try is the Student Conservation Association, which contains detailed information for high school and college students about conservation careers. Their Web site http://www.sca-inc.org/ offers internships, volunteer positions, and seasonal opportunities.

2. Consult http://eelink.net/, the site for environmental education on the Internet. It is geared to support educators who work with K–12 students. It can give you an idea of professional resources, environmental projects, and grants and jobs.

3. Visit a local nature center and participate in an educational program that interests you. Observe the Naturalist who presents the program, and then speak to him or her after the event to learn more about the career.

4. Take courses in science such as biology, environmental studies, conservation, or botany.

5. Gain teaching experience by working as a teaching assistant for a science course or tutoring children in the sciences.

DIRECTOR OF CONSERVATION

CAREER PROFILE

Duties: Directs conservation education and advocacy for an environmental organization; helps to preserve environment and set policy

Alternate Title(s): Director of Science, Conservationist, Director of Policy

Salary Range: $35,000 to $65,000

Employment Prospects: Fair

Advancement Prospects: Fair

Best Geographical Location(s): All, particularly regions with parks, water, and conservation needs, and policy groups in Washington, D.C.

Prerequisites:

Education or Training—Undergraduate degree in conservation, natural resources, or science; graduate degree highly preferred

Experience—Three to 10 years working for environmental organizations

Special Skills and Personality Traits—Excellent written and verbal communication skills; knowledge of conservation; good teaching and research skills; strong analytical skills

CAREER LADDER

Executive Director or President

Director of Conservation

Teacher, Naturalist, or Educational Director

Position Description

In order to assure the longevity of the millions of species of plants and animals throughout our country, someone must advocate on their behalf. Someone must monitor the environment and the laws—and how the two intersect—to ensure preservation and conservation. The professional who plays a major role in this process is often a Director of Conservation.

Directors of Conservation work for environmental and conservation organizations to develop and implement policy that will preserve the environment. They research and formulate positions on issues for their organization such as land preservation, endangered species, and others. They may develop conservation priorities for their region, state, or even the nation, depending on their organization. Their roles are multifaceted and include education, advocacy, policy making, and research.

Conservation organizations are often asked about the stand they take on particular legal issues. For example, legislators and the media might contact an organization such as the Audubon Society to find out their position on regulating wetlands in a particular region and how it might affect the flora and fauna.

Directors of Conservation are the professionals who determine the stand of their organizations. They conduct research and have a strong knowledge base of natural resources to understand how the environment will be affected by various legal decisions. One of their major responsibilities is meeting with the board of directors and advising them on policy issues. They must determine both what the major policy issues are, as well as the position their organization will take.

Directors of Conservation also work closely with the education and advocacy departments within their organization.

They often teach classes, work with schoolchildren, and present to the community about various nature and conservation topics. They may help students with activities such as conservation projects. Furthermore, they often serve on the board or committees of many related local conservation groups, participating in outreach and collaborative efforts.

The important topics for conservation vary depending on the geographical location where the organization is located. For example, each organization may focus on different types of endangered species. In an area native to eagles, Directors of Conservation may make decisions whether or not building a ball field in open space will be detrimental to the eagle population. If wetlands exist, they may decide how they need to be regulated. Their main goal is to preserve the natural environment in the best possible way. By educating lawmakers and the community, as well as the board and staff of their own organization, about the issues at stake, Directors of Conservation gain buy-in for their decisions.

Their duties may include:

- Answering telephone calls and e-mails from the public, board members, and policy makers
- Mobilizing community members to take action on issues
- Writing and editing conservation plans
- Establishing land management efforts and techniques
- Developing goals for conservation targets
- Designing protection strategies
- Overseeing projects
- Writing grants and participating in fund-raising
- Negotiating transactions with private landowners
- Supervising staff
- Partnering with other conservation and ecological groups

Directors of Conservation typically work between 40 and 50 hours per week. Their work schedule may include some evenings and weekends to accommodate the public hours of nature centers, tours, and groups. While they spend some of their time working in an office, they also spend time outdoors, leading groups and analyzing preservation sites and habitats. They may travel frequently to determine ecological status of various locations.

Salaries

Salaries for Directors of Conservation will vary depending on the size and budget of their organization. Another factor affecting salary is whether the organization is local or national in scope. Insiders say that a typical salary range is from $35,000 to $65,000 per year.

Employment Prospects

Employment prospects are fair for Directors of Conservation. As more species make the endangered list and the public faces the prospect of losing them forever, awareness has increased for the importance of conservation. There is a steady stream of positions available for those who have paid their dues in the field and have worked their way up. Opportunities are often found through professional associations and networking in the field.

Advancement Prospects

Advancement prospects are also fair. Directors of Conservation are usually at a high level within their organizations, so to advance they often will move from a smaller organization to a larger one. They may also seek positions as presidents or executive directors once they have built up at least 10 years of experience. Others may choose to work as consultants, lobbyists, or grant writers.

Education and Training

To become a Director of Conservation, one must hold a bachelor's degree, usually in conservation, biology, ecology, natural resources, or resources management. Additional courses or majors in life and natural sciences are also valuable. This is particularly important at larger, national organizations and for advancement.

Most Directors of Conservation also have graduate degrees, most frequently at the master's level. Subjects include biology, wildlife management, nonprofit administration, and resources management.

Experience, Skills, and Personality Traits

According to insiders, there is a specific path and experience needed to find a job in conservation, and academic degrees are not enough to land a position. It is critical for students to volunteer at an environmental organization while in college and/or graduate school. Even just several hours per week will provide an understanding about the field as well as a potential entry to the organization. This experience will help students circulate their names around and gain essential exposure to the field and professional contacts. Networking matters here, and those students who have established professionals making inquiries on their behalf will have a distinct edge over their competition.

Furthermore, after gaining volunteer experience, aspiring professionals should consider seasonal opportunities. Many conservation organizations hire employees for temporary positions funded through small grants, such as conducting research on a particular endangered species that comes to this habitat only in the summer.

Directors of Conservation typically have between three and 10 years of experience. They should be excellent public speakers, able to teach children and adults alike, as well as communicate with board members and policy makers. They need to be knowledgeable about science, nature, and conservation. As strong researchers, Directors of Conservation understand public policy and how to determine issues of major importance. Creative thinking enables them to find sometimes nontraditional solutions to complex problems. Above all, they should feel passionate about conservation and preservation and be committed to the cause of their organization.

Unions and Associations

Directors of Conservation may belong to the Society for Conservation Biology, the Wildlife Society, the Nature Conservancy, the Audubon Society, wildlife management associations by state, and the Sierra Club, among others. Students interested in conservation careers can join the Student Conservation Association, which provides service opportunities, outdoor skills and leadership training to thousands of young people each year.

Tips for Entry

1. There are many online resources to search for conservation jobs. Consult http://www.environetwork.com and http://www.ecojobs.com, which lists a number of jobs for free and then more by subscription.

2. Take a look at the Web site for The Nature Conservancy at http://nature.org/. According to their site, it is their mission to "preserve the plants, animals and natural communities that represent the diversity of life on Earth by protecting the lands and waters they need to survive." They have career information, as well as details about conservation issues.

3. The Student Conservation Association has detailed information for high school and college students about how to get involved in conservation careers. Their Web site http://www.sca-inc.org/ lists internships, volunteer positions, and seasonal opportunities as well.

4. Learn more about environmental policy by looking at the Web sites for major conservation organizations. For example, the National Audubon Society (http://www.audubon.org) has a section on the front page of their site for issues and action.

5. Research various conservation organizations that interest you. Rather than depending only on existing internship descriptions, be proactive and contact them yourself to find out if they have positions.

OUTDOOR INSTRUCTOR

CAREER PROFILE

Duties: Leads groups on wilderness trips that may include mountaineering, kayaking, or rafting; ensures safety and delivers curriculum

Alternate Title(s): Wilderness Instructor, Outdoor Trip Leader, Field Staff

Salary Range: $55 to $150 per day for seasonal staff; $26,000 to $40,000 per year for full-time staff

Employment Prospects: Excellent

Advancement Prospects: Good

Best Geographical Location(s): Wilderness locations with multiple national parks, mountains, and rivers

Prerequisites:

    Education or Training—No particular educational requirements, but many hold bachelor's degrees or higher; first aid training; CPR training

    Experience—Must be 21 years of age; some prior wilderness experience necessary; teaching experience helpful

    Special Skills and Personality Traits—Technical skills in climbing, kayaking, or rafting; adventurous spirit; good judgment; wilderness competence; sense of humor; team player; excellent interpersonal skills

    Licensure/Certification—May require Wilderness First Response (WFR) certification

CAREER LADDER

```
┌─────────────────────────────────┐
│        Course Director          │
└─────────────────────────────────┘

┌─────────────────────────────────┐
│       Outdoor Instructor        │
└─────────────────────────────────┘

┌─────────────────────────────────┐
│ Logistics Coordinator or Teacher,│
│        Ski Instructor,           │
│    or Recent College Graduate    │
└─────────────────────────────────┘
```

Position Description

Are you fearless in the wilderness and confident about your skills in rock climbing, kayaking, or backpacking? Do you feel committed to preserving the environment and helping others to gain appreciation for nature while building their self-esteem? If you cannot get enough of the great outdoors and you want to share your passion with other people, explore working as an Outdoor Instructor. Outdoor Instructors lead youth, teens, and adults on worldwide wilderness adventures ranging from sailing in New England and hiking the Austrian Alps to desert canyoneering in Utah and whitewater canoeing in Mexico. Trips may last between five days and one semester (72 days). During this time, Outdoor Instructors deliver curriculum and help their groups to work together, brave the elements, and overcome obstacles, promoting personal growth while taking in the scenery.

Usually, two Outdoor Instructors and a course director are assigned to each group. Groups consist of up to 12 people and are frequently called "patrols." The course director does not have full involvement with the trip, since he or she is often supervising other adventures as well. It is up to the Outdoor Instructors to work together to create a team environment that will enable their patrol to get the most from their experience.

Before a trip begins, the Outdoor Instructors that will be working together meet to discuss their teaching styles, educational methodologies, and other specifics about the trip, in addition to overseeing the packing of equipment and food. A key aspect of preparation is the review of student forms before the students actually arrive. They examine the medical and behavioral forms completed during student registration in order to gain an initial understanding of group dynamics, student strengths and weaknesses, and issues or concerns that may come up during the expedition.

Once the trip is in full swing, Outdoor Instructors may act as teachers, counselors, mentors, parents, and guides all at once. They take their responsibility seriously and are knowledgeable enough to know how to challenge their groups without putting them at risk. At all times, they adhere to high safety standards and ensure course quality. They carry out their planned curriculum and itinerary, but they are flexible and tailor activities to meet the needs of each specific patrol. Always they are aware of not only the entire group, but also each individual and how he or she is responding to the program. They run through exercises and initiatives to develop empowering student experiences.

Their duties are diverse and may include:

- Specializing with specific populations such as troubled youth
- Developing curriculum and exercises for building teams and self-esteem
- Fostering group cohesiveness
- Handling natural and medical emergency situations
- Empowering people to take risks
- Carrying equipment, cooking, and pitching tents
- Administering first aid and CPR
- Learning about the flora and fauna of particular regions

Furthermore, outdoor expertise areas often include:

- Rafting
- Canoeing
- Kayaking
- Rock climbing
- Skiing/Snowboarding/Snowshoeing
- Hiking/Mountaineering
- Backpacking
- Sailing
- Canyoneering
- Dogsledding

Most Outdoor Instructors do not lead trips full-time; they work an average of 40 days per year in this capacity. Their work is contracted and seasonal depending upon their area of expertise. During the year, many Outdoor Instructors are public school teachers, ski instructors, or college/graduate students. However, when they are working it is a 24-hour job. When a natural crisis such as a lightning storm occurs and the Outdoor Instructors are unable to get any sleep, business resumes as usual when the sun comes up. There is no such thing as sick days or vacation days when a trip is in full swing.

A pitfall of working as an Outdoor Instructor is that the work can be physically draining, as well as transient. One Outdoor Instructor mentioned the phenomenon of living out of his car, common among instructors who do not set up a permanent residence if they are traveling six months out of the year. For these reasons, most Outdoor Instructors do not spend more than three to five years doing this kind of work, as they want to establish more permanence in their lives. However, since it is such a passion for many, it may be something they do on a limited basis as they can for the rest of their lives. Many Outdoor Instructors say the opportunity to do what they love, combined with the satisfaction they get from seeing their students' sense of accomplishment, is unparalleled in other professions.

Salaries

Most Outdoor Instructors are not year-round staff members, so they get paid per day, rather than annually. Entry-level salaries begin at $55 per day and can go up to $150 per day for an experienced instructor teaching multiple courses. The average salary is approximately $80 per day. Outward Bound, the leading adventure-based education program, uses a credit system in which employees can earn salary credits for good performance, college degrees, and personal wilderness accomplishments such as climbing Mount Kilimanjaro during their own time. These credits can be applied to increase salary levels.

However, there has been a recent movement in organizations such as Outward Bound to create more full-time field staff positions for those who want to make this work their career. Full-time Outdoor Instructors earn between $26,000 and $30,000, while program directors can earn between $30,000 and $40,000.

Employment Prospects

Employment prospects for Outdoor Instructors are excellent. There are numerous adventure-based programs located throughout the United States, and they strive to hire good candidates with the necessary skill sets. Usually one area of outdoor expertise is needed, and then programs will provide the necessary training to learn others.

Advancement Prospects

Advancement prospects are good overall for Outdoor Instructors. Finding full-time work in the field is the most challenging, but they may be able to stay with adventure-based education programs to move into management positions such as course director, program director, or manager, where they can supervise instructors and run logistics or operations. Furthermore, the experience of being an Outdoor

Instructor is often well respected by employers in other organizations. It tells them a candidate is responsible and confident, a good leader as well as a team player. Groups such as Outward Bound have programs for alumni that enable them to participate in community outreach and speak about their experiences. For this reason, Outdoor Instructors can capitalize on their experience to move on within the nonprofit sector as educators and leaders.

Education and Training

Outdoor Instructors come from a variety of educational backgrounds. Although college degrees are not required, many Outdoor Instructors are college graduates, which may help them earn a higher salary. Experience teaching, counseling, leading groups, and working with people is helpful, in addition to prior wilderness training. Since Outdoor Instructors need to be at least 21 years old to get hired, younger candidates may gain experience by working in logistics for the organization—packing food, driving, and carrying equipment.

All Outdoor Instructors are required to come in with a core set of competencies, but they also receive extensive training before leading their first group. Training for new instructors may last up to two weeks, where they complete a full orientation and training curriculum.

Special Requirements

A variety of programs offer the Wilderness First Responder (WFR) course leading to certification. This is a first-aid certification course lasting 70 to 80 hours, which trains outdoor leaders, guides, and rangers to deal with crises in remote settings. It prepares individuals to respond to medical emergencies and issues such as treating hypothermia, administering CPR, and using rescue skills through education and role-playing. Many schools nationwide offer the WFR; two such programs include http://www.soloschools.com/wfr.html and http://www.cboutdoors.com/wilderness_first_responder.htm.

Experience, Skills, and Personality Traits

Required experience and skills vary depending on the type of wilderness trip each Outdoor Instructor will run. For example, mountaineering courses may require a minimum of 50 days of prior backpacking experience and the ability to carry a load of up to 70 pounds, while kayaking and raft-ing courses might require instructors to have past documented experience with Class III rapids and with boat operations. It is safe to say that the more outdoor competencies one has, the better for finding opportunities.

In addition to wilderness skills and experience, Outdoor Instructors need to be natural leaders, teachers, and counselors as well. Part of the mission of many adventure programs is to instill self-reliance and environmental understanding. Outdoor Instructors must be gregarious, confident, and competent. They must have the ability to stay calm in stressful situations and to inspire leadership and respect. They should care about people and be able to minimize conflict within their groups by promoting teamwork. Also, a sense of humor helps to make the trips fun and adventurous, an experience the students will always remember.

Unions and Associations

Professional associations for Outdoor Instructors include the Association for Experiential Education, which focuses on gaining direct experience to increase knowledge, develop skills, and clarify values, and the Outdoor Industry Association, which represents companies and organizations that supply outdoor goods.

Tips for Entry

1. Check out the Web site of Outward Bound, the leading nonprofit adventure-based education program in the world: http://www.outwardbound.org.
2. Follow your passion in terms of the outdoors, whether it is snowboarding, canoeing, or ice climbing, and gain expertise in that area. Pursue the activity and get instruction from trained professionals to bring you to an advanced level.
3. Take a first-aid course, get certified in CPR, and learn more about the WFR certification.
4. If you have the opportunity to participate in a wilderness expedition, take it. It will help you learn a lot about yourself, as well as the work that goes into leading a group. In addition to programs such as Outward Bound, many colleges offer programs to incoming undergraduate and graduate students to participate in a short-term adventure before classes begin. Check out the information on your campus.

PARK RANGER

CAREER PROFILE

Duties: Protects the flora and fauna of national and state parks; educates and assures safety of park visitors

Alternate Title(s): Forester, Ranger

Salary Range: $18,000 to $40,000 and up

Employment Prospects: Fair

Advancement Prospects: Good

Best Geographical Location(s): Wilderness and rural areas; urban areas with parks and recreation centers and nature preserves

Prerequisites:

Education or Training—Bachelor's degree, or a high school diploma and a minimum of three years of experience in park services

Experience—Internship or part-time seasonal work as a Park Ranger

Special Skills and Personality Traits—Flexibility; love of the outdoors; leadership skills; strong communication ability; physical stamina and outdoor technical skills

Licensure/Certification—Positions with the federal government are open to United States citizens only; they may also have age limitations, require first-aid certification, and require a valid driver's license

CAREER LADDER

```
┌─────────────────────────────────┐
│  District Ranger, Park Manager,  │
│       or Staff Specialist        │
└─────────────────────────────────┘

┌─────────────────────────────────┐
│          Park Ranger             │
└─────────────────────────────────┘

┌─────────────────────────────────┐
│       Intern, Volunteer,         │
│  or Seasonal/Part-time Ranger    │
└─────────────────────────────────┘
```

Position Description

Few landscapes in the United States surpass the beauty of national and state parks. Spanning coast to coast, they range from lush verdant mountains to sandy arid deserts to manicured urban oases. Overall, there are 316 national parks in the country, and more than 110,000 state and local parks where people come to hike, swim, ski, fish, boat, and find sanctuary from their busy lives. In order for these parks to retain their beauty and their natural resources, they need to be well protected and cared for. Park Rangers watch over plants and wildlife, as well as visitors to these spots of relaxation and recreation, to ensure conservation and safety alike.

The responsibilities of Park Rangers fall into several areas. One area is interpretation, which includes the process of educating visitors about the parks. In addition to knowing the resources of their particular park inside and out, Park Rangers have a wealth of knowledge, encompassing botany, ecology, geology, history, and wildlife. They share this knowledge through tours and other public programs such as lectures and workshops. The mission of education is vast. In one week, a Park Ranger may lead a group on a hike that explains all the plant life along the way; lead a nature walk to see specific animals such as birds of prey; give a lecture about ecosystems and forestry; and complete a nature project with an elementary school group. Also, they may staff a visitor's center, where they answer any questions from the public about park services, as well as park history. Sometimes, they may plan and prepare permanent and alternating educational exhibits in mini-museums at these centers.

Another major component of being a Park Ranger is search and rescue. Park Rangers are trained in first aid,

CPR, rescue operations, and other emergency medical techniques in order to respond to emergencies. They must constantly be aware of weather and environmental conditions leading to disasters such as forest fires or avalanches. If hikers do not return by dark or boaters get lost at sea, it is the Park Ranger who puts a plan into action, searching for the missing visitors and mobilizing teams. They investigate all accidents, determining causes and prevention. This is difficult work and requires patience, composure, and physical stamina.

In a related role, Park Rangers also serve as law enforcement for their parks. They enforce park regulations and in most cases, have the authority to arrest and remove those park guests who break the law. They often must deal with vandals, trespassers, the drunk and disorderly, and the disrespectful visitors who abuse the natural resources. They prevent people from committing acts both intentional and unintentional that will interfere with conservation, such as cutting down trees for firewood, littering, and feeding wildlife.

Furthermore, Park Rangers also handle park maintenance and administration. They answer questions and help establish park policy and procedure. They maintain trails, manage and perform trash collection, and ensure natural resources and habitats remain unspoiled. They may also work in the front office and operate campgrounds.

Additional duties may include:

- Developing conservation programs
- Writing brochures
- Preparing natural, cultural, and historical exhibits
- Studying wildlife behavior
- Answering correspondence
- Hiking on trails
- Monitoring air and water quality
- Restoring natural habitats
- Performing safety inspections
- Investigating violations

Park Rangers typically work a 40-hour workweek, including evenings, weekends, and holidays, but those hours vary greatly and afford some flexibility. For example, someone may work four 10-hour shifts per week, rather than five eight-hour shifts, or they may alternate between 35-hour weeks and 45-hour weeks. Some Park Rangers choose to work some night shifts, often at the park until 3:00 A.M., in order to free up day schedules. Flexibility is important as Park Rangers at the national level often get moved around several times during their careers, working in different parks. Preferences are taken into consideration, but cannot always be accommodated.

Although some parks may close in the winter, most Park Rangers work year round, using the winter months for landscaping, planning exhibits, and preparing for the upcoming

season. Furthermore, most Park Rangers have generous vacation time, ranging from four to six weeks depending on experience, and they often take this vacation during the wintertime.

Parks do not only encompass wilderness areas, but also include forests, lakeshores, seashores, historic buildings, battlefields, archaeological properties, and recreation areas. While many Park Rangers work for the National Parks Service (http://www.nps.gov/personnel/), they may also be employed by state and local parks.

Salaries

Park Rangers enter the field at various salary grades, depending on their education and experience. According to the National Parks Service, the starting salary for summer Park Ranger hires with a college degree is a GS-4 ($18,687); permanent Park Ranger hires are GS-5 ($20,908) to GS-9 ($31,680) depending on college degrees and experience. These entry-level salaries may go up into the mid-$40,000 range and above with five to 10 years of service.

Employment Prospects

Job openings for Park Rangers are quite competitive. The low pay is balanced out by the desirable lifestyle and ability to spend much time outdoors, leading to many applicants for few positions. Internships and various volunteer programs within the parks are excellent ways to gain entry, as are seasonal or part-time positions. Organizations and programs offering internships include the Student Conservation Association (http://www.sca-inc.org) and the Cultural Resources Diversity Program (http://www.cr.nps.gov/crdi/).

Advancement Prospects

Once hired, Park Rangers have good opportunity for advancement. According to the National Parks Service, they may move up through the ranks to become district rangers, park managers, and staff specialists in interpretation, park planning, resource management, and related areas. Also, as they gain more experience and increase their influence over more staff and area, their responsibilities and independence will increase as well. Upper-level Park Rangers are hired for being strong leaders and managers.

Education and Training

While three years of parks service experience will compensate for a four-year college degree, the vast majority of Park Rangers hold a bachelor's degree. Because of the diversity of their responsibilities and knowledge areas, they may study geology, ecology, environmental science, biology, history, archaeology, botany, parks and recreation management, law enforcement, natural resource management, forestry, public administration, museum studies, or business. Many also hold a master's degree in these areas in order to develop specializations.

Upon hiring, Park Rangers at national parks undergo extensive training through the National Parks Service. State and local Park Rangers are hired and trained by comparable state and local associations.

Special Requirements

Since Park Rangers hired by the National Parks Service are federal government employees, the jobs have stringent requirements and detailed applications. You must be 18 years old and a United States citizen to apply, and some positions have an age cutoff at 37 years old. Certain positions may require law enforcement credentials, and all require a valid driver's license. Others may require first-aid certifications including CPR and Emergency Medical Technician (EMT). Background checks and drug testing are also required. Check the National Parks Service Web site for more information at http://www.nps.gov. State and local parks have their own set of requirements that differ from the federal government and need to be checked individually.

Experience, Skills, and Personality Traits

In order to deal with the public on a daily basis, Park Rangers must be very customer-service focused and enjoy working with people. They must be strong leaders and excellent communicators, skilled at explaining and engaging visitors. Also, they should have outdoor skills such as hiking, boating, and camping, as well as good physical stamina. Park Rangers are good team players, but they also work well independently.

As a group, Park Rangers generally have extremely high job satisfaction. They spend their days in beautiful surroundings outdoors, doing what they love. However, they need to be comfortable with somewhat stringent regulations of the job, including wearing uniforms and working within a hierarchy. They need to be comfortable with both acting as an authority as well as listening to authority.

To break into the field, internships or volunteer work in parks services is very helpful. Seasonal work is a way to pay your dues, gaining experience while helping with basic desk and maintenance work such a answering phones and picking up trash. People also come into the field with prior experience in law enforcement, museums, construction, or grounds management.

Unions and Associations

Park Rangers may belong to associations such as the Association of National Park Rangers, the National Recreation and Park Association, and the National Association of State Park Directors, as well as local and state organizations.

Tips for Entry

1. Visit the Web site http://www.usajobs.opm.gov/, the official job site of the United States federal government. This will explain the procedure of completing an application to work for the National Parks Service.

2. Learn more about conservation and natural resource management by visiting Web sites such as http://palimpsest.stanford.edu/, http://www.eco-index.org/, and http://www.iisd.org/natres/.

3. Explore graduate programs in parks and recreation management such as the program at Indiana University-Bloomington (http://www.indiana.edu/~recpark/grad_overview.html) and North Carolina State University in Raleigh (http://www.cfr.ncsu.edu/prtm/masters.htm).

4. In addition to the National Parks Service, Park Rangers are also employed at the national level by the United States Department of Agriculture (USDA) Forest Service. Take a look at their Web site at http://www.fs.fed.us/.

5. Visit national, state, and local parks and speak to Park Rangers about their job. Hone your experience in your favorite outdoor skill area.

ZOOLOGIST

CAREER PROFILE

Duties: Studies the origins, behavior, and life cycles of animals; studies animals in both their natural habitat and in the laboratory

Alternate Title(s): Animal Scientist, Animal Biologist, Wildlife Biologist, Ornithologist (bird specialist), Mammalogist (mammal specialist), Herpetologist (reptile specialist), Ichthyologist (fish specialist)

Salary Range: $35,000 to $55,000

Employment Prospects: Fair

Advancement Prospects: Fair

Best Geographical Location(s): Cities with many colleges and universities, zoos, and aquariums; rural research centers

Prerequisites:

Education or Training—Minimum of bachelor's degree; master's or Ph.D. required for research positions

Experience—Some education-related research and field experience

Special Skills and Personality Traits—Love for animals; scientific mind and intellectual curiosity; analytical and numerical skills; keen observation ability

CAREER LADDER

```
┌─────────────────────────────┐
│  Director, Research Team,    │
│  Head Zoologist, or Zoologist│
│  at a larger institution     │
└─────────────────────────────┘

┌─────────────────────────────┐
│                              │
│  Zoologist                   │
│                              │
└─────────────────────────────┘

┌─────────────────────────────┐
│  Lab Technician, Field Assistant, │
│  or Research Assistant       │
└─────────────────────────────┘
```

Position Description

Zoologists are biological scientists who study animals. Aspects of animal life they examine may range from nutrition and habitats to mating rituals and aggression. Working in both the field and the laboratory, they observe and record details, then analyze their findings. The discoveries they make and reports they generate can influence conservation and animal care.

To initiate a research study, Zoologists pose a question, such as "What is the typical diet of a horned owl?" or "How do white-tailed deer select their mates?" Research projects must be carefully planned in order to secure funding and make sure there is a sufficient budget. Zoologists often write proposals for these research grants. They also must ensure that they have the proper staff support and equipment to carry out the project.

When in the field, Zoologists may study animals as individuals or in groups. They may face inclement weather conditions and must be prepared for occasionally strenuous outdoor activity and handling of animals. For example, hiking may be required to reach a particular habitat, and once there, Zoologists may need to stay in a specific position for as long as is needed, regardless of discomfort.

Also, Zoologists may need to trap animals for observation. While trapping is done humanely so as not to harm the creatures, Zoologists may be trained to handle some dangerous species that the average person needs to avoid. They use equipment such as binoculars, field journals, Global Positioning Systems (GPS), and scales to record details such as age, sex, size, and more.

In the lab, Zoologists make sense of their observations. They are skilled at data analysis techniques such as crunching numbers and working on statistical spreadsheets. The results are ultimately generated into reports and papers that may be submitted to scientific and zoological journals.

In addition to colleges and universities, Zoologists may be employed at zoos, aquariums, and conservation parks. At zoos, they may have a number of responsibilities unique to their setting. Frequently, Zoologists are involved in some public education programs where they make presentations about animals to visitors and answer questions. They also might have some zookeeping duties that involve maintaining and caring for animals. For instance, they may make recommendations for diet or habitat based upon their observations.

At zoos, Zoologists may also perform curatorial and administrative work where they make decisions in the best interest of the animals, as well as to further the future of the park. They may collaborate with other zoos on animal exchanges and visiting exhibits, participate in breeding plans, attend meetings, and work on public relations or fund-raising. These activities further the mission of zoos to promote conservation awareness.

Whenever you visit a zoo, you may be aware of the ecological messages about environmental protection featured on most exhibits. Zoologists are committed to conservation and are advocates for conservation issues. They understand the importance of maintaining biodiversity for they can see the consequences resulting from the loss of species.

Their duties may include:

- Identifying animal species
- Studying animal bones
- Attending professional conferences
- Publishing scientific articles
- Generating research reports
- Improving practices to eliminate animal disease
- Developing and testing new drugs
- Investigating areas such as in-vitro fertilization and cryogenics
- Working with other animal care personnel including zookeepers, veterinarians, and technicians
- Working on biodiversity exhibits and projects

The study of animals is widely diverse as they range from one-celled amoebas to massive elephants. Most Zoologists have specialty areas and are experts on particular species or groups. As new species are constantly being identified, insiders feel their field is limitless and exciting. There is opportunity to travel for fieldwork and conferences. Zoologists also enjoy being a part of an international scientific network and community.

Hours can be extensive and nontraditional, but most Zoologists are passionate about their research and do not mind. Some Zoologists in zoos are required to wear uniforms, but many do not. However, this is not a field of high fashion. Comfortable and water-resistant clothing is a necessity, particularly for fieldwork.

Salaries

According to the Bureau of Labor Statistics (BLS), the median annual earnings for Zoologists in 2002 were $47,740. This figure may vary depending on the work setting and additional responsibilities of the Zoologist. Those Zoologists who are university professors tend to earn more than their colleagues at zoos and wildlife parks do. However, Zoologists often get additional funding and grants for travel and research studies.

Employment Prospects

Employment prospects are fair for Zoologists, since their employment options are somewhat limited compared to other professions. Competition is tight for existing jobs, and positions are often found through professional networks. Overall, the BLS predicts average growth for Zoologists over the next 10 years. In the future, the conservation movement will grow as the loss of species to our ecosystem is becoming recognized as an international problem. This may create continued opportunities for Zoologists who help protect endangered species.

Advancement Prospects

Advancement prospects are also fair for Zoologists. For many who lead their own research teams, they are where they want to be in their careers and are looking to continue their research, rather than seeking higher positions. Some Zoologists may move from zoos to universities or vice-versa, or to more geographically desirable regions as opportunities open up. Others may give lectures or publish articles and papers.

Education and Training

Most Zoologists begin their careers as undergraduate biology majors. They may also study wildlife biology or zoology if their school offers the programs; if not, they supplement biology with course work in animal behavior. In addition to all types of biology, courses in chemistry, physics, ecology, and population studies are useful, as are courses that hone research and writing skills, such as English and the social sciences.

With a bachelor's degree, entry-level opportunities may be available as a field or laboratory technician. These types of positions generally involve animal care, habitat management, or data collection. Recent graduates may also work as research assistants on existing zoological studies. However, it is impossible to lead a research team or conduct independent research without an advanced degree.

While some may stop at the master's degree level, most Zoologists have a doctoral degree that enables them to work in many settings, initiate studies, and conduct all types of research. It is at the graduate level that Zoologists specialize and often begin studying zoology. Students may choose a graduate program based on a particular professor's research interest, as well as proximity to zoos, aquariums, specific regions, or research centers.

Experience, Skills, and Personality Traits

A love for animals alone is not enough experience to become a Zoologist. Prior to school or during their education, aspiring Zoologists work on ranches, on farms, in veterinary clinics, and in zoos and aquariums. They are familiar with animal behavior in and out of their natural environments.

Zoologists are scientists with analytical minds. They have the numerical skills to analyze complex data and the problem-solving skills to understand results. Furthermore, they need to be excellent observers. There is an art to studying other living creatures that requires an innate talent in noticing minute details and changes.

Also, Zoologists need to be flexible. Animals do not follow schedules, and their behavior can be unpredictable. Zoologists must be able to go with the flow and be up for the challenges of studying live creatures.

Unions and Associations

Zoologists may belong to a variety of professional associations depending on their areas of expertise such as the American Zoo and Aquarium Association and the Society for Integrative and Comparative Biology. Those Zoologists involved with zookeeping may belong to the American Association of Zookeepers, Inc. Other specialty organizations include the Society for the Study of Amphibians and Reptiles, the American Society of Mammalogists, and the American Society of Ichthyologists and Herpetologists.

Tips for Entry

1. Learn more about schools offering the graduate degree in zoology or wildlife science. Take a look at the list at the following site: http://www.gradschools. com/programs/zoology.html.
2. Visit your local zoo or aquarium and take note of animal habitats, locations, and behavior. Sometimes information about research studies is displayed as part of the exhibits.
3. Speak to a Zoologist to learn more about his or her career. Find out what a typical day is like, as well as the career path.
4. Take courses in the biological sciences. Determine which aspects are the most interesting to you. Try to find a position as a research assistant for a professor who is involved with an applicable study.
5. Volunteer to work with animals at a farm, ranch, shelter, zoo, or veterinary office.

ENVIRONMENTAL ACTIVIST

CAREER PROFILE

Duties: Promotes environmental causes and works to influence public policy; encourages activism from individuals and communities and organizes campaigns

Alternate Title(s): Environmental Advocate, Community Organizer, Grassroots Organizer, Field Organizer, Canvass Director, Campaign Director

Salary Range: $0 to $50,000 and up

Employment Prospects: Good

Advancement Prospects: Good

Best Geographical Location(s): Major cities for headquarters work; Washington, D.C., for lobbying work; and nationwide for grassroots organizing work

Prerequisites:

Education or Training—No specific requirements, but most have bachelor's degrees in an environmental science field

Experience—Prior volunteer or activism work

Special Skills and Personality Traits—Dedication and commitment to environmental causes; excellent verbal and written communication skills; persistence; good organizational skills; persuasive and leadership ability

CAREER LADDER

```
┌─────────────────────────────────────┐
│  Program Director, Director of Public │
│  Policy, Director of Government       │
│  Relations, or Director              │
│  of Community Organizing             │
└─────────────────────────────────────┘

┌─────────────────────────────────────┐
│      Environmental Activist          │
└─────────────────────────────────────┘

┌─────────────────────────────────────┐
│          Volunteer                   │
└─────────────────────────────────────┘
```

Position Description

Are you passionate about saving the environment? Above all, Environmental Activists are motivated to influence change. They work as volunteers, program coordinators, coalition builders, and communicators to make individuals, corporations, and the government aware about how decisions they make can affect natural resources. Environmental Activists generally feel it is their duty and responsibility to take action against any injustice toward the Earth and its creatures.

Environmental Activists work to influence public policy. They seek to make positive changes to conditions that may be harmful to the public as well as the environment. They can affect public policy through acting as direct advocates themselves, working directly with the legislators. Additionally, Environmental Activists may serve as community or grassroots organizers who motivate and empower citizens to take action to solve problems. They develop campaigns built around a specific cause and determine a strategy and plan.

Always a step ahead of the news and well-informed about important issues, Environmental Activists scan the media for new developments that will affect the environment. They read press releases, receive e-mail bulletins, and check activism Web sites several times each day. Additionally, they are experts about cause and effect of environmental actions. They know how the acts of car manufacturers and pesticide companies will affect particular species and can provide details to back up their positions. By adopting a position on issues affecting the environment, they work to support this stance through facts and consequences.

Each week, most major environmental organizations send out "action alerts." These are brief blurbs that inform people about major issues currently causing concern. Not only do they explain what the problem is, but they also suggest a course of action to combat it. For example, if an oil drill is scheduled that will affect wildlife, the action alert might offer a form letter that a reader can sign, which will get forwarded to the appropriate congressperson or policy maker. Environmental Activists read these alerts and plan accordingly, as well as write these alerts for their organizations.

Another role of many Environmental Activists is coalition building. These are alliances of concerned parties that join together to combine resources and efforts. Coalitions can effectively create targeted strategies, lobby the government, and motivate people to get involved. By working together, they send a unified and well-structured message that can have a stronger impact than an individual voice.

Environmental Activists also work at the grassroots level, in the communities. They energize those who live in areas directly affected by environmental factors, as well as those citizens who feel strongly about environmental issues, to contact policy makers on behalf of their organization. They may provide form letters, telephone numbers, or Web sites to facilitate this process. Furthermore, Environmental Activists may hold meetings to motivate and inform people about consequences of environmental problems, as well as activism techniques.

Their duties may include:

* Meeting with members of Congress and other policy makers
* Conducting community outreach
* Designing publicity materials
* Drafting letters and Web site content
* Devising long- and short-term activism strategies
* Writing proposals, presentations, and press releases
* Organizing events
* Performing fund-raising activities

There are virtually thousands of local, state, and national environmental organizations for which Environmental Activists may work. These groups range from huge international organizations in major cities to community groups in small towns with staffs of less than 10. At the entry level, they may perform administrative work as they learn the ropes. However, as they take on more responsibility, Environmental Activists can conduct research, develop strategies, and take on strong leadership roles, meeting with high-level government and business officials to present the position for their organization.

To lead a campaign, Environmental Activists must be skilled at management and organization. A major task might be to recruit and manage volunteers. By tapping into groups who are concerned about the environment and committed to the cause, they double or triple their workforce and voices.

Also, Environmental Activists must be flexible and available to work nontraditional hours. They may be required to travel or visit different communities. Because anyone who goes into this field does so because of his or her passion for social justice and a better world, this is rarely a problem.

Salaries

Environmental Activists range can be volunteers who are passionate about a cause and advocate for issues for free while they are employed elsewhere, or they may be full-time employees of environmental organizations who are compensated for their efforts. Jobs at environmental organizations tend to pay in the $30,000 to $40,000 range for entry-level activism positions. Those who advance to director-level positions can earn considerably more.

Also, there are some part-time paid positions in addition to numerous unpaid internships and volunteer jobs. These may pay anywhere between $8 and $30 per hour.

Employment Prospects

For Environmental Activists who are geographically flexible, there are a number of employment opportunities. While positions at the headquarters of major organizations such as the Sierra Club may be hard to come by, regional positions such as field organizer are available nationwide. As the importance of environmental issues grows in our country, so will the need for professionals to fight for these rights.

New groups spring up constantly needing staff to get them off the ground. However, the availability of funding to pay salaries for these positions depends on philanthropy and the current political and economic climate of the United States.

Advancement Prospects

With a background in environmental activism, there are several places one can go to advance. Positions in government relations and public policy for environmental organizations are high level and high responsibility. Those Environmental Activists with the right combination of education and experience—usually a master's or professional degree and five years of activism work—may seek this path.

Others may become leaders of community organizing or direct specific programs. Additionally, Environmental Activists may become full-time lobbyists, working with state and federal legislators on behalf of their causes.

Education and Training

While anyone can be an activist in his or her own community, a minimum of a bachelor's degree is required for employment at major environmental organizations. Courses that emphasize environmental science, conservation, biology, natural resources, and ecology are helpful, as are classes in communications, public policy and administration, nonprofit management, and ethics.

Many colleges and universities offer individual courses in environmental advocacy, but few grant degrees in this area. However, there are several graduate programs that offer specialization in environmental leadership, advocacy, or organizing. Notable graduate programs include the Environmental Advocacy and Organizing program at Antioch New England Graduate School in Keene, N.H. (http://esdept.antiochne.edu/advocacy/default.html), the Environment and Community program at Antioch University Seattle in Seattle, Wash. (http://www.antiochsea.edu/academics/enviro/index.html), and the M.A. program in Environmental Leadership at Naropa University in Boulder, Colo. (http://www.naropa.edu/envma/index.html).

Numerous other schools, such as Loyola University in Chicago, Ill. (http://www.luc.edu/depts/envsci/certificate_program.html) offer certificate and training programs. The Web site http://www.EnviroEducation.com offers additional information. Other Environmental Activists have graduate degrees in law, public policy or administration, or nonprofit management.

In addition to education, there are several hands-on training programs that help to prepare Environmental Activists. One such program, the Environmental Leadership Training Program, is offered through Green Corps (http://www.greencorps.org) and is a one-year, paid internship program for recent college graduates. Other environmental organizations may offer additional training and resources.

Experience, Skills, and Personality Traits

Many Environmental Activists get started with their activism through campus organizing while in college. They have a background in volunteering that may include activities as basic as stuffing envelopes and going door-to-door or as sophisticated as starting their own group, partnering with national organizations, and arranging conferences, summits, and presentations to lawmakers.

Activism requires skills in planning, leadership, conflict resolution, organizing, and team building. Environmental Activists must coach and motivate others, with the ability to persuade people about the worth of their cause. In order to do this, they must be excellent communicators who can articulate themselves well both verbally and in writing. With determination and persistence, they must be self-starters who can work independently as well as with a team. Also important is the ability to be flexible. Knowledge of environmental issues is a must.

Unions and Associations

Environmental Activists may belong to the National Association of Environmental Professionals and the National Organizers Alliance. Furthermore, they may work for, belong to, or be affiliated with environmental organizations such as the Sierra Club, the Nature Conservancy, or Greenpeace.

Tips for Entry

1. Get involved in campus organizing. You can join an existing group at your school, or begin your own if there is an issue you would like to see covered. The following links offers some tips on campus organizing to help you get started: http://environment.about.com/gi/dynamic/offsite.htm?zi=1/XJ&sdn=environment&zu=http://protest.net/activists_handbook/ and http://www.campusactivism.org/.

2. Stay informed about environmental issues and become aware of action alerts. Make it a habit to regularly check Web sites such as http://actionnetwork.org/.

3. The Rockwood Leadership Program trains activists in all aspects of social changes and works with many nonprofit organizations. Read about their programs at: http://www.rockwoodfund.org/.

4. For ideas about employment, check out the National Environmental Directory. This is the most comprehensive environmental directory in the country, including more than 13,000 organizations. It is available on the Internet at http://environmentaldirectory.net/.

5. Visit the Web site of Greenpeace, an international nonprofit environmental activism organization. Register there as a cyberactivist: http://act.greenpeace.org/.

BIORESOURCE ENGINEER

CAREER PROFILE

Duties: Designs, constructs, operates, and maintains systems that contain biological components; also works on the technological construction of these systems

Alternate Title(s): Environmental Engineer, Civil Engineer, Water Resources Engineer, Agricultural Engineer

Salary Range: $40,000 to $70,000 and up

Employment Prospects: Fair to Good

Advancement Prospects: Fair

Best Geographical Location(s): Developing countries, rural areas

Prerequisites:

Education or Training—Bachelor's degree in related engineering discipline; many positions also require master's degree in engineering

Experience—Several years of related work experience or internships

Special Skills and Personality Traits—Excellent analytical skills; good scientific and mathematical ability; able to work independently as well as part of a team; creativity; good communication skills; strong technology skills

Licensure/Certification—Licensure as a registered professional engineer (PE) may be required

CAREER LADDER

```
┌─────────────────────────────┐
│   Director of Engineering    │
│     or Project Director      │
└─────────────────────────────┘

┌─────────────────────────────┐
│    Bioresource Engineer      │
└─────────────────────────────┘

┌─────────────────────────────┐
│   Junior Engineer or Intern  │
└─────────────────────────────┘
```

Position Description

Bioresource engineering is a multidisciplinary field that involves utilizing natural resources to develop systems that benefit society. The common thread between the systems constructed in this field is that they all contain biological components. Knowledge of mathematics, as well as physical and biological sciences is used to solve problems related to plants, animals, waste, food, and the natural environment. Bioresource Engineers combine biology and environmental science and seek to make the environment safer for technology.

Bioresource Engineers are involved with constructing these systems with biological components. There are a number of sub-fields and systems exist on a wide range of scales. For example, Bioresource Engineers may analyze the watershed issues of a major river, looking at both the soil and the water and strategizing how to meet human needs while sustaining the river ecologically. On the other hand, they may build farm machines to be used in agribusiness or develop biochemical agents to be used for crop protection. They may analyze food production and the technology used for storage. Although the scales and systems vary, they are linked by their biological orientation.

A number of specialties within bioresource engineering can include:

- Soil and water engineering
- Bioenvironmental engineering
- Food and bioprocess engineering
- Agricultural engineering

Depending on their specialty, Bioresource Engineers have a number of work options in the nonprofit sector. In terms of agriculture, they may work for U.S. agencies or international development organizations. Here, they may identify diseases found in crops and forests, work with facilities where biological products are grown, and handle waste management and sanitation issues.

In international development organizations, one of the goals is often economic development. For developing nations to become self-sufficient, the economy needs to be stable, people need work training, and systems must be in working order. Bioresource Engineers who specialize in agriculture can be a major part of this process. By working with local farmers and teaching them the most effective ways to grow crops, they can make a substantial impact on food production. They also work with the land and soil to make sure it is viable for farming.

With an environmental focus, the role of Bioresource Engineers emphasizes conservation. They look to find ways to treat waste organically and protect and develop land. Also, they work to develop systems that conserve soil and water quality. They examine pollution and the use of pesticides and fertilizers. Always, Bioresource Engineers look to the safety of humans and animals as a prime concern with the systems they design.

Another nonprofit option for Bioresource Engineers is working at colleges and universities. As professors, they can teach students and conduct research. They also may work on projects for government and business, as well as have involvement with professional associations.

Additional duties may include:

- Developing plans for drainage, waste management, land improvements, and irrigation
- Advising people on how best to use available resources
- Improving methods and operations
- Designing food processing plants and related mechanical systems
- Advising people on water quality and treatment issues
- Making recommendations regarding waste management systems where waste interacts with the land and surrounding water
- Visit various sites and observing environmental problems
- Conducting research and various safety/environmental studies

Bioresource Engineers use the same engineering principles regardless of the scale of the project; the basic application is the same. They become knowledgeable about many different areas including watersheds, soil, water flow, waste management, food production, and others. Throughout the process, they consider how their work will affect various ecosystems and contribute to making society environmentally responsible.

Work conditions often involve long hours spent outdoors. Bioresource Engineers should like working outside in all types of weather conditions. They spend time working independently as well as working as part of a team.

Salaries

Salaries for Bioresource Engineers are usually in the $50,000 to $70,000 range. Compensation varies depending on the nonprofit employment setting. The Bureau of Labor Statistics (BLS) has data on median annual earnings for the two most closely related engineering fields to bioresource engineering, civil engineering and environmental engineering. According to the BLS, median annual earnings of civil engineers were $60,070 in 2002, and median annual earnings of environmental engineers were $61,410 in 2002. Earnings in business and government are at the high end of the spectrum.

Employment Prospects

While the Bureau of Labor Statistics (BLS) predicts a slower than average growth for all engineers through 2012, the growth pattern varies depending on engineering specialty. The BLS forecasts growth for environmental engineers to be faster than average, and this statistic is closest to Bioresource Engineers.

Because Bioresource Engineers work on environmental issues, which continue to grow in importance throughout the world, their job opportunities will be better. It is important for them to stay current on new technologies and developments in the field to enhance their employment opportunities. Those who are looking to work in international aid and development will be needed for their technical expertise that many other professionals in that field lack.

In addition to full-time employment, some Bioresrouce Engineers do project work, particularly in international aid and development. They are called in to provide immediate assistance to a region in need and move on when the project is complete.

Advancement Prospects

Bioresource Engineers can advance by moving to different types of organizations. They also may seek additional education and training to specialize further, increasing their employment options. Furthermore, they may work as consultants to nonprofits, government, and private businesses.

Education and Training

The minimum requirement for work as a Bioresource Engineer is a bachelor's degree in an engineering discipline. Some schools offer the degree in bioresource engineering, while others come into the field with degrees in civil engineering, environmental engineering, and agricultural engineering. An engineering education provides a solid framework in mathematics, science, and computer technology.

According to the BLS, approximately 340 colleges and universities offer bachelor's degree programs in engineering that are accredited by the Accreditation Board for Engineering and Technology (ABET). Also, 240 colleges offer accredited bachelor's degree programs in engineering technology. For more information, see http://www.abet.org/about.html.

In addition to the bachelor's degree, many Bioresource Engineers have a master's degree in engineering as well. It is not uncommon for engineers to have their bachelor's degree and master's degree in different engineering disciplines.

Special Requirements

The BLS states that "all 50 States and the District of Columbia require licensure for engineers who offer their services directly to the public. Engineers who are licensed are called Professional Engineers (PE). This licensure generally requires a degree from an ABET-accredited engineering program, 4 years of relevant work experience, and successful completion of a State examination." For more information, see ABET's Web site at http://www.abet.org/about.html.

Experience, Skills, and Personality Traits

Bioresource Engineers must be excellent problem solvers, with superior analytical skills. They need good technology knowledge with extensive computer skills. Furthermore, they should be excellent communicators who are well organized and pay close attention to detail. At the same time, they must be creative and able to visualize projects from start to completion.

Depending upon their work area, Bioresource Engineers may need additional types of experience. For example, international experience and language skills may be helpful for international aid and development work, as is knowledge of agricultural engineering. A strong background in environmental issues is crucial for work with environmental organizations.

Unions and Associations

While there is currently no professional association specifically for Bioresource Engineers, they frequently belong to the American Academy of Environmental Engineers, the American Society of Agricultural Engineers, or the American Society of Civil Engineers.

Tips for Entry

1. Learn more about Engineers Without Borders, a group whose mission is to "partner with disadvantaged communities to improve their quality of life through implementation of environmentally and economically sustainable engineering projects, while developing internationally responsible engineering students." You can take a look at internship and volunteer opportunities through their Web site at http://www.ewb-usa.org/.

2. The Peace Corps is always looking for engineers with technical expertise to join their program, a terrific way to make a strong contribution, develop valuable skills, and form a lifelong network. Learn more by visiting http://www.peacecorps.gov.

3. Explore more about Bioresource Engineers by typing "bioresource engineering" into a search engine such as Google or Yahoo.

4. Take courses in different engineering disciplines including civil, mechanical, environmental, electrical, and agricultural engineering.

5. Investigate job opportunities for engineers at sites such as http://www.engineerjobs.com/, http://www.engcen.com/, http://www.ecojobs.com, and http://www.developmentex.com/job_opportunities/opp_summary.asp.

INTERNATIONAL
RELATED POSITIONS

TRANSLATOR/INTERPRETER

CAREER PROFILE

Duties: Converts written, oral, or sign language text into another language.

Alternate Title(s): Translator deals with written language; Interpreter deals with spoken language only

Salary Range: $30,000 to $65,000 and up

Employment Prospects: Good

Advancement Prospects: Fair

Best Geographical Location(s)s: Urban areas, cities with large international or multilingual populations

Prerequisites:

Education or Training—Fluency in two or more languages is required. An undergraduate or graduate degree in foreign languages or culture is helpful.

Experience—Familiarity with foreign countries and culture; work experience in settings where translation and interpretation are common such as education, medicine, or diplomacy

Special Skills and Personality Traits—Cultural sensitivity and awareness, superior verbal and written communication skills

CAREER LADDER

```
┌─────────────────────────────────┐
│  Consultant or Head of Translation/ │
│    Interpretation Services       │
└─────────────────────────────────┘

┌─────────────────────────────────┐
│    Translator or Interpreter     │
└─────────────────────────────────┘

┌─────────────────────────────────┐
│            Student               │
└─────────────────────────────────┘
```

Position Description

If you've ever heard the saying "lost in translation," you may have an idea about the challenging job of a Translator or Interpreter. These professionals link people together by enabling them to communicate. Whether helping patients and their families understand the care they need or assisting with aid in a disaster relief situation, Translators and Interpreters bridge the barriers sometimes created by language to place all people in a situation on a level playing field.

Translators deal exclusively with written documents. They evaluate pieces of writing and make sure they not only convert the words into another language, but that they also retain the original meaning. They may translate different types of publications, including articles, books, and even Web sites. To do their jobs, it is important for Translators to have an excellent grasp of grammar, punctuation, idioms, and word usage in their native language, as well as at least one foreign language.

Interpreters are responsible for listening to live speech and converting what the speakers say into a language others can understand. This can be a foreign language or sign language. They may interpret consecutively, where they wait for a speaker to pause, or simultaneously, where they begin interpreting while the speaker is talking. If they are interpreting for the hearing impaired, Interpreters convert spoken language into the hand signals of sign language.

Interpreters are often used at large meetings, conferences, and question-and-answer sessions. It is helpful for them to review background information on the topic at hand before they begin an interpretation session. They must listen carefully and think quickly. Interpreters must be so familiar with both languages that they can anticipate what will come next.

Environments in which Translators and Interpreters can work are numerous. Nonprofit settings include large international organizations such as the United Nations, nongovernmental organizations (NGOs), universities, and hospitals.

They may also work for nonprofit agencies providing legal or social service assistance to immigrant populations. Also, they may serve as tour guides or assistants for groups and individuals.

Their duties may include:

- Attending meetings, conferences, or events where more than one language is spoken
- Reviewing information on topic to be discussed before an interpreting session
- Listening to statements of speaker to ascertain meaning
- Using electronic audio systems to transcribe language
- Reading written material, such as legal documents, scientific works, or news reports
- Rewriting material into specified language, according to established rules of grammar
- Consulting dictionaries and other reference materials for word usage
- Speaking with people to ensure language comprehension

Translators and Interpreters may work irregular hours that include evenings or weekends. Travel may be required depending on the position.

Salaries

Translators and Interpreters can earn different salaries depending on their employment setting. According to *Compensation in Nonprofit Organizations, 16th Edition,* a 2003 survey report of 131 benchmark jobs from Abbott, Langer & Associates, Inc., the median income for an Interpreter working in the nonprofit sector is $38,804. Salaries can range from $30,000 to $60,000 and up.

Those Translators and Interpreters who work independently charge hourly rates, often ranging from $15 to $60 per hour. The Bureau of Labor Statistics (BLS) states that individuals classified as language specialists for the federal government earned an average of $64,234 annually in 2003.

Employment Prospects

As the working world becomes increasingly global, job opportunities for Translators and Interpreters are expected to grow faster than average. Many organizations require Interpreters for large events, as well as day-to-day work with foreign clients, patients, or constituents. Also, they will be needed for international aid and development work.

Opportunities will also vary depending upon the language specialties of the Translators and Interpreters. Certain languages are more in demand than others are, particularly at different times in world events. For example, during specific world conflict situations, professionals are needed who have expertise in those languages. Also, languages that are spoken by many of the world's people such as Asian languages are often in high demand.

Currently, computer software has been developed that can provide translation services, but it is limited and is not expected to affect job opportunities. Computers may assist with literal translation, but will not be able to convey the meaning with the ease and precise skill of an experienced professional.

Advancement Prospects

Most Translators and Interpreters work independently or for large international organizations. Advancement occurs with seniority and experience. Freelancing enables Translators and Interpreters to build their own client bases and work on flexible schedules. Furthermore, many Translators and Interpreters with significant experience may become consultants on language and culture for nonprofit and business organizations.

Education and Training

While no formal training or education is required to become a Translator or Interpreter, most Translators and Interpreters have at least a four-year college degree. Many also hold an advanced degree, which is helpful for professional advancement. Degrees are often in specific foreign languages and culture.

A limited number of schools offer certificate or degree programs in translating or interpreting. Check with the American Translators Association for more information (http://www.atanet.org/).

In addition to their native language, Translators and Interpreters must be fluent in at least one foreign language; many professionals are fluent in more than two languages. This training can come from formal course work, intensive language institutes, or personal experience such as travel.

Experience, Skills, and Personality Traits

Translators and Interpreters must have a skill for written and spoken language. They must be excellent communicators and have a strong grasp of grammar and word usage. Translators and Interpreters must be able to work independently. It is crucial that they process information easily and think quickly and creatively.

Also important is the ability to understand and appreciate different cultures. Translators and Interpreters have often lived and studied in different parts of the world and are sensitive to diversity.

Unions and Associations

For Translators and Interpreters, the main professional association is the American Translators Association. Other associations include the Translators and Interpreters Guild, a nationwide union for Translators and Interpreters, and the American Association of Language Specialists. For those professionals whose specialty is interpreting sign language, the Registry of Interpreters for the Deaf is a national nonprofit professional association.

Tips for Entry

1. Find opportunities to apply languages being studied academically. Volunteer with international student organizations to practice your skills and have conversations with foreign language speakers.
2. Attend an event where you can observe Interpreters at work. Pay close attention to their body language, mannerisms, and fluency.
3. Research the history and cultures of foreign countries to gain a stronger perspective beyond language.
4. Get intensive training through a language institute. Middlebury College in Middlebury, Vermont, is known for their programs (http://cat.middlebury.edu/ls/introduction.html).
5. Consider opportunities offered at the United Nations. For employment, a candidate must have a bachelor of arts in his or her main language, as well as passing a test and being skilled in three of the six official United Nations languages. For more information, see http://www.un.org.

PEACE WORKER

CAREER PROFILE

Duties: Works to eliminate violence and promote world peace through research, education, and advocacy

Alternate Title(s): Peace and International Security Analyst, Foreign Policy Analyst, Mediator, Conflict Resolution Specialist, Peace Educator

Salary Range: $0 to $70,000 and up

Employment Prospects: Fair

Advancement Prospects: Fair

Best Geographical Location(s): Major cities; regions of need worldwide

Prerequisites:

Education or Training—While educational requirements will vary depending on the position, most jobs require graduate degrees and coursework in international affairs, political science, and history

Experience—Varies from entry-level to several years of postgraduate school experience

Special Skills and Personality Traits—Excellent research and writing skills; tact and diplomacy; cultural sensitivity and understanding; strong communication skills

CAREER LADDER

```
┌─────────────────────────────────────────┐
│  Senior positions including Department    │
│   Chairperson, Research Analyst,          │
│     or Education Director                  │
└─────────────────────────────────────────┘

┌─────────────────────────────────────────┐
│             Peace Worker                  │
└─────────────────────────────────────────┘

┌─────────────────────────────────────────┐
│               Intern                      │
└─────────────────────────────────────────┘
```

Position Description

The world constantly struggles with a number of terrible problems and threats to peace such as terrorism, genocide, and civil war. While everyone can acknowledge the severity and awfulness of these problems, some people feel incredibly passionate about working to reduce and eradicate these threats. These individuals are Peace Workers, and they contribute to reducing violence and conflict in order to promote a peaceful world. There are many roles that Peace Workers can take in order to help make the world a better place.

On an international level, Peace Workers often focus in on specific areas related to violence. They may work to solve issues of war and peace, studying and analyzing security policy, nuclear weapons, and the arms trade. They consider not just issues of national security, but also issues of human security that affect people worldwide. Furthermore, they may specialize in different areas of foreign policy working for nongovernmental organizations (NGOs) such

as the United Nations or organizations through the European Union.

Also, some Peace Workers do international development work. They may work with specific ethnic groups or regions that have recently experienced or are currently experiencing violence or war, such as Kosovo, Somalia, and the Middle East. They address suffering and help the members of these countries deal with the atrocities they have faced and rebuild their communities. They provide aid to those in need and work to create policy that will minimize future conflict.

Peace Workers often are mediators and educators who try to encourage dialogue between conflicting groups. Their goal is to foster understanding and to get beyond the animosity that inhibits reconciliation. Through direct work with people, they educate and facilitate discussion and programming designed to develop common bonds. For example, an organization called Seeds of Peace (http://www.seedsofpeace.org) prepares teenagers from areas of conflict (primarily from the Middle East) with leadership skills that will be critical to promoting coexistence and peace in their homelands.

Many professors of peace studies teach about positive peace versus negative peace in their courses, a common theme in contemporary peace research. Whereas negative peace is the absence of war and violence, positive peace is one that goes beyond the elimination of war to where relationships have actually been transformed. Some Peace Workers strive to not only stop ongoing war, but also to reconstruct the root sources of conflict. They analyze the history of the conflict and determine causes. Then they use this information as a method of education to bring about positive change.

Their duties may include:

- Analyzing world economics and the way it affects peace
- Conducting research and advocacy work
- Writing papers, proposals, and promotional materials to promote peace and draw attention to issues
- Studying the United States military budget and priorities
- Learning about causes of violence
- Teaching courses on peace studies
- Visiting regions of world conflict
- Documenting issues of violence
- Examining efforts of various countries to reduce conflict
- Developing peace-building activities, trainings, and peace curriculum
- Determining policy and procedure for peace education
- Working with groups of people to foster better communication
- Writing grant proposals for peace programs
- Working through their religious affiliation to promote peace

Those who become Peace Workers are idealists who want to translate their idealism into something tangible. They strongly believe in human rights and the right of every individual to live in peace. Since their work can be carried out in many ways, people make their contribution to the field with all sorts of professional backgrounds, including lawyers, psychologists, professors, and journalists. They may be employed by NGOs, think tanks, the U.S. government, relief organizations such as the Red Cross, human rights organization such as Amnesty International, the United Nations, and many other nonprofit organizations worldwide. Most Peace Workers can expect to travel and have the option to be based in a variety of world regions in the United States and abroad, depending on their specialty.

Salaries

Since the jobs of Peace Workers vary so much, salaries vary as well. Someone may begin in the field as an unpaid intern, but go on to head a department at a large international think tank, become a lawyer specializing in international peace issues or mediation, train to be a psychologist working with war victims, or study to be a professor of peace studies, all commanding potential salaries of $70,000 and up. Salaries at peace-related nonprofit organizations are typically in the $30,000 to $40,000 range.

Employment Prospects

Employment prospects are fair, in that it is difficult to find salaried positions for Peace Workers, particularly those focused on research and analysis. Many Peace Workers begin as interns or volunteers to gain entry to an organization. Most opportunities are available in foreign policy work and through the government, working for the State Department or on Capitol Hill. Currently, there are also many opportunities for those who focus on terrorist activity and are experts on nuclear weapon threats.

Advancement Prospects

Advancement prospects are also fair since positions are scarce. Most Peace Workers advance by continuing their education or seeking additional training in order to take on a more specific role within the field. They also may move from smaller organizations to larger ones, and to different world regions.

Education and Training

Many students feel passionate about world peace but are unsure how this idealism translates into actual job opportunity. Most Peace Workers have a minimum of a master's degree, commonly in international affairs, international public policy, or political science. However, their education starts at the undergraduate level, through course work in history, international affairs, and political science. This provides a foundation to better understand how the United States interacts with the world, as well as the historical background behind the political relationships between countries. Courses in political economy help to further this understanding. It is important for Peace Workers to understand the impact of globalization and the role economics plays in world relationships. Philosophy courses cover issues on peace and justice that are also essential. Many schools also offer courses in national and international security, coping with international conflict, defense and arms control, human rights, and causes of war and peace.

A relatively new discipline is that of "Peace Studies." One such program is the Five College Program in Peace and World Security Studies (PAWSS), a multidisciplinary program through a consortium of schools in Massachusetts—Amherst, Hampshire, Mount Holyoke, and Smith Colleges, and the University of Massachusetts at Amherst. Faculty members at these five schools established this program in order to enhance undergraduate education in peace and international security studies. The program, as well as others like it, encourage and inform students about internship opportunities to combine hands-on training with academics. According to the PAWSS Web site, graduate programs fall into six major divisions (often combining elements):

- Peace and justice in the religious context
- General peace and conflict studies
- Mediation and conflict resolution
- Citizen participation in socioeconomic development
- Arms control and international security
- Public interest law and alternative dispute resolution

For those who want to focus on conflict resolution, programs include George Mason University's Institute for Conflict Analysis & Resolution (http://www.gmu.edu/departments/ICAR/) in Fairfax, Va., which offers bachelor's degrees, master's degrees, and doctoral degrees.

Experience, Skills, and Personality Traits

For the most part, Peace Workers are committed and passionate, as they find practical outlets to feed their humanitarian urges. They are excellent researchers, writers, and communicators, with an ability to work with many types of people without judgment. They are tactful and diplomatic, especially those involved with education and mediation.

In order to break into the field, internships and volunteer experience is crucial, providing an understanding and inside perspective of the field. Language skills are also helpful, as is experience living in different parts of the world.

Unions and Associations

Peace Workers can belong to a variety of professional associations, including the Arms Control Association, the Inter-national Peace Research Association, the International Studies Association, PUGWASH (an organization offering conferences for scholars concerned with reducing the danger of armed conflict), Peace Action and the Peace Education Fund, and the Peace and Justice Studies Association.

Tips for Entry

1. Take a look at the Web site for the Five College Program in Peace and World Security Studies (PAWSS): http://pawss.hampshire.edu/. It offers information about undergraduate and graduate programs, as well as careers and internships.
2. Consider a study abroad program. Whether for a semester, a summer, or even more short-term, living and learning in another country provides invaluable cross-cultural knowledge and understanding.
3. Explore internship resources. In addition to listings available through your own campus, many Web sites list information and opportunities, including http://www.forusa.org/programs/internships/internships.html, http://www.csbsju.edu/peacestudies/Internships/Internships.htm, http://www.idealist.org, and http://www.peace-action.org/abt/jobs.html.
4. Learn more about conflict resolution and mediation studies by visiting sites such as http://peace.fresno.edu/, http://www.cclsweb.org/MidnightFiles/Peace/peacecon.htm, and http://members.aol.com/Altdisres/General.html.
5. What are you passionate about? Because peace studies is a large field, choose an issue and focus your internship and academic efforts in that area, whether it is education, conflict resolution, foreign policy, aid and relief, or reducing the arms risk.

HUMAN RIGHTS ACTIVIST

CAREER PROFILE

Duties: Works to promote and protect international human rights through policy, programming, advocacy, research, and/or education

Alternate Title(s): Human Rights Advocate, Program Director, Program Officer, Policy Analyst, Specialist, Humanitarian Officer

Salary Range: $20,000 to $100,000

Employment Prospects: Fair to good

Advancement Prospects: Fair to good

Best Geographical Location(s): Major cities, college towns, and international locations

Prerequisites:

Education or Training—Varies by type of position, but most jobs require a bachelor's degree and many prefer graduate training

Experience—Varies depending on the position from two to five years

Special Skills and Personality Traits—Knowledge of human rights issues; excellent research, writing, and communication skills; commitment to human rights issues; international experience including languages and work/study abroad

CAREER LADDER

```
┌─────────────────────────────────────┐
│   Director of Human Rights Issues,   │
│  Executive Director, Legal Counsel   │
│   or comparable upper-level position │
└─────────────────────────────────────┘

┌─────────────────────────────────────┐
│                                      │
│        Human Rights Activist         │
│                                      │
└─────────────────────────────────────┘

┌─────────────────────────────────────┐
│    Intern, Community Organizer,      │
│       or Program Coordinator         │
└─────────────────────────────────────┘
```

Position Description

The field of international human rights aims to make a difference in the world. It addresses injustices and promotes the concept that every individual on the planet is entitled to the same basic equalities. According to the New Encyclopaedia Britannica Ready Reference, human rights are rights that belong to an individual as a consequence of being human. These rights are civil, political, economic, social, and cultural. Human Rights Activists work in many ways to protect these rights as various declarations and treaties define them.

Human Rights Activists want to make changes in the international spectrum and alter the way people are treated. They believe that human rights are universal and cannot be denied. They want to promote current social justice efforts and as well as expand them with new initiatives. In this multidisciplinary field, there are a number of different approaches Human

Rights Activists can take to achieve their goals. Career opportunities can include public policy, advocacy and legal aid, economic development, research and scholarship, fund-raising, education and programming, and other direct services.

Unfortunately, the injustices in the world are exhaustive. Human Rights Activists can specialize to work with many different populations who need advocates to give voice to their issues. The issues facing these groups can relate to freedom, inequality, democratization, health, aid and development, public policy, ethics, and more. Human Rights Activists work to effect change for groups internationally, including:

- Women
- Minorities
- Children
- Refugees

- Prisoners
- Sweatshop workers or laborers
- Those persecuted for religious reasons

In terms of public policy, Human Rights Activists influence the formulation of policy. They examine the laws that govern how we respond to people or situations in crisis. They may work directly for the government, regional organizations, or international organizations. In this arena, Human Rights Activists often have advanced degrees that make them experts in particular subcategories of human rights.

Advocates work as champions for those who cannot adequately speak for themselves. Human Rights Activists working as advocates may focus on a particular world region (such as Central America) or a specific issue (such as violence against women). They may represent their cause through legal action such as fighting against both individual abuses and national policy making. They may also work for non-governmental organizations (commonly called NGOs) where they can develop ideas for programs that will improve quality of life for individuals and groups through research and outreach. Another part of their job can be the implementation of these programs through staffing, training, and site visits.

Economic rights are basic human rights that can be violated by denying individuals the means to support themselves. Without viable work and income, people cannot provide for their health, education, food, and environmental conditions. Human Rights Activists involved with economic and political development work on these issues.

Human Rights Activists can also pursue a career path of research and scholarship. Many conduct research and teach as part of university programs or institutes on human rights. These centers are often a collaboration of scholars, policy makers, and other activists who make a living promoting international human rights. Through research, Human Rights Activists can provide documentation of injustices, giving credence to their work. By producing concrete evidence, their work gains credibility that can help effect change.

Like all other fields in the nonprofit sector, Human Rights Activists can make a career out of raising funds to support human rights issues. Funding is crucial to sustain regular operations as well as special programs and initiatives. They may write proposals, conduct outreach, make presentations, and meet with corporations, individuals, and foundations.

Through education, Human Rights Activists can promote awareness of international human rights at many levels. Teaching opportunities abound at the K–12 level as well as at college programs. Education can be an opportunity to mobilize volunteers and provide outreach as well. Some Human Rights Activists may coordinate volunteers and provide educational programs for populations in need. Others may manage programs and allocate funds for educational projects.

Human Rights Activists can be involved with providing many direct services to people or communities in need. Services can include the legal, educational, medical, social, and psychological, among others. Human Rights Activists may be involved with running the programs, providing the services, or mobilizing volunteers. An example of a U.S.-based direct service program is Bellevue/NYU's Program for Survivors of Torture in New York City (http://www.survivorsoftorture.org). It offers medical, psychological, and legal/asylum services for more than 1,500 men, women, and children from more than 70 countries worldwide. Other Human Rights Activists may work directly in the countries in need.

Duties for Human Rights Activists in these various specialties may include:

- Organizing fact-finding missions
- Writing grant proposals
- Conducting research
- Monitoring legislation
- Lobbying for issues
- Implementing public education campaigns
- Promoting justice
- Organizing at the grassroots level
- Building coalitions and ongoing relationships
- Collaborating with teams that may include policy makers, officials, service providers, and volunteers
- Supervising volunteers or interns

Depending on their specialty area, Human Rights Activists may work for the government, for intergovernmental organizations such as the United Nations, or for NGOs. Settings may also include research/policy institutes, universities, religious-affiliated institutions, foundations that provide grants to support international human rights issues, and other international organizations. Human Rights Activists may be based domestically or internationally. Some positions require extensive travel and/or a combination of domestic and international work.

Salaries

Because the roles and responsibilities of Human Rights Activists vary greatly, so do their salaries. Entry-level positions such as program coordinators and community organizers often attract recent college graduates and pay in the low $20,000 range. For those with graduate degrees and experience in the field, salaries can be considerably higher. Depending on the position and requirements, administrative positions may pay from the mid $30,000s to more than $100,000 at large organizations.

Employment Prospects

Employment prospects vary depending on education, experience, and type of work setting. Overall, opportunities are fair to good, as world recognition of human rights issues and abuses are growing in importance. Entry-level positions in areas such as grassroots organizing offer the chance to get exposure to the field. Internships and volunteer work are another good way to gain entry. Higher-level positions are reserved for those with graduate degrees and considerable experience, and are often found through networking within the human rights community.

Advancement Prospects

Because the field is so diverse, Human Rights Activists have a variety of options for advancement. Many advancement prospects involve graduate training in law, public policy, international relations, or other related fields. Human Rights Activists who want to further their careers often find a niche and become experts in a particular topic, either specializing in the needs of a particular group or world region. They may go on to direct human rights activities, including legal issues, policy making, communications, grant writing, and more for various international organizations.

Education and Training

Human Rights Activists come to the field from a variety of different backgrounds. While in some small, grassroots organizations it would be possible for a Human Rights Activist not to have a college degree, the vast majority of positions require a bachelor's degree or higher.

In addition to a liberal arts curriculum, a number of helpful courses or majors might include international relations, anthropology, public policy, economics, political science, history, and education. Human rights and social justice courses are becoming more commonplace and are offered at many schools. Study of these subjects can be further expanded upon at the graduate level. Many Human Rights Activists involved in legal issues also have a law degree.

Many graduate programs in public policy or administration offer a specialization in human rights. Additionally, there are a number of both undergraduate and graduate programs nationwide that specifically focus on human rights issues. A list of these programs can be found at http://www.derechos.net/links/edu/index.html. This site also includes excellent information about human rights training programs, scholarships, and internships.

Since much of the work of Human Rights Activists is very hands-on; internships, fellowships, and volunteer work are an important way to gain training in the field. While graduate programs may set up their students with research and policy internships or fellowships at large organizations, undergraduates can volunteer their time at domestic and international organizations in need of support. For more information, consult the *Human Rights Internship Book* (Career Education Institutes. Winston-Salem, N.C., 1999). The following Web sites are also helpful: http://www.derechos.net/links/act/intern.html, http://www.hrusa.org/jobs/listings.php?catid=3, and http://www.idealist.org.

Experience, Skills, and Personality Traits

Above all, Human Rights Activists are passionate about their work. Regardless of their field and specialization, they are committed to promoting equality and justice whether it is through research, education, or direct service. They demonstrate their enthusiasm and mobilize others to take action. Even against opposition, which is often the case, they are persistent.

Human Rights Activists should be excellent communicators, with superb writing, research, and public speaking skills. They need to be well informed about human rights issues, world affairs, and politics. It is important for them to be able to put human rights abuses in a historical context and understand the background. In addition to being innovative and creative, it is necessary for them to be collaborators and team players.

Furthermore, Human Rights Activists need cross-cultural experience to work in the international sector. They should have spent time living, working, or studying abroad. Foreign language skills are extremely helpful; many Human Rights Activists are proficient in several languages.

Unions and Associations

Human Rights Activists may be members of a variety of organizations, depending on their interest area. While there are no specific professional associations, those in the field may participate in conferences, events, and forums organized through organizations such as Derechos Human Rights, Women's Human Rights Net, Idealist.org, and the Human Rights Internet.

Tips for Entry

1. Learn more about the Universal Declaration of Human Rights, adopted by the United Nations General Assembly in 1948 (http://www.unhchr.ch/udhr/index.htm). Adopted in the wake of the human rights abuses of World War II, this was the first declaration that mentioned human rights by name, launching it as a field.
2. There are many Web sites that offer more information about human rights as a field. Try some of these links to gather more information:
   - The Human Rights Research Center: http://www.hrusa.org/default.htm
   - Derechos Human Rights: http://www.derechos.org
   - The Columbia University Center for the Study of Human Rights: http://www.columbia.edu/cu/humanrights/
   - Human Rights Watch: http://www.hrw.org/
   - Institute for Global Communications: http://www.igc.org/
   - The University of Minnesota Human Rights Library: http://www1.umn.edu/humanrts/

- Women's Human Rights Net: http://www.whrnet.org/
- One World: http://www.oneworld.net/
- Action Without Borders, Idealist.org: http://www.idealist.org
- Human Rights Internet: http://www.hri.ca/index.aspx

3. Take a look at organizations that focus on various aspects of the human rights field. Amnesty International works to protect human rights worldwide (http://www.amnesty.org) and CARE fights global poverty (http://www.care.org). Witness focuses on using video and technology to fight for human rights (http://www.witness.org/), the National Network for Immigrant and Refugee Rights works to help immigrants and refugees (http://www.nnirr.org/), and Earth Rights International focuses on human rights and the environment (http://www.earthrights.org/).

4. What issues are you passionate about? Explore your interests and volunteer your time to help people in need, whether directly or indirectly. Consider international community service programs by checking out sites such as http://www.globalroutes.org/.

DIRECTOR OF INTERNATIONAL ACTIVITIES

CAREER PROFILE

Duties: Oversees international relationships, projects, and programs for an association or other nonprofit organization

Alternate Title(s): Director of International Programs, International Project Manager, Director of International Affairs, Director of International Relations

Salary Range: $50,000 to $100,000 and up

Employment Prospects: Fair to Good

Advancement Prospects: Good

Best Geographical Location(s): Major cities

Prerequisites:

Education or Training—Bachelor's degree; master's degree in international affairs or related field often preferred

Experience—Three to seven years depending upon the position; international experience such as work or study abroad

Special Skills and Personality Traits—Cultural sensitivity and diplomacy; understanding of international issues; foreign language skills

CAREER LADDER

```
┌─────────────────────────────────────────┐
│   Director of International Activities    │
│   (larger organization) or Vice President │
└─────────────────────────────────────────┘

┌─────────────────────────────────────────┐
│   Director of International Activities     │
└─────────────────────────────────────────┘

┌─────────────────────────────────────────┐
│        International Relations            │
│  Coordinator/Manager or other position    │
│   that includes international activities   │
└─────────────────────────────────────────┘
```

Position Description

As the working world becomes increasingly more global, managing domestic and international relationships is an important part of the work of many nonprofit organizations. Whether they are a professional membership association with overseas chapters or a cultural institution hosting millions of foreign visitors annually, the link between nonprofits and the international realm is crucial. Nonprofits may define their international engagement differently, with some actually working in a variety of countries and others focusing on creating ties, but one thing is clear. Organizations with international interests depend on the Director of International Activities to manage, build, and nurture these mutually beneficial relationships in order to achieve their greater goals.

Directors of International Activities often play many roles within an organization, all geared at bringing together international aspects of their work. Their jobs may entail several or many of the following components. They often participate in public outreach, tapping into the appropriate international markets to gain support for programs and projects. Additionally, if they are involved with planning meetings, they ensure that topics have an international flavor and that programs are publicized to and well attended by international members. Another aspect may be to coordinate international projects and bring appropriate chapters together for collaboration. Furthermore, they might create partnerships with non-U.S. sister organizations.

In professional or trade associations, Directors of International Activities work as liaisons with their international counterparts and are involved with the international chapters and membership bases. They work with chapter leaders from other countries on issues such as determining common concerns, developing relevant programs, and brainstorming about new member recruiting and member retention. Since many professions face global issues affecting all members, Directors of International Activities may research these areas and set up educational programming for members worldwide. They are well informed about what is going on in their profession and the world, as well as the implications of new trends and developments.

Improving communication is another goal for Directors of International Activities. They may plan meetings and phone conferences in order to improve interaction. E-mail has certainly brought the world closer together and is usually the quickest and easiest way for international correspondence. Directors of International Activities may work to develop Web site content related to international issues to facilitate this communication.

Within domestic nonprofits, Directors of International Activities help to gain worldwide support for their issues. For example, a local women's foundation may participate in an international women's network in order to join together with women from all over the globe with the goal of improving their lives. Together they may identify regions in particular need of activism and focus their energies on education and raising funds for particular programs to help these women.

Their duties may include:

- Monitoring international trends
- Focusing on international development and philanthropy
- Marketing programs and projects internationally
- Recruiting international members
- Coordinating translation of publications and other materials
- Developing an international certification program
- Maintaining a global policy and procedures manual
- Creating awareness of world affairs and international opportunities
- Providing guidance internally to assist other departments with international components of their work
- Fostering relationships with international institutions and/or committees
- Supervising staff
- Managing different types of international exchange programs

Many Directors of International Activities happen into their positions from other roles in the nonprofit sector that have evolved to include international responsibilities. For instance, a membership director may find that he or she spends much time cultivating international members and enjoying this aspect of the job, creating a niche. After several years, this could lead to a position as a Director of International Activities.

People who find satisfaction in this role are fascinated by the world around them. They have traveled and seen different cultures, and they strive to bring people together with common understanding. Also, they are savvy about international politics and affairs. Directors of International Activities can expect some travel with their jobs, which is an attractive feature for many considering the field, although the amount of travel will vary depending on the organization. They may work for professional and trade organizations, international nonprofits, domestic nonprofits, and colleges and universities, among others.

Salaries

According to the 2003 *ASAE Association Executive Compensation and Benefits Study,* which the American Society of Association Executives publishes every two years, the average total compensation for a Director of International Activities is $100,450. However, this figure is for executive-level professionals at large organizations. Salaries will vary depending upon the size, location, budget, and type of organization. A range may be anywhere from $50,000 to $100,000 and up.

Employment Prospects

Overall, employment prospects are fair to good for Directors of International Activities. Jobs may be hard to find since not all nonprofits are large enough to have budgets for these positions. However, in spite of this, they are growing in importance, as the mission of many organizations becomes more global.

Advancement Prospects

Directors of International Activities hone a set of research and communication skills that can be applied to many different settings. They may not find much movement within their current organizations, since their position is usually at a relatively high level, but they can use their skills to springboard into other areas of the nonprofit sector, moving from trade associations to international aid and development, running university programs, or taking leadership roles at large multinational organizations.

Education and Training

In addition to a bachelor's degree, most Directors of International Activities have a master's degree in international affairs, international relations, or related fields. Those who conduct more educational programming often hold a master's degree in international education. Undergraduate study that includes courses in international affairs, economics, world politics, and communication is also helpful.

Experience, Skills, and Personality Traits

In order to be a successful Director of International Activities, it is crucial to have experience living, working, or studying abroad. Even just one summer taking courses helps, but having spent more time working or studying abroad is even better. The cultural exposure and understanding that comes from living in another country is experience that can never be duplicated by academics alone.

Directors of International Activities must possess cultural sensitivity and diplomacy. They should be excellent communicators and researchers, with a strong understanding of international issues. They are not ethnocentric and respect that other cultures have different methods of communication and interaction, as well as values. Foreign language skills are also very useful.

Unions and Associations

Directors of International Activities may belong to professional associations, including the American Society of Association Executives and the Institute of International Education (IIE), a global higher education and professional exchange agency. They may also belong to other international affairs associations depending upon their organization. Those affiliated with universities may belong to the Association of Professional Schools of International Affairs (APSIA).

Tips for Entry

1. Consider study abroad programs. If you are unable to dedicate a year or a semester, look into summer programs. Opportunities are available to meet every major, course of study, and budget, some offering financial assistance packages. Visit your campus study abroad office or search the many sites on the Internet, including http://www.studiesabroad.com/, http://www.studyabroad.com/, http://www.goabroad. com/, and http://www.studyabroadlinks.com/.

2. Many Web sites are dedicated to overseas experience. The Council on International Educational Exchange (CIEE) at http://www.ciee.org offers study and work abroad programs that provide necessities for short-term jobs such as work permits and housing information. Also see http://www.transitionsabroad.com for more about work, study, travel, and volunteer experience.

3. Hone your foreign language skills through intensive study and course work. Surround yourself with books and media to further immerse yourself in the language you are learning.

4. Volunteer to work with international students on your campus. Many schools offer mentoring programs where you can help students learn English and become acclimated to American culture, while you gain a better appreciation for their culture as well.

5. Read international newspapers such as the *New York Times* that focus on world affairs to gain a better understanding of current events and world politics.

INTERNATIONAL AID WORKER

CAREER PROFILE

Duties: Performs humanitarian work in nations worldwide in times of disaster and conflict; offers long-term assistance to improve quality of life in developing nations

Alternate Title(s): International Relief Worker, International Development Coordinator

Salary Range: $0 to $50,000 and up

Employment Prospects: Poor to Fair

Advancement Prospects: Fair to Good

Best Geographical Location(s): Developing nations for fieldwork, and major world cities for headquarters work

Prerequisites:

Education or Training—Varies depending on position ranging from no formal education to specific technical advanced degrees

Experience—Previous international experience

Special Skills and Personality Traits—Flexibility; ability to remain calm when faced with stressful situations; good decision-making skills; excellent communication skills; cultural sensitivity; commitment and passion; foreign language skills

CAREER LADDER

```
┌─────────────────────────────┐
│      Country Director        │
└─────────────────────────────┘

┌─────────────────────────────┐
│   International Aid Worker   │
└─────────────────────────────┘

┌─────────────────────────────┐
│         Volunteer            │
└─────────────────────────────┘
```

Position Description

Despite all the technical advances of the 21st century, many nations throughout the world suffer and struggle. Disease, famine, and natural disasters sweep through regions, as do manmade disasters of war and conflict. The field of international aid and development exists to provide support to these nations. International Aid Workers are on the front lines, offering their help in a variety of ways.

One way that International Aid Workers can contribute is through humanitarian work. In these situations, they are sent to nations faced with emergency problems such as those listed above—war, conflict, and natural disaster. International Aid Workers coordinate and distribute emergency assistance, including food, shelter, and medical aid. They are the logisticians, setting up refugee camps, providing fuel and blankets.

By training, some International Aid Workers have specific technical backgrounds to perform their jobs. They include physicians, nurses, nutritionists, health educators, and civil, environmental, and water engineers. However, not all International Aid Workers come from other professions. Many choose this career as their primary profession and become project managers. Instead of a specific technical skill, project managers are skilled at organizing people, and they manage the international aid process. They may specialize in the coordination of a particular area, such as emergency services.

Another area in which International Aid Workers are employed is in development. Development refers to the long-term process of improving the standard of living in developing countries. Rather than going in for crisis control, they look at the big picture and analyze needs over time. They examine issues such as agriculture, environment concerns, education, and economic development.

International Aid Workers with development responsibilities often serve as advisers. They make recommendations to the local government, other international agencies, and local communities, and attend meetings with these groups. Also, they provide technical assistance to improve engineering, health, and agricultural difficulties.

Furthermore, International Aid Workers help to set up new programs in developing nations. By researching and assessing their current site, they design projects that are appropriate and will bring results. As managers, International Aid Workers have many human resources responsibilities, such as budgeting, writing reports and proposals, and taking care of the staff.

Their duties may include:

- Addressing water and sanitation needs of people faced with disaster
- Setting up campsites and cooking
- Driving all-terrain vehicles to distribute food and other goods
- Reading and learning about the history and politics of their region
- Keeping informed of new developments and government changes
- Conducting research
- Writing reports and grant and program proposals
- Creating and delivering educational programs in different communities
- Offering and coordinating medical assistance programs
- Attending meetings
- Training volunteers and other staff members
- Working with institutional and grant donors
- Analyzing and strategizing development plans

International Aid Workers may work in the humanitarian or development sphere; they may also move between the two areas at different points during their careers.

Additionally, International Aid Workers in the field may face hazardous conditions on a regular basis.

They must be prepared for living situations that are quite different from those to which they are accustomed. Comforts of home that can be absent include indoor plumbing, heat/air conditioning, a variety of food choices, and access to shopping, entertainment, and other amenities. Yet, most International Aid Workers do not mind these sacrifices because they find their jobs tremendously rewarding.

Salaries

The international aid and development field is made up of people with a wide variety of professional backgrounds and salaries vary accordingly. Many people try a short-term stint as an International Aid Worker volunteering for little or no pay. For example, organizations such as Doctors Without Borders and the Peace Corps offer a stipend that covers room and board to their volunteer participants.

However, those who pursue careers as International Aid Workers can earn between $25,000 and $50,000 for a mid-level position, according to insiders. Experts say that many nongovernmental organizations (NGOs) pay in the $40,000 range for employees with three years of experience and a master's degree. Other benefits may include housing. The United Nations and local governments tend to pay better than NGOs.

If International Aid Workers advance to become country directors, a typical salary range could be $70,000 to $80,000 per year.

Employment Prospects

Employment prospects are competitive for International Aid Workers. Unlike other fields, each candidate competes with a global workforce, which can be overwhelming.

While those looking to volunteer are always welcome, people looking to make a career in the field find it to be a close-knit and closed community. According to International Aid Workers, networking is a key way to find a position. Since the stakes are so high for the work they do, those in charge like to hire people they already know and trust. Many jobs are contracted for a few years only, and opportunities come and go depending on donor money.

A common way to begin is through well-known volunteer programs such as the Peace Corps. In addition to gaining valuable experience, it is also an excellent way to make contacts in the development field.

Advancement Prospects

It is much easier to advance than it is to find initial employment. Once someone gets into the field, prospects for advancement are good, particularly for those International Aid Workers who work in the field, rather than at headquarters. This is especially true for those International Aid Workers who work in dangerous regions. While these positions might not be appealing to some, for those who enjoy risk and feel committed to their mission, advancement can be a reward for International Aid Workers who are comfortable with peril.

For a career in NGOs, International Aid Workers may advance to become country directors of a specific nation. Country directors have two main roles that are both internal and external. First, they are responsible for all operations of their agency in their country. This includes budgeting, staffing, and logistics. Their second role is diplomatic. Country directors serve as the face of their agency for their country of employment. They negotiate with donors, meet with officials, and maintain relationships with the community and other organizations and agencies in the area.

Additionally, International Aid Workers can find advancement through work as consultants to international nonprofit relief agencies.

Education and Training

There are no formal educational requirements for general international aid and development work, although most International Aid Workers have a minimum of a bachelor's degree. However, many International Aid Workers do need specific backgrounds for certain positions and jobs with particular agencies.

Many International Aid Workers at NGOs and at organizations such as the United Nations have a master's degree. Fields of study may include business, humanitarian assistance, public health, public administration, international education, international affairs, or development studies.

The best training for work as an International Aid Worker comes through volunteer programs in the field.

Furthermore, many have come through the Peace Corps, where they gain valuable experience as well as go through an extensive training program. Also, many organizations offer in-service training to their International Aid Workers.

Experience, Skills, and Personality Traits

To achieve a mid-level position in international aid, three years of experience and an advanced degree are typical. International experience is a necessity, and most professionals speak and/or understand several foreign languages. While the ideal experience comes from volunteering, working, living, or studying abroad, a background in working with other cultures within the United States is paramount for those who are unable to go overseas.

Some International Aid Workers bring specific technical skills such as medicine, engineering, information technology (IT) and computer programming, or teaching to their work. Others have useful skills gained through their education, such as research and writing that can be equally helpful.

All International Aid Workers must be resilient, flexible, and adventurous. Their work requires them to live in places that are not their home, and the element of conflict and difficult governments can make the situation even more confusing. They must be strong-willed, determined, and calm people who can take crisis in stride.

Above all, International Aid Workers are deeply committed to improving the lives of others. Compassionate but not condescending, they are dedicated to helping people and must be sensitive to the diverse situations people face throughout the world.

Unions and Associations

While there are no specific professional associations for International Aid Workers, a number of Web communities and sites offer valuable information. These include:

Aid Workers Network: http://www.aidworkers.net
The Development Executive Group: http://www.developmentex.com
DevNetJobs: http://www.devnetjobs.org
InterAction: http://www.interaction.org
People In Aid: http://www.peopleinaid.org
Relief Web: http://www.reliefweb.int

Tips for Entry

1. Networking is essential for finding positions in international aid and development. One International Aid Worker recommends persistence as a key element. Do not hesitate to send multiple e-mails and call contacts several times if there is a position that interests you.

2. International experience demonstrates that you can perform in different world regions. Consider international volunteer programs such as the Peace Corps (http://www.peacecorps.gov), Cross-Cultural Solutions (http://www.crossculturalsolutions.org/intvol/resources.cfm), and the International Rescue Committee (http://www.theirc.org/index.cfm/wwwID/1864/topicID/60/locationID/0).

3. To learn more about the realities of international development work, consult Leanne Olson's book *A Cruel Paradise: Journals of an International Relief Worker* (Insomniac Press, 2000).

4. Explore some of the nonprofits working in the area of relief. Try CARE (http://www.care.org), the American Red Cross (https://www.redcross.org/), and Catholic Relief Services (http://www.catholicrelief.org/).

5. Think globally, but begin locally. Volunteer at home to show your passion for a cause and your commitment to helping others.

6. Determine your best skills for international relief work and market them. Even if you do not have specific technical training in a field like engineering, think about what you have gained from your education. Make sure to demonstrate skills such as research, writing, communication, and problem solving on job applications, your résumé, and interviews.

INTERNATIONAL EDUCATOR

Duties: Participates in furthering international education in any number of ways including advising foreign students in the United States, helping U.S. students study and work abroad, administering language programs in other countries, and creating educational programs in developing nations.

Alternate Title(s): International Student Adviser, Program Coordinator, ESL Teacher or Administrator, Study Abroad Coordinator, Educational Program Administrator, Communications Specialist

Salary Range: $35,000 to $60,000 and up

Employment Prospects: Fair to Good

Advancement Prospects: Fair to Good

Best Geographical Location(s): Large U.S. cities with international populations; developing nations

Prerequisites:

Education or Training—Minimum of a bachelor's degree; master's degree usually required

Experience—Prior experience teaching; studying, living, or working abroad

Special Skills and Personality Traits—Excellent verbal and written communication skills; cultural sensitivity; patience; good organizational skills; knowledge of other cultures and language ability

Licensure/Certification—Some positions may require teacher certification

```
┌─────────────────────────────────┐
│  Director of Educational Programs,│
│       Student Advising,          │
│   or International Exchange       │
└─────────────────────────────────┘

┌─────────────────────────────────┐
│     International Educator        │
└─────────────────────────────────┘

┌─────────────────────────────────┐
│      Volunteer or Intern         │
└─────────────────────────────────┘
```

Position Description

Encompassing international educational exchanges, development of educational programs throughout the world, and providing advice to students on all sides of the globe, the field of international education has many components. Working both domestically and abroad, International Educators are committed to promoting education and the exchange of ideas and knowledge between cultures. There are a variety of settings in which they work and roles they play in order to accomplish these goals.

International Educators may work as foreign student advisers. The most common employers for these International Educators are colleges and universities, as well as non-profits that provide services for foreign students studying in the United States. They help students navigate the educational and cultural differences that come from foreign study.

A major area of their work involves dealing with immigration issues and making sure students have the proper documentation and visas to study in the United States. Their objective is to help students study and work legally while they are in this country. International Educators work with students while they are in their home countries (often through e-mail) as well as once they matriculate into a domestic program.

As advisers, International Educators also help foreign students acclimate to life in the United States. They present workshops and programs designed to encourage cultural understanding and adjustment. Programming usually begins with orientation programs once they arrive. Often, they arrange trips for the students to experience life in the particular city in which they are studying, including theater, museums, and sporting events. International Educators also help students seek aid for any academic problems they may face.

Furthermore, International Educators also help American students who want to study in foreign countries. Also employed mainly by colleges and universities, as well as other educational exchange organizations, they help students select academic programs that match their interests. If a student wants to work or intern while abroad, International Educators may help them with the documentation and legality of making this happen. Another part of this job is marketing study abroad programs to get students interested and excited about foreign study.

International Educators may also work for nonprofit organizations that provide cross-cultural training and solutions for individuals and businesses. Each year, millions of U.S. employees must travel overseas and may be unaware of appropriate customs and cultural norms. International Educators can work as trainers or consultants to teach people what to expect in various countries throughout the world. They also help foster tolerance and understanding, promoting good relations for themselves, their business, and the United States in general.

In addition to these domestic roles, many International Educators also work overseas. Another facet of international education is aid and development work. International Educators may develop curriculum, offer teacher training, and monitor and evaluate existing programs for effectiveness. They also develop new programs based on the needs of the region, with many specializations including girls' education, health education, and literacy.

As program administrators as well as technical specialists, they supervise staff, manage a budget, and ensure that teachers have the necessary tools and supplies to do their jobs. Often employed by nongovernmental organizations (NGOs), they partner with government agencies and the local community to increase educational awareness and emphasize the benefits that will come to the community with education.

Another aspect of international education that enables International Educators to work domestically or internationally is administering English as a second language (ESL) programs. In the United States, many for-profit programs exist to help new immigrants learn English, but there are also language programs through universities and nonprofits that are geared at helping them to acclimate as well. Additionally, in countries throughout the world, programs exist to help children and adults learn English, whether for travel later on, or for their own interest. International Educators

may teach, develop curriculum, supervise teachers, and create new programs.

Additional duties may include:

- Working with refugees in resettlement areas
- Coordinating community service projects
- Arranging housing and home stays for foreign students in the United States and vice versa
- Creating marketing materials such as brochures, flyers, and posters
- Developing curriculum and training materials to promote cultural awareness
- Researching different world regions to understand customs and culture
- Keeping up on international educational issues
- Working on international educational reform and advocacy
- Writing grant proposals for educational programs
- Providing conflict resolution and mediation
- Administering international fellowship and scholarship positions

Whether helping a Korean student find an internship to complement her educational program in Boston or developing a campaign for education reform in Kenya, International Educators are committed to promoting education as a tool to combat world problems such as injustice and prejudice. By fostering cultural understanding in all settings in which they work, they are advocates for human rights and find their work very rewarding. Positions may follow a traditional nine-to-five schedule, or they may vary to include evening and weekend programs that meet the needs of students and other participants.

Salaries

International Educators typically earn in the $40,000 to $50,000 range, depending on the position. Large universities tend to pay at the high end of the spectrum, particular for those professionals with experience. NGOs also are known to offer competitive pay. The low end usually comes from jobs at international community agencies with poor program funding.

International Educators sometimes supplement their salaries by working as consultants to various organizations and offering private tutoring services.

Employment Prospects

Employment prospects for International Educators are fair to good. The number of possible work environments provides many job prospects for those who are flexible. Worldwide education is growing in importance, with special attention being paid to girls' education in developing countries. However, positions (particularly those abroad) are often dependent on the grant money to fund them. International Educators may find project work that is rewarding, but does not provide job security.

Opportunities in colleges and universities are often the most plentiful. Jobs can be found through networking with other International Educators through graduate school programs and professional associations.

Advancement Prospects

International Educators may advance to direct international centers, international student services, or a variety of programs. An advance degree is usually a prerequisite for advancement, as is personal international experience. Management and leadership skills are needed for director-level work. Also, International Educators may become self-employed as consultants and cross-cultural trainers.

Education and Training

According to the Association of International Educators (NAFSA), most careers as an International Educator require a bachelor's degree. A graduate degree is increasingly preferred. Students study many international and education-related fields, including liberal arts, psychology, teaching, counseling, public affairs, foreign languages and cultures, and international relations.

Graduate programs in the field of international education are becoming more popular and valuable for the profession. The following Web site includes universities with international education graduate programs: http://listserv.acsu. buffalo.edu/cgi-bin/wa?A2=ind0302&L=secuss-l&P= R24848&I=-3.

Special Requirements

Some work settings may require International Educators to be licensed teachers of English as a second language. See the TESOL (Teachers of English to Speakers of Other Languages) Web site at http://www.tesol.org/s_tesol/index.asp.

Experience, Skills, and Personality Traits

Above all, respect for diversity and tolerance is important for work as an International Educator. International Educators work with people who are often different from them, and they must have patience and strong listening skills to hear their concerns and not get frustrated by language barriers. They must also have excellent communication skills as articulate speakers and writers.

Furthermore, International Educators need some prior international experience. Whether they have studied, worked, or lived abroad, they bring a solid familiarity with other cultures. Teaching experience is also very valuable, both domestic and international. It is helpful for International Educators to be fluent or proficient in at least one foreign language.

Unions and Associations

The Association of International Educators (NAFSA) is the main professional association for those involved with international education. International Educators may also be members of Teachers of English to Speakers of Other Languages (TESOL) and the Alliance for International and Cultural Exchange.

Tips for Entry

1. The Institute of International Education (IIE) is a nonprofit organization that creates and implements study, training, and exchange programs for students all over the world. In addition to conducting policy research and advising students, IIE also administers such prestigious fellowship programs as the Fulbright. For more information, visit http://www.iie.org.
2. Organizations that encourage communication between different groups are also good options for employment. Take a look at Global Nomads Group (http:// www.gng.org/), which fosters dialogue among the world's youth.
3. The Association of International Educators (NAFSA) has excellent career information on their Web site. Explore their links at http://www.nafsa.org.
4. Do you live or attend school in a region with a large immigrant population? If so, volunteer to work with this group as a teacher, tutor, counselor, or literacy trainer.
5. Another major player in the field of cultural exchange is Council on International Educational Exchange. Spend time on their Web site at http://www.ciee.org to learn about programs and view job listings.

APPENDIXES

APPENDIX I
GRADUATE SCHOOL
AND CERTIFICATE PROGRAMS

A. NONPROFIT MANAGEMENT

The following schools offer graduate degree or certificate programs in nonprofit management. Some programs are part of schools of business, while others are within schools of public administration or other academic departments. For more information, check out Web sites such as http://www.nonprofits.org/misc/acad.html and http://pirate.shu.edu/~mirabero/Kellogg.html; which include compiled lists on this topic.

ALABAMA

Auburn University at Montgomery
Department of Political Science and
  Public Administration
Certificate in Nonprofit Management and
  Leadership
P.O. Box 244023
Montgomery, AL 36124-4023
Phone: (334) 244-3698
http://sciences.aum.edu/popa/cert_nonprofit.
  html

ARIZONA

Arizona State University
Center for Nonprofit Leadership
  and Management
College of Public Programs
P.O. Box 874703
Tempe, AZ 85287-4703
Phone: (480) 965-0607
Fax: (480) 727-8878
http://www.asu.edu/copp/nonprofit/

ARKANSAS

University of Arkansas at Little Rock
UALR Institute of Government
Graduate Certificate in Nonprofit
  Management
Sixth Floor, Ross Hall
2801 South University
Little Rock, AR 72204
Phone: (501) 569-8026
Fax: (501) 569-8514
http://www.ualr.edu/npgc/

CALIFORNIA

Hope International University
School of Graduate Studies
Program in Business Administration
Nonprofit Management
Fullerton, CA 92831-3138
Phone: (800) 762-1294
http://www.hiu.edu

San Francisco State University
Graduate Division
College of Behavioral and Social
  Sciences
Public Administration Program
San Francisco, CA 94132-1722
Phone: (415) 338-2023
http://www.sfsu.edu

University of San Francisco
College of Professional Studies
Department of Public Management
Institute for Nonprofit Administration
San Francisco, CA 94117-1080
Phone: (415) 422-6000
http://www.usfca.edu

CONNECTICUT

Yale University
School of Management
Nonprofit Concentration
135 Prospect Street
P.O. Box 208200
New Haven, CT 06520-8200
Phone: (203) 432-5932
Fax: (203) 432-7004
http://mba.yale.edu/

COLORADO

Regis University
School of Professional Studies
Program in Nonprofit Management
Denver, CO 80221-1099
Phone: (800) 677-9270
http://www.regis.edu

DISTRICT OF COLUMBIA

Georgetown University
Center for Public and Nonprofit
  Leadership
Nonprofit Management Executive
  Certificate
3240 Prospect Street, NW, Lower Level
Washington, DC 20007
Phone: (202) 687-0500
http://gppi.georgetown.edu/

The George Washington University
School of Business and Public
  Management
Department of Public Administration
Washington, DC 20052
Phone: (202) 994-6584
http://www.gwu.edu

Trinity College
School of Professional Studies
Programs in Administration
Washington, DC 20017-1094
Phone: (202) 884-9400
http://www.trinitydc.edu

FLORIDA

Florida Atlantic University
School of Public Administration
Master of Nonprofit Management

FAU/BCC Higher Education Complex
111 East Las Olas Boulevard
Fort Lauderdale, FL 33301
Phone: (954) 762-5650
Fax: (954) 762-5693
http://www.fau.edu/divdept/caupa/spa

University of Central Florida
College of Health and Public Affairs
Program in Public Administration
Orlando, FL 32816
Phone: (407) 823-2604
http://www.ucf.edu

GEORGIA

Georgia State University
Andrew Young School of Policy Studies
Nonprofit Studies Program
University Placeaza
Atlanta, GA 30303-3083
Phone: (404) 651-3990
http://www.gsu.edu/~wwwsps/nonprofit/
index.htm

ILLINOIS

DePaul University
College of Liberal Arts and Sciences
Program in Public Service
Chicago, IL 60604-2287
Phone: (312) 362-5367
http://www.depaul.edu

North Central College
Graduate Programs
Department of Leadership Studies
Naperville, IL 60566-7063
Phone: (630) 637-5840
http://www.noctrl.edu

Northwestern University
Kellogg Graduate School of Management
Programs in Management
Evanston, IL 60208
Phone: (847) 491-3300
http://www.nwu.edu

Roosevelt University
School of Policy Studies, College of Arts
and Sciences
Certificate in Nonprofit Management
430 South Michigan Avenue
Chicago, IL 60605
Phone: (312) 341-3744
http://www.roosevelt.edu/cas/sps/
cert-npm.htm

St. Xavier University Chicago
Graham School of Management
Master of Science in Public and
Non-Profit Management
3700 West 103rd Street
Chicago, IL 60655
Phone: (773) 298-3000
http://www.sxu.edu

University of Illinois at Chicago
College of Urban Planning and Public
Affairs
Certificate in Nonprofit Management
412 South Peoria, Suite 115
Chicago, IL 60607-7064
Phone: (312) 413-8088
Fax: (312) 413-8095
http://www.uic.edu/cuppa/

INDIANA

Indiana University
School of Public and Environmental
Affairs
Master of Public Affairs, Concentration in
Nonprofit Management
1315 East Tenth Street
Bloomington, IN 47405
Phone: (800) 765-7755
http://www.iu.edu/~speaweb/public/master/
nonprofit.html

Indiana University Northwest
Division of Public and Environmental
Affairs
Gary, IN 46408-1197
Phone: (219) 980-6737
http://www.iun.indiana.edu

**Indiana University–Purdue University
Indianapolis**
Center on Philanthropy
MA in Philanthropic Studies
Indianapolis, IN 46202
Phone: (317) 274-4200
http://www.iupui.edu

LOUISIANA

University of New Orleans
College of Urban and Public Affairs
The International Project for Nonprofit
Leadership
2000 Lakeshore Drive
New Orleans, LA 70148
Phone: (504) 280-6277
Fax: (504) 280-6272
http://www.uno.edu/~cupa/

MARYLAND

**The College of Notre Dame
of Maryland**
Master of Arts in Nonprofit Management
4701 North Charles Street
Baltimore, MD 21210
Phone: (410) 435-0100
http://www.ndm.edu/graduatestudies/
majors/gs_maNonProfManagement.cfm

MASSACHUSETTS

Boston University
School of Management
Program in Public and Nonprofit
Management
Boston, MA 02215
Phone: (612) 353-2312
http://www.bu.edu

Brandeis University
Heller Graduate School-Program in
Management
Master of Management in Human
Services
Hornstein Program in Jewish Communal
Service
Waltham, MA 02454-9110
Phone: (800) 279-4105
http://www.brandeis.edu

Lesley University
School of Management
Cambridge, MA 02138-2790
Phone: (617) 349-8690
http://www.lesley.edu

Suffolk University
Frank Sawyer School of Management
Department of Public Management
Boston, MA 02108-2770
Phone: (617) 573-8302
http://www.suffolk.edu

Tufts University
Division of Graduate and Continuing
Studies and Research
Professional and Continuing Studies
Management of Community
Organizations Program
Medford, MA 02155
Phone: (617) 627-3700
http://www.tufts.edu

Worcester State College
Graduate Studies
Program in Non-Profit Management
Worcester, MA 01602-2597

Phone: (508) 929-8120
http://www.worcester.edu

MICHIGAN

Grand Valley State University
School of Public and Nonprofit
    Administration
401 West Fulton Street
Grand Rapids, MI 49504
Phone: (616) 331-6575
Fax: (616) 331-7120
http://www.gvsu.edu/spna/

University of Michigan, Flint
Master of Public Administration
    Program
Specialization in Administration of
    Nonprofit Agencies
310 French Hall
303 East Kearsley Street
Flint, MI 48502
Phone: (810) 762-3470
http://graduateprograms.umflint.edu/pub_
    admin.htm

MINNESOTA

Hamline University
Graduate School of Public Administration
    and Management
St. Paul, MN 55104-1284
Phone: (651) 523-2284
http://www.hamline.edu

Metropolitan State University
College of Management
St. Paul, MN 55106-5000
Phone: (612) 373-2724
http://www.metrostate.edu

St. Cloud State University
School of Graduate Studies
College of Social Studies
Program in Public and Nonprofit
    Institutions
St. Cloud, MN 56301-4498
Phone: (320) 255-2113
http://www.stcloudstate.edu

**St. Mary's University of Minnesota
    (Winona)**
Graduate and Professional Programs
Master of Arts in Philanthropy and
    Development
700 Terrace Heights
Winona, MN 55987-1399
Phone: (800) 635-5987

Fax: (507) 452-4430
http://www.smumn.edu/sitepages/pid311.
    php

University of St. Thomas
Graduate Studies
Graduate School of Business
St. Paul, MN 55105-1096
Phone: (651) 962-4226
http://www.stthomas.edu

MISSOURI

University of Missouri, Columbia
Truman School of Public Affairs
Specialization in Nonprofit Management
105 Middlebush Hall
Columbia, MO 65211-6100
Phone: (573) 882-3304
Fax: (573) 884-4872
http://www.truman.missouri.edu/
    AcademicPrograms/nonprof.html

University of Missouri–St. Louis
Nonprofit Management & Leadership
    Program
Public Policy Administration
One University Boulevard, 406 Tower
St. Louis, MO 63121-4499
Phone: (314) 516-5145
Fax: (314) 516-5210
http://www.umsl.edu/%7Econted/npml/

NEW HAMPSHIRE

Antioch University New England
Graduate School of Organization and
    Management
Master in Human Services Administration
40 Avon Street
Keene, NH 03431-3516
Phone: (603) 357-3122
Fax: (603) 357-0718
http://omdept.antiochne.edu/OMDegrees/
    mhsa

NEW JERSEY

Seton Hall University
College of Arts and Sciences
Center for Public Service
Program in Management of Nonprofit
    Organizations
South Orange, NJ 07079-2697
Phone: (973) 761-9510
http://www.shu.edu

NEW YORK

The College of St. Rose
Graduate Studies
School of Business
Not for Profit Management Department
Albany, NY 12203-1419
Phone: (518) 454-5137
http://www.strose.edu

New School University
Robert J. Milano Graduate School
    of Management and Urban Policy
Program in Nonprofit Management
New York, NY 10011-8603
Phone: (212) 229-5462
http://www.newschool.edu

New York University
Robert F. Wagner Graduate School
    of Public Service
Program in Public Administration
New York, NY 10012-1019
Phone: (212) 998-7414
http://www.nyu.edu

Pace University
White Plains Campus
Dyson College of Arts and Sciences
Department of Public Administration
White Plains, NY 10603
Phone: (914) 422-4283
http://www.pace.edu

The Sage Colleges
Department of Management
Certificate Programs—Managing
    Not-for-Profit Organizations
45 Ferry Street
Troy, NY 12180
Phone: (518) 244-2000
http://www.sage.edu

NORTH CAROLINA

**University of North Carolina
    at Charlotte**
Graduate Certificate in Nonprofit
    Management
9201 University City Boulevard
Charlotte, North Carolina 28223-0001
Phone: (704) 687-2577
http://www.mpa.uncc.edu/
    graduatecertificate. htm

**University of North Carolina
    at Greensboro**
Department of Political Science

Nonprofit Management Certificate
Greensboro, NC 27402
Phone: (336) 256-0510
http://www.uncg.edu/psc/Npinfo.htm

OHIO

Case Western Reserve University
Weatherhead School of Management
Mandel Center for Nonprofit Organizations
Cleveland, OH 44106
Phone: (216) 368-2000
http://www.cwru.edu

OKLAHOMA

Oral Roberts University
School of Business
Tulsa, OK 74171-0001
Phone: (918) 495-6236
http://www.oru.edu

OREGON

University of Oregon
School of Architecture and Allied Arts
Certificate Program in Not-For-Profit
    Management
119 Hendricks Hall, 1209
    University of Oregon
Eugene, OR 97403-1209
Phone: (541) 346-3635
Fax: (541) 346-2040
http://utopia.uoregon.edu/ppm/ppm_
    certificate.htm

Willamette University
George H. Atkinson Graduate School
    of Management
Salem, OR 97301-3931
Phone: (503) 370-6167
http://www.willamette.edu

PENNSYLVANIA

Carlow College
Division of Professional Leadership

Pittsburgh, PA 15213-3165
Phone: (412) 578-8764
http://www.carlow.edu

Eastern College
Graduate Business Programs
Program in Nonprofit Management
St. Davids, PA 19087-3696
Phone: (610) 341-5972
http://www.eastern.edu

Marywood University
Public Administration Program,
    Concentration in Nonprofit
    Management
2300 Adams Avenue
Scranton, PA 18509
Phone: (570) 348-6211
http://www.marywood.edu/departments/
    publicadm/nonprofit.htm

University of Pennsylvania
Fels Institute of Government
5-Course Nonprofit Administration
    Certificate
3814 Walnut Street
Philadelphia, PA 19104-6197
Phone: (215) 898-8216
Fax: (215) 898-1202
http://www.fels.upenn.edu/

TENNESSEE

Tennessee State University
Institute of Government
Certificate in Non-Profit Management
330 Tenth Avenue North
Campus Box 140
Nashville, TN 37203
Phone: (615) 963-7241
Fax: (615) 963-7245
http://www.tnstate.edu/IOG/
    CNPMhomepage.htm

University of Memphis
Division of Public and Nonprofit
    Administration
136 McCord Hall

Memphis, TN 38152
Phone: (901) 678-3360
Fax: (901) 678-2981
http://padm.memphis.edu/

University of Tennessee at Chattanooga
Political Science Department
Nonprofit Certificate and Concentration
615 McCallie Avenue
Chattanooga, TN 37403-2594
Phone: (423) 425-4068
http://www.utc.edu/Academic/MPA/

TEXAS

St. Edward's University
College of Professional and Graduate
    Studies
Program in Business Administration
Austin, TX 78704-6489
Phone: (512) 448-8600
http://www.stedwards.edu

VIRGINIA

Virginia Commonwealth University
School of Government and Public Affairs
Graduate Certificate in Nonprofit
    Management
P.O. Box 842028
923 West Franklin Street, Room 518
Richmond, VA 23284-2028
Phone: (804) 828-8041
Fax: (804) 828-2171
http://www.has.vcu.edu/pos/NPgraduate_
    certificate.htm

WASHINGTON

Seattle University
College of Arts and Sciences
Institute of Public Service
Program in Not-for-Profit Leadership
Seattle, WA 98122
Phone: (206) 296-5900
http://www.seattleu.edu

B. PUBLIC POLICY, AFFAIRS, AND ADMINISTRATION

Many schools offer graduate programs in public affairs, public administration, and public policy, which train professionals to be leaders in public service, nonprofit management, and government. The most common degree available is the M.P.A. (master of public administration), while others who are more interested in policy than management choose the M.P.P. (master of public policy). Yet other programs offer doctoral degrees and other master's degrees. See the Web sites of the National Association of Schools of Public Affairs and Administration (http://naspaa.org/) as well as the Association for Public Policy Analysis and Management (http://www.appam.org) for completely updated listings.

ALABAMA

Auburn University at Auburn
Department of Political Science
Graduate Programs in Public
 Administration and Policy
8030 Haley Center
Auburn, AL 36849
Phone: (334) 844-5371
http://www.auburn.edu/mpa

Auburn University at Montgomery
Department of Political Science
 and Public Administration
Graduate Programs in Public
 Administration
P.O. Box 244023
Montgomery, AL 36124-4023
Phone: (334) 244-3698
Fax: (334) 244-3826
http://sciences.aum.edu/popa/index.htm

Birmingham-Southern College
Office of Graduate Programs
Master of Arts in Public and Private
 Management
900 Arkadelphia Road
P.O. Box 549052
Birmingham, AL 35254
Phone: (205) 226-4841
http://www.bsc.edu/academics/business/
 mppm/index.htm

University of Alabama at Birmingham
The Graduate School
Public Administration Graduate Program
1530 3rd Avenue South
Birmingham, AL 35294-3350
Phone: (205) 934-4653
http://www.uab.edu/govt/mpa

University of Alabama, Tuscaloosa
Political Science Department
Master of Public Administration
P.O. Box 870213
Tuscaloosa, AL 35487-0213
Phone: (205) 348-3800
http://www.as.ua.edu/psc/grad.htm

University of South Alabama
Department of Political Science/Criminal
 Justice
Master of Public Administration
Mobile, AL 36688-0002
Phone: (251) 460-7161
Fax: (251) 460-6567
http://www.southalabama.edu/
 graduateprograms/artsandsci.html

ALASKA

University of Alaska
College of Business and Public Policy
Masters of Public Administration
3211 Providence Drive
Anchorage, AK 99508
Phone: (907) 786-4127
Fax: (907) 786-4115
http://www.cbpp.uaa.alaska.edu/dept/
 dept.asp?page=public

University of Alaska Southeast
Master of Public Administration Program
11120 Glacier Highway
Juneau, AK 99801
Phone: (800) 478-9069; (877) 465-6402
Fax: (877) 465-6549
http://www.uas.alaska.edu/uas/mpa/

ARIZONA

Arizona State University
School of Public Affairs
Graduate Programs in Public
 Administration
P.O. Box 870603
Tempe, AZ 85287-0603
Phone: (480) 965-3926
http://spa.asu.edu/acadprog.htm

The University of Arizona
School of Public Administration and
 Policy
Master of Public Administration and
 Ph.D. in Management
McClelland Hall, 405

P.O. Box 210108
Tucson, Arizona 85721-0108
Phone: (520) 621-3634
http://www.bpa.arizona.edu/~spap/

ARKANSAS

Arkansas State University
Department of Political Science
Master of Public Administration
P.O. Box 1750
State University, AR 72467-1750
Phone: (870) 972-3048
http://polsci.astate.edu/
 Degree%20Information/mpapage.htm

University of Arkansas, Fayetteville
Department of Political Science
M.P.A. Program
428 Old Main
Fayetteville, AR 72701
Phone: (479) 575-3356
Fax: (479) 575-6432
http://plsc.uark.edu/grad/

University of Arkansas, Little Rock
The Clinton School of Public Service
Master in Public Service Program
4301 West Markham Street #820
Little Rock, AR 72205
Phone: (501) 526-6619
Fax: (501) 526-6658
http://clintonschool.uasys.edu/

University of Arkansas, Little Rock
UALR Institute of Government
Master in Public Administration
2801 South University
Little Rock, AR 72204
Phone: (501) 569-8514
http://www.ualr.edu/iog/mpa.html

CALIFORNIA

California State Polytechnic University
Political Science Department
Masters in Public Administration
 Program

3801 West Temple Avenue
Pomona, CA 91768-4055
Phone: (909) 869-4739
http://www.csupomona.edu/~lnelson/
    mpaprogram/

California State University, Bakersfield
School of Business and Public
    Administration
Master of Public Administration
9001 Stockdale Highway
Bakersfield, CA 93311-1099
Phone: (661) 664-2326
http://www.csubbpa.com/index.cfm?
    fuseaction=page&page_id=11

California State University, Chico
School of Graduate, International, and
    Sponsored Programs
Master of Public Administration
Tehama Hall Room 211
Chico, CA 95929-0875
Phone: (530) 898-5734
Fax: (530) 898-6889
http://www.csuchico.edu/gisp/gs/
    programs/mpa/index.html

**California State University,
    Dominguez Hills**
School of Business and Public Policy
Master of Public Administration Program
1000 East Victoria Street
Carson, CA 90747
Phone: (310) 243-3661
http://som.csudh.edu/mpaoncampus/

California State University, Fresno
Division of Graduate Studies
Department of Political Science
Master of Public Administration
5340 North Campus Drive M/S SS19
Fresno, CA 93740-8019
Phone: (559) 278-2988
http://www.csufresno.edu/gradstudies/
    narratives/publicad-prog.htm

California State University, Fullerton
Division of Criminal Justice and Political
    Science
Masters in Public Administration Program
Fullerton, CA 92834
Phone: (714) 278-2168
http://hss.fullerton.edu/polisci/MPAprog.
    htm

California State University, Hayward
Department of Public Administration
25800 Carlos Bee Boulevard
Hayward, CA 94542

Phone: (510) 885-3282
http://www.csuhayward.edu

**California State University,
    Long Beach**
Graduate Center for Public Policy
    and Administration
1250 Bellflower Boulevard
Long Beach, CA 90840-4602
Phone: (562) 985-4178
Fax: (562) 985-4672
http://www.csulb.edu/~beachmpa/

California State University, Los Angeles
School of Natural and Social Sciences,
    Department of Political Science
M.S. in Public Administration
5151 State University Drive
Los Angeles, CA 90032-8226
Phone: (323) 343-2232
http://www.calstatela.edu/dept/pol_sci/
    MSPA1.html

California State University, Northridge
College of Extended Learning
Master of Public Administration
18111 Nordhoff Street
Northridge, CA 91330
Phone: (818)-677-5635
http://www.csun.edu/exl/program/mpa/
    index.htm

**California State University,
    Sacramento**
Master of Public Policy and
    Administration (M.P.P.A.)
6000 J Street
Sacramento, CA 95819
Phone: (916) 278-6557
http://www.csus.edu/mppa

**California State University,
    San Bernadino**
College of Business and Public
    Administration
MPA Program
Jack H. Brown Hall
5500 University Parkway
San Bernadino, CA 92407-2397
Phone: (909) 880-5758
Fax: (909) 880-7517
http://www.sbpa.csusb.edu/pa/mpa/

California State University, Stanislaus
Department of Politics & Public
    Administration
Master of Public Administration
801 West Monte Vista Avenue
Turlock, CA 95382

Phone: (209) 667-3388
Fax: (209) 667-3724
http://www.csustan.edu/ppa/index.html

**The Frederick S. Pardee RAND
    Graduate School**
Ph.D. in Policy Analysis
1700 Main Street
P.O. Box 2138
Santa Monica, CA 90407-2138
Phone: (310) 393-0411, x7690
Fax: (310) 451-6978
http://www.rgs.edu/index.html

Golden Gate University
Executive Master of Public
    Administration
536 Mission Street
San Francisco, CA 94105-2968
Phone: (800) 448-4968
Fax: (415) 442-7807
http://www.ggu.edu/school_of_
    business/programs_degrees/public_
    administration/executive_mpa

**The Monterey Institute
    of International Studies**
Graduate School of International Policy
    Studies
425 Van Buren Street
Monterey, CA 93940
Phone: (831) 647-6543
http://www.miis.edu/gsips-progs-
    degcertover.html

Pepperdine University
School of Public Policy
24255 Pacific Coast Highway
Malibu, CA 90263-7490
Phone: (310) 506-7493
Fax: (310) 506-7494
http://publicpolicy.pepperdine.edu/
    academics/mpp/

San Diego State University
School of Public Administration and
    Urban Studies
5500 Campanile Drive
San Diego, CA 92182-4505
Phone: (619) 594-6224
Fax: (619) 594-1165
http://psfa.sdsu.edu/spaus/

San Francisco State University
College of Behavioral and Social
    Sciences
Public Administration Program
1600 Holloway Avenue
San Francisco, CA 94132

Phone: (415) 338-2985
Fax: (415) 338-1194
http://bss.sfsu.edu/~mpa/

San Jose State University
Political Science Department
Master of Public Administration
One Washington Square
San Jose, CA 95192
Phone: (408) 924-5550
http://info.sjsu.edu/web-
    dbgen/catalog/departments/POLS-
    section-5.html

University of California, Berkeley
Richard & Rhoda Goldman
    School of Public Policy
2607 Hearst Avenue
Berkeley, CA 94720-7320
Phone: (510) 642-4670
Fax: (510) 643-9657
http://socrates.berkeley.edu/~gspp/

University of California, Los Angeles
School of Public Policy and Social
    Research
3250 Public Policy Building
P.O. Box 951656
Los Angeles, CA 90095-1656
Phone: (310) 206-7568
http://www.sppsr.ucla.edu/main.cfm

University of La Verne
College of Business & Public
    Management
Landis Academic Center
1950 3rd Street
La Verne, CA 91750
Phone: (909) 593-3511 ext. 4058/4192;
    (877) 558-4858
Fax: (909) 392-2704
http://www.ulv.edu/cbpm/pa/

University of San Francisco
College of Professional Studies
Graduate Program in Public
    Administration
2130 Fulton Street
San Francisco, CA 94117-1080
Phone: (415) 422-6000
http://www.cps.usfca.edu/prospective/
    MPA.html

University of Southern California
School of Policy, Planning, and
    Development
Graduate Programs in Public
    Management and Public Policy
Lewis Hall 312
Los Angeles, CA 90089-0626

Phone: (213) 740-6842
http://www.usc.edu/sppd/

COLORADO

University of Colorado at Denver
Graduate School of Public Affairs
P.O. Box 173364 – Campus Box 142
Denver, CO 80217-3364
Phone: (303) 556-5970
Fax: (303) 556-5971
http://carbon.cudenver.edu/public/gspa/
    home.html

University of Denver
Institute for Public Policy Studies
2199 South University Boulevard
Denver, CO 80208
Phone: (303) 871-2468
Fax: (303) 871-3066
http://www.du.edu/ipps/

CONNECTICUT

University of Connecticut
Department of Public Policy
Master of Public Administration Program
421 Whitney Road, U-1106
Storrs, CT 06269-1106
Phone: (860) 486-4518
http://www.mpa.uconn.edu/

DELAWARE

University of Delaware
Graduate School of Urban Affairs
    and Public Policy
182 Graham Hall
Newark, DE 19716
Phone: (302) 831-1687
Fax: (302) 831-3587
http://www.udel.edu/suapp/

DISTRICT OF COLUMBIA

American University
School of Public Affairs
Graduate Programs in Public
    Administration and in Public Policy
4400 Massachusetts Avenue, NW
Washington, DC 20016
Phone: (202) 885-6230
http://www.american.edu/academic.depts/
    spa/dpa/programs/

Georgetown University
Georgetown Public Policy Institute
Master of Public Policy and Master
    of Policy Management Programs

3520 Prospect Street, NW, 4th Floor
Washington, DC 20007
Phone: (202) 687-5932
Fax: (202) 687-5544
http://gppi.georgetown.edu/

George Washington University
School of Public Policy and Public
    Administration
M.P.A., M.P.P., and Ph.D. Programs
805 21st Street, NW
Media and Public Affairs Building,
    Room 602
Washington, DC 20052
Phone: (202) 994-8500
http://www.gwu.edu/~spppa/

Howard University
Department of Political Science
Master of Arts in Public Administration
4th and College Streets, NW
Washington, DC 20059
Phone: (202) 806-6800
Fax: (202) 462-4053
http://www.gs.howard.edu/gradprograms/
    political.htm

FLORIDA

Florida Atlantic University
School of Public Administration
FAU/BCC Higher Education Complex
111 East Las Olas Boulevard
Fort Lauderdale, FL 33301
Phone: (954) 762-5650
Fax: (954) 762-5693
http://www.fau.edu/divdept/caupa/spa/

Florida Gulf Coast University
College of Professional Studies
Master of Public Administration
19501 Ben Hill Griffin Parkway
Fort Myers, FL 33965-6565
Phone: (239) 590-1000
http://www.fgcu.edu/

Florida International University
College of Health and Urban Affairs
School of Policy and Management
University Park, PCA 257
11200 Southwest 8th Street
Miami, FL 33199
Phone: (305) 348-5890
Fax: (305) 348-5348
http://chua2.fiu.edu/pa/

Florida State University
Askew School of Public Administration
    & Policy

Tallahassee, FL 32306-2250
Phone: (850) 644-3525
Fax: (850) 644-7617
http://askew.fsu.edu/

Nova Southeastern University
H. Wayne Huizenga School of Business
    and Entrepreneurship
Masters and Doctoral Programs in Public
    Administration
3301 College Avenue
Fort Lauderdale, FL 33314
Phone: (954) 262-5000; (800) 672-7223
http://www.huizenga.nova.edu/programs/
    masters.cfm

University of Central Florida
Division of Graduate Studies
Department of Public Administration
Millican Hall, Suite 230
P.O. Box 160112
Orlando, FL 32816-0112
Phone: (407) 823-2766
Fax: (407) 823-6442
http://www.cohpa.ucf.edu/pubadm/index.
    cfm

University of Miami
School of Business Administration
M.P.A. Program
Coral Gables, FL 33124-3220
Phone: (305) 284-4154
http://www.miami.edu

University of North Florida
Department of Political Science and
    Public Administration
4567 St. Johns Bluff Road
Jacksonville, FL 32224
Phone: (904) 620-1000
http://www.unf.edu/graduatestudies/
    programs/coas/mpa.html

University of South Florida
Public Administration Program
4202 East Fowler Avenue
Tampa, FL 33620
Phone: (813) 974-2011
http://www.usf.edu

University of West Florida
Division of Administrative Studies
Master of Public Administration
11000 University Parkway
Building 54 Room 119
Phone: (850) 474-2592
http://cops.uwf.edu/copsweb/adminstd/
    medmpa.cfm

GEORGIA
Albany State University
Department of History, Science,
    and Public Administration
Master of Public Administration
504 College Drive
Albany, GA 31705
Phone: (921) 430-4870
Fax: (912) 430-7895
http://asuweb.asurams.edu/artsci/History/
    index.html

Augusta State University
Department of Political Science
Master of Public Administration Program
2500 Walton Way
Augusta, GA 30904-2200
Phone: (706) 729-2256
Fax: (706) 667-4083
http://www.aug.edu/mpa/

Clark Atlanta University
Department of Public Administration
223 James P. Brawley Drive
    at Fair Street, SW
Atlanta, GA 30314
Phone: (404) 880-6650
http://www.cau.edu/

Columbus State University
Department of Political Science
Master of Public Administration
4225 University Avenue
Columbus, GA 31907
Phone: (706) 568-2027
Fax: (706) 565-3469
http://polsci.colstate.edu/mparequire.htm

Georgia College and State University
College of Arts and Sciences
Master of Public Administration and
    Master of Public Affairs
Milledgeville, GA 31061-0490
Phone: (478) 445-5004
http://www.gcsu.edu/acad_affairs/grad_
    school/arts.html

Georgia Institute of Technology
College of Liberal Arts, School
    of Public Policy
M.S. and Ph.D. in Public Policy
781 Marietta Street
Atlanta, GA 30318
Phone: (404) 894-1727
Fax: (404) 894-8573
http://www.spp.gatech.edu

Georgia Southern University
Department of Political Science

Masters in Public Administration
Carroll Building / P.O. Box 8101
Statesboro, GA 30460-8101
Phone: (912) 681-5698
Fax: (912) 681-5348
http://class.georgiasouthern.edu/polisci/
    index.html

Georgia State University
Andrew Young School of Policy Studies
Department of Public Administration
    and Urban Studies
University Plaza
Atlanta, GA 30303-3083
Phone: (404) 651-3350
Fax: (404) 651-1378
http://www.gsu.edu/~wwwpau/

Kennesaw State University
Department of Political Science and
    International Affairs
Master of Public Administration
Mail Box #2302
1000 Chastain Road
Kennesaw, GA 30144
Phone: (770) 423-6631
http://www.kennesaw.edu/pols/mpa/

Savannah State University
College of Liberal Arts and Social
    Sciences
Master of Public Administration
P.O. Box 20385
Savannah, GA 31404
Phone: (912) 356-2966
Fax: (912) 353-3299
http://www.savstate.edu/class/Politsci/mpa/
    index.html

State University of West Georgia
Department of Political Science and
    Planning
Master of Public Administration
Carrollton, GA 30118
Phone: (770) 836-6504
http://www.westga.edu/~polisci/mpa.html

University of Georgia
School of Public and International Affairs
Department of Public Administration
    & Policy
204 Baldwin Hall
Athens, GA 30602-1615
Phone: (706) 542-9660
Fax: (706) 583-0610
http://www.uga.edu/spia/home/index.htm

Valdosta State University
Department of Political Science
Master of Public Administration

101 West Hall
Valdosta, GA 31698-0001
Phone: (229) 293-6058
Fax: (229) 293-6075
http://www.valdosta.edu/mpa/

GUAM

University of Guam
College of Professional Studies
School of Business and Public
    Administration
UOG Station
Mangilao, GU, USA 96923
Phone: (671) 735-2550
Fax: (671) 734-5362
http://www.uog.edu/cbpa/

HAWAII

University of Hawaii at Manoa
College of Social Sciences
Masters in Public Administration
Saunders Hall 631
2424 Maile Way
Honolulu, HI 96822
Phone: (808) 956-8260
Fax: (808) 956-9571
http://www.puba.hawaii.edu

IDAHO

Boise State University
Department of Public Policy and
    Administration
Public Affairs and Art West Building,
    Room 127
Boise, ID 83725-1935
Phone: (208) 426-1476
Fax: (208) 426-4370
http://ppa.boisestate.edu/

University of Idaho
College of Letters, Arts, and Social
    Sciences
Department of Political Science and
    Public Affairs Research
Administration 205
P.O. Box 443165
Moscow, ID 83844-3165
Phone: (208) 885-6328
Fax: (208) 885-5102
http://www.uidaho.edu/bpar/mpa.html

ILLINOIS

DePaul University
College of Liberal Arts and Sciences
Program in Public Service
25 East Jackson Boulevard
Chicago, IL 60604-2287
Phone: (312) 362-8441
http://condor.depaul.edu/~pubserv/
    welcome.html

Governors State University
College of Business and Public
    Administration
Master of Public Administration Program
1 University Parkway
University Park, IL 60466-0975
Phone: (708) 534-5000
http://www.govst.edu/cbpa/t_cbpa_pgm_
    MSMPA.asp?id=244

Illinois Institute of Technology
College of Science and Letters
Master of Public Administration
3300 South Federal Street
Chicago, IL 60616-3793
Phone: (312) 567-3000
http://www.grad.iit.edu/bulletin/programs/
    pubadmin.html#mpa

Northern Illinois University
Division of Public Administration
DeKalb, IL 60115
Phone: (815) 753-0184
http://www.niu.edu/pub_ad/paweb.html

Roosevelt University
School of Policy Studies, College of Arts
    and Sciences
Master of Public Administration
430 South Michigan Avenue
Chicago, IL 60605
Phone: (312) 341-3744
http://www.roosevelt.edu/cas/sps/mpa.htm

Southern Illinois University, Carbondale
Department of Political Science
Master of Public Administration
Mailcode 4501
Carbondale, IL 62901
Phone: (618) 536-2371
Fax: (618) 453-3163
http://www.siu.edu/departments/cola/
    polysci/index.htm#

**Southern Illinois University,
    Edwardsville**
Department of Public Administration and
    Policy Analysis
M.P.A. Program
Edwardsville, IL 62026
Phone: (618) 650-3762
http://www.siue.edu/PAPA/

University of Chicago
Harris Graduate School of Public Policy
    Studies
1155 East 60th Street
Chicago, IL 60637
Phone: (773) 702-8401
http://harrisschool.uchicago.edu/academic/

University of Illinois at Chicago
College of Urban Planning
    and Public Affairs
412 South Peoria, Suite 115
Chicago, IL 60607-7064
Phone: (312) 413-8088
Fax: (312) 413-8095
http://www.uic.edu/cuppa/

University of Illinois at Springfield
Public Administration M.P.A.
One University Plaza
Springfield, IL 62703
Phone: (217) 206-6600
http://www.uis.edu/admissions/applyGrad/
    PublicAdminMPA/index.html#mpa

INDIANA

Indiana University, Bloomington
School of Public and Environmental Affairs
SPEA Building 441
Bloomington, IN 47405
Phone: (812) 855-2457
http://www.indiana.edu/~speaweb/

Indiana University Northwest
School of Public and Environmental
    Affairs
3400 Broadway
Lindenwood Hall 114
Gary, IN 46408
Phone: (219) 980-6695
Fax: (219) 980-6737
http://www.iun.edu/~speanw/

**Indiana University–Purdue University,
    Fort Wayne**
School of Public and Environmental
    Affairs
Neff Hall 260
2101 Coliseum Boulevard East
Fort Wayne, IN 46805-1499
Phone: (260) 481-6351
Fax: (260) 481-6346
http://www.ipfw.edu/spea/GRADPRO.
    HTM

Indiana University–Purdue University, Indiananapolis
School of Public and Environmental
    Affairs
801 West Michigan Street
Indianapolis, IN 46202
Phone: (317) 274-4656
Fax: (317) 274-5153
http://www.spea.iupui.edu/Contact/index.
    asp

Indiana University South Bend Campus
School of Public and Environmental
    Affairs
Wiekamp Hall
1800 Mishawaka Avenue
South Bend, IN 46615
Phone: (574) 237-4131
http://www.iusb.edu/~sbspea/

IOWA

Drake University
College of Business and Public
    Administration
Aliber Hall
2507 University Avenue
Des Moines, IA 50311-4505
Phone: (515) 271-3142
http://www.cbpa.drake.edu/

Iowa State University
Public Policy and Administration
    Program
503 Ross Hall
Ames, IA 50011-1204
Phone: (515) 294-3764
http://www.iastate.edu/~mpa/

KANSAS

University of Kansas
Department of Public Administration
The Edwin O. Stene Graduate Program
    in Public Administration
Blake Hall
1541 Lilac Lane #318
Lawrence, KS 66045-3177
Phone: (785) 864-3527
Fax: (785) 864-5208
http://www.ku.edu/~kupa/

Wichita State University
Hugo Wall School of Urban
    and Public Affairs
Master of Public Administration
1845 Fairmount
Wichita, KS 67260-0155
Phone: (316) 978-7240

Fax: (316) 978-6533
http://www.hugowallschool.com/

KENTUCKY

Eastern Kentucky University
Department of Government
Master of Public Administration
521 Lancaster Avenue
113 McCreary Hall
Richmond, KY 40475
Phone: (859) 622-1000
http://www.government.eku.edu/
    WebPages/mpahome.htm

Kentucky State University
School of Public Administration
400 East Main Street
Frankfort, KY 40601
Phone: (502) 597-6000
http://www.kysu.edu/colleges_schools/
    cps/school_of_public_admin/

Murray State University
Department of Government,
    Law & International Affairs
Master of Public Administration
5A Faculty Hall
Murray, KY 42071
Phone: (270) 762-2661
Fax: (270) 762-2688
http://www.murraystate.edu/chfa/glia/
    MPA.htm

Northern Kentucky University
College of Arts and Sciences
Master of Public Administration
Nunn Drive
Highland Heights, KY 41099
Phone: (859) 572-5326
http://www.nku.edu/~mpa/

University of Kentucky
Martin School of Public Policy &
    Administration
415 Patterson Office Tower
Lexington, KY 40506-0027
Phone: (859) 257-5741
Fax: (859) 323-1937
http://www-martin.uky.edu/

University of Louisville
Graduate School
Master of Public Administration
105 Houchens Building
University of Louisville
Louisville, KY 40292
Phone: (502) 852-3101
http://graduate.louisville.edu/

Western Kentucky University
Department of Political Science
Public Administration Program
1 Big Red Way
Bowling Green, KY 42101
Phone: (270) 745-4558
Fax: (270) 745-2945
http://www.wku.edu/Dept/Academic/
    AHSS/politicalscience/

LOUISIANA

Grambling State University
Department of Political Science
    and Public Administration
P.O. Box 4266
Phone: (318) 274-2714; (318) 274-2310
Fax: (318) 274-3427
http://www.gram.edu/Colleges_Schools/
    Liberal%20Arts/Poly%20Sci/masters.
    htm

Louisiana State University
E. J. Ourso College of Business
    Administration
Public Administration Institute
3200 CEBA Building
Baton Rouge, LA 70803-6312
Phone: (225) 578-6743
Fax: (225) 578-9078
http://www.bus.lsu.edu/pai/

Southern University
Nelson Mandela School of Public Policy
    & Urban Affairs
410 Higgins Hall
Baton Rouge, LA 70813
Phone: (225) 771-3092
Fax: (225) 771-3105
http://publicpolicy.subr.edu/

University of New Orleans
College of Urban and Public Affairs
308 Math Building
2000 Lakeshore Drive
New Orleans, LA 70148
Phone: (504) 280-6277
Fax: (504) 280-6272
http://www.uno.edu/~cupa/

MAINE

University of Maine
Department of Public Administration
5754 North Stevens Hall
Orono, ME 04469-5754
Phone: (207) 581-1872
Fax: (207) 581-3039
http://www.umaine.edu/pubadmin/

University of Southern Maine
Edmund S. Muskie School of Public
    Service
96 Falmouth Street
P.O. Box 9300
Portland, ME 04104-9300
Phone: (207) 780-4430
Fax: (207) 780-4417
http://muskie.usm.maine.edu/

MARYLAND

Johns Hopkins University
Institute for Policy Studies
Master of Arts in Public Policy Program
Wyman Building
3400 North Charles Street
Baltimore, MD 21218-2696
Phone: (410) 516-4167
Fax: (410) 516-8233
http://www.jhu.edu/~ips/maps/

University of Baltimore
Master of Public Administration Program
St. Paul, Room 121
1420 North Charles Street
Baltimore, MD 21201
Phone: (410) 837-6118
http://www.ubalt.edu/cla_spa/mpa/

**University of Maryland,
    Baltimore County**
Maryland Institute for Policy Analysis
    and Research
Department of Public Policy
1000 Hilltop Circle
Baltimore, MD 21250
Phone: (410) 455-1080
Fax: (410) 455-1184
http://www.umbc.edu/posi/

University of Maryland, College Park
School of Public Policy
Van Munching Hall
College Park, MD 20742-1821
Phone: (301) 405-6330
http://www.publicpolicy.umd.edu/

MASSACHUSETTS

Bridgewater State College
Department of Political Science
Master of Public Administration Program
Summer Street House
180 Summer Street
Bridgewater, MA 02325
Phone: (508) 531-1387
http://www.bridgew.edu/PoliSci/

Clark University
College of Professional and Continuing
    Education
Master of Public Administration
950 Main Street
Worcester, Massachusetts 01610
Phone: (508) 793-7217
http://copace.clarku.edu/master_degrees.
htm

Harvard University
John F. Kennedy School of Government
Programs in Public Administration and
    Public Policy
79 JFK Street
Cambridge, MA 02138
Phone: (617) 495-1100
http://www.ksg.harvard.edu/apply/

Northeastern University
Department of Political Science
Master of Public Administration
303 Meserve Hall
Boston, MA 02115-5000
Phone: (617) 373-2796
Fax: (617) 373-5311
http://www.casdn.neu.edu/%7Epolisci/

Suffolk University
Sawyer School of Management
Public Administration Department
8 Ashburton Place, 10th Floor
Boston, MA 02108
Phone: (617) 573-8330
Fax: (617) 227-4618
http://www.suffolkpad.org/

University of Massachusetts, Amherst
Center for Public Policy and
    Administration
Thompson Hall
Amherst, MA 01003
Phone: (413) 545-3940
Fax: (413) 545-1108
http://www.masspolicy.org/future/default.
htm

University of Massachusetts at Boston
John W. McCormack Institute of Public
    Affairs
100 Morrissey Boulevard
Boston, MA 02125
Phone: (617) 287-5543
Fax: (617) 287-5544
http://www.mccormack.umb.edu/MSPA/

MICHIGAN

Central Michigan University
Political Science Department
M.P.A. Program
247 Anspach Hall
Mount Pleasant, MI 48859
Phone: (989) 774-3442
Fax: (989) 774-1136
http://www.chsbs.cmich.edu/political%
    5Fscience/mpa/

Eastern Michigan University
Political Science Department
Public Administration Program
202 Welch Hall
Ypsilanti, Michigan 48197
Phone: (734) 487-0042
http://www.emich.edu/public/polisci/
    pubad/about.htm

Grand Valley State University
School of Public and Nonprofit
    Administration
401 West Fulton Street
Grand Rapids, MI 49504
Phone: (616) 331-6575
Fax: (616) 331-7120
http://www.gvsu.edu/spna/

Michigan State University
Program in Public Policy and
    Administration
303 South Kedzie Hall
East Lansing, MI 48824-1032
Phone: (517) 353-3290
Fax: (517) 432-1091
http://polisci.msu.edu/~mpa/

Northern Michigan University
Master of Public Administration
1401 Presque Isle Avenue
Marquette, MI 49855
Phone: (906) 227-1823
http://www.nmu.edu/mpa/

Oakland University
Department of Political Science
Master of Public Administration Program
418 Varner Hall
Rochester, MI 48309-4488
Phone: (248) 370-2352
http://www4.oakland.edu/mpa/

University of Michigan, Ann Arbor
Gerald R. Ford School of Public Policy
440 Lorch Hall
Ann Arbor, MI 48109-1220
Phone: (734) 764-3490

Fax: (734) 763-9181
http://www.fordschool.umich.edu/

University of Michigan, Dearborn
Department of Social Sciences
Master's of Public Policy
2140 SSB
4901 Evergreen Road
Dearborn, MI 48128
Phone: (313) 593-5096
http://casl.umd.umich.edu/MPP/

University of Michigan, Flint
Master of Public Administration Program
310 French Hall
303 East Kearsley Street
Flint, MI 48502
Phone: (810) 762-3470
http://graduateprograms.umflint.edu/pub_
    admin.htm

Wayne State University
Department of Political Science
Master of Public Administration Program
2040 Faculty/Administration Building
Detroit, MI 48202
Phone: (313) 577-2630
Fax: (313) 993-3435
http://www.cla.wayne.edu/polisci/

Western Michigan University
School of Public Affairs and
    Administration
1903 West Michigan Avenue
Kalamazoo, MI 49008-5440
Phone: (269) 387-8930
Fax: (269) 387-8935
http://www.wmich.edu/spaa/

MINNESOTA

Hamline University
Graduate School of Public Administration
    and Management (GPAM)
1536 Hewitt Avenue, MS-A1740
Saint Paul, MN 55104-1284
Phone: (651) 523-2284
http://web.hamline.edu/graduate/gpam/
    index.htm

University of Minnesota
Hubert H. Humphrey Institute of Public
    Affairs
301 19th Avenue South
Minneapolis, MN 55455
Phone: (612) 626-8910
http://www.hhh.umn.edu/

MISSISSIPPI

Jackson State University
Department of Public Policy and
    Administration
3825 Ridgewood Road, Box 18
Jackson, MS 39217
Phone: (601) 432-6277
Fax: (601) 432-6322
http://www.jsums.edu/liberalarts/
    pubpolicy/index.html

Mississippi State University
Department of Political Science
Master of Public Policy and
    Administration Program
P.O. Box PC
Mississippi State, MS 39762-6003
Phone: (662) 325-2711
Fax: (662) 325-2716
http://www.msstate.edu/dept/
    politicalscience/programs/MPPA.
    program1.html

MISSOURI

Park University
Master of Public Affairs
934 Wyandotte, 4th Floor
Kansas City, MO 64105
Phone: (816) 421-1125
Fax: (816) 471-1658
http://www.park.edu/MPA/index.asp

Southwest Missouri State University
Department of Political Science
Master of Public Administration Program
901 South National Avenue
Springfield, MO 65804
Phone: (417) 836-5630
Fax: (417) 836-6655
http://www.smsu.edu/polsci/MPA.htm

University of Missouri, Columbia
Truman School of Public Affairs
105 Middlebush Hall
Columbia, MO 65211-6100
Phone: (573) 882-3304
Fax: (573) 884-4872
http://www.truman.missouri.edu/

University of Missouri, Kansas City
Cookingham Institute of Public Affairs
305 Bloch School
5110 Cherry Street
Kansas City, MO 64110-2499
Phone: (816) 235-2894
http://www.bloch.umkc.edu/cookingham

University of Missouri, St. Louis
Master of Public Policy Administration
One University Boulevard, 406 Tower
St. Louis, MO 63121-4499
Phone: (314) 516-5145
Fax: (314) 516-5210
http://www.umsl.edu/divisions/graduate/
    mppa/

MONTANA

Montana State University
Department of Political Science
Master's of Public Administration
Room 2-143 Wilson Hall
Bozeman, MT 59717
Phone: (406) 994-4141
Fax: (406) 994-6692
http://www.montana.edu/wwwpo/
    mpaprogram/

NEBRASKA

University of Nebraska at Omaha
School of Public Administration
6001 Dodge Street
Omaha, NE 68182
Phone: (402) 554-2800
http://spa.unomaha.edu/

NEVADA

University of Nevada, Las Vegas
Greenspun College of Urban Affairs
4505 Maryland Parkway, Box 456026
Las Vegas, NV 89154-6026
Phone: (702) 895-4828
Fax: (702) 895-1813
http://www.unlv.edu/Colleges/Urban/
    pubadmin/

NEW JERSEY

Fairleigh Dickinson University
Public Administration Institute
New College of General and Continuing
    Studies
285 Madison Avenue
Madison, NJ 07940
Phone: (973) 443-8500
http://www.fduinfo.com/gradbull/
    ncpa-mpa-pubadmin.php

Kean University
College of Business and Public
    Administration
1000 Morris Avenue
Union, NJ 07083

Phone: (908) 737-KEAN
http://www.kean.edu/cbpa.html

Princeton University
Woodrow Wilson School of Public and
  International Affairs
Robertson Hall
Princeton, NJ 08544-1013
Phone: (609) 258-4800
Fax: (609) 258-1418
http://www.wws.princeton.edu/

Rutgers University, Camden
Graduate Department of Public Policy
  and Administration
401 Cooper Street
Camden, NJ 08102
Phone: (856) 225-6359
Fax: (856) 225-6559
http://www.camden.rutgers.edu/dept-pages/
  pubpol/

Rutgers University, Newark
Graduate Department of Public
  Administration
360 ML King Boulevard
701 Hill Hall
Newark, NJ 07102
Phone: (973) 393-5093
Fax: (973) 393-5907
http://pubadmin.newark.rutgers.edu/

Seton Hall University
The John C. Whitehead School of
  Diplomacy and International Relations
400 South Orange Avenue
South Orange, NJ 07079
Phone: (973) 275-2515
Fax: (973) 275-2519
http://diplomacy.shu.edu/

NEW MEXICO

New Mexico State University
Department of Government
Masters of Public Administration
Las Cruces, NM 88001
Phone: (505) 646-3539
http://www.nmsu.edu/~mpa/

University of New Mexico
School of Public Administration
Albuquerque, NM 87131
Phone: (505) 277-0111
http://spa.mgt.unm.edu/

NEW YORK

Baruch College, CUNY
School of Public Affairs
One Bernard Baruch Way, Box D-0901
New York, NY 10010-5585
Phone: (212) 802-5900
Fax: (212) 802-5903
http://www.baruch.cuny.edu/spa/index.jsp

Binghamton University
Graduate School
Master of Public Administration Program
P.O. Box 6000
Binghamton, NY 13902-6000
Phone: (607) 777-2719
http://mpa.binghamton.edu/

Columbia University
School of International and Public Affairs
420 West 118th Street
New York, NY 10027
Phone: (212) 854-6216
Fax: (212) 864-4847
http://www.sipa.columbia.edu

Cornell University
Cornell Institute for Public Affairs
294 Caldwell Hall
Ithaca, NY 14853-3501
Phone: (607) 255-8018
Fax: (607) 255-5240
http://www.cipa.cornell.edu/

**John Jay College for Criminal Justice,
  CUNY**
Department of Public Management
899 Tenth Avenue
New York, NY 10019
Phone: (212) 237-8000
http://web.jjay.cuny.edu/~pub-mgt/
  intranet.html

Long Island University, Brooklyn
School of Business, Public Administration
  and Information Sciences
1 University Plaza – H700
Brooklyn, NY 11201
Phone: (718) 488-1070
Fax: (718) 488-1125
http://www.brooklyn.liu.edu/sbpais/index.
  html

**Long Island University, C.W. Post
  Campus**
School of Public Service
720 Northern Boulevard
Brookville, NY 11548
Phone: (516) 299-2716
Fax: (516) 299-3912

http://www.cwpost.liunet.edu/cwis/cwp/
  colofman/programs/grad15.html

Marist College
School of Management
Master of Public Administration
3399 North Road
Poughkeepsie, NY 12601
Phone: (845) 575-3800
http://www.marist.edu/management/mpa/

New School University
Milano Graduate School of Management
  and Urban Policy
72 Fifth Avenue
New York, NY 10011
Phone: (212) 229-5311
Fax: (212) 229-5354
http://www.newschool.edu/milano/index.
  htm

New York University
Robert F. Wagner Graduate School of
  Public Service
295 Lafayette Street
New York, NY 10012-9604
Phone: (212) 998-7400
http://www.nyu.edu/wagner/academics/

Pace University
Dyson College of Arts & Sciences
Master of Public Administration
One Martine Avenue, Room 324
White Plains, New York 10606
Phone: (914) 422-4298
Fax: (914) 422-4361
http://appserv.pace.edu/execute/page.cfm?
  doc_id=3308

The Sage Colleges
Department of Management
Master of Science in Public Administration
45 Ferry Street
Troy, NY 12180
Phone: (518) 244-2000
http://www.sage.edu

**State University of New York (SUNY)
  at Albany**
Rockefeller College of Public Affairs
  & Policy
Milne Hall, 135 Western Avenue
Albany, NY 12222
Phone: (518) 442-5244
Fax: (518) 442-5298
http://www.albany.edu/rockefeller/

**State University of New York (SUNY)
  College at Brockport**
Department of Public Administration

350 New Campus Drive
Brockport, NY 14420-2961
Phone: (585) 395-2375
Fax: (585) 395-2242
http://www.brockport.edu/pubadmin/

Syracuse University
The Maxwell School
Department of Public Administration
200 Eggers Hall
Syracuse, NY 13244-1090
Phone: (315) 443-2252
Fax: (315) 443-3385
http://www.maxwell.syr.edu/pa/

NORTH CAROLINA

Appalachian State University
Department of Political Science
  and Criminal Justice
Master of Public Administration
Boone, NC 28608
Phone: (828) 262-3085
http://www.acs.appstate.edu/dept/ps-cj/
  checkst/degreeg.html

Duke University
Terry Sanford Institute of Public Policy
P.O. Box 90239
Durham, NC 27708-0239
Phone: (919) 613-7401
Fax: (919) 613-7403
http://www.pubpol.duke.edu

East Carolina University
Political Science Department
M.P.A. Program
Greenville, NC 27858
Phone: (252) 328-6030
http://www.ecu.edu/polsci/mpa/

North Carolina Central University
College of Arts and Science
Department of Public Administration
1801 Fayetteville Street
Durham, NC 27707
Phone: (919) 530-6100
http://www.nccu.edu/artsci/publicadmin/

North Carolina State University
Public Administration Program
NCSU Box 8102
Raleigh, NC 27695-8101
Phone: (919) 515-5159
Fax: (919) 515-7333
http://www.chass.ncsu.edu/pa/MPA.htm

**University of North Carolina
  at Chapel Hill**
Department of Public Policy
Abernethy Hall
CB #3435
Chapel Hill, NC 27599-3435
Phone: (919) 962-1600
Fax: (919) 962-5824
http://www.unc.edu/depts/pubpol/index.
  html

**University of North Carolina
  at Charlotte**
Master of Public Administration Program
9201 University City Boulevard
Charlotte, NC 28223-0001
Phone: (704) 687-3366
http://www.mpa.uncc.edu/

**University of North Carolina
  at Greensboro**
Department of Political Science
Master of Public Affairs Program
234 Graham Building
Greensboro, NC 27402
Phone: (336) 256-0510
http://www.uncg.edu/psc/mpa.htm

**University of North Carolina
  at Pembroke**
Master of Public Administration Program
P.O. Box 1510
Pembroke, NC 28372-1510
Phone: (800) 949-UNCP (8627); (910)
  521-6000
http://www.uncp.edu/catalog/html/mpa.htm

**University of North Carolina
  at Wilmington**
Masters of Public Administration
  Program
601 South College Road
Wilmington, NC 28403
Phone: (910) 962-3385
http://www.uncwil.edu/mpa/

Western Carolina University
Department of Political Science
Master of Public Affairs Program
210 University Center
Cullowhee, NC 28723
Phone: (828) 227-3855
http://www.wcu.edu/as/politicalscience/
  MPA.html

NORTH DAKOTA

University of North Dakota
Graduate Programs in Public
  Administration
P.O. Box 8379
Grand Forks, ND 58202
Phone (701) 777-3831
Fax: (701) 777-2085
http://www.und.edu/dept/grad/depts/public_
  admin/

OHIO

Bowling Green State University
Department of Political Science
Master of Public Administration Program
Bowling Green, OH 43403
Phone: (419) 372-2921
http://www.bgsu.edu/colleges/gradcol/
  programs/MPA.html

Cleveland State University
Maxine Goodman Levin College of
  Urban Affairs
Master of Public Administration Program
2121 Euclid Avenue
Cleveland, OH 44115
Phone: (216) 687-2135
http://urban.csuohio.edu/

Kent State University
Department of Political Science
Master of Public Administration Program
302 Bowman Hall
Kent, OH 44242-0001
Phone: (330) 672-2060
Fax: (330) 672-3362
http://dept.kent.edu/mpa/

Ohio State University
School of Public Policy and Management
300 Fisher Hall
2100 Neil Avenue
Columbus, OH 43210-1144
Phone: (614) 292-8696
Fax: (614) 292-2548
http://ppm.ohio-state.edu/

Ohio University
Department of Political Science
Master of Public Administration
Bentley Annex 266
Athens, OH 45701
Phone: (740) 597-1348
http://www.ohiou.edu/pols/PUBADMIN.
  HTML

University of Akron
Department of Public Administration and
     Urban Studies
Buchtel College of Arts and Sciences
The Polsky Building 265
Akron, OH 44325-7904
Phone: (330) 972-7618
Fax: (330) 972-6376
http://www.uakron.edu/colleges/artsci/
     depts/paus

University of Dayton
Master of Public Administration Program
Dayton, OH 45469-1425
Phone: (937) 229-3651
Fax: (937) 229-3900
http://www.udayton.edu/~mpa/

University of Toledo
College of Arts & Sciences
Political Science and Public
     Administration
1032 Scott Hall
Toledo, OH 43606
Phone: (419) 530-4151
http://www.politicalscience.utoledo.edu/
     grad/mpa.htm

Wright State University
Department of Urban Affairs and
     Geography
Master of Public Administration
3640 Colonel Glenn Highway
Dayton, OH 45435
Phone: (937) 775-2941
Fax: (937) 775-2422
http://www.wright.edu/cupa/graduate.htm

OKLAHOMA

University of Oklahoma
Programs in Public Administration
455 West Lindsey Street, Room 305
Norman, OK 73019-2003
Phone: (405) 325-6432
Fax: (405) 325-3733
http://www.ou.edu/cas/psc/pa/

OREGON

Portland State University
College of Urban and Public Affairs
Mark O. Hatfield School of Government
Public Administration Division
URBN 650
506 Southwest Mill Street
Portland, OR 97207
Phone: (800) 547-8887, extension 3920
http://www.publicadmin.pdx.edu/

University of Oregon
School of Architecture and Allied Arts
Department of Planning Public Policy
     & Management
119 Hendricks Hall, 1209 University
     of Oregon
Eugene, OR 97403-1209
Phone: (541) 346-3635
Fax: (541) 346-2040
http://utopia.uoregon.edu/ppm/
     PPMDescription.htm

PENNSYLVANIA

Carnegie Mellon University
H. John Heinz III School of Public Policy
     and Management
Hamburg Hall 1108
5000 Forbes Avenue
Pittsburgh, PA 15213-3890
Phone: (800) 877-3498
http://www.heinz.cmu.edu/

Marywood University
Public Administration Program
2300 Adams Avenue
Scranton, PA 18509
Phone: (570) 348-6211
http://www.marywood.edu/departments/
     publicadm/index.htm

**Pennsylvania State University
     at Harrisburg**
School of Public Affairs
777 West Harrisburg Pike
W-160 Olmsted Building
Middletown, PA 17057
Phone: (717) 948-6058
http://www.hbg.psu.edu/hbg/programs/
     gradprog/padm.html

Shippensburg University
Department of Political Science
Master of Public Administration
1871 Old Main Drive
Shippensburg, PA 17257
Phone: (717) 477-1718
http://www.ship.edu/~polisci/

University of Pennsylvania
Fels Institute of Government
3814 Walnut Street
Philadelphia, PA 19104-6197
Phone: (215) 898-8216
Fax: (215) 898-1202
http://www.fels.upenn.edu/

University of Pittsburgh
Graduate School of Public and
     International Affairs
3601 Posvar Hall
Pittsburgh, PA 15260
Phone: (412) 648-7640
http://www.gspia.pitt.edu/

Villanova University
Department of Political Science
Master of Public Administration
800 Lancaster Avenue
Villanova, PA 19085
Phone: (610) 519-4518
Fax: (610) 519-7487
http://www.gradartsci.villanova.edu/mpa/

Widener University
Master of Public Administration Program
One University Place
Chester, PA 19013
Phone: (610) 499-1120
http://www.widener.edu/mpa

RHODE ISLAND

University of Rhode Island
Department of Political Science
M.P.A. Program
206 Washburn Hall
Kingston, RI 02881-0817
Phone: (401) 874-2183
Fax: (401) 874-4072
http://www.uri.edu/artsci/psc/graduate/grad.
     html#mpa

SOUTH CAROLINA

Clemson University
University of South Carolina
The Joint MPA Degree Program
The University Center, P.O. Box 5616
Greenville, SC 29606
Phone: (864) 250-8880
http://business.clemson.edu/mpa/

University of Charleston
Joseph P. Riley, Jr. Institute for Public
     Affairs and Policy Studies
M.P.A. Program
Charleston, SC 29424
Phone: (843) 953-6105
http://www.cofc.edu/~puba/

SOUTH DAKOTA

University of South Dakota
Department of Arts and Sciences,
    Political Science
Master of Public Administration
414 East Clark Street
Vermillion, SD 57069
Phone: (605) 677-5701
Fax: (605) 677-6302
http://www.usd.edu/polsci/

TENNESSEE

East Tennessee State University
College of Business & Technology
Master of Public Management Program
P.O. Box 70699
Johnson City, TN 37614
Phone: (423) 439-5314
Fax: (423) 439-5274
http://business.etsu.edu/grad/mpm.htm

Tennessee State University
Institute of Government
330 Tenth Avenue North
Campus Box 140
Nashville, TN 37203
Phone: (615) 963-7241
Fax: (615) 963-7245
http://www.tnstate.edu/IOG/instgov.html

University of Memphis
Division of Public and Nonprofit
    Administration
136 McCord Hall
Memphis, TN 38152
Phone: (901) 678-3360
Fax: (901) 678-2981
http://padm.memphis.edu/

University of Tennessee at Chattanooga
Political Science Department
M.P.A. Program
615 McCallie Avenue
Chattanooga, TN 37403-2594
Phone: (423) 425-4068
http://www.utc.edu/Academic/MPA/

University of Tennessee at Knoxville
Department of Political Science
M.P.A. Program
1001 McClung Tower
Knoxville, TN 37996-0410
Phone: (865) 974-2261
Fax: (865) 974-7037
http://web.utk.edu/~polisci/

TEXAS

Midwestern State University
Department of Health and Public
    Administration
3410 Taft Boulevard
Wichita Falls, TX 76308
Phone: (940) 397-4752
Fax: (940) 397-6291
http://hs2.mwsu.edu/healthandpublic/
    index.asp

Stephen F. Austin State University
Department of Political Science,
    Georaphy and Public Administration
P.O. Box 13045 SFA Station
Nacogdoches, TX 75962
Phone: (936) 468-3903
http://www.sfasu.edu/polisci/

Texas State University, San Marcos
Department of Political Science
Master of Public Administration Program
San Marcos, TX 78666
Phone: (512) 245-2143
http://www.polisci.swt.edu/public_
    administration/public_admin.html

Texas Tech University
Master of Public Administration Program
Holden Hall 116
Lubbock, TX 79409-1015
Phone: (806) 742-3125
Fax: (806) 742-0850
http://www.depts.ttu.edu/politicalscience/
    mpa/

University of Houston
Political Science Department
Master of Public Administration Program
447 Phillip G. Hoffman Hall
Houston, TX 77204-3011
Phone: (713) 743-3931
http://crystal.cpp.uh.edu/uhmpa/

University of North Texas
Department of Public Administration
366 Wooten Hall
P.O. Box 310617
Denton, TX 76203-0617
Phone: (940) 565-2165
Fax: (940) 565-4466
http://www.unt.edu/padm/

University of Texas at Arlington
School of Urban and Public Affairs
P.O. Box 19588
601 South Nedderman Drive
Arlington, TX 76019
Phone: (817) 272-3071

Fax: (817) 272-5008
http://www.uta.edu/supa/

University of Texas at Austin
LBJ School of Public Affairs
P.O. Box Y
Austin, TX 78713-8925
Phone: (512) 471-0801
Fax: (512) 471-8455
http://www.utexas.edu/lbj/

University of Texas at Dallas
School of Social Sciences
Master of Public Affairs
P.O. Box 830688
Richardson, TX 75083-0688
Phone: (972) 883-2935
http://www.utdallas.edu/dept/socsci/
    graduate_programs.html

University of Texas–Pan American
College of Social and Behavioral
    Sciences
Public Administration Program
1201 West University Drive
Edinburg, TX 78539-2999
Phone: (956) 381-3341
Fax: (956) 381-8805
http://www.panam.edu/dept/mpa/

University of Texas at San Antonio
College of Public Policy
501 West Durango Boulevard
San Antonio, TX 78207
Phone: (210) 458-2700
Fax: (210) 458-2424
http://copp.utsa.edu/

University of Texas at Tyler
Public Administration Program
3900 University Boulevard
Tyler, TX 75799
Phone: (903) 566-7434
http://www.uttyl.edu/socialsciences/mpa.
    htm

UTAH

Brigham Young University
George W. Romney Institute
    of Public Management
M.P.A. Program
730 TNRB
Provo, UT 84602-3113
Phone: (801) 422-9173
http://marriottschool.byu.edu/mpa/

University of Utah
Center for Public Policy and
    Administration

260 South Central Campus Drive, Room #214
Salt Lake City, UT 84112-9154
Phone: (801) 581-6781
http://www.cppa.utah.edu/mpa/

VERMONT

University of Vermont
The Graduate College
Master of Public Administration Program
Morrill Hall
Burlington, VT 05405
Phone: (802) 656-2606
Fax: (802) 656-1423
http://www.uvm.edu/cdae/mpa/

VIRGINIA

College of William and Mary
The Thomas Jefferson Program in Public Policy
P.O. Box 8795
Williamsburg, VA 23187
Phone: (757) 221-2368
Fax: (757) 221-2390
http://www.wm.edu/tjppp/

George Mason University
Master of Public Administration
Robinson A201 – MSN 3F4
Fairfax, VA 22030
Phone: (703) 993-1411
Fax: (703) 993-1399
http://www.gmu.edu/departments/mpa/

George Mason University
School of Public Policy
4400 University Drive, MS 3C6
Finley Building
Fairfax, VA 22030
Phone: (703) 993-2280
http://policy.gmu.edu/

James Madison University
Department of Political Science
Master of Public Administration
MSC 1101
Harrisonburg, VA 22807
Phone: (540) 568-6149; 6031
http://www.jmu.edu/polisci/mpa/index.htm

Old Dominion University
College of Business and Public Administration
Constant Hall
Norfolk, VA 23529
Phone: (757) 683-3961
http://www.odu-cbpa.org/mpa.htm

Virginia Commonwealth University
School of Government and Public Affairs
Master of Public Administration
P.O. Box 842028
923 West Franklin Street, Room 518
Richmond, VA 23284-2028
Phone: (804) 828-8041
Fax: (804) 828-2171
http://www.has.vcu.edu/pos/mpa.htm

Virginia Polytechnic Institute and State University
Center for Public Administration & Policy
104 Draper Road
Blacksburg, VA 24060
Phone: (540) 231-5133
Fax: (540) 231-7067
http://www.cpap.vt.edu/

WASHINGTON

Eastern Washington University
Graduate Program in Public Administration
668 North Riverpoint Boulevard, Suite A
Spokane, WA 99202-1660
Phone: (509) 358-2248
http://www.cbpa.ewu.edu/~pa/

Evergreen State College
Master of Public Administration Program
2700 Evergreen Parkway, NW
Olympia, WA 98505
Phone: (360) 867-6554
http://www.evergreen.edu/mpa/

Seattle University
Institute of Public Service
901 12th Avenue
P.O. Box 222000
Seattle, WA 98122-1090
Phone: (206) 296-6000
http://www.seattleu.edu/artsci/ips/

University of Washington
Daniel J. Evans School of Public Affairs
P.O. Box 353055
Seattle, WA 98195-3055
Phone: (206) 543-4900
Fax: (206) 543-1096
http://www.evansuw.org/mpa/index.html

WEST VIRGINIA

West Virginia University
School of Applied Social Sciences
Division of Public Administration
P.O. Box 6322
Morgantown, WV 26506-6322
Phone: (304) 293-2614
Fax: (304) 293-8814
http://www.as.wvu.edu/pubadm/

WISCONSIN

University of Wisconsin, Madison
Robert M. La Follette School of Public Affairs
1225 Observatory Drive
Madison, WI 53706
Phone: (608) 262-3581
Fax: (608) 265-3233
http://www.lafollette.wisc.edu/

University of Wisconsin, Milwaukee
Master of Public Administration Program
P.O. Box 413
Milwaukee, WI 53201
Phone: (414) 229-4732
Fax: (414) 229-5021
http://www.uwm.edu/Dept/MPA/

University of Wisconsin, Oshkosh
Political Science Department
Master of Public Administration Program
800 Algoma Boulevard
Oshkosh, WI 54901
Phone: (920) 424-3230
Fax: (920) 424-2319
http://www.uwosh.edu/departments/mpa/

WYOMING

University of Wyoming
Department of Political Science
Public Administration Program
Department 3197
1000 East University Avenue
Laramie, WY 82071
Phone: (307) 766-6484
http://uwadmnweb.uwyo.edu/Pols/

C. PUBLIC HEALTH, COMMUNITY HEALTH EDUCATION, AND COMMUNITY HEALTH/PREVENTIVE MEDICINE

The following programs include schools of public health and other graduate public health programs that have been accredited by the Council on Education for Public Health. They prepare students to work in a variety of health-related nonprofit roles, as educators, advocates, analysts, and policy makers. For more information, see the Council's Web site at http://www.ceph.org.

ALABAMA

University of Alabama at Birmingham
School of Public Health
1530 Third Avenue, South
RPHB 140
Birmingham, AL 35294-0022
Phone: (205) 975-7742
http://www.uab.edu/PublicHealth/

ARIZONA

University of Arizona, Arizona State University, and Northern Arizona University
Mel and Enid Zuckerman Arizona
    College of Public Health
1501 North Campbell Avenue
P.O. Box 245163
Tucson, AZ 85724-5163
Phone: (520) 626-7083
http://www.publichealth.arizona.edu

ARKANSAS

University of Arkansas for Medical Sciences
College of Public Health
4301 West Markham, #820
Little Rock, AR 72205-7199
Phone: (501) 526-6600
http://www.uams.edu/coph

CALIFORNIA

California State University, Fresno
MPH Program
College of Health and Human Services
2345 East San Ramon Avenue
Fresno, CA 93740-0030
Phone: (559) 278-4014
http://www.csufresno.edu/mph

California State University, Long Beach
MPH and MS Programs in Community
    Health Education
College of Health & Human Services
1250 Bellflower Boulevard
Long Beach, CA 90840
Phone: (562) 985-4057
http://www.csulb.edu/depts/hs/htdocs/

California State University, Northridge
MPH Program in Community Health
    Education
College of Health & Human
    Development
18111 Nordhoff Street
Northridge, CA 91330
Phone: (818) 677-2997
http://publichealth.sdsu.edu/

Loma Linda University
School of Public Health
Loma Linda, CA 92350
Phone: (909) 558-4578
http://www.llu.edu/llu/sph/

San Diego State University
Graduate School of Public Health
San Diego, CA 92182-4162
Phone: (619) 594-1255
http://www.publichealth.sdsu.edu

San Francisco State University
MPH Program in Community Health
    Education
Department of Health Education
1600 Holloway Avenue – HSS 326
San Francisco, CA 94132-4161
Phone: (415) 338-1413
http://www.sfsu.edu/~hed/

San Jose State University
MPH Program in Community Health
    Education
Department of Health Science
School of Applied Sciences and Arts
San Jose, CA 95192
Phone: (408) 924-2970
http://www.sjsu.edu/health

University of California, Berkeley
School of Public Health
19 Earl Warren Hall
Berkeley, CA 94720
Phone: (510) 642-2082
http://ist-socrates.berkeley.edu/~sph/

University of California, Los Angeles
School of Public Health
Center for the Health Sciences
P.O. Box 951772
Los Angeles, CA 90095
Phone: (310) 825-6381
http://www.ph.ucla.edu

University of Southern California
MPH Program
Keck School of Medicine
Department of Preventive Medicine
1000 South Fremont Avenue, Unit 8,
    Room 5133
Alhambra, CA 91803
Phone: (626) 457-6678
http://www.usc.edu/medicine/mph

COLORADO

University of Colorado Health Sciences Center
MSPH Program
Department of Preventive Medicine &
    Biometrics
4200 East Ninth Avenue,
    Mail Stop B-119
Denver, CO 80262
Phone: (303) 315-8350
http://www.uchsc.edu/pmb/pmb

University of Northern Colorado
MPH Program in Community Health
    Education
Department of Community Health &
    Nutrition
College of Health & Human Sciences
Greeley, CO 80639
Phone: (970) 351-2755
http://www.unco.edu/hhs/chn/chn.htm

CONNECTICUT

Southern Connecticut State University
MPH Program in Community Health
    Education

Department of Public Health
144 Farnham Avenue
New Haven, CT 06515-1355
Phone: (203) 392-6954
http://www.southernct.edu/departments/
    publichealth

University of Connecticut
Graduate Program in Public Health
Department of Community Medicine
    and Health Care
School of Medicine
Farmington, CT 06030-6325
Phone: (860) 679-1510
http://grad.uchc.edu/

Yale University
Department of Epidemiology
    and Public Health
School of Medicine
P.O. Box 208034
60 College Street
New Haven, CT 06520-8034
Phone: (203) 785-2867
http://info.med.yale.edu/eph/

DISTRICT OF COLUMBIA

The George Washington University
School of Public Health and Health
    Services
2300 Eye Street, NW
Washington, DC 20037
Phone: (202) 994-5179
http://www.gwumc.edu/sphhs

FLORIDA

Florida A & M University
MPH Program
Institute of Public Health
Science Research Center, Room 207D
Tallahassee, FL 32307
Phone: (850) 599-3254
http://www.famu.edu/

Florida International University
Graduate Program in Public Health
Robert R. Stempel School of Public Health
11200 Southwest 8th Street, VH 216
Miami, FL 33199
Phone: (305) 348-7158
http://ssph.fiu.edu

Nova Southeastern University
MPH Program
College of Osteopathic Medicine
3200 South University Drive
Fort Lauderdale, FL 33328

Phone: (954) 262-1613
http://www.nova.edu/ph

University of Miami
MPH Program
Department of Epidemiology
    and Public Health
P.O. Box 016069 (R669)
Miami, FL 33101
Phone: (305) 243-6759
http://www.epidemiology.med.miami.edu/

University of South Florida
College of Public Health
13201 Bruce B. Downs Boulevard
    (MDC-56)
Tampa, FL 33612-3805
Phone: (813) 974-6603
http://www.hsc.usf.edu/publichealth/

GEORGIA

Armstrong Atlantic State University
MPH Program in Community Health
    Education
Department of Health Sciences
11935 Abercorn Street
Savannah, GA 31419-1997
Phone: (912) 921-5480
http://www.armstrong.edu/Administration/
    grad_catalog/cat/hp/science/mph.htm

Emory University
Rollins School of Public Health
1518 Clifton Road, NE
Atlanta, GA 30322
Phone: (404) 727-8720
http://www.sph.emory.edu

Morehouse School of Medicine
MPH Program
Department of Community Health
    and Preventive Medicine
720 Westview Drive, SW
Atlanta, GA 30310-1495
Phone: (404) 752-1831
http://www.msm.edu

HAWAII

University of Hawaii
MPH Program
John A. Burns School of Medicine
Department of Public Health Sciences
    and Epidemiology
1960 East West Road
Honolulu, HI 96822
Phone: (808) 956-5739
http://www.hawaii.edu/publichealth/

IDAHO

Idaho State University
MPH Program in Community Health
    Education
Kasiska College of Health Professions
Department of Health & Nutrition
    Sciences
Campus Box 8109
Pocatello, ID 83209-8109
Phone: (208) 282-2729
http://www.isu.edu/departments/chp

ILLINOIS

Northern Illinois University
MPH Program Public and Community
    Health Programs
School of Allied Health Professions
DeKalb, IL 60115-2854
Phone: (815) 753-1384
http://www.ahp.niu.edu/ph

Northwestern University
MPH Program
Feinberg School of Medicine
Department of Preventive Medicine
680 North Lake Shore Drive, Suite 1102
Chicago, IL 60611
Phone: (312) 503-0027
http://www.publichealth.northwestern.
    edu/

University of Illinois at Chicago
School of Public Health
1603 West Taylor Street, MC: 923
Chicago, IL 60612-4394
Phone: (312) 996-6620
http://www.uic.edu/sph/

INDIANA

Indiana University at Bloomington
MPH Program in Community Health
    Education
Department of Applied Health Science
School of Health, Physical Education
    and Recreation
Bloomington, IN 47405-4801
Phone: (812) 855-3627
http://www.indiana.edu/~aphealth

Indiana University–Indianapolis
MPH Program
School of Medicine
Department of Public Health
1050 Wishard Boulevard, 4th Floor,
    Room 4167
Indianapolis, IN 46202-2872

Phone: (317) 278-0337
http://www.pbhealth.iupui.edu

IOWA

**Des Moines University–Osteopathic
    Medical Center**
Public Health Program
3200 Grand Avenue
Des Moines, IA 50312
Phone: (515) 271-1720
http://www.dmu.edu/dhm/mph/index.htm

University of Iowa
College of Public Health
200 Hawkins Drive, E220HI GH
Iowa City, IA 52242
Phone: (319) 384-5452
http://www.public-health.uiowa.edu

KANSAS

**University of Kansas School
    of Medicine**
KU-MPH Program
Departments of Preventive Medicine and
    Public Health
1010 North Kansas
Wichita, KS 67214-3199
Phone: (316) 293-2627
http://www.kumc.edu/mph

Wichita State University
MPH Program
Department of Public Health Sciences
1845 North Fairmount
P.O. Box 152
Wichita, KS 67260-0152
Phone: (316) 978-3060
http://wichita.edu/PHS

KENTUCKY

Western Kentucky University
MPH Program
Department of Public Health
1 Big Red Way
Bowling Green, KY 42101
Phone: (270) 745-4797
http://www.wku.edu/Dept/Academic/chhs
    /publichealth/

LOUISIANA

**Louisiana State University Health
    Sciences Center**
MPH Program

Department of Public Health and
    Preventive Medicine
1600 Canal Street, 8th Floor
New Orleans, LA 70112
Phone: (504) 599-1396
http://publichealth.lsuhsc.edu

Tulane University
Health Sciences Center
School of Public Health
    and Tropical Medicine
1440 Canal Street, Suite 2430
New Orleans, LA 70112-2715
Phone: (504) 588-5397
http://www.sph.tulane.edu

MARYLAND

Johns Hopkins University
Bloomberg School of Public Health
615 North Wolfe Street
Baltimore, MD 21205-2179
Phone: (410) 955-3540
http://www.jhsph.edu

Morgan State University
Public Health Program
School of Graduate Studies
1700 East Cold Spring Lane
Jenkins Building 343
Baltimore, MD 21251
Phone: (443) 885-4012
http://php.morgan.edu/ionedit/content/
    masters_program.asp?id=366

**Uniformed Services University
    of the Health Sciences**
MPH, MTM&H, MSPH Programs
Department of Preventive Medicine and
    Biometrics
School of Medicine
4301 Jones Bridge Road
Bethesda, MD 20814-4799
Phone: (301) 295-3050
http://cim.usuhs.mil/geo/
    preventivemedicine. htm

University of Maryland, College Park
MPH Program in Community Health
    Education
Department of Public and Community
    Health
Valley Drive, Suite 2387
College Park, MD 20742-2611
Phone: (301) 405-2464
http://www.hhp.umd.edu/dpch/

MASSACHUSSETTS

Boston University
School of Public Health
715 Albany Street
Boston, MA 02118
Phone: (617) 638-4640
http://www.bumc.bu.edu/SPH

Harvard University
School of Public Health
677 Huntington Avenue
Boston, MA 02115
Phone: (617) 432-1025
http://www.hsph.harvard.edu

Tufts University School of Medicine
Graduate Programs in Public Health
Department of Family Medicine and
    Community Health
136 Harrison Avenue
Boston, MA 02111
Phone: (617) 636-0935
http://www.tufts.edu/med/gpph/index.html

University of Massachusetts Amherst
School of Public Health
    and Health Sciences
715 North Pleasant Street
108 Arnold House
Amherst, MA 01003-9304
Phone: (413) 545-1303
http://www.umass.edu/sphhs

MICHIGAN

University of Michigan
School of Public Health
109 South Observatory Street
Ann Arbor, MI 48109-2029
Phone: (734) 763-5454
http://www.sph.umich.edu/

MINNESOTA

University of Minnesota
School of Public Health
Mayo Mail Code 197
420 Delaware Street, SE
Minneapolis, MN 55455-0381
Phone: (612) 624-6669
http://www.sph.umn.edu

MISSISSIPPI

University of Southern Mississippi
MPH Program
Center for Community Health
College of Health & Human Sciences

P.O. Box 5122
Hattiesburg, MS 39406-5122
Phone: (601) 266-5437
http://www.usm.edu/chs

MISSOURI

Saint Louis University
School of Public Health
3545 Lafayette Avenue, Suite 300
St. Louis, MO 63104-1314
Phone: (314) 977-8100
http://publichealth.slu.edu

NEBRASKA

University of Nebraska Medical Center
University of Nebraska at Omaha
MPH Program
Collaborating Center for Public Health
   and Community Service
115 South 49th Avenue
Omaha, NE 68132
Phone: (402) 561-7566
http://www.unmc.edu/mph/

NEW HAMPSHIRE

Dartmouth Medical School
MPH Program
Center for Evaluative Clinical Sciences
Department of Educational Programs
Hinman Box 7252, MML Building
Hanover, NH 03755-3871
Phone: (603) 650-1782
http://www.dartmouth.edu/~cecs/
   gradprograms/degree_programs.html

NEW JERSEY

**University of Medicine and Dentistry
   of New Jersey**
Rutgers, The State University of New
   Jersey
New Jersey Institute of Technology
School of Public Health
683 Hoes Lane West
P.O. Box 9
Piscataway, NJ 08854
Phone: (732) 235-9700
http://sph.umdnj.edu

NEW MEXICO

New Mexico State University
MPH Program in Community Health
   Education
College of Health and Social Services

P.O. Box 30001, Department 3HLS
Las Cruces, NM 88003-8001
Phone: (505) 646-4300
http://www.nmsu.edu/~hlthdpt/

University of New Mexico
MPH Program
School of Medicine
1 University of New Mexico, MSC 09 5060
Albuquerque, NM 87131
Phone: (505) 272-4173
http://hsc.unm.edu/fcm/MPH

NEW YORK

**Brooklyn College – City University
   of New York**
Department of Health and Nutrition
   Sciences
2900 Bedford Avenue
Brooklyn, NY 11210
Phone: (718) 951-5026
http://academic.brooklyn.cuny.edu/hns/
   health_sciences/graduate/mph/index.
   htm

Columbia University
Mailman School of Public Health
722 West 168th Street, 14th Floor
New York, NY 10032
Phone: (212) 305-3929
http://mailman.hs.columbia.edu

**Hunter College, City University
   of New York**
MPH Program in Urban Public Health
School of Health Sciences
CUNY, 425 East 25th Street
New York, NY 10010
Phone: (212) 481-5111
http://www.hunter.cuny.edu/health/uph

New York Medical College
School of Public Health
Valhalla, NY 10595
Phone: (914) 594-4531
http://www.nymc.edu/sph/

New York University
MPH Program in Community Health
   Education
Department of Nutrition, Food Studies
   and Public Health
Steinhardt School of Education
35 West 4th Street, Suite 1200
New York, NY 10012
Phone: (212) 998-5780
http://www.nyu.edu/education/health/
   healthed/

**University at Albany, State University
   of New York**
School of Public Health
One University Place
Rensselaer, NY 12144-3456
Phone: (518) 402-0283
http://www.albany.edu/sph/

University of Rochester
MPH Program
School of Medicine and Dentistry
Department of Community and
   Preventive Medicine
601 Elmwood Avenue
P.O. Box 644
Rochester, NY 14642
Phone: (585) 275-7882
http://www.urmc.rochester.edu/smd/cpm/
   education/index.html

NORTH CAROLINA

**University of North Carolina,
   Chapel Hill**
School of Public Health
170 Rosenau Hall
CB #7400
Chapel Hill, NC 27599-7400
Phone: (919) 966-3215
http://www.sph.unc.edu/

**University of North Carolina,
   Greensboro**
MPH Program in Community Health
   Education
Department of Public Health Education
Health and Human Performance
   Building, Suite 437
Greensboro, NC 27402-6169
Phone: (336) 334-5532
http://www.uncg.edu/phe

OHIO

**Bowling Green State University
Medical University of Ohio
University of Toledo**
Northwest Ohio Consortium MPH
   Program c/o Medical College of Ohio
Department of Public Health
4412 Collier Building
3015 Arlington Avenue
Toledo, OH 43614
Phone: (419) 383-4107
http://www.mco.edu/allh/mph/index.html

**Northeastern Ohio Universities College
   of Medicine, University of Akron,
   Cleveland State University, Kent**

State University, Youngstown State University, and Northeastern Ohio Universities
MPH Program Division of Community Medicine and Health Sciences
4209 State Route 44
P.O. Box 95
Rootstown, OH 44272-0095
Phone: (330) 325-6179
http://darla.neoucom.edu/MPH/

Ohio State University
School of Public Health
College of Medicine and Public Health
M-116 Starling Loving Hall
320 West 10th Avenue
Columbus, OH 43210-1240
Phone: (614) 293-3913
http://www.sph.ohio-state.edu

OKLAHOMA

University of Oklahoma
College of Public Health
P.O. Box 26901
801 Northeast 13th Street
Oklahoma City, OK 73104-5072
Phone: (405) 271-2232
http://w3.ouhsc.edu/coph/

OREGON

Portland State University, Oregon Health and Science University, and Oregon State University
Oregon MPH Program
Portland State University
P.O. Box 751
Portland, OR 97201-0751
Phone: (503) 725-5106
http://www.oregonmph.org

PENNSYLVANIA

Drexel University
School of Public Health
Mail Stop 660
245 North 15th Street
Philadelphia, PA 19102-1192
Phone: (215) 762-4110
http://www.drexel.edu/pubhealth/default.html

East Stroudsburg University
MPH Program in Community Health Education
Health Department
East Stroudsburg, PA 18301

Phone: (570) 422-3702
http://www.esu.edu/mph

Temple University
MPH Program in Community Health Education
Department of Public Health
304 Vivacqua Hall
P. O. Box 2843
Philadelphia, PA 19122
Phone: (215) 204-8726
http://www.temple.edu/publichealth

University of Pittsburgh
Graduate School of Public Health
A-624 Crabtree Hall
130 DeSoto Street
Pittsburgh, PA 15261
Phone: (412) 624-3001
http://www.publichealth.pitt.edu

West Chester University
MPH Program
Department of Health
West Chester, PA 19383
Phone: (610) 436-2931
http://health-sciences.wcupa.edu/health/mph.htm

PUERTO RICO

University of Puerto Rico
Graduate School of Public Health
Medical Sciences Campus
P. O. Box 365067
San Juan, PR 00936
Phone: (787) 764-5975
http://www.rcm.upr.edu/

RHODE ISLAND

Brown University
MPH Program
Department of Community Health
P. O. Box G-A4
Providence, RI 02912
Phone: (401) 863-2059
http://bms.brown.edu/pubhealth/mph/

SOUTH CAROLINA

University of South Carolina
Arnold School of Public Health
800 Sumter Street
109 Health Sciences Building (#76)
Columbia, SC 29208
Phone: (803) 777-5032
http://www.sph.sc.edu/

TENNESSEE

East Tennessee State University
MPH Program
Department of Public Health
P. O. Box 70674
Johnson City, TN 37614-0674
Phone: (423) 439-4332
http://www.etsu.edu/cpah/pubheal/

University of Tennessee
MPH Program
Department of Health & Exercise Science
1914 Andy Holt Avenue
Knoxville, TN 37996-2710
Phone: (865) 974-6674
http://hes.utk.edu/grad/public_health.html

TEXAS

Texas A&M University System Health Science Center
School of Rural Public Health
1266 TAMU
College Station, TX 77843-1266
Phone: (979) 845-2387
http://tamushsc.tamu.edu/SRPH

University of North Texas
Health Science Center
School of Public Health
3500 Camp Bowie Boulevard
Fort Worth, TX 76107-2699
Phone: (817) 735-2323
http://www.hsc.unt.edu/education/sph

University of Texas
School of Public Health
P. O. Box 20186
Houston, TX 77225
Phone: (713) 500-9050
http://www.sph.uth.tmc.edu/

University of Texas Medical Branch at Galveston
Graduate Program in Public Health
Department of Preventive Medicine and Community Health
301 University Boulevard
1.116 Ewing Hall
Galveston, TX 77555-1150
Phone: (409) 772-1128
http://www.utmb.edu/pmch/mph/default.htm

UTAH

University of Utah
MPH and MSPH Programs

Department of Family and Preventive
   Medicine
Public Health Programs
375 Chipeta Way, Suite A
Salt Lake City, UT 84108
Phone: (801) 587-3315
http://www.med.utah.edu/dfpm/mph.htm

VIRGINIA

**Eastern Virginia Medical School
   and Old Dominion University**
Graduate Program of Public Health
Eastern Virginia Medical School
P. O. Box 1980
Norfolk, VA 23501-1980
Phone: (757) 446-6120
http://www.evms.edu/hlthprof/mph/index.
   html

Virginia Commonwealth University
MPH Program

Department of Preventive Medicine and
   Community Health
P. O. Box 980212
Richmond, VA 23298-0212
Phone: (804) 828-9785
http://www.commed.vcu.edu/

WASHINGTON

University of Washington
School of Public Health and Community
   Medicine
P. O. Box 357230
Seattle, WA 98195
Phone: (206) 543-1144
http://sphcm.washington.edu

WEST VIRGINIA

West Virginia University
MPH Program
Department of Community Medicine
P. O. Box 9190

Morgantown, WV 26506-9190
Phone: (304) 293-2502
http://www.hsc.wvu.edu/som/cmed/

WISCONSIN

Medical College of Wisconsin
MPH Programs
Division of Public Health
8701 Watertown Plank Road
Milwaukee, WI 53226
Phone: (414) 456-4510
http://instruct.mcw.edu/prevmed/

University of Wisconsin – La Crosse
MPH Program in Community Health
   Education
Department of Health Education and
   Health Promotion
203 Mitchell Hall
La Crosse, WI 54601
Phone: (608) 785-8163
http://perth.uwlax.edu/hper/HEHP/

D. SOCIAL WORK

The Council on Social Work Education maintains a list on their Web site (http://www.cswe.org/) of accredited master's (MSW) and bachelor's (BSW) degree programs. The master's degree programs are listed below, but check the site for BSW programs and for new additions of programs that have recently become accredited.

ALASKA

University of Alaska Anchorage
School of Social Work
College of Health and Social Welfare
3211 Providence Drive
Anchorage, AK 99508-8230
Phone: (907) 786-6900
Fax: (907) 786-6912
http://www.uaa.alaska.edu/socwork/

ALABAMA

Alabama A&M University
Graduate Social Work Department
P.O. Box 1417
Normal, AL 35762
Phone: (256) 372-5478
Fax: (256) 372-5484
http://www.aamu.edu

University of Alabama
School of Social Work
P.O. Box 870314
Tuscaloosa, AL 35487-0314
Phone: (205) 348-7027

Fax: (205) 348-9419
http://www.ua.edu/academic/colleges/
   socwork

ARKANSAS

University of Arkansas at Little Rock
School of Social Work
2801 South University Avenue
Little Rock, AR 72204
Phone: (501) 569-3240
Fax: (501) 569-3184
http://www.ualr.edu/~swdept/

ARIZONA

Arizona State University
School of Social Work
P.O. Box 871802
Tempe, AZ 85287-1802
Phone: (480) 965-2795
Fax: (480) 965-2799
http://ssw.asu.edu

Arizona State University West
College of Human Services

Department of Social Work-MC: 3251
P.O. Box 3251
Phoenix, AZ 85069-7100
Phone: (602) 543-4679
Fax: (602) 543-6612
http://www.west.asu.edu/chs/

CALIFORNIA

**California State University,
   Bakersfield**
Social Work Program
9001 Stockdale Highway
Bakersfield, CA 93311-1099
Phone: (661) 664-3434
Fax: (661) 665-6928
http://www.csub.edu/SocialWork/

California State University, Fresno
Department of Social Work Education
5310 North Campus Drive, PH 102
Fresno, CA 93740-8019
Phone: (559) 278-3992
Fax: (559) 278-7191
http://www.csufresno.edu

California State University, Long Beach
Department of Social Work
1250 Bellflower Boulevard
Long Beach, CA 90840-4602
Phone: (562) 985-2110
Fax: (562) 985-5514
http://www.csulb.edu/depts/socialwk/

**California State University,
    Los Angeles**
School of Social Work
5151 State University Drive
Los Angeles, CA 90008
Phone: (323) 343-4680
Fax: (323) 343-6312
http://www.calstatela.edu/dept/soc_work/
    index.htm

**California State University,
    Sacramento**
Division of Social Work
6000 J Street
Sacramento, CA 95819-6090
Phone: (916) 278-6943
Fax: (916) 278-7167
http://www.hhs.csus.edu/SWRK/

**California State University, San
    Bernardino**
Department of Social Work
5500 University Parkway
San Bernardino, CA 92407-2397
Phone: (909) 880-5501
Fax: (909) 880-7029
http://socialwork.csusb.edu

**California State University,
    Stanislaus**
Social Work Department
801 West Monte Vista Avenue
Turlock, CA 95382
Phone: (209) 667-3091
Fax: (209) 667-3869
http://www.csustan.edu/Social_Work/
    index.htm

Loma Linda University
Department of Social Work
Griggs Hall
Loma Linda, CA 92350
Phone: (909) 558-8548
Fax: (909) 558-0450
http://www.llu.edu/llu/

San Diego State University
School of Social Work
5500 Campanile Drive
San Diego, CA 92182-4119
Phone: (619) 594-6865

Fax: (619) 594-5991
http://chhs.sdsu.edu/sw/

San Francisco State University
School of Social Work
1600 Holloway Avenue
San Francisco, CA 94132
Phone: (415) 338-1003
Fax: (415) 338-0591
http://www.sfsu.edu/~socwork/

San Jose State University
College of Social Work
One Washington Square
Suite 215
San Jose, CA 95192-0124
Phone: (408) 924-5800
Fax: (408) 924-5892
http://www.sjsu.edu/depts/SocialWork/

University of California at Berkeley
School of Social Welfare
120 Haviland Hall
Berkeley, CA 94720-7400
Phone: (510) 642-4341
Fax: (510) 643-6126
http://socialwelfare.berkeley.edu

University of California at Los Angeles
Department of Social Welfare
School of Public Policy and Social
    Research
3250 Public Policy Building
P.O. Box 951656
Los Angeles, CA 90095-1656
Phone: (310) 825-2892
Fax: (310) 206-7564
http://www.sppsr.ucla.edu/sw

University of Southern California
School of Social Work
MRF Building, Room 214
699 West 34th Street
Los Angeles, CA 90089-0411
Phone: (213) 740-2711
Fax: (213) 740-3301
http://www.usc.edu/dept/socialwork/

COLORADO

Colorado State University
School of Social Work
127 Education Building
Fort Collins, CO 80523-1586
Phone: (970) 491-6612
Fax: (970) 491-7280
http://www.cahs.colostate.edu/sw/

University of Denver
Graduate School of Social Work
2148 South High Street
Denver, CO 80208-2886
Phone: (303) 871-2203
Fax: (303) 871-2845
http://www.du.edu/gssw/

CONNECTICUT

Southern Connecticut State University
Graduate Social Work Program
Department of Social Work
101 Farnham Avenue
New Haven, CT 06515
Phone: (203) 392-6551
Fax: (203) 392-6580
http://www.southernct.edu

University of Connecticut
School of Social Work
1798 Asylum Avenue
West Hartford, CT 06117
Phone: (860) 570-9141
Fax: (860) 570-9264
http://www.ssw.uconn.edu

DISTRICT OF COLUMBIA

Catholic University of America
National Catholic School of Social
    Service
Shahan Hall-Cardinal Station
Washington, DC 20064
Phone: (202) 319-5458
Fax: (202) 319-5093
http://ncsss.cua.edu

Gallaudet University
Department of Social Work
800 Florida Avenue, NE
Washington, DC 20002-3695
Phone: (202) 651-5160
Fax: (202) 651-5817
http://depts.gallaudet.edu/social.work/

Howard University
School of Social Work
601 Howard Place, NW
Washington, DC 20059
Phone: (202) 806-7300
Fax: (202) 387-4309
http://www.socialwork.howard.edu

DELAWARE

Delaware State University
Master of Social Work Program

Department of Social Work
1200 North DuPont Highway
Dover, DE 19901
Phone: (302) 857-6770
Fax: (302) 857-6794
http://www.dsc.edu

FLORIDA

Barry University
School of Social Work
11300 Northeast 2nd Avenue
Miami Shores, FL 33161
Phone: (305) 899-3900
Fax: (305) 899-3934
http://www.barry.edu/socialwork/

**Florida Agricultural and Mechanical
    University**
Department of Social Work
301 Ware-Rhaney Building
Tallahassee, FL 32307-3500
Phone: (850) 561-2251
Fax: (850) 599-3215
http://www.famu.edu

Florida Atlantic University
School of Social Work
777 Glades Road
Boca Raton, FL 33431-0091
Phone: (561) 297-3234
Fax: (561) 297-2866
http://www.fau.edu/ssw/

Florida Gulf Coast University
Division of Social Work
College of Professional Studies
10501 FGCU Boulevard South
Fort Myers, FL 33965-6565
Phone: (239) 590-7825
Fax: (239) 590-7842
http://cps.fgcu.edu/sw/

Florida International University
School of Social Work
11200 Southwest 8th Street
ECS 460
Miami, FL 33199
Phone: (305) 348-5880
Fax: (305) 348-5313
http://w3.fiu.edu/sw/

Florida State University
School of Social Work
UCC 2505
Tallahassee, FL 32306-2570
Phone: (850) 644-4751
Fax: (850) 644-9750
http://ssw.fsu.edu

University of Central Florida
School of Social Work
P.O. Box 163358
Orlando, FL 32828
Phone: (407) 823-2114
Fax: (407) 823-5697
http://www.cohpa.ucf.edu/social/

University of South Florida
School of Social Work
MGY 132
4202 East Fowler Avenue
Tampa, FL 33620-8100
Phone: (813) 974-2063
Fax: (813) 974-4675
http://www.cas.usf.edu/social_work/index.
    html

GEORGIA

Clark Atlanta University
Whitney M. Young, Jr., School of Social
    Work
223 James P. Brawley Drive, Southwest
Atlanta, GA 30314-4391
Phone: (404) 880-8311
Fax: (404) 880-6434
http://www.cau.edu

Georgia State University
School of Social Work
College of Health and Human Sciences
MSC 8L0381
33 Gilmer Street, SE Unit 8
Atlanta, GA 30303-3083
Phone: (404) 651-3526
Fax: (404) 651-1863
http://www.gsu.edu

Savannah State University
Master's Department of Social Work
College of Liberal Arts and Social
    Sciences
P.O. Box 20553
Savannah, GA 31404
Phone: (912) 356-2410
Fax: (912) 356-2458
http://www.savstate.edu

University of Georgia
School of Social Work
Tucker Hall
Athens, GA 30602-7016
Phone: (706) 542-3364
Fax: (706) 542-3282
http://www.uga.edu

Valdosta State University
Division of Social Work

1500 Patterson Street
Valdosta, GA 31698
Phone: (229) 249-4864
Fax: (229) 245-4341
http://www.valdosta.peachnet.edu/sowk/

HAWAII

University of Hawaii at Manoa
School of Social Work
1800 East-West Road
Honolulu, HI 96822
Phone: (808) 956-6123
Fax: (808) 956-5964
http://www2.hawaii.edu/sswork/welcome.
    html

IDAHO

Boise State University
School of Social Work
1910 University Drive
Boise, ID 83725-1940
Phone: (208) 426-1568
Fax: (208) 426-4291
http://www.idbsu.edu/socwork

IOWA

St. Ambrose University
School of Social Work
518 West Locust Street
Davenport, IA 52803
Phone: (563) 333-6379
Fax: (563) 333-6097
http://www.sau.edu/msw

University of Iowa
School of Social Work
308 North Hall
Iowa City, IA 52242-1223
Phone: (319) 335-1250
Fax: (319) 335-1711
http://www.uiowa.edu/~socialwk/

University of Northern Iowa
Master of Social Work Program
Department of Social Work
30 Sabin Hall
Cedar Falls, IA 50614-0405
Phone: (319) 273-6249
Fax: (319) 273-6976
http://www.uni.edu/socialwork/

ILLINOIS

Aurora University
School of Social Work

George Williams College
347 South Gladstone Avenue
Aurora, IL 60506-4892
Phone: (630) 844-5419
Fax: (630) 844-4923
http://www.aurora.edu/socialwork/

Chicago State University
Department of Social Work
Williams Science Center 315
9501 South King Drive
Chicago, IL 60628-1598
Phone: (773) 995-2207
Fax: (773) 821-2420
http://www.csu.edu

Dominican University
Graduate School of Social Work
Priory Campus
7200 West Division Street
River Forest, IL 60305-1066
Phone: (708) 366-3463
Fax: (708) 366-3446
http://www.dom.edu

Governors State University
College of Health Professions
Masters of Social Work Program
University Park, IL 60466
Phone: (708) 235-3997
Fax: (708) 235-2196
http://www.govst.edu

Illinois State University
School of Social Work
Campus Box 4650
Normal, IL 61790-4650
Phone: (309) 438-3631
Fax: (309) 438-5880
http://www.socialwork.illstu.edu

Loyola University of Chicago
School of Social Work
820 North Michigan Avenue
Chicago, IL 60611
Phone: (312) 915-7005
Fax: (312) 915-7645
http://www.luc.edu/schools/socialwork/

**Southern Illinois University
    Carbondale**
School of Social Work
Quigley Hall, Room 6
Mail Code 4329
Carbondale, IL 62901-4329
Phone: (618) 453-2243
Fax: (618) 453-4291
http://www.siu.edu/~socwork/

**Southern Illinois University
    Edwardsville**
Department of Social Work
College of Arts and Sciences, Peck Hall,
    Room 1306
P.O. Box 1450
Edwardsville, IL 62026-1450
Phone: (618) 650-5758
Fax: (618) 650-3509
http://www.siue.edu/SOCIAL/

University of Chicago
School of Social Service Administration
969 East 60th Street
Chicago, IL 60637
Phone: (773) 702-1250
Fax: (773) 834-1582
http://www.uchicago.edu

University of Illinois at Chicago
Jane Addams College of Social Work
M/C 309
1040 West Harrison Street
Chicago, IL 60607-7134
Phone: (312) 996-3219
Fax: (312) 996-1802
http://www.uic.edu/jaddams/college/

**University of Illinois
    at Urbana–Champaign**
School of Social Work
1207 West Oregon Street
Urbana, IL 61801
Phone: (217) 333-2261
Fax: (217) 244-5220
http://www.social.uiuc.edu

INDIANA

Indiana University
School of Social Work
902 West New York Street
ES 4138
Indianapolis, IN 46202-5156
Phone: (317) 274-6705
Fax: (317) 274-8630
http://socialwork.iu.edu

University of Southern Indiana
Social Work Department
8600 University Boulevard
Evansville, IN 47712
Phone: (812) 464-1843
Fax: (812) 465-1116
http://www.usi.edu/EDU/SOC_WORK/
    SOCIAL.asp

KANSAS

Newman University
Social Work Program
3100 McCormick Avenue
Wichita, KS 67213-2097
Phone: (316) 942-4291, ext. 216
Fax: (316) 942-4483
http://www.newmanu.edu

University of Kansas
School of Social Welfare
1545 Lilac Lane
Lawrence, KS 66044-3184
Phone: (785) 864-4720
Fax: (785) 864-5277
http://www.socwel.ukans.edu/

Washburn University
Department of Social Work
1700 College Avenue
Topeka, KS 66621-0001
Phone: (785) 231-1010, ext. 1616
Fax: (785) 231-1027
http://www.washburn.edu/sas/social-work/
    index.html

Wichita State University
School of Social Work
P.O. Box 154
1845 Fairmount
Wichita, KS 67620-0154
Phone: (316) 978-7250
Fax: (316) 978-3328
http://www.wichita.edu

KENTUCKY

Spalding University
School of Social Work
851 South Fourth Street
Louisville, KY 40203-2115
Phone: (502) 585-9911, ext. 2183
Fax: (502) 992-2413
http://www.spalding.edu

University of Kentucky
College of Social Work
619 Patterson Office Tower
Lexington, KY 40506-0027
Phone: (859) 257-6654
Fax: (859) 323-1030
http://www.uky.edu/SocialWork/welcome.
    html

University of Louisville
Raymond A. Kent School of Social Work
Oppenheimer Hall
Louisville, KY 40292

Phone: (502) 852-6402
Fax: (502) 852-0422
http://www.louisville.edu/kent/

LOUISIANA

Grambling State University
School of Social Work
P.O. Box 907
Grambling, LA 71245
Phone: (318) 274-3388
Fax: (318) 274-3254
http://www.gram.edu/socialwork/default.asp

Louisiana State University
School of Social Work
311 Huey P. Long Field House
Baton Rouge, LA 70803
Phone: (225) 578-1351
Fax: (225) 578-1357
http://www.socialwork.lsu.edu/

Southern University at New Orleans
School of Social Work
6400 Press Drive
New Orleans, LA 70126
Phone: (504) 286-5376
Fax: (504) 286-5387
http://www.suno.edu

Tulane University
School of Social Work
6823 St. Charles Avenue
New Orleans, LA 70118-5672
Phone: (504) 865-5314
Fax: (504) 862-8727
http://www.tulane.edu/~tssw/

MASSACHUSSETTS

Boston College
Graduate School of Social Work
McGuinn Hall
140 Commonwealth Avenue
Chestnut Hill, MA 02467-3807
Phone: (617) 552-4020
Fax: (617) 552-2374
http://www.bc.edu/gssw

Boston University
School of Social Work
264 Bay State Road
Boston, MA 02215
Phone: (617) 353-3750
Fax: (617) 353-5612
http://www.bu.edu/ssw/

Salem State College
School of Social Work
352 Lafayette Street

Salem, MA 01970
Phone: (978) 542-6650
Fax: (978) 542-6936
http://www.salemstate.edu/socialwork/

Simmons College
School of Social Work
300 The Fenway
Boston, MA 02115
Phone: (617) 521-3900
Fax: (617) 521-3980
http://www.simmons.edu/programs/ssw/

Smith College
School for Social Work
Lilly Hall
Northampton, MA 01063
Phone: (413) 585-7950
Fax: (413) 585-7994
http://www.smith.edu/ssw/

Springfield College
School of Social Work
263 Alden Street
Springfield, MA 01109-3797
Phone: (413) 748-3065
Fax: (413) 748-3069
http://www.spfldcol.edu

Wheelock College
Division of Social Work
200 The Riverway
Boston, MA 02215
Phone: (617) 879-2331
Fax: (617) 879-2352
http://www.wheelock.edu

MARYLAND

University of Maryland–Baltimore
School of Social Work
Louis L. Kaplan Hall
525 West Redwood Street
Baltimore, MD 21201-1777
Phone: (410) 706-7794
Fax: (410) 706-0273
http://www.ssw.umaryland.edu

MAINE

University of Maine
School of Social Work
5770 Social Work Building
Orono, ME 04469
Phone: (207) 581-2389
Fax: (207) 581-2396
http://www.ume.maine.edu/~soclwork/

University of New England
School of Social Work

716 Stevens Avenue
Portland, ME 04103
Phone: (207) 797-7688, ext. 4513
Fax: (207) 878-4719
http://www.une.edu/chp/socialwork/index.html

University of Southern Maine
Department of Social Work
96 Falmouth Street
P.O. Box 9300
Portland, ME 04104-9300
Phone: (207) 780-4120
Fax: (207) 780-4902
http://www.usm.maine.edu

MICHIGAN

Andrews University
Department of Social Work
Nethery Hall
Berrien Springs, MI 49104
Phone: (269) 471-6196
Fax: (269) 471-3686
http://www.andrews.edu

Eastern Michigan University
M.S.W. Program Office
317 Marshall Building
Ypsilanti, MI 48197
Phone: (734) 487-4169
Fax: (734) 487-6832
http://www.emich.edu/public/swk/swkhome.htm

Grand Valley State University
School of Social Work
3rd Floor, DeVos Center
401 West Fulton Street
Grand Rapids, MI 49504
Phone: (616) 331-6550
Fax: (616) 331-6570
http://www.gvsu.edu/ssw/

Michigan State University
School of Social Work
254 Baker Hall
East Lansing, MI 48824
Phone: (517) 353-8632
Fax: (517) 353-3038
http://www.ssc.msu.edu/~sw/

University of Michigan
School of Social Work
1080 South University
Ann Arbor, MI 48109-1106
Phone: (734) 764-5340
Fax: (734) 764-9954
http://www.ssw.umich.edu

Wayne State University
School of Social Work
4756 Cass Avenue
201 Thompson Home
Detroit, MI 48202
Phone: (313) 577-4400
Fax: (313) 577-8770
http://www.socialwork.wayne.edu

Western Michigan University
School of Social Work
1903 Western Avenue
Kalamazoo, MI 49008-5354
Phone: (269) 387-3170
Fax: (269) 387-3183
http://www.wmich.edu/hhs/sw/

MINNESOTA

Augsburg College
Department of Social Work
2211 Riverside Avenue
Minneapolis, MN 55454
Phone: (612) 330-1189
Fax: (612) 330-1493
http://www.augsburg.edu

**College of Saint Catherine/University
    of Saint Thomas**
School of Social Work
Mail LOR 406
2115 Summit Avenue
St Paul, MN 55105
Phone: (651) 962-5810
Fax: (651) 962-5819
http://www.stthomas.edu/socialwork/

University of Minnesota–Duluth
Department of Social Work
220 Bohannon Hall
Duluth, MN 55812-2496
Phone: (218) 726-7245
Fax: (218) 726-7185
http://www.d.umn.edu/sw/

University of Minnesota–Twin Cities
School of Social Work
105 Peters Hall
1404 Gortner Avenue
St. Paul, MN 55108
Phone: (612) 625-1220
Fax: (612) 624-3744
http://ssw.che.umn.edu/

MISSOURI

Saint Louis University
School of Social Service
3550 Lindell Boulevard

St. Louis, MO 63103
Phone: (314) 977-2712
Fax: (314) 977-2731
http://www.slu.edu/colleges/SOCSVC/

Southwest Missouri State University
School of Social Work
Professional Building, Suite 200
901 South National Avenue
Springfield, MO 65804
Phone: (417) 836-6953
Fax: (417) 836-7688
http://www.smsu.edu/swk/

University of Missouri–Columbia
School of Social Work
729 Clark Hall
Columbia, MO 65211-4470
Phone: (573) 882-4447
Fax: (573) 882-8926
http://web.missouri.edu/~sswmain/

University of Missouri–Kansas City
School of Social Work
4825 Troost, Suite 106
Kansas City, MO 64110-2499
Kathylene F. Siska, Dean
Phone: (816) 235-6308
Fax: (816) 235-6573
http://www.umkc.edu

University of Missouri–St. Louis
Department of Social Work
College of Arts and Sciences
8001 Natural Bridge Road
St. Louis, MO 63121-4499
Phone: (314) 516-6385
Fax: (314) 516-5816
http://www.umsl.edu/~socialwk/

Washington University
George Warren Brown School of Social
    Work
One Brookings Drive
Campus Box 1196
St. Louis, MO 63130-4899
Phone: (314) 935-6693
Fax: (314) 935-8511
http://gwbweb.wustl.edu

MISSISSIPPI

Jackson State University
School of Social Work
3825 Ridgewood Road, Suite 9
Jackson, MS 39211
Phone: (601) 432-6819
Fax: (601) 432-6827
http://www.jsums.edu

University of Southern Mississippi
School of Social Work
P.O. Box 5114
Hattiesburg, MS 39406
Phone: (601) 266-4163
Fax: (601) 266-4165
http://www.usm.edu

NORTH CAROLINA

East Carolina University
School of Social Work
Ragsdale Building, Room 104-C
Greenville, NC 27858-4353
Phone: (252) 328-4208
Fax: (252) 328-4196
http://www.ecu.edu

**University of North Carolina
    at Chapel Hill**
School of Social Work
Tate-Turner-Kuralt Building, CB 3550
301 Pittsboro Street
Chapel Hill, NC 27599-3550
Phone: (919) 962-1225
Fax: (919) 962-0890
http://ssw.unc.edu

**University of North Carolina
    at Greensboro/North Carolina A&T
    State University**
Joint Master of Social Work Program
P.O. Box 26170
Greensboro, NC 27402-6170
Phone: (336) 334-4100
Fax: (336) 334-5210
http://www.uncg.edu/swk/jmsw/jmsw.
    html

NORTH DAKOTA

University of North Dakota
Department of Social Work
Gillette Hall
P.O. Box 7135
Grand Forks, ND 58202-7135
Phone: (701) 777-2669
Fax: (701) 777-4257
http://www.und.nodak.edu/

NEBRASKA

**University of Nebraska
    at Omaha**
School of Social Work
Annex 40
60th and Dodge Streets
Omaha, NE 68182-0293
Phone: (402) 554-2793

Fax: (402) 554-3788
http//socialwork.unomaha.edu/

NEW HAMPSHIRE

University of New Hampshire
Department of Social Work
Pettee Hall
55 College Road
Durham, NH 03824-3596
Phone: (603) 862-1799
Fax: (603) 862-4374
http://www.unh.edu/social-work/index.html

NEW JERSEY

Kean University
Department of Social Work
Master of Social Work Program
1000 Morris Avenue
Hutchinson Hall, Room 305
Union, NJ 07083-7131
Phone: (908) 737-4030
Fax: (908) 737-4064
http://www.kean.edu

Monmouth University
Social Work Department
Norwood and Cedar Avenue
West Long Branch, NJ 07764-1898
Phone: (732) 571-3543
Fax: (732) 263-5217
http://www.monmouth.edu/socialwork

Rutgers, The State University of New Jersey
School of Social Work
536 George Street
New Brunswick, NJ 08901-1167
Phone: (732) 932-7253
Fax: (732) 932-8915
http://www.rutgers.edu

NEW MEXICO

New Mexico Highlands University
School of Social Work
Box 9000
Las Vegas, NM 87701
Phone: (505) 454-3563
Fax: (505) 454-3454
http://www.nmhu.edu/academics/schsocwork/

New Mexico State University
School of Social Work
P.O. Box 30001, MSC 3SW
Las Cruces, NM 88003-8001
Phone: (505) 646-2143
Fax: (505) 646-4116
http://www.nmsu.edu~/socwork/

NEVADA

University of Nevada, Las Vegas
School of Social Work
4505 Maryland Parkway
P.O. Box 455032
Las Vegas, NV 89154-5032
Phone: (702) 895-4338
Fax: (702) 895-4079
http://www.nscee.edu/unlv/Colleges/Urban/

University of Nevada, Reno
School of Social Work
Business Building, Room 523
Mail Stop 090
Reno, NV 89557-0068
Phone: (775) 784-6542
Fax: (775) 784-4573
http://www.unr.edu/SocialWork/

NEW YORK

Adelphi University
School of Social Work
South Avenue
Garden City, NY 11530
Phone: (516) 877-4355
Fax: (516) 877-4436
http://www.adelphi.edu/socialwork/

Columbia University
School of Social Work
622 West 113th Street
New York, NY 10025
Phone: (212) 854-5189
Fax: (212) 854-4585
http://www.columbia.edu/cu/ssw

Fordham University
Graduate School of Social Service
113 West 60th Street, Room 726
Lincoln Center Campus
New York, NY 10023-7479
Phone: (212) 636-6600
Fax: (212) 636-7876
http://www.fordham.edu

Greater Rochester Collaborative M.S.W. Program
55 St. Paul Street
2nd Floor
Rochester, NY 14604
Phone: (585) 327-7450

Fax: (585) 232-8603
http://www.brockport.edu/grcmsw/

Hunter College of the City University of New York
School of Social Work
129 East 79th Street
New York, NY 10021
Phone: (212) 452-7085
Fax: (212) 452-7150
http://www.hunter.cuny.edu/socwork/

New York University
Shirley M. Ehrenkranz School of Social Work
One Washington Square North
New York, NY 10003
Phone: (212) 998-5959
Fax: (212) 995-4172
http://www.nyu.edu

Roberts Wesleyan College
Master of Social Work Program
2301 Westside Drive
Rochester, NY 14624-1997
Phone: (585) 594-6410
Fax: (585) 594-6480
http://www.rwc.edu/academic/social_w_s/index.htm

State University of New York at Stony Brook
School of Social Welfare
Health Sciences Center
Level 2, Room 093
Stony Brook, NY 11794-8231
Phone: (631) 444-2139
Fax: (631) 444-8908
http://www.uhmc.sunysb.edu/socwelf/

State University of New York, University at Buffalo
School of Social Work
685 Baldy Hall
P.O. Box 601050
Buffalo, NY 14260-1050
Phone: (716) 645-3381, ext. 221
Fax: (716) 645-3883
http://www.socialwork.buffalo.edu

Syracuse University
School of Social Work
Sims Hall
Syracuse, NY 13244-1230
Phone: (315) 443-5550
Fax: (315) 443-5576
http://www.social.syr.edu

University at Albany, State University of New York
School of Social Welfare
135 Western Avenue
Albany, NY 12222
Phone: (518) 442-5329
Fax: (518) 442-5380
http://www.albany.edu/ssw/index.html

Yeshiva University
Wurzweiler School of Social Work
Belfer Hall
2495 Amsterdam Avenue
New York, NY 10033
Phone: (212) 960-0820
Fax: (212) 960-0822
http://www.yu.edu/wurzweiler/

OHIO

Case Western Reserve University
Mandel School of Applied Social Sciences
10900 Euclid Avenue
Cleveland, OH 44106-7164
Phone: (216) 368-2256
Fax: (216) 368-2850
http://msass.cwru.edu

Cleveland State University/University of Akron
Joint Master of Social Work Program
School of Social Work
College of Fine and Applied Arts
Akron, OH 44325-8001
Phone: (330) 972-5275
Fax: (330) 972-5739
http://www.csuohio.edu

Ohio State University
College of Social Work
300 Stillman Hall
1947 College Road
Columbus, OH 43210-1162
Phone: (614) 292-2972
Fax: (614) 292-6940
http://www.csw.ohio-state.edu

Ohio University
Department of Social Work
Master's Degree Social Work Program
Morton Hall 416
Athens, OH 45701-2979
Phone: (740) 593-1291
Fax: (740) 593-0427
http://www.socialwork.ohiou.edu/

University of Cincinnati
School of Social Work

P.O. Box 210108
Cincinnati, OH 45221-0108
Phone: (513) 556-4615
Fax: (513) 556-2077
http://www.uc.edu/socialwork/

OKLAHOMA

University of Oklahoma
School of Social Work
1005 Jenkins Avenue
Norman, OK 73019
Phone: (405) 325-2821
Fax: (405) 325-7072
http://www.ou.edu

OREGON

Portland State University
Graduate School of Social Work
P.O. Box 751
Portland, OR 97207-0751
Phone: (503) 725-4712
Fax: (503) 725-5545
http://www.pdx.edu

PENNSYLVANIA

Bryn Mawr College
Graduate School of Social Work and Social Research
300 Airdale Road
Bryn Mawr, PA 19010-1697
Phone: (610) 520-2600
Fax: (610) 520-2655
http://www.brynmawr.edu

California University of Pennsylvania
Department of Social Work and Gerontology
MSW Program
P.O. Box 90
California, PA 15419-1394
Phone: (724) 938-4022
Fax: (724) 938-1651
http://www.cup.edu/ugcatalog/Programs/SocialWork/

Marywood University
School of Social Work
2300 Adams Avenue
Scranton, PA 18509-1598
Phone: (570) 348-6282, ext. 2388
Fax: (570) 961-4742
http://www.marywood.edu

Temple University
School of Social Administration

1301 Cecil B. Moore Avenue
Ritter Hall Annex, Room 555
Philadelphia, PA 19122
Phone: (215) 204-8623
Fax: (215) 204-9606
http://www.temple.edu/socialwork/

University of Pennsylvania
School of Social Work
3701 Locust Walk
Philadelphia, PA 19104-6214
Phone: (215) 898-5511
Fax: (215) 573-2099
http://www.ssw.upenn.edu

University of Pittsburgh
School of Social Work
2117 Cathedral of Learning
Pittsburgh, PA 15260
Phone: (412) 624-6304
Fax: (412) 624-6323
http://www.pitt.edu/~pittssw/

West Chester University
Department of Graduate Social Work
Reynolds Hall
West Chester, PA 19383
Phone: (610) 436-2664
Fax: (610) 738-0375
http://www.wcupa.edu

Widener University
Center for Social Work Education
One University Place
Chester, PA 19013
Phone: (610) 499-1153
Fax: (610) 499-4617
http://www.widener.edu

PUERTO RICO

Universidad Interamericana de Puerto Rico, Recinto Metropolitano
School of Social Work
P.O. Box 191293
San Juan, PR 00919-1293
Phone: (787) 250-1912, ext. 235
Fax: (787) 250-6843
http://www.metro.inter.edu

University of Puerto Rico, Rio Piedras Campus
Beatriz Lassalle Graduate School of Social Work
P.O. Box 23345
San Juan, PR 00931-3345
Phone: (787) 764-0000, ext. 2218
Fax: (787) 772-1482
http://www.rrp.upr.edu

RHODE ISLAND

Rhode Island College
School of Social Work
Providence, RI 02908
Phone: (401) 456-8042
Fax: (401) 456-8620
http://www.ric.edu/socwk/

SOUTH CAROLINA

University of South Carolina
College of Social Work
Columbia, SC 29208
Phone: (803) 777-5291
Fax: (803) 777-3498
http://www.sc.edu/cosw/

TENNESSEE

University of Tennessee
College of Social Work
221 Henson Hall
Knoxville, TN 37996-3333
Phone: (865) 974-3176
Fax: (865) 974-4803
http://www.csw.utk.edu

TEXAS

Baylor University
School of Social Work
P.O. Box 97320
Waco, TX 76798-7320
Phone: (254) 710-6400
Fax: (254) 710-6455
http://www.baylor.edu

Our Lady of the Lake University
Worden School of Social Service
411 Southwest 24th Street
San Antonio, TX 78207-4689
Phone (210) 434-3969
Fax: (210) 431-4028
http://www.ollusa.edu/academic/worden/
    worden.htm

Stephen F. Austin State University
Master of Social Work Program
School of Social Work
P.O. Box 6104
SFA Station
Nacogdoches, TX 75962-6104
Phone: (936) 468-5105
Fax: (936) 468-7201
http://www.sfasu.edu/aas/socwk/

Texas State University – San Marcos
School of Social Work
601 University Drive
San Marcos, TX 78666-4616
Phone: (512) 245-8833
Fax: (512) 245-8097
http://www.health.swt.edu/SOWK/SOWK.
    html

University of Houston
Graduate School of Social Work
237 Social Work Building
Houston, TX 77204-4013
Phone: (713) 743-8085
Fax: (713) 743-3267
http://www.sw.uh.edu

University of Texas at Arlington
School of Social Work
UTA Box 19129
Arlington, TX 76019-0129
Phone: (817) 272-3613
Fax: (817) 272-2016
http://www2.uta.edu/ssw/

University of Texas at Austin
School of Social Work
1 University Station D3500
Austin, TX 78712-0358
Phone: (512) 471-1937
Fax: (512) 471-7268
http://www.utexas.edu/ssw/

University of Texas–Pan American
Department of Social Work
1201 West University Drive
Edinburg, TX 78541-2999
Phone: (956) 381-3575
Fax: (956) 381-3516
http://www.panam.edu/dept/socialwork/

UTAH

Brigham Young University
School of Social Work
2190 Joseph F. Smith Building (JFSB)
Provo, UT 84602
Phone: (801) 422-3282
Fax: (801) 422-0624
http://fhss.byu.edu/socwork/

University of Utah
College of Social Work
395 South 1500 East
Room 111
Salt Lake City, UT 84112-0260
Phone: (801) 581-6192
Fax: (801) 585-3219
http://www.socwk.utah.edu/

VIRGINIA

Norfolk State University
Ethelyn R. Strong School of Social Work
700 Park Avenue
Norfolk, VA 23504
Phone: (757) 823-8668
Fax: (757) 823-2556
http://www.nsu.edu/Academics/social/
    socwork.htm

Radford University
School of Social Work
P.O. Box 6958
Radford, VA 24142
Phone: (540) 831-7689
Fax: (540) 831-7670
http://www.runet.edu~sowk-web/

Virginia Commonwealth University
School of Social Work
1001 West Franklin Street
P.O. Box 842027
Richmond, VA 23284-2027
Phone: (804) 828-1030
Fax: (804) 828-7541
http://www.vcu.edu/slwweb/index.html

VERMONT

University of Vermont
Department of Social Work
443 Waterman Building
85 South Prospect Street
Burlington, VT 05405-0160
Phone: (802) 656-8800
Fax: (802) 656-8565
http://www.uvm.edu

WASHINGTON

Eastern Washington University
School of Social Work and Human
    Services
203 Senior Hall
Cheney, WA 99004-2441
Phone: (509) 359-6481
Fax: (509) 359-6475
http://sswhs.ewu.edu

University of Washington
School of Social Work
4101 15th Avenue, NE
Seattle, WA 98105-6299
Phone: (206) 685-1660
Fax: (206) 221-3910
http://depts.washington.edu/sswweb/

Walla Walla College
Graduate School of Social Work
204 South College Avenue
College Place, WA 99324-1198
Phone: (509) 527-2883
Fax: (509) 527-2434
http://www.wcu.edu

WISCONSIN

University of Wisconsin–Madison
School of Social Work
1350 University Avenue
Madison, WI 53706-1510
Phone: (608) 263-3561

Fax: (608) 263-3836
http://www.wisc.edu

University of Wisconsin–Milwaukee
Helen Bader School of Social Welfare
P.O. Box 786
Milwaukee, WI 53201
Phone: (414) 229-4400
Fax: (414) 229-5311
http://www.uwm.edu/Dept/SSW/

WEST VIRGINIA

West Virginia University
School of Applied Social Sciences

Division of Social Work
P.O. Box 6830
Morgantown, WV 26506-6830
Phone: (304) 293-3501, ext. 3128
Fax: (304) 293-5936
http://www.wvu.edu/~socialwk/

WYOMING

University of Wyoming
Division of Social Work
P.O. Box 3632
Laramie, WY 82071
Phone: (307) 766-6112
Fax: (307) 766-6839
http://uwacadweb.uwyo.edu/SocialWork/

E. COUNSELING

A degree in counseling provides training in helping, listening, and psychology that can be useful in many nonprofit settings. The following list of graduate programs are accredited by the Council for Accreditation of Counseling and Related Educational Programs (CACREP). Be advised that not all institutions seek accreditation for each of their counseling degree programs, and one can still become licensed as a Nationally Certified Counselor without attending an accredited program. If you are interested in attending a school that is not on this list, visit the school's Web site directly to see if they offer programs in counseling. Available programs include M.A. degrees, M.S. degrees, M.Ed. degrees, Ed.D degrees, and Ph.D. degrees. Consult the CACREP Web site (http://www.cacrep.org) and the National Board for Certified Counselor's Web site (http://www.nbcc.org) for more information.

ALABAMA

Auburn University
Counseling & Counseling Psychology
2084 Haley Center
Auburn University, AL 36849-5222
Phone: (334) 844-2880
http://www.auburn.edu/ccp

Troy State University–Phenix City
Department of Counseling and
  Psychology
One University Place
Phenix City, AL 36869
Phone: (334) 448-5146
http://www.tsupc.edu/dep-cp.htm

The University of Alabama
Program in Counselor Education
P.O. Box 870231
Tuscaloosa, AL 35487-0231
Phone: (205) 348-7579
http://education.ua.edu/psych/counselor/
  index.html

University of Montevallo
Department of Counseling, Leadership
  and Foundations
College of Education
Station 6380
Montevallo, AL 35115
Phone: (205) 665-6380
http://www.montevallo.edu

ARIZONA

Arizona State University
College of Education
MC 0611
Payne Hall, Room 302
Tempe, AZ 85287-0611
Phone: (480) 965-6104
http://seamonkey.ed.asu.edu/~gail/
  programs/mc.htm

Northern Arizona University
Center for Excellence in Education
Educational Psychology
College of Education
P.O. Box 5774, CEE

Flagstaff, AZ 86011-5774
Phone: (928) 523-6534
http://www.nau.edu/~cee/academics/EPS/

University of Phoenix
Phoenix and Tucson Campuses
Department of Counselor Education
4635 East Elwood Street
Phoenix, AZ 85040
Phone: (480) 537-2179
http://www.phoenix.edu

ARKANSAS

Arkansas State University
Department of Psychology and
  Counseling
P.O. Box 1560
State University, AR 72467-1560
Phone: (870) 972-3064
http://www.clt.astate.edu/psycoun/

University of Arkansas
Educational Leadership, Counseling and
  Foundations

136 Graduate Education Building
Fayetteville, AR 72701
Phone: (479) 575-7311
http://www.uark.edu/depts/cned/web/
    counselhome.html

CALIFORNIA

California Polytechnic State University
Psychology and Human Development
    Department
San Luis Obispo, CA 93407
Phone: (805) 756-1617
http://www.calpoly.edu/~psychhd/masters.
    html

California State University–Fresno
Department of Counseling & Special
    Education
School of Education and Human
    Development
5005 North Maple Avenue, M/S3
Fresno, CA 93740-8025
Phone: (559) 278-0328
http://education.csufresno.edu/cser/

California State University–Los Angeles
Division of Administration and
    Counseling
King Hall C-1065
5151 State University Drive
Los Angeles, CA 90032
Phone: (323) 343-4250
http://www.calstatela.edu/dept/edac/

California State University–Northridge
Educational Psychology & Counseling
18111 Nordhoff Street
Northridge, CA 91330-8265
Phone: (818) 677-4976
http://www.csun.edu/edpsy

San Francisco State University
Department of Counseling
1600 Holloway Avenue
Burk Hall 524
San Francisco, CA 94132
Phone: (415) 328-2005
http://www.sfsu.edu/~counsel

Sonoma State University
Masters in Counseling
1801 East Cotati Avenue, Room N220
Rohnert Park, CA 94928
Phone: (707) 664-2340 or 2754
http://www.sonoma.edu/counseling/

COLORADO

Adams State College
Department of Psychology and Counselor
    Education
ES 309 – Box J
Alamosa, CO 81102
Phone: (719) 587-7873
http://counselored.adams.edu/

Colorado State University
Education 215
Counseling and Career Development
Fort Collins, CO 80523
Phone: (970) 491-6879
http://ccd.colostate.edu

Denver Seminary
Counseling Department
3401 South University Boulevard
Englewood, CO 80110
Phone: (303) 762-6950
http://www.denverseminary.edu

**University of Colorado at Colorado
Springs**
1420 Austin Bluffs Parkway
College of Education
Department of Counseling and
    Leadership
Colorado Springs, CO 80933-7150
Phone: (719) 262-4095
http://web.uccs.edu/education

University of Colorado – Denver
Counseling Psychology and Counselor
    Education
Campus Box 106
P.O. Box 173364
Denver, CO 80217-3364
Phone: (303) 556-6032
http://soe.cudenver.edu/

University of Northern Colorado
Division of Professional Psychology
McKee Hall #248, Box 131
Greeley, CO 80639
Phone: (970) 351-2544
http://www.unco.edu/coe/ppsy/

CONNECTICUT

Fairfield University
Counselor Education Department
Graduate School of Education and Allied
    Professions
Fairfield, CT 06430-7524
Phone: (203) 254-4000 ext. 3228
http://www.fairfield.edu

Southern Connecticut State University
Counseling and School Psychology
    Department
501 Crescent Street
New Haven, CT 06515
Phone: (203) 392-5913
http://www.soe.scsu.ctstateu.edu

Western Connecticut State University
Education Department
Westside Campus
Danbury, CT 06810
Phone: (203) 837-8513
http://www.wcsu.ctstateu.edu/sps

DELAWARE

Wilmington College
New Castle and Georgetown Campuses
320 DuPont Highway
New Castle, DE 19720
Phone: (302) 655-5400
http://www.wilmcoll.edu/
    behavioralscience/mcc-prog.html

DISTRICT OF COLUMBIA

Gallaudet University
Department of Counseling
800 Florida Avenue, NE
Washington, DC 20002
Phone: (202) 651-5515
http://depts.gallaudet.edu/counseling/
    schoolprograms.htm

George Washington University
Department of Counseling
Human and Organizational Studies
Graduate School of Education and
    Human Development
2134 G Street, NW
Washington, DC 20052
Phone: (202) 994-6856
http://www.gwu.edu/~chaos/

FLORIDA

Barry University
Miami Shores and Orlando Campuses
ADSOE/Counseling Program
11300 Northeast Second Avenue
Miami Shores, FL 33161-6695
Phone: (305) 899-371
http://www.barry.edu/ed/counseling/
    default.htm

Florida International University
Department of Educational and
    Psychological Studies

FIU – University Park Campus
ZEB 214A
Miami, FL 33119
Phone: (305) 348-2094
http://www.fiu.edu/~edpsy/
counseloredhome.htm

Florida State University
215 Stone Building
College of Education
Tallahassee, FL 32306
Phone: (850) 644-9439
http://www.epls.fsu.edu/psych_services.
index.htm

Rollins College
Graduate Studies in Counseling
1000 Holt Avenue, Box 2726
Winter Park, FL 32789-4499
Phone: (407) 646-2132
http://www.rollins.edu/holt/counsel.html

Stetson University
Department of Counselor Education
421 North Woodland Boulevard
Unit 8389
DeLand, FL 32720
Phone: (386) 822-7239
http://www.stetson.edu/counselored

University of Central Florida
Department of Child Family and
Community Sciences
Counselor Education Program
Educational Services Department
P.O. Box 161250
400 Central Boulevard
Orlando, FL 32816
Phone: (407) 823-2052
http://edcollege.ucf.edu/

University of Florida
Counselor Education Department
1215 Norman Hall
Gainesville, FL 32611
Phone: (352) 392-0731 ext.234
http://www.coe.ufl.edu/counselor/

University of North Florida
Counselor Education Program
College of Education and Human Services
St. Johns Bluff Road South
Jacksonville, FL 32224-2645
Phone: (904) 620-2838
http://www.unf.edu/coehs/grad/listings.html

GEORGIA

Columbus State University
Department of Counseling, Educational
Leadership, and Professional Studies
4225 University Avenue
Columbus, GA 31907-5645
Phone: (706) 568-2301
http://celps.colstate.edu

Georgia State University
Counseling and Psychological Services
College of Education
30 Pryor Street, Suite 950
Atlanta, GA 30303-3083
Phone: (404) 651-2550
http://education.gsu.edu/cps/

State University of West Georgia
Department of Counseling and
Educational Psychology
Education Center Annex #237
Carrollton, GA 30118-5170
Phone: (770) 836-6554
http://www.westga.edu/~cep/

University of Georgia
Counseling & Human Development
Services
402 Aderhold Hall
Athens, GA 30602-7142
Phone: (706) 542-4103
http://www.coe.uga.edu/echd/

HAWAII

University of Hawaii at Manoa
Department of Counselor Education
College of Education
1776 University Avenue
Wist Addition Room 221
Honolulu, HI 96822
Phone: (808) 956-4389
http://www2.hawaii.edu/~dce/

IDAHO

Boise State University
Counselor Education Department
Education Building, Room 612
1910 University
Boise, ID 83725-1720
Phone: (208) 426-1821
http://education.boisestate.edu/counseling/

Idaho State University
Department of Counseling
P.O. Box 8120
Pocatello, ID 83209-8120

Phone: (208) 282-3156
http://www.isu.edu/departments/hpcounsl/

Northwest Nazarene University
Counseling Program
623 Holly Street
Nampa, ID 83686
Phone: (208) 467-8428
http://www.nnu.edu/

University of Idaho
Division of Adult, Counselor, and
Technology Education
P.O. Box 443083
Moscow, ID 83844-3083
Phone: (208) 885-7476
http://www.uidaho.edu/ed/acte/counseling/
index.html

ILLINOIS

Bradley University
Department of Educational Leadership
and Human Development
1501 West Bradley Avenue
Westlake Hall
Peoria, IL 61625
Phone: (309) 677-3193
http://www.bradley.edu

Chicago State University
Psychology Department of the College
of Arts and Sciences
Harold Washington Hall 328
9501 South King Drive
Chicago, IL 60629
Phone: (773) 995-2210
http://www.csu.edu/Psychology/grad.
htm

Concordia University
Psychology Department
7400 Augusta
River Forest, IL 60305-1499
Phone: (708) 209-3059
http://www.curf.edu

Eastern Illinois University
Department of Counseling and Student
Development
600 Lincoln Avenue
Charleston, IL 61920-3099
Phone: (217) 581-7800
http://www.eiu.edu/~eiucsd/

Governors State University
Division of Psychology & Counseling
College of Education
University Park, IL 60466

Phone: (708) 534-4393
http://www.govst.edu/users/gpsych/PandC.
html

Northeastern Illinois University
Counselor Education Program
5500 North St. Louis Avenue
Chicago, IL 60625-4699
Phone: (773) 442-5552
http://www.neiu.edu

Northern Illinois University
Department of Counseling, Adult and
Health Education
Graham Hall 223
DeKalb, IL 60115-2854
Phone: (815) 753-8462
http://www.cedu.niu.edu/cahe/index.html

Roosevelt University
Counseling and Human Services
College of Education
430 South Michigan Avenue
Chicago, IL 60605
Phone: (312) 341-2436
http://www.roosevelt.edu/education/chs-
ma.htm

**Southern Illinois University
at Carbondale**
Counseling Programs
Educational Psychology and Special
Education Department
Wham Building, Room 223
Carbondale, IL 62901-4618
Phone: (618) 536-7763
http://www.siu.edu/departments/coe/epse/

University of Illinois at Springfield
Human Development Counseling
Program
Brookens 359
Springfield, IL 62794-9243
Phone: (217) 206-6504
http://www.uis.edu/~bcrowley/department.
html

Western Illinois University
Department of Counselor Education
WIU – QC Center
3561 60th Street
Moline, IL 61265-5881
Phone: (309) 762-1876
http://www.wiu.edu/users/miscp/

INDIANA

Ball State University
Department of Counseling Psychology
and Guidance Services
Teachers College – Room 622
Muncie, IN 47306-0585
Phone: (765) 285-8040
http://www.bsu.edu/web/counselingpsych/

Butler University
Counselor Education Program
JH246
4600 Sunset Avenue
Indianapolis, IN 46208
Phone: (317) 940-9490
http://www.butler.edu/educ/grad.scmain.
html

Grace College
M.A. in Counseling Program
200 Seminary Drive
Winona Lake, IN 46590
Phone: (574) 372-5100 x6055
http://www.grace.edu

Indiana State University
Department of Counseling
School of Education, Room 1517
Terre Haute, IN 47809
Phone: (812) 237-4389
http://counseling.indstate.edu/

Indiana University
Department of Counseling and
Educational Psychology
Wright Education Building
201 North Rose Avenue
Bloomington, IN 47405-1006
Phone: (812) 856-8344
http://www.indiana.edu/~counsel

Indiana Wesleyan University
Graduate Counseling
4201 South Washington Street
Marion, IN 46953
Phone: (765) 677-2995
http://GraduateCounseling.indwes.edu/

Purdue University
Department of Educational Studies
Beering Hall of Liberal Arts and
Education
100 North University
West Lafayette, IN 47907-1446
Phone: (765) 494-9742
http://www.edst.purdue.edu/cd/
development/cdmain.html

IOWA

University of Northern Iowa
Educational Leadership, Counseling and
Postsecondary Education
508 Schindler Education Center
Cedar Falls, IA 50614-0604
Phone: (319) 273-2605
http://www.uni.edu/coe/elcpe/counseling/
index.shtml

The University of Iowa
Counseling, Rehabilitation and Student
Development
N338 Lindquist Center North
Iowa City, IA 52242-1529
Phone: (319) 335-5275
http://www.education.uiowa.edu/crsd

KANSAS

Emporia State University
Division of Counselor Education and
Rehabilitation Programs
Campus Box 4036
1200 Commercial Street
Emporia, KS 66801
Phone: (620) 341-5220
http://www.emporia.edu/counre/

Kansas State University
Department of Counseling and
Educational Psychology
323 Bluemont Hall
1100 Mid Campus Drive
Manhattan, KS 66506-5312
Phone: (785) 532-5937
http://www.educ.ksu.edu/Departments/
EdPsych/overbieew.html

Pittsburg State University
Department of Psychology and
Counseling
Pittsburg, KS 66762-7551
Phone: (316) 235-4530
http://www.pittstate.edu/psych/

KENTUCKY

Eastern Kentucky University
Counseling and Educational Leadership
406 Lancaster Avenue
Richmond, KY 40475
Phone: (859) 622-1124
http://www.education.eku.edu/CEL/

Lindsey Wilson College
210 Lindsey Wilson Street
Columbia, KY 42728

Phone: (502) 384-8121
http://www.lwccounseling.org/

Murray State University
Educational Leadership and Counseling
P.O. Box 9
Murray, KY 42071
Phone: (270) 762-2795
http://www.murraystate.edu/coe/elc/

LOUISIANA

Louisiana State University
120 Peabody Hall
ELRC, Counselor Education
Baton Rouge, LA 70803
Phone: (225) 388-2199
http://asterix.ednet.lsu.edu/~elrcweb/

Loyola University New Orleans
Department of Education and Counseling
6363 St. Charles Avenue, Campus Box 66
New Orleans, LA 70118
Phone: (504) 864-7859
http://www.loyno.edu/education/
counseling/

Northwestern State University
College of Education
Student Personnel Services Program
Natchitoches, LA 71497
Phone: (318) 357-6289
http://www.education.nsula.edu/sps/

Our Lady of Holy Cross College
Humanities, Education, and Counseling
4123 Woodland Drive
New Orleans, LA 70131
Phone: (504) 398-2214
http://www.olchh.edu/olhcc/Academics/
HEC/index.htm

Southeastern Louisiana University
Counseling, Family Studies, and
Educational Leadership
SLU Box 10863
Hammond, LA 70402
Phone: (504) 549-2309
http://www.selu.edu/Academics/Education/
dhd/index.htm

University of Louisiana at Monroe
Department of Educational Leadership
and Counseling
700 University Avenue
Monroe, LA 71209-0230
Phone: (318) 342-1246
http://www.ulm.edu

University of New Orleans
Counselor Education Graduate Program
Department of Educational Leadership,
Counseling and Foundations
348 Education Building
New Orleans, LA 70148-2515
Phone: (504) 280-6662
http://www.ed.uno.edu/~EDFR/

MAINE

University of Southern Maine
Department of Human Resource
Development
400 Bailey Hall
Gorham, ME 04038-1083
Phone: (207) 780-5317
http://www.usm.maine.edu/cehd/

MARYLAND

Loyola College in Maryland
Graduate Program in Pastoral Counseling
and Spiritual Care
8890 McGraw Road, Suite 380
Columbia, MD 21045
Phone: (410) 617-7617
http://www.loyola.edu/academics/
alldepartmets/pastoralcounseling

Loyola College in Maryland
School Counseling Program
Timonium Graduate Center
2034 Greenspring Drive
Timonium, MD 21093
Phone: (410) 617-1509
http://www.loyola.edu/education/
counseling/

University of Maryland at College Park
Counseling and Personnel Services
3214 Benjamin Building
College of Education
College Park, MD 20742
Phone: (301) 405-8904
http://www.education.umd.edu/edcp/

MICHIGAN

Andrews University
Educational & Counseling Psychology
Bell Hall 160
Berrien Springs, MI 49104-0104
Phone: (616) 471-3466
http://www.educ.andrews.edu

Eastern Michigan University
Department of Leadership and
Counseling
John W. Porter Building, Suite 304
Ypsilanti, MI 48197
Phone: (734) 487-0255
http://www.emich.edu/coe/leadcons/

Oakland University
Department of Counseling
Room 478 O'Dowd Hall
Rochester, MI 48309-4494
Phone: (248) 370-2841
http://www.oakland.edu/sehs/organi/depts/
cns/index.html

University of Detroit Mercy
Department of Counseling and Addiction
Studies
4001 West McNichols Road
234 Reno Hall
Detroit, MI 48219
Phone: (313) 578-0436
http://www.udmercy.edu

Wayne State University
Counselor Education/College of
Education
311 Education Building
5429 Gullen Mall
Detroit, MI 48202
Phone: (313) 577-2435
http://www.coe.wayne.edu/org/TBF/tbf.
html

Western Michigan University
Counselor Education and Counseling
Psychology
3102 Sangren Hall
1903 West Michigan Avenue
Kalamazoo, MI 49008-5195
Phone: (269) 387-5114
http://www.wmich.edu/cecp

MINNESOTA

Capella University
School of Human Services
222 South 9th Street, 20th Floor
Minneapolis, MN 55402
Phone: (612) 659-5325
http://www.capella.edu/counselor-
education

Minnesota State University Mankato
Counseling and Student Personnel,
Box 52
107 Armstrong Hall
Mankato, MN 56002-8400

Phone: (507) 389-2423
http://www.coled.mankato.msus.edu/csp/
   index.asp

Minnesota State University Moorhead
Counseling and Student Affairs
209 Lommen Hall
1104 7th Avenue South
Moorhead, MN 56563
Phone: (218) 477-2009
http://www.mnstate.edu/cnsa/

St. Cloud State University
Department of Educational Research,
   School Counseling, and Rehabilitation
720 4th Avenue South
St. Cloud, MN 56301
Phone: (320) 308-2992
http://condor.stcloudstate.edu/~ceep/

University of Minnesota Duluth
Department of Psychology
   and Mental Health
320 Bohannon Hall
10 University Drive
Duluth, MN 55812
Phone: (218) 726-8196
http://www.d.umn.edu/cehsp/

Winona State University
(Winona and Rochester Campuses)
Counselor Education Department
132 Gildemeister Hall
P.O. Box 5838
Rochester, MN 55987-5838
Phone: (800) 336-5418 x7137
http://www.winona.msus.edu/
   counseloreducation/

MISSISSIPPI

Delta State University
Division of Behavioral Sciences
Ewing 335
P.O. Box 3142
Cleveland, MS 38733
Phone: (662) 846-4357
http://www.deltast.edu/academics/educ/
   behavsci/public_html/index.html

Mississippi College
Psychology and Counseling Department
P.O. Box 4013
Clinton, MS 39058
Phone: (601) 925-3841
http://www.mc.edu/campus/academics/psy/

Mississippi State University
Counselor Education & Educational
   Psychology
P.O. Box 9727
Mississippi State, MS 39762
Phone: (662) 325-3426
http://www.msstate.edu/Dept/COE/
   CEdEPy/cedepy.html

University of Mississippi
Department of Leadership and Counselor
   Education
Suite 200, School of Education
P.O. Box 1848
University, MS 38677-1848
Phone: (662) 915-7069
http://www.olemiss.edu/depts/edu_
   school2/couned/main.htm

University of Southern Mississippi
Department of Psychology
Southern Station Box 5025
Hattiesburg, MS 39406-5025
Phone: (601) 266-4177
http://www.usm.edu/psy/counseling/
   masters_counseling.htm

MISSOURI

Southeast Missouri State University
Department of Educational
   Administration and Counseling
One University Placeaza, Mail Stop 5550
Cape Girardeau, MO 63701-4799
Phone: (573) 986-2399
http://www4.semo.edu/counsel/

Truman State University
Counselor Preparation
Division of Education
100 East Normal
Kirksville, MO 63501
Phone: (816) 785-4399
http://www.gradschool.truman.edu/
   counseling.stm

University of Missouri – St. Louis
Division of Counseling and Family
   Therapy
College of Education
469 Marillac Hall
8001 Natural Bridge Road
St. Louis, MO 63121-4499
Phone: (314) 516-5782
http://www.umsl.edu/~educate/counseling/
   main.html

MONTANA

Montana State University –
   Bozeman
Health and Human Development
218 Herrick Hall
Bozeman, MT 59717
Phone: (406) 994-3299
http://www.montana.edu/wwwhhd

NEBRASKA

University of Nebraska Kearney
Department of Counseling and School
   Psychology
Founders Hall
Kearney, NE 68849
Phone: (308) 865-8358
http://www.unk.edu/acad/csp

University of Nebraska at Omaha
Counseling Department
6001 Dodge Street
Kayser Hall 421
College of Education
Omaha, NE 68182-0167
Phone: (402) 554-2727
http://www.unocoe.unomaha.edu/coun.
   htm

NEVADA

University of Nevada, Las Vegas
Department of Counseling
4505 Maryland Parkway, Box 453045
Las Vegas, NV 89154-3045
Phone: (702) 895-1392
http://www.unlv.edu/Colleges/Urban/
   Counseling/

University of Nevada, Las Vegas
Educational Psychology and School
   Counseling
4505 South Maryland Parkway
Las Vegas, NV 89154-3003
Phone: (702) 895-0909
http://www.education.unlv.edu/EP/grad/
   couns.htm

University of Nevada, Reno
Counseling & Educational Psychology
Department 281
Reno, NV 89557-0213
Phone: (775) 784-1772
http://www.unr.edu/educ/cep/cepindex.
   html

NEW JERSEY

The College of New Jersey
Department of Counselor Education
Forcina Hall 337
P.O. Box 7718
Ewing, NJ 08620-0718
Phone: (609) 771-2119
http://www.tcnj.edu/~educat/cpsindex.htm

Kean University
Department of Special Education and
    Counseling
1000 Morris Avenue
Union, NJ 07083
Phone: (908) 737-3842
http://www.kean.edu

Rider University
Department of Graduate Education
    and Human Services/Counseling
    Services Program
2083 Lawrenceville Road
Lawrenceville, NJ 08648-3099
Phone: (609) 895-5487
http://www.rider.edu

William Paterson University
Department of Special Education and
    Counseling
300 Pompton Road, Raubinger Hall
Wayne, NJ 07170
Phone: (973) 720-3085
http://www.wpunj.edu/COE/Departments/
    sped/default.htm

NEW MEXICO

New Mexico State University
Counseling and Educational Psychology
O'Donnell, Room 205
Las Cruces, NM 88003
Phone: (505) 646-4092
http://education.nmsu.edu/cep/

University of New Mexico
Counselor Education Program
College of Education
Simpson Hall
Albuquerque, NM 87131-1246
Phone: (505) 277-8933
http://www.unm.edu/~divbse/couns/
    counselor.htm

NEW YORK

Long Island University C. W. Post
Department of Counseling and
    Development
Library Room 320
720 Northern Boulevard
Brookville, NY 11548-1300
Phone: (516) 299-2814
http://www.cwpost.liu.edu/cwis/cwp/

**Plattsburgh State University
    of New York**
Counselor Education Department
101 Broad Street, Ward Hall
Plattsburgh, NY 12901
Phone: (518) 564-4177
http://www.plattsburgh.edu/clg/

St. John's University
Jamaica and Staten Island Campuses
Human Services and Counseling
8000 Utopia Parkway
Jamaica, NY 11439
Phone: (718) 990-1562
http://www.stjohns.edu/pls/portal30/sjudev.
    school.home?p_siteid=36&p_navbar=
    269&p_id=50785

SUNY at Brockport
Department of Counselor Education
184 Faculty Office
350 New Campus Drive
Brockport, NY 14420-2953
Phone: (585) 395-2258
http://www.brockport.edu/~counsele/CE.
    HTM

Syracuse University
Counseling and Human Services
259 Huntington Hall
Syracuse, NY 13244-3240
Phone: (315) 443-2266
http://soeweb.syr.edu/chs/counhumserv.
    html

University of Rochester
Department Counseling and Human
    Development
Margaret Warner Graduate School of
    Education and Human Development
Rochester, NY 14627
Phone: (585) 275-5077
http://www.rochester.edu/warner

NORTH CAROLINA

Appalachian State University
Human Development and Psychological
    Counseling
Boone, NC 28608
Phone: (828) 262-2055
http://www.hpc.appstate.edu/

North Carolina A & T State University
Human Development and Services
212 Hudgin Hall
Greensboro, NC 27411-1066
Phone: (336) 334-7280
http://prometheus.educ.ncat.edu/users/adsv/

North Carolina State University
Counselor Education Department
520 Poe Hall
P.O. Box 7801
Raleigh, NC 27695-7801
Phone: (919) 515-6358
http://www2.ncsu.edu/ncsu/cep/

**University of North Carolina
    at Chapel Hill**
School Counseling Program
CB #3500 Peabody Hall
School of Education
Chapel Hill, NC 27599-3500
Phone: (919) 962-9196
http://www.unc.edu/depts/ed/med_sch_
    counseling/

**The University of North Carolina
    at Charlotte**
Department of Counseling, Special
    Education, and Child Development
Counselor Education
9201 University City Boulevard
Charlotte, NC 28223-0001
Phone: (704) 687-4726
http://education.uncc.edu/counseling/

**The University of North Carolina
    at Greensboro**
Department of Counseling & Educational
    Development
P.O. Box 26171
Greensboro, NC 27402-6170
Phone: (336) 334-3425
http://www.uncg.edu/ced

Wake Forest University
Counselor Education Program
P.O. Box 7266 Reynolds Station
Winston-Salem, NC 27109
Phone: (336) 758-4932
http://www.wfu.edu/cep

Western Carolina University
Department of Human Services
204 Killian Building
Cullowhee, NC 28723
Phone: (828) 227-3292
http://ceap.wcu.edu/counseling/

NORTH DAKOTA

North Dakota State University
Counselor Education Program
School of Education
Family Life Center 210
Fargo, ND 58105-5057
Phone: (701) 231-7204
http://www.ndsu.nodak.edu/adsu/School_
    of_education/counsed/index.html

OHIO

Cleveland State University
CASAL Department
2121 Euclid Avenue
1419 Rhodes Tower
Cleveland, OH 44115
Phone: (216) 687-4605
http://www.csuohio.edu/casal

John Carroll University
Department of Education
    & Allied Studies
20700 North Park Boulevard
University Heights
Cleveland, OH 44118-4581
Phone: (216) 397-1710 or 3001
http://www.jcu.edu

Kent State University
Counseling & Human Development
    Services
310 White Hall
Kent, OH 44242-0001
Phone: (330) 672-0696
http://chds.educ.kent.edu/

Ohio University
Counselor Education
201 McCracken Hall
Athens, OH 45701
Phone: (740) 593-4460
http://www.ohio.edu/che/index.html

University of Akron
Counseling and Special Education
127 Carroll Hall
Akron, OH 44325-5007
Phone: (330) 972-5515
http://www.uakron.edu/colleges/educ/
    Counseling/index.php

University of Cincinnati
Counseling Program
Division of Human Services
P.O. Box 210002
Cincinnati, OH 45221-0002
Phone: (513) 556-3347
http://homepages.uc.edu/counseling/

University of Toledo
Department of Counseling and Mental
    Health Services
MS 119
2801 West Bancroft Street
Toledo, OH 43606-3390
Phone: (419) 530-4775
http://cmhs.utoledo.edu/

Wright State University
Department of Human Services
M052 Creative Arts Center
3640 Colonel Glenn Highway
Dayton, OH 45435-0001
Phone: (937) 775-4467
http://www.ed.wright.edu/departments/hs/

Youngstown State University
Department of Counseling
One University Plaza
Youngstown, OH 44555-0001
Phone: (330) 941-3257
http://www.cc.ysu.edu/counseling/

OREGON

Oregon State University
Counselor Education Program
100 Education Hall
School of Education
Corvallis, OR 97331
Phone: (541) 737-8204
http://oregonstate.edu/education/counselor.
    html

Portland State University
Department of Special Education and
    Counselor Education Programs
Graduate School of Education
P.O. Box 751
Portland, OR 97207-0751
Phone: (503) 725-4611
http://www.ed.pdx.edu/spedcoun/
    counpgrm.html

Southern Oregon University
Master in Applied Psychology
1250 Siskiyou Boulevard
Ashland, OR 97520
Phone: (541) 552-6958
http://www.sou.edu/

PENNSYLVANIA

Duquesne University
Department of Counseling, Psychology
    and Special Education
School of Education
Canevin Hall
Pittsburgh, PA 15282

Phone: (412) 396-6099
http://www.education.duq.edu/counselored

Edinboro University of Pennsylvania
Professional Studies Department
Centennial Hall 3rd Floor
Edinboro, PA 16444
Phone: (814) 732-1116
http://www.edinboro.edu/cwis/education/
    counseling/main_menu.html

Marywood University
Dr. John C. Boylan
Department of Counseling
2300 Adams Avenue
Scranton, PA 18509
Phone: (570) 348-6211 x2319
http://www.marywood.edu/departments/
    counseling/index.htm

The Pennsylvania State University
Counselor Education, Counseling
    Psychology and Rehabilitation
    Services
327 CEDAR Building
University Park, PA 16828
Phone: (814) 863-2412
http://www.ed.psu.edu/cned/ced.asp

Shippensburg University
Department of Counseling
1871 Old Main Drive
Shippensburg, PA 17257
Phone: (717) 477-1658
http://www.ship.edu/~counsel

Slippery Rock University
Counseling and Educational Psychology
006 McKay Education Building
Slippery Rock, PA 16057
Phone: (724) 738-2274
http://www.sru.edu/depts/educatio/cedp.
    html

University of Pittsburgh
Department of Psychology in Education
5C01 WWPH
Pittsburgh, PA 15260
Phone: (412) 624-7226
http://www.education.pitt.edu/pie/index.
    htm

University of Scranton
Department of Counseling and Human
    Services
Panuska College of Professional Studies
Scranton, PA 18510-4523
Phone: (570) 941-4129
http://academics.scranton.edu/department/
    chs/

SOUTH CAROLINA

Clemson University

Department of Counseling and
    Educational Leadership
College of Health, Education and Human
    Development
330 Tillman Hall, Box 340710
Clemson, SC 29634-0710
Phone: (864) 656-4506
http://www.hehd.clemson.edu/c&el

University of South Carolina

Counselor Education
Department of Educational Psychology
College of Education
266 Wardlaw Hall
Columbia, SC 29208
Phone: (803) 777-1936
http://edpsych.ed.sc.edu/ce/

Winthrop University

Department of Counseling and
    Leadership
Richard W. Riley College of Education
143 Withers Building,
    701 Oakland Avenue
Rockhill, SC 29733
Phone: (803) 323-4725
http://www.coe.winthrop.edu

SOUTH DAKOTA

South Dakota State University

College of Education and Counseling
P.O. Box 507 Wenona Hall
Brookings, SD 57007-0095
Phone: (605) 688-4321
http://www.sdstate.edu/~wedc/http/CHRD.
    htm

University of South Dakota

Division of Counseling and Psychology
    in Education
Delzell School of Education
414 East Clark Street
Vermillion, SD 57069
Phone: (605) 677-5257
http://www.usd.edu/cpe/indexcg.htm

TENNESSEE

East Tennessee State University

Department of Human Development
    and Learning
College of Education, P.O. Box 70548
Johnson City, TN 37614-0548
Phone: (423) 439-4197
http://coe.etsu.edu/department/hdal/index.
    htm

Middle Tennessee State University

Department of Psychology
P.O. Box 87
Murfreesboro, TN 37132
Phone: (615) 898-2559
http://www.mtsu.edu/~psych/counsel.htm

The University of Memphis

Counseling, Educational Psychology, and
    Research
Ball Hall, Room 100
Memphis, TN 38152-0001
Phone: (901) 678-2814
http://cepr.memphis.edu.coun_menu.asp

The University of Tennessee

Counselor Education and Counseling
    Psychology
College of Education
Knoxville, TN 37996-3400
Phone: (423) 974-4207
http://cehhs.utk.edu/index_degrees.html

University of Tennessee at Chattanooga

Graduate Studies
615 McCallie Avenue
Department 4154
Chattanooga, TN 37403
Phone: (423) 425-4544
http://www.utc.edu/

Vanderbilt University

Human Development Counseling Program
P.O. Box 22-GPC
Nashville, TN 37203
Phone: (615) 322-8484
http://peabody.vanderbilt.edu/depts/hod/
    hodweb/grad/hdc.html

TEXAS

St. Mary's University

Department of Counseling and Human
    Services
One Camino Santa Marie
San Antonio, TX 78228
Phone: (210) 436-3226
http://www.stmarytx.edu/acad/counseling/

Stephen F. Austin State University

Department of Counseling and Special
    Educational Programs
P.O. Box 13019
Nacogdoches, TX 75962-3019
Phone: (936) 468-1079
http://www.sfasu.edu/hs/counseli.htm

Texas A & M University – Commerce

Department of Counseling
202 Education North

Commerce, TX 75429-3011
Phone: (903) 886-5637
http://www7.tamu-
    commerce.edu/counseling/

Texas A & M University – Corpus Christi

Counseling and Educational Psychology
6300 Ocean Drive
Corpus Christi, TX 78412
Phone: (361) 825-2307
http://www.tamucc.edu/

Texas State University

Department of Educational
    Administration & Psychology
    Services
601 University Drive
San Marcos, TX 78666-4615
Phone: (512) 245-3757
http://www.eaps.swt.edu/counseling.html

Texas Tech University

Counselor Education Program
P.O. Box 41071
Administration Building
College of Education
Lubbock, TX 79409-1071
Phone: (806) 742-1997 x263
http://www.educ.ttu.edu/cdce/

Texas Woman's University

Department of Family Sciences
P.O. Box 425769
Denton, TX 76204-5769
Phone: (940) 898-2694
http://www.twu.edu/cope/famsci/

University of Mary Hardin-Baylor

Graduate Psychology and Counseling
900 College Street
UMHB Box 8014
Belton, TX 76513
Phone: (254) 295-4555
http://www.umhb.edu

University of North Texas

Program in Counselor Education
P.O. Box 311337
Denton, TX 76203-1337
Phone: (940) 565-2910
http://www.coe.unt.edu/cdhe/cnslored.
    htm

UTAH

Brigham Young University

Department of Counseling Psychology
    and Special Education
David O. McKay School of Education

320-A McKay Building
Provo, UT 84602-4839
Phone: (801) 422-1311
http://www.byu.edu/cse

University of Phoenix – Utah
College of Counseling and Human
    Services
Salt Lake City, UT 84123
Phone: (801) 263-1444 ext.4222
http://www.university-of-phoenix-adult-
    education.com/University_of_Phoenix_
    counseling.html

VERMONT

University of Vermont
Counseling Program
Mann Hall
208 Cockchester Avenue
Burlington, VT 05405-0160
Phone: (802) 656-3888
http://www.uvm.edu/~cslgprog

VIRGINIA

The College of William and Mary
School of Education
P.O. Box 8795
Williamsburg, VA 23187-8795
Phone: (757) 221-4001
http://www.wm.edu/education.programs/
    space/html

Eastern Mennonite University
Graduate Counseling Program
1200 Park Road
Harrisonburg, VA 22802
Phone: (540) 432-4244
http://www.emu.edu/graduatecounseling/

James Madison University
Counselor Education Program
School Psychology
MSC 7401
Harrisonburg, VA 22807
Phone: (540) 568-6522
http://cep.jmu.edu/counselpsyc/

Lynchburg College
Department of Counselor Education
School of Education and Human
    Development
1501 Lakeside Drive
Lynchburg, VA 24501-3199
Phone: (434) 544-8150
http://www.lynchburg.edu/GraduateStudies/
    SchooleducationHuman.htm

Marymount University
Department of Psychology
School of Education and Human Services
2807 North Glebe Road
Arlington, VA 22207
Phone: (703) 284-1633
http://www.marymount.edu/academic/sehs/
    ps/gprog.html

Old Dominion University
Counseling Program
College of Education
Norfolk, VA 23529
Phone: (757) 783-5308
http://odu.edu/webroot/orgs/educ/elc/elc.
    nsf/pages/grad_coun

Radford University
Counselor Education Department
709 Howe Street
P.O. Box 6994
Radford, VA 24142
Phone: (540) 831-6755
http://www.runet.edu

Regent University
School of Counseling
    and Human Services
1000 Regent University Drive
Virginia Beach, VA 23464-9800
Phone: (757) 226-4293
http://www.regent.edu

University of Virginia
Curry School of Education
405 Emmet Street, 169 Ruffner Hall
P.O. Box 400269
Charlottesville, VA 22903-2495
Phone: (434) 243-8717
http://curry.edschool.Virginia.EDU/
    counsed/

**Virginia Polytechnic Institute
    and State University**
Counselor Education
308 East Eggleston – 0302
ELPS Department
Blacksburg, VA 24061-0302
Phone: (703) 538-8483
http://www.chre.vt.edu/thohen/index.html

WASHINGTON

Eastern Washington University
Department of Counselor Education and
    Developmental Psychology
705 West First Avenue
Spokane, WA 99202-1660
Phone: (509) 623-4225

http://cehd.ewu.edu/cedpsite/cedpdocs/
    master/Cnslschool/cnssclhome.htm

Western Washington University
Department of Psychology
516 High Street
Bellingham, WA 98225-9089
Phone: (360) 650-3523
http://www.ac.wwu.edu/~psych

WEST VIRGINIA

West Virginia University
Department of Counseling, Rehabilitation
    Counseling, and Counseling
    Psychology
502 Allen Hall
P.O. Box 6122
Morgantown, WV 26506-6122
Phone: (304) 293-3807 x1213
http://www.wvu.edu/~crc/couns/

WISCONSIN

University of Wisconsin Oshkosh
Counselor Education Department
800 Algoma Boulevard
Oshkosh, WI 54901
Phone: (920) 424-1475
http://www.coehs.uwosh.edu/departments.
    counselor_ed/index.php

University of Wisconsin Superior
Department of Counseling &
    Psychological Professions
McCaskill Hall, Room 111
Belknap & Catlin Avenue
P.O. Box 2000
Superior, WI 54880
Phone: (715) 394-8151
http://www.umsuper.edu/catalog/general/
    2002-2004/graduate/ccp.html

University of Wisconsin Whitewater
Counselor Education Department
800 West Main Street
Whitewater, WI 53190
Phone: (262) 472-1452
http://academics/uww.edu/counseled/

WYOMING

University of Wyoming
Counselor Education
College of Education
P.O. Box 3374
University Station
Laramie, WY 82071
Phone: (307) 766-4002
http://ed.uwyo.edu/Departments/
    depcounsel/index.htm

F. ARTS ADMINISTRATION

Graduate programs in arts administration prepare professionals for leadership roles in arts and cultural institutions, such as museums, theaters, symphonies, and arts organizations. The following programs are listed at http://www. petersons. com for offering graduate degrees in the field. Also check out the Association of Arts Administration Educators (AAAE) at http://www.artsnet.org/aaae/aaaemain.html for additional program listings.

ALABAMA

University of Alabama
The Department of Theatre and Dance
MFA in Theatre Management
P. O. Box 870239
Tuscaloosa, AL 35487
Phone: (205) 348-4442
Fax: (205) 348-9048
http://www.as.ua.edu/theatre/theatman.html

CALIFORNIA

University of Southern California
School of Fine Arts
Program in Public Art Studies
Los Angeles, CA 90089
Phone: (213) 740-2787
Fax: (213) 749-9703
http://finearts.usc.edu/

DISTRICT OF COLUMBIA

American University
College of Arts and Sciences
Department of Performing Arts
Program in Arts Management
Kreeger Building
400 Massachusetts Avenue, NW
Washington, DC 20016-8001
Phone: (202) 885-3420
Fax: (202) 885-1092
http://american.edu/cas/department_
    performingarts.shtml

FLORIDA

Florida State University
Graduate Studies
School of Visual Arts and Dance
Tallahassee, FL 32306
Phone: (850) 644-5473
http://www.fsu.edu/gradstudies/
    collegesandschools/visualartsanddance.
    shtml

ILLINOIS

Columbia College Chicago
Graduate School
Department of Arts Entertainment
    and Media Management
Chicago, IL 60605-1996
Phone: (312) 344-7654
Fax: (312) 344-8047
http://www.colum.edu/graduate/gradaemm.
    html

School of the Art Institute of Chicago
Program in Arts Administration
37 South Wabash
Chicago, Illinois 60603
Phone: (312) 899-5219; (800) 232-7242
http://www.artic.edu

INDIANA

Indiana University Bloomington
College of Arts and Sciences
Program in Arts Administration
Bloomington, IN 47405
Phone: (812) 855-0282
Fax: (812) 855-8679
http://www.indiana.edu/~artsadm/

LOUISIANA

University of New Orleans
Graduate School
College of Liberal Arts
Program in Arts Administration
New Orleans, LA 70148
Phone: (504) 280-6158
http://www.uno.edu/%7Earta/

MARYLAND

Goucher College
Graduate Program in Arts Administration
Baltimore, MD 21204-2794
Phone: (410) 337-6200
Fax: (410) 337-6085
http://www.goucher.edu/maaa/index.
    cfm

MASSACHUSSETTS

Boston University
Metropolitan College
Arts Administration Program
808 Commonwealth Avenue
Boston, MA 02215
Phone: (617) 353-4064
Fax: (617) 358-1230
http://www.bu.edu/artsadmin

Northeastern University
College of Arts and Sciences
Program in Law, Policy, and Society
202 Holmes Hall
Boston, MA 02115
Phone: (617) 373-3644
Fax: (617) 373-4691
http://www.lps.neu.edu

MICHIGAN

Eastern Michigan University
College of Arts and Sciences
Department of Communication and
    Theatre Arts
Ypsilanti, MI 48197
Phone: (734) 487-3131
http://www.emich.edu/academics/
    programs/ arts.htm

MINNESOTA

**Saint Mary's University
    of Minnesota**
Graduate School
Program in Arts Administration
Winona, MN 55987-1399
Phone: (612) 728-5146
Fax: (612) 728-5121
http://www.smumn.edu/sitepages/pid98.
    php

MISSOURI

Webster University
Leigh Gerdine College of Fine Arts
Department of Art
Program in Arts Management and
    Leadership
St. Louis, MO 63119-3194
Phone: (314) 968-6983
Fax: (314) 968-7116
http://www.webster.edu/acadaffairs/
    acadprogs.html#mfa

NEW JERSEY

Seton Hall University
Graduate Department of Public and
    Healthcare Administration
Program in Arts Administration
400 South Orange Avenue
South Orange, NJ 07079
Phone: (973) 761-9510
Fax: (973) 275-2463
http://artsci.shu.edu%2fcps

NEW YORK

Fashion Institute of Technology
School of Graduate Studies E315
Program in Gallery and Retail Arts
    Administration
Seventh Avenue at 27th Street
New York, NY 10001-5992
Phone: (212) 217-5714
Fax: (212) 217-5156
http://www.fitnyc.edu

New York University
The Steinhardt School of Education
Department of Art and Art Professions
Program in Visual Arts Administration
New York, NY 10012-1019
Phone: (212) 998-5030
Fax: (212) 995-4328
http://www.nyu.edu/education/steinhardt/
    db/programs/10

New York University
The Steinhardt School of Education
Department of Music and Performing
    Arts Professions
Program in Performing Arts
    Administration
New York, NY 10012-1019
Phone: (212) 998-5030
Fax: (212) 995-4328
http://www.nyu.edu/education/steinhardt/
    db/programs/30

Pratt Institute
Program in Design Management
200 Willoughby Avenue
Brooklyn, NY 11205
Phone: (718) 636-3669 or 3514;
    (800) 331-0834
Fax: (718) 636-3670
http://www.pratt.edu

Pratt Institute
School of Art and Design
Program in Arts and Cultural
    Management
Brooklyn, NY 11205-3899
Phone: (718) 636-3669

Fax: (718) 636-3670
http://www.pratt.edu

Teachers College
    of Columbia University
Program in Arts Administration
525 West 120th Street, Box 302
New York, NY 10027
Phone: (212) 678-3710
http://www.tc.columbia.edu%2fdiscover

NORTH CAROLINA

North Carolina School of the Arts
Performing Arts Management Program
1533 South Main Street
Winston-Salem, NC 27127-2188
Phone: (336) 770-1346
Fax: (336) 770-3213
http://www.ncarts.edu/

**University of North Carolina at
    Charlotte**
Graduate School
College of Arts and Sciences
Program in Arts Administration
Charlotte, NC 28223-0001
Phone: (704) 687-3366
Fax: (704) 687-3279
http://www.uncc.edu/gradmiss/gs_arts_
    admin.html

OHIO

Ohio State University
College of the Arts
Department of Art Education
Program in Arts Policy and
    Administration
Columbus, OH 43210
Phone: (614) 688-4346
Fax: (614) 688-8217
http://arts.osu.edu/ArtEducation/APA/
    index. php

University of Akron
College of Fine and Applied Arts
School of Dance, Theatre, and Arts
    Administration
Program in Arts Administration
Akron, OH 44325-0001
Phone: (330) 972-5905
http://www3.uakron.edu/dtaa/index.html

University of Cincinnati
Division of Research and Advanced
    Studies
Conservatory of Music
Divisions of Opera, Musical Theater,
    Drama, and Arts Administration

Cincinnati, OH 45221
Phone: (513) 556-4383
Fax: (513) 556-0202
http://www.ccm.uc.edu/arts_admin/

OKLAHOMA

Oklahoma City University
Meinders School of Business
Program in Business Administration
    (specialization in arts management)
Oklahoma City, OK 73106-1402
Phone: (800) 633-7242 ext. 4
Fax: (405) 521-5356
http://www.okcu.edu/business/msb_
    graduate/mba.asp

OREGON

University of Oregon
Graduate School
School of Architecture and Allied Arts
Program in Arts and Administration
Eugene, OR 97403-5230
Phone: (541) 346-3639
Fax: (541) 346-3626
http://aad.uoregon.edu/

PENNSYLVANIA

Carnegie Mellon University
The Institute for Management
    of Creative Enterprises
Master of Arts Management
Pittsburgh, PA 15213-3891
Phone: (412) 268-8436
Fax: (412) 268-3590
http://www.artsnet.org/mam/

Drexel University
College of Media Arts and Design
Department of Performing Arts
Philadelphia, PA 19104-2875
Phone: (215) 895-2451
Fax: (215) 895-2452
http://www.drexel.edu/academics/comad/
    performingarts/index.html

TEXAS

Southern Methodist University
Meadows School of the Arts
Division of Arts Administration
P.O. Box 750356
Dallas, TX 75275
Phone: (214) 768-3765
Fax: (214) 768-3272
http://www.smu.edu/meadows/artsadmin/

VIRGINIA

George Mason University
College of Visual and Performing Arts
Master of Arts Management
4400 University Drive, MS 4C1
Fairfax, VA 22030
Phone: (703) 993-8381
http://artsmanagement.gmu.edu/

Shenandoah University
Shenandoah Conservatory Program in
    Arts Administration
1460 University Avenue
Winchester, VA 22601-5195

Phone: (540) 665-1290
Fax: (540) 665-4627
http://www.su.edu/conservatory/scon/
    Academics/ArtsManagement/index.
    htm

**Virginia Polytechnic Institute
    and State University**
College of Arts and Sciences
Department of Theatre Arts
School of the Arts Graduate Program
    in Arts Administration
213 Performing Arts Building
Blacksburg, VA 24061
Phone: (540) 231-1854

Fax: (540) 231-7321
http://www.sota.vt.edu/artsadmin.html

WISCONSIN

University of Wisconsin–Madison
School of Business
Program in Arts Administration
3150 Grainger Hall of Business
975 University Avenue
Madison, WI 53706-1380
Phone: (608) 262-4000
Fax: (608) 265-4192
http://www.bus.wisc.edu/graduateprograms/

G. HIGHER EDUCATION/STUDENT PERSONNEL ADMINISTRATION

The following is a *Directory of Graduate Programs Preparing Student Affairs Professionals,* developed by the Professional Preparation Commission of the American College Personnel Association. These schools offer programs that prepare students for positions within college and university administration, including both student and academic affairs.

The departments are often within schools of education and offer master's and/or doctoral degrees. For a complete updated listing, go to: http://www.acpa.nche.edu/c12/directory.htm. Those interested in counseling, teaching, and other education-related graduate programs may find these links useful as well.

ARIZONA

Arizona State University
School of Education
Programs in Psychology and Education
    and Educational Leadership and
    Policy Studies
Tempe, AZ 85287
Phone: (480) 965-9011
http://coe.asu.edu/elps/

Northern Arizona University
School of Education
Master's in Education with Student
    Affairs emphasis
South San Francisco Street
Flagstaff, AZ 86011
Phone: (888) 667-3628
http://coe.nau.edu/academics/EPS/

The University of Arizona
School of Education
Center for the Study of Higher Education
Tucson, AZ 85721
Phone: (520) 621-2211
http://www.ed.arizona.edu/hed/index.html

ARKANSAS

Arkansas Tech University
School of Education
Master of Science in College Personnel
1509 North Boulder Avenue
Russellville, AR 72801

Phone: (800) 582-6953
http://education.atu.edu/

University of Arkansas
School of Education
Department of Educational Leadership,
    Counseling and Foundations
Fayetteville, AR 72701
Phone: (479) 575-2000
http://www.uark.edu/depts/coehp/ELCF.
    htm

CALIFORNIA

Azusa Pacific University
School of Education and Behavioral
    Studies
Department of Higher Education and
    Organizational Leadership
901 East Alosta Avenue, P.O. Box 7000
Azusa, CA 91702-7000
Phone: (800) 825-5278
http://www.apu.edu/educabs/graduate/

California State University, Long Beach
College of Education
Master of Science in Student
    Development in Higher Education
1250 Bellflower Boulevard
Long Beach, CA 90840
Phone: (562) 985-1609
http://www.ced.csulb.edu/edpac/
    academic/sdhe/index.cfm

Claremont Graduate University
School of Educational Studies
Master's and Ph.D. program in education
    with emphasis on higher
    education/adult development
150 East Tenth Street
Claremont, CA 91711-6160
Phone: (909) 621-8317
http://www.cgu.edu/ses/highered.htm

San Diego State University
College of Education
Master's Degree in Postsecondary
    Educational Leadership with a
    Specialization in Student Affairs
5500 Campanile Drive
San Diego, CA 92182
Phone: (619) 594-6091
http://edweb.sdsu.edu/newedweb/index.
    php

University of Southern California
USC Rossier School of Education
Master's in Postsecondary Administration
    and Student Affairs
Certificate in the Management of College
    Student Services
University Park Campus
Los Angeles, CA 90089
Phone: (213) 740-2311
http://www.usc.edu/dept/education/

COLORADO

Colorado State University
School of Education
Master of Science Degree in Student
    Affairs in Higher Education
Fort Collins, CO 80523
Phone: (970) 491-1963
http://welcome.colostate.edu/

University of Denver
College of Education
Higher Education Program
2199 South University Boulevard
Denver, CO 80208
Phone: (303) 871-2000
http://www.du.edu/education/

University of Northern Colorado
Division of Educational Leadership
    and Policy Studies
Program in Higher Education and Student
    Affairs Leadership
McKee Hall 418, Campus Box 103
Greeley, CO 80639
Phone: (970) 351-2861
Fax: (970) 351-3334
http://www.unco.edu/coe/elps/

CONNECTICUT

University of Connecticut
NEAG School of Education
Master's Program in Student Affairs
249 Glenbrook Road
Storrs, CT 06269
Phone: (860) 486-6278
Fax: (860) 486-4028
http://www.education.uconn.edu/

DELAWARE

University of Delaware
College of Human Services, Education,
    & Public Policy
M.A. in Student Affairs Practice in
    Higher Education
184 Graham Hall
Newark, DE 19716
Phone: (302) 831-2394
Fax: (302) 831-4605
http://www.udel.edu/chep/

DISTRICT OF COLUMBIA

George Washington University
Graduate School of Education and
    Human Development
Programs in Higher Education
    Administration and Student Affairs
    Administration
2121 Eye Street, NW
Washington, DC 20052
Phone: (202) 994-1000
http://gsehd.gwu.edu/gsehd/

FLORIDA

Florida International University
College of Education, Department of
    Educational Leadership and Policy
    Studies
Graduate Programs in Higher Education
Sanford and Dolores Ziff and Family
    Building (ZEB)
FIU-University Park
11200 Southwest 8 Street
Miami, FL 33199
Phone: (305) 348-3418
http://education.fiu.edu/

Florida State University
College of Education, Department
    of Educational Leadership
    and Policy Studies
Programs in Higher Education
Tallahassee, FL 32306
Phone: (850) 644-7077
http://www.fsu.edu/%7Eelps/

University of Florida
College of Education
Department of Educational Leadership,
    Policy and Foundations
P.O. Box 117049, Norman 258
Gainesville, FL 32611-7049
Phone: (352) 392-2391, ext. 300
Fax: (352) 392-0038
http://www.coe.ufl.edu/Leadership/
    programs/programs.html

University of Miami
School of Education
M.S.Ed. and Certificate Program in
    Higher Education/Enrollment
    Management
5202 University Drive
Coral Gables, FL 33146
Phone: (305) 284-5013
http://www.education.miami.edu/
    organization/organizations_detail.asp?
    Organization_ID=12

University of South Florida
College of Education
College Student Affairs M.S.Ed. Program
4202 East Fowler Avenue, ADM151
Tampa, FL 33620
Phone: (813) 974-9095
Fax: (813) 974-7436
http://csa.sa.usf.edu/

GEORGIA

University of Georgia
College of Education
Programs in Higher Education and
    College Student Affairs
    Administration
G-3 Aderhold Hall
Athens, GA 30602
Phone: (706) 542-6446
Fax: (706) 542-0360
http://www.coe.uga.edu/graduate.html

ILLINOIS

Eastern Illinois University
Department of Counseling and Student
    Development
MS in Student Affairs
2102 Buzzard Hall
600 Lincoln Avenue
Charleston, IL 61920-3099
Phone: (217) 581-2400
http://www.eiu.edu/~eiucsd/csd/
    studentAffairs.html

Illinois State University
School of Education
Programs in Educational Administration
    and Foundations
DeGarmo Hall
Mail Box Code: 5300
Normal, IL 61790-5300
Phone: (309) 438-5415
Fax: (309) 438-3813
http://www.coe.ilstu.edu/eafdept/
    programs/

Loyola University Chicago
School of Education
Master's and Doctoral Programs in
    Higher Education
820 North Michigan Avenue
Chicago, IL 60611
Phone: (312) 915-6800
Fax: (312) 915-6660
http://www.luc.edu/schools/education/
    degree/degree.shtml

**Southern Illinois University
    at Carbondale**
College of Education and Human
    Services

Department of Educational
   Administration and Higher Education
131 Pulliam Hall
Carbondale, IL 62901-4606
Phone: (618) 536-4434
http://www.siu.edu/departments/coe/
   eahe/

Western Illinois University
School of Graduate Studies
Program in College Student Personnel
Horrabin Hall 80
Macomb, IL 61455-1390
Phone: (309) 298-1183
Fax: (309) 298-2222
http://www.wiu.edu/grad/catalog/csp.shtml

INDIANA

Ball State University
Teachers College
Department of Educational Studies
Graduate Program in Student Affairs
   Administration in Higher Education
2000 University Avenue
Muncie, IN 47306-0610
Phone: (765) 285-5461
Fax: (765) 285-5489
http://www.bsu.edu/web/edstudies/

Indiana State University
Department of Counseling
Student Affairs and Higher Education
   Graduate Program
1518 College of Education
Indiana State University
Terre Haute, IN 47809
Phone: (812) 237-2832
Fax: (812) 237-2729
http://counseling.indstate.edu/saa/

Indiana University
School of Education
Higher Education and Student Affairs
   Program
201 North Rose Avenue #4228
Bloomington, IN 47405-1006
Phone: (812) 856-8364
http://www.indiana.edu/~hesa/

Purdue University
Office of Graduate Studies, School of
   Education
Programs in College Student Affairs and
   Higher Education Administration
100 North University Street
Room 6104
West Lafayette, IN 47907-2067
Phone: (765) 494-2345

Fax: (765) 494-5832
http://www.edci.purdue.edu/gradoffice/

IOWA

Iowa State University
College of Education, Department
   of Educational Leadership
   and Policy Studies
Program in Higher Education
N247D Lagomarcino Hall
Ames, IA 50011-3195
Phone: (515) 294-7113
Fax: (515) 294-4942
http://www.educ.iastate.edu/elps/hged/
   homepage.htm

University of Iowa
College of Education
Department of Counseling, Rehabilitation
   and Student Development
Graduate Programs in Student Affairs
N338 Lindquist Center
Iowa City, IA 52242-1529
Phone: (319) 335-5275
Fax: (319) 335-5291
http://coe164.education.uiowa.edu:8180/
   crsd/sdp/Default.htm

University of Northern Iowa
Graduate College, College of Education
Department of Educational Leadership,
   Counseling, and Postsecondary
   Education
Program in Postsecondary Education
Cedar Falls, IA 50614
Phone: (319) 273-2605
Fax: (319) 273-5175
http://www.uni.edu/coe/elcpe/

KANSAS

Emporia State University
School of Graduate Studies
The Teachers College
Department of Counselor Education and
   Rehabilitation Programs
MS in Student Personnel
Emporia, KS 66801-5087
Phone: (620) 341-5220
http://www.emporia.edu/counre/student_
   personnel.htm

Kansas State University
College of Education, Department of
   Counseling and Educational
   Psychology
Program in Student Personnel Services in
   Higher Education

6 Bluemont Hall
Manhattan, KS 66506
Phone: (785) 532-5541
Fax: (785) 532-7304
http://www.educ.ksu.edu/Departments/Ed
   Psych/Overview.html

University of Kansas
School of Education
Department of Teaching and Leadership
MS in Higher Education
Lawrence, KS 66045
Phone: (785) 864-4437
Fax: (785) 864-5207
http://www.soe.ku.edu/depts/tl/graduate/
   gr_programs.html

KENTUCKY

University of Louisville
College of Education and Human
   Development
Department of Leadership, Foundations
   and Human Resource Education
MA in Higher Education
Louisville, KY 40292-0001
Phone: (502) 852-0617
Fax: (502) 852-4563
http://www.louisville.edu/edu/elfh/
   programs/mahe_online.html

Western Kentucky University
Department of Counseling
   and Student Affairs
M.A.E.. in Student Affairs
Tate Page Hall 409
1 Big Red Way
Bowling Green, KY 42101
Phone: (270) 745-4953
Fax: (270) 745-5445
http://edtech.cebs.wku.edu/~counsel/sa/
   sa-index.htm

LOUISIANA

Northwestern State University
College of Education
Master of Arts Program in Student
   Personnel Services
Natchitoches, LA 71497
Phone: (318) 357-6289
http://education.nsula.edu/sps/

MAINE

University of Maine
College of Education and Human
   Development

Program in Higher Education
Orono, ME 04469
Phone: (207) 581-3218
Fax: (207) 581-3232
http://www.umaine.edu/edhd/academic/
grad/highered.htm

MARYLAND

University of Maryland, College Park
University of Maryland, College Park
College of Education, Department of
Counseling and Personnel Services
Program in College Personnel
College Park, MD 20742
Phone: (301) 405-4190
Fax: (301) 314-9305
http://www.education.umd.edu/EDCP/CSP/

MASSACHUSETTS

Boston College
Lynch Graduate School of Education
Higher Education Program
Chestnut Hill, MA 02467-3800
Phone: (617) 552-4214
Fax: (617) 552-0812
http://www.bc.edu/schools/lsoe/highered/

Harvard University
Graduate School of Education
Higher Education Master's Program
13 Longfellow Hall
Appian Way
Cambridge, MA 02138
Phone: (617) 495-3414
Fax: (617) 496-3577
http://www.gse.harvard.edu/~highered/

Northeastern University
Bouvé College of Health Sciences
Department of Counseling and Applied
Educational Psychology
MS in College Student Development and
Counseling
123 Behrakis Health Sciences Center
Boston, MA 02115
Phone: (617) 373-2708
Fax: (617) 373-4701
http://www.bouve.neu.edu/Graduate/
Health/counsel_csd.html

Springfield College
Department of Psychology &
Counseling
Programs in Student Personnel
Administration
263 Alden Street
Springfield, MA 01109-3797

Phone: (413) 748-3329
Fax: (413) 748-3854
http://www.spfldcol.edu/home.nsf/
academics/graduate

Suffolk University
College of Arts and Sciences
Department of Education and Human
Services
M.Ed. in Administration of Higher
Education
41 Temple Street
Boston, MA 02114
Phone: (617) 573-8261
Fax: (617) 305-1743
http://www.suffolk.edu/cas/ehs/grad_
AdminEducation.html

University of Massachusetts–Amherst
School of Education
Department of Educational Policy,
Research and Administration
Program in Higher Education
Amherst, MA 01003
Phone: (413) 545-4184
http://www.umass.edu/education/
departments/main_epra.htm

MICHIGAN

Eastern Michigan University
College of Education
Department of Leadership and
Counseling
Programs in Higher Education and
Student Affairs
Suite 304 John W. Porter Building
Ypsilanti, MI 48197
Phone: (734) 487-0255
Fax: (734) 487-4608
http://www.emich.edu/coe/leadcons/index.
html

Grand Valley State University
School of Education
College Student Affairs Leadership
Allendale, MI 49401-9403
Phone: (616) 331-2025
Fax: (616) 331-2000
http://www.gvsu.edu/csal/

Michigan State University
College of Education
Department of Higher, Adult
and Lifelong Education
134 Erickson Hall
East Lansing, MI 48824
Phone: (517) 353-9680
Fax: (517) 432-2718

http://ed-web3.educ.msu.edu/ead/HALE/
Halehome.htm

University of Michigan
School of Education
Higher Education Graduate Programs
610 East University Avenue
Ann Arbor, MI 48109-1259
Phone: (734) 764-7563
http://www.soe.umich.edu/highereducation/
index.html

Western Michigan University
School of Education
Department of Counselor Education and
Counseling Psychology
Programs in Student Affairs in Higher
Education
3102 Sangren Hall
Kalamazoo, MI 49008-5102
Phone: (269) 387-5100
http://www.wmich.edu/cecp/programs/

MINNESOTA

Minnesota State University–Mankato
College of Education
Department of Counseling & Student
Personnel
107 Armstrong Hall
Mankato, MN 56001
Phone: (507) 389-2423
Fax: (507) 389-5074
http://www.coled.mnsu.edu/departments/
csp/

**Minnesota State
University–Moorhead**
College of Education and Human
Services
Department of Counseling and Student
Affairs
Moorhead, MN 56563
Phone: (218) 577-2297
http://www.mnstate.edu/cnsa/

University of St. Thomas
School of Education: Leadership, Policy
& Administration
1000 LaSalle Avenue, MOH 217
Minneapolis, MN 55403
Phone: (651) 962-4550; (800) 328-6819
Fax: (651) 962-4169
http://www.stthomas.edu/education/elanda/
index.html#anchor2

MISSISSIPPI

Mississippi State University
College of Education
Doctoral Program in Community College
  Leadership
Department of Instructional Systems,
  Leadership, and Workforce
  Development
P.O. Box 9730
Mississippi State, MS 39762
Phone: (662) 325-3041
http://www.msstate.edu/dept/grad/

University of Mississippi
School of Education
Graduate Program in Higher Education
  Leadership
SOE #200
University, MS 38677
Phone: (662) 915-7070
Fax: (662) 915-7230
http://www.olemiss.edu/depts/educ_
  school2/highed/main.htm

University of Southern Mississippi
College of Education & Psychology
Department of Education Leadership
  and Research and Department
  of Psychology
Programs in Higher Education and
  College Student Personnel
P.O. Box 5023
Hattiesburg, MS 39406-5023
Phone: (601) 266-4568
http://www.usm.edu/colleges/cep/

MISSOURI

Central Missouri State University
College of Education
  and Human Services
Department of Educational Leadership
  and Human Development
Program in School Administration &
  Higher Education
Warrensburg, MO 64093
Phone: (660) 543-4272
http://www.cmsu.edu/elhd/SchoolAdmin/
  index.htm

Southeast Missouri State University
Department of Educational
  Administration and Counseling
Master of Arts in Higher Education
  Administration
Graduate Studies, Memorial Hall 106
One University Plaza MS 4400
Cape Girardeau, MO 63701

Phone: (573) 651-2430
http://www.semo.edu/gradschool/
  academics/ study.htm

St. Louis University
College of Public Service
Department of Educational Leadership
  and Higher Education
Master of Arts in College Student
  Personnel
McGannon Hall
3750 Lindell Boulevard
St. Louis, MO 63108-3342
Phone: (314) 977-2508
Fax: (314) 977-3214
http://www.slu.edu/colleges/cops/elhe/ma_
  stud_personnel.pdf

University of Missouri-Columbia
College of Education, Department
  of Educational Leadership
  and Policy Analysis
M.A. Program with emphasis in Higher
  Education
202 Hill Hall
Columbia, MO 65211-2190
Phone: (573) 882-8221
Fax: (573) 884-5714
http://elpa.coe.missouri.edu/

NEBRASKA

University of Nebraska at Lincoln
College of Education and Human
  Sciences
Graduate Programs in Educational
  Administration
Lincoln, NE 68588
Phone: (402) 472-0889
http://cehsdept.unl.edu/index.php?Page=
  1010

University of Nebraska at Omaha
College of Education, Department of
  Counseling
M.S. with Concentration in Student
  Affairs in Higher Education
Kayser Hall 421, 60th and Dodge Street
Omaha, NE 68182
Phone: (402) 554-2727
Fax: (402) 554-3684
http://www.unocoe.unomaha.edu/couns/
  programs.htm

NEVADA

University of Nevada, Las Vegas
Department of Educational Leadership
College of Education

Programs in Student Personnel and
  Higher Education Leadership
4505 Maryland Parkway
Las Vegas, NV 89154-3002
Phone: (702) 895-1432
Fax: (702) 895-3492
http://education.unlv.edu/Educational_
  Leadership/higheredadmin/
  higheredadmin.htm

University of Nevada, Reno
College of Education
Department of Counseling and
  Educational Psychology
Program in College Student Development
Mail Stop 281
Reno, NV 89577-0213
Phone: (775) 784-6637 ext. 2067
Fax: (775) 784-1990
http://www.unr.edu/colleges/educ/cep/
  cepindex.html

NEW JERSEY

Seton Hall University
College of Education and Human
  Services
Department of Education Leadership,
  Management, and Policy
Programs in College Student Personnel
  Administration and Higher Education
400 South Orange Avenue
South Orange, NJ 07079
Phone: (973) 761-9397
Fax: (973) 761-7642
http://education.shu.edu/academicprograms/
  edadmin/index.html

NEW YORK

Canisius College
College of Education and Human Services
Program in College Student Personnel
  Administration
2001 Main Street
Buffalo, NY 14208
Phone: (716) 888-2760
Fax: (716) 888-3299
http://www.canisius.edu/cspa/

Columbia University
Teacher's College
Program in Higher and Postsecondary
  Education
525 West 120th Street
New York, NY 10027
Phone: (212) 678-3750
Fax: (212) 678-3743

http://www.tc.columbia.edu/academic/
o&ldept/highered

New York University
Steinhardt School of Education
Department of Administration,
Leadership, & Technology
M.A. in Student Affairs; Ph.D. in Higher
Education
239 Greene Street, Suite 300
New York, NY 10003
Phone: (212) 998-5520
Fax: (212) 995-4041
http://www.nyu.edu/education/alt/highered/

State University of New York at Buffalo
Graduate School of Education
Program in Higher Education
Administration
Office of Graduate Admissions
366 Baldy Hall
P.O. Box 601000
Buffalo, NY 14260
Phone: (716) 645-2110
Fax: (716) 645-7937
http://www.gse.buffalo.edu/dc/eoap/he.htm

Syracuse University
School of Education
Higher Education Program
350 Huntington Hall
Syracuse, NY 13244-2340
Phone: (315) 443-4763
Fax: (315) 443-9218
http://soeweb.syr.edu/HigherEd/
HIGHEREDU.HTML

NORTH CAROLINA

Appalachian State University
Reich College of Education
The Department of Human Development
and Psychological Counseling
Master of Arts in College Student
Development
730 Rivers Street
Boone, NC 28608
Phone: (828) 262-2232
http://www.hpc.appstate.edu/Programs.htm

North Carolina State University
College of Education
Department of Adult and Community
College Education
Program in Student Affairs in Higher
Education
310-H Poe Hall, Campus Box 7801
Raleigh, NC 27695-7801
Phone: (919) 515-6240

http://www2.ncsu.edu:8010/ncsu/ced/acce/
grad.html

Western Carolina University
College of Education and Allied
Professions
Department of Educational Leadership
and Foundations
Program in College Student Personnel
460 HFR
Cullowhee, NC 28723
Phone: (828) 227-7147
Fax: (828) 227-7036
http://www.wcu.edu/rgs

OHIO

Bowling Green State University
College of Education and Human
Development
Division of Higher Education and Student
Affairs
M.A. in College Student Personnel, Ph.D.
in Higher Education Administration
330 Education Building
Bowling Green, OH 43403-0249
Phone: (419) 372-7305
Fax: (419) 372-9382
http://www.bgsu.edu/colleges/edhd/LPS/
HESA/csp
http://www.bgsu.edu/colleges/edhd/LPS/
HESA/hied

Kent State University
College and Graduate School
of Education
Department of Teaching, Leadership, and
Curriculum Studies – Educational
Administration
Higher Education Administration &
Student Personnel Programs
Kent, OH 44242
Phone: (330) 672-2580; (330) 672-0654
Fax: (330) 672-3246
http://hied.educ.kent.edu/

Miami University
College of Education
and Allied Professions
Department of Educational Leadership
Program in College Student Personnel
350 McGuffey Hall
Oxford, OH 45056
Phone: (513) 529-6851
Fax: (513) 529-1729
http://www.muohio.edu/csp/

Ohio State University
College of Education

Department of Educational
Policy & Leadership
Program in Higher Education and Student
Affairs
301 Ramseyer Hall
29 West Woodruff Avenue
Columbus, OH 43210
Phone: (614) 292-4322
Fax: (614) 292-7020
http://www.coe.ohio-state.edu/edpl/eahe/
hesa/spa/spa~1.htm

Ohio University
College of Education
Department of Counseling and Higher
Education
Program in College Student Personnel
McCracken Hall
Athens, OH 45701
Phone: (740) 593-4454; (740) 593-0847
Fax: (740) 593-0477
http://www.ohiou.edu/che/index.html
http://www.ohiou.edu/che/csp/
csp-welcome.html

University of Akron
College of Education
Department of Educational Foundations
and Leadership
Program in Higher Education
Administration
Zook Hall
Akron, OH 44325-4201
Phone: (330) 972-7680
Fax: (330) 972-5636
http://www2.uakron.edu/higher-ed/

University of Dayton
School of Education and Allied Professions
Department of Counselor Education and
Human Services
M.Ed. in Higher Education
Administration,
M.Ed. in College Student Personnel
300 College Park
Dayton, OH 45469-1300
Phone: (937) 229-3644
Fax: (937) 229-1055
http://soeap.udayton.edu/academic/edc/

University of Toledo
College of Education
Program in Higher Education
Snyder Memorial, Mail Stop 106
Toledo, OH 43609
Phone: (419) 530-2695
Fax: (419) 530-4912
http://education.utoledo.edu/ed_leadership/
higher_ed/

Wright State University
College of Education and Human Services
Department of Educational Leadership
Program in Student Affairs and Higher
    Education
377 Allyn Hall
Wright State University
Dayton, OH 45435
Phone: (937) 775-3286
Fax: (937) 775-2099
http://www.wright.edu/cehs/sa/

Youngstown State University
Counseling Department
Program in Higher Education Student
    Services
One University Plaza
Youngstown, OH 44555
Phone: (330) 941-3257
http://www.ysu.edu/counseling/
    HigherEdWeb/highered.htm

OREGON

Oregon State University
School of Education
Department of Adult and Higher
    Education
Program in College Student Services
    Administration
Corvallis, OR 97331
Phone: (541) 737-4317
Fax: (541) 737-8971
http://oregonstate.edu/education/programs/
    cssa.html

PENNSYLVANIA

Bucknell University
College of Arts and Sciences
Department of Education
Master of Science in Education, College
    Student Personnel
Lewisburg, PA 17837
Phone: (570) 577-1324
Fax: (570) 577-3184
http://www.departments.bucknell.edu/
    education/

Edinboro University of Pennsylvania
School of Education
Department of Professional Studies
Program in Student Personnel Services
Centennial Hall Room 311
Edinboro, PA 16444
Phone: (814) 732-2260
Fax: (814) 732-2233
http://www.edinboro.edu/cwis/profstudies/
    CounMain.html

Indiana University of Pennsylvania
College of Education
Program in Student Affairs in Higher
    Education
206 Stouffer Hall
Indiana, PA 15705
Phone: (724) 357-1251
Fax: (724) 357-7821
http://www.iup.edu/sahe

Kutztown University
College of Graduate Studies
Department of Counseling and Human
    Services
Program in Student
    Affairs/Administration and Student
    Affairs/College Counseling
Kutztown, PA 19530-0730
Phone: (610) 683-4223
Fax: (610) 683-1585
http://www.kutztown.edu/academics/
    graduate/programs/index.shtml

Pennsylvania State University
College of Education
Department of Counselor Education,
    Counseling Psychology, and
    Rehabilitation Services
Program in Student Affairs
327 CEDAR Building
University Park, PA 16802
Phone: (814) 863-2410
Fax: (814) 863-7750
http://www.ed.psu.edu/cned/csp/index.asp

Shippensburg University
College of Education & Human Services
Department of Counseling – CEC
Program in College Student Personnel
1871 Old Main Drive
Shippensburg, PA 17257
Phone: (717) 477-1676
Fax: (717) 477-4056
http://ark.ship.edu

Slippery Rock University
College of Education
Department of Counseling and
    Educational Psychology
Program in College Student Personnel
Slippery Rock, PA 16057
Phone: (724) 738-2276
Fax: (724) 738-4859
http://www.sru.edu/pages/4974.asp

University of Pennsylvania
Graduate School of Education
Program in Higher Education
    Management

3700 Walnut Street
Philadelphia, PA 19104-6216
Phone: (215) 898-2444
http://www.gse.upenn.edu/degrees_
    programs/hed_masters.php

RHODE ISLAND

University of Rhode Island
Department of Human Development
    and Family Studies
Master's in College Student Personnel
Transition Center, Lower College Road
Kingston, RI 02881
Phone: (401) 874-2150
Fax: (401) 874-4020
http://www.uri.edu/hss/csp/

SOUTH CAROLINA

Clemson University
College of Health, Education, and Human
    Development, School of Education
Department of Counselor Education and
    Educational Leadership
M.Ed.-Counselor Education, Student
    Affairs, Ph.D.-Educational Leadership
330 Tillman Hall Box 340710
Clemson, SC 29634-0710
Phone: (864) 656-0328; (864) 656-3484
Fax: (864) 656-1322
http://www.hehd.clemson.edu/schoolofed/
    index.html

University of South Carolina
College of Education
Department of Educational Leadership &
    Policies
M.Ed. in Higher Education and Student
    Affairs; Ph.D. in Higher Education
    Administration
Wardlaw College, Suite 310
Columbia, SC 29208
Phone: (803) 777-5240
Fax: (803) 777-3090
http://www.ed.sc.edu/edlp/hesa.asp

SOUTH DAKOTA

South Dakota State University
College of Education and Counseling
Educational Leadership Department
Adult and Higher Education
    Administration Program
Brookings, SD 57007
Phone: (800) 952-3541
http://learn.sdstate.edu/edgrad/ahedad.
    html

TENNESSEE

University of Memphis
College of Education
Programs in Higher and Adult Education
    and Student Personnel Counseling
Ball Hall 100
Memphis, TN 38152
Phone: (901) 678-2841
Fax: (901) 678-5114
http://coe.memphis.edu/

University of Tennessee, Knoxville
Department of Educational
    Administration and Policy Studies
College of Education, Health, and Human
    Sciences
Master of Science in College Student
    Personnel
1126 Volunteer Boulevard
A325 Claxton Complex
Knoxville, TN 37996-3430
Phone: (865) 974-2216
Fax: (865) 974-6146
http://web.utk.edu/~eaps;
    http://web.utk.edu/~collsp/

TEXAS

Baylor University
School of Education, Department of
    Educational Administration
Master of Science in Education in Student
    Services Administration
Waco, TX 76798
Phone: (254) 710-7912
Fax: (254) 710-2213
http://www.baylor.edu/soe/ed_admin/

Texas A & M University
College of Education
Department of Educational
    Administration and Human Resource
    Development
Master's Program in Student Affairs
    Administration in Higher Education
511 Harrington Tower
4226 TAMU
College Station, TX 77843-4226
Phone: (979) 845-2716
Fax: (979) 862-4347
http://www.coe.tamu.edu/~saahe/;
    http://coe.tamu.edu:81/eahr/programs/
    hied.php

Texas State University – San Marcos
College of Education
Department of Educational Administration
    and Psychological Services

Counseling and Guidance – Student
    Affairs Emphasis
601 University Drive
San Marcos, TX 78666
Phone: (512) 245-2152
Fax: (512) 245-7979
http://www.vpsa.txstate.edu/Graduate/
    index.htm

Texas Tech University
College of Education
Department of Educational Psychology
    and Leadership
Program in Higher Education
P.O. Box 41071 COE
Lubbock, TX 79409-1071
Phone: (806) 742-1997 x266
Fax: (806) 742-2179
http://www.educ.ttu.edu/edhe

University of North Texas
College of Education
Department of Counseling, Development,
    and Higher Education
Program in Higher Education
University of North Texas
P.O. Box 310829
Denton, TX 76203-0829
Phone: (940) 565-2910
http://www.unt.edu/highered/

UTAH

University of Utah
College of Education, Department of
    Educational Leadership and Policy
Program in Educational Leadership and
    Policy/Higher Education Emphasis
1705 Campus Center Drive, Room 339
Salt Lake City, UT 84112-9254
Phone: (801) 581-6714
Fax: (801) 581-6756
http://www.ed.utah.edu/elp/

VERMONT

University of Vermont
College of Education and Social Services
Higher Education and Student Affairs
    Program
Mann Hall
208 Colchester Avenue
Burlington, VT 05405
Phone: (802) 656-2030
Fax: (802) 656-3173
http://www.uvm.edu/~uvmhesa;
    http://www.uvm.edu/~cess/edlps.html

VIRGINIA

College of William and Mary
School of Education
Department of Educational Policy,
    Planning and Leadership
Programs in Higher Education
    Administration
P.O. Box 8795
Williamsburg, VA 23187
Phone: (757) 221-2317
Fax: (757) 221-2293
http://www.wm.edu/education/programs/
    eppl/index.php

James Madison University
College of Integrated Science and
    Technology
Department of Graduate Psychology
M.Ed. in College Student Personnel
    Administration
MSC 2401
Harrisonburg, VA 22807
Phone: (540) 568-6275
Fax: (540) 568-6280
http://www.jmu.edu/cspa

Old Dominion University
Darden College of Education
Department of Educational Leadership
    and Counseling
M.S Ed in Higher Education, Ed.S. in
    Higher Education, Ph.D. in
    Community College
Leadership, Fall 2004: Ph.D. in Education
    with a Higher Education Specialty
    (pending approval)
110 Education Building
Norfolk, VA 23529
Phone: (757) 683-3702
Fax: (757) 683-5756
M.S.Ed.: http://www.odu.edu/highered
Ed.S.: http://web.odu.edu/webroot/orgs/
    Educ/ELC/elc.nsf/pages/edshighered
Ph.D.: http://www.odu.edu/webroot/orgs/
    educ/elc/elc.nsf/pages/ccleadership

Radford University
College of Education and Human
    Development
Department of Counselor Education
Program in College Counseling and
    Student Affairs
P. O. Box 6994
Radford, VA 24142
Phone: (540) 831-5214
http://www.radford.edu/~edcs-web/

University of Virginia
Curry School of Education

Programs in Higher Education and
Counselor Education – Student Affairs
P.O. Box 400261
Charlottesville, VA 22904-4261
Phone: (434) 924-3334
Fax: (434) 924-0747
http://curry.edschool.virginia.edu/
academics/

**Virginia Polytechnic Institute & State
University**
College of Liberal Arts and Human
Sciences
Department of Educational Leadership
and Policy Studies
Program in Higher Education and Student
Affairs
308 East Eggleston Hall (0302)
Blacksburg, VA 24061
Phone: (540) 231-5106
Fax: (540) 231-7845

http://filebox.vt.edu/chre/elps/hesa

WASHINGTON

Seattle University
School of Education/Student
Development Administration Program
Department of Professional Studies
M.A., M.Ed. in Student Development
Administration
900 Broadway
Seattle, WA 98122-4340
Phone: (206) 296-6061; (206) 296-6170
Fax: (206) 296-2053
http://www.seattleu.edu/soe/sda/

Western Washington State University
College of Education
M.Ed. in Student Affairs Administration
in Higher Education

Department of Educational Leadership,
MS 9087
516 High Street
Bellingham, WA 98225-9087
Phone: (360) 650-6552
Fax: (360) 650-7516
http://www.wce.wwu.edu/Depts/SPA/

WISCONSIN

University of Wisconsin–La Crosse
College of Health, Physical Education,
Recreation and Teacher Education
Program in College Student Development
and Administration
1741 State Street, 212 Cartwright
La Crosse, WI 54601
Phone: (608) 785-8889
Fax: (608) 785-6575
http://www.uwlax.edu/csda

H. INTERNATIONAL AFFAIRS

Graduate programs in international affairs offer a multidisciplinary education combining courses in economics, policy, and history in order to prepare professionals for work in the international community. The Association of Professional Schools of International Affairs (APSIA) maintains on their Web site a list of schools that offer graduate programs in international affairs, including international relations and international policy. Check their Web site for updated listings at http://www.apsia.org.

ARIZONA

**Thunderbird, The American Graduate
School of International Management**
15249 North 59th Avenue
Glendale, AZ 85306
Phone: (602) 978-7784
Fax: (602) 547-1356
http://www.t-bird.edu

CALIFORNIA

**Monterey Institute on International
Studies**
Graduate School of International Policy
Studies
425 Van Buren Street
Monterey, CA 93940
Phone: (831) 647-6696
Fax: (831) 647-6650
http://www.miis.edu/gsips-about-
dean.html

University of California, San Diego
Graduate School of International
Relations and Pacific Studies (IR/PS)
9500 Gilman Drive, 0520

La Jolla, CA 92093-0520
Phone: (858) 534-5914
Fax: (858) 534-3939
http://www.irps.ucsd.edu

University of Southern California
School of International Relations
Von KleinSmid Center
University Park
Los Angeles, CA 90089-0043
Phone: (213) 740-2136
Fax: (213) 742-0281
E-mail: sir@usc.edu
http://www.usc.edu/dept/LAS/ir

COLORADO

University of Denver
Graduate School of International Studies
Ben Cherrington Hall, 325
South Gaylord Street
Denver, CO 80208-0280
Phone: (303) 871-2544
Fax: (303) 871-3585
E-mail: gsisadm@du.edu
http://www.du.edu/gsis

CONNECTICUT

Yale University
Yale Center for International
and Area Studies
Henry R. Luce Hall
34 Hillhouse Avenue
New Haven, CT 06520
Phone: (203) 432-3410
Fax: (203) 432-9383
E-mail: ycias@yale.edu
http://www.yale.edu/ycias

DISTRICT OF COLUMBIA

American University
School of International Service
4400 Massachusetts Avenue, NW
Washington, DC 20016-8071
Phone: (202) 885-1600
Fax: (202) 885-1027
E-mail: sisgrad@american.edu
http://www.american.edu/sis

Georgetown University
Edmund A. Walsh School of Foreign
Service

301 InterCultural Center
37th & O Streets, NW
Washington, DC 20057
Phone: (202) 687-5696
Fax: (202) 687-1431
E-mail: gradmail@georgetown.edu
http://www.georgetown.edu/sfs

George Washington University
1957 E Street, NW
Elliott School of International Affairs
Washington, DC 20052
Phone: (202) 994-6240
Fax: (202) 994-0335
E-mail: elliott@gwu.edu
http://www.gwu.edu/~elliott

Howard University
Ralph J. Bunche International Affairs
    Center
4th and College Streets, NW
Washington, DC 20059
Phone: (202) 806-6800
Fax: (202) 462-4053
http://www.howard.edu

**National Foreign Affairs Training
    Center**
Foreign Service Institute
Department of State
Washington, DC 20522-4201
Phone: (703) 302-6703
Fax: (703) 302-7461
http://www.state.gov/m/fsi

FLORIDA

Florida International University
Department of International Relations
DM 432, University Park Campus
Miami, FL 33199
Phone: (305) 348-2556
Fax: (305) 348-2197
http://www.fiu.edu/~intlrel

University of Miami
Department of International and
    Comparative Studies
Coral Gables, FL 33124-2211
Phone: (305) 284-4303
Fax: (305) 284-1596
http://www.miami.edu/MAIA/

ILLINOIS

DePaul University
International Studies Program
990 West Fullerton Avenue
Chicago, IL 60614

Phone: (773) 325-7877
Fax: (773) 325-7556
http://www.depaul.edu/~intstuds

University of Chicago
Committee on International Relations
5828 South University Avenue, Room
    301
Chicago, IL 60637
Phone: (773) 702-8054
Fax: (773) 702-5140
http://www.cir.uchicago.edu

MARYLAND

Johns Hopkins University
Paul H. Nitze School of Advanced
    International Studies
1740 Massachusetts Avenue, NW
Washington, DC 20036
Phone: (202) 663-5600
Fax: (202) 663-5621
http://www.sais-jhu.edu

University of Maryland
School of Public Policy
2101 Van Munching Hall
College Park, MD 20742-1811
Phone: (301) 405-6331
Fax: (301) 403-4675
E-mail: puaf-
    admissions@umail.umd.edu
http://www.puaf.umd.edu

MASSACHUSSETTS

Harvard University
John F. Kennedy School of Government
79 John F. Kennedy Street
Cambridge, MA 02138
Phone: (617) 495-1100
Fax: (617) 496-9118
http://www.ksg.harvard.edu

Tufts University
The Fletcher School of Law and
    Diplomacy
160 Packard Avenue
Medford, MA 02155
Phone: (617) 627-3700
Fax: (617) 627-3712
http://www.fletcher.tufts.edu

MICHIGAN

University of Michigan
Gerald R. Ford School of Public Policy
440 Lorch Hall
Ann Arbor, MI 48109-1220

Phone: (734) 764-3490
Fax: (734) 763-9181
http://www.spp.umich.edu

MINNESOTA

University of Minnesota
Hubert H. Humphrey Institute
    of Public Affairs
301 19th Avenue South
Minneapolis, MN 55455
Phone: (612) 626-8910
Fax: (612) 625-3513
http://www.hhh.umn.edu

NEW JERSEY

Princeton University
Woodrow Wilson School of Public
    and International Affairs
Robertson Hall
Princeton, NJ 08544-1013
Phone: (609) 258-4800
Fax: (609) 258-1418
http://www.wws.princeton.edu

**Rutgers, The State University
    of New Jersey**
Center for Global Change and
    Governance
123 Washington Street, Suite 510
Newark, NJ 07102-3094
Phone: (973) 353-5585
Fax: (973) 353-5074
http://www.cgcg.rutgers.edu

Seton Hall University
John C. Whitehead School of Diplomacy
    and International Relations
400 South Orange Avenue
South Orange, NJ 07079
Phone: (973) 275-2514
Fax: (973) 275-2519
http://www.diplomacy.shu.edu

NEW YORK

Columbia University
School of International and Public Affairs
420 West 118th Street
New York, NY 10027
Phone: (212) 854-6216
Fax: (212) 864-4847
E-mail: sipa_admission@columbia.edu
http://www.sipa.columbia.edu

Fordham University
Graduate Program in International
    Political Economy and Development

Dealy Hall, Room E-511
441 East Fordham Road
Bronx, NY 10458
Phone: (718) 817-4064
Fax: (718) 817-4565
E-mail: iped@fordham.edu
http://www.fordham.edu/iped

Syracuse University
The Maxwell School's International
   Relations Degree Program
200 Eggers Hall
Syracuse, NY 13244-1090
Phone: (315) 443-2252
Fax: (315) 443-3385
http://www.maxwell.syr.edu

NORTH CAROLINA

Duke University
Terry Sanford Institute of Public Policy
P.O. Box 90239
Durham, NC 27708-0239

Phone: (919) 613-7401
Fax: (919) 613-7403
E-mail: ppsinfo@duke.edu
http://www.pubpol.duke.edu

PENNSYLVANIA

University of Pittsburgh
Graduate School of Public and
   International Affairs
3G38 Posvar Hall
Pittsburgh, PA 15260
Phone: (412) 648-7600
Fax: (412) 648-2605
E-mail: gspia@pitt.edu
http://www.gspia.pitt.edu

VIRGINIA

George Mason University
International Commerce and Policy
   Program
3401 North Fairfax Drive, Room 201

Arlington, VA 22201
Phone: (703) 993-8200
Fax: (703) 993-8215
http://www.gmu.edu/departments/t-icp

WASHINGTON

University of Washington
Henry M. Jackson School of International
   Studies
P.O. Box 353650
Seattle, WA 98195-3650
Phone: (206) 543-4370
Fax: (206) 685-0668
E-mail: jsis@u.washington.edu
http://www.isis.artsci.washington.edu

APPENDIX II
PROFESSIONAL ASSOCIATIONS

A. NONPROFIT MANAGEMENT

GENERAL

Alliance for Nonprofit Management
1899 L Street, NW
6th Floor
Washington, DC 20036
Phone: (202) 955-8406
Fax: (202) 721-0086
http://www.allianceonline.org/

American Society of Association Executives
1575 I Street, NW
Washington, DC 20005
Phone: (202) 626-2723
http://www.asaenet.org/

National Council of Nonprofit Associations
1030 15th Street, NW
Suite 870
Washington, DC 20005-1525
Phone: (202) 962-0322
Fax: (202) 962-0321
http://www.ncna.org/

Society for Nonprofit Organizations
5820 Canton Center Road
Suite 165
Canton, MI 48187
Phone: (734) 451-3582
Fax: (734) 451-5935
http://danenet.wicip.org/snpo/

FUND-RAISING AND DEVELOPMENT

American Association of Fundraising Counsel
4700 West Lake Avenue
Glenview, IL 60025
Phone: (847) 375-4709
Fax: (866) 263-2491
http://www.aafrc.org

The American Association of Grant Professionals (AAGP)
http://www.grantprofessionals.org
E-mail: info@grantprofessionals.org

Association of Fundraisers and Direct Sellers
5775-G Peachtree-Dunwoody Road
Atlanta, GA 30342
Phone: (404) 252-3663
Fax: (404) 252-0774
http://www.afrds.org

Association of Fundraising Professionals
1101 King Street
Suite 700
Alexandria, VA 22314
Phone: (703) 684-0410
Fax: (703) 684-0540
http://www.afpnet.org/

Association of Professional Researchers for Advancement
40 Shuman Boulevard
Suite 325
Naperville, IL 60563
Phone: (630) 717-8160
Fax: (630) 717-8354
http://www.aprahome.org/

Women in Development, New York, Inc.
211 West 56th Street
Suite 7J
New York, NY 10019
Phone: (212) 265-7650
http://www.widny.org/

SPECIAL EVENTS

International Association for Exhibition Management
Physical Address:
8111 LBJ Freeway
Suite 750
Dallas, TX 75251-1313
Mailing Address:
P.O. Box 802425
Dallas, TX 75380-2425
Phone: (972) 458-8002
Fax: (972) 458-8119
http://www.iaem.org/

International Special Events Society (ISES)
401 North Michigan Avenue
Chicago, IL 60611-4267
Phone: (312) 321-6853; (800) 688-ISES (4737)
http://www.ises.com/

MARKETING AND COMMUNICATIONS

American Management Association
1601 Broadway
New York, NY 10019
Phone: (212) 586-8100
Fax: (212) 903-8168
http://www.amanet.org

American Marketing Association
311 South Wacker Drive
Suite 5800
Chicago, IL 60606
Phone: (312) 542-9000
Fax: (312) 542-9001
http://www.ama.org

International Association of Business Communicators
One Hallidie Plaza
Suite 600
San Francisco, CA 94102
Phone: (415) 544-4700; (800) 776-4222
Fax: (415) 544-4747
http://www.iabc.com

Newsletters and Electronic Publishers Association
1501 Wilson Boulevard
Suite 509
Arlington, VA 22209
Phone: (703) 527-2333; (800) 356-9302
Fax: (703) 841-0629
http://www.newsletters.org

Public Affairs Council
2033 K Street, NW
Suite 700
Washington, DC 20006

Phone: (202) 872-1790
Fax: (202) 835-8343
http://www.pac.org

Public Relations Society of America
33 Irving Place
New York, NY 10003-2376
Phone: (212) 995-2230
Fax: (212) 995-0757
http://www.prsa.org/

Sales and Marketing Executives International
5500 Interstate North Parkway #545
Atlanta, GA 30328
Phone: (770) 661-8500
Fax: (770) 661-8512
http://www.smei.org

Small Publishers, Artists & Writers Network
PMB 123
323 East Matilija Street
Suite 110
Ojai, CA 93023
Phone: (818) 886-4281
Fax: (818) 886-3320
http://www.spawn.org

VOLUNTEER MANAGEMENT

Association for Volunteer Administration
P.O. Box 32092
Richmond, VA 23294-2092
Phone: (804) 672-3353
Fax: (804) 672-3368
http://www.avaintl.org/

FINANCE

The American Institute of Certified Public Accountants
1211 Avenue of the Americas
New York, NY 10036
Phone: (212) 596-6200
Fax: (212) 596-6213
http://www.aicpa.org/index.htm

Association for Financial Professionals
7315 Wisconsin Avenue
Suite 600 West
Bethesda, MD 20814
Fax: (301) 907-2864
Phone: (301) 907-2862
http://www.afponline.org

Financial Management Association International
College of Business Administration
University of South Florida
Tampa, FL 33620-5500
Phone: (813) 974-2084
Fax: (813) 974-3318
http://www.fma.org

Institute of Management Accountants
10 Paragon Drive
Montvale, NJ 07645-1759
Phone: (800) 638-4427; (201) 573-9000
http://www.imanet.org/

National Association of State Auditors, Comptrollers, and Treasurers
2401 Regency Road
Suite 302
Lexington, KY 40503-2914
Phone: (859) 276-1147
Fax: (859) 278-0507
http://www.nasact.org/coalition.htm

RESEARCH

Association for Research on Nonprofit Organizations and Voluntary Action (ARNOVA)
550 West North Street
Suite 301
Indianapolis, IN 46202
Phone: (317) 684-2120
Fax: (317) 684-2128
http://www.arnova.org/

Association of Professional Researchers for Advancement
40 Shuman Boulevard
Suite 325
Naperville, IL 60563
Phone: (630) 717-8160
Fax: (630) 717-8354
http://www.aprahome.org/

ADMINISTRATIVE

International Association of Administrative Professionals
10502 Northwest Ambassador Drive
P.O. Box 20404
Kansas City, MO 64195-0404
Phone: (816) 891-6600
Fax: (816) 891-9118
http://www.iaap-hq.org

The National Association of Executive Secretaries and Administrative Assistants
900 South Washington Street
Suite G-13
Falls Church, VA 22046
Phone: (703) 237-8616
Fax: (703) 533-1153
http://www.naesaa.com/

INFORMATION TECHNOLOGY/COMPUTERS

The Internet Society
1775 Wiehle Avenue
Suite 102
Reston, VA 20190-5108
Phone: (703) 326-9880
Fax: (703) 326-9881
http://www.isoc.org/

The World Organization of Webmasters
9580 Oak Avenue Parkway
Suite 7-177
Folsom, CA 95630
Phone: (916) 989-2933
Fax: (916) 987-3022
http://www.joinwow.org

BOARD OF DIRECTORS

boardnetUSA
http://www.boardnetusa.org

BoardSource
1828 L Street, NW
Suite 900
Washington, DC 20036-6299
Phone: (202) 452-6262 or (800) 883-6262
Fax: (202) 452-6299
http://www.boardsource.org/

Management Assistance Program for Nonprofits (MAP)
2233 University Avenue West
Suite 360
St. Paul, MN 55114
Phone: (651) 647-1216
http://mapnp.nonprofitoffice.com/

B. BUSINESS, PROFESSIONAL, AND TRADE ASSOCIATIONS

GENERAL

The American Society of Association Executives (ASAE)
The ASAE Building
1575 I Street, NW
Washington, DC 20005-1103
Phone: (888) 950-2723, (202) 371-0940
Fax: (202) 371-8315
http://www.asaenet.org

LIBRARIANS

American Library Association
50 East Huron
Chicago, IL 60611
Phone: (800) 545-2433
http://www.ala.org

Association for Library and Information Science Education (ALISE)
1009 Commerce Park Drive
Suite 150
P.O. Box 4219
Oak Ridge, TN 37830

Phone: (865) 425-0155
Fax: (865) 481-0390
http://www.alise.org

Special Libraries Association
331 South Patrick Street
Alexandria, VA 22314-3501
Phone: (703) 647-4900
Fax: (703) 647-4901
http://www.sla.org

EDITORS

The Council of Editors of Learned Journals
http://www.celj.org/

The Council of Science Editors
c/o Drohan Management Group
12100 Sunset Hills Road
Suite 130
Reston, VA 20190
Phone: (703) 437-4377
Fax: (703) 435-4390
http://www.cbe.org/

Society for Technical Communication
901 North Stuart Street
Suite 904
Arlington, VA 22203
Phone: (703) 522-4114
http://www.stc.org/

Society of American Business Editors and Writers, Inc.
Missouri School of Journalism
134 Neff Annex
Columbia, MO 65211-1200
Phone: (573) 882-7862
Fax: (573) 884-1372
http://www.sabew.org/

Society of Professional Journalists
Eugene S. Pulliam National Journalism Center
3909 North Meridian Street
Indianapolis, IN 46208
Phone: (317) 927-8000
Fax: (317) 920-4789
http://www.spj.org/

C. FOUNDATIONS

Association of Small Foundations
4905 Del Ray Avenue
Suite 308
Bethesda, MD 20814
Phone: (301) 907-3337
Fax: (301) 907-0980
http://www.smallfoundations.org/

The Council on Foundations
1828 L Street, NW
Washington, DC 20036
Phone: (202) 466-6512
Fax: (202) 785-3926
http://www.cof.org

Emerging Practitioners in Philanthropy (EPIP)
666 West End Avenue
Suite 1B
New York, NY 10025
Phone: (212) 497-7544/7
Fax: (212) 472-0508
http://www.epip.org

The Foundation Center
79 Fifth Avenue
New York, NY 10003
Phone: (212) 620-4230
Fax: (212) 691-1828
http://fdncenter.org/

Grantmakers for Education
720 Southwest Washington Street
Suite 605
Portland, OR 97205
Phone: (503) 595-2100
Fax: (503) 595-2102
http://www.edfunders.com/

Grantmakers for Effective Organizations
1413 K Street, NW
2nd Floor
Washington, DC 20005
Phone: (202) 898-1840
Fax: (202) 898-0318
http://www.geofunders.org/

Grantmakers in Health
1100 Connecticut Avenue, NW
Suite 1200
Washington, DC 20036
Phone: (202) 452-8331
Fax: (202) 452.8340
http://www.gif.org

The Grant Managers Network
141 Homestead Avenue
Metairie, LA 70005

Phone: (504) 834-9656
http://www.gmnetwork.org/

National Center for Family Philanthropy
1818 N Street, NW
Suite 300
Washington, DC 20036
Phone: (202) 293-3424
Fax: (202) 293-3395
http://www.ncfp.org/

Regional Association of Grantmakers—New York office
(with chapters nationwide)
505 Eighth Avenue
Suite 1805
New York, NY 10018-6505
Phone: (212) 714-0699
Fax: (212) 239-2075
http://www.nyrag.org/

Women's Funding Network
1375 Sutter Street
Suite 406
San Francisco, CA 94109
Phone: (415) 441-0706
http://www.wfnet.org/

D. HEALTH AND SCIENCE

PUBLIC HEALTH, INCLUDING HEALTH EDUCATION AND EPIDEMIOLOGY

American Alliance for Health, Physical Education, Recreation & Dance
1900 Association Drive
Reston, VA 20191-1598
Phone: (703) 476-3400; (800) 213-7193
http://www.aahperd.org/

American College of Epidemiology
1500 Sunday Drive
Suite 102
Raleigh, NC 27607
Phone: (919) 861-5573
Fax: (919) 787-4916
http://www.acepidemiology.org/

American Epidemiology Society
http://www.acepidemiology.org/societies/
AES.shtml

American Public Health Association
800 I Street, NW
Washington, DC 20001
Phone: (202) 777-2742
Fax: (202) 777-2534
http://www.apha.org

Association of Schools of Public Health
1101 15th Street, NW
Suite 910
Washington, DC 20005
Phone: (202) 296-1099
Fax: (202) 296-1252
http://www.asph.org

National Commission for Health Education Credentialing, Inc.
1541 Alta Drive
Suite 303
Whitehall, PA 18052-5642
Phone: (484) 223-0770;
(888) 624-3248
Fax: (800) 813-0727
http://www.nchec.org

Society for Epidemiological Research (SER)
P.O. Box 990
Clearfield, UT 84098
Phone: (801) 525-0231
Fax: (801) 774-9211
http://www.epiresearch.org/

Society for Public Health Education
750 First Street, NE
Suite 910
Washington, DC 20002-4242
Phone: (202) 408-9804
Fax: (202) 408-9815
http://www.sophe.org

HOSPITAL/HEALTH CARE ADMINISTRATION

American College of Healthcare Administrators
300 North Lee Street
Suite 301
Alexandria, VA 22314
Phone: (703) 739-7900;
(888) 88-ACHCA
Fax: (703) 739-7901
http://www.achca.org/

American College of Healthcare Executives
One North Franklin
Suite 1700
Chicago, IL 60606-4425
Phone: (312) 424-2800
Fax: (312) 424-0023
http://www.ache.org/

The Association of University Programs in Health Administration (AUPHA)
2000 North 14th Street
Suite 780
Arlington, VA 22201
Phone: (703) 894-0940
Fax: (703) 894-0941
http://www.aupha.org

E. SOCIAL SERVICES AND RELIGIOUS ORGANIZATIONS

GENERAL

National Organization for Human Service Education
5601 Brodie Lane
Suite 620-215
Austin, TX 78745
Phone: (512) 692-9361
Fax: (512) 692-9445
http://www.nohse.org

REHABILITATION COUNSELING

American Rehabilitation Counseling Association (ARCA)
5999 Stevenson Avenue
Alexandria, VA 22304-3300
Phone: (800) 545-2223
Fax: (703) 823-0252
http://www.nchrtm.okstate.edu/arca/

International Association of Rehabilitation Professionals
3540 Soquel Avenue
Suite A
Santa Cruz, CA 95062
Phone: (831) 464-4892; (800) 240-9059
Fax: (831) 576-1417
http://www.rehabpro.org/

National Council on Rehabilitation Education
http://www.rehabeducators.org/

National Employment Counseling Association
5999 Stevenson Avenue
Alexandria, VA 22304
Phone: (800) 347-6647 x222
http://www.geocities.com/
employmentcounseling/neca.html

National Rehabilitation Counseling Association
8807 Sudley Road
Suite 102
Manassas, VA 22110-4719
Phone: (703) 361-2077
Fax: (703) 361-2489
http://nrca-net.org/

SOCIAL WORK

**The American Association
  of State Social Work Boards**
400 South Ridge Parkway
Suite B
Culpeper, VA 22701
Phone: (800) 225-6880; (540) 829-6880
Fax: (540) 829-0142
http://www.aswb.org

Council on Social Work Education
1600 Duke Street
Alexandria, VA 22314
Phone: (703) 683-8080
http://www.cswe.org

**National Association
  of Social Workers**
750 First Street, NE
Suite 700
Washington, DC 20002-4241
Phone: (800) 742-4089
http://www.naswdc.org/

PSYCHOLOGY

**American Board of Professional
  Psychology, Inc.**
300 Drayton Street
3rd Floor
Savannah, GA 31401
Phone: (912) 234-5477; (800) 255-7792
Fax: (912) 234-5120
http://www.abpp.org

American Psychological Association
750 1st Street, NE
Washington, DC 20002
Phone: (800) 374-2721; (202) 336-5500
http://www.apa.org

**Association of State and Provincial
  Psychology Boards**
P.O. Box 241245
Montgomery, AL 36124-1245
Phone: (334) 832-4580
Fax: (334) 269-6379
http://www.asppb.org

**National Association of School
  Psychologists**
4340 East West Highway
Suite 402
Bethesda, MD 20814
Phone: (301) 657-0270
Fax: (301) 657-0275
http://www.nasponline.org

HUMAN SERVICES

**American Public Human Services
  Association (APHSA)**
810 First Street, NE
Suite 500
Washington, DC 20002
Phone: (202) 682-0100
Fax: (202) 289-6555
http://www.aphsa.org/

**Council for Standards in Human
  Services Education**
Harrisburg Area Community College,
  Human Services Program
One HACC Drive
Harrisburg, PA 17110-2999
http://www.cshse.org

**National Organization for Human
  Services**
5601 Brodie Lane
Suite 620-215
Austin, TX 78745
Phone: (512) 692-9361
Fax: (512) 692-9445
http://www.nohse.org

RELIGIOUS ORGANIZATIONS

**African American Ministers
  Association**
http://www.covchurch.org

American Association of Rabbis
350 Fifth Avenue
Suite 3304
New York, NY 10118
Phone: (212) 244-3350

Catholic Online
P.O. Box 9686
Bakersfield, CA 93389
Phone: (661) 869-1000
Fax: (661) 869-0461
http://www.catholic.org

**Center for Applied Research
  in the Apostolate (CARA)**
Georgetown University
2300 Wisconsin Avenue, NW
Suite 400
Washington, DC 20007
Phone: (202) 687-8080
Fax: (202) 687-8083
http://cara.georgetown.edu

**Hebrew Union College-Jewish Institute
  of Religion**
One West 4th Street
New York, NY 10012
Phone: (212) 674-5300
Fax: (212) 388-1720
http://www.huc.edu

**Jewish Theological Seminary
  of America**
3080 Broadway
New York, NY 10027
Phone: (212) 678-8000
http://www.jtsa.edu

**National Conference of Diocesan
  Vocation Directors**
450 Hewett Street
Neillsville, WI 54456
Phone: (715) 254-0830
Fax: (715) 254-0831
http://www.ncdvd.org/

**The National Federation
  for Catholic Youth Ministry**
415 Michigan Avenue, NE
Suite 40
Washington, DC 20017-4503
Phone: (202) 636-3825
Fax: (202) 526-7544
http://www.nfcym.org

F. ADVOCACY AND COMMUNITY DEVELOPMENT

URBAN PLANNING

American Planning Association
122 South Michigan Avenue
Suite 1600
Chicago, IL 60603
Phone: (312) 431-9100
Fax: (312) 431-9985
and
1776 Massachusetts Avenue, NW
Washington, DC 20036-1904
Phone: (202) 872-0611
Fax: (202) 872-0643
http://www.planning.org

**Association of Collegiate Schools
    of Planning**
6311 Mallard Trace
Tallahassee, FL 32312
Phone: (850) 385-2054
Fax: (850) 385-2084
http://www.acsp.org/

Urban Land Institute
1025 Thomas Jefferson Street, NW
Suite 500 West
Washington, DC 20007
Phone: (202) 624-7000; (800) 321-5011
Fax: (202) 624-7140
http://www.uli.org

LOBBYING

**American Association of Political
    Consultants**
600 Pennsylvania Avenue, SE
Suite 330
Washington, DC 20003
Phone: (202) 544-9815
Fax: (202) 544-9816
http://www.theaapc.org/

American League of Lobbyists
P.O. Box 30005
Alexandria, VA 22310
Phone: (703) 960-3011
Fax: (703) 960-4070
http://www.alldc.org

Women in Government Relations
801 North Fairfax Street
Suite 211
Alexandria, VA 22314-1757
Phone: (703) 299-8546
Fax: (703) 299-9233
http://www.wgr.org/

GRASSROOTS ORGANIZING

The National Organizers Alliance
715 G Street, SE
Washington, DC 20003
Phone: (202) 543-6603
Fax: (202) 543-2462
http://www.noacentral.org/

COMMUNITY DEVELOPMENT

The Community Development Society
1123 North Water Street
Milwaukee, WI 53202
Phone: (414) 276-7106
Fax: (414) 276-7704
http://www.comm-dev.org

**InterAction (American Council
    for Voluntary International Action)**
1717 Massachusetts Avenue, NW
Suite 801
Washington, DC 20036
Phone: (202) 667-8227
Fax: (202) 667-8236
http://www.interaction.org

**National Association of Community
    Action Agencies**
1100 17th Street, NW
Suite 500
Washington, DC 20036
Phone: (202) 265-7546
Fax: (202) 265-8850
http://www.nacaa.org

**National Community Reinvestment
    Coalition**
733 15th Street, NW
Suite 540
Washington, DC 20005
Phone: (202) 628-8866
Fax: (202) 628-9800
http://www.ncrc.org

**National Congress for Community
    Economic Development (NCEED)**
1030 15th Street, NW
Suite 325
Washington, DC 20005
Phone: (202) 289-9020
Fax: (202) 289-7051
http://www.ncced.org

National Neighborhood Coalition
1875 Connecticut Avenue, NW
Suite 410
Washington, DC 20009
Phone: (202) 986-2096
Fax: (202) 986-1941
http://www.neighborhoodcoalition.org

YOUTH ORGANIZING

American Youth Policy Forum
1836 Jefferson Place, NW
Washington, DC 20036
Phone: (202) 775-9731
Fax: (202) 775-9733
http://www.aypf.org/index.htm

**America's Promise – The Alliance
    for Youth**
909 North Washington Street
Suite 400
Alexandria, VA 22314-1556
Phone: (703) 684-4500
Fax: (703) 535-3900
http://www.americaspromise.org

**The Center for Teen
    Empowerment, Inc.**
48 Rutland Street
Boston, MA 02118
Phone: (617) 536-4266
http://teenempowerment.org/

**National Assembly of Health and
    Human Services Organizations**
1319 F Street, NW
Suite 402
Washington, DC 20004
Phone: (202) 347-2080
Fax: (202) 393-4517
http://www.nassembly.org

ECONOMICS

**American Agricultural Economics
    Association**
415 South Duff Avenue
Suite C
Ames, IA 50010-6600
Phone: (515) 233-3202
Fax: (515) 233-3101
http://www.aaea.org

American Economics Association
2014 Broadway
Suite 305
Nashville, TN 37203

Phone: (615) 322-2595
Fax: (615) 343-7590
http://www.vanderbilt.edu/AEA/index.
  htm

**American Real Estate and Urban
  Economics Association**
P.O. Box 9958
Richmond, VA 23228
Phone: (866) 273-8321
Fax: (877) 273-8323
http://www.areuea.org/

**Association of Environmental and
  Resource Economists**
1616 P Street, NW
Room 510
Washington, DC 20036
Phone: (202) 328-5077
Fax: (202) 939-3460
http://www.aere.org/

**National Association for Business
  Economics**
1233 20th Street, NW
Suite 505

Washington, DC 20036
Phone: (202) 463-6223
Fax: (202) 463-6239
http://www.nabe.com/

The Society of Labor Economists
5807 South Woodlawn Avenue
Chicago, IL 60637
Phone: (773) 702-8607
Fax: (773) 834-2009
http://gsbwww.uchicago.edu/labor/sole.
  htm

G. ARTS AND CULTURE

GENERAL

Americans for the Arts
1000 Vermont Avenue, NW
6th Floor
Washington, DC 20005
Phone: (202) 371-2830
Fax: (202) 371-0424
http://www.artsusa.org/

Arts & Business Council Inc.
520 Eighth Avenue
3rd Floor
Suite 319
New York, NY 10018
Phone: (212) 279-5910
Fax: (212) 279-5915
http://www.artsandbusiness.org/

MUSEUMS

American Association of Museums
1575 Eye Street, NW
Suite 400
Washington, DC 20005
Phone: (202) 289-1818
Fax: (202) 289-6578
http://www.aam-us.org/

**Association of Science-Technology
  Centers Incorporated**
1025 Vermont Avenue, NW
Suite 500
Washington, DC 20005-3516
Phone: (202) 783-7200
Fax: (202) 783-7207
http://www.astc.org

**New York City Museum Educator's
  Roundtable (NYCMER)**
c/o Allison Day, Youth and Family
  Programs Manager
The Brooklyn Museum of Art
200 Eastern Parkway
Brooklyn, NY 11238
http://www.nycmer.org/

Regional Alliance for Preservation
http://www.rap-arcc.org/

**Standing Professional Committee
  on Education (EdCom)**
http://www.edcom.org/about/welcome.
  shtml

THEATER

Actors' Equity Association
165 West 46th Street
New York, NY 10036
Phone: (212) 869-8530
Fax: (212) 719-9815
http://www.actorsequity.org/home.html

**International Society for the
  Performing Arts Foundation**
17 Purdy Avenue
P.O. Box 909
Rye, NY 10580
Phone: (914) 921-1550
Fax: (914) 921-1593
http://www.ispa.org/

The League of Resident Theatres
1501 Broadway
Suite 2401
New York, NY 10036
Phone: (212) 944-1501, ext. 19
Fax (212) 768-0785
http://www.lort.org/

**Society of Stage Directors and
  Choreographers**
1501 Broadway
Suite 1701
New York, NY 10036
Phone: (212) 391-1070
Fax: (212) 302-6195
http://www.ssdc.org/

Theatre Communications Group
520 Eighth Avenue
24th Floor
New York, NY 10018-4156
Phone: (212) 609-5900
Fax: (212) 609-5901
http://www.tcg.org/

PUBLIC RADIO

**American Federation of Television
  and Radio Artists**
New York National Office
260 Madison Avenue
New York, NY 10016-2401
Phone: (212) 532-0800
Fax: (212) 532-2242
http://www.aftra.com

Americans for Radio Diversity
http://www.radiodiversity.com

**American Women in Radio
  and Television**
8405 Greensboro Drive
Suite 800
McLean, VA 22102
Phone: (703) 506-3290
Fax: (703) 506-3266
http://www.awrt.org

Corporation for Public Broadcasting
401 Ninth Street, NW
Washington, DC 20004-2129
Phone: (202) 879-9600; (800) 272-2190
http://www.cpb.org

National Association of Broadcasters
1771 N Street, NW
Washington, DC 20036
Phone: (202) 429-5300
Fax: (202) 429-4199
http://www.nab.org

Public Radio News Directors, Inc.
http://www.prndi.org/

**Public Radio Programmer's
    Association, Inc.**
517 Ocean Front Walk
Suite 10
Venice, CA 90291
Phone: (310) 664-1591
Fax: (310) 664-1592
http://www.prpd.org/

HISTORIANS

**American Association for State and
    Local History**
1717 Church Street
Nashville, TN 37203-2991
Phone: (615) 320-3203
Fax: (615) 327-9013
http://www.aaslh.org/

American Historical Association
400 A Street, SE
Washington, DC 20003-3889
Phone: (202) 544-2422
Fax: (202) 544-8307
http://www.historians.org/

National Council on Public History
425 University Boulevard
Indianapolis, IN 46202
Phone: (317) 274-2716
http://www.ncph.org

**National Trust for Historic
    Preservation**
1785 Massachusetts Avenue, NW
Washington, DC 20036-2117
Phone: (202) 588-6000
http://www.nationaltrust.org

Organization of American Historians
112 North Bryan Avenue
P.O. Box 5457
Bloomington, IN 47408-5457
Phone: (812) 855-7311
Fax: (812) 855-0696
http://www.oah.org

Society of American Archivists
527 South Wells Street
5th Floor
Chicago, IL 60607
Phone: (312) 922-0140
Fax: (312) 347-1452
http://www.archivists.org

H. COLLEGES AND UNIVERSITIES

GENERAL HIGHER
EDUCATION

**American College Personnel
    Association**
One Dupont Circle, NW
Suite 300
Washington, DC 20036
Phone: (202) 235-ACPA
http://www.myacpa.org/

**National Association of College and
    University Business Officers
    (NACUBO)**
2501 M Street, NW
Suite 400
Washington, DC 20037
Phone: (202) 861-2500
Fax: (202) 861-2583
http://www.nacubo.org

**National Association of Student
    Personnel Administrators**
1875 Connecticut Avenue, NW
Suite 418
Washington DC 20009
Phone: (202) 265-7500
Fax: (202) 797-1157
http://www.naspa.org/

CAREER COUNSELING

American Counseling Association
5999 Stevenson Avenue
Alexandria, VA 22304
Phone: (800) 347-6647
Fax: (800) 473-2329
http://www.counseling.org

**National Association of Colleges and
    Employers**
62 Highland Avenue
Bethlehem, PA 18017-9085
Phone: (610) 868-1421 or
    (800) 544-5272
Fax: (610) 868-0208
http://www.naceweb.org

**National Career Development
    Association**
c/o Creative Management Alliance
10820 East 45th Street
Suite 210
Tulsa, OK 74146
Phone: (918) 663-7060; (866) 367-6232
Fax: (918) 663-7058
http://www.ncda.org

**National Employment Counseling
    Association**
5999 Stevenson Avenue

Alexandria, VA 22304
Phone: (800) 347-6647 x222
http://www.employmentcounseling.org

ACADEMIC ADVISING

**National Academic Advising
    Association**
Kansas State University
2323 Anderson Avenue
Suite 225
Manhattan, KS 66502-2912
Phone: (785) 532-5717
Fax: (785) 532-7732
http://www.nacada.ksu.edu/

**National Association of Academic
    Advisors for Athletes**
14606 Woodlake Trace
Louisville, KY 40245
Phone: (502) 253-9530
Fax: (502) 253-9533
http://www.nfoura.org

ADMISSIONS

**American Association of Collegiate
    Registrars and Admissions Officers**
One Dupont Circle, NW
Suite 520

Washington, DC 20036
Phone: (202) 293-9161
Fax: (202) 872-8857
http://www.aacrao.org/

The College Board
45 Columbus Avenue
New York, NY 10023-6992
Phone: (212) 713-8000
http://www.collegeboard.com/splash

**National Association of College
    Admissions Counselors**
1631 Prince Street
Alexandria, VA 22314-2818
Phone: (703) 836-2222
Fax: (703) 836-8015
http://www.nacac.com/index.html

FINANCIAL AID

The College Board
45 Columbus Avenue
New York, NY 10023-6992

Phone: (212) 713-8000
http://www.collegeboard.com/splash

**National Association of Student
    Financial Aid Administrators
    (NASFAA)**
1129 20th Street, NW
Suite 400
Washington, DC 20036-3453
Phone: (202) 785-0453
Fax: (202) 785-1487
http://www.nasfaa.org

REGISTRARS

**American Association of Collegiate
    Registrars and Admissions
    Officers**
One Dupont Circle, NW
Suite 520
Washington, DC 20036
Phone: (202) 293-9161
Fax: (202) 872-8857
http://www.aacrao.org/

ACADEMIA/PROFESSORS

**American Association of Community
    Colleges**
One Dupont Circle, NW
Washington, DC 20036
Phone: (202) 728-0200
Fax: (202) 833-2467
http://www.aacc.nche.edu/

**American Association of University
    Professors**
1012 Fourteenth Street, NW
Suite 500
Washington, DC 20005
Phone: (202) 737-5900
Fax: (202) 737-5526
http://www.aaup.org

**Association of American Colleges and
    Universities**
1818 R Street, NW
Washington, DC 20009
Phone: (202) 387-3760
Fax: (202) 265-9532
http://www.aacu-edu.org

I. ENVIRONMENT, NATURE, AND CONSERVATION

GENERAL

**Association for Environmental
    and Outdoor Education (AEOE)**
P.O. Box 2555
Wrightwood, CA 92397-2555
http://aeoe.org/

Association for Experiential Education
3775 Iris Avenue
Suite 4
Boulder, CO 80301-2043
Phone: (303) 440-8844; (866) 522-8337
Fax: (303) 440-9581
http://www.aee.org

Association of National Park Rangers
http://www.anpr.org/actions2.htm

**National Association of Environmental
    Professionals**
P.O. Box 2086
Bowie, MD 20718
Phone: (888) 251-9902; (301) 860-1140
Fax: (301) 860-1141
http://www.naep.org/

**National Association of State Park
    Directors**
Philip K. McKnelly—
    NASPD Executive Director

8829 Woodyhill Road
Raleigh, NC 27613
Phone: (919) 971-9300
http://www.naspd.org/

National Audubon Society
700 Broadway
New York, NY 10003
Phone: (212) 979-3000
Fax: (212) 979-3188
http://www.audubon.org

**National Recreation and Park
    Association**
22377 Belmont Ridge Road
Ashburn, VA 20148
Phone: (703) 858-0784
Fax: (703) 858-0794
http://www.nrpa.org/

**National Science Teachers Association
    (NSTA)**
1840 Wilson Boulevard
Arlington, VA 22201-3000
Phone: (703) 243-7100
http://www.nsta.org

The Nature Conservancy
4245 North Fairfax Drive
Suite 100

Arlington, VA 22203-1606
Phone: (800) 628-6860; (703) 841-4850
http://nature.org

**North American Association for
    Environmental Education (NAAEE)**
2000 P Street, NW
Suite 540
Washington, DC 20036
Phone: (202) 419-0412
Fax: (202) 419-0415
http://naaee.org/

Outdoor Industry Association
4909 Pearl East Circle
Suite 200
Boulder, CO 80301
Phone: (303) 444-3353
Fax: (303) 444-3284
http://www.outdoorindustry.org

Sierra Club National Headquarters
85 Second Street
2nd Floor
San Francisco, CA 94105
Phone: (415) 977-5500
Fax: (415) 977-5799
http://www.sierraclub.org

Society for Conservation Biology
4245 North Fairfax Drive
Suite 400
Arlington, VA 22203-1651
Phone: (703) 276-2384
Fax: (703) 995-4633
http://www.conbio.org

The Wildlife Society
5410 Grosvenor Lane
Suite 200
Bethesda, MD 20814-2144
Phone: (301) 897-9770
Fax: (301) 530-2471
http://www.wildlife.org

ZOOLOGY

American Association of Zookeepers (AAZK), Inc.
3601 Southwest 29th Street
Suite 133
Topeka, KS 66614-2054
http://www.aazk.org

American Society of Ichthyologists and Herpetologists
Florida International University
Biological Sciences
11200 Southwest 8th Street
Miami, FL 33199
Phone: (305) 348-1235
Fax: (305) 348-1986
http://www.asih.org/contact.html

American Society of Mammalogists
http://www.mammalsociety.org/

TRANSLATION/ INTERPRETATION

The American Association of Language Specialists
http://www.taals.net/

American Translators Association
225 Reinekers Lane
Suite 590
Alexandria, VA 22314
Phone: (703) 683-6100
Fax: (703) 683-6122
http://www.atanet.org

Registry of Interpreters for the Deaf, Inc.
333 Commerce Street
Alexandria, VA 22314

American Zoo and Aquarium Association
8403 Colesville Road
Suite 710
Silver Spring, MD 20910-3314
Phone: (301) 562-0777
Fax: (301) 562-0888
http://www.aza.org

Society for Integrative and Comparative Biology
1313 Dolley Madison Boulevard
Suite 402
McLean, VA 22101
Phone: (703) 790-1745;
(800) 955-1236
Fax: (703) 790-2672
http://www.sicb.org

Society for the Study of Amphibians and Reptiles
http://www.ssarherps.org

ACTIVISM

Greenpeace USA
702 H Street, NW
Suite 300
Washington DC 20001
Phone: (202) 462-1177
Fax: (202) 462-4507
http://www.greenpeace.org

The National Organizers Alliance
715 G Street, SE
Washington, DC 20003
Phone: (202) 543-6603

J. INTERNATIONAL RELATED

Phone: (703) 838-0030
TTY: (703) 838-0459
Fax: (703) 838-0454
http://www.rid.org

The Translators and Interpreters Guild
962 Wayne Avenue
Suite 500
Silver Spring, MD 20910
Phone: (301) 563-6450; (800) 992-0367
Fax: (301) 563-6020
http://www.ttig.org/

PEACE STUDIES

Arms Control Association
1150 Connecticut Avenue, NW
Suite 620

Fax: (202) 543-2462
http://www.noacentral.org/

ENGINEERING

American Academy of Environmental Engineers
130 Holiday Court
Suite 100
Annapolis, MD 21401
Phone: (410) 266-3311
Fax: (410) 266-7653
http://www.aaee.net

American Society of Agricultural Engineers
2950 Niles Road
St Joseph, MI 49085
Phone: (269) 429-0300
Fax: (269) 429-3852
http://www.asae.org

American Society of Civil Engineers
1801 Alexander Bell Drive
Reston, VA 20191-4400
Phone: (703) 295-6300; (800) 548-2723
Fax: (703) 295-6222
http://www.asce.org

Engineers Without Borders – USA
1880 Industrial Circle
Suite B3
Longmont, CO 80501
Phone: (303) 772-2723
http://www.ewb-usa.org/

Washington, DC 20036
Phone: (202) 463-8270
Fax: (202) 463-8273
http://www.armscontrol.org

The International Peace Research Association (IPRA)
http://www.human.mie-u.ac.jp/peace/index.htm

The International Studies Association
324 Social Sciences Building
University of Arizona
Tucson, AZ 85721
Phone: (520) 621-7715
Fax: (520) 621-5780
http://www.isanet.org

Peace Action and the Peace Action Education Fund
1100 Wayne Avenue
Suite 1020
Silver Spring, MD 20910
Phone: (301) 565-4050
Fax: (301) 565-0850
http://www.peace-action.org

Peace and Justice Studies Association
The Evergreen State College
Mailstop: SEM 3127
Olympia, WA 98505
http://www.peacejusticestudies.org

PUGWASH
11 Dupont Circle, NW
Suite 900
Washington, DC 20036
Phone: (202) 478-3440
http://www.pugwash.org

INTERNATIONAL AFFAIRS

Association of Professional Schools of International Affairs (APSIA)
http://www.apsia.org

Institute of International Education
809 United Nations Plaza
New York, NY 10017-3580
Phone: (212) 883-8200
Fax: (212) 984-5452
http://www.iie.org

HUMAN RIGHTS

Action Without Borders (Idealist.org)
79 Fifth Avenue
17th Floor
New York, NY 10003
Phone: (212) 843-3973
Fax: (212) 564-3377
http://www.idealist.org

Derechos Human Rights
http://www.derechos.org

Human Rights Internet
8 York Street
Suite 302
Ottawa, ON KI N5S6
Phone: (613) 789-7407
Fax: (613) 789-7414
http://www.hri.ca/index.aspx

Human Rights Watch
350 Fifth Avenue
34th Floor
New York, NY 10118-3299
Phone: (212) 290-4700
Fax: (212) 736-1300
http://www.hrw.org/

One World
http://www.oneworld.net/

Women's Human Rights Net
http://www.whrnet.org/

EDUCATION

Alliance for International and Cultural Exchange
1776 Massachusetts Avenue, NW
Suite 620
Washington, DC 20036-1912
Phone: (202) 293-6141
Fax: (202) 293-6144
http://www.alliance-exchange.org/

Association of International Educators (NAFSA)
1307 New York Avenue, NW
8th Floor
Washington, DC 20005-4701
Phone: (202) 737-3699
Fax: (202) 737-3657
http://www.nafsa.org

Teachers of English to Speakers of Other Languages (TESOL)
700 South Washington Street
Suite 200
Alexandria, VA 22314
Phone: (703) 836-0774;
(888) 547-3369
Fax: (703) 836-7864 or
(703) 836-6447
http://www.tesol.org/s_tesol/index.asp

APPENDIX III
LIST OF NONPROFIT ORGANIZATIONS

Each year, the *NonProfit Times* (http://www.nptimes.com), the leading business publication for nonprofit management, puts together a list of 100 largest nonprofit organizations. The nonprofits included in this list from 2004, known as the "NPT 100," raise at least 10 percent of their total revenue from public sources such as donations and grants. While this list omits grant-making organizations such as foundations and groups like the United Way, it does represent the great diversity of the nonprofit sector. Organizations fall in all industry categories, including social services, education, health, arts and culture, conservation, international, associations, and religious organizations. You will also see that they are scattered in locations across the country. The addresses listed here are the national headquarters of these organizations; many have additional branches in other locations.

This list may serve as a starting point for you to explore opportunities at different nonprofits. Visit their Web sites to learn more about their missions, programs, and job listings. Keep in mind that there are thousands more nonprofits to meet all interest areas. Your local phone book can introduce you to those in your community.

1. YMCAs in the United States
101 North Wacker Drive
Chicago, IL 60606
Phone: (312) 977-0031
http://www.ymca.net

2. American Red Cross
2025 E Street, NW
Washington, DC 20006
Phone: (202) 303-4498
http://www.redcross.org

3. Catholic Charities USA
1731 King Street
Alexandria, VA 22314
Phone: (703) 549-1390
Fax: (703) 549-1656
http://www.catholiccharitiesusa.org/

4. Salvation Army
615 Slaters Lane
P.O. Box 269
Alexandria, VA 22313
http://www.salvationarmyusa.org/

5. United Jewish Communities
P.O. Box 30
Old Chelsea Station
New York, NY 10113
Phone: (212) 284-6500
http://www.ujc.org/

6. Goodwill Industries International
15810 Indianola Drive
Rockville, MD 20855
Phone: (301) 530-6500
http://www.goodwill.org/

7. Shriners Hospitals for Children
International Headquarters
2900 Rocky Point Drive
Tampa, FL 33607-1460
Phone: (813) 281-0300
http://www.shrinershq.org/

8. Boys and Girls Club of America
1230 West Peachtree Street, NW
Atlanta, GA 30309
Phone: (404) 487-5700
http://www.bgca.org/

9. American Cancer Society
1599 Clifton Road
Atlanta, GA 30329
Phone: (800) ACS-2345
http://www.cancer.org

10. Gifts in Kind International
333 North Fairfax Street
Alexandria, VA 22314
Phone: (703) 836-2121
Fax: (703) 549-1481
http://www.giftsinkind.org/

11. Habitat for Humanity International
121 Habitat Street
Americus, GA 31709-3498
Phone: (229) 924-6935, ext. 2551 or 2552
http://www.habitat.org/

12. Boy Scouts of America
National Council
P.O. Box 152079

Irving, TX 75015-2079
http://www.scouting.org/

13. Planned Parenthood Federation of America
434 West 33rd Street
New York, NY 10001
Phone: (212) 541-7800
Fax: (212) 245-1845
http://www.plannedparenthood.org

14. The Nature Conservancy
4245 North Fairfax Drive
Suite 100
Arlington, VA 22203-1606
Phone: (703) 841-5300
http://www.nature.org/

15. YWCA of the USA
1015 18th Street, NW
Suite 1100
Washington, DC 20036
Phone: (202) 467-0801
Fax: (202) 467-0802
http://www.ywca.org

16. Volunteers of America
National Office
1660 Duke Street
Alexandria, VA 22314-3421
Phone: (703) 341-5000; (800) 899-0089
http://www.volunteersofamerica.org

17. Easter Seals
230 West Monroe Street
Suite 1800
Chicago, IL 60606

Phone: (312) 726-6200; (800) 221-6827
Fax: (312) 726-1494
http://www.easterseals.com

18. AmeriCARES Foundation
88 Hamilton Avenue
Stamford, CT 06902
Phone: (800) 486-HELP
http://www.americares.org/

19. World Vision
800 West Chestnut Avenue
Monrovia, CA 91016-3198
http://www.wvi.org/

20. Girl Scouts of the USA
420 Fifth Avenue
New York, NY 10018-2798
Phone: (212) 852-8000; (800) 478-7248
http://www.girlscouts.org

21. Feed the Children
P.O. Box 36
Oklahoma City, OK 73101-0036
Phone: (405) 942-0228; (800) 627-4556
Fax: (405) 945-4177
http://www.feedthechildren.org/

22. CARE USA
151 Ellis Street
Atlanta, GA 30303
Phone: (404) 681-2552
Fax: (404) 589-2651
http://www.careusa.org

23. American Heart Association
National Center
7272 Greenville Avenue
Dallas, TX 75231
Phone: (800) AHA-USA-1
http://www.americanheart.org

24. Catholic Relief Services
209 West Fayette Street
Baltimore, MD 21201-3443
Phone: (410) 625-2220; (800) 736-3467
http://www.catholicrelief.org/

25. Public Broadcasting Services
1320 Braddock Place
Alexandria, VA 22314
Phone: (703) 739-5400
http://www.pbs.org

26. America's Second Harvest
35 East Wacker Drive, #2000
Chicago, IL 60601
Phone: (312) 263-2303; (800) 771-2303
http://www.secondharvest.org/

27. Food for the Poor
550 SW 12th Avenue
Department 9662
Deerfield Beach, FL 33442
Phone: (954) 427-2222
http://www.foodforthepoor.org

28. ALSAC-St. Jude's Children's Research Hospital
St. Jude Children's Research Hospital
332 North Lauderdale
Memphis, TN 38105
Phone: (901) 495-3300
http://www.stjude.org

29. Dana Farber Cancer Institute
44 Binney Street
Boston, MA 02115
Phone: (866) 408-DFCI
http://www.dfci.harvard.edu/

30. City of Hope
National Medical Center
1500 East Duarte Road
Duarte, CA 91010
Phone: (626) 256-HOPE; (626) 301-8200 (Jobline)
http://www.cityofhope.org

31. Campus Crusade for Christ, Inc.
100 Lake Hart Drive
Orlando, FL 32832
Phone: (407) 826-2000
http://www.ccci.org

32. Smithsonian Institution
750 9th Street, NW
Suite 6100
Washington DC 20560-0912
Phone: (202) 275-1102; (202) 287-3102 (Jobline)
http://www.si.edu/

33. United Cerebral Palsy Association
1660 L Street, NW
Suite 700
Washington, DC 20036
Phone: (202) 776-0406; (800) 872-5827
Fax: (202) 776-0414
http://www.ucp.org/

34. U.S. Fund for UNICEF
333 East 38th Street
New York, NY 10016
Phone: (212) 686-5522
Fax: (212) 779-1670
http://www.unicefusa.org

35. Save the Children Federation, Inc.
54 Wilton Road
Westport, CT 06880
Phone: (203) 221-4030; (800) 728-3843
http://www.savethechildren.org

36. Fred Hutchinson Cancer Research Center
1100 Fairview Avenue North
P.O. Box 19024
Seattle, WA 98109-1024
Phone: (206) 667-5000
Fax: (206) 667-4051
http://www.fhcrc.org/

37. Metropolitan Museum of Art
1000 Fifth Avenue
New York, NY 10028-0198
Phone: (212) 535-7710
http://www.metmuseum.org

38. Special Olympics International, Inc.
1133 19th Street, NW
Washington, DC 20036
Phone: (202) 628-3630
Fax: (202) 824-0200
http://www.specialolympics.org

39. Big Brothers/Big Sisters of America
National Office
230 North 13th Street
Philadelphia, PA 19107
Phone: (215) 567-7000
http://www.bbsa.org

40. March of Dimes
1275 Mamaroneck Avenue
White Plains, NY 10605
Phone: (914) 997-4629
http://www.marchofdimes.com

41. WGBH Education Foundation
P.O. Box 200
Boston, MA 02134
Phone: (617) 300-5400
http://www.wgbh.org/

42. Samaritan's Purse
P.O. Box 3000
Boone, NC 28607
Phone: (828) 262-1980
http://www.wgbh.org/

43. Metropolitan Opera Association, Inc.
Lincoln Center
New York, NY 10023
Phone: (212) 799-3100
http://www.metopera.org

44. The Christian Missionary Alliance
P.O. Box 35000
Colorado Springs, CO 80935-3500
Phone: (719) 599-5999
http://www.cmalliance.org

45. American Diabetes Association
1701 North Beauregard Street
Alexandria, VA 22311
Phone: (800) DIABETES
http://www.diabetes.org

46. National Multiple Sclerosis Society
733 Third Avenue
New York, NY 10017
Phone: (800) 344-4867
http://www.nationalmssociety.org

47. Art Institute of Chicago
111 South Michigan Avenue
Chicago, IL 60603-6110
Phone: (312) 443-3600
Fax: (312) 443-0849
http://www.artic.edu/

48. Trinity Broadcasting Network
P. O. Box A
Santa Ana, CA 92711
Phone: (714) 832-2950
http://www.tbn.org/

49. Christian Broadcasting Network
977 Centerville Turnpike
Virginia Beach, VA 23463
Phone: (757) 226-7000
http://www.cbn.com

50. Christian Aid Ministries
P.O. Box 360
Berlin, OH 44610
Phone: (330) 893-2428
Fax: (905) 871-5165
http://www.christianaid.ca/

51. Scholarship America
One Scholarship Way
St. Peter, MN 56082
Phone: (800) 537-4180
http://www.scholarshipamerica.org/

52. American Lung Association
61 Broadway
6th Floor
New York, NY 10006
Phone: (212) 315-8700
http://www.lungusa.org

53. Ducks Unlimited, Inc.
One Waterfowl Way
Memphis, TN 38120
Phone: (901) 758-3825
http://www.ducks.org/

54. Leukemia & Lymphoma Society
1311 Mamaroneck Avenue
White Plains, NY 10605
Phone: (914) 949-5213
Fax: (914) 949-6691
http://www.leukemia.org

55. Muscular Dystrophy Association
3300 East Sunrise Drive
Tucson, AZ 85718
Phone: (800) 572-1717
http://www.mdausa.org/

56. Girls and Boys Town
378 Bucher Drive
Boys Town, NE 68010
Phone: (800) 321-4171
http://www.girlsandboystown.org

57. Map International, Inc.
2200 Glynco Parkway
Brunswick, GA 31525
Phone: (912) 265-6010
Fax: (912) 265-6170
http://www.map.org

58. Educational Broadcasting Corporation
450 West 33rd Street
6th Floor
New York, NY 10001
Phone: (212) 560-1313
http://www.wnet.org/

59. Institute of International Education
809 United Nations Plaza
New York, NY 10017-3580
Phone: (212) 883-8200
Fax: (212) 984-5452
http://www.iie.org

60. Young Life
P.O. Box 520
Colorado Springs, CO 80901
Phone: (719) 381-1800
http://www.younglife.org

61. Sesame Workshop
One Lincoln Plaza
New York, NY 10023
Phone: (212) 595-3456
Fax: (212) 875-6088
http://www.sesameworkshop.org

62. Alzheimer's Disease & Related Disorders Association
225 North Michigan Avenue
Floor 17
Chicago, IL 60601-7633
Phone: (312) 335-8700; (800) 272-3900
Fax: (312) 335-1110
http://www.alz.org

63. Girls Incorporated
120 Wall Street
New York, NY 10005-3902
Phone: (800) 374-4475
http://www.girlsinc.org

64. International Rescue Committee
122 East 42nd Street
New York, NY 10168
Phone: (212) 551-3000
http://www.theirc.org

65. Cystic Fibrosis Foundation
6931 Arlington Road
Bethesda, MD 20814
Phone: (301) 951-4422; (800) FIGHT CF
Fax: (301) 951-6378
http://www.cff.org

66. National Mental Health Association
2001 North Beauregard Street
12th Floor
Alexandria, VA 22311
Phone: (703) 684-7722
Fax: (703) 684-5968
http://www.nmha.org

67. National Association for the Exchange of Industrial Resources
560 McClure Street
Galesburg, IL 61401
Phone: (800) 562-0955
Fax: (309) 343-0862
http://www.naeir.org/

68. Wildlife Conservation Society
2300 Southern Boulevard
Bronx, NY 10460
Phone: (718) 220-5100
http://www.wcs.org/

69. Trust for Public Land
116 New Montgomery Street
4th Floor
San Francisco, CA 94105
Phone: (415) 495-4014
Fax: (415) 495-4103
http://www.tpl.org/

70. Compassion International
Colorado Springs, CO 80997
Phone: (800) 336-7676
http://www.compassion.com

71. Christian Children's Fund
2821 Emerywood Parkway
Richmond, VA 23294
Phone: (800) 776-6767
http://www.christianchildrensfund.org/

72. National Gallery of Art
2000B South Club Drive
Landover, MD 20785
Phone: (202) 737-4215; (202) 842-6298
(Jobline)
http://www.nga.gov

73. Make a Wish Foundation
3550 North Central Avenue
Suite 300
Phoenix, AZ 85012-2127
Phone: (602) 279-WISH; (800) 722-
WISH
Fax: (602) 279-0855
http://www.wish.org

74. Junior Achievement, Inc.
One Education Way
Colorado Springs, CO 80906
Phone: (719) 540-8000
Fax: (719) 540-6299
http://www.ja.org

**75. Juvenile Diabetes Foundation
International**
120 Wall Street
New York, NY 10005-4001
Phone: (800) 533-CURE
Fax: (212) 785-9595
http://www.jdf.org/

76. Catholic Medical Mission Board
10 West 17th Street
New York, NY 10011-5765
Phone: (212) 242-7757; (800) 678-5659
Fax: (212) 807-9161
http://www.cmmb.org

**77. Susan G. Komen Breast Cancer
Foundation**
5005 LBJ Freeway
Suite 250
Dallas, TX 75244
Phone: (972) 855-1600
Fax: (972) 855-1605
http://www.komen.org

78. United Negro College Fund, Inc.
8260 Willow Oaks Corporate Drive

P.O. Box 10444
Fairfax, VA 22031-8044
Phone: (800) 331-2244
http://www.uncf.org

79. Brother's Brother Foundation
1200 Galveston Avenue
Pittsburgh, PA 15233
Phone: (412) 321-3160
Fax: (412) 321-3325
http://www.brothersbrother.org/

80. Focus on the Family
Colorado Springs, CO 80995
Phone: (719) 531-3400;
(800) AFAMILY
Fax: (719) 531-3424
http://www.family.org/

81. The Carter Center
One Copenhill
453 Freedom Parkway
Atlanta, GA 30307
Phone: (404) 420-5100
http://www.cartercenter.org

82. Project HOPE
255 Carter Hall Lane
Millwood, VA 22646
Phone: (540) 837-2100
Fax: (540) 837-9052
http://www.projecthope.org/

**83. Jewish Board of Family and
Children's Services**
120 West 57th Street
New York, NY 10019
Phone: (212) 582-9100
Fax: (212) 956-0526
http://www.jbfcs.org/

84. Arthritis Foundation
P.O. Box 7669
Atlanta, GA 30357-0669
Phone: (404) 965-7888; (800) 568-4045
http://www.arthritis.org/

85. Covenant House
460 West 41st Street
New York, NY 10036-6801
Phone: (212) 613-0300
http://www.covenanthouse.org

86. National Public Radio, Inc.
635 Massachusetts Avenue, NW
Washington, DC 20001
Phone: (202) 513-2000
Fax: (202) 513-3329
http://www.npr.org

**87. National Wildlife Foundation and
Endowment**
11100 Wildlife Center Drive
Reston, VA 20190-5362
Phone: (800) 822-9919
http://www.nwf.org

88. Disabled American Veterans
3725 Alexandria Pike
Cold Spring, KY 41076
Phone: (859) 441-7300
Mailing Address
P.O. Box 14301
Cincinnati, OH 45250-0301
http://www.dav.org

**89. John F. Kennedy Center for the
Performing Arts**
2700 F Street, NW
Washington, DC 20566
Phone: (202) 416-8000
http://www.kennedy-center.org/

90. Mercy Corps International
Dept W
3015 Southwest First
Portland, OR 97201
Phone: (800) 852-2100
http://www.mercycorps.org

91. Museum of Modern Art
11 West 53 Street
New York, NY 10019-5497
Phone: (212) 708-9400
http://www.moma.org

**92. American Museum of Natural
History**
Central Park West at 79th Street
New York, NY 10024-5192
Phone: (212) 769-5100
http://www.amnh.org/

93. Wycliffe Bible Translators
P.O. Box 628200
Orlando, FL 32862-8200
Phone: (407) 852-3600; (800) 992-5433
Fax: (407) 852-3601
http://www.wycliffe.org

**94. Rotary Foundation of Rotary
International**
One Rotary Center
1560 Sherman Avenue
Evanston, IL 60201
Phone: (847) 866-3000
Fax: (847) 328-8554 or (847) 328-8281
http://www.rotary.org/foundation/index.html

95. Billy Graham Evangelistic Association
1 Billy Graham Parkway
Charlotte, NC 28201
Phone: (704) 401-2432
http://www.billygraham.org/

96. Museum of Fine Arts, Boston
Avenue of the Arts
465 Huntington Avenue
Boston, MA 02115-5597
Phone: (617) 267-9300
http://www.mfa.org

97. World Wildlife Fund
1250 24th Street, NW
Washington, DC 20037
Phone: (202) 293-4800
http://www.worldwildlife.org

98. National Jewish Medical and Research Center
1400 Jackson Street
Denver, CO 80206
Phone: (800) 222-LUNG
http://www.njc.org

99. Colonial Williamsburg Foundation
P. O. Box 1776
Williamsburg, VA 23187-1776
Phone: (757) 229-1000
http://www.history.org/

100. Direct Relief International
27 South La Patera Lane
Santa Barbara, CA 93117
Phone: (805) 964-4767
Fax: (805) 681-4838
http://www.directrelief.org

APPENDIX IV
USEFUL WEB SITES

The following Web sites contain useful information about the nonprofit sector. While most maintain job listings, others were included because of the valuable career insight they offer. They are broken down in similar categories to the rest of the book, where one can search by industry or general nonprofit job function.

Also, many nonprofits list their internal jobs directly on their own Web sites. From the home page of organizations that interest you, look for links that say "jobs," "employment," or "about us."

As Web sites become outdated very quickly, do not be discouraged if a link is no longer active. Just by typing something as generic as "nonprofit jobs" into a search engine such as Google or Yahoo, you will find that many new sites have sprung up.

A. GENERAL NONPROFIT

America's Job Bank
http://www.ajb.dni.us/

CareerBuilder.com
http://www.careerpath.com

CharityChannel
http://charitychannel.com/

Community Career Center
http://www.nonprofitjobs.org

Good Works
http://goodworksfirst.org/

GuideStar—The National Database of Nonprofit Organizations
http://www.guidestar.org/

Idealist.org: Action Without Borders
http://www.idealist.org

Minnesota Council of Nonprofits Nonprofit Job Board
http://www.mncn.org/jobs/jobs.htm

New York Regional Association of Grant Makers
http://www.nyrag.org

Nonprofit Career Network
http://www.nonprofitcareer.com

Nonprofit Directions
http://www.nonprofitdirections.org/

nonprofitemployment.com
http://www.nonprofitemployment.com/

Nonprofit Oyster
http://www.nonprofitoyster.com

The NonProfit Times
http://nptimes.com/

NPO.net Jobs Service
http://www.itresourcecenter.org/nponet/jobs/

On-Line Sources for Nonprofit Jobs
http://www.mapnp.org/library/gen_rsrc/jobs/np_jobs.htm

OpportunityKnocks.org
http://www.opportunitynocs.org/index.jsp

PNNOnline: the nonprofit news and information resource
http://pnnonline.org

B. FUND-RAISING

Association of Fundraising Professionals—Jobs
http://www.afpnet.org/jobs

Charity People
http://www.charitypeople.com/

Global Fundraising Jobs
http://www.globalfundraisingjobs.com/s-index

C. FOUNDATIONS AND PHILANTHROPY

The Chronicle of Philanthropy
http://philanthropy.com/

The Foundation Center
http://www.fdncenter.org

Philanthropy Journal
http://philanthropyjournal.org/

D. HEALTH AND SCIENCE

All Health Jobs
http://www.allhealthjobs.com/job_links.htm

American Public Health Association
http://www.apha.org/career/

Association of Schools of Public Health Career & Employment Links
http://www.asph.org/document.cfm?page=733

The Association of State and Territorial Health Officials
http://www.astho.org/index.php?template=employment.php&PHPSESSID=bafb6ad

Health Careers
http://www.medsearch.com/

Medical Jobs/Healthcare Jobs
http://www.nationjob.com/medical/

National Institutes of Health Research & Training Opportunities
http://www.nih.gov/science/opportunities.html

Partners in Information Access for the Public Health Workplace
http://www.phpartners.org/jobs.html

Public Health Employment Connection
http://www.cfusion.sph.emory.edu/PHEC/
phec.cfm

PublicHealthJobs.net
http://www.publichealthjobs.net/

Public Health Jobs Worldwide
http://www.jobspublichealth.com/

E. SOCIAL SERVICE AND RELIGIOUS ORGANIZATIONS

ChurchJobs.net
http://www.churchjobs.net/

Human Service Jobs
http://www.hspeople.com

Human Services Career Network
http://www.hscareers.com/

The Clearinghouse for Jewish Communal Jobs
http://www.jewishjobs.com/jj/jobseekers.
shtml

Ministry Search
http://www.ministrysearch.com/

The New Social Worker Online
http://www.socialworker.com/home/
menu/Social_Work_Jobs_&_Career_
Development/

The Social Service Job Site
http://www.socialservice.com/

Social Work and Social Services Jobs Online
http://gwbweb.wustl.edu/jobs/

SocialWorkJobBank
http://www.socialworkjobbank.com/

F. ADVOCACY AND COMMUNITY DEVELOPMENT

Alliance for Justice
http://www.afj.org/

Community Development Society
http://www.comm-dev.org

Essential Information
http://www.essential.org/

Habitat for Humanity International
http://www.habitat.org/

NeighborWorks
http://www.nw.org

Pratt Institute Center for Community and Environmental Development
http://www.picced.org/index.php

SERVEnet
http://www.servenet.org

G. ARTS AND CULTURE

American Association of Museums
Museum Careers
http://www.aam-us.org/aviso/index.cfm

Association of Science – Technology Centers
http://www.astc.org/profdev/jobs/jobs.htm

Global Museum—The International Museum Webzine
http://www.globalmuseum.org/

Museum Careers
http://www4.wave.co.nz/~jollyroger/
GM2/jobs/jobs.htm

Museum Employment Resource Center
http://www.museum-employment.com/

MuseumJobs.com
http://www.museumjobs.com

H. COLLEGES AND UNIVERSITIES

Academic Employment Network
http://www.academploy.com/

Academic360.com
http://www.academic360.com

American College Personnel Association (ACPA) Ongoing Placement
http://www.acpa.nche.edu/placemnt/
placemnt.htm

The Chronicle of Higher Education
http://www.chronicle.com

Higher Education Jobs
http://www.higheredjobs.com

National Association of Colleges and Employers
http://www.naceweb.org

Student Affairs Administrators in Higher Education
http://www.naspa.org/

I. ENVIRONMENT, NATURE, AND CONSERVATION

Cyber-Sierra's Natural Resources Job Search
http://www.cyber-sierra.com/nrjobs/

EarthNet
http://www.envirocitizen.org/enet/jobs/
index.asp

Earthworks-jobs.com
http://www.earthworks-jobs.com/

ECEA (Environmental, Construction, Engineering, Architectural) Jobs Online
http://www.eceajobs.com/

EnviroEducation.com
http://www.enviroeducation.com/careers-
jobs/

EnvironmentalCareer.com
http://www.environmentalcareer.com/

Environmental Career Opportunities
http://www.ecojobs.com/

The Environmental Careers Organization
http://www.eco.org

Environmental Expert
http://www.environmental-center.
com/jobs.asp

Environmental Jobs and Careers
http://www.ejobs.org

Green Dream Jobs
http://www.sustainablebusiness.com/jobs/
index.cfm

North American Association for Environmental Education
http://eelink.net/eejobs.html

Society for Conservation Biology
http://www.conbio.org/SCB/Services/Jobs/

The Student Conservation Association
http://www.thesca.org/

**J. INTERNATIONAL RELATED,
INTERNATIONAL
DEVELOPMENT,
AND HUMAN RIGHTS**

Cross-Cultural Solutions
http://www.crossculturalsolutions.org/

DEVJOBS
http://www.devjobsmail.com/main/
    homepage.html

DevNetJobs.org
http://www.devnetjobs.org/

Foreign Policy Association Job Board
http://www.fpa.org/jobs_contact2423/jobs
    _contact.htm

Going Global
http://www.goinglobal.com/

**The Institute for International
    Cooperation and Development**
http://www.iicd-
    volunteer.org/noflash.html

InterAction.org
http://www.interaction.org/

International Jobs Center
http://www.internationaljobs.org/

International Volunteer Program
http://www.ivpsf.org/

OverseasJobs.com
http://www.overseasjobs.com/

Peace Corps
http://www.peacecorps.gov/index.cfm

ReliefWeb
http://www.reliefweb.int/vacancies/

BIBLIOGRAPHY

GENERAL NONPROFIT

Christiano, Richard. *Volunteer! The Comprehensive Guide to Voluntary Service in the U.S. and Abroad.* New York: Council on International Educational Exchange, 1995.

Cohen, Lilly, and Dennis R. Young. *Careers for Dreamers and Doers: A Guide to Management Careers in the Nonprofit Sector.* New York: The Foundation Center, 1989.

Colvin, Donna, ed. *Good Works: A Guide to Careers in Social Change.* Preface by Ralph Nader. New York: Barricade Books, 1994.

Crosby, Olivia. "Paid Jobs in Charitable Nonprofits," *Occupational Outlook Quarterly* (Summer 2001): 11–23.

Duronio, Margaret A., and Eugene R. Tempel. *Fund Raisers: Their Careers, Stories, Concerns, and Accomplishments.* San Francisco: Jossey-Bass, 1996.

Eberts, Marjorie. *Careers for Good Samaritans and Other Humanitarian Types.* 2nd ed. New York: McGraw-Hill/Contemporary Books, 1998.

Everett, Melissa. *Making a Living While Making a Difference.* British Columbia: New Society Publishers, 1999.

Hamilton, Leslie, and Robert Tragert. *100 Best Nonprofits to Work For.* Stamford, Conn.: Thomson Learning, 2000.

Hopkins, Bruce R. *Starting and Managing a Nonprofit Organization: A Legal Guide,* 3rd ed. New York: John Wiley & Sons, 2001.

Lewis, David. *Management of Non-Governmental Development Organizations: An Introduction (Routledge Studies in the Management of Voluntary and Non-Profit Organizations).* Oxford: Routledge, 2001.

Lowell, Stephanie. *The Harvard Business School Guide to Careers in the Nonprofit Sector.* Boston: Harvard Business School Press, 2000.

Jebens, Harley. *100 Jobs in Social Change.* New York: Macmillan, 1996.

King, Richard M. *From Making a Profit to Making a Difference: How to Launch Your New Career in Nonprofits.* Gardena, Calif.: SCB Distributors, 2000.

Klein, Kim. *Fundraising for Social Change,* 4th ed. San Francisco: Jossey Bass, 2001.

Krannich, Ron, and Caryl Krannich. *Jobs and Careers with Nonprofit Organizations.* Manassas Park, Va.: Impact Publications, 1999.

Lauber, Daniel. *Non-Profits' and Education Job Finder.* River Forest, Ill.: Planning/Communications, 1997.

Rowh, Mark. *Opportunites in Fund-Raising Careers.* Chicago: VGM Career Books, 2000.

Slesinger, Larry. *Search: Winning Strategies to Get Your Next Job in the Nonprofit World.* Glen Echo, Md.: Piemonte Press, 2004.

Wagner, Lilya D. *Careers in Fundraising (AFP/Wiley Fund Development Series).* New York: John Wiley, 2001.

Wet Feet. *The WetFeet Insider Guide to Careers in Non-Profits and Government Agencies.* San Francisco: Wet Feet Press, reissue edition, 2003.

BUSINESS, PROFESSIONAL, AND TRADE ASSOCIATIONS

Axelrod-Contrada, Joan, and John Kerry. *Career Opportunities in Politics, Government, and Activism.* New York: Facts On File, 2003.

Encyclopedia of Associations. Farmington Hills, Mich.: Gale Group, 1999.

International Handbook on Association Management. 2nd ed. Washington, D.C.: American Society of Association Executives, 2004.

FOUNDATIONS, GRANT-MAKING ORGANIZATIONS, AND PHILANTHROPY

Sealander, Judith. *Private Wealth and Public Life: Foundation Philanthropy and the Reshaping of American Social Policy from the Progressive Era to the New Deal.* Baltimore: Johns Hopkins University Press, 1997.

HEALTH AND SCIENCE

Caldwell, Carol Coles. *Opportunities in Nutrition Careers.* New York: McGraw-Hill, 1999.

Damp, Dennis V., and Erin M. Taylor, eds. *Health Care Job Explosion!: High Growth Health Care Careers and Job Locator.* 2nd ed. Ashland, Ohio: Bookhaven Press, 1998.

DeBuono, Barbara A. *Advancing Healthy Populations: The Pfizer Guide to Careers in Public Health.* New York: Pfizer Pharmaceuticals Group, 2002.

Echaore-McDavid, Susan. *Career Opportunities in Science.* New York: Checkmark Books, 2003.

Field, Shelly, and Arthur E. Weintraub. *Career Opportunities in Health Care.* 2nd ed. New York: Checkmark Books, 2002.

Karni, Karen. *Opportunities in Clinical Laboratory Science Careers, Revised Edition.* 2nd ed. New York: McGraw-Hill/Contemporary Books, 2002.

Osborn, Garth, and Patricia Ohmans. *Finding Work in Global Health.* Saint Paul, Minn.: Health Advocates Press, 1999.

Snook, Donald. *Opportunities in Hospital Administration Careers.* New York: McGraw-Hill, 1997.

270 Ways to Put Your Talent to Work in the Health Field. Washington, D.C.: National Health Council, 1998.

Wischnitzer, Dr. Saul, and Edith Wischnitzer. *Health-Care Careers for the 21st Century.* Indianapolis: JIST Works, 2000.

SOCIAL SERVICE AND RELIGIOUS ORGANIZATIONS

Burger, William R., et al. *The Helping Professions: A Careers Sourcebook.* Stamford, Conn.: Wadsworth Publishing, 1999.

Collison, Brooke B., ed., and Nancy J. Garfield. *Careers in Counseling and Human Services.* 2nd ed. New York: Taylor & Francis, 1996.

Garner, Geraldine. *Careers in Social and Rehabilitation Services.* 2nd ed. New York: McGraw-Hill/Contemporary Books, 2001.

Ginsberg, Leon H. *Careers in Social Work.* 2nd ed. Upper Saddle River, N.J.: Pearson Allyn & Bacon, 2000.

Grobman, Linda May. *Days in the Lives of Social Workers: 50 Professionals Tell "Real-Life" Stories from Social Work Practice.* 2nd ed. Harrisburg, Pa.: White Hat Communications, 1999.

Nelson, John Oliver. *Opportunities in Religious Service Careers.* New York: McGraw-Hill, 2003.

Paradis, Adrian. *Careers for Caring People & Other Sensitive Types.* 2nd ed. McGraw-Hill, 2003.

Sternberg, Robert J. *Career Paths in Psychology. Where Your Degree Can Take You.* Washington, D.C.: American Psychology Association, 1997.

Wallner, Rosemary. *Human Services Worker (Career Exploration).* Mankato, Minn.: Capstone Press, 2000.

Williams, Ellen. *Opportunities in Gerontology and Aging Services Careers, Revised Edition.* New York: McGraw-Hill/Contemporary Books; 2002.

ADVOCACY AND COMMUNITY DEVELOPMENT

Bobo, Kimberley A., et al. *Organizing for Social Change: Midwest Academy: Manual for Activists.* 3rd ed. Washington, D.C.: Seven Locks Press, 2001.

DeBroff, Stacy M., Jill P. Martyn, and Alexa Shabecoff. *Public Interest Job Search Guide 2001–2002: Harvard Law School's Handbook & Directory for Law Students and Lawyers Seeking Public Service Work,* 12th ed. Cambridge, Mass.: Harvard Law School, 2001.

Kretzmann, John P., and John L. McKnight. *Building Communities from the Inside Out: A Path toward Finding and Mobilizing a Community's Assets.* Chicago: ACTA Publications, 1997.

Shabecoff, Alice, and Paul C. Brophy. *A Guide to Careers in Community Development.* Washington, D.C.: Island Press, 2001.

Shaw, Randy. *The Activist's Handbook: A Primer, Updated Edition with a New Preface.* Berkeley: University of California Press, 2001.

Sen, Rinku, and Kim Klein. *Stir It Up: Lessons in Community Organizing and Advocacy.* San Francisco: Jossey-Bass, 2003.

ARTS AND CULTURE

Camenson, Blythe. *Opportunities in Museum Careers.* New York: McGraw-Hill 1996.

Danilov, Victor J. *Museum Careers and Training: A Professional Guide.* Westport, Conn.: Greenwood Press, 1994.

Eberts, Marjorie, and Margaret Gisler. *Careers for Culture Lovers & Other Artsy Types.* 2nd ed. New York: McGraw-Hill/Contemporary Books, 1999.

Field, Shelly. *Career Opportunities in Theater and the Performing Arts.* 2nd ed. New York: Facts On File, 1999.

Haubenstock, Susan H., and David Joselit. *Career Opportunities in Art.* 3rd ed. New York: Facts On File, 2001.

COLLEGES AND UNIVERSITIES

Barr, Margaret J., and Mary K. Desler. *The Handbook of Student Affairs Administration: A Publication of the National Association of Student Personnel Administrators.* 2nd ed. San Francisco: Jossey-Bass, 2000.

Goldsmith, John A., John Komlos, and Peggy Schine Gold. *The Chicago Guide to Your Academic Career: A Portable Mentor for Scholars from Graduate School through Tenure.* Chicago: University of Chicago Press, 2001.

ENVIRONMENT, NATURE, AND CONSERVATION

American Hiking Society. *Helping Out in the Outdoors: A Directory of Volunteer Work and Internships on America's Public Lands.* Washington, D.C.: American Hiking Society, 1999.

DeGalan, Julie, and Bryon Middlekauff. *Great Jobs for Environmental Science Majors.* McGraw-Hill, 2002.

Doyle, Kevin, ed. Environmental Careers Organization. *The Complete Guide to Environmental Careers in the 21st Century.* Washington, D.C.: Island Press, 1999.

Environmental Careers Organization. *The ECO Guide to Careers that Make a Difference: Environmental Work for a Sustainable World.* Washington, D.C.: Island Press, 2004.

Fanning, Odom. *Opportunities in Environmental Careers.* 2nd ed. New York: McGraw-Hill, 2002.

Fasulo, Mike, and Jane Kinney. *Careers for Enviromental Types & Others Who Respect the Earth.* Chicago: VGM Career Books, 2002.

Miller, Louise. *Careers for Nature Lovers and Other Outdoor Types.* New York: McGraw-Hill, 2001.

National Wildlife Federation. Conservation Directory. Published and updated annually. Washington, D.C. (http://www.nwf.org/about/communication.cfm)

Quintana, Debra. *100 Jobs in the Environment.* New York: Macmillan, 1997.

Shenk, Ellen. *Outdoor Careers.* Mechanicsburg, Pa.: Stackpole Books, 2000.

Student Conservation Association. *Earth Work: Resource Guide to Nationwide Green Jobs.* New York: HarperCollins West, 1994.

Student Conservation Association Staff, comp. and Scott D. Izzo. *Guide to Graduate Environmental Programs.* Washington D.C.: Island Press, 1997.

INTERNATIONAL AID AND DEVELOPMENT

Bell, Arthur H. *Great Jobs Abroad.* New York: McGraw-Hill, 2000.

Carland, Maria Pinto, and Lisa Gihring, eds. 7th ed. *Careers in International Affairs.* Washington, D.C.: Georgetown University Press, 2003.

Christie, Sally. *Vault Guide to International Careers.* New York: Vault Reports 2004.

Giese, Filomena. *Alternative to the Peace Corps—A Directory of Third World & U. S. Volunteer Opportunities.* Oakland, Calif.: Food First Books, 1999.

Griffith, Susan. *Work Your Way around the World.* Oxford: Vacation Work, 2001.

Human Rights Organizations & Periodicals Directory 2003–2004. Berkeley, Calif.: Meiklejohn Civil Liberties Institute, 2003.

Kocher, Eric, and Nina Segal. *International Jobs: Where They Are, How to Get Them.* 6th ed. Reading, Mass.: Perseus Books, 2003.

Kruempelmann, Elizabeth. *The Global Citizen: A Guide to Creating an International Life and Career.* Berkeley, Calif.: Ten Speed Press, 2002.

Lauber, Daniel, with Kraig Rice. *International Job Finder: Where the Jobs Are Worldwide.* River Forest, Ill.: Planning/Communications, 2002.

Mueller, Nancy. *Work Worldwide: International Career Strategies for the Adventurous Job Seeker.* Emeryville, Calif.: Avalon Travel Publishing, 2000.

Seelye, H. Ned, and J. Laurence Day. *Careers for Foreign Language Aficionados & Other Multilingual Types.* 2nd ed. New York: McGraw-Hill Companies, 2001.

GENERAL REFERENCE

Career Information Center. 7th ed. 13 vols. New York: Macmillan, 1999.

Encyclopedia of Careers and Vocational Guidance. 11th ed. 4 vols. Chicago: Ferguson, 2000.

Farr, Michael, and Laurence Shatkin. *Enhanced Occupational Outlook Handbook.* Indianapolis: JIST Publishing, 2002.

U.S. Department of Labor, Bureau of Labor Statistics. *Occupational Outlook Handbook. 2004–2005.* Indianapolis: JIST Publishing, 2004.

CAREER EXPLORATION AND SELF-ASSESSMENT

Bernstein, Alan B., and Nicholas R. Schaffzin. *The Princeton Review Guide to Your Career.* 4th ed. New York: Princeton Review Publishing, 2000.

Boldt, Laurence G. *Zen and the Art of Making a Living: A Practical Guide to Creative Career Design.* New York: Penguin Books, 1999.

Bolles, Richard Nelson. *The 2004 What Color is Your Parachute?* Berkeley, Calif.: Ten Speed Press, 2004.

Edwards, Paul and Sarah. *Finding Your Perfect Work.* Rev. ed. New York: Jeremy P. Tarcher, 2003.

Gurvis, Sandra. *Careers for Nonconformists: A Practical Guide to Finding and Developing a Career Outside the Mainstream.* New York: Marlowe & Company, 2000.

Jansen, Julie. *I Don't Know What I Want, but I Know It's Not This: A Step-By-Step Guide to Finding Gratifying Work.* New York: Penguin Books, 2003.

Lore, Nicholas. *The Pathfinder: How to Choose or Change Your Career for a Lifetime of Satisfaction and Success.* New York: Fireside, 1998

Nemko, Marty and Paul & Sarah Edwards. *Cool Careers for Dummies.* New York, Wiley, 2001.

Sher, Barbara. *Live the Life You Love: In Ten Easy Step-By Step Lessons.* New York: Dell, 1997.

Tieger, Paul D., and Barbara Barron-Tieger. *Do What You Are: Discover the Perfect Career for You through the Secrets of Personality Type.* 3rd ed. Boston: Little Brown, 2001.

JOB SEARCH

Criscito, Pat. *Resumes in Cyberspace: Your Complete Guide to a Computerized Job Search.* Hauppauge, N.Y.: Barron's Educational Series, 2000.

Crispin, Gerry, and Mark Mehler. *Careerxroads 2000: The Directory of Job, Resume and Career Management Sites on the World Wide Web.* Indianapolis: JIST Works, 2000.

Dixon, Pam. *Job Searching Online for Dummies.* 2nd ed. Indianapolis: IDG Books, 2000.

Figler, Howard. *The Complete Job-Search Handbook: Everything You Need to Know to Get the Job You Really Want.* 3rd ed. New York: Owl Books, 1999.

Petras, Kathryn, and Ross Petras. *The Only Job Hunting Guide You'll Ever Need: The Most Comprehensive Guide for Job Hunters and Career Switchers.* New York: Simon & Schuster, 1995.

Yate, Martin. *Careersmarts: Jobs With a Future.* New York: Ballantine Books, 1997.

INDEX

Page numbers in **boldface** indicate major treatment of a topic.